# HOW TO BE AN ANTIRACIST

# HOW TO
# BE AN
# ANTIRACIST

## IBRAM X.
## KENDI

ONE WORLD
NEW YORK

Published in the United States by One World, an imprint of Random House,
a division of Penguin Random House LLC, New York.

ONE WORLD is a registered trademark and its colophon is a trademark
of Penguin Random House LLC.

LIBRARY OF CONGRESS CATALOGING-IN-PUBLICATION DATA
Names: Kendi, Ibram X., author.
Title: How to be an antiracist / Ibram X. Kendi.
Description: New York : One World, 2019. | Includes index.
Identifiers: LCCN 2018058619 | ISBN 9780525509288 |
ISBN 9780525509295 (ebook)
Subjects: LCSH: Anti-racism—United States. | Racism—Psychological
aspects. | United States—Race relations. | Kendi, Ibram X.
Classification: LCC E184.A1 K344 2019 | DDC 305.800973—dc23
LC record available at https://lccn.loc.gov/2018058619

Printed in the United States of America on acid-free paper

randomhousebooks.com

16  18  20  19  17

*Book design by Jo Anne Metsch*

TO SURVIVAL

# TABLE OF CONTENTS

# HOW TO BE AN ANTIRACIST

# MY RACIST INTRODUCTION

DESPISED SUITS AND ties. For seventeen years I had been surrounded by suit-wearing, tie-choking, hat-flying church folk.
My teenage wardrobe hollered the defiance of a preacher's kid.

It was January 17, 2000. More than three thousand Black
people—with a smattering of White folks—arrived that Monday
morning in their Sunday best at the Hylton Memorial Chapel in
Northern Virginia. My parents arrived in a state of shock. Their
floundering son had somehow made it to the final round of the
Prince William County Martin Luther King Jr. oratorical contest.

I didn't show up with a white collar under a dark suit and
matching dark tie like most of my competitors. I sported a racy
golden-brown blazer with a slick black shirt and bright color-
streaked tie underneath. The hem of my baggy black slacks crested
over my creamy boots. I'd already failed the test of respectability
before I opened my mouth, but my parents, Carol and Larry,
were all smiles nonetheless. They couldn't remember the last time
they saw me wearing a tie and blazer, however loud and crazy.

But it wasn't just my clothes that didn't fit the scene. My competitors were academic prodigies. I wasn't. I carried a GPA lower than 3.0; my SAT score barely cracked 1000. Colleges were recruiting my competitors. I was riding the high of having received surprise admission letters from the two colleges I'd halfheartedly applied to.

A few weeks before, I was on the basketball court with my high school team, warming up for a home game, cycling through layup lines. My father, all six foot three and two hundred pounds of him, emerged from my high school gym's entrance. He slowly walked onto the basketball court, flailing his long arms to get my attention—and embarrassing me before what we could call the "White judge." Classic Dad. He couldn't care less what judgmental White people thought about him. He rarely if ever put on a happy mask, faked a calmer voice, hid his opinion, or avoided making a scene. I loved and hated my father for living on his own terms in a world that usually denies Black people their own terms. It was the sort of defiance that could have gotten him lynched by a mob in a different time and place—or lynched by men in badges today.

I jogged over to him before he could flail his way right into our layup lines. Weirdly giddy, he handed me a brown manila envelope.

"This came for you today."

He motioned me to open the envelope, right there at half-court as the White students and teachers looked on.

I pulled out the letter and read it: I had been admitted to Hampton University in southern Virginia. My immediate shock exploded into unspeakable happiness. I embraced Dad and exhaled. Tears mixed with warm-up sweat on my face. The judging White eyes around us faded.

I thought I was stupid, too dumb for college. Of course, intelligence is as subjective as beauty. But I kept using "objective" standards, like test scores and report cards, to judge myself. No wonder I sent out only two college applications: one to Hampton and the other to the institution I ended up attending, Florida A&M University. Fewer applications meant less rejection—and I fully expected those two historically Black universities to reject me. Why would any university want an idiot on their campus who can't understand Shakespeare? It never occurred to me that maybe I wasn't really trying to understand Shakespeare and that's why I dropped out of my English II International Baccalaureate class during my senior year. Then again, I did not read much of anything in those years.

Maybe if I'd read history then, I'd have learned about the historical significance of the new town my family had moved to from New York City in 1997. I would have learned about all those Confederate memorials surrounding me in Manassas, Virginia, like Robert E. Lee's dead army. I would have learned why so many tourists trek to Manassas National Battlefield Park to relive the glory of the Confederate victories at the Battles of Bull Run during the Civil War. It was there that General Thomas J. Jackson acquired his nickname, "Stonewall," for his stubborn defense of the Confederacy. Northern Virginians kept the stonewall intact after all these years. Did anyone notice the irony that at this Martin Luther King Jr. oratorical contest, my free Black life represented Stonewall Jackson High School?

THE DELIGHTFUL EVENT organizers from Delta Sigma Theta sorority, the proud dignitaries, and the competitors were all seated on the pulpit. (The group was too large to say we were seated in the pulpit.) The audience sat in rows that curved around the long, arched pulpit, giving room for speakers to pace to the far sides of the chapel while delivering their talks; five stairs also allowed us to descend into the crowd if we wanted.

The middle schoolers had given their surprisingly mature speeches. The exhilarating children's choir had sung behind us. The audience sat back down and went silent in anticipation of the three high school orators.

I went first, finally approaching the climax of an experience that had already changed my life. From winning my high school competition months before to winning "best before the judges" at a countywide competition weeks before—I felt a special rainstorm of academic confidence. If I came out of the experience dripping with confidence for college, then I'd entered from a high school drought. Even now I wonder if it was my poor sense of self that first generated my poor sense of my people. Or was it my poor sense of my people that inflamed a poor sense of myself? Like the famous question about the chicken and the egg, the answer is less important than the cycle it describes. Racist ideas make people of color think less of themselves, which makes them more vulnerable to racist ideas. Racist ideas make White people think more of themselves, which further attracts them to racist ideas.

I thought I was a subpar student and was bombarded by messages—from Black people, White people, the media—that told me that the reason was rooted in my race . . . which made me more discouraged and less motivated as a student . . . which only further reinforced for me the racist idea that Black people just weren't very studious . . . which made me feel even more despair or indifference . . . and on it went. At no point was this cycle interrupted by a deeper analysis of my own specific circumstances and shortcomings or a critical look at the ideas of the society that judged me—instead, the cycle hardened the racist ideas inside me until I was ready to preach them to others.

I REMEMBER THE MLK competition so fondly. But when I recall the racist speech I gave, I flush with shame.

"What would be Dr. King's message for the millennium? Let's visualize an angry seventy-one-year-old Dr. King . . ." And I began my remix of King's "I Have a Dream" speech.

It was joyous, I started, our emancipation from enslavement. But "now, one hundred thirty-five years later, the Negro is still not free." I was already thundering, my tone angry, more Malcolm than Martin. "Our youth's minds are still in captivity!"

I did not say our youth's minds are in captivity of racist ideas, as I would say now.

"They think it's okay to be those who are most feared in our society!" I said, as if it was their fault they were so feared.

"They think it's okay not to think!" I charged, raising the classic racist idea that Black youth don't value education as much as their non-Black counterparts. No one seemed to care that this well-traveled idea had flown on anecdotes but had never been grounded in proof. Still, the crowd encouraged me with their applause. I kept shooting out unproven and disproven racist ideas about all the things wrong with Black youth—ironically, on the day when all the things right about Black youth were on display.

I started pacing wildly back and forth on the runway for the pulpit, gaining momentum.

"They think it's okay to climb the high tree of pregnancy!" Applause. "They think it's okay to confine their dreams to sports and music!" Applause.

Had I forgotten that I—not "Black youth"—was the one who had confined his dreams to sports? And I was calling Black youth "they"? Who on earth did I think I was? Apparently, my placement on that illustrious stage had lifted me out of the realm of ordinary—and thus inferior—Black youngsters and into the realm of the rare and extraordinary.

In my applause-stoked flights of oratory, I didn't realize that to say something is wrong about a racial group is to say something is inferior about that racial group. I did not realize that to say something is inferior about a racial group is to say a racist idea. I thought I was serving my people, when in fact I was serving up racist ideas about my people to my people. The Black judge seemed to be eating it up and clapping me on my back for more. I kept giving more.

"Their minds are being held captive, and our adults' minds are right there beside them," I said, motioning to the floor. "Because they somehow think that the cultural revolution that began on the day of my dream's birth is over.

"How can it be over when many times we are unsuccessful because we lack intestinal fortitude?" Applause.

"How can it be over when our kids leave their houses not

knowing how to make themselves, only knowing how to not make themselves?" Applause.

"How can it be over if all of this is happening in our community?" I asked, lowering my voice. "So I say to you, my friends, that even though this cultural revolution may never be over, I still have a dream . . ."


I STILL HAVE a nightmare—the memory of this speech whenever I muster the courage to recall it anew. It is hard for me to believe I finished high school in the year 2000 touting so many racist ideas. A racist culture had handed me the ammunition to shoot Black people, to shoot myself, and I took and used it. Internalized racism is the real Black on Black crime.

I was a dupe, a chump who saw the ongoing struggles of Black people on MLK Day 2000 and decided that Black people themselves were the problem. This is the consistent function of racist ideas—and of any kind of bigotry more broadly: to manipulate us into seeing people as the problem, instead of the policies that ensnare them.

The language used by the forty-fifth president of the United States offers a clear example of how this sort of racist language and thinking works. Long before he became president, Donald Trump liked to say, "Laziness is a trait in Blacks." When he decided to run for president, his plan for making America great again: defaming Latinx immigrants as mostly criminals and rapists and demanding billions for a border wall to block them. He promised "a total and complete shutdown of Muslims entering the United States." Once he became president, he routinely called his Black critics "stupid." He claimed immigrants from Haiti "all have AIDS," while praising White supremacists as "very fine people" in the summer of 2017.

Through it all, whenever someone pointed out the obvious, Trump responded with variations on a familiar refrain: "No, no. I'm not a racist. I'm the least racist person that you have ever interviewed," that "you've ever met," that "you've ever encountered." Trump's behavior may be exceptional, but his denials are normal. When racist ideas resound, denials that those ideas are racist typically follow. When racist policies resound, denials that those policies are racist also follow.

Denial is the heartbeat of racism, beating across ideologies, races, and nations. It is beating within us. Many of us who strongly call out Trump's racist ideas will strongly deny our own. How often do we become reflexively defensive when someone calls something we've done or said racist? How many of us would agree with this statement: " 'Racist' isn't a descriptive word. It's a pejorative word. It is the equivalent of saying, 'I don't like you.'" These are actually the words of White supremacist Richard Spencer, who, like Trump, identifies as "not racist." How many of us who despise the Trumps and White supremacists of the world share their self-definition of "not racist"?

What's the problem with being "not racist"? It is a claim that signifies neutrality: "I am not a racist, but neither am I aggressively against racism." But there is no neutrality in the racism struggle. The opposite of "racist" isn't "not racist." It is "antiracist." What's the difference? One endorses either the idea of a racial hierarchy as a racist, or racial equality as an antiracist. One either believes problems are rooted in groups of people, as a racist, or locates the roots of problems in power and policies, as an antiracist. One either allows racial inequities to persevere, as a racist, or confronts racial inequities, as an antiracist. There is no in-between safe space of "not racist." The claim of "not racist" neutrality is a mask for racism. This may seem harsh, but it's important at the outset that we apply one of the core principles of antiracism, which is to return the word "racist" itself back to its proper usage. "Racist" is not—as Richard Spencer argues—a pejorative. It is not the worst word in the English language; it is not the equivalent of a slur. It is descriptive, and the only way to undo racism is to consistently identify and describe it—and then dismantle it. The attempt to turn this usefully descriptive term into an almost unusable slur is, of course, designed to do the opposite: to freeze us into inaction.

· · ·

THE COMMON IDEA of claiming "color blindness" is akin to the notion of being "not racist"—as with the "not racist," the color-blind individual, by ostensibly failing to see race, fails to see racism and falls into racist passivity. The language of color blindness—like the language of "not racist"—is a mask to hide racism. "Our Constitution is color-blind," U.S. Supreme Court Justice John Harlan proclaimed in his dissent to *Plessy v. Ferguson,* the case that legalized Jim Crow segregation in 1896. "The white race deems itself to be the dominant race in this country," Justice Harlan went on. "I doubt not, it will continue to be for all time, if it remains true to its great heritage." A color-blind Constitution for a White-supremacist America.

THE GOOD NEWS is that racist and antiracist are not fixed identities. We can be a racist one minute and an antiracist the next. What we say about race, what we do about race, in each moment, determines what—not who—we are.

I used to be racist most of the time. I am changing. I am no longer identifying with racists by claiming to be "not racist." I am no longer speaking through the mask of racial neutrality. I am no longer manipulated by racist ideas to see racial groups as problems. I no longer believe a Black person cannot be racist. I am no longer policing my every action around an imagined White or Black judge, trying to convince White people of my equal humanity, trying to convince Black people I am representing the race well. I no longer care about how the actions of other Black individuals reflect on me, since none of us are race representatives, nor is any individual responsible for someone else's racist ideas. And I've come to see that the movement from racist to antiracist is always ongoing—it requires understanding and snubbing racism based on biology, ethnicity, body, culture, behavior, color, space, and class. And beyond that, it means standing ready to fight at racism's intersections with other bigotries.

. . .

THIS BOOK IS ultimately about the basic struggle we're all in, the struggle to be fully human and to see that others are fully human. I share my own journey of being raised in the dueling racial consciousness of the Reagan-era Black middle class, then right-turning onto the ten-lane highway of anti-Black racism— a highway mysteriously free of police and free on gas—and veering off onto the two-lane highway of anti-White racism, where gas is rare and police are everywhere, before finding and turning down the unlit dirt road of antiracism.

After taking this grueling journey to the dirt road of antiracism, humanity can come upon the clearing of a potential future: an antiracist world in all its imperfect beauty. It can become real if we focus on power instead of people, if we focus on changing policy instead of groups of people. It's possible if we overcome our cynicism about the permanence of racism.

We know how to be racist. We know how to pretend to be not racist. Now let's know how to be antiracist.

## CHAPTER 1

# DEFINITIONS

**RACIST:** One who is supporting a racist policy through their actions or inaction or expressing a racist idea.

**ANTIRACIST:** One who is supporting an antiracist policy through their actions or expressing an antiracist idea.

OUL LIBERATION SWAYED onstage at the University of Illinois arena, rocking colorful dashikis and Afros that shot up like balled fists—an amazing sight to behold for the eleven thousand college students in the audience. Soul Liberation appeared nothing like the White ensembles in suits who'd been sounding hymns for nearly two days after Jesus's birthday in 1970.

Black students had succeeded in pushing the InterVarsity Christian Fellowship, the U.S. evangelical movement's premier college organizer, to devote the second night of the conference to Black theology. More than five hundred Black attendees from across the country were on hand as Soul Liberation began to perform. Two of those Black students were my parents.

They were not sitting together. Days earlier, they had ridden on the same bus for twenty-four hours that felt like forty-two, from Manhattan through Pennsylvania, Ohio, and Indiana, before arriving in central Illinois. One hundred Black New Yorkers converged on InterVarsity's Urbana '70.

My mother and father had met during the Thanksgiving break weeks earlier when Larry, an accounting student at Manhattan's Baruch College, co-organized a recruiting event for Urbana '70 at his church in Jamaica, Queens. Carol was one of the thirty people who showed up—she had come home to Queens from Nyack College, a small Christian school about forty-five miles north of her parents' home in Far Rockaway. The first meeting was uneventful, but Carol noticed Larry, an overly serious student with a towering Afro, his face hidden behind a forest of facial hair, and Larry noticed Carol, a petite nineteen-year-old with dark freckles sprayed over her caramel complexion, even if all they did was exchange small talk. They'd independently decided to go to Urbana '70 when they heard that Tom Skinner would be preaching and Soul Liberation would be performing. At twenty-eight years old, Skinner was growing famous as a young evangelist of Black liberation theology. A former gang member and son of a Baptist preacher, he reached thousands via his weekly radio show and tours, where he delivered sermons at packed iconic venues like the Apollo Theater in his native Harlem. In 1970, Skinner published his third and fourth books, *How Black Is the Gospel?* and *Words of Revolution*.

Carol and Larry devoured both books like a James Brown tune, like a Muhammad Ali fight. Carol had discovered Skinner through his younger brother, Johnnie, who was enrolled with her at Nyack. Larry's connection was more ideological. In the spring of 1970, he had enrolled in "The Black Aesthetic," a class taught by legendary Baruch College literary scholar Addison Gayle Jr. For the first time, Larry read James Baldwin's *The Fire Next Time,* Richard Wright's *Native Son,* Amiri Baraka's wrenching plays, and the banned revolutionary manifesto *The Spook Who Sat by the Door* by Sam Greenlee. It was an awakening. After Gayle's class, Larry started searching for a way to reconcile his faith with his newfound Black consciousness. That search led him to Tom Skinner.

SOUL LIBERATION LAUNCHED into their popular anthem, "Power to the People." The bodies of the Black students who had surged to the front of the arena started moving almost in unison with the sounds of booming drums and heavy bass that, along with the syncopated claps, generated the rhythm and blues of a rural Southern revival.

The wave of rhythm then rushed through the thousands of White bodies in the arena. Before long, they, too, were on their feet, swaying and singing along to the soulful sounds of Black power.

Every chord from Soul Liberation seemed to build up anticipation for the keynote speaker to come. When the music ended, it was time: Tom Skinner, dark-suited with a red tie, stepped behind the podium, his voice serious as he began his history lesson.

"The evangelical church . . . supported the status quo. It supported slavery; it supported segregation; it preached against any attempt of the Black man to stand on his own two feet."

Skinner shared how he came to worship an elite White Jesus Christ, who cleaned people up through "rules and regulations," a savior who prefigured Richard Nixon's vision of law and order. But one day, Skinner realized that he'd gotten Jesus wrong. Jesus wasn't in the Rotary Club and he wasn't a policeman. Jesus was a "radical revolutionary, with hair on his chest and dirt under his fingernails." Skinner's new idea of Jesus was born of and committed to a new reading of the gospel. "Any gospel that does not . . . speak to the issue of enslavement" and "injustice" and "inequality—any gospel that does not want to go where people are hungry and poverty-stricken and set them free in the name of Jesus Christ—is not the gospel."

Back in the days of Jesus, "there was a system working just like today," Skinner declared. But "Jesus was dangerous. He was dangerous because he was changing the system." The Romans locked up this "revolutionary" and "nailed him to a cross" and killed and buried him. But three days later, Jesus Christ "got up out of the grave" to bear witness to us today. "Proclaim liberation to the captives, preach sight to the blind" and "go into the world and tell men who are bound mentally, spiritually, and physically, 'The liberator has come!'"

The last line pulsated through the crowd. "The liberator has come!" Students practically leapt out of their seats in an ovation—taking on the mantle of this fresh gospel. The liberators had come.

My parents were profoundly receptive to Skinner's call for evangelical liberators and attended a series of Black caucuses over the week of the conference that reinforced his call every night. At Urbana '70, Ma and Dad found themselves leaving the civilizing and conserving and racist church they realized they'd been part of. They were saved into Black liberation theology and joined the churchless church of the Black Power movement. Born in the days of Malcolm X, Fannie Lou Hamer, Stokely Carmichael, and other antiracists who confronted segregationists and assimilationists in the 1950s and 1960s, the movement for Black solidarity, Black cultural pride, and Black economic and political self-determination had enraptured the entire Black world. And now, in 1970, Black power had enraptured my parents. They stopped thinking about saving Black people and started thinking about liberating Black people.

In the spring of 1971, Ma returned to Nyack College and helped form a Black student union, an organization that challenged racist theology, the Confederate flags on dorm-room doors, and the paucity of Black students and programming. She started wearing African-print dresses and wrapped her growing Afro in African-print ties. She dreamed of traveling to the motherland as a missionary.

Dad returned to his church and quit its famed youth choir. He began organizing programs that asked provocative questions: "Is Christianity the White man's religion?" "Is the Black church relevant to the Black community?" He began reading the work of James Cone, the scholarly father of Black liberation theology and author of the influential *Black Theology & Black Power* in 1969.

One day in the spring of 1971, Dad struck up the nerve to go up to Harlem and attend Cone's class at Union Theological Seminary. Cone lectured on his new book, *A Black Theology of Liberation*. After class, Dad approached the professor.

"What is your definition of a Christian?" Dad asked in his deeply earnest way.

Cone looked at Dad with equal seriousness and responded: "A Christian is one who is striving for liberation."

James Cone's working definition of a Christian described a Christianity of the enslaved, not the Christianity of the slaveholders. Receiving this definition was a revelatory moment in Dad's life. Ma had her own similar revelation in her Black student union—that Christianity was about struggle and liberation. My parents now had, separately, arrived at a creed with which to shape their lives, to be the type of Christians that Jesus the revolutionary inspired them to be. This new definition of a word that they'd already chosen as their core identity naturally transformed them.

MY OWN, STILL-ONGOING journey toward being an antiracist began at Urbana '70. What changed Ma and Dad led to a changing of their two unborn sons—this new definition of the Christian life became the creed that grounded my parents' lives and the lives of their children. I cannot disconnect my parents' religious strivings to be Christian from my secular strivings to be an antiracist. And the key act for both of us was defining our terms so that we could begin to describe the world and our place in it. Definitions anchor us in principles. This is not a light point: If we don't do the basic work of defining the kind of people we want to be in language that is stable and consistent, we can't work toward stable, consistent goals. Some of my most consequential steps toward being an antiracist have been the moments when I arrived at basic definitions. To be an antiracist is to set lucid definitions of racism/antiracism, racist/antiracist policies, racist/antiracist ideas, racist/antiracist people. To be a racist is to constantly redefine racist in a way that exonerates one's changing policies, ideas, and personhood.

So let's set some definitions. What is racism? Racism is a marriage of racist policies and racist ideas that produces and normalizes racial inequities. Okay, so what are racist policies and ideas? We have to define them separately to understand why they are married and why they interact so well together. In fact, let's take one step back and consider the definition of another important phrase: racial inequity.

Racial inequity is when two or more racial groups are not standing on approximately equal footing. Here's an example of racial inequity: 71 percent of White families lived in owner-occupied homes in 2014, compared to 45 percent of Latinx families and 41 percent of Black families. Racial equity is when two or more racial groups are standing on a relatively equal footing. An example of racial equity would be if there were relatively equitable percentages of all three racial groups living in owner-occupied homes in the forties, seventies, or, better, nineties.

A racist policy is any measure that produces or sustains racial inequity between racial groups. An antiracist policy is any measure that produces or sustains racial equity between racial groups. By policy, I mean written and unwritten laws, rules, procedures, processes, regulations, and guidelines that govern people. There is no such thing as a nonracist or race-neutral policy. Every policy in every institution in every community in every nation is producing or sustaining either racial inequity or equity between racial groups.

Racist policies have been described by other terms: "institutional racism," "structural racism," and "systemic racism," for instance. But those are vaguer terms than "racist policy." When I use them I find myself having to immediately explain what they mean. "Racist policy" is more tangible and exacting, and more likely to be immediately understood by people, including its victims, who may not have the benefit of extensive fluency in racial terms. "Racist policy" says exactly what the problem is and where the problem is. "Institutional racism" and "structural racism" and "systemic racism" are redundant. Racism itself is institutional, structural, and systemic.

"Racist policy" also cuts to the core of racism better than "racial discrimination," another common phrase. "Racial discrimination" is an immediate and visible manifestation of an underlying racial policy. When someone discriminates against a person in a racial group, they are carrying out a policy or taking advantage of the lack of a protective policy. We all have the power to discriminate. Only an exclusive few have the power to make policy. Focusing on "racial discrimination" takes our eyes off the central agents of racism: racist policy and racist policymakers, or what I call racist power.

Since the 1960s, racist power has commandeered the term "racial discrimination," transforming the act of discriminating on the basis of race into an inherently racist act. But if racial discrimination is defined as treating, considering, or making a distinction in favor or against an individual based on that person's race, then racial discrimination is not inherently racist. The defining question is whether the discrimination is creating equity or inequity. If discrimination is creating equity, then it is antiracist. If discrimination is creating inequity, then it is racist. Someone reproducing inequity through permanently assisting an overrepresented racial group into wealth and power is entirely different than someone challenging that inequity by temporarily assisting an underrepresented racial group into relative wealth and power until equity is reached.

The only remedy to racist discrimination is antiracist discrimination. The only remedy to past discrimination is present discrimination. The only remedy to present discrimination is future discrimination. As President Lyndon B. Johnson said in 1965, "You do not take a person who, for years, has been hobbled by chains and liberate him, bring him up to the starting line of a race and then say, 'You are free to compete with all the others,' and still justly believe that you have been completely fair." As U.S. Supreme Court Justice Harry Blackmun wrote in 1978, "In order to get beyond racism, we must first take account of race. There is no other way. And in order to treat some persons equally, we must treat them differently."

The racist champions of racist discrimination engineered to

maintain racial inequities before the 1960s are now the racist opponents of antiracist discrimination engineered to dismantle those racial inequities. The most threatening racist movement is not the alt right's unlikely drive for a White ethnostate but the regular American's drive for a "race-neutral" one. The construct of race neutrality actually feeds White nationalist victimhood by positing the notion that any policy protecting or advancing non-White Americans toward equity is "reverse discrimination."

That is how racist power can call affirmative action policies that succeed in reducing racial inequities "race conscious" and standardized tests that produce racial inequities "race neutral." That is how they can blame the behavior of entire racial groups for the inequities between different racial groups and still say their ideas are "not racist." But there is no such thing as a not-racist idea, only racist ideas and antiracist ideas.

So what is a racist idea? A racist idea is any idea that suggests one racial group is inferior or superior to another racial group in any way. Racist ideas argue that the inferiorities and superiorities of racial groups explain racial inequities in society. As Thomas Jefferson suspected a decade after declaring White American independence: "The blacks, whether originally a distinct race, or made distinct by time and circumstances, are inferior to the whites in the endowments both of body and mind."

An antiracist idea is any idea that suggests the racial groups are equals in all their apparent differences—that there is nothing right or wrong with any racial group. Antiracist ideas argue that racist policies are the cause of racial inequities.

Understanding the differences between racist policies and antiracist policies, between racist ideas and antiracist ideas, allows us to return to our fundamental definitions. Racism is a powerful collection of racist policies that lead to racial inequity and are substantiated by racist ideas. Antiracism is a powerful collection of antiracist policies that lead to racial equity and are substantiated by antiracist ideas.

. . .

ONCE WE HAVE a solid definition of racism and antiracism, we can start to make sense of the racialized world around us, before us. My maternal grandparents, Mary Ann and Alvin, moved their family to New York City in the 1950s on the final leg of the Great Migration, happy to get their children away from violent Georgia segregationists and the work of picking cotton under the increasingly hot Georgia sun.

To think, they were also moving their family away from the effects of climate change. Do-nothing climate policy is racist policy, since the predominantly non-White global south is being victimized by climate change more than the Whiter global north, even as the Whiter global north is contributing more to its acceleration. Land is sinking and temperatures are rising from Florida to Bangladesh. Droughts and food scarcity are ravishing bodies in Eastern and Southern Africa, a region already containing 25 percent of the world's malnourished population. Human-made environmental catastrophes disproportionately harming bodies of color are not unusual; for instance, nearly four thousand U.S. areas—mostly poor and non-White—have higher lead poisoning rates than Flint, Michigan.

I am one generation removed from picking cotton for pocket change under the warming climate in Guyton, outside Savannah. That's where we buried my grandmother in 1993. Memories of her comforting calmness, her dark green thumb, and her large trash bags of Christmas gifts lived on as we drove back to New York from her funeral. The next day, my father ventured up to Flushing, Queens, to see his single mother, also named Mary Ann. She had the clearest dark-brown skin, a smile that hugged you, and a wit that smacked you.

When my father opened the door of her apartment, he smelled the fumes coming from the stove she'd left on, and some other fumes. His mother nowhere in sight, he rushed down the hallway and into her back bedroom. That's where he found his mother, as if sleeping, but dead. Her struggle with Alzheimer's, a disease more prevalent among African Americans, was over.

There may be no more consequential White privilege than

life itself. White lives matter to the tune of 3.5 additional years over Black lives in the United States, which is just the most glaring of a host of health disparities, starting from infancy, where Black infants die at twice the rate of White infants. But at least my grandmothers and I met, we shared, we loved. I never met my paternal grandfather. I never met my maternal grandfather, Alvin, killed by cancer three years before my birth. In the United States, African Americans are 25 percent more likely to die of cancer than Whites. My father survived prostate cancer, which kills twice as many Black men as it does White men. Breast cancer disproportionately kills Black women.

Three million African Americans and four million Latinx secured health insurance through the Affordable Care Act, dropping uninsured rates for both groups to around 11 percent before President Barack Obama left office. But a staggering 28.5 million Americans remained uninsured, a number primed for growth after Congress repealed the individual mandate in 2017. And it is becoming harder for people of color to vote out of office the politicians crafting these policies designed to shorten their lives. Racist voting policy has evolved from disenfranchising by Jim Crow voting laws to disenfranchising by mass incarceration and voter-ID laws. Sometimes these efforts are so blatant that they are struck down: North Carolina enacted one of these targeted voter-ID laws, but in July 2016 the Court of Appeals for the Fourth Circuit struck it down, ruling that its various provisions "target African Americans with almost surgical precision." But others have remained and been successful. Wisconsin's strict voter-ID law suppressed approximately two hundred thousand votes— again primarily targeting voters of color—in the 2016 election. Donald Trump won that critical swing state by 22,748 votes.

We are surrounded by racial inequity, as visible as the law, as hidden as our private thoughts. The question for each of us is: What side of history will we stand on? A racist is someone who is supporting a racist policy by their actions or inaction or expressing a racist idea. An antiracist is someone who is supporting an antiracist policy by their actions or expressing an antiracist idea. "Racist" and "antiracist" are like peelable name tags that are placed and replaced based on what someone is doing or not doing, supporting or expressing in each moment. These are not permanent tattoos. No one becomes a racist or antiracist. We can only strive to be one or the other. We can unknowingly strive to be a racist. We can knowingly strive to be an antiracist. Like fighting an addiction, being an antiracist requires persistent self-awareness, constant self-criticism, and regular self-examination.

Racist ideas have defined our society since its beginning and can feel so natural and obvious as to be banal, but antiracist ideas remain difficult to comprehend, in part because they go against the flow of this country's history. As Audre Lorde said in 1980, "We have all been programmed to respond to the human differences between us with fear and loathing and to handle that difference in one of three ways: ignore it, and if that is not possible, copy it if we think it is dominant, or destroy it if we think it is subordinate. But we have no patterns for relating across our human differences as equals." To be an antiracist is a radical choice in the face of this history, requiring a radical reorientation of our consciousness.

# DUELING CONSCIOUSNESS

**ASSIMILATIONIST:** One who is expressing the racist idea that a racial group is culturally or behaviorally inferior and is supporting cultural or behavioral enrichment programs to develop that racial group.

**SEGREGATIONIST:** One who is expressing the racist idea that a permanently inferior racial group can never be developed and is supporting policy that segregates away that racial group.

**ANTIRACIST:** One who is expressing the idea that racial groups are equals and none needs developing, and is supporting policy that reduces racial inequity.

M Y PARENTS HAD not seen each other since the bus ride to Urbana '70. Christmas approached in 1973. Soul Liberation held a concert at the iconic Broadway Presbyterian Church in Harlem that turned into a reunion of sorts for the New York attendees of Urbana '70. Dad and Ma showed up. Old friends beckoned, and something new. After the chords of Soul Liberation fell silent, my parents finally spoke again and a spark finally lit.

Days later, Dad called. He asked Ma out. "I've been called to the mission field," Ma responded. "Leaving in March."

Ma and Dad persevered, even after Ma left to teach in a rural Liberian village outside Monrovia for nine months. Eight years later they were married, daring to name me, their second son, "exalted father" when I arrived in a world not in the practice of exalting Black bodies. Just before that arrival, as my pregnant mother celebrated her thirty-first birthday on June 24, 1982, President Reagan declared war on her unborn baby. "We must put drug abuse on the run through stronger law enforcement," Reagan said in the Rose Garden.

It wasn't drug abuse that was put on the run, of course, but people like me, born into this regime of "stronger law enforcement." The stiffer sentencing policies for drug crimes—not a net increase in crime—caused the American prison population to quadruple between 1980 and 2000. While violent criminals typically account for about half of the prison population at any given time, more people were incarcerated for drug crimes than violent crimes every year from 1993 to 2009. White people are more likely than Black and Latinx people to sell drugs, and the races consume drugs at similar rates. Yet African Americans are far more likely than Whites to be jailed for drug offenses. Nonviolent Black drug offenders remain in prisons for about the same length of time (58.7 months) as violent White criminals (61.7 months). In 2016, Black and Latinx people were still grossly overrepresented in the prison population at 56 percent, double their percentage of the U.S. adult population. White people were still grossly underrepresented in the prison population at 30 percent, about half their percentage of the U.S. adult population.

Reagan didn't start this so-called war, as historian Elizabeth Hinton recounts. President Lyndon B. Johnson first put us on the run when he named 1965 "the year when this country began a thorough, intelligent, and effective war on crime." My parents were in high school when Johnson's war on crime mocked his undersupported war on poverty, like a heavily armed shooter mocking the underresourced trauma surgeon. President Richard Nixon announced his war on drugs in 1971 to devastate his harshest critics—Black and antiwar activists. "We could arrest their leaders, raid their homes, break up their meetings, and vilify them night after night on the evening news," Nixon's domestic-policy chief, John Ehrlichman, told a *Harper's* reporter years later. "Did we know we were lying about the drugs? Of course we did."

Black people joined in the vilification, convinced that homicidal drug dealers, gun toters, and thieving heroin addicts were flushing "down the drain" all "the hard won gains of the civil rights movement," to quote an editorial in *The Washington Afro-American* in 1981. Some, if not most, Black leaders, in an effort to appear as saviors of the people against this menace, turned around and set the Black criminal alongside the White racist as the enemies of the people.

Seemingly contradictory calls to lock up and to save Black people dueled in legislatures around the country but also in the minds of Americans. Black leaders joined with Republicans from Nixon to Reagan, and with Democrats from Johnson to Bill Clinton, in calling for and largely receiving more police officers, tougher and mandatory sentencing, and more jails. But they also called for the end of police brutality, more jobs, better schools, and drug-treatment programs. These calls were less enthusiastically received.

By the time I came along in 1982, the shame about "Black on Black crime" was on the verge of overwhelming a generation's pride about "Black is beautiful." Many non-Black Americans looked down on Black addicts in revulsion—but too many Black folk looked down on the same addicts in shame.

Both of my parents emerged from poor families, one from Northern urban projects, one from Southern rural fields. Both framed their rise from poverty into the middle class in the 1980s as a climb up the ladder of education and hard work. As they climbed, they were inundated with racist talking points about Black people refusing to climb, the ones who were irresponsibly strung out on heroin or crack, who enjoyed stealing and being criminally dependent on the hard-earned money of climbing Americans like them.

In 1985, adored civil-rights lawyer Eleanor Holmes Norton took to *The New York Times* to claim the "remedy . . . is not as simple as providing necessities and opportunities," as antiracists argued. She urged the "overthrow of the complicated, predatory ghetto subculture." She called on people like my parents with "ghetto origins" to save "ghetto males" and women by impressing on them the values of "hard work, education, respect for family" and "achieving a better life for one's children." Norton provided no empirical evidence to substantiate her position that certain "ghetto" Blacks were deficient in any of these values.

But my parents, along with many others in the new Black middle class, consumed these ideas. The class that challenged racist policies from the 1950s through the 1970s now began challenging other Black people in the 1980s and 1990s. Antiracism seemed like an indulgence in the face of the self-destructive behavior they were witnessing all around them. My parents followed Norton's directive: They fed me the mantra that education and hard work would uplift me, just as it had uplifted them, and would, in the end, uplift all Black people. My parents—even from within their racial consciousness—were susceptible to the racist idea that it was laziness that kept Black people down, so they paid more attention to chastising Black people than to Reagan's policies, which were chopping the ladder they climbed up and then punishing people for falling.

The Reagan Revolution was just that: a radical revolution for the benefit of the already powerful. It further enriched high-income Americans by cutting their taxes and government regulations, installing a Christmas-tree military budget, and arresting the power of unions. Seventy percent of middle-income Blacks said they saw "a great deal of racial discrimination" in 1979, before Reagan revolutionaries rolled back enforcement of civil-rights laws and affirmative-action regulations, before they rolled back funding to state and local governments whose contracts and jobs had become safe avenues into the single-family urban home of the Black middle class. In the same month that Reagan announced his war on drugs on Ma's birthday in 1982, he cut the safety net of federal welfare programs and Medicaid, sending more low-income Blacks into poverty. His "stronger law enforcement" sent more Black people into the clutches of violent cops, who killed twenty-two Black people for every White person in the early 1980s. Black youth were four times more likely to be unemployed in 1985 than in 1954. But few connected the increase in unemployment to the increase in violent crime.

Americans have long been trained to see the deficiencies of people rather than policy. It's a pretty easy mistake to make: People are in our faces. Policies are distant. We are particularly poor at seeing the policies lurking behind the struggles of people. And so my parents turned away from the problems of policy to look at the problems of people—and reverted to striving to save and civilize Black people rather than liberate them. Civilizer theology became more attractive to my parents, in the face of the rise of crack and the damage it did to Black people, as it did to so many children of civil rights and Black power. But in many ways, liberation theology remained their philosophical home, the home they raised me in.

DEEP DOWN, MY parents were still the people who were set on fire by liberation theology back in Urbana. Ma still dreamed of globetrotting the Black world as a liberating missionary, a dream her Liberian friends encouraged in 1974. Dad dreamed of writing liberating poetry, a dream Professor Addison Gayle encouraged in 1971.

I always wonder what would have been if my parents had not let their reasonable fears stop them from pursuing their dreams. Traveling Ma helping to free the Black world. Dad accompanying her and finding inspiration for his freedom poetry. Instead, Ma settled for a corporate career in healthcare technology. Dad settled for an accounting career. They entered the American middle class—a space then as now defined by its disproportionate White majority—and began to look at themselves and their people not only through their own eyes but also "through the eyes of others." They joined other Black people trying to fit into that White space while still trying to be themselves and save their people. They were not wearing a mask as much as splitting into two minds.

This conceptual duple reflected what W.E.B. Du Bois indelibly voiced in *The Souls of Black Folk* in 1903. "It is a peculiar sensation, this double-consciousness, this sense of always looking at one's self through the eyes of others," Du Bois wrote. He would neither "Africanize America" nor "bleach his Negro soul in a flood of white Americanism." Du Bois wished "to be both a Negro and an American." Du Bois wished to inhabit opposing constructs. To be American is to be White. To be White is to not be a Negro.

What Du Bois termed double consciousness may be more precisely termed *dueling* consciousness. "One ever feels his two-ness," Du Bois explained, "an American, a Negro; two souls, two thoughts, two unreconciled strivings; two warring ideals in one dark body, whose dogged strength alone keeps it from being torn asunder." Du Bois also explained how this war was being waged within his own dark body, wanting to be a Negro and wanting to "escape into the mass of Americans in the same way that the Irish and Scandinavians" were doing.

These dueling ideas were there in 1903, and the same duel overtook my parents—and it remains today. The duel within Black consciousness seems to usually be between antiracist and assimilationist ideas. Du Bois believed in both the antiracist concept of racial relativity, of every racial group looking at itself with its own eyes, and the assimilationist concept of racial standards, of "looking at one's self through the eyes" of another racial group—in his case, White people. In other words, he wanted to liberate Black people from racism but he also wanted to change them, to save them from their "relic of barbarism." Du Bois argued in 1903 that racism and "the low social level of the mass of the race" were both "responsible" for the "Negro's degradation." Assimilation would be part of the solution to this problem.

Assimilationist ideas are racist ideas. Assimilationists can position any racial group as the superior standard that another racial group should be measuring themselves against, the benchmark they should be trying to reach. Assimilationists typically position White people as the superior standard. "Do Americans ever stop to reflect that there are in this land a million men of Negro blood . . . who, judged by any standard, have reached the full measure of the best type of modern European culture? Is it fair, is it decent, is it Christian . . . to belittle such aspiration?" Du Bois asked in 1903.

THE DUELING CONSCIOUSNESS played out in a different way for my parents, who became all about Black self-reliance. In 1985, they were drawn to Floyd H. Flake's Allen African Methodist Episcopal Church in Southside Queens. Flake and his equally magnetic wife, Elaine, grew Allen into a megachurch and one of the area's largest private-sector employers through its liberated kingdom of commercial and social-service enterprises. From its school to its senior-citizen housing complex to its crisis center for victims of domestic abuse, there were no walls to Flake's church. It was exactly the type of ministry that would naturally fascinate those descendants of Urbana '70. My father joined Flake's ministerial staff in 1989.

My favorite church program happened every Thanksgiving. We would arrive as lines of people were hugging the church building, which smelled particularly good that day. Perfumes of gravy and cranberry sauce warmed the November air. The aromas multiplied in deliciousness as we entered the basement fellowship hall, where the ovens were. I usually found my spot in the endless assembly line of servers. I could barely see over the food. But I strained up on my toes to help feed every bit of five thousand people. I tried to be as kind to these hungry people as my mother's peach cobbler. This program of Black people feeding Black people embodied the gospel of Black self-reliance that the adults in my life were feeding me.

Black self-reliance was a double-edged sword. One side was an abhorrence of White supremacy and White paternalism, White rulers and White saviors. On the other, a love of Black rulers and Black saviors, of Black paternalism. On one side was the antiracist belief that Black people were entirely capable of ruling themselves, of relying on themselves. On the other, the assimilationist idea that Black people should focus on pulling themselves up by their baggy jeans and tight halter tops, getting off crack, street corners, and government "handouts," as if those were the things partially holding their incomes down. This dueling consciousness nourished Black pride by insisting that there was nothing wrong with Black people, but it also cultivated shame with its implication that there was something behaviorally wrong with Black people . . . well, at least those other Black people. If the problem was in our own behavior, then Reagan revolutionaries were not keeping Black people down—we were keeping ourselves down.

WHITE PEOPLE HAVE their own dueling consciousness, between the segregationist and the assimilationist: the slave trader and the missionary, the proslavery exploiter and the antislavery civilizer, the eugenicist and the melting pot–ter, the mass incarcerator and the mass developer, the Blue Lives Matter and the All Lives Matter, the not-racist nationalist and the not-racist American.

Assimilationist ideas and segregationist ideas are the two types of racist ideas, the duel within racist thought. White assimilationist ideas challenge segregationist ideas that claim people of color are incapable of development, incapable of reaching the superior standard, incapable of becoming White and therefore fully human. Assimilationists believe that people of color can, in fact, be developed, become fully human, just like White people. Assimilationist ideas reduce people of color to the level of children needing instruction on how to act. Segregationist ideas cast people of color as "animals," to use Trump's descriptor for Latinx immigrants—unteachable after a point. The history of the racialized world is a three-way fight between assimilationists, segregationists, and antiracists. Antiracist ideas are based in the truth that racial groups are equals in all the ways they are different, assimilationist ideas are rooted in the notion that certain racial groups are culturally or behaviorally inferior, and segregationist ideas spring from a belief in genetic racial distinction and fixed hierarchy. "I am apt to suspect the negroes and in general all the other species of men (for there are four or five different kinds) to be naturally inferior to the whites," Enlightenment philosopher David Hume wrote in 1753. "There never was a civilized nation of any other complexion than white. . . . Such a uniform and constant difference could not happen, in so many countries and ages, if nature had not made an original distinction between these breeds of men."

David Hume declared that all races are created unequal, but Thomas Jefferson seemed to disagree in 1776 when he declared "all men are created equal." But Thomas Jefferson never made the antiracist declaration: All racial groups are equals. While segregationist ideas suggest a racial group is permanently inferior, assimilationist ideas suggest a racial group is temporarily inferior. "It would be hazardous to affirm that, equally cultivated for a few generations," the Negro "would not become" equal, Jefferson once wrote, in assimilationist fashion.

The dueling White consciousness fashioned two types of racist policies, reflecting the duel of racist ideas. Since assimilationists posit cultural and behavioral hierarchy, assimilationist policies and programs are geared toward developing, civilizing, and integrating a racial group (to distinguish from programs that uplift individuals). Since segregationists posit the incapability of a racial group to be civilized and developed, segregationist policies are geared toward segregating, enslaving, incarcerating, deporting, and killing. Since antiracists posit that the racial groups are already civilized, antiracist policies are geared toward reducing racial inequities and creating equal opportunity.

White people have generally advocated for both assimilationist and segregationist policies. People of color have generally advocated for both antiracist and assimilationist policies. The "history of the American Negro is the history of this strife," to quote Du Bois—the strife between the assimilationist and the antiracist, between mass civilizing and mass equalizing. In Du Bois's Black body, in my parents' Black bodies, in my young Black body, this double desire, this dueling consciousness, yielded an inner strife between Black pride and a yearning to be White. My own assimilationist ideas stopped me from noticing the racist policies really getting high during Reagan's drug war.

THE DUELING WHITE consciousness has, from its position of relative power, shaped the struggle within Black consciousness. Despite the cold truth that America was founded "by white men for white men," as segregationist Jefferson Davis said on the floor of the U.S. Senate in 1860, Black people have often expressed a desire to be American and have been encouraged in this by America's undeniable history of antiracist progress, away from chattel slavery and Jim Crow. Despite the cold instructions from the likes of Nobel laureate Gunnar Myrdal to "become assimilated into American culture," Black people have also, as Du Bois said, desired to remain Negro, discouraged by America's undeniable history of racist progress, from advancing police violence and voter suppression, to widening racial inequities in areas ranging from health to wealth.

History duels: the undeniable history of antiracist progress, the undeniable history of racist progress. Before and after the Civil War, before and after civil rights, before and after the first Black presidency, the White consciousness duels. The White body defines the American body. The White body segregates the Black body from the American body. The White body instructs the Black body to assimilate into the American body. The White body rejects the Black body assimilating into the American body—and history and consciousness duel anew.

The Black body in turn experiences the same duel. The Black body is instructed to become an American body. The American body is the White body. The Black body strives to assimilate into the American body. The American body rejects the Black body. The Black body separates from the American body. The Black body is instructed to assimilate into the American body—and history and consciousness duel anew.

But there is a way to get free. To be antiracist is to emancipate oneself from the dueling consciousness. To be antiracist is to conquer the assimilationist consciousness and the segregationist consciousness. The White body no longer presents itself as the American body; the Black body no longer strives to be the American body, knowing there is no such thing as the American body, only American bodies, racialized by power.

## CHAPTER 3

# POWER

**RACE:** A power construct of collected or merged difference that lives socially.

W E PULLED INTO the parking lot, looking for signs of life. But the daily life of the school had ended hours ago. It was pushing four o'clock on that warm April day in 1990, on Long Island, New York.

The car was parked and I could see the unease in my parents' faces as they freed themselves from their seatbelts. Maybe they were just trying to wrap their heads around making this thirty-minute drive out to Long Island twice a day, every weekday, year after year—on top of their hour-long job commutes to Manhattan. I sensed their discomfort and felt my own. Nerves about changing schools. Wishing P.S. 251 went past second grade. Feeling sick being so far from home in this foreign neighborhood. My seven-year-old feelings were roiling.

Several public elementary schools resided within walking distance of my house in Queens Village. But Black New Yorkers with the wherewithal to do it were separating their children from poor Black children in poor Black neighborhoods, just like White New Yorkers were separating their children from Black children. The dueling consciousness of White parents did not mind spending more money on housing in order to send their kids to White public schools—and keep them away from the purportedly bad schools and bad children. The dueling consciousness of Black parents did not mind paying for private Black schools to keep their children away from those same public schools and children.

A Black woman greeted us at the front door of Grace Lutheran School. She had been waiting. She was the school's third-grade teacher, and after a quick greeting, she took us down a corridor. Classrooms stood on both sides, but I fixated on the class photos outside the rooms: all those adult White faces and young Black faces looking back at us. We occasionally peeked inside nicely decorated classrooms. No sounds. No students. No teachers. Just footsteps.

She took us to her third-grade classroom, a long throw from the entrance. We could see the materials laid out for a science project, the details of which she explained to us. I couldn't care less about raising chicks. Then she took us over to a round table and asked if we had any questions. Sitting down, my mother asked a question about the curriculum. I did not care much about that, either. I started looking more intently around the classroom. A pause in the discussion caught my attention—Dad had just asked about the racial makeup of the student body. Majority Black. I took note. My mind drifted away again, this time wandering around the classroom and around the school, trying to imagine the students and teachers, remembering those pictures in the hallway. A pause caught my attention again. A question popped out of me.

"Are you the only Black teacher?"

"Yes, but—"

I cut her off. "Why are you the only Black teacher?"

Puzzled, she looked away at my parents. My parents exchanged curious looks. I kept staring at the teacher, wondering why she was looking at my parents. Ma ended the awkward silence. "He has been reading biographies of Black leaders."

Ma was talking about the critically acclaimed Junior Black Americans of Achievement series, promoted by Coretta Scott

King. Dad had bought a stack of these biographies, towering over one hundred now. Martin Luther King Jr. Frederick Douglass. Mary McLeod Bethune. Richard Allen. Ida B. Wells. Dad kept urging me to pull from the tower for every writing project.

These gripping biographies were as exciting to me as new video games on my Sega Genesis. Once I started reading, I could not stop. Discovering through these books the long history of harm done to Black Americans left me seething and brought to life a kind of racial consciousness for the first time.

"He is very much aware of being Black," Ma made sure to add, looking at Dad. She did not look for confirmation. Dad nodded in agreement anyway, as I stared at the teacher, awaiting my answer.

In that classroom, on that April day in 1990, my parents discovered that I had entered racial puberty. At seven years old, I began to feel the encroaching fog of racism overtaking my dark body. It felt big, bigger than me, bigger than my parents or anything in my world, and threatening. What a powerful construction race is—powerful enough to consume us. And it comes for us early.

But for all of that life-shaping power, race is a mirage, which doesn't lessen its force. We are what we see ourselves as, whether what we see exists or not. We are what people see us as, whether what they see exists or not. What people see in themselves and others has meaning and manifests itself in ideas and actions and policies, even if what they are seeing is an illusion. Race is a mirage but one that we do well to see, while never forgetting it is a mirage, never forgetting that it's the powerful light of racist power that makes the mirage.

So I do not pity my seven-year-old self for identifying racially as Black. I still identify as Black. Not because I believe Blackness, or race, is a meaningful scientific category but because our societies, our policies, our ideas, our histories, and our cultures have rendered race and made it matter. I am among those who have been degraded by racist ideas, suffered under racist policies, and who have nevertheless endured and built movements and cultures to resist or at least persist through this madness. I see myself culturally and historically and politically in Blackness, in being an African American, an African, a member of the forced and unforced African diaspora. I see myself historically and politically as a person of color, as a member of the global south, as a close ally of Latinx, East Asian, Middle Eastern, and Native peoples and all the world's degraded peoples, from the Roma and Jews of Europe to the aboriginals of Australia to the White people battered for their religion, class, gender, transgender identity, ethnicity, sexuality, body size, age, and disability. The gift of seeing myself as Black instead of being color-blind is that it allows me to clearly see myself historically and politically as being an antiracist, as a member of the interracial body striving to accept and equate and empower racial difference of all kinds.

Some White people do not identify as White for the same reason they identify as not-racist: to avoid reckoning with the ways that Whiteness—even as a construction and mirage—has informed their notions of America and identity and offered them privilege, the primary one being the privilege of being inherently normal, standard, and legal. It is a racial crime to be yourself if you are not White in America. It is a racial crime to look like yourself or empower yourself if you are not White. I guess I became a criminal at seven years old.

It is one of the ironies of antiracism that we must identify racially in order to identify the racial privileges and dangers of being in our bodies. Latinx and Asian and African and European and Indigenous and Middle Eastern: These six races—at least in the American context—are fundamentally power identities, because race is fundamentally a power construct of blended difference that lives socially. Race creates new forms of power: the power to categorize and judge, elevate and downgrade, include and exclude. Race makers use that power to process distinct individuals, ethnicities, and nationalities into monolithic races.

. . .

THE FIRST GLOBAL power to construct race happened to be the first racist power and the first exclusive slave trader of the constructed race of African people. The individual who orchestrated this trading of an invented people was nicknamed the "Navigator," though he did not leave Portugal in the fifteenth century. The only thing he navigated was Europe's political-economic seas, in order to create the first transatlantic slave-trading policies. Hailed for something he was not (and ignored for what he was)—it is fitting that Prince Henry the Navigator, the brother and then uncle of Portuguese kings, is the first character in the history of racist power.

Prince Henry lived in me. The name Henry had traveled down through the centuries and over the Atlantic Ocean and eventually into my father's family. After my mother gave my older brother a middle name from her family, Dad chose a middle name for me from his family. He chose the name of his enslaved great-great-grandfather, Henry. Dad did not know that this ancestor shared the name of the Navigator, but when I learned the history, I knew it had to go. My middle name is now Xolani, meaning peace, the very thing Henry's slave traders snatched from Africa (and the Americas and Europe), the thing they snatched from my ancestor Henry.

Until his death in 1460, Prince Henry sponsored Atlantic voyages to West Africa by the Portuguese, to circumvent Islamic slave traders, and in doing so created a different sort of slavery than had existed before. Premodern Islamic slave traders, like their Christian counterparts in premodern Italy, were not pursuing racist policies—they were enslaving what we now consider to be Africans, Arabs, and Europeans alike. At the dawn of the modern world, the Portuguese began to exclusively trade African bodies. Prince Henry's sailors made history when they navigated past the feared "black" hole of Cape Bojador, off Western Sahara, and brought enslaved Africans back to Portugal.

Prince Henry's first biographer—and apologist—became the first race maker and crafter of racist ideas. King Afonso V commissioned Gomes de Zurara, a royal chronicler and a loyal commander in Prince Henry's Military Order of Christ, to compose a glowing biography of the African adventures of his "beloved uncle." Zurara finished *The Chronicle of the Discovery and Conquest of Guinea* in 1453, the first European book on Africa.

One of Zurara's stories chronicled Prince Henry's first major slave auction in Lagos, Portugal, in 1444. Some captives were "white enough, fair to look upon, and well proportioned," while others were "like mulattoes" or "as black as Ethiops, and so ugly." Despite their different skin colors and languages and ethnic groups, Zurara blended them into one single group of people, worthy of enslavement.

Unlike babies, phenomena are typically born long before humans give them names. Zurara did not call Black people a race. French poet Jacques de Brézé first used the term "race" in a 1481 hunting poem. In 1606, the same diplomat who brought the addictive tobacco plant to France formally defined race for the first time in a major European dictionary. "Race . . . means descent," Jean Nicot wrote in the *Trésor de la langue française.* "Therefore, it is said that a man, a horse, a dog, or another animal is from a good or bad race." From the beginning, to make races was to make racial hierarchy.

Gomes de Zurara grouped all those peoples from Africa into a single race for that very reason: to create hierarchy, the first racist idea. Race making is an essential ingredient in the making of racist ideas, the crust that holds the pie. Once a race has been created, it must be filled in—and Zurara filled it with negative qualities that would justify Prince Henry's evangelical mission to the world. This Black race of people was lost, living "like beasts, without any custom of reasonable beings," Zurara wrote. "They had no understanding of good, but only knew how to live in a bestial sloth."

After Spanish and Portuguese colonizers arrived in the Americas in the fifteenth century, they took to race making all the different indigenous peoples, calling them one people, "Indians," or *negros da terra* (Blacks from the land) in sixteenth-century Brazil.

Spanish lawyer Alonso de Zuazo in 1510 contrasted the beastly race of Blacks as "strong for work, the opposite of the natives, so weak who can work only in undemanding tasks." Both racist constructions normalized and rationalized the increased importing of the supposedly "strong" enslaved Africans and the ongoing genocide of the supposedly "weak" Indians in the Americas.

The other races, save Latinx and Middle Easterners, had been completely made and distinguished by the Age of Enlightenment in the eighteenth century. Beginning in 1735, Carl Linnaeus locked in the racial hierarchy of humankind in *Systema Naturae*. He color-coded the races as White, Yellow, Red, and Black. He attached each race to one of the four regions of the world and described their characteristics. The Linnaeus taxonomy became the blueprint that nearly every enlightened race maker followed and that race makers still follow today. And, of course, these were not simply neutral categories, because races were never meant to be neutral categories. Racist power created them for a purpose.

Linnaeus positioned *Homo sapiens europaeus* at the top of the racial hierarchy, making up the most superior character traits. "Vigorous, muscular. Flowing blond hair. Blue eyes. Very smart, inventive. Covered by tight clothing. Ruled by law." He made up the middling racial character of *Homo sapiens asiaticus*: "Melancholy, stern. Black hair; dark eyes. Strict, haughty, greedy. Covered by loose garments. Ruled by opinion." He granted the racial character of *Homo sapiens americanus* a mixed set of atttributes: "Ill-tempered, impassive. Thick straight black hair; wide nostrils; harsh face; beardless. Stubborn, contented, free. Paints himself with red lines. Ruled by custom." At the bottom of the racial hierarchy, Linnaeus positioned *Homo sapiens afer*: "Sluggish, lazy. Black kinky hair. Silky skin. Flat nose. Thick lips. Females with genital flap and elongated breasts. Crafty, slow, careless. Covered by grease. Ruled by caprice."

FROM 1434 TO 1447, Gomes de Zurara estimated, 927 enslaved Africans landed in Portugal, "the greater part of whom were turned into the true path of salvation." It was, according to Zur-ara, Prince Henry's paramount achievement, an achievement blessed by successive popes. No mention of Prince Henry's royal fifth (*quinto*), the 185 or so of those captives he was given, a for-tune in bodies.

The obedient Gomes de Zurara created racial difference to convince the world that Prince Henry (and thus Portugal) did not slave-trade for money, only to save souls. The liberators had come to Africa. Zurara personally sent a copy of *The Chronicle of the Discovery and Conquest of Guinea* to King Afonso V with an intro-ductory letter in 1453. He hoped the book would "keep" Prince Henry's name "before" the "eyes" of the world, "to the great praise of his memory." Gomes de Zurara secured Prince Henry's memory as surely as Prince Henry secured the wealth of the royal court. King Afonso was accumulating more capital from selling enslaved Africans to foreigners "than from all the taxes levied on the entire kingdom," observed a traveler in 1466. Race had served its purpose.

Prince Henry's racist policy of slave trading came first—a cun-ning invention for the practical purpose of bypassing Muslim traders. After nearly two decades of slave trading, King Afonso asked Gomes de Zurara to defend the lucrative commerce in human lives, which he did through the construction of a Black race, an invented group upon which he hung racist ideas. This cause and effect—a racist power creates racist policies out of raw self-interest; the racist policies necessitate racist ideas to justify them—lingers over the life of racism.

FROM THE JUNIOR Black Americans of Achievement series on-ward, I had been taught that racist ideas cause racist policies. That ignorance and hate cause racist ideas. That the root problem of racism is ignorance and hate.

But that gets the chain of events exactly wrong. The root problem—from Prince Henry to President Trump—has always been the self-interest of racist power. Powerful economic, political, and cultural self-interest—the primitive accumulation of capital in the case of royal Portugal and subsequent slave traders—has been behind racist policies. Powerful and brilliant intellectuals in the tradition of Gomes de Zurara then produced racist ideas to justify the racist policies of their era, to redirect the blame for their era's racial inequities away from those policies and onto people.

THE TEACHER SOON overcame her surprise at a seven-year-old questioning her about the paucity of Black teachers. After searching my parents' faces, she looked back at me. "Why are you asking that question?" she asked nicely.

"If you have so many Black kids, you should have more Black teachers," I said.

"The school hasn't hired more Black teachers."

"Why?"

"I don't know."

"Why don't you know?"

My parents could see my agitation growing. Dad changed the subject. I didn't mind. My train of thought had taken me away, anyway. I was thinking about what Ma had just said. I am Black. I am Black.

I ended up attending a private Lutheran school closer to home, White third-grade teacher and all. I did not mind until I noticed.

## CHAPTER 4

# BIOLOGY

**BIOLOGICAL RACIST:** One who is expressing the idea that the races are meaningfully different in their biology and that these differences create a hierarchy of value.

**BIOLOGICAL ANTIRACIST:** One who is expressing the idea that the races are meaningfully the same in their biology and there are no genetic racial differences.

CANNOT RECALL HER name. So very odd. I can recite the names of my Black fourth-, fifth-, and sixth-grade teachers. But the name of my White third-grade teacher is lost in my memory like the names of so many racist White people over the years who interrupted my peace with their sirens. Forgetting her may have been a coping mechanism. People of color sometimes cope with abuse from individual Whites by hiding those individuals behind the generalized banner of Whiteness. "She acted that way," we say, "because she is White."

But generalizing the behavior of racist White individuals to all White people is as perilous as generalizing the individual faults of people of color to entire races. "He acted that way because he is Black. She acted that way because she is Asian." We often see and remember the race and not the individual. This is racist categorizing, this stuffing of our experiences with individuals into color-marked racial closets. An antiracist treats and remembers individuals as individuals. "She acted that way," we should say, "because she is racist."

I know that now, but that knowledge won't bring back the

specific memory of that teacher. My parents do not remember her name, either. All we remember is what she did.

My third-grade class was mostly made up of Black kids, with a handful of Asian and Latinx kids. Three White kids—two girls and a boy—kept to themselves and sat toward the front of the class. I sat toward the back near the door, where I could see everything. I could see when the White teacher overlooked raised non-White hands and called on White hands. I could see her punish non-White students for something she didn't punish White students for doing.

This was not a problem specific to my school or my childhood—it's a problem that cuts from private to public schools and through time. During the 2013–14 academic year, Black students were four times more likely than White students to be suspended from public schools, according to Department of Education data.

Back in my third-grade class, the unfair punishments and overlooking did not seem to bother the other Black students, so I did not let them bother me. But one day, before Christmas break in 1990, it became unavoidable.

A tiny and quiet girl—tinier and quieter than me—sat on the other side of the back of the room. The teacher asked a question and I saw her slowly raise her dark-skinned hand, which was a rare occurrence. Her shyness, or something else, generally kept her mouth closed and arm down. But something roused her today. I smiled as I saw her small hand rising for the teacher's attention.

The teacher looked at her, looked away, and instead called on a White hand as soon as it was raised. As the Black girl's arm came down, I could see her head going down. As I saw her head going down, I could see her spirits going down. I turned and looked up at the teacher, who, of course, was not looking at me. She was too busy engaging a favored White child to notice what was happening in the back row—neither my fury nor the sadness of the girl registered for her.

Scholars call what I saw a "microaggression," a term coined by eminent Harvard psychiatrist Chester Pierce in 1970. Pierce employed the term to describe the constant verbal and nonverbal abuse racist White people unleash on Black people wherever we go, day after day. A White woman grabs her purse when a Black person sits next to her. The seat next to a Black person stays empty on a crowded bus. A White woman calls the cops at the sight of Black people barbecuing in the park. White people telling us that our firmness is anger or that our practiced talents are natural. Mistaking us for the only other Black person around. Calling the cops on our children for selling lemonade on the street. Butchering Ebonics for sport. Assuming we are the help. Assuming the help isn't brilliant. Asking us questions about the entire Black race. Not giving us the benefit of the doubt. Calling the cops on us for running down the street.

As an African American, Pierce suffered from and witnessed this sort of everyday abuse. He identified these individual abuses as microaggressions to distinguish from the macroaggressions of racist violence and policies.

Since 1970, the concept of microaggressions has expanded to apply to interpersonal abuses against all marginalized groups, not just Black people. In the last decade, the term has become popular in social-justice spaces through the defining work of psychologist Derald Wing Sue. He defines microaggressions as "brief, everyday exchanges that send denigrating messages to certain individuals because of their group membership."

I don't think it's coincidental that the term "microaggression" emerged in popularity during the so-called post-racial era that some people assumed we'd entered with the election of the first Black president. The word "racism" went out of fashion in the liberal haze of racial progress—Obama's political brand—and conservatives started to treat racism as the equivalent to the N-word, a vicious pejorative rather than a descriptive term. With the word itself becoming radioactive to some, passé to others, some well-meaning Americans started consciously and perhaps unconsciously looking for other terms to identify racism. "Microaggression" became part of a whole vocabulary of old and new words—like "cultural wars" and "stereotype" and "implicit bias" and "economic anxiety" and "tribalism"—that made it easier to talk about or around the R-word.

I do not use "microaggression" anymore. I detest the post-racial platform that supported its sudden popularity. I detest its component parts—"micro" and "aggression." A persistent daily low hum of racist abuse is not minor. I use the term "abuse" because aggression is not as exacting a term. Abuse accurately describes the action and its effects on people: distress, anger, worry, depression, anxiety, pain, fatigue, and suicide.

What other people call racial microaggressions I call racist abuse. And I call the zero-tolerance policies preventing and punishing these abusers what they are: antiracist. Only racists shy away from the R-word—racism is steeped in denial.


BACK IN THE classroom, I needed some time to think about the racist abuse I saw. I watched my dejected classmate with her head down when we all began the walk through the long hall that led to the adjoining chapel, where we were to have our weekly service. Her sadness did not seem to let up. My fury did not, either.

The chapel had a postmodern design but was simple inside: a small pulpit and dozens of rows of brown pews, with a cross looming over it all from the back wall. When the morning service ended, the teacher began motioning my classmates out. I didn't move. I sat at the edge of the pew and stared at the teacher as she approached.

"Ibram, time to go," she said pleasantly.

"I'm not going anywhere!" I faintly replied, and looked straight ahead at the cross.

"What?"

I looked up at her, eyes wide and burning: "I'm not going anywhere!"

"No! You need to leave, right now."

Looking back, I wonder, if I had been one of her White kids would she have asked me: "What's wrong?" Would she have wondered if I was hurting? I wonder. I wonder if her racist ideas chalked up my resistance to my Blackness and therefore categorized it as misbehavior, not distress. With racist teachers, misbehaving kids of color do not receive inquiry and empathy and legitimacy. We receive orders and punishments and "no excuses," as if we are adults. The Black child is ill-treated like an adult, and the Black adult is ill-treated like a child.

My classmates were nearly out of the chapel. An observant handful stopped near the door, gazing and speculating. Irate and perplexed at this disruption, the teacher tried again to command me. She failed again. She grabbed my shoulder.

"Don't touch me!" I yelled.

"I'm calling the principal," she said, turning toward the exit.

"I don't care! Call her! Call her right now," I shouted, looking straight ahead as she walked away behind me. I felt a single tear falling from each eye.

It was chapel-quiet now. I wiped my eyes. I started rehearsing what I was going to tell the principal. When she came, she offered more commands that she thought could move me. She learned her lesson like her predecessor. I was not going to move until I recited my first dissertation on racism, until I had a chance to defend our Blackness.


OUR BLACKNESS. I am Black. I looked at the girl's dark skin and saw my skin color. Saw her kinky hair, split down the middle in cornrows held by barrettes, and saw my kinky hair, my small Afro. Saw her broad nose and saw my nose. Saw her thicker lips and saw my lips. Heard her talk and heard the way I talk. I did not see a mirage. We were the same. Those three favored White kids—they were different to my eight-year-old racial understanding. Their whiter skin color, straighter hair, skinnier noses and lips, their different way of speaking, even the way they wore their uniforms—all marked a different species to me. The difference was not skin deep.

No one taught me that these differences were meaningless to

our underlying humanity—the essence of biological antiracism. Adults had in so many ways taught me that these superficial differences signified different forms of humanity—the essence of biological racism.

Biological racists are segregationists. Biological racism rests on two ideas: that the races are meaningfully different in their biology and that these differences create a hierarchy of value. I grew up believing the first idea of biological racial difference. I grew up disbelieving the second idea of biological racial hierarchy, which conflicted with the biblical creation story I'd learned through religious study, in which all humans descend from Adam and Eve. It also conflicted with the secular creed I'd been taught, the American creation story that "all men are created equal."

My acceptance of biological racial distinction and rejection of biological racial hierarchy was like accepting water and rejecting its wetness. But that is precisely what I learned to do, what so many of us have learned to do in our dueling racial consciousness.

Biological racial difference is one of those widely held racist beliefs that few people realize they hold—nor do they realize that those beliefs are rooted in racist ideas. I grew up hearing about how Black people had "more natural physical ability," as half of respondents replied in a 1991 survey. How "Black blood" differed from "White blood." How "one drop of Negro blood makes a Negro" and "puts out the light of intellect," as wrote Thomas Dixon in *The Leopard's Spots* (1902). How Black people have natural gifts of improvisation. How "if blacks have certain inherited abilities, such as improvisational decision making, that could explain why they predominate in certain fields such as jazz, rap, and basketball, and not in other fields, such as classical music, chess, and astronomy," suggested Dinesh D'Souza in his 1995 book with the laughably dishonest title *The End of Racism*. How Black women had naturally large buttocks and Black men had naturally large penises. How the "increase of rape of white women" stems from the "large size of the negro's penis" and their "birthright" of "sexual madness and excess," as a doctor wrote in a 1903 issue of *Medicine*.

How Black people are biologically distinct because of slavery. At the 1988 American Heart Association conference, a Black hypertension researcher said African Americans had higher hypertension rates because only those able to retain high levels of salt survived consuming the salt water of the Atlantic Ocean during the Middle Passage. "I've bounced this off a number of colleagues and . . . it seems certainly plausible," Clarence Grim told swooning reporters. Plausibility became proof, and the slavery/hypertension thesis received the red carpet in the cardiovascular community in the 1990s. Grim did not arrive at the thesis in his research lab. It came to him as he read *Roots* by Alex Haley. Who needs scientific proof when a biological racial distinction can be imagined by reading fiction? By reading the Bible?

THE SAME BIBLE that taught me that all humans descended from the first pair also argued for immutable human difference, the result of a divine curse. "The people who were scattered over the earth came from Noah's three sons," according to the story of the biblical Great Flood in the ninth chapter of Genesis. Noah planted a vineyard, drank some of its wine, and fell asleep, naked and drunk, in his tent. Ham saw his father's nakedness and alerted his brothers. Shem and Japheth refused to look at Noah's nakedness, walked backward into his tent, and covered him. When Noah awoke, he learned that Ham, the father of Canaan, had viewed him in all his nakedness. "May a curse be put on Canaan," Noah raged. "May Canaan be the slave of Shem."

Who are the cursed descendants of Canaan? In 1578, English travel writer George Best provided an answer that, not coincidentally, justified expanding European enslavement of African people. God willed that Ham's son and "all his posteritie after him should be so blacke and loathsome," Best writes, "that it might remain a spectacle of disobedience to all the worlde."

Racist power at once made biological racial distinction and biological racial hierarchy the components of biological racism. This curse theory lived prominently on the justifying lips of slaveholders until Black chattel slavery died in Christian countries in the nineteenth century. Proof did not matter when biological racial difference could be created by misreading the Bible.

But science can also be misread. After Christopher Columbus discovered a people unmentioned in the Bible, speculations arose about Native Americans and soon about Africans descending from "a different Adam." But Christian Europe regarded polygenesis—the theory that the races are separate species with distinct creations—as heresy. When Isaac La Peyrère released *Men Before Adam* in 1655, Parisian authorities threw him in prison and burned his books. But powerful slaveholders in places like Barbados "preferred" the proslavery belief that there existed a "race of Men, not derivable from Adam" over "the Curse of Ham."

Polygenesis became a source of intellectual debate throughout the Age of Enlightenment. The debate climaxed in the 1770s, during the first transatlantic antislavery movement. In 1776, Thomas Jefferson came down on the side of monogenesis. But over the next few decades, polygenesis came to rule racial thought in the United States through scholars like Samuel Morton and Louis Agassiz, prompting biologist Charles Darwin to write in the opening pages of *The Origin of Species* in 1859, "The view which most naturalists entertain, and which I formerly entertained—namely, that each species has been independently created—is erroneous." He offered a theory of natural selection that was soon used as another method to biologically distinguish and rank the races.

The naturally selected White race was winning the struggle, was evolving, was headed toward perfection, according to social Darwinists. The only three outcomes available for the "weaker" races were extinction, slavery, or assimilation, explained the social Darwinist who founded American sociology. "Many fear the first possibility for the Indians," Albion Small co-wrote in 1894; "the second fate is often predicted for the negroes; while the third is anticipated for the Chinese and other Eastern peoples."

The transatlantic eugenics movement, powered by Darwin's half cousin Francis Galton, aimed to speed up natural selection with policies encouraging reproduction among those with superior genes and re-enslaving or killing their genetic inferiors. Global outrage after the genocidal eugenics-driven policies of Nazi Germany in the mid-twentieth century led to the marginalization of biological racism within academic thought for the first time in four hundred years. Biological racism—curse theory, polygenesis, and eugenics—had held strong for that long. And yet marginalization in academic thought did not mean marginalization in common thought, including the kind of common thinking that surrounded me as a child.

SCIENTISTS AND APPLAUSE accompanied the president of the United States as he walked into the East Room of the White House on June 26, 2000. Bill Clinton took his position behind a podium in the middle of two screens featuring this headline: DECODING THE BOOK OF LIFE / A MILESTONE FOR HUMANITY. Geneticists had started decoding the book of life in 1990, the same year I identified myself in that book as Black.

After thanking politicians and scientists from around the world, Clinton harkened back two hundred years, to the day Thomas Jefferson "spread out a magnificent map" of the continental United States "in this room, on this floor."

"Today, the world is joining us here in the East Room to behold a map of even greater significance," Clinton announced. "We are here to celebrate the completion of the first survey of the entire human genome. Without a doubt, this is the most important, most wondrous map ever produced by humankind." When scientists finished drawing the map of "our miraculous genetic code," when they stepped back and looked at the map, one of the "great truths" they saw was "that in genetic terms, all human beings, regardless of race, are more than 99.9 percent the same," Clinton declared. "What that means is that modern science has confirmed what we first learned from ancient faiths. The most important fact of life on this Earth is our common humanity."

No one told me the defining investigation in modern human

history was unfolding behind the racial wars of the 1990s. It was arguably one of the most important scientific announcements ever made by a sitting head of state—perhaps as important to humans as landing on the moon—but the news of our fundamental equality was quickly overtaken by more-familiar arguments.

"Scientists planning the next phase of the human genome project are being forced to confront a treacherous issue: the genetic differences between human races," science writer Nicholas Wade reported in *The New York Times* not long after Clinton's announcement. In his 2014 bestseller, *A Troublesome Inheritance,* Wade made the case that "there is a genetic component to human social behavior." This connecting of biology to behavior is the cradle of biological racism—it leads to biological ranking of the races and the supposition that the biology of certain races yields superior behavioral traits, like intelligence.

But there is no such thing as racial ancestry. Ethnic ancestry does exist. Camara Jones, a prominent medical researcher of health disparities, explained it this way to bioethics scholar Dorothy Roberts: "People are born with ancestry that comes from their parents but are assigned a race." People from the same ethnic groups that are native to certain geographic regions typically share the same genetic profile. Geneticists call them "populations." When geneticists compare these ethnic populations, they find there is more genetic diversity between populations within Africa than between Africa and the rest of the world. Ethnic groups in Western Africa are more genetically similar to ethnic groups in Western Europe than to ethnic groups in Eastern Africa. Race is a genetic mirage.

Segregationists like Nicholas Wade figure if humans are 99.9 percent genetically alike, then they must be 0.1 percent distinct. And this distinction must be racial. And that 0.1 percent of racial distinction has grown exponentially over the millennia. And it is their job to search heaven and earth for these exponentially distinct races.

Assimilationists have accepted a different job, which has been in the works for decades. "What should we be teaching inside our churches and beyond their four walls?" Christian fundamentalist Ken Ham, the co-author of *One Race One Blood,* asked in an op-ed in 2017. "For one, point out the common ground of both evolutionists and creationists: the mapping of the human genome concluded that there is only one race, the human race."

Singular-race makers push for the end of categorizing and identifying by race. They wag their fingers at people like me identifying as Black—but the unfortunate truth is that their well-meaning post-racial strategy makes no sense in our racist world. Race is a mirage but one that humanity has organized itself around in very real ways. Imagining away the existence of races in a racist world is as conserving and harmful as imagining away classes in a capitalistic world—it allows the ruling races and classes to keep on ruling.

Assimilationists believe in the post-racial myth that talking about race constitutes racism, or that if we stop identifying by race, then racism will miraculously go away. They fail to realize that if we stop using racial categories, then we will not be able to identify racial inequity. If we cannot identify racial inequity, then we will not be able to identify racist policies. If we cannot identify racist policies, then we cannot challenge racist policies. If we cannot challenge racist policies, then racist power's final solution will be achieved: a world of inequity none of us can see, let alone resist. Terminating racial categories is potentially the last, not the first, step in the antiracist struggle.

The segregationist sees six biologically distinct races. The assimilationist sees one biological human race. But there is another way of looking, through the lens of biological antiracism. To be antiracist is to recognize the reality of biological equality, that skin color is as meaningless to our underlying humanity as the clothes we wear over that skin. To be antiracist is to recognize there is no such thing as White blood or Black diseases or natural Latinx athleticism. To be antiracist is to also recognize the living, breathing reality of this racial mirage, which makes our skin colors more meaningful than our individuality. To be antiracist is to focus on ending the racism that shapes the mirages, not to ignore the mirages that shape peoples' lives.

THE PRINCIPAL FINALLY sat down next to me. Maybe she suddenly saw me not as the misbehaving Black boy but as a boy, a student under her care, with a problem. Maybe not. In any case, I was allowed to speak. I defended my dissertation. I did not use terms like "racist abuse" and "racist ideas." I used terms like "fair" and "unfair," "sad" and "happy." She listened and surprised me with questions. My one-boy sit-in ended after she heard me out and agreed to talk to that teacher.

I expected to be punished when the principal summoned Ma that afternoon. After describing what happened, the principal told her my behavior was prohibited at the school. Ma did not say it would never happen again, as the principal expected. Ma told her she would have to speak to me.

"If you are going to protest, then you're going to have to deal with the consequences," Ma said that night, as she would on future nights after my demonstrations.

"Okay," I replied. But no consequences came this time. And the teacher eased up on the non-White students.

Third grade ended it. My parents took me out of that school. One year was enough. They looked for a Christian private school that better validated my racial identity. They found the Black teaching staff at St. Joseph's Parish Day School, an Episcopalian school closer to our home in Queens Village, where I attended fourth, fifth, and sixth grades.

For seventh grade and the yearlong comedy show that kept my eighth-grade classroom filled with laughs and hurt feelings, I transferred to a private Lutheran school around the corner from St. Joseph's. Almost all my Black eighth-grade classmates were jokesters. Almost everyone got joked on for something. But one joke stung more than others.

## CHAPTER 5

# ETHNICITY

**ETHNIC RACISM:** A powerful collection of racist policies that lead to inequity between racialized ethnic groups and are substantiated by racist ideas about racialized ethnic groups.

**ETHNIC ANTIRACISM:** A powerful collection of antiracist policies that lead to equity between racialized ethnic groups and are substantiated by antiracist ideas about racialized ethnic groups.

WE DISSED SPEEDO because he was so uptight. We rode camel jokes on another boy for the divot on the top of his head. We pointed mercilessly at one girl's skyscrapers for legs. "You expecting?" we kept asking the obese boy. "We know you expecting," we kept saying to the obese girl. They renamed me Bonk, after the video-game character whose only weapon was his insanely large head, which made a rhythmic "Bonk. Bonk. Bonk" as he attacked his enemies.

I dished out as many jokes as anyone—the eight-year-old third-grade dissident had turned into a popular teenager with a penchant for cruel jokes. Maybe my empathetic sensibilities would have been rekindled if I'd gotten on the bus and Million Man–marched in Washington, D.C., that fall of 1995. But my father, caring for his ailing sibling, did not take us.

None of us attended that fall's other big event, either: the O. J. Simpson trial in Los Angeles. Two weeks before the Million Man March, I sat in my eighth-grade classroom, waiting patiently with my Black classmates, listening to the radio. When "not guilty" sliced the silence like a cleaver, we leapt from behind our desks, shouting, hugging each other, wanting to call our friends and parents to celebrate. (Too bad we didn't have cellphones.)

Over in Manhattan, my father assembled with his accounting co-workers in a stuffed, stiff, and silent conference room to watch the verdict on television. After the not-guilty verdict was read, my father and his Black co-workers migrated out of the room with grins under their frowns, leaving their baffled White co-workers behind.

Back in my classroom, amid the hugging happiness, I glanced over at my White eighth-grade teacher. Her red face shook as she held back tears, maybe feeling that same overwhelming sensation of hopelessness and discouragement that Black people feel all too many times. I smiled at her—I didn't really care. I wanted O.J. to run free. I had been listening to what the Black adults around me had been lecturing about for months in 1995. They did not think O.J. was innocent of murder any more than they thought he was innocent of selling out his people. But they knew the criminal-justice system was guilty, too. Guilty for freeing the White cops who beat Rodney King in 1991 and the Korean storekeeper who killed fifteen-year-old Latasha Harlins that same year after falsely accusing her of stealing orange juice. But the O.J. verdict didn't stop justice from miscarrying when it came to Black bodies—all kinds of Black bodies. New Yorkers saw it two years later, when NYPD officers inside a Brooklyn police station rammed a wooden stick up the rectum of a thirty-year-old Haitian immigrant named Abner Louima, after viciously beating him on the ride to the station. And two years after that, the justice system freed another group of NYPD officers who'd blasted forty-one bullets at the body of Amadou Diallo, an unarmed twenty-three-year-old immigrant from Guinea. It did not matter if Black people breathed first in the United States or abroad. In the end, racist violence did not differentiate.

But back in my eighth-grade class, my fellow African Americans did differentiate. Kwame probably bore the nastiest beating of jokes. He was popular, funny, good-looking, athletic, and cool—yet his Ghanaian ethnicity trumped all. We relentlessly joked on Kwame like he was Akeem, from the kingdom of Za-munda, and we were Darryl, Lisa's obnoxious boyfriend, in the 1988 romantic comedy *Coming to America*. After all, we lived in Queens, where Akeem came in search of a wife and fell for Lisa in the movie.

In *Coming to America,* Darryl, Lisa, Akeem, and Patrice (Lisa's sister) are sitting in the stands, watching a basketball game. "Wear-ing clothes must be a new experience for you," Darryl quips with a glance at Akeem. An annoyed Lisa, sitting between the two men, changes the subject. Darryl brings it back. "What kind of games do y'all play in Africa? Chase the monkey?" Darryl grins. African Americans in the audience were expected to grin with Darryl and laugh at Akeem. Back in our classrooms, we para-phrased Darryl's jokes about barbaric and animalistic Africans to the Kwames in our midst.

These were racist jokes whose point of origin—the slave trade—was no laughing matter. When Black people make jokes that dehumanize other branches of the African diaspora, we allow that horror story to live again in our laughs. Ethnic racism is the resurrected script of the slave trader.

The origins of ethnic racism can be found in the slave trade's supply-and-demand market for human products. Different en-slavers preferred different ethnic groups in Africa, believing they made better slaves. And the better slaves were considered the bet-ter Africans. Some French planters thought of the Congolese as "magnificent blacks" since they were "born to serve." Other French planters joined with Spanish planters and considered cap-tives from Senegambia "the best slaves." But most planters in the Americas considered the ethnic groups from the Gold Coast— modern-day Ghana—to be "the best and most faithful of our slaves," as relayed by one of Antigua's wealthiest planters and gov-ernors, Christopher Codrington.

Planters and slave traders least valued Angolans, considering them the worst slaves, the lowest step on the ladder of ethnic rac-ism, just above animals. In the 1740s, captives from the Gold Coast were sold for nearly twice as much as captives from Angola.

Maybe Angolans' low value was based on their oversupply: Angolans were traded more than any other African ethnic group. The twenty or so captives hauled into Jamestown, Virginia, in August 1619, beginning African American history, were Angolan.

Planters had no problem devising explanations for their ethnic racism. "The Negroes from the Gold Coast, Popa, and Whydah," wrote one Frenchman, "are born in a part of Africa which is very barren." As a result, "they are obliged to go and cultivate the land for their subsistence" and "have become used to hard labor from their infancy," he wrote. "On the other hand . . . Angola Negroes are brought from those parts of Africa . . . where everything grows almost spontaneously." And so "the men never work but live an indolent life and are in general of a lazy disposition and tender constitution."

My friends and I may have been following an old script when it came to ethnic racism, but our motivations weren't the same as those old planters'. Under our laughs at Kwame and Akeem was probably some anger at continental Africans. "African chiefs were the ones waging war on each other and capturing their own people and selling them," President Yoweri Museveni of Uganda told a 1998 crowd that included President Bill Clinton, taking a page out of African American memory of the slave trade. I still remember an argument I had with some friends in college years later—they told me to leave them alone with my "Africa shit." Those "African motherfuckers sold us down the river," they said. They sold their "own people."

The idea that "African chiefs" sold their "own people" is an anachronistic memory, overlaying our present ideas about race onto an ethnic past. When European intellectuals created race between the fifteenth and eighteenth centuries, lumping diverse ethnic groups into monolithic races, it didn't necessarily change the way the people saw themselves. Africa's residents in the seventeenth and eighteenth centuries didn't look at the various ethnic groups around them and suddenly see them all as one people, as the same race, as African or Black. Africans involved in the slave trade did not believe they were selling their own people—

they were usually selling people as different to them as the Europeans waiting on the coast. Ordinary people in West Africa—like ordinary people in Western Europe—identified themselves in ethnic terms during the life of the slave trade. It took a long time, perhaps until the twentieth century, for race making to cast its pall over the entire globe.

THROUGHOUT THE 1990S, the number of immigrants of color in the United States grew, due to the combined effects of the Immigration and Nationality Act of 1965, the Refugee Act of 1980, and the Immigration Act of 1990. Taken together, these bills encouraged family reunification, immigration from conflict areas, and a diversity visa program that spiked immigration from countries outside Europe. Between 1980 and 2000, the Latinx immigrant population ballooned from 4.2 million to 14.1 million. As of 2015, Black immigrants accounted for 8.7 percent of the nation's Black population, nearly triple their share in 1980. As an early-eighties baby, I witnessed this upsurge of immigrants of color firsthand.

While some African Americans were wary of this immigrant influx from the Black world, my parents were not. A Haitian couple with three boys lived across the street from us, and I befriended the youngest boy, Gil, and his cousin Cliff. I spent many days over there eating rice and peas, fried plantains, and chicken dishes with names I couldn't pronounce. I learned a little Haitian Creole. Gil's father pastored a Haitian church in Flatbush, Brooklyn, the heart of New York's West Indian community. I often joined them for church, taking in large helpings of Haitian American culture along with the day's sermon.

Gil and Cliff held me close, but Gil's parents did not. They were nice and accommodating, but there was always a distance between us. I never felt part of the family, despite how many times I ate at their dinner table. Maybe they kept me at arm's length because I was African American, at a time when Haitian immigrants were feeling the sting of African American bigotry.

Maybe not. Maybe I am making something out of nothing. But that same feeling recurred in other encounters. West Indian immigrants tend to categorize African Americans as "lazy, unambitious, uneducated, unfriendly, welfare-dependent, and lacking in family values," Mary C. Waters found in her 1999 interview-rich study of West Indian attitudes. African Americans tended to categorize West Indians as "selfish, lacking in race awareness, being lackeys of whites, and [having] a sense of inflated superiority."

I grew up with different kinds of Black people all around me—I never knew anything else. But being surrounded by Black immigrants was new for my parents' and grandparents' generations.

The loosening immigration laws of the 1960s through 1990s were designed to undo a previous generation of immigration laws that limited non-White immigration to the United States. The 1882 Chinese Restriction Act was extended to an even broader act, encompassing a larger "Asiatic Barred Zone," in 1917. The 1921 Emergency Quota Act and the Immigration Act of 1924 severely restricted the immigration of people from Africa and Eastern and Southern Europe and practically banned the immigration of Asians until 1965. "America must be kept American," President Calvin Coolidge said when he signed the 1924 law. Of course, by then "American" included millions of Negro, Asian, Native, Middle Eastern, and Latinx peoples (who would, at least in the case of Mexican Americans, be forcibly repatriated to Mexico by the hundreds of thousands). But Coolidge and congressional supporters determined that only immigrants from northeastern Europe—Scandinavia, the British Isles, Germany— could keep America American, meaning White. The United States "was a mighty land settled by northern Europeans from the United Kingdom, the Norsemen, and the Saxon," proclaimed Maine representative Ira Hersey, to applause, during debate over the Immigration Act of 1924.

Nearly a century later, U.S. senator Jeff Sessions lamented the growth of the non-native-born population. "When the numbers reached about this high in 1924, the president and Congress changed the policy. And it slowed down significantly," he told Breitbart's Steve Bannon in 2015. "We then assimilated through to 1965 and created really the solid middle class of America with assimilated immigrants. And it was good for America." A year later, as attorney general, Sessions began carrying out the Trump administration's anti-Latinx, anti-Arab, and anti–Black immigrant policies geared toward making America White again. "We should have more people from places like Norway," Trump told lawmakers in 2018. There were already enough people of color like me, apparently.

THE CURRENT ADMINISTRATION's throwback to early-twentieth-century immigration policies—built on racist ideas of what constitutes an American—were meant to roll back the years of immigration that saw America dramatically diversify, including a new diversity within its Black population, which now included Africans and West Indians in addition to the descendants of American slaves. But regardless of where they came from, they were all racialized as Black.

The fact is, all ethnic groups, once they fall under the gaze and power of race makers, become racialized. I am a descendant of American slaves. My ethnic group is African American. My race, as an African American, is Black. Kenyans are racialized as a Black ethnic group, while Italians are White, Japanese are Asian, Syrians are Middle Eastern, Puerto Ricans are Latinx, and Choctaws are Native American. The racializing serves the core mandate of race: to create hierarchies of value.

Across history, racist power has produced racist ideas about the racialized ethnic groups in its colonial sphere and ranked them—across the globe and within their own nations. The history of the United States offers a parade of intra-racial ethnic power relationships: Anglo-Saxons discriminating against Irish Catholics and Jews; Cuban immigrants being privileged over Mexican immigrants; the model-minority construction that includes East Asians and excludes Muslims from South Asia. It's a history that began with early European colonizers referring to the Cherokee, Chickasaw, Choctaw, Creek, and Seminole as the "Five Civilized Tribes" of Native Americans, as compared to other "wild" tribes. This ranking of racialized ethnic groups within the ranking of the races creates a racial-ethnic hierarchy, a ladder of ethnic racism within the larger schema of racism.

We practice ethnic racism when we express a racist idea about an ethnic group or support a racist policy toward an ethnic group. Ethnic racism, like racism itself, points to group behavior, instead of policies, as the cause of disparities between groups. When Ghanaian immigrants to the United States join with White Americans and say African Americans are lazy, they are recycling the racist ideas of White Americans about African Americans. This is ethnic racism.

The face of ethnic racism bares itself in the form of a persistent question:

"Where are you from?"

I am often asked this question by people who see me through the lens of ethnic racism. Their ethnic racism presumes I—a college professor and published writer—cannot be a so-called lowly, lazy, lackluster African American.

"I am from Queens, New York," I respond.

"No, no, where are you really from?"

"I am really from New York."

Frustrated, the person slightly alters the line of inquiry. "Where are your parents from?" When I say, "My dad's family is from New York, and my ma's family is from Georgia," the questioner freezes up in confusion. When I add, "I am a descendant of enslaved Africans in the United States," the questions cease. They finally have to resign themselves to the fact that I am an African American. Perhaps the next move is for the person to look at me as extraordinary—not like those ordinary inferior African Americans—so they can leave quietly, their ethnic-racist lens intact.

But sometimes they do not leave quietly. Sometimes they take the opportunity to lecture down at my ethnic group, like a bold

Ghanaian student early in my professorial career in upstate New York. He delivered a monologue to a classroom full of African Americans that touched on everything from our laziness to our dependence on welfare. I offered data that disproved his ethnic racism—e.g., the facts that the majority of Americans on welfare are not African American and the majority of African Americans eligible for welfare refuse it. But he held tightly to his ethnic racism and spoke on as the snickering of the African American students slowly turned to anger (while many of the children of Black immigrants remained quiet). To calm my African American students, I recited the ethnically racist ideas African Americans express about West Africans, to show them that the absurdity of ethnic racism is universal. It backfired. They all started nodding their heads to the litany of stereotypes about African immigrants.

To be antiracist is to view national and transnational ethnic groups as equal in all their differences. To be antiracist is to challenge the racist policies that plague racialized ethnic groups across the world. To be antiracist is to view the inequities between all racialized ethnic groups as a problem of policy.

The Ghanaian student confronted me after class as I packed up (and as some of his African American classmates glared sharply at him while leaving the room). When he finished his second monologue to me, I asked if he minded answering some questions. He agreed to. I really just wanted to keep him talking to me for a while longer, in case there were any angry students still waiting for him outside the classroom. Fights—or worse—were occasionally erupting between Black ethnic groups in New York, just as they had a century prior between White ethnic groups.

"What are some of the racist ideas the British say about Ghanaians?" I asked.

He offered a blank stare before blurting out, "I don't know."

"Yes, you do. Tell me some. It's okay."

He was silent for a moment and then started speaking again, now much more slowly and nervously than in his earlier rants, seemingly wondering where this was going. When he finished listing racist ideas, I spoke again.

"Now, are those ideas true?" I asked. "Are the British superior to Ghanaians?"

"No!" he said proudly. I was proud, too, that he had not internalized these racist ideas about his own racialized ethnic group.

"When African Americans repeat British racist ideas about Ghanaians, do you defend your people?"

"Yes. Because they are not true!"

"So these ideas about African Americans: Who did you get these ideas from?"

He thought. "My family, my friends, and my observations," he said.

"Who do you think your fellow Ghanaian Americans got these ideas about African Americans from?"

He thought much longer this time. From the side of his eye he saw another student waiting to speak to me, which seemed to rush his thoughts—he was a polite kid in spite of his urge to lecture. But I did not rush him. The other student was Jamaican and listening intently, maybe thinking about who Jamaicans got their ideas about Haitians from.

"Probably American Whites," he said, looking me straight in the eye for the first time.

His mind seemed open, so I jumped on in. "So if African Americans went to Ghana, consumed British racist ideas about Ghanaians, and started expressing those ideas to Ghanaians, what would Ghanaians think about that? What would you think about that?"

He smiled, surprising me. "I got it," he said, turning to walk out of the classroom.

"Are you sure?" I said, raising my voice over the Jamaican student's head.

He turned back to me. "Yes, sir. Thanks, Prof."

I respected him for his willingness to reflect on his own hypocrisy. And I didn't want to overreact when he trashed African Americans, because I knew where he was coming from: I had been there myself. When I learned the history of ethnic racism, of African Americans commonly degrading Africans as "barbaric" or routinely calling West Indians in 1920s Harlem "monkey chasers"—or when I remembered my own taunts of Kwame back in eighth grade—I tried not to run away from the hypocrisy, either. How can I get upset at immigrants from Africa and South America for looking down on African Americans when African Americans have historically looked down on immigrants from Africa and South America? How can I critique their ethnic racism and ignore my ethnic racism? That is the central double standard in ethnic racism: loving one's position on the ladder above other ethnic groups and hating one's position below that of other ethnic groups. It is angrily trashing the racist ideas about one's own group but happily consuming the racist ideas about other ethnic groups. It is failing to recognize that racist ideas we consume about others came from the same restaurant and the same cook who used the same ingredients to make different degrading dishes for us all.

WHEN STUDIES STARTED to show that the median family income of African Americans was far lower than that of foreign-born Blacks and that African Americans had higher rates of poverty and unemployment, numerous commentators wondered why Black immigrants do so much better than Blacks born in America. They also answered their own questions: Black immigrants are more motivated, more hardworking, and "more entrepreneurial than native-born blacks," wrote one commentator in *The Economist* in 1996. Their success shows "that racism does not account for all, or even most, of the difficulties encountered by native-born blacks."

Ethnically racist ideas, like all racist ideas, cover up the racist policies wielded against Black natives and immigrants. Whenever Black immigrants compare their economic standing to that of Black natives, whenever they agree that their success stories show that antiracist Americans are overstating racist policies against African Americans, they are tightening the handcuffs of racist policy around their own wrists. Black immigrants' comparisons with

Black natives conceal the racial inequities between Black immigrants and non-Black immigrants.

Despite studies showing Black immigrants are, on average, the most educated group of immigrants in the United States, they earn lower wages than similarly trained non-Black immigrants and have the highest unemployment rate of any immigrant group. An ethnic racist asks, Why are Black immigrants doing better than African Americans? An ethnic antiracist asks, Why are Black immigrants not doing as well as other immigrant groups?

The reason Black immigrants generally have higher educational levels and economic pictures than African Americans is not that their transnational ethnicities are superior. The reason resides in the circumstances of human migration. Not all individuals migrate, but those who do, in what's called "immigrant self-selection," are typically individuals with an exceptional internal drive for material success and/or they possess exceptional external resources. Generally speaking, individual Black and Latinx and Asian and Middle Eastern and European immigrants are uniquely resilient and resourceful—not because they are Nigerian or Cuban or Japanese or Saudi Arabian or German but because they are immigrants. In fact, immigrants and migrants of all races tend to be more resilient and resourceful when compared with the natives of their own countries and the natives of their new countries. Sociologists call this the "migrant advantage." As sociologist Suzanne Model explained in her book on West Indian immigrants, "West Indians are not a black success story but an *immigrant* success story." As such, policies from those of Calvin Coolidge to Donald Trump's limiting immigration to the United States from China or Italy or Senegal or Haiti or Mexico have been self-destructive to the country. With ethnic racism, no one wins, except the racist power at the top. As with all racism, that is the entire point.

THERE WERE NO winners in eighth grade, either. In class, I'd randomly shout, *"Ref!"* A friend would scream, *"Uuuuuu!"* Another friend would scream, *"Geeeeee!"* And the whole class of African Americans would burst out laughing as the three of us pointed at Kwame and chanted, *"Ref-u-gee! Ref-u-gee! Ref-u-gee!"* The smirking White teacher would tell us to be quiet. Kwame would break the quietness with defensive jokes. The cycle would repeat, day after day.

Kwame never seemed to let the jokes bother him. In that way, he resembled Akeem in *Coming to America,* a prince so powerful, so sophisticated, so self-assured, that he was able to ignore demeaning jokes like an elite athlete ignoring a hostile crowd. Kwame had a smugness about him that maybe, subconsciously, we were trying to shatter by pulling him down to earth. As scholar Rosemary Traoré found in a study of an urban high school, "African students wondered why their fellow African American brothers and sisters treated them as second-class citizens, while the African Americans wondered why the African students [seemed] to feel or act so superior to them." The tensions created by ethnic racism didn't produce any winners, just confusion and hurt on both sides.

Don't get me wrong, Kwame joked back. Kwame and others never let me forget that I had a big-ass head. I never knew why. My head wasn't that big—maybe a little out of proportion.

But a high school growth spurt was coming.

CHAPTER 6

# BODY

**BODILY RACIST:** One who is perceiving certain racialized bodies as more animal-like and violent than others.

**BODILY ANTIRACIST:** One who is humanizing, deracializing, and individualizing nonviolent and violent behavior.

DONE. FINISHED WEARING uniforms. Through with attending chapel service. The older I became, the more I despised the conformity of private schooling and churching. After eighth grade, I was finally free of them. I enrolled in John Bowne High School, a public school that my Haitian neighbor Gil attended. It was in Flushing, in central Queens, just across the street from Queens College. We bathed in the ambient noise of the nearby Long Island Expressway.

In the mid-1950s, public-housing authorities allowed my grandmother to move into the predominantly White Pomonok Houses, due south of John Bowne. Dad went through all of his local elementary schooling in the late 1950s without noticing another Black student, only the kids of working-class White families, who were even then fixing to flee to suburban Long Island. By 1996 they were nearly all gone.

After school, John Bowne students jammed into public buses like clothes jammed into a drawer. As my bus made its way toward Southside Queens, it slowly emptied. On this day, I stood near the back door, facing a teenage boy we called Smurf, a nickname he earned from his short, skinny frame, blue-black skin, thick ears, and big round eyes that nearly met in the center of his face.

As I stood near him, Smurf reached into his pants and pulled out a black pistol. He stared at it and I stared at it, too. Everyone did. Smurf looked up and pointed the gun—loaded or unloaded?—directly at me. "You scared, yo?" he asked with almost brotherly warmth, a smirk resting on his face.

"BLACKS MUST UNDERSTAND and acknowledge the roots of White fear in America," President Bill Clinton said in a speech on October 16, 1995, the same day as the Million Man March. He'd escaped the march and the Black men assembling practically on the White House lawn for the campus of the University of Texas. "There is a legitimate fear of the violence that is too prevalent in our urban areas," he added. "By experience or at least what people see on the news at night, violence for those White people too often has a Black face."

History tells the same story: Violence for White people really has too often had a Black face—and the consequences have landed on the Black body across the span of American history. In 1631, Captain John Smith warned the first English colonizers of New England that the Black body was as devilish as any people in the world. Boston pastor Cotton Mather preached compliance to slavery in 1696: Do not "make yourself infinitely Blacker than you are already." Virginia lieutenant-governor Hugh Drysdale spoke of "the Cruel disposition of those Creatures" who planned a freedom revolt in 1723. Seceding Texas legislators in 1861 complained of not receiving more federal "appropriations for protecting . . . against ruthless savages." U.S. senator Benjamin Tillman told his colleagues in 1903, "The poor African has become a fiend, a wild beast, seeking whom he may devour." Two leading criminologists posited in 1967 that the "large . . . criminal display of the violence among minority groups such as Negroes" stems from their "subculture-of-violence." Manhattan Institute fellow

Heather Mac Donald wrote "The core criminal-justice population is the black underclass" in *The War on Cops* in 2016.

This is the living legacy of racist power, constructing the Black race biologically and ethnically and presenting the Black body to the world first and foremost as a "beast," to use Gomes de Zurara's term, as violently dangerous, as the dark embodiment of evil. Americans today see the Black body as larger, more threatening, more potentially harmful, and more likely to require force to control than a similarly sized White body, according to researchers. No wonder the Black body had to be lynched by the thousands, deported by the tens of thousands, incarcerated by the millions, segregated by the tens of millions.

WHEN I FIRST picked up a basketball, at around eight years old, I also picked up on my parents' fears for my Black body. My parents hated when I played ball at nearby parks, worried I'd get shot, and tried to discourage me by warning me of the dangers waiting for me out there. In their constant fearmongering about Black drug dealers, robbers, killers, they nurtured in me a fear of my own Black neighbors. When I proposed laying concrete in our grassy backyard and putting up a basketball hoop there, my father built a court faster than a house flipper, a nicer one than the courts at nearby parks. But the new basketball court could not keep me away from my own dangerous Black body. Or from Smurf on the bus.

"NAW, YO," I coolly responded to Smurf's question about my fear. My eyes locked on the gun.

"Whatever, man," he snickered. "You scared, yo." Then he jammed the gun in my ribs and offered a hard smile.

I looked him straight in the eye, scared as hell. "Naw, yo," I said, giggling a little, "but that's a nice piece, though."

"It is, ain't it?"

Satisfied, Smurf turned, gun in hand, and looked for somebody else to scare. I exhaled relief but knew I could have been harmed that day, as I could have other days. Especially, I thought, inside John Bowne High School, surrounded by other Black and Latinx and Asian teens.

Moving through John Bowne's hallways, eyes sharper than my pencils, I avoided stepping on new sneakers like they were land mines (though when I did accidentally step on one, nothing exploded). I avoided bumping into people, worried a bump could become a hole in my head (though when I did inevitably bump into someone, my head stayed intact). I avoided making eye contact, as if my classmates were wolves (though when I did, my body did not get attacked). I avoided crews, fearing they would flock at me at any moment (though when I did have to pass through a crew, I didn't get jumped). What could happen based on my deepest fears mattered more than what did happen to me. I believed violence was stalking me—but in truth I was being stalked inside my own head by racist ideas.

Crews ran my high school—like crews run America—and I considered joining the Zulu Nation, awed by its history and reach. Witnessing an initiation changed my mind. The perverse mix of punches and stomps, handshakes and hugs, turned me off. But I did have an informal crew, bound by an ironclad loyalty that required us to fight for each other, should the occasion arise.

One day we met another crew on a block near the Long Island Expressway—maybe five of us and fifteen of them, all staring menacingly at each other as we approached. This was new to me, the showdown, the curses flying and landing, the escalating displays of anger. Threats slamming like fists. I was in the mix with the rest of them—but passing drivers glancing over could not see that I was fighting my nervousness more than anything.

One threat led to another. No one rushed me, as small and unassuming as I was. I saw big Gil fighting off punches. I wanted to help him, but then I saw a tall, skinny, solitary teen looking around nervously. He reminded me of myself. I crept up behind him and jump-threw a vicious right hook. He went down hard on the pavement and I skittered off. Soon we heard sirens and scattered like ants, fearful of getting smashed by the NYPD.

WE WERE UNARMED, but we knew that Blackness armed us even though we had no guns. Whiteness disarmed the cops—turned them into fearful potential victims—even when they were approaching a group of clearly outstrapped and anxious high school kids. Black people comprise 13 percent of the U.S. population. And yet, in 2015, Black bodies accounted for at least 26 percent of those killed by police, declining slightly to 24 percent in 2016, 22 percent in 2017, and 21 percent in 2018, according to *The Washington Post*. Unarmed Black bodies—which apparently look armed to fearful officers—are about twice as likely to be killed as unarmed White bodies.

Gil and I ran over the Long Island Expressway overpass and hopped onto a departing bus, feeling lucky, catching our breath. I could have gone to jail, or worse, that day.

More than the times I risked jail, I am still haunted by the times I did not help the victims of violence. My refusal to help them jailed me in fear. I was as scared of the Black body as the White body was scared of me. I could not muster the strength to do right. Like that time on another packed bus after school. A small Indian teen—tinier than me!—sat near me at the back of the bus that day. My seat faced the back door, and the Indian teen sat in the single seat right next to the back door. I kept staring at him, trying to catch his eye so I could give him a nod that would direct him to the front of the bus. I saw other Black and Indian kids on the bus trying to do the same with their eyes. We wanted so badly for him to move. But he was fixated on whatever was playing on his fresh new Walkman. His eyes were closed and his head bobbed.

Smurf and his boys were on the bus that day, too. For the moment, they were blocked from the Indian teen by the bodies of other kids—they couldn't see him sitting there. But when the bus cleared enough for them to have a clear lane to him, Smurf, as expected, focused in on the thing we didn't want him to see.

He did not have his pistol that day. Or maybe he did.

Smurf motioned to his boys and stood up. He walked a few feet and stood over the Indian teen, his back to me, his head turned to face his boys.

"What the fuck!"

He pointed his finger, gun-like, at the seated teen's head. "Look at this motherfucker!"

IN 1993, A bipartisan group of White legislators introduced the Violent Crime Control and Law Enforcement Act. They were thinking about Smurf—and me. The Congressional Black Caucus was also thinking about Smurf and me. They asked for $2 billion more in the act for drug treatment and $3 billion more for violence-prevention programs. When Republicans called those items "welfare for criminals" and demanded they be scaled back for their votes, Democratic leaders caved. Twenty-six of the thirty-eight voting members of the Congressional Black Caucus caved, too. After all, the bill reflected their fear for my Black body—and of it. The policy decision reflected their dueling consciousness—and their practical desire to not lose the prevention funding entirely in a rewrite of the bill. On top of its new prisons, capital offenses, minimum sentences, federal three-strike laws, police officers, and police weaponry, the law made me eligible, when I turned thirteen in 1995, to be tried as an adult. "Never again should Washington put politics and party above law and order," President Bill Clinton said upon signing the bipartisan, biracial bill on September 13, 1994.

"YO, NIGGA, RUN that Walkman," Smurf said rather gently. The kid did not look up, still captivated by the beat coming from his headphones. Smurf punch-tapped him on the shoulder. "Yo, nigga, run that Walkman," he shouted.

I wanted to stand up and yell, "Leave that nigga alone. Why you always fucking with people, Smurf? What the fuck is wrong with you?" But my fear caged me. I remained seated and quiet.

The kid finally looked up, startled. "What!" The shock of Smurf looming over him and the loudness of the music made him raise his voice. I shook my head but without shaking my head. I remained still.

CLINTON DEMOCRATS THOUGHT they had won the political turf war to own crime as an issue—to war on the Black body for votes. But it took little time for racist Americans to complain that even the most expensive crime bill in human history was not enough to stop the beast, the devil, the gun, Smurf, me. Around Thanksgiving in 1995, Princeton political scientist John J. DiIulio Jr. warned of the "coming of the super-predators," especially young bodies like mine in "Black inner-city neighborhoods." DiIulio later said he regretted using the term. But DiIulio never had to internalize this racist idea and look at his own body in fear. He never had to deal with being hunted. My friends at John Bowne did. I did. In 1996, I turned fourteen. A super-predator was growing in me, in Smurf, they said. I believed what I heard.

"Most inner-city children grow up surrounded by teenagers and adults who are themselves deviant, delinquent or criminal," DiIulio wrote. Watch out. "A new generation of street criminals is upon us—the youngest, biggest and baddest generation any society has ever known," he warned. My band of "juvenile 'super-predators'" were "radically impulsive, brutally remorseless youngsters, including ever more preteenage boys, who murder, assault, rape, rob, burglarize, deal deadly drugs, join gun-toting gangs and create serious communal disorders." We, the young Black super-predators, were apparently being raised with an unprecedented inclination toward violence—in a nation that presumably did not raise White slaveholders, lynchers, mass incarcerators, police officers, corporate officials, venture capitalists, financiers, drunk drivers, and war hawks to be violent.

This swarm of super-predators never materialized in the late 1990s. Violent crime had already begun its dramatic decline by the time I stared at Smurf demanding that Walkman in 1996. Homicides had dropped to their lowest levels since the Reagan era, when intense crack-market competition and unregulated gun trafficking spiked the rate.

But crime bills have never correlated to crime any more than fear has correlated to actual violence. We are not meant to fear suits with policies that kill. We are not meant to fear good White males with AR-15s. No, we are to fear the weary, unarmed Latinx body from Latin America. The Arab body kneeling to Allah is to be feared. The Black body from hell is to be feared. Adept politicians and crime entrepreneurs manufacture the fear and stand before voters to deliver them—messiahs who will liberate them from fear of these other bodies.

"NIGGA, YOU DIDN'T hear me!" Smurf fumed. "I said run that fucking Walkman!"

In my mind I tried to devise a strategy for the poor kid, imagining myself in his place. I had a bit of a gift for staying calm and defusing potentially volatile situations, which served me well whether I was dealing with the violently finicky Smurfs of the world or capriciously violent police officers. I learned to disarm or avoid the Smurfs around town—kids bent on mayhem. But I also saw that strangers were doing the same calculations when they saw me coming—I'd see the fear in their eyes. They'd see me and decide they were looking at Smurf. We scared them just the same—all they saw were our dangerous Black bodies. Cops seemed especially fearful. Just as I learned to avoid the Smurfs of the world, I had to learn to keep racist police officers from getting nervous. Black people are apparently responsible for calming the fears of violent cops in the way women are supposedly responsible for calming the sexual desires of male rapists. If we don't, then we are blamed for our own assaults, our own deaths.

But at that point, the kid across from me was out of options—

there was probably no way to defuse the situation. "Run that fucking Walkman!" Smurf yelled, now turning heads at the front of the bus and most likely prompting the bus driver to call the ruckus in. The shocked teen started to stand up, saying nothing, just shaking his head. He probably intended to relocate to the front, near the relative safety of the bus driver. But as soon as he straightened his body, Smurf landed a side haymaker to the kid's temple—his head bounced into the window and then onto the bus's floor. Smurf snatched the tumbling Walkman, and then his boys got up to join in. The kid covered his face when the stomps from Timberland boots came pummeling down. It all happened right in front of me. I did nothing. I did nothing.

The bus stopped. The back door opened. Smurf and his boys leapt off and ran away, lighthearted, grinning. But I noticed that four-eyes from Smurf's crew remained on the bus, lurking and looking, seemingly waiting for somebody to help this kid laid out in agony. I did nothing.

THE RESPONSIBILITY OF keeping myself safe followed me like the stray dogs in my neighborhood, barking fear into my consciousness. I never wanted to arrive home to my parents with empty pockets and no shoes, with a leaking, beaten body like the Indian kid. Or worse, no arrival at all, only a letter from the police reporting my murder, or a phone call from the hospital. I convinced my parents (or so I thought) I was safe. But I did not convince myself. The acts of violence I saw from Smurf and others combined with the racist ideas all around me to convince me that more violence lurked than there actually was. I believed that violence didn't define just Smurf but all the Black people around me, my school, my neighborhood. I believed it defined me—that I should fear all darkness, up to and including my own Black body.

Those of us Black writers who grew up in "inner city" Black neighborhoods too often recall the violence we experienced more than the nonviolence. We don't write about all those days we were not faced with guns in our ribs. We don't retell all those days we did not fight, the days we didn't watch someone get beaten in front of us. We become exactly like the nightly local-news shows—if it bleeds, it leads—and our stories center on violent Black bodies instead of the overwhelming majority of nonviolent Black bodies. In 1993, near the height of urban violent crime, for every thousand urban residents, seventy-four, or 7.4 percent, reported being victims of violent crime, a percentage that declined further thereafter. In 2016, for every thousand urban residents, about thirty, or 3 percent, reported being victims of violent crimes. These numbers are not precise. Researchers estimate that more than half of violent crimes from 2006 to 2010 went unreported to law enforcement. And even being around violent crime can create adverse effects. But the idea that directly experienced violence is endemic and everywhere, affecting everyone, or even most people—that Black neighborhoods, as a whole, are more dangerous than "war zones," to use President Trump's term—is not reality.

It all makes sense that this is the story we so often tell—the fist-swinging and gunshots and early deaths cling to us like a second skin, while the hugs and dances and good times fall away. But the writer's work reflects, and the reader consumes, those vivid, searing memories, not the everyday lived reality of the Black body.

As many moments as I had of anxiety and fear from other Black bodies, I probably lived many more moments in serenity and peace. As much as I feared that violence stalked me, my daily life was not organized around that fear. I played baseball for years with White kids on Long Island and always wondered why they never wanted to visit my neighborhood, my home. When I would ask, the looks of horror on their faces, and even more on their parents' faces, startled and confused me. I knew there were dangers on my block; I also thought it was safe.

I did not connect the whole or even most of Southside Queens with violence, just as I did not connect all or even most of my Black neighbors with violence. Certain people like Smurf, cer-

tain blocks, and certain neighborhoods I knew to avoid. But not because they were Black—we were almost all Black. I knew in a vague way that Black neighborhoods with high-rise public housing like 40P (the South Jamaica Houses) or Baisley Park Houses were known to be more violent than neighborhoods like mine, Queens Village, with more single-family homes, but I never really thought about why. But I knew it wasn't Blackness—Blackness was a constant.

A study that used National Longitudinal Survey of Youth data from 1976 to 1989 found that young Black males engaged in more violent crime than young White males. But when the researchers compared only employed young males of both races, the differences in violent behavior vanished. Or, as the Urban Institute stated in a more recent report on long-term unemployment, "Communities with a higher share of long-term unemployed workers also tend to have higher rates of crime and violence."

Another study found that the 2.5 percent decrease in unemployment between 1992 and 1997 resulted in a decrease of 4.3 percent for robbery, 2.5 percent for auto theft, 5 percent for burglary, and 3.7 percent for larceny. Sociologist Karen F. Parker strongly linked the growth of Black-owned businesses to a reduction in Black youth violence between 1990 and 2000. In recent years, the University of Chicago Crime Lab worked with the One Summer Chicago Plus jobs program and found a 43 percent reduction in violent-crime arrests for Black youths who worked eight-week-long part-time summer jobs, compared with a control group of teens who did not.

In other words, researchers have found a much stronger and clearer correlation between violent-crime levels and unemployment levels than between violent crime and race. Black neighborhoods do not all have similar levels of violent crime. If the cause of the violent crime is the Black body, if Black people are violent demons, then the violent-crime levels would be relatively the same no matter where Black people live. But Black upper-income and middle-income neighborhoods tend to have less violent crime than Black low-income neighborhoods—as is the case in non-Black communities. But that does not mean low-income Black people are more violent than high-income Black people. That means low-income neighborhoods struggle with unemployment and poverty—and their typical byproduct, violent crime.

For decades, there have been three main strategies in reducing violent crime in Black neighborhoods. Segregationists who consider Black neighborhoods to be war zones have called for tough policing and the mass incarceration of super-predators. Assimilationists say these super-predators need tough laws and tough love from mentors and fathers to civilize them back to nonviolence. Antiracists say Black people, like all people, need more higher-paying jobs within their reach, especially Black youngsters, who have consistently had the highest rates of unemployment of any demographic group, topping 50 percent in the mid-1990s.

There is no such thing as a dangerous racial group. But there are, of course, dangerous individuals like Smurf. There is the violence of racism—manifest in policy and policing—that fears the Black body. And there is the nonviolence of antiracism that does not fear the Black body, that fears, if anything, the violence of the racism that has been set on the Black body.

Perceptions of danger and actual threats met me each day at John Bowne, in various forms. There was the dangerous disinterest of some teachers. Or the school's dangerous overcrowding: three thousand students packed into a school built for far fewer. The classes were so large—twice as large as in my private schools—that detached students like me were able to hold our own back-of-the-room classes before detached teachers. I do not remember a single teacher or class or lesson or assignment from ninth grade. I was checked out—following the lead of most of the teachers, administrators, and politicians who were ostensibly in charge of my education. I attended John Bowne like someone who clocked in to his job with no intention of working. I only worked hard on my first love.

# CULTURE

**CULTURAL RACIST:** One who is creating a cultural standard and imposing a cultural hierarchy among racial groups.

**CULTURAL ANTIRACIST:** One who is rejecting cultural standards and equalizing cultural differences among racial groups.

M Y DAD DRAGGED me to see the 1994 documentary *Hoop Dreams,* a film about the perils of two young boys pursuing the exceedingly unlikely possibility of a lucrative NBA career. His intervention failed, like the dreams of the kids in the film. For me, basketball was life.

It was a cool early-winter day in 1996 and I sat warm in the locker room after practice, getting dressed and exchanging jokes with my new teammates on John Bowne's junior-varsity basketball team. Suddenly, our White coach burst into the locker room like something was wrong. We muted the jokes as he looked hopelessly at our dark faces. He leaned against a locker as if a lecture was building up inside him.

"You all need to post two Cs and three Ds to remain on the team. Okay? Okay?" Everyone nodded or stared back, perhaps expecting more. But that was all he had to say. Our jokes resumed again.

I had neither loved nor hated middle school. But a few months in high school had changed me. I cannot pinpoint what triggered my hatred of school. My difficulty separating the harassing cop from the harassing teacher? A heightened sensitivity to the glares from teachers who saw my Black body not as a plant to be cultivated but as a weed to be plucked out of their school and thrown into their prison? Freshman year I posted what grades I needed to stay on the basketball team: two Cs and three Ds. Only basketball and parental shame stopped me from dropping out and staying home all day like some other teens.

When I climbed onto the crowded public buses after school, I felt like a runaway. Most days, Smurf was nowhere to be found. Stopping and going, the bus headed south, until the last stop—my cultural home away from home.

We called the central artery of Southside Queens the Ave, the place where Jamaica Avenue crosses 164th Street. On weekends, I'd walk out of my house, strut a block up 209th Street to Jamaica Avenue, and hail a dollar cab down those three dozen blocks to the Ave. One dollar, one ride, one random driver. Little did I know, similar privately run cheap cars or vans, stuffed with sweating and content and tired and recharged and traumatized Black bodies, were hurrying through neighborhoods all over the Black world. I have since traveled on these fast-moving cultural products in other parts of the world, from Ghana to Jamaica (the island nation, not the Ave). The ride always takes me back to Queens.

Nothing compared to arriving at the Ave. A couple dozen city blocks lined with stores, this enormous shopping district was crowded with wide-eyed teens. We never knew what we were going to see—what kicks (sneakers) were going to be on sale; what beef (conflict) was going to be cooking; what guads (boys) and shorties (girls) were going to be rocking (wearing). Excuse my Ebonics—a term coined by psychologist Robert Williams in 1973 to replace racist terms like "Nonstandard Negro English." I must use the language of the culture to express the culture.

Some Americans despised my Ebonics in 1996. In that year the Oakland school board recognized Black people like me as bilingual, and in an act of cultural antiracism recognized "the legitimacy and richness" of Ebonics as a language. They resolved to use Ebonics with students "to facilitate their acquisition and mas-

tery of English language skills." The reaction was fierce. Jesse Jackson at first called it "an unacceptable surrender, bordering on disgrace. It's teaching down to our children."

Was it? It helps to dig back into the origins of Ebonics. Enslaved Africans formulated new languages in nearly every European colony in the Americas, including African American Ebonics, Jamaican Patois, Haitian Creole, Brazilian Calunga, and Cubano. In every one of these countries, racist power—those in control of government, academia, education, and media—has demeaned these African languages as dialects, as "broken" or "improper" or "nonstandard" French, Spanish, Dutch, Portuguese, or English. Assimilationists have always urged Africans in the Americas to forget the "broken" languages of our ancestors and master the apparently "fixed" languages of Europeans—to speak "properly." But what was the difference between Ebonics and so-called "standard" English? Ebonics had grown from the roots of African languages and modern English just as modern English had grown from Latin, Greek, and Germanic roots. Why is Ebonics broken English but English is not broken German? Why is Ebonics a dialect of English if English is not a dialect of Latin? The idea that Black languages outside Africa are broken is as culturally racist as the idea that languages inside Europe are fixed.


WHEN THE REACTION to the Nazi Holocaust marginalized biological racism, cultural racism stepped into its place. "In practically all its divergences," African American culture "is a distorted development, or a pathological condition, of the general American culture," Gunnar Myrdal wrote in *An American Dilemma,* his 1944 landmark treatise on race relations, which has been called the "bible" of the civil-rights movement. Myrdal's scripture standardized the general (White) American culture, then judged African American culture as distorted or pathological from that standard. Whoever makes the cultural standard makes the cultural hierarchy. The act of making a cultural standard and hierarchy is what creates cultural racism.

To be antiracist is to reject cultural standards and level cultural difference. Segregationists say racial groups cannot reach their superior cultural standard. Assimilationists say racial groups can, with effort and intention, reach their superior cultural standards. "It is to the advantage of American Negroes as individuals and as a group to become assimilated into American culture" and "to acquire the traits held in esteem by the dominant white Americans," Myrdal suggested. Or, as President Theodore Roosevelt said in 1905, the goal should be to assimilate "the backward race . . . so it may enter into the possession of true freedom, while the forward race is enabled to preserve unharmed the high civilization wrought out by its forefathers."

Even Alexander Crummell, the stately Episcopalian priest who founded the first formal Black intellectual society in 1897, urged his fellow Black Americans to assimilate. He agreed with those racist Americans who classed Africans as fundamentally imitative. "This quality of imitation has been the grand preservative of the Negro in all the lands of his thraldom," Crummell preached in 1877.

WE CERTAINLY WEREN'T imitating anything on the Ave—to the contrary. The wider culture was avidly imitating and appropriating from us; our music and fashion and language were transforming the so-called mainstream. We did not care if older or richer or Whiter Americans despised our nonstandard dress like our nonstandard Ebonics. We were fresh like they just took the plastic off us, as Jadakiss rapped. Fresh baggy jeans sagging down. Fresh button-down shirts or designer sweatshirts in the winter under our bubble coats. Fresh T's or sports jerseys in the summer above our baggy jean shorts. Dangling chains shining like our smiles. Piercings and tattoos and bold colors told the mainstream world just how little we wanted to imitate them.

Freshness was about not just getting the hottest gear but devising fresh ways to wear it, in the best tradition of fashion: experimentation, elaboration, and impeccable precision. Timberland boots and Nike Air Force 1s were our cars of choice in New York City. It seems as if everyone—girl or boy—had wheat-colored Tims in their closets if they could afford or snatch them. Our black Air Force 1s had to be blacker than the prison populations. Our white Air Force 1s had to be whiter than the NYPD. Had to be as smooth as baby skin. No blemishes. No creases. We kept them black or white through regular touch-ups from paint sticks. We stuffed our shoes at night with paper or socks to ward off creasing in the front. Time to put on the shoes in the morning. Many of us knew the trick to keep the creases away all day. Put on a second sock halfway and fold the other half twice on top of my toes to fill the front of the sneaker. It hurt like those tight Guess jeans around the waists of shorties. But who cared about pain when fresh brought so much joy.

Jason Riley, a *Wall Street Journal* columnist, did not see us or our disciples in the twenty-first century as fresh cultural innovators. "Black culture today not only condones delinquency and thuggery but celebrates it to the point where black youths have adopted jail fashion in the form of baggy, low-slung pants and oversize T-shirts." But there was a solution. "If blacks can close the civilization gap, the race problem in this country is likely to become insignificant," Dinesh D'Souza once reasoned. "Civilization" is often a polite euphemism for cultural racism.


I HATED WHAT they called civilization, represented most immediately by school. I loved what they considered dysfunctional—African American culture, which defined my life outside school. My first taste of culture was the Black church. Hearing strangers identify as sister and brother. Listening to sermonic conversations, all those calls from preachers, responses from congregants. Bodies swaying in choirs like branches on a tree, following the winds and twists of a soloist. The Holy Ghost mounting women for wild shouts and basketball sprints up and down aisles. Flying hats covering the new wigs of old ladies who were keeping it fresh for Jee-susss-sa. Funerals livelier than weddings. Watching Ma dust

off her African garb and Dad his dashikis for Kwanzaa celebra-
tions livelier than funerals.

I loved being in the midst of a culture created by my ancestors,
who found ways to re-create the ideas and practices of their ancestors with what was available to them in the Americas, through
what psychologist Linda James Myers calls the "outward physical
manifestations of culture." These outward physical manifestations
our ancestors encountered included Christianity, the English language, and popular European food, instruments, fashion, and
customs. Culturally racist scholars have assumed that since African Americans exhibit outward physical manifestations of European culture, "North American negroes . . . in culture and
language" are "essentially European," to quote anthropologist
Franz Boas in 1911. "It is very difficult to find in the South today
anything that can be traced directly back to Africa," attested sociologist Robert Park in 1919. "Stripped of his cultural heritage,"
the Negro's reemergence "as a human being was facilitated by his
assimilation" of "white civilization," wrote sociologist E. Franklin
Frazier in 1939. As such, "the Negro is only an American, and
nothing else," argued sociologist Nathan Glazer in 1963. "He has
no values and culture to guard and protect." In the final analysis,
"we are not Africans," Bill Cosby told the NAACP in 2004.

It is difficult to find the survival and revival of African cultural
forms using our surface-sighted cultural eyes. Those surface-
sighted eyes assess a cultural body by its skin. They do not look
behind, inside, below. Those surface-sighted eyes have historically looked for traditional African religions, languages, foods,
fashion, and customs to appear in the Americas just as they appear
in Africa. When they did not find them, they assumed African
cultures had been overwhelmed by the "stronger" European cultures. Surface-sighted people have no sense of what psychologist
Wade Nobles calls "the deep structure of culture," the philosophies and values that change outward physical forms. It is this
"deep structure" that transforms European Christianity into a
new African Christianity, with mounting spirits, calls and re-

sponses, and Holy Ghost worship; it changes English into Ebonics, European ingredients into soul food. The cultural African survived in the Americans, created a strong and complex culture with Western "outward" forms "while retaining inner [African] values," anthropologist Melville Herskovits avowed in 1941. The same cultural African breathed life into the African American culture that raised me.

THE AVE. I just loved being surrounded by all those Black people—or was it all that culture?—moving fast and slow, or just standing still. The Ave had an organic choir, that interplay of blasting tunes from the store to the car trunk, to the teen walking by, practicing her rhymes, to the cipher of rappers on the corners. Gil would freestyle; I would listen and bob my head. The sound of hip-hop was all around us.

"Son, they shook / Cause ain't no such things as halfway crooks / Scared to death, scared to look, they shook." "Shook Ones" was the Queens anthem in the mid-nineties from the self-proclaimed "official Queensbridge murderers"—Mobb Deep. They promised to get their listeners "stuck off the realness," and indeed I was. I despised the teen actors hiding their fear under a tough veneer. They seemed so real to racist cops and outsiders, who could not make distinctions among Black bodies, anyway. But we could tell. "He ain't a crook son / he's just a shook one."

I heard the booming rhymes of Queens's finest: Nas, Salt-N-Pepa, Lost Boyz, A Tribe Called Quest, Onyx, and LL Cool J's "Hey lover, hey lover / This is more than a crush"; and a couple of Brooklyn cats like Biggie Smalls and the whole Junior M.A.F.I.A. and the newbie Jay-Z; and that ill Staten Island crew, the Wu-Tang Clan, learning "life is hell / living in the world no different from a cell"; and that Harlem genius, Big L; and those guads from outside the city, from Queen Latifah setting it off, to Bone Thugs-N-Harmony fast-rapping—"Wake up, wake up, wake up it's the first of tha month"—to Tupac Shakur writing a letter to his mama. I related when Tupac confessed, "I hung around with the thugs, and even though they sold drugs / They showed a young brother love."

Hip-hop has had the most sophisticated vocabulary of any American musical genre. I read endlessly its poetic text. But parents and grandparents did not see us listening to and memorizing gripping works of oral poetry and urban reporting and short stories and autobiographies and sexual boasting and adventure fantasies. They saw—and still see—words that would lead my mind into deviance. "By reinforcing the stereotypes that long hindered blacks, and by teaching young blacks that a thuggish adversarial stance is the properly 'authentic' response to a presumptively racist society, rap retards black success," linguist John McWhorter once claimed. C. Delores Tucker campaigned against rap in the mid-1990s. "You can't listen to all that language and filth without it affecting you," Tucker liked to say—just like our parents and grandparents liked to say. The sixty-six-year-old chair of the National Political Congress of Black Women, the venerable veteran of the civil rights movement, kept coming at us like a Biggie Smalls battle rap.

THE NEXT YEAR we left Queens, left the Ave behind, to start our new life in the South. At the end of a school day sometime in the fall of 1997, I nervously made my way to the gymnasium to see who'd made the cut for Stonewall Jackson High School's junior-varsity basketball team.

I walked over to the gym alone. I hated being alone all the time. I did not have any friends at my new high school in Manassas, Virginia. I'd arrived weeks before at our new house in a predominantly White suburban neighborhood. Manassas wasn't the Deep South, but it was unquestionably south of Jamaica, Queens. Our first night there, I stayed up all night, occasionally looking out the window, worried the Ku Klux Klan would arrive any minute. Why did Aunt Rena have to move here and entice my parents?

The word had spread quickly in school that the quiet, skinny kid wearing baggy clothes, Air Force 1s, and Tims, with a weird accent and a slow strut, was from New York. Girls and boys alike were fascinated—but not necessarily reaching out to be my friend. Basketball was my only companion.

I opened a door to the gym, walked slowly across the dark court to the other side, and came upon the JV list. I confidently looked for my name. I did not see it. Startled, I looked again, pointing my index finger as I slowly read each name. I did not see my name.

Tears welled up. I turned around and fast-walked away, holding back my tears. I made my way to the school bus and plopped down like I've never plopped down on a seat before.

My sadness about being cut was overwhelmed by a deeper agony: Not making the team had fully cut off my one route to finding friends in my new school. I was suffering but held it together on my short walk home from the bus stop.

When I opened the front door, I saw Dad coming down the stairs of our split-level home—I stepped inside and fell into his surprised arms. We sat down together on the stairs, the front door still flung open. I cried uncontrollably, alarming my father. After a few minutes, I gathered myself and said, "I didn't make the team," only to start crying again and blurt out, "Now I'm never going to have any friends!"

Basketball had been life. It all changed when those tears finally passed.


AT FIFTEEN, I was an intuitive believer in multiculturalism, unlike assimilationist sociologists such as Nathan Glazer, who lamented the idea in his book that year, *We Are All Multiculturalists Now*. I opposed racist ideas that belittled the cultures of urban Black people, of hip-hop—of me. I sensed that to ridicule the Black cultures I knew—urban culture, hip-hop culture—would be to ridicule myself.

At the same time, though, as an urban Black Northerner, I

looked down on the cultures of non-urban Blacks, especially
Southerners, the very people I was now surrounded by. I mea-
sured their beloved go-go music—then popular in D.C. and
Virginia—against what I considered to be the gold standard of
Black music, Queens hip-hop, and despised it like C. Delores
Tucker despised hip-hop. The guys in Virginia could not dress. I
hated their Ebonics. I thought the basketball players were scrubs
who I had to patronize, a belief that cost me the spot on the JV
squad. I walked around during those early months at Stonewall
Jackson with an unspoken arrogance. I suspect potential friends
heard my nonverbal cues of snobbery and rightly stayed away.

When we refer to a group as Black or White or another racial
identity—Black Southerners as opposed to Southerners—we are
racializing that group. When we racialize any group and then
render that group's culture inferior, we are articulating cultural
racism. When I defended Black culture in my mind, I was treating culture in a general sense, not a specific sense, just as I understood race in a general sense, not a specific sense. I knew it was
wrong to say Black people were culturally inferior. But I was
quick to judge specific Black cultures practiced by specific Black
racial groups. Judging the culture I saw in Manassas from the cultural standards of Black New York was no different than White
New York judging Black New York from White New York's
cultural standards. That is no different than White America judging Latinx America from White America's cultural standards.
That is no different than Europe judging the rest of the world
from European cultural standards, which is where the problem
started, back during the so-called Age of Enlightenment.

"That every practice and sentiment is barbarous, which is not
according to the usages of modern Europe, seems to be a fundamental maxim with many of our critics and philosophers," wrote
critical Scottish Enlightenment philosopher James Beattie in
1770. "Their remarks often put us in mind of the fable of the
man and the lion." In the fable, a man and lion travel together,
arguing over who is superior. They pass a statue that shows a lion
strangled by a man. The man says, "See there! How strong we are,

and how we prevail over even the king of beasts." The lion replies, "This statue was made by one of you men. If we lions knew how to erect statues, you would see the man placed under the paw of the lion." Whoever creates the cultural standard usually puts themself at the top of the hierarchy.

"All cultures must be judged in relation to their own history, and all individuals and groups in relation to their cultural history, and definitely not by the arbitrary standard of any single culture," wrote Ashley Montagu in 1942, a clear expression of cultural relativity, the essence of cultural antiracism. To be antiracist is to see all cultures in all their differences as on the same level, as equals. When we see cultural difference, we are seeing cultural difference—nothing more, nothing less.

It took me a while. Months of loneliness—really almost two years, if we are talking about making true friends. But I slowly but surely started to respect African American culture in Northern Virginia. I slowly but surely came down from the clouds of my culturally racist conceit. But I could not rise above my behaviorally racist insecurity.

## CHAPTER 8

# BEHAVIOR

**BEHAVIORAL RACIST:** One who is making individuals responsible for the perceived behavior of racial groups and making racial groups responsible for the behavior of individuals.

**BEHAVIORAL ANTIRACIST:** One who is making racial group behavior fictional and individual behavior real.

DID EVENTUALLY MAKE friends, an interracial group who arrived just as my old gear from the Ave became too small for my growing body. I lost the purity of my New York accent and jump shot, but I found living, breathing, laughing friends, like Chris, Maya, Jovan, and Brandon.

My schoolwork did not recover. I never bothered much with class back in Queens—I skipped classes at John Bowne to play spades in the lunchroom and tuned out teachers like they were bad commercials, doing just enough classwork to stay married to basketball. I was definitely not living up to my academic potential—and as a Black teenager in the nineties, my shortcomings didn't go unnoticed or unjudged. The first to notice were the adults around me of my parents' and grandparents' generation. As legal scholar James Forman Jr. documents, the civil-rights generation usually evoked Martin Luther King Jr. to shame us. "Did Martin Luther King successfully fight the likes of Bull Connor so that we could ultimately lose the struggle for civil rights to misguided or malicious members of our own race?" asked Washington, D.C., prosecutor Eric Holder at an MLK birthday celebration in 1995. "You are costing everybody's freedom," Jesse Jackson told a group of Alabama prisoners that year. "You can rise above this if you change your mind," he added. "I appeal to you. Your mother appealed to you. Dr. King died for you."

The so-called "first Black president" followed suit. "It isn't racist for Whites to say they don't understand why people put up with gangs on the corner or in the projects or with drugs being sold in the schools or in the open," said President Clinton in 1995. "It's not racist for Whites to assert that the culture of welfare dependency, out of wedlock pregnancy, and absent fatherhood cannot be broken by social programs, unless there is first more personal responsibility."

Black people needed to stop playing "race cards," the phrase Peter Collier and David Horowitz used to brand "talk of race and racism" in 1997. The issue was personal irresponsibility.

Indeed, I was irresponsible in high school. It makes antiracist sense to talk about the personal irresponsibility of individuals like me of all races. I screwed up. I could have studied harder. But some of my White friends could have studied harder, too, and their failures and irresponsibility didn't somehow tarnish their race.

My problems with personal irresponsibility were exacerbated—or perhaps even caused—by the additional struggles that racism added to my school life, from a history of disinterested, racist teachers, to overcrowded schools, to the daily racist attacks that fell on young Black boys and girls. There's no question that I could have hurdled that racism and kept on running. But asking every nonathletic Black person to become an Olympic hurdler, and blaming them when they can't keep up, is racist. One of racism's harms is the way it falls on the unexceptional Black person who is asked to be extraordinary just to survive—and, even worse, the Black screwup who faces the abyss after one error, while the White screwup is handed second chances and empathy. This shouldn't be surprising: One of the fundamental values of racism to White people is that it makes success attainable for even unexceptional Whites, while success, even moderate success, is usually reserved for extraordinary Black people.

How do we think about my young self, the C or D student, in antiracist terms? The truth is that I should be critiqued as a student—I was undermotivated and distracted and undisciplined. In other words, a bad student. But I shouldn't be critiqued as a bad *Black* student. I did not represent my race any more than my irresponsible White classmates represented their race. It makes racist sense to talk about personal irresponsibility as it applies to an entire racial group. Racial-group behavior is a figment of the racist's imagination. Individual behaviors can shape the success of individuals. But policies determine the success of groups. And it is racist power that creates the policies that cause racial inequities.

Making individuals responsible for the perceived behavior of racial groups and making whole racial groups responsible for the behavior of individuals are the two ways that behavioral racism infects our perception of the world. In other words, when we believe that a racial group's seeming success or failure redounds to each of its individual members, we've accepted a racist idea. Likewise, when we believe that an individual's seeming success or failure redounds to an entire group, we've accepted a racist idea. These two racist ideas were common currency in the 1990s. Progressive Americans—the ones who self-identified as "not racist"—had abandoned biological racism by the mid-1990s. They had gone further: Mostly they'd abandoned ethnic racism, bodily racism, and cultural racism. But they were still sold on behavioral racism. And they carried its torch unwaveringly, right up to the present.

The same behavioral racism drove many of the Trump voters whom these same "not racist" progressives vociferously opposed in the 2016 election. They, too, ascribed qualities to entire groups—these were voters whose political choice correlated with their belief that Black people are ruder, lazier, stupider, and crueler than White people. "America's Black community . . . has turned America's major cities into slums because of laziness, drug use, and sexual promiscuity," fancied Reverend Jamie Johnson, director of a faith-based center in Trump's Department of Homeland Security, after the election. "Although black civil rights leaders like to point to a supposedly racist criminal justice system to explain why our prisons house so many black men, it's been obvious for decades that the real culprit is black behavior," argued Jason Riley in 2016.

Every time someone racializes behavior—describes something as "Black behavior"—they are expressing a racist idea. To be an antiracist is to recognize there is no such thing as racial behavior. To be an antiracist is to recognize there is no such thing as Black behavior, let alone irresponsible Black behavior. Black behavior is as fictitious as Black genes. There is no "Black gene." No one has ever scientifically established a single "Black behavioral trait." No evidence has ever been produced, for instance, to prove that Black people are louder, angrier, nicer, funnier, lazier, less punctual, more immoral, religious, or dependent; that Asians are more subservient; that Whites are greedier. All we have are stories of individual behavior. But individual stories are only proof of the behavior of individuals. Just as race doesn't exist biologically, race doesn't exist behaviorally.

But what about the argument that clusters of Black people in the South, or Asian Americans in New York's Chinatown, or White people in the Texas suburbs seem to behave in ways that follow coherent, definable cultural practices? Antiracism means separating the idea of a culture from the idea of behavior. Culture defines a group tradition that a particular racial group might share but that is not shared among all individuals in that racial group or among all racial groups. Behavior defines the inherent human traits and potential that everyone shares. Humans are intelligent and lazy, even as that intelligence and laziness might appear differently across the racialized cultural groups.

BEHAVIORAL RACISTS SEE it differently from antiracists, and even from each other. In the decades before the Civil War, behavioral racists argued over whether it was freedom or slavery that caused supposed mediocre Black behavior. To proslavery theorists, Black behavioral deficiencies stemmed from freedom, either in Africa or among emancipated slaves in America. In the states that "retained the ancient relation" between White mastery and Black slavery, Blacks "had improved greatly in every respect—in numbers, comfort, intelligence, and morals," Secretary of State John C. Calhoun explained to a British critic in 1844. This proslavery position held after slavery. Freed Blacks "cut off from the spirit of White society"—their civilizing masters—had degenerated into the "original African type," with behavioral traits ranging from hypersexuality, immorality, criminality, and laziness to poor parenting, Philip Alexander Bruce maintained in his popular 1889 book, *The Plantation Negro as a Freeman*.

In contrast, abolitionists, including Benjamin Rush in 1773, argued, "All the vices which are charged upon the Negroes in the southern colonies and the West-Indies, such as Idleness, Treachery, Theft, and the like, are the genuine offspring of slavery." A year later, Rush founded the budding nation's first White antislavery society. Prefacing Frederick Douglass's slave narrative in 1845, abolitionist William Lloyd Garrison stated that slavery degraded Black people "in the scale of humanity. . . . Nothing has been left undone to cripple their intellects, darken their minds, debase their moral nature, obliterate all traces of their relationship to mankind."

Abolitionists—or, rather, progressive assimilationists—conjured what I call the oppression-inferiority thesis. In their well-meaning efforts to persuade Americans about the horrors of oppression, assimilationists argue that oppression has degraded the behaviors of oppressed people.

This belief extended into the period after slavery. In his address to the founding meeting of Alexander Crummell's American Negro Academy in 1897, W.E.B. Du Bois pictured "the first and greatest step toward the settlement of the present friction between the races . . . lies in the correction of the immorality, crime, and laziness among the Negroes themselves, which still remains as a heritage of slavery." This framing of slavery as a demoralizing force was the mirror image of the Jim Crow historian's framing of slavery as a civilizing force. Both positions led Americans toward behavioral racism: Black behavior demoralized by freedom—or freed Black behavior demoralized by slavery.

The latest expression of the oppression-inferiority thesis is known as post-traumatic slave syndrome, or PTSS. Black "infighting," materialism, poor parenting, colorism, defeatism, rage—these "dysfunctional" and "negative" behaviors "as well as many others are in large part related to trans-generational adaptations associated with the past traumas of slavery and on-going oppression," maintains psychologist Joy DeGruy in her 2005 book, *Post Traumatic Slave Syndrome*. (Some people believe, based on misleading studies, that these trans-generational adaptations are genetic.)

DeGruy claimed "many, many" African Americans suffer from PTSS. She built this theory on anecdotal evidence and modeled it on post-traumatic stress disorder (PTSD). But studies show that many, many people who endure traumatic environments don't contract post-traumatic stress disorder. Researchers found that among soldiers returning from Iraq and Afghanistan, PTSD rates ranged from 13.5 to 30 percent.

Black individuals have, of course, suffered trauma from slavery and ongoing oppression. Some individuals throughout history have exhibited negative behaviors related to this trauma. DeGruy is a hero for ushering the constructs of trauma, damage, and healing into our understanding of Black life. But there is a thin line between an antiracist saying individual Blacks have suffered trauma and a racist saying Blacks are a traumatized people. There is similarly a thin line between an antiracist saying slavery was debilitating and a racist saying Blacks are a debilitated people. The latter constructions erase whole swaths of history: for instance, the story of even the first generation of emancipated Black people, who moved straight from plantations into the Union army, into politics, labor organizing, Union leagues, artistry, entrepreneurship, club building, church building, school building, community building—buildings more commonly razed by the fiery hand of racist terrorism than by any self-destructive hand of be-havioral deficiencies derived from the trauma of slavery.

Increasingly in the twentieth century, social scientists replaced slavery with segregation and discrimination as the oppressive hand ravaging Black behavior. Psychoanalysts Abram Kardiner and Lionel Ovesey expressed this alarm in their 1951 tome, *The Mark of Oppression: A Psychosocial Study of the American Negro.* "There is not one personality trait of the Negro the source of which cannot be traced to his difficult living conditions," they wrote. "The final result is a wretched internal life," a crippled "self-esteem," a vicious "self-hatred," "the conviction of unlov-ability, the diminution of affectivity, and the uncontrolled hostil-ity." Widely taken as scientific fact, these sweeping generalizations were based on the authors' interviews with all of twenty-five sub-jects.

AS A STRUGGLING Black teenager in the nineties, I felt suffocated by a sense of being judged, primarily by the people I was closest to: other Black people, particularly older Black people who wor-ried over my entire generation. The Black judge in my mind did not leave any room for the mistakes of Black individuals—I didn't just have to deal with the consequences of my personal failings, I had the added burden of letting down the entire race. Our mis-takes were generalized as the mistakes of the race. It seemed that White people were free to misbehave, make mistakes. But if we failed—or failed to be twice as good—then the Black judge handed down a hard sentence. No probation or parole. There was no middle ground—we were either King's disciples or thugs kill-ing King's dream.

But, of course, while that may have felt true in a larger social sense, individual Black parents responded as individuals. My own parents privately etched out probationary middle grounds for their own children. I did not make Ma and Dad proud. But they didn't treat me as a thug and lock me away—they kept trying. When I was in eleventh grade at Stonewall Jackson, my parents nudged me into International Baccalaureate (IB) classes, and even though I didn't have particularly high expectations for myself, I went along with it. I entered the sanctimonious world of IB, surrounded by a sea of White and Asian students. This environment only made my hatred of school more intense, if now for a different reason. I felt stranded, save for an occasional class with my friend Maya, a Black teen preparing for Spelman College. None of my White and Asian classmates came to save me. Rarely opening my lips or raising my hand, I shaped myself according to what I thought they believed about me. I felt like a person in a leaky boat as they sailed by me every day on their way to standardized-test prep sessions, Ivy League dreams, and competitions for teachers' praises. I saw myself through their eyes: an impostor, deserving of invisibility. My drowning in the supposed sea of advanced intelligence was imminent.

I internalized my academic struggles as indicative of something wrong not just with my behavior but with Black behavior as a whole, since I represented the race, both in their eyes—or what I thought I saw in their eyes—and in my own.

The so-called Nation's Report Card told Americans the same story. It first reported the math scores of eighth- and fourth-graders in 1990, the year I entered third grade. Asian fourth-graders scored thirty-seven points, Whites thirty-two points, and Latinx twenty-one points higher than Black fourth-graders on the standardized math test. By 2017, the scoring gaps in fourth-grade mathematics had slightly narrowed. The racial "achievement gap" in reading between White and Black fourth-graders also narrowed between 1990 and 2017 but widened between White and Black twelfth-graders. In 2015, Blacks had the lowest mean SAT scores of any racial group.

As a high school student, I believed standardized tests effectively measured smarts and therefore my White and Asian classmates were smarter than me. I thought I was a fool. Clearly, I needed another shaming lesson about how King died for me.

. . .

NOT UNTIL MY senior year in college did I realize I was a fool for thinking I was a fool. I was preparing for my last major standardized test, the Graduate Record Exam, or GRE. I had already forked over $1,000 for a preparatory course, feeding the U.S. test-prep and private tutoring industry that would grow to $12 billion in 2014 and is projected to reach $17.5 billion in 2020. The courses and private tutors are concentrated in Asian and White communities, who, not surprisingly, score the highest on standardized tests. My GRE prep course, for instance, was not taught on my historically Black campus. I had to trek over to the campus of a historically White college in Tallahassee.

I sat surrounded by White students before a White teacher at Florida State University, a flashback to my lonely boat at Stonewall Jackson. I wondered why I was the only Black student in the room and about my own economic privilege and the presumed economic privilege of my fellow students. I wondered about another stratum of students, who weren't even in the room, the ones who could pay for private tutoring with this teacher.

The teacher boasted the course would boost our GRE scores by two hundred points, which I didn't pay much attention to at first—it seemed an unlikely advertising pitch. But with each class, the technique behind the teacher's confidence became clearer. She wasn't making us smarter so we'd ace the test—she was teaching us *how* to take the test.

On the way home from the class, I typically stopped by the gym to lift weights. When I first started weight lifting, I naturally assumed the people lifting the heaviest weights were the strongest people. I assumed wrong. To lift the most required a combination of strength and the best form; one was based on ability, the other on access to the best information and training. Well-trained lifters with exquisite form lifted heavier weights than similarly or even better-endowed lifters with poorer form.

This regular commute from the GRE prep course to the weight room eventually jarred me into clarity: The teacher was not making us stronger. She was giving us form and technique so we'd know precisely how to carry the weight of the test.

It revealed the bait and switch at the heart of standardized tests—the exact thing that made them unfair: She was teaching test-taking form for standardized exams that purportedly measured intellectual strength. My classmates and I would get higher scores—two hundred points, as promised—than poorer students, who might be equivalent in intellectual strength but did not have the resources or, in some cases, even the awareness to acquire better form through high-priced prep courses. Because of the way the human mind works—the so-called "attribution effect," which drives us to take personal credit for any success—those of us who prepped for the test would score higher and then walk into better opportunities thinking it was all about us: that we were better and smarter than the rest and we even had inarguable, quantifiable proof. Look at our scores! Admissions counselors and professors would assume we were better qualified and admit us to their graduate schools (while also boosting their institutional rankings). And because we're talking about featureless, objective numbers, no one would ever think that racism could have played a role.

The use of standardized tests to measure aptitude and intelligence is one of the most effective racist policies ever devised to degrade Black minds and legally exclude Black bodies. We degrade Black minds every time we speak of an "academic-achievement gap" based on these numbers. The acceptance of an academic-achievement gap is just the latest method of reinforcing the oldest racist idea: Black intellectual inferiority. The idea of an achievement gap means there is a disparity in academic performance between groups of students; implicit in this idea is that academic achievement as measured by statistical instruments like test scores and dropout rates is the only form of academic "achievement." There is an even more sinister implication in achievement-gap talk—that disparities in academic achievement accurately reflect disparities in intelligence among racial groups. Intellect is the linchpin of behavior, and the racist idea of the achievement gap is the linchpin of behavioral racism.

Remember, to believe in a racial hierarchy is to believe in a racist idea. The idea of an achievement gap between the races—with

Whites and Asians at the top and Blacks and Latinx at the bottom—creates a racial hierarchy, with its implication that the racial gap in test scores means something is wrong with the Black and Latinx test takers and not the tests. From the beginning, the tests, not the people, have always been the racial problem. I know this is a hard idea to accept—so many well-meaning people have tried to "solve" this problem of the racial achievement gap—but once we understand the history and policies behind it, it becomes clear.

The history of race and standardized testing begins in 1869, when English statistician Francis Galton—a half cousin of Charles Darwin—hypothesized in *Hereditary Genius* that the "average intellectual standard of the negro race is some two grades below our own." Galton pioneered eugenics decades later but failed to develop a testing mechanism that verified his racist hypothesis. Where Galton failed, France's Alfred Binet and Theodore Simon succeeded, when they developed an IQ test in 1905 that Stanford psychologist Lewis Terman revised and delivered to Americans in 1916. These "experimental" tests would show "enormously significant racial differences in general intelligence, differences which cannot be wiped out by any scheme of mental culture," the eugenicist said in his 1916 book, *The Measurement of Intelligence.*

Terman's IQ test was first administered on a major scale to 1.7 million U.S. soldiers during World War I. Princeton psychologist Carl C. Brigham presented the soldiers' racial scoring gap as evidence of genetic racial hierarchy in *A Study of American Intelligence,* published three years before he created the Scholastic Aptitude Test, or SAT, in 1926. Aptitude means natural ability. Brigham, like other eugenicists, believed the SAT would reveal the natural intellectual ability of White people.

Physicist William Shockley and psychologist Arthur Jensen carried these eugenic ideas into the 1960s. By then, genetic explanations—if not the tests and the achievement gap itself—had largely been discredited. Segregationists pointing to inferior genes had been overwhelmed in the racist debate over the cause of the achievement gap by assimilationists pointing to inferior environments.

Liberal assimilationists shifted the discourse to "closing the achievement gap," powering the testing movement into the nineties, when *The Bell Curve* controversy erupted in 1994 over whether the gap could be closed. "It seems highly likely to us that both genes and the environment have something to do with racial differences" in test scores, wrote Harvard psychologist Richard Herrnstein and political scientist Charles Murray in *The Bell Curve*. The racist idea of an achievement gap lived on into the new millennium through George W. Bush's No Child Left Behind Act and Obama's Race to the Top and Common Core—initiatives that further enlarged the role of standardized testing in determining the success and failure of students and the schools they attended. Through these initiatives and many, many others, education reformers banged the drum of the "achievement gap" to get attention and funding for their equalizing efforts.

But what if, all along, these well-meaning efforts at closing the achievement gap have been opening the door to racist ideas? What if different environments lead to different kinds of achievement rather than different levels of achievement? What if the intellect of a low-testing Black child in a poor Black school is different from—and not inferior to—the intellect of a high-testing White child in a rich White school? What if we measured intelligence by how knowledgeable individuals are about their own environments? What if we measured intellect by an individual's desire to know? What if we realized the best way to ensure an effective educational system is not by standardizing our curricula and tests but by standardizing the opportunities available to all students?

In Pennsylvania, a recent statewide study found that at any given poverty level, districts with a higher proportion of White students receive significantly more funding than districts with more students of color. The chronic underfunding of Black schools in Mississippi is a gruesome sight to behold. Schools lack basic supplies, basic textbooks, healthy food and water. The lack of resources leads directly to diminished opportunities for learning. In other words, the racial problem is the opportunity gap, as antiracist reformers call it, not the achievement gap.

. . .

BACK IN HIGH school, those final days in 1999 were taking forever. I sat bored during free time in my government class. As my mind wandered, my eyes wandered and latched on to Angela, sitting behind me. Brown-skinned with high cheekbones and a sweet disposition, Angela appeared to be writing intently.

"What are you doing?" I asked.

"I'm writing my speech," she said with her usual smile, not looking up from her writing.

"Speech for what?"

"For the MLK contest. You haven't heard?"

I shook my head, and so she told me all about the Prince William County Martin Luther King Jr. oratorical contest. Stonewall Jackson participants would give their speeches in two days. Stonewall's winner would go on to the county competition. The top three finalists would speak at the Hylton Chapel on MLK Day in 2000.

She urged me to participate. At first, I declined. But by the time she finished with me, I was in. The prompt for the contest was "What would be Dr. King's message for the millennium?" and what came to my pen were all the racist ideas about Black youth behavior circulating in the 1990s that, without realizing, I had deeply internalized. I started writing an anti-Black message that would have filled King with indignity—less like King himself and more like the shaming speeches about King that I heard so often from adults of my parents' generation. If only I'd spent more time listening to King instead of all the adults who claimed to speak for him. "We must no longer be ashamed of being Black," King would have told me, as he told a gathering of Black people in 1967. "As long as the mind is enslaved, the body can never be free."

As long as the mind thinks there is something behaviorally wrong with a racial group, the mind can never be antiracist. As long as the mind oppresses the oppressed by thinking their oppressive environment has retarded their behavior, the mind can never be antiracist. As long as the mind is racist, the mind can never be free.

To be antiracist is to think nothing is behaviorally wrong or right—inferior or superior—with any of the racial groups. Whenever the antiracist sees individuals behaving positively or negatively, the antiracist sees exactly that: individuals behaving positively or negatively, not representatives of whole races. To be antiracist is to deracialize behavior, to remove the tattooed stereotype from every racialized body. Behavior is something humans do, not races do.

I FINISHED A draft of the speech that night. "Let me hear it!" Angela excitedly asked the next day, before our government class.

"Hear what?" I said shyly, turning around, knowing exactly what.

"Your speech!" She beamed. "I know you got it there. Let me hear it!"

Feeling obligated, I slowly recited my speech. The more I read, the more confidence I felt. The racist ideas sounded so good, so right, as racist ideas normally do. When I finished, Angela was ecstatic.

"You're going to win! You're going to win!" she chanted softly as class started. I kept turning around and telling her to stop. Angela saw my smiles and did not.

I did not sleep much that night. Between fine-tuning my speech and quieting my nerves and fears, I had too much going in my mind. I fell eventually into a deep sleep, so deep I did not hear my alarm. When I awoke, I realized I had missed the competition. Upset but also relieved, I made my way to school.

Angela was waiting for me at the competition all morning. After the last participant had spoken to the Stonewall judges, Angela demanded they reconvene when I arrived at school and she did not take no from them—the same as she didn't take no from me.

And sure enough, when I got to school, the judges reconvened for me. Hearing all that Angela did, a storm surge of gratitude washed away my fears and nerves. I was determined to give the speech of my life. And I did. I won, racist ideas and all.

WINNING STARTED TO melt away the shame I felt for myself and my race regarding my academic struggles. The Black judge was proud of me. I was more than proud of myself. But my racist insecurity started transforming into racist conceit. The transformation had actually already started when I decided to attend Florida A&M University. "It felt right," I told people. I did not disclose to anyone or myself why this historically Black university felt right.

On my visit during the summer of 1999, everyone gushed about Florida A&M as the biggest and baddest HBCU—historically Black college and university—in the land. *Time* magazine and *The Princeton Review* had named it College of the Year in 1997. For the second time in three years, Florida A&M had outpaced Harvard in its recruitment of National Achievement Scholars (the best of the best of Black high school students). President Frederick S. Humphries, a six-foot-five-inch bundle of charisma, had personally recruited many of those students, while growing his university into the nation's largest HBCU.

Whenever we say something just feels right or wrong we're evading the deeper, perhaps hidden, ideas that inform our feelings. But in those hidden places, we find what we really think if we have the courage to face our own naked truths. I did not look within myself to see why Florida A&M just felt right—a reason beyond my desire to be around Black excellence. The truth is, I wanted to flee misbehaving Black folk.

Florida A&M became for me the best of Blackness, all right. I never could have imagined the enrapturing sound of Blackness at its peak. Two weeks after landing on campus, I heard it in all its glory.

# COLOR

**COLORISM:** A powerful collection of racist policies that lead to inequities between Light people and Dark people, supported by racist ideas about Light and Dark people.

**COLOR ANTIRACISM:** A powerful collection of antiracist policies that lead to equity between Light people and Dark people, supported by antiracist ideas about Light and Dark people.

M Y VOICE CREAKED like an old staircase. My arms flailed sluggishly as I stood on the highest of the seven hills in Tallahassee, Florida. I wasn't tired from climbing on that September day in 2000. I'd been on campus for a few weeks and the school spirit had already mounted me and worn me out, just as it had the thousands of people around me—my fellow Rattlers of Florida A&M University. We called our school FAMU, pronounced as in "family," FAM-YOU.

I looked again at Bragg Stadium's football scoreboard. FAMU 39. MORGAN STATE 7. But I had no time to rest my tiring arms and screams. Halftime approached.

I should have saved my energy, but as a freshman I did not know any better. I had never seen a performance by the Marching 100, the high-stepping pride of FAMU, arguably the most accomplished marching band in history and certainly the most imitated marching band in the land. I'm biased, but see my receipts. William P. Foster had just retired after fifty-two years of raising what *Sports Illustrated* dubbed "the best college marching band in the country." FAMU band members hit the Grammy

Awards stage in 2006. But nothing compared to that Super Bowl in 2007, when I bragged incessantly and danced horribly as my friends and I watched the Marching 100 play for Prince.

Back in 2000, though, the Marching 100 confused me on first sight in the first quarter. Winter-clothed in thick pants and long-sleeved orange, green, and white uniforms, adorned with capes and towering hats, they made me hot just watching them roast in the Florida sun. They played off the heat like jam sessions between plays. But nothing prepared me for what I was about to see at halftime.

My roommate, Clarence, stood next to me. Clarence and I arrived at FAMU from different places, had come running from different trails that converged in friendship. Him: an academic titan from Birmingham, Alabama. Me: an academic minion from up north. My daring, untethered ideas complemented his methodical analyses. My fuzzy sense of self and direction embraced his clarity. Clarence considered FAMU a pit stop on a mapped-out trail to a top law school and corporate law and wealth. I considered FAMU an inclusive Black commune to explore and find myself. My explorations amused Clarence. But nothing entertained him more than my eyes.

Clarence's hazelnut skin matched his hazel eyes, an eye color that is rare for anyone around the world but most commonly found among people of Southern and Eastern European heritage, not African Americans. When I first saw his lighter eyes, I assumed they were fake. It turned out, his genes provided him what I had to buy.

Before arriving at FAMU, I'd started wearing "honey" contact lenses, or "orange eyes," as my friends called them. My colored contacts were hard to miss on me. Hazel contacts were perhaps the most popular colored contact lens among Black folk, but I picked one shade even lighter. It seemed okay to me to play with my eye color. I knew some Black people who wore blue or green contacts, which I thought was shameful. I saw them—but not me—as straining to look White.

Above my orange eyes, Clarence did not see a low haircut,

sometimes with fading up the back and sides, all times a brush flattening the kinks that struggled to stand and band in freedom before the next killa haircut. I started cornrowing my hair in college, twisting them up in small locs, or letting the kinks stretch out, hardly caring that racists judged these hairstyles as the unprofessional uniform of thugs. My cornrows signified an antiracist idea. My honey eyes a capitulation to assimilation. Together, they braided the assimilationist and antiracist ideas of my dueling consciousness.

Did I think my honey eyes meant I was striving to be White? No way. I was simply refining a cuter version of myself, which studies show is the explanation of most buyers of artificial eyes, complexion, hair, or facial features. I never asked myself the antiracist question. Why? Why did I think lighter eyes were more attractive on me? What did I truly want?

I wanted to be Black but did not want to look Black. I looked up to the new post-racial beauty ideal, an outgrowth of the old White beauty ideal. Lightening eye color. Killing kinks. Lightening skin color. Thinning or thickening facial features. All to reach an ideal we did not label White. This post-racial beauty ideal is Lightness: the race of lighter skin and eyes, straighter hair, thinner noses, and semi-thick lips and buttocks, perceived as biracial or racially ambiguous.

The dueling consciousness of antiracist pride in one's own race and assimilationist desire to be another race stirs this paradoxical post-racial beauty ideal. "It is simultaneously inclusive, multicultural, and new, while remaining exclusive, Eurocentric, and . . . old-fashioned." It is "white beauty repackaged with dark hair," sociologist Margaret Hunter explains.

I had no idea my light eyes embodied the latest form of "colorism," a term coined by novelist Alice Walker in 1983. The post-racial beauty ideal hides colorism, veils it in euphemism. Colorism is a form of racism. To recognize colorism, we must first recognize that Light people and Dark people are two distinct racialized groups shaped by their own histories. Dark people—the unidentified racial group of darker skins, kinky hair, broader noses and lips—span many races, ethnicities, and nationalities. Light people sometimes pass for White and may yet be accepted into Whiteness so that White people can maintain majorities in countries like the United States, where demographic trends threaten to relegate them to minority status. Some reformers project Light people as the biracial key to racial harmony, an embodiment of a post-racial future.

Colorism is a collection of racist policies that cause inequities between Light people and Dark people, and these inequities are substantiated by racist ideas about Light and Dark people. Colorism, like all forms of racism, rationalizes inequities with racist ideas, claiming the inequities between Dark people and Light people are not due to racist policy but are based in what is wrong or right with each group of people. Colorist ideas are also assimilationist ideas, encouraging assimilation into—or transformation into something close to—the White body.

To be an antiracist is to focus on color lines as much as racial lines, knowing that color lines are especially harmful for Dark people. When the gains of a multicolored race disproportionately flow to Light people and the losses disproportionately flow to Dark people, inequities between the races mirror inequities within the races. But because inequities between the races overshadow inequities within the races, Dark people often fail to see colorism as they regularly experience it. Therefore, Dark people rarely protest policies that benefit Light people, a "skin color paradox," as termed by political scientists Jennifer L. Hochschild and Vesla Weaver.

Anti-Dark colorism follows the logic of behavioral racism, linking behavior to color, studies show. White children attribute positivity to lighter skin and negativity to Dark skin, a colorism that grows stronger as they get older. White people usually favor lighter-skinned politicians over darker-skinned ones. Dark African Americans are disproportionately at risk of hypertension. Dark African American students receive significantly lower GPAs than Light students. Maybe because racist Americans have higher expectations for Light students, people tend to remember educated Black men as Light-skinned even when their skin is Dark. Is that why employers prefer Light Black men over Dark Black men regardless of qualifications? Even Dark Filipino men have lower incomes than their lighter peers in the United States. Dark immigrants to the United States, no matter their place of origin, tend to have less wealth and income than Light immigrants. When they arrive, Light Latinx people receive higher wages, and Dark Latinx people are more likely to be employed at ethnically homogeneous jobsites.

Dark sons and Light daughters receive higher-quality parenting than Light sons and Dark daughters. Skin color influences perceptions of attractiveness most often for Black women. As skin tone lightens, levels of self-esteem among Black women rise, especially among low- and middle-income Black women.

Dark African Americans receive the harshest prison sentences and more time behind bars. White male offenders with African facial features receive harsher sentences than their all-European peers. Dark female students are nearly twice as likely to be suspended as White female students, while researchers found no disparity between Light and White female students. Inequities between Light and Dark African Americans can be as wide as inequities between Black and White Americans.

THE SECOND QUARTER ticked away. I stared as the world's longest multicolored Rattler uncurled itself. The Marching 100 should have been named the Marching 400. Hundreds of band members slowly stepped onto the field, one after another, into lines of instruments, into a rhythmic strut. Lines low-stepped behind FAMU's team on our side of the field, to the other side of the field behind Morgan State's team, and into the end zones. The line colors draped over the green field like strokes of paint on a canvas. Skin color didn't matter in this procession. It never should have mattered.

I watched the spreading lines of cymbals, trumpets, trombones, saxophones, clarinets, French horns, flutes, and those big tubas. Instruments rhythmically swayed in unison with bodies. The half ended. Football players ran through band lines and departed the field. Instead of a rush out to the concession stands, people rushed to their seats to stand and wait.

Some male students didn't care about watching the Marching 100's first performance of the season and instead prowled inside the shaded concourse or outside the stadium, searching for a new friend, hoping they had more game than football. If they were anything like my friends, then Light women were their favorite, and it showed up in the words they spit. "Ugly-Black," they called darker women. "Nappy-headed." But straight and long hair was "good hair."

"She's cute . . . for a Dark girl," was the best some of them could muster for darker-skinned women. Even Dark gay men heard it: "I don't normally date Dark-skin men, but . . ."

The first woman I dated at FAMU was lighter than me, with almost caramel-colored skin. Straight hair fell down her petite body. I liked her (or did I like that she liked me?). But I did not like how my friends fawned over her and overlooked her darker roommate and best friend. The more my friends ignored or denigrated the Dark woman, the more I resented myself for liking the Light woman. After a few months, I had enough. I abruptly cut off the Light woman. My friends thought I had lost my mind. To this day, they deem the Light woman the prettiest woman I dated at FAMU. After her, they say, I rolled downhill into the Dark abyss.

They are right about the darkness—if not the abyss. That first Light college girlfriend ended up being the last at FAMU. I pledged to date only Dark women. Only my Light friend Terrell did not think I had lost my mind. He preferred Dark women, too. I looked down on the rest—anyone who did not prefer Dark women, as well. I hardly realized my own racist hypocrisy: I was turning the color hierarchy upside down, but the color hierarchy remained. Dark people degraded and alienated Light people with names: light bright, high yellow, redbone. "You're never Black enough," a Light woman once told Oprah about her feelings of rejection. Light people constantly report their struggle to integrate with Dark people, to prove their Blackness to Dark people, as if Dark people are the judge and standard of Blackness. The irony is that many Dark people—read me, circa 2000—do think of themselves as the judge and standard of Blackness, while at the same time meekly aspiring to the standard of Lightness or Whiteness.

White people and Dark people reject and envy Light people. White people have historically employed the one-drop rule—that even one drop of Black blood makes you Black—to bar Light people from pure Whiteness. Dark people employ the two-drop rule, as I call it—two drops of White blood make you less Black—to bar Light people from pure Blackness. Light people employ the three-drop rule, as I call it—three drops of Black blood mean you're too Dark—to bar Dark people from pure Lightness. The "drop" rules of racial purity were mirages, just like the races themselves and the idea of racial blood. No racial group was pure.

When people look at my chocolate-brown skin, broad nose, thick lips, and the long hair I locked during my junior year at FAMU, around the time I retired my orange eyes for good, they do not see a biracial man. They do not see my White great-great-grandfather.

Nothing has been passed down about this White man except that he impregnated my great-great-grandmother, who bore him a Light child named Eliza in 1875. In the 1890s, Eliza married the Dark-skinned Lewis, who had recently arrived in Guyton, Georgia, from Sylvania, West Virginia. In 1920, they bore my grandfather Alvin. Eliza, Alvin, and Ma, all lighter-skinned, all married Dark people.

An ancestral pull toward Dark people? Wishful thinking to exonerate my anti-Light colorism. I had antiracist intentions, unmindful that the car of racism can drive just as far with the right intentions. To be an antiracist is not to reverse the beauty standard. To be an antiracist is to eliminate any beauty standard based on skin and eye color, hair texture, facial and bodily features shared by groups. To be an antiracist is to diversify our standards of beauty like our standards of culture or intelligence, to see beauty equally in all skin colors, broad and thin noses, kinky and straight hair, light and dark eyes. To be an antiracist is to build and live in a beauty culture that accentuates instead of erases our natural beauty.


"FOR IT IS well known," attested Anglican missionary Morgan Godwyn in an antislavery pamphlet in 1680, "that the Negro's . . . do entertain as high thoughts of themselves and of their Complexion, as our Europeans do." Johann Joachim Winckelmann, the so-called "father" of Western art history, endeavored, like his fellow Enlightenment intellectuals, to bring down my ancestors' high thoughts. African people must accept the "correct conception" of beauty, Winckelmann demanded in *History of the Art of Antiquity* in 1764. "A beautiful body will be all the more beautiful the whiter it is."

The slaveholder's philosophy extended this further: A body will be all the more superior the Whiter it is—an enslaved body will be closer to the slaveholder the Whiter it is. Large slaveholders more often worked Light people in the house and Dark people in the fields, reasoning that Light people were suited for skilled tasks and Dark people for more physically demanding tasks. A body will be all the more animalistic the darker it is. Slaveholders crafted a hierarchy that descended from the intellectually strong White down to the Light, then to the Dark, and, finally, to the physically strong Animal. "Ferocity and stupidity are the characteristics of those tribes in which the peculiar Negro features are found most developed," intoned one writer.

The U.S. father of colorism is Samuel Stanhope Smith, a longtime theologian who taught at and then presided over Princeton University in early America. In early 1787, the young Princeton professor gave the annual oration to the new nation's most distinguished scholarly group, the American Philosophical Society. He spoke before the White men who wrote the U.S. Constitution that year, pledging to use "the genuine light of truth." Smith's racist light: "domestic servants . . . who remain near the [White] persons" have "advanced far before the others in acquiring the regular and agreeable features." Since "field slaves" live "remote from . . . their superiors," their bodies "are, generally, ill shaped," and their kinky hair is "the farthest removed from the ordinary laws of nature." In an 1850 book, Peter Browne leaned on his unrivaled human-hair collection to classify the "hair" of Whites and "wool" of Blacks, to swear, "The hair of the white man is more perfect than that of the Negro."

Some enslavers considered Dark people more perfect than the so-called human mule, or mulatto. The biracial "hybrid" is "a degenerate, unnatural offspring, doomed by nature to work out its own destruction," wrote Alabama physician Josiah Nott in the *Boston Medical and Surgical Journal* in 1843.

Enslavers' public racist ideas sometimes clashed with their private racist ideas, which typically described Light women as smarter, kinder, gentler, and more beautiful than Dark women. Slaveholders paid much more for enslaved Light females than for their Dark counterparts. From long before the United States even existed until long after American slavery ended, White men cast these "yaller gals" and "Jezebels" as seductresses, unable to admit their centuries of attempted and actual rapes.

Some abolitionists framed biracial Light people as "tragic mulattoes," imprisoned by their "one drop" of "Black blood." In Harriet Beecher Stowe's 1852 bestseller, *Uncle Tom's Cabin,* the only four runaways are the only four biracial captives. Stowe contrasts the biracial runaway George, "of fine European features and a high, indomitable spirit," with a docile "full Black" named Tom. "Sons of white fathers . . . will not always be bought and sold and traded," Tom's slaveholder says.

Freed sons of White fathers will always be "more likely to enlist themselves under the banners of the whites," *Charleston Times* editor Edwin Clifford Holland contended in 1822. Maybe Holland had the Brown Fellowship Society in mind, a biracial mutual-aid organization dedicated to "Social Purity" in Charleston. Or maybe he foresaw the White and Light only barbershops owned by Light people in Washington, D.C., before the Civil War.

When emancipation in 1865 thrust all Black people into the land of freedom, White communities built higher walls of segregation to keep Black people out. Light communities, too, built higher walls of segregation to keep Dark people out. To maintain Light privilege, the segregated Light people further segregated their Dark brothers and sisters, preserving prewar racial disparities between Light and Dark people. After slavery, Light people were wealthier than Dark people and more likely to have good-paying jobs and schooling.

By the end of the nineteenth century, dozens of cities had "Blue Vein" societies, which barred Dark people "not white enough to show blue veins," as Charles Chesnutt put it in an 1898 short story. Light people reproduced the paper-bag test, pencil test, door test, and comb test to bar Dark people from their churches, businesses, parties, organizations, schools, and HBCUs.

But these segregators were still segregated from Whiteness. In 1896, shoemaker Homer Plessy—of the *Plessy v. Ferguson* case, which deemed constitutional "equal but separate accommodations"—hailed from a proud Light community in New Orleans. But Mississippi professor Charles Carroll considered the interracial intercourse of the White human and the Black "beast" the most diabolical of all sins. Naturally rebellious Light men were raping White women, leading to lynchings, Carroll warned in his 1900 book, *The Negro a Beast.* In 1901, North Carolina State University president George T. Winston disagreed, framing Dark people as committing "more horrible crimes." Sociologist Edward Byron Reuter added to Winston's position, declaring that biracial people were responsible for all Black achievements, in his 1918 book, *The Mulatto in the United States.* Reuter made Light people a sort of racial middle class, below White people and above Dark people.

Reuter defended Light people from the wrath of eugenicists demanding "racial purity" and from Dark people challenging their colorism. By the final days of 1920, the famous grandson of a biracial man had enough of Dark activists, especially Marcus Garvey and his fast-growing Universal Negro Improvement Association. "American Negroes recognize no color line in or out of the race, and they will in the end punish the man who attempts to establish it," W.E.B. Du Bois declared in *The Crisis*. This from a man who probably heard the Black children's rhyme: "If you're white, you're right / If you're yellow, you're mellow / If you're brown, stick around / If you're black, get back." This from a man who in his own "Talented Tenth" essay in 1903 listed twenty-one Black leaders, all but one of whom was biracial. This from a man who heard Light people say over and over again that the Dark masses needed "proper grooming," as imparted by North Carolina educator Charlotte Hawkins Brown, who took pride in her English ancestry.

Du Bois's avowal of a post-color Black America after the presidential election of Warren G. Harding in 1920 was as out of touch as John McWhorter's avowal of a post-racial America after Barack Obama's presidential election in 2008. Either racist policies or Black inferiority explains why White people are wealthier, healthier, and more powerful than Black people today. Either racist policies or Dark inferiority explained why Light people were wealthier, healthier, and more powerful than Dark people in 1920. Du Bois snubbed the existence of colorism, claiming it had been "absolutely repudiated by every thinking Negro."

Du Bois had changed his thinking by the 1930s, moving closer to the deported Garvey. He replaced Garvey as the chief antiracist critic of the NAACP, which initially shied away from defending the Dark and poor Scottsboro Boys, who were falsely accused of raping two Alabama White women in 1931. Du Bois could not stand the NAACP's new executive secretary, Walter White. The blue-eyed, blond-haired son of biracial parents had advocated assimilation and reportedly believed that "unmixed" Negroes were "inferior, infinitely inferior now." In *The Crisis* in 1934, months before leaving the NAACP, Du Bois bristled: "Walter White is white."

Entrepreneurs were hard at work figuring out a way for Black people, through changing their color and hair, to pass as Light or White, as Walter White had in his earlier investigations of lynchings. The post–World War I craze of the conk—short for the gel called congolene—made it as fashionable for Black men to straighten their hair as for Black women. "I had joined that multitude of Negro men and women in America" trying "to look 'pretty' by white standards," Malcolm X recalled after receiving his first conk as a teenager. Skin-lightening products received a boost after the discovery in 1938 that monobenzyl ether of hydroquinone (HQ) lightened Dark skin.

By the early 1970s, Black power activists inspired by Malcolm X and Angela Davis—including my parents—were liberating their kinks. No more killa cuts for the Black men. No more straight hair for Black women. The higher the better was in. Not many men had a higher Afro than my father. Dark people like my father were saying it loud: "I'm Dark and I'm proud."

SOME DARK PEOPLE took too much pride in Darkness, inverting the color hierarchy as I did at FAMU, deploying the two-drop rule to disavow the Blackness of Light people even as they adored the Light Malcolm X, Angela Davis, Huey P. Newton, and Kathleen Cleaver. And, eventually, the Light ideal came back with a vengeance, if it had ever left. In his 1988 film *School Daze,* Spike Lee satirized his experiences in the late 1970s at historically Black Morehouse College as a battle between the Dark-skinned "jigaboos" and the Light-skinned "wannabes." My father slowly cut his Afro over the years, and my mother straightened her kinks by the time I arrived.

In the 1980s, Light children were adopted first, had higher incomes, and were less likely to be trapped in public housing and prisons. "The lighter the skin, the lighter the sentence" became a popular antiracist saying as the era of mass incarceration surged in the 1990s. In 2007, MSNBC's Don Imus compared

Rutgers's Dark basketball players—"that's some nappy-headed hos there"—to Tennessee's Light players—"they all look cute"—after they played in the NCAA women's championship. In a 2014 casting call for the movie *Straight Outta Compton,* the Sandi Alesse Agency ranked extras: "A GIRLS: . . . Must have real hair . . . B GIRLS: . . . You should be light-skinned . . . C GIRLS: These are African American girls, medium to light skinned with a weave . . . D GIRLS: These are African American girls . . . Medium to dark skin tone. Character types."

By then, singer Michael Jackson had paved the skin-bleaching boulevard traveled by rapper Lil' Kim, baseball player Sammy Sosa, and so many more. Skin-bleaching products were raking in millions for U.S. companies. In India, "fairness" creams topped $200 million in 2014. Today, skin lighteners are used by 70 percent of women in Nigeria; 35 percent in South Africa; 59 percent in Togo; and 40 percent in China, Malaysia, the Philippines, and South Korea.

Some White people have their own skin-care "addiction" to reach a post-racial ideal: tanning. In 2016, the United States elected the "orange man," as NeNe Leakes calls Trump, who reportedly uses a tanning bed every morning. Paradoxically, some tanning White people look down on bleaching Black people, as if there's a difference. Surveys show that people consider tanned skin—the replica color of Light people—more attractive than naturally pale skin and Dark skin.

HALFTIME ARRIVED. LINES of musicians linked together and outlined the entire football field. The largest human-made rectangle I had ever seen. Colored orange and green. Not Dark and Light. My eyes widened in awe at the length of the FAMU Rattler. On the far side, seven tall and slender drum majors, five yards apart, slowly low-stepped to the center of the field as announcer Joe Bullard yelled their names over our screams. They stopped when they reached the center of the field, facing us. Slowly, they twirled. The drum line sounded. The drum majors sat and then stood, leading the band in a twerk, twerk, twerk, twerk, twerk. We went mad.

"Please welcome what has become known as America's band," Bullard said as the band played and high-stepped around the field, knees folding into their chests with the ease of folding chairs.

"The innnnn-credible, the maaaaagnificent, the number-one band innnnnnnn the woooorld. The faaaantastic Florida A&M University Marching Band!"

Band members stopped in straight lines and faced us. They kissed their instruments.

"First the souuund!"

*Daaaa . . . da, da, daaaaaaaa*—the trumpets blew Twentieth Century Fox's thunderous movie introduction, blasting our ears off.

Then the show. High-stepping band members changed in and out of intricate formations and played choruses by Destiny's Child, Carl Thomas, and Sisqó, as the tens of thousands of people sang backup as the world's biggest choir. The R&B ballads warmed us up for the climax—the rap songs. Bucking and twerking and twisting and jumping and swaying all in unison, the band and the backup dancers were one as the crowd rapped. I kept rubbing my eyes, thinking they were deceiving me. I could not play an instrument and could barely dance. How could all these heavy-coated students play tough songs and dance sophisticated routines in harmony? Ludacris, Trick Daddy, Three 6 Mafia, Outkast—the band paraded these Southern rappers before high-stepping off the field to the theme song of *Good Times,* to our deafening applause. Utterly exhilarated, I don't know if I ever clapped and stomped harder and louder.

Halftime over, the exodus out of the stands startled me. The people had come to see what the people had come to see.

I HAD COME to see Clarence. I walked into our off-campus apartment, all giddy, like after watching the Marching 100 that first time. Quietness shrouded the afternoon. Dirty dishes sat in the open kitchen. Clarence had to be in his room, finishing homework.

The door was open; I knocked on it anyway, disturbing him at his desk. He looked up in wonder. We had roomed together for nearly two years. Clarence had gotten used to my midday interruptions. He braced himself for my latest epiphany.

CHAPTER 10

# WHITE

**ANTI-WHITE RACIST:** One who is classifying people of European descent as biologically, culturally, or behaviorally inferior or conflating the entire race of White people with racist power.

STOOD IN THE doorframe, sometime in March 2002. Clarence probably sensed another argument coming. We were tailor-made to argue against each other. Intensely cynical, Clarence seemed to believe nothing. Intensely gullible, I was liable to believe anything, a believer more than a thinker. Racist ideas love believers, not thinkers.

"So what you want to tell me?" Clarence asked.

"I think I figured White people out," I said.

"What is it now?"

I'D ARRIVED AT FAMU trying to figure Black people out. "I had never seen so many Black people together with positive motives," I wrote in an English 101 essay in October 2000. The sentence seemed out of place, sandwiched nastily between "I had never heard the world famous 'Marching 100' perform" and "This was my first ever college football game." The idea—even more out of place. How did I overlook all those Black people who came together with positive motives in all those places and spaces of my upbringing? How did I become the Black judge? Racist ideas suspend reality and retrofit history, including our individual histories.

Anti-Black racist ideas covered my freshman eyes like my orange contacts when I first moved into Gibbs Hall at FAMU. When you entered the lobby, to the right you'd see a busy, tired-looking office. If you took a slight left, you'd find yourself walking down the hallway to my dorm room; a sharper left would take you to the television room, where our dorm's cluster of basketball fans regularly lost bitter arguments to the army of football fans over television rights.

There were no arguments on, or games on, in the television room on the evening of November 7, 2000. We still had our game faces on, though. Rookie voters, we were watching the election results unfold, hoping that our votes would help keep the brother of Florida's governor out of the White House. Black Floridians had not forgotten Jeb Bush's termination of affirmative-action programs earlier in the year. We had voted to save the rest of America from the racist Bushes.

The election was coming down to the winner of Florida. The polls closed, and before long we saw Al Gore's winning face flash on the screen. Game over. We rejoiced. I joined a joyful exodus out of the television room. We marched to our dorm rooms like fans streaming from the stadium when the Marching 100's half-time show ended. The people had come to see what the people had come to see.

The next morning, I awoke to learn that George W. Bush somehow held a narrow lead in Florida of 1,784 votes. Too close to call, and Jeb Bush's appointees were overseeing the recount.

The unfairness of it all crashed on me that November. My anti-Black racist ideas were no consolation. I walked out of my dorm room that morning into a world of anguish. In the weeks that followed, I heard and overheard, read and reread, angry, tearful, first- and secondhand stories of FAMU students and their families back home not being able to vote. Complaints from Black citizens who'd registered but never received their registration cards. Or their voting location had been changed. Or they were unlawfully denied a ballot without a registration card or ordered to leave the long line when polls closed. Or they were told that as convicted felons they could not vote. Earlier in the year, Florida purged fifty-eight thousand alleged felons from the voting rolls. Black people were only 11 percent of registered voters but comprised 44 percent of the purge list. And about twelve thousand of those people purged were not convicted felons.

Reporters and campaign officials seemed more focused on Floridians whose votes were not counted or counted the wrong way. Palm Beach County used confusing ballots that caused about nineteen thousand spoiled ballots and perhaps three thousand Gore voters to mistakenly vote for Pat Buchanan. Gadsden County, next to Tallahassee, had Florida's highest percentage of Black voters and the highest spoilage rate. Blacks were ten times more likely than Whites to have their ballots rejected. The racial inequity could not be explained by income or educational levels or bad ballot design, according to a *New York Times* statistical analysis. That left one explanation, one that at first I could not readily admit: racism. A total of 179,855 ballots were invalidated by Florida election officials in a race ultimately won by 537 votes.

A twenty-nine-year-old Ted Cruz served on Bush's legal team that resisted efforts at manual recounts in Democratic counties that could have netted Gore tens of thousands of votes while pushing for manual recounts in Republican counties that netted Bush 185 additional votes.

Watching this horror flick unfold, I recoiled in fear for days after the election. But not some of my peers at FAMU. They amassed the courage I did not have, that all antiracists must have. "Courage is not the absence of fear, but the strength to do what is right in the face of it," as the anonymous philosopher tells us. Some of us are restrained by fear of what could happen to us if we resist. In our naïveté, we are less fearful of what could happen to us—or is already happening to us—if we don't resist.

On November 9, 2000, FAMU's courageous student-government leaders directed a silent march of two thousand students from campus to Florida's nearby capitol, where they conducted a sit-in. The sit-in lasted for about twenty-four hours, but the witch hunt we launched back at campus lasted for weeks, if not months. We hunted out those thousands of FAMU students who did not vote. We shamed those nonvoters with stories of people who marched so we could vote. I participated in this foolish hunt—one seems to recur every time an election is lost. The shaming ignores the real source of our loss and heartbreak. The fact was that Black people delivered enough voters to win, but those voters were sent home or their votes spoiled. Racist ideas often lead to this silly psychological inversion, where we blame the victimized race for their own victimization.

When on December 12, 2000, the U.S. Supreme Court stopped Florida's recount, I no longer saw the United States as a democracy. When Gore conceded the next day, when White Democrats stood aside and let Bush steal the presidency on the strength of destroyed Black votes, I was shot back into the binary thinking of Sunday school, where I was taught about good and evil, God and the Devil. As Bush's team transitioned that winter, I transitioned into hating White people.

White people became devils to me, but I had to figure out how they came to be devils. I read "The Making of Devil," a chapter in Elijah Muhammad's *Message to the Blackman in America,* written in 1965. Muhammad led the unorthodox Nation of Islam (NOI) from 1934 until his death in 1975. According to the theology he espoused, more than six thousand years ago, in an all-Black world, a wicked Black scientist named Yakub was exiled alongside his 59,999 followers to an island in the Aegean Sea. Yakub plotted his revenge against his enemies: "to create upon the earth a devil race."

Yakub established a brutal island regime of selective breeding—eugenics meeting colorism. He killed all Dark babies and forced Light people to breed. When Yakub died, his followers carried on, creating the Brown race from the Black race, the Red race from the Brown race, the Yellow race from the Red race, and the White race from the Yellow race. After six hundred years, "on the island of Patmos was nothing but these blond, pale-skinned, cold-blue-eyed devils—savages."

White people invaded the mainland and turned "what had been a peaceful heaven on earth into a hell torn by quarreling and fighting." Black authorities chained the White criminals and marched them to the prison caves of Europe. When the Bible says, "Moses lifted up the serpent in the wilderness," NOI theologians say the "serpent is symbolic of the devil white race Moses lifted up out of the caves of Europe, teaching them civilization" to rule for the next six thousand years.

Aside from the White rule for six thousand years, this history of White people sounded eerily similar to the history of Black people I'd learned piecemeal in White schools of racist thought. White racists cast Black people as living in the bushes of Africa, instead of in caves, until Moses, in the form of White enslavers and colonizers, arrived as a civilizer. Slavery and colonization ended before Black people—and Africa—became civilized in the ways of White people. Black people descended into criminality and ended up lynched, segregated, and mass-incarcerated by noble officers of the law in "developed" White nations. "Developing" Black nations became riddled with corruption, ethnic strife, and incompetence, keeping them poor and unstable, despite all sorts of "aid" from the former mother countries in Europe. The NOI's history of White people was the racist history of Black people in Whiteface.

According to NOI mythology, during World War I, God appeared on earth in the form of Wallace Fard Muhammad. In 1931, Fard sent Elijah Muhammad on the divine mission to save the "Lost-Found Nation of Islam" in the United States—to redeem Black people with knowledge of this true history.

My first time reading this story, I sat there in my dorm room, sweating, mesmerized, scared. It felt like I had climbed up and consumed forbidden fruit. Every White person who'd maltreated me, since my third-grade teacher, suddenly rushed back into my memory like a locomotive blaring its horn in the middle of the forest. But my attention remained focused on all those Whites who'd railroaded the election of 2000 in Florida. All those White policemen intimidating voters, White poll officials turning away voters, White state officials purging voters, White lawyers and judges defending the voter suppression. All those White politicians echoing Gore's call to, "for the sake of our unity as a people and the strength of our democracy," concede the election to Bush. White people showed me they did not actually care about national unity or democracy, only unity among and democracy for White people!

I lay in my dorm room, staring up at the ceiling, silently raging at the White people walking away into the wilderness to plan Bush's presidency.

ELIJAH MUHAMMAD'S WHITE creation story made so much sense to me. Half a century earlier, it also made sense to a calculating, cursing, and crazy young Black prisoner nicknamed "Satan." One day, in 1948, Satan's brother, Reginald, whispered to him during a visit, "The white man is the devil." When he returned to his Massachusetts cell, a line of White people appeared before his eyes. He saw White people lynching his activist father, committing his activist mother to an insane asylum, splitting up his siblings, telling him being a lawyer was "no realist goal for a nigger," degrading him on eastern railroads, trapping him for the police, sentencing him to eight to ten years for robbery because his girlfriend was White. His brothers and sisters, clutching their sore necks from a similar rope of White racism, had already converted to the Nation of Islam. In no time, they turned Satan back into Malcolm Little, and Malcolm Little into Malcolm X.

Malcolm X left prison in 1952 and quickly began to grow Elijah Muhammad's Nation of Islam, through his powerful speaking and organizing. The suddenly resurgent NOI caught the attention of the media, and in 1959 Louis Lomax and Mike Wallace produced a television documentary on the NOI, *The Hate That Hate Produced,* which ran on CBS. It made Malcolm X a household name.

In 1964, after leaving the Nation of Islam, Malcolm X made the hajj to Mecca and changed his name again, to el-Hajj Malik el-Shabazz, and converted to orthodox Islam. "Never have I witnessed such" an "overwhelming spirit of true brotherhood as is practiced by people of all colors and races here in this Ancient Holy Land," he wrote home on April 20. Days later, he began to "toss aside some of my previous conclusions [about white people] . . . You may be shocked by these words coming from me. But . . . I have always been a man who tries to face facts, and to accept the reality of life as new experience and new knowledge unfolds it." On September 22, 1964, Malcolm made no mistake about his conversion. "I totally reject Elijah Muhammad's racist philosophy, which he has labeled 'Islam' only to fool and misuse gullible people, as he fooled and misused me," he wrote. "But I blame only myself, and no one else for the fool that I was, and the harm that my evangelic foolishness in his behalf has done to others."

Months before being assassinated, Malcolm X faced a fact many admirers of Malcolm X still refuse to face: Black people can be racist toward White people. The NOI's White-devil idea is a classic example. Whenever someone classifies people of European descent as biologically, culturally, or behaviorally inferior, whenever someone says there is something wrong with White people as a group, someone is articulating a racist idea.

The only thing wrong with White people is when they embrace racist ideas and policies and then deny their ideas and policies are racist. This is not to ignore that White people have massacred and enslaved millions of indigenous and African peoples, colonized and impoverished millions of people of color around the globe as their nations grew rich, all the while producing racist ideas that blame the victims. This is to say their history of pillaging is not the result of the evil genes or cultures of White people. There's no such thing as White genes. We must separate the warlike, greedy, bigoted, and individualist cultures of modern empire and racial capitalism (more on that later) from the cultures of White people. They are not one and the same, as the resistance within White nations shows, resistance admittedly often tempered by racist ideas.

To be antiracist is to never mistake the global march of White racism for the global march of White people. To be antiracist is to never mistake the antiracist hate of White racism for the racist hate of White people. To be antiracist is to never conflate racist people with White people, knowing there are antiracist Whites and racist non-Whites. To be antiracist is to see ordinary White people as the frequent victimizers of people of color and the frequent victims of racist power. Donald Trump's economic policies are geared toward enriching White male power—but at the expense of most of his White male followers, along with the rest of us.

We must discern the difference between racist power (racist policymakers) and White people. For decades, racist power contributed to stagnating wages, destroying unions, deregulating banks and corporations, and steering funding for schools into prison and military budgets, policies that have often drawn a backlash from some White people. White economic inequality, for instance, soared to the point that the so-called "99 percenters" occupied Wall Street in 2011, and Vermont senator Bernie Sanders ran a popular presidential campaign against the "billionaire class" in 2016.

Of course, ordinary White people benefit from racist policies, though not nearly as much as racist power and not nearly as much as they could from an equitable society, one where the average White voter could have as much power as superrich White men to decide elections and shape policy. Where their kids' business-class schools could resemble the first-class prep schools of today's superrich. Where high-quality universal healthcare could save millions of White lives. Where they could no longer face the cronies of racism that attack them: sexism, ethnocentrism, homophobia, and exploitation.

Racist power, hoarding wealth and resources, has the most to lose in the building of an equitable society. As we've learned, racist power produces racist policies out of self-interest and then produces racist ideas to justify those policies. But racist ideas also suppress the resistance to policies that are detrimental to White people, by convincing average White people that inequity is rooted in "personal failure" and is unrelated to policies. Racist power manipulates ordinary White people into resisting equalizing policies by drilling them on what they are losing with equalizing policies and how those equalizing policies are anti-White. In 2017, most White people identified anti-White discrimination as a serious problem. "If you apply for a job, they seem to give the Blacks the first crack at it," said sixty-eight-year-old Tim Hershman of Ohio to an NPR reporter. African Americans are getting unfair handouts, "and it's been getting worse for Whites," Hershman said. Hershman was complaining of losing a promotion to a Black finalist, even though it was actually another White person who got the job.

Claims of anti-White racism in response to antiracism are as old as civil rights. When Congress passed the (first) Civil Rights Act of 1866, it made Black people citizens of the United States, stipulated their civil rights, and stated that state law could not "deprive a person of any of these rights on the basis of race." President Andrew Johnson reframed this antiracist bill as a "bill made to operate in favor of the colored against the white race." Racist Americans a century later framed supporters of affirmative action as "hard-core racists of reverse discrimination," to quote former U.S. solicitor general Robert Bork in *The Wall Street Journal* in 1978. When Alicia Garza typed "Black Lives Matter" on Facebook in 2013 and when that love letter crested into a movement in 2015, former New York City mayor Rudy Giuliani called the movement "inherently racist."

White racists do not want to define racial hierarchy or policies that yield racial inequities as racist. To do so would be to define their ideas and policies as racist. Instead, they define policies not rigged for White people as racist. Ideas not centering White lives are racist. Beleaguered White racists who can't imagine their lives not being the focus of any movement respond to "Black Lives Matter" with "All Lives Matter." Embattled police officers who can't imagine losing their right to racially profile and brutalize respond with "Blue Lives Matter."

Ordinary White racists function as soldiers of racist power. Dealing each day with these ground troops shelling out racist abuse, it is hard for people of color not to hate ordinary White people. Anti-White racist ideas are usually a reflexive reaction to White racism. Anti-White racism is indeed the hate that hate produced, attractive to the victims of White racism.

And yet racist power thrives on anti-White racist ideas—more hatred only makes their power greater. When Black people recoil from White racism and concentrate their hatred on everyday White people, as I did freshman year in college, they are not fighting racist power or racist policymakers. In losing focus on racist power, they fail to challenge anti-Black racist policies, which means those policies are more likely to flourish. Going after White people instead of racist power prolongs the policies harming Black life. In the end, anti-White racist ideas, in taking some or all of the focus off racist power, become anti-Black. In the end, hating White people becomes hating Black people.

IN THE END, hating Black people becomes hating White people.

On October 15, 2013, workers unveiled a twelve-by-twenty-four-foot sign near a major roadway in Harrison, Arkansas, known in those parts as Klan territory. The same sign showed up on billboards overlooking major roadways from Alabama to Oregon. Passing drivers saw bold black letters against a yellow background: ANTI-RACIST IS A CODE WORD FOR ANTI-WHITE.

Robert Whitaker, who ran for vice president of the United States in 2016 on the American Freedom Party's ticket, popularized this declaration in a 2006 piece called "The Mantra." This mantra has become scripture to the self-identified "swarm" of White supremacists who hate people of color and Jews and fear the "ongoing program of genocide against my race, the white race," as Whitaker claimed.

History tells a different story. Contrary to "the mantra," White supremacists are the ones supporting policies that benefit racist power against the interests of the majority of White people. White supremacists claim to be pro-White but refuse to acknowledge that climate change is having a disastrous impact on the earth White people inhabit. They oppose affirmative-action programs, despite White women being their primary beneficiaries. White supremacists rage against Obamacare even as 43 percent of the people who gained lifesaving health insurance from 2010 to 2015 were White. They heil Adolf Hitler's Nazis, even though it was the Nazis who launched a world war that destroyed the lives of more than forty million White people and ruined Europe. They wave Confederate flags and defend Confederate monuments, even though the Confederacy started a civil war that ended with more than five hundred thousand White American lives lost—more than every other American war combined. White supremacists love what America used to be, even though America used to be—and still is—teeming with millions of struggling White people. White supremacists blame non-White people for the struggles of White people when any objective analysis of their plight primarily implicates the rich White Trumps they support.

White supremacist is code for anti-White, and White supremacy is nothing short of an ongoing program of genocide against the White race. In fact, it's more than that: White supremacist is code for anti-human, a nuclear ideology that poses an existential threat to human existence.

I CARRIED THE White hate into my sophomore year, as anti-Muslim and anti-Arab hate filled the American atmosphere like a storm cloud after 9/11. Many Americans did not see any problem with their growing hate of Muslims in the spring of 2002. And I did not see any problem with my growing hate of White people. Same justifications. "They are violent evildoers." "They hate our freedoms."

I kept reading, trying to find the source of White evil. I found more answers in Senegalese scholar Cheikh Anta Diop's two-cradle theory, long before I learned about his antiracist work on the African ancestry of the ancient Egyptians. Diop's two-cradle theory suggested the harsh climate and lack of resources in the northern cradle nurtured in Europeans barbaric, individualistic, materialist, and warlike behaviors, which brought destruction to the world. The amenable climate and abundance of resources in the southern cradle nurtured the African behaviors of community, spirituality, equanimity, and peace, which brought civilization to the world.

I blended Diop's environmental determinism with Michael Bradley's version of the same, his theory in *The Iceman Inheritance* that the White race's ruthlessness is the product of its upbringing in the Ice Age. But I still felt thirsty for biological theories. How we frame the problem—and who we frame as the problem—shapes the answers we find. I was looking for a biological theory of why White people are evil. I found it in *The Isis Papers* by psychiatrist Frances Cress Welsing.

The global White minority's "profound sense of numerical inadequacy and color inferiority" causes their "uncontrollable sense of hostility and aggression," Welsing wrote. White people are defending against their own genetic annihilation. Melanin-packing "color always 'annihilates' . . . the non-color, white." Ironically, Welsing's theory reflects fears of genetic annihilation that White supremacists around the Western world have been expressing these days in their fears of "white genocide"—an idea with a deep history, as in the work of eugenicists like Lothrop Stoddard and his 1920 bestseller, *The Rising Tide of Color Against White World-Supremacy*.

I devoured Welsing, but later, when I learned melanin did not give me any Black superpower, I felt deflated. It turns out, it's the racist one-drop rule that made Black identity dominant in biracial people, not any genetic distinction or melanin superpower. My search continued.

. . .

I DID NOT knock on Clarence's door that day to discuss Welsing's "color confrontation theory." Or Diop's two-cradle theory. He had snickered at those theories many times before. I came to share another theory, the one that finally figured White people out.

"They are aliens," I told Clarence, confidently resting on the doorframe, arms crossed. "I just saw this documentary that laid out the evidence. That's why they are so intent on White supremacy. That's why they seem to not have a conscience. They are aliens."

Clarence listened, face expressionless.

"You can't be serious."

"I'm dead serious. This explains slavery and colonization. This explains why the Bush family is so evil. This explains why Whites don't give a damn. This explains why they hate us so damn much. They are aliens!" I'd lifted off the doorframe and was in full argumentative mode.

"You really are serious about this," Clarence said with a chuckle. "If you're serious, then that has got to be the dumbest thing I ever heard in my life! I mean, seriously, I can't believe you are that gullible." The chuckle turned to a grimace.

"Why do you spend so much time trying to figure out White people?" he asked after a long pause. Clarence had asked this question before. I always answered the same way.

"Because figuring them out is the key! Black people need to figure out what we are dealing with!"

"If you say so. But answer me this: If Whites are aliens, why is it that Whites and Blacks can reproduce? Humans can't reproduce with animals on this planet, but Black people can reproduce with aliens from another planet? Come on, man, let's get real."

"I am being real," I replied. But I really had no comeback. I stood and turned around awkwardly, walked to my room, plopped down on my bed, and returned to staring at the ceiling. Maybe White people were not aliens. Maybe they became this way on earth. Maybe I needed to read more Frances Cress Welsing. I looked over at *The Isis Papers* on my nightstand.

. . .

BY THE FALL of 2003, Clarence had graduated and I decided to share my ideas with the world. I began my public writing career on race with a column in FAMU's student newspaper, *The Famuan*. On September 9, 2003, I wrote a piece counseling Black people to stop hating Whites for being themselves. Really, I was counseling myself. "I certainly understand blacks who have been wrapped up in a tornado of hate because they could not escape the encircling winds of truth about the destructive hand of the white man." Wrapped in this tornado, I could not escape the fallacious idea that "Europeans are simply a different breed of human," as I wrote, drawing on ideas in *The Isis Papers*. White people "make up only 10 percent of the world's population" and they "have recessive genes. Therefore they're facing extinction." That's why they are trying to "destroy my people," I concluded. "Europeans are trying to survive and I can't hate them for that."

The piece circulated widely in Tallahassee, alarming White readers. Their threats hit close to home. My new roommates, Devan, Brandon, and Jean, half-jokingly urged me to watch my back from the Klan. FAMU's new president, Fred Gainous, called me into his office to scold me. I scolded him back, calling him Jeb's boy.

The editor of the *Tallahassee Democrat* summoned me to his office, too. I needed to complete this required internship to graduate with my journalism degree. I walked into his office in fear. It felt like walking into a termination, the termination of my future. And, indeed, something would be terminated that day.

## CHAPTER 11

# BLACK

**POWERLESS DEFENSE:** The illusory, concealing, disempowering, and racist idea that Black people can't be racist because Black people don't have power.

WALKED INTO HIS office. Every time I looked at Mizell Stewart, the *Tallahassee Democrat* editor, in the autumn of 2003, I saw the tall, slim, light-skinned actor Christopher Duncan. His tense energy reminded me of Braxton, Duncan's character on *The Jamie Foxx Show.*

I sat down. He swiveled back in his chair. "Let's talk about this piece," he said.

He darted from critique to critique, surprised at my defenses. I could debate without getting upset. So could he. Black people were problematic to me, but he realized White evil ached in the forefront of my mind.

He became quiet, clearly mulling something over. I was not going to confront him, just defend myself as respectfully as I could. He held my graduation in his hands.

"You know, I have a nice car," he said slowly, "and I hate it when I get pulled over and I'm treated like I am one of them niggers."

I took a deep inaudible breath, turned my lips inside, licked them, and mentally ordered my silence. "Them niggers" hung in the air between our probing eye contact. He waited for my response. I stayed silent.

I wanted to stand up and point and yell, "Who the fuck do you think you are?" I would have cut off his answer: "Clearly you don't think you are a nigger! What makes them niggers and you not a nigger? Am I one of 'them niggers'?" My air quotes struck the air over his head.

He separated himself from "them niggers," racialized them, looked down on them. He directed his disdain not toward the police officers who racially profiled him, who mistreated him, but to "them niggers."

NO ONE POPULARIZED this racial construct of "them niggers" quite like comedian Chris Rock in his 1996 HBO special, *Bring the Pain*. Rock began the show on an antiracist note, mocking reactions among White people to the O. J. Simpson verdict. He then turned to talk about Black people and "our own personal civil war." He picked a side: "I love Black people, but I hate niggers." It was a familiar refrain for me—my own dueling consciousness had often settled on the same formula, adding after the 2000 election: "I love Black people, but I hate niggers and White people."

While hip-hop artists recast "nigga" as an endearing term, "nigger" remained a derisive term outside and inside Black mouths. Rock helped Black people remake the racial group "niggers" and assigned qualities to this group, as all race makers have done. "Niggers" always stop Black people from having a good time, Rock said. Niggers are too loud. Niggers are always talking, demanding credit for taking care of their kids and staying out of prison. "The worst thing about niggers is that they love to not know," Rock teased. "Books are like Kryptonite to a nigger." He rejected the antiracist claim that "the media has distorted our image to make us look bad." Forget that! It was niggers' fault. When he'd go to get money, he wasn't "looking over my shoulders for the media. I'm looking for niggers."

We were laughing as Chris Rock shared the great truth that the nigger is not equal to the Black man (a remix of "the great truth that the negro is not equal to the white man," expressed by Confederate vice president Alexander Stephens in 1861). Racist Whites had schooled us well in generalizing the individual characteristics we see in a particular Black person. We were not seeing and treating Black people as individuals, some of whom do bad things: We created a group identity, niggers, that in turn created a hierarchy, as all race making does. We added the hypocritical audacity of raging when White people called all of us niggers (Chris Rock stopped performing this routine when he saw White people laughing too hard).

We did not place loud people who happened to be Black into an interracial group of loud people—as antiracists. We racialized the negative behavior and attached loudness to niggers, like White racists, as Black racists. We did not place negligent Black parents into an interracial group of negligent parents—as antiracists. We racialized the negative behavior and attached negligent parenting to niggers, like White racists, as Black racists. We did not place Black criminals into an interracial group of criminals—as antiracists. We racialized the negative behavior and attached criminality to niggers, like White racists, as Black racists. We did not place lazy Blacks into an interracial group of lazy people—as antiracists. We racialized the negative behavior and attached laziness to niggers, like White racists, as Black racists.

And after all that, we self-identified as "not-racist," like White racists, as Black racists.

Chris Rock met Black Americans where all too many of us were at the turn of the millennium, stationed within the dueling consciousness of assimilationist and antiracist ideas, distinguishing ourselves from them niggers as White racists were distinguishing themselves from us niggers. We felt a tremendous antiracist pride in Black excellence and a tremendously racist shame in being connected to them niggers. We recognized the racist policy we were facing and were ignorant of the racist policy them niggers were facing. We looked at them niggers as felons of the race when our anti-Black racist ideas were the real Black on Black crime.

In 2003, as I sat in the Black editor's office, 53 percent of Black people were surveyed as saying that something other than racism mostly explained why Black people had worse jobs, income, and housing than Whites, up from 48 percent a decade earlier. Only 40 percent of Black respondents described racism as the source of these inequities in 2003. By 2013, in the middle of Obama's presidency, only 37 percent of Black people were pointing to "mostly racism" as the cause of racial inequities. A whopping 60 percent of Black people had joined with the 83 percent of White people that year who found explanations other than racism to explain persisting racial inequities. The internalizing of racist ideas was likely the reason.

Black minds were awakened to the ongoing reality of racism by the series of televised police killings and flimsy exonerations that followed the Obama election, the movement for Black Lives, and the eventual racist ascendancy of Donald Trump. By 2017, 59 percent of Black people expressed the antiracist position that racism is the main reason Blacks can't get ahead (compared to 35 percent of Whites and 45 percent of Latinx). But even then, about a third of Black people still expressed the racist position that struggling Blacks are mostly responsible for their own condition, compared to 54 percent of Whites, 48 percent of Latinx, and 75 percent of Republicans.

Clearly, a large percentage of Black people hold anti-Black racist ideas. But I still wanted to believe Stewart's "them niggers" comment was abnormal. The truth is, though, Stewart had put up a mirror. I had to face it. I hated what I saw. He was saying what I had been thinking for years. He had the courage to say it. I hated him for that.

How was his criticism of Black people different than my criticism of Black people when we blamed them for their own votes being stolen or accused them of lethargy and self-sabotage? How was our criticism of Black people any different from the anti-Black criticism of White racists? I learned in that office that day that every time I say something is wrong with Black people, I am simultaneously separating myself from them, essentially saying "them niggers." When I do this, I am being a racist.

I THOUGHT ONLY White people could be racist and that Black people could not be racist, because Black people did not have power. I thought Latinx, Asians, Middle Easterners, and Natives could not be racist, because they did not have power. I had no sense of the reactionary history of this construction, of its racist bearing.

This powerless defense, as I call it, emerged in the wake of racist Whites dismissing antiracist policies and ideas as racist in the late 1960s. In subsequent decades, Black voices critical of White racism defended themselves from these charges by saying, "Black people can't be racist, because Black people don't have power."

Quietly, though, this defense shields people of color in positions of power from doing the work of antiracism, since they are apparently powerless, since White people have all the power. This means that people of color are powerless to roll back racist policies and close racial inequities even in their own spheres of influence, the places where they actually do have some power to effect change. The powerless defense shields people of color from charges of racism even when they are reproducing racist policies and justifying them with the same racist ideas as the White people they call racist. The powerless defense shields its believers from the history of White people empowering people of color to oppress people of color and of people of color using their limited power to oppress people of color for their own personal gain.

Like every other racist idea, the powerless defense underestimates Black people and overestimates White people. It erases the small amount of Black power and expands the already expansive reach of White power.

The powerless defense does not consider people at all levels of power, from policymakers like politicians and executives who have the power to institute and eliminate racist and antiracist policies, to policy managers like officers and middle managers empowered to execute or withhold racist and antiracist policies. Every single person actually has the power to protest racist and antiracist policies, to advance them, or, in some small way, to stall them. Nation-states, sectors, communities, institutions are run by policymakers and policies and policy managers. "Institutional power" or "systemic power" or "structural power" is the policymaking and managing power of people, in groups or individually. When someone says Black people can't be racist because Black people don't have "institutional power," they are flouting reality.

The powerless defense strips Black policymakers and managers of all their power. The powerless defense says the more than 154 African Americans who have served in Congress from 1870 to 2018 had no legislative power. It says none of the thousands of state and local Black politicians have any lawmaking power. It says U.S. Supreme Court justice Clarence Thomas never had the power to put his vote to antiracist purposes. The powerless defense says the more than seven hundred Black judges on state courts and more than two hundred Black judges on federal courts have had no power during the trials and sentencing processes that built our system of mass incarceration. It says the more than fifty-seven thousand Black police officers do not have the power to brutalize and kill the Black body. It says the three thousand Black police chiefs, assistant chiefs, and commanders have no power over the officers under their command. The powerless defense says the more than forty thousand full-time Black faculty at U.S. colleges and universities in 2016 did not have the power to pass and fail Black students, hire and tenure Black faculty, or shape the minds of Black people. It says the world's eleven Black billionaires and the 380,000 Black millionaire families in the United States have no economic power, to use in racist or antiracist ways. It says the sixteen Black CEOs who've run Fortune 500 companies since 1999 had no power to diversify their workforces. When a Black man stepped into the most powerful office in the world in 2009, his policies were often excused by apologists who said he didn't have executive power. As if none of his executive orders were carried out, neither of his Black attorneys general had any power to roll back mass incarceration, or his Black national security adviser had no power. The truth is: Black people can be racist because Black people do have power, even if limited.

Note that I say *limited* Black power rather than no power. White power controls the United States. But not absolutely. Absolute power necessitates complete control over all levels of power. All policies. All policy managers. All minds. Ironically, the only way that White power can gain full control is by convincing us that White people already have all the power. If we accept the idea that we have no power, we are falling under the sort of mind control that will, in fact, rob us of any power to resist. As Black History Month father Carter G. Woodson once wrote: "When you control a man's thinking you do not have to worry about his actions. You do not have to tell him not to stand here or go yonder. He will find his 'proper place' and will stay in it."

Racist ideas are constantly produced to cage the power of people to resist. Racist ideas make Black people believe White people have all the power, elevating them to gods. And so Black segregationists lash out at these all-powerful gods as fallen devils, as I did in college, while Black assimilationists worship their all-powerful White angels, strive to become them, to curry their favor, reproducing their racist ideas and defending their racist policies.

Aside from Justice Clarence Thomas's murderous gang of anti-Black judgments over the years, perhaps the most egregious Black on Black racist crime in recent American history decided the 2004 presidential election. George W. Bush narrowly won reelection by taking Ohio with the crucial help of Ohio's ambitious Black Secretary of State, Ken Blackwell, who operated simultaneously as Bush's Ohio campaign co-chair.

Blackwell directed county boards to limit voters' access to the provisional ballots that ensured that anyone improperly purged from voting rolls could cast their ballot. He ordered voter-registration forms accepted only on expensive eighty-pound stock paper, a sly technique to exclude newly registered voters (who he almost certainly knew were more likely to be Black). Under Blackwell's supervision, county boards were falsely telling former prisoners they could not vote. County boards allocated fewer voting machines to heavily Democratic cities. Black Ohio voters on average waited fifty-two minutes to vote, thirty-four minutes longer than White voters, according to one post-election study. Long lines caused 3 percent of Ohio voters to leave before voting, meaning approximately 174,000 potential votes walked away, larger than Bush's 118,000 margin of victory. "Blackwell made Katherine Harris look like a cupcake," Representative John Conyers said after investigating Ohio's voter suppression, referring to the Florida secretary of state who certified Bush as winner of the election in 2000. But according to the theory that Black people can't be racist because they lack power, Blackwell didn't have the power to suppress Black votes. Remember, we are all either racists or antiracists. How can Florida's Katherine Harris be a racist in 2000 and Blackwell be an antiracist in 2004?

After unsuccessfully running for Ohio governor in 2006 and chairman of the Republican National Committee in 2009, Blackwell joined Trump's Presidential Advisory Commission on Election Integrity in May 2017. The commission had clearly been set up, although Trump would never admit it, to find new ways to suppress the voting power of Trump's opponents, especially the Democratic Party's most loyal voters: Black people. Clearly, even thirteen years later, Trump officials had not forgotten Blackwell's state-of-the-art racist work suppressing Black votes for Bush's re-election.

With the popularity of the powerless defense, Black on Black criminals like Blackwell get away with their racism. Black people call them Uncle Toms, sellouts, Oreos, puppets—everything but the right thing: racist. Black people need to do more than revoke their "Black card," as we call it. We need to paste the racist card to their foreheads for all the world to see.

The saying "Black people can't be racist" reproduces the false duality of racist and not-racist promoted by White racists to deny their racism. It merges Black people with White Trump voters who are angry about being called racist but who want to express racist views and support their racist policies while being identified as not-racist, no matter what they say or do. By this theory, Black people can hate them niggers, value Light people over Dark people, support anti-Latinx immigration policies, defend the anti-Native team mascots, back bans against Middle Eastern Muslims, and still escape charges of racism. By this theory, Latinx, Asians, and Natives can fear unknown Black bodies, support mass-incarcerating policies, and still escape charges of racism. By this theory, I can look upon White people as devils and aliens and still escape charges of racism.

When we stop denying the duality of racist and antiracist, we can take an accurate accounting of the racial ideas and policies we support. For the better part of my life I held both racist and antiracist ideas, supported both racist and antiracist policies; I've been antiracist one moment, racist in many more moments. To say Black people can't be racist is to say all Black people are being antiracist at all times. My own story tells me that is not true. History agrees.

THE RECORDED HISTORY of Black racists begins in 1526 in *Della descrittione dell'Africa (Description of Africa),* authored by a Moroccan Moor who was kidnapped after he visited sub-Saharan Africa. His enslavers presented him to Pope Leo X, who converted him to Christianity, freed him, and renamed him Leo Africanus. *Description of Africa* was translated into multiple European languages and emerged as the most influential book of anti-Black racist ideas in the sixteenth century, when the British, French, and Dutch were diving into slave trading. "Negroes . . . leade a beastly kind of life, being utterly destitute of the use of reason, of dexterities of wit, and of all arts," Africanus wrote. "They so behave themselves, as if they had continually lived in a Forrest among wild beasts." Africanus may have made up his travels to sub-Saharan Africa to secure favor from the Italian court.

Englishman Richard Ligon may have made up the stories in *A*

*True and Exact History of the Island of Barbadoes,* published in 1657. Led by Sambo, a group of slaves disclose a plot for a slave revolt. They refuse their master's rewards. A confused master asks why, Ligon narrates. It was "but an act of Justice," Sambo says, according to Ligon. Their duty. They are "sufficiently" rewarded "in the Act."

Slavery was justified in Sambo's narrative, because some Black people believed they were supposed to be enslaved. The same was true of Ukawsaw Gronniosaw, who authored the first known slave narrative, in 1772. Born to Nigerian royalty, Gronniosaw was enslaved at fifteen by an ivory merchant, who sold him to a Dutch captain. "My master grew very fond of me, and I loved him exceedingly" and "endeavored to convince him, by every action, that my only pleasure was to serve him well." The ship reached Barbados. A New Yorker purchased Gronniosaw and brought him home, where he came to believe there was "a black man call'd the Devil that lived in hell." Gronniosaw was sold again to a minister, who transformed him from "a poor heathen" into an enslaved Christian. He was apparently happy to escape the Black Devil.

Slaveowners welcomed ministers preaching the gospel of eternal Black enslavement, derived from the reading of the Bible where all Black people were the cursed descendants of Ham. A fifty-one-year-old free Black carpenter had to first teach away these racist ideas in 1818 as he began recruiting thousands of enslaved Blacks to join his slave revolt around Charleston, South Carolina. Denmark Vesey set the date of the revolt for July 14, 1822, the anniversary of the storming of the Bastille during the French Revolution. The aim of the revolt was to take down slavery, as in the successful 1804 Haitian revolution that inspired Vesey.

But the revolt had to remain a secret, even from some slaves. Don't mention it "to those waiting men who receive presents of old coats from their masters," Vesey's chief lieutenants told recruiters. "They'll betray us." One recruiter did not listen and told house slave Peter Prioleau, who promptly told his master in May.

By late June 1822, South Carolina enslavers had destroyed Vesey's army, which one estimate placed as high as nine thousand strong. Vesey, hung on July 2, 1822, remained defiant to the very end.

The South Carolina legislature emancipated Peter Prioleau on Christmas Day, 1822, and bestowed on him a lifetime annual pension. By 1840, he'd acquired seven slaves of his own and lived comfortably in Charleston's free Light community. Even when he was a slave, this Black man had no desire to get rid of his master. He used his power to spoil one of the most well-organized slave revolts in American history. He used his power to fully take on the qualities of his master, to become him: slaves, racist ideas, and all.

PETER PRIOLEAU RESEMBLED William Hannibal Thomas, a nineteenth-century Black man who wanted to be accepted by White people as one of their own. But as Jim Crow spread in the 1890s, Thomas was shoved more deeply into Blackness. He finally deployed the tactic self-interested Black racists have been using from the beginning to secure White patronage: He attacked Black people as inferior. When Thomas's *The American Negro* appeared weeks before Booker T. Washington's *Up from Slavery* in 1901, *The New York Times* placed Thomas "next to Mr. Booker T. Washington, the best American authority on the negro question."

Blacks are an "intrinsically inferior type of humanity," Thomas wrote. Black history is a "record of lawless existence." Blacks are mentally retarded, immoral savages, "unable practically to discern between right and wrong," Thomas wrote. Ninety percent of Black women are "in bondage to physical pleasure." The "social degradation of our freedwomen is without parallel in modern civilization." In the end, Thomas's "list of negative qualities of Negroes seemed limitless," as his biographer concluded.

Thomas believed himself to be among a minority of Light people who had overcome their inferior biological heritage. But this "saving remnant" was set "apart from their white fellow-men." We show, Thomas pleaded to White people, that "the redemption of the negro is . . . possible and assured through a thorough assimilation of the thought and ideals of American civilization." To speed up this "national assimilation," Thomas advised restricting the voting rights of corrupt Blacks, intensely policing natural Black criminals, and placing all Black children with White guardians.

Black people stamped William Hannibal Thomas as the "Black Judas." Black critics ruined his credibility and soon White racists could no longer use him, so they tossed him away like a paper plate, as White racists have done to so many disposable Black racists over the years. Thomas found work as a janitor, before dying in obscurity in 1935.

Black people would be betrayed by Black on Black criminals again and again in the twentieth century. In the 1960s, the diversifying of America's police forces was supposed to alleviate the scourge of police brutality against Black victims. The fruit of decades of antiracist activism, a new crop of Black officers were expected to treat Black citizens better than their White counterparts did. But reports immediately surfaced in the 1960s that Black officers were as abusive as White officers. One report noted "in some places, low-income Negroes prefer white policemen because of the severe conduct of Negro officers." A 1966 study found Black officers were not as likely to be racist as Whites, but a significant minority expressed anti-Black racist ideas like, "I'm telling you these people are savages. And they're real dirty." Or the Black officer who said, "There have always been jobs for Negroes, but the f—— people are too stupid to go out and get an education. They all want the easy way out."

To color police racism as White on the pretext that only White people can be racist is to ignore the non-White officer's history of profiling and killing "them niggers." It is to ignore that the police killer in 2012 of Brooklyn's Shantel Davis was Black, that three of the six officers involved in the 2015 death of Freddie Gray were Black, that the police killer in 2016 of Charlotte's Keith Lamont Scott was Black, and that one of the police killers in 2018 of Sacramento's Stephon Clark was Black. How can the White officers involved in the deaths of Terence Crutcher, Sandra Bland, Walter L. Scott, Michael Brown, Laquan McDonald, and Decynthia Clements be racist but their Black counterparts be antiracist?

To be fair, one survey of nearly eight thousand sworn officers in 2017 makes strikingly clear that White officers are far and away more likely to be racist than Black officers these days. Nearly all (92 percent) of White officers surveyed agreed with the postracial idea that "our country has made the changes needed to give Blacks equal rights with Whites." Only 6 percent of White officers co-signed the antiracist idea that "our country needs to continue making changes to give Blacks equal rights with Whites," compared to 69 percent of Black officers. But the disparity shrinks concerning deadly police encounters. Black officers (57 percent) are only twice as likely as White officers (27 percent) to say "the deaths of Blacks during encounters with police in recent years are signs of a broader problem."

The new crop of Black politicians, judges, police chiefs, and officers in the 1960s and subsequent decades helped to create a new problem. Rising levels of violent crime engulfed impoverished neighborhoods. Black residents bombarbed their politicians and crime fighters with their racist fears of *Black* criminals as opposed to criminals. Neither the residents nor the politicians nor the crime fighters wholly saw the heroin and crack problem as a public-health crisis or the violent-crime problem in poor neighborhoods where Black people lived as a poverty problem. Black people seemed to be more worried about other Black people killing them in drug wars or robberies by the thousands each year than about the cancers, heart diseases, and respiratory diseases killing them by the hundreds of thousands each year. Those illnesses were not mentioned, but "Black on Black crime has reached a critical level that threatens our existence as a people," wrote *Ebony* publisher John H. Johnson, in a 1979 special issue on the topic. The Black on Black crime of internalized racism had indeed reached a critical level—this new Black-abetted focus on the crisis of "Black crime" helped feed the growth of the movement toward mass incarceration that would wreck a generation.

The rise of mass incarceration was partially fueled by Black people who, even as they adopted racist ideas, did so ostensibly out of trying to save the Black community in the 1970s. But the 1980s brought a more premeditated form of racism, as channeled through the Black administrators Ronald Reagan appointed to his cabinet. Under Clarence Thomas's directorship from 1980 to 1986, the Equal Employment Opportunity Commission doubled the number of discrimination cases it dismissed as "no cause." Samuel Pierce, Reagan's secretary of the Department of Housing and Urban Development (HUD), redirected billions of dollars in federal funds allotted for low-income housing to corporate interests and Republican donors. Under Pierce's watch in the first half of the 1980s, the number of public-housing units in non-White neighborhoods dropped severely. Poor Black people faced a housing crisis in the 1980s that Pierce made worse, even though he had the power to alleviate it, setting the stage for future secretaries of HUD like Trump's appointee, Ben Carson. These were men who used the power they'd been given—no matter how limited and conditional—in inarguably racist ways.

AS THE EDITOR and I stared each other down, I had a heated conversation—and conversion—in my mind. Eventually, the silence broke and the editor excused me from his office. I received an ultimatum before the end of the workday: Terminate my race column for *The Famuan* or be terminated from my internship at the *Tallahassee Democrat*. I terminated my column in absolute bitterness, feeling as if I terminated a part of myself.

And I did begin to terminate a part of myself—for the better. I began to silence one half of the war within me, the duel between antiracism and assimilation that W.E.B. Du Bois gave voice to, and started embracing the struggle toward a single consciousness of antiracism. I picked up a second major, African American studies.

I took my first Black history course that fall of 2003, the first of four African and African American history courses I would take over three semesters with FAMU professor David Jackson. His precise, detailed, engaging, but somehow funny lectures systematically walked me back through history for the first time. I had imagined history as a battle: on one side Black folks, on the other a team of "them niggers" and White folks. I started to see for the first time that it was a battle between racists and antiracists.

Ending one confusion started another: what to do with my life. As a senior in the fall of 2004, I found that sports journalism no longer moved me. At least not like this thrilling new history I was discovering. I ended up abandoning the press box for what Americans were saying was the most "dangerous" box.

## CHAPTER 12

# CLASS

**CLASS RACIST:** One who is racializing the classes, supporting policies of racial capitalism against those race-classes, and justifying them by racist ideas about those race-classes.

**ANTIRACIST ANTICAPITALIST:** One who is opposing racial capitalism.

EXCITED TO BEGIN graduate school in African American studies at Temple University, I moved to North Philadelphia in the early days of August 2005. Hunting Park to be exact, steps away from Allegheny Avenue and the neighborhood of Allegheny West. My second-floor one-bedroom apartment overlooked North Broad Street: White people driving by, Black people walking by, Latinx people turning right on Allegheny. None of the people outside my building, a drab chocolate tenement adjoining an Exxon station, could tell that a few windows up over its vacant ground-floor storefront was home to a real human life. Its covered windows looked like shut eyes in a casket.

Death resided there, too, apparently. My new Black neighbors had been told for years that Hunting Park and Allegheny West were two of the most dangerous neighborhoods in Philadelphia— the poorest, with the highest reported rates of violent crime.

I unpacked myself in the "ghetto," as people flippantly called my new neighborhood. The ghetto had expanded in the twentieth century as it swallowed millions of Black people migrating from the South to Western and Northern cities like Philadelphia. White flight followed. The combination of government welfare—in the form of subsidies, highway construction, and loan guarantees—along with often racist developers opened new wealth-building urban and suburban homes to the fleeing Whites, while largely confining Black natives and new Black migrants to the so-called ghettos, now overcrowded and designed to extract wealth from their residents. But the word "ghetto," as it migrated to the Main Street of American vocabulary, did not conjure a series of racist policies that enabled White flight and Black abandonment—instead, "ghetto" began to describe unrespectable Black behavior on the North Broad Streets of the country.

"The dark ghetto is institutionalized pathology; it is chronic, self-perpetuating pathology; and it is the futile attempt by those with power to confine that pathology so as to prevent the spread of its contagion to the 'larger community,'" wrote psychologist Kenneth Clark in his 1965 book, *Dark Ghetto*. "Pathology," meaning a deviation from the norm. Poor Blacks in the "ghetto" are pathological, abnormal? Abnormal from whom? What group is the norm? White elites? Black elites? Poor Whites? Poor Latinx? Asian elites? The Native poor?

All of these groups—like the group "Black poor"—are distinct race-classes, racial groups at the intersection of race and class. Poor people are a class, Black people a race. Black poor people are a race-class. When we say poor people are lazy, we are expressing an elitist idea. When we say Black people are lazy, we are expressing a racist idea. When we say Black poor people are lazier than poor Whites, White elites, and Black elites, we are speaking at the intersection of elitist and racist ideas—an ideological intersection that forms class racism. When Dinesh D'Souza writes, "the behavior of the African American underclass . . . flagrantly violates and scandalizes basic codes of responsibility, decency, and civility," he is deploying class racism.

When a policy exploits poor people, it is an elitist policy. When a policy exploits Black people, it is a racist policy. When a policy exploits Black poor people, the policy exploits at the intersection of elitist and racist policies—a policy intersection of class racism. When we racialize classes, support racist policies against those race-classes, and justify them by racist ideas, we are engaging in class racism. To be antiracist is to equalize the race-classes. To be antiracist is to root the economic disparities between the equal race-classes in policies, not people.

Class racism is as ripe among White Americans—who castigate poor Whites as "White trash"—as it is in Black America, where racist Blacks degrade poor Blacks as "them niggers" who live in the ghetto. Constructs of "ghetto Blacks" (and "White trash") are the most obvious ideological forms of class racism. Pathological people made the pathological ghetto, segregationists say. The pathological ghetto made pathological people, assimilationists say. To be antiracist is to say the political and economic conditions, not the people, in poor Black neighborhoods are pathological. Pathological conditions are making the residents sicker and poorer while they strive to survive and thrive, while they invent and reinvent cultures and behaviors that may be different but never inferior to those of residents in richer neighborhoods. But if the elite race-classes are judging the poor race-classes by their own cultural and behavioral norms, then the poor race-classes appear inferior. Whoever creates the norm creates the hierarchy and positions their own race-class at the top of the hierarchy.

DARK GHETTO WAS a groundbreaking study of the Black poor during President Johnson's war on poverty in the 1960s, when scholarship on poverty was ascendant, like the work of anthropologist Oscar Lewis. Lewis argued that the children of impoverished people, namely poor people of color, were raised on behaviors that prevented their escape from poverty, perpetuating generations of poverty. He introduced the term "culture of poverty" in a 1959 ethnography of Mexican families. Unlike other economists, who explored the role of policy in the "cycle of poverty"—predatory exploitation moving in lockstep with meager income and opportunities, which kept even the hardest-working people in poverty and made poverty expensive—Lewis reproduced the elitist idea that poor behaviors keep poor people poor. "People with a culture of poverty," Lewis wrote, "are a marginal people who know only their own troubles, their own local conditions, their own neighborhood, their own way of life."

White racists still drag out the culture of poverty. "We have got this tailspin of culture in our inner cities in particular of men not working, and just generations of men not even thinking about working, and not learning the value and the culture of work," Wisconsin representative Paul Ryan said in 2015. "So there's a real culture problem here that has to be dealt with."

Unlike Lewis and Ryan, Kenneth Clark presented the hidden hand of racism activating the culture of poverty, or what he called "pathology." In Clark's work, the dueling consciousness of the oppression-inferiority thesis resurfaced. First slavery, then segregation, and now poverty and life in the "ghetto" made Black people inferior, according to this latest update of the thesis. Poverty became perhaps the most enduring and popular injustice to fit into the oppression-inferiority thesis.

Something was making poor people poor, according to this idea. And it was welfare. Welfare "transforms the individual from a dignified, industrious, self-reliant *spiritual* being into a dependent animal creature without his knowing it," U.S. senator Barry Goldwater wrote in *The Conscience of the Conservative* in 1960. Goldwater and his ideological descendants said little to nothing about rich White people who depended on the welfare of inheritances, tax cuts, government contracts, hookups, and bailouts. They said little to nothing about the White middle class depending on the welfare of the New Deal, the GI Bill, subsidized suburbs, and exclusive White networks. Welfare for middle- and upper-income people remained out of the discourse on "handouts," as welfare for the Black poor became the true oppressor in the conservative version of the oppression-inferiority thesis. "The evidence of this failure is all around us," wrote Heritage Foundation president Kay Coles James in 2018. "Being black and the daughter of a former welfare recipient, I know firsthand the unintended harm welfare has caused."

Kenneth Clark was an unrelenting chronicler of the racist policies that made "the dark ghetto," but at the same time he reinforced the racial-class hierarchy. He positioned the Black poor as inferior to Black elites like himself, who had also long lived "within the walls of the ghetto," desperately attempting "to escape its creeping blight." Clark considered the Black poor less stable than the White poor. "The white poor and slum dweller have the advantage of . . . the belief that they can rise economically and escape from the slums," he wrote. "The Negro believes himself to be closely confined to the pervasive low status of the ghetto." Obama made a similar case during his campaign speech on race in 2008. "For all those who scratched and clawed their way to get a piece of the American Dream, there were many who didn't make it—those who were ultimately defeated, in one way or another, by discrimination. That legacy of defeat was passed on to future generations—those young men and increasingly young women who we see standing on street corners or languishing in our prisons, without hope or prospects for the future." This stereotype of the hopeless, defeated, unmotivated poor Black is without evidence. Recent research shows, in fact, that poor Blacks are more optimistic about their prospects than poor Whites are.

For ages, racist poor Whites have enriched their sense of self on the stepladder of racist ideas, what W.E.B. Du Bois famously called the "wage" of Whiteness. I may not be rich, but at least I am not a nigger. Racist Black elites, meanwhile, heightened their sense of self on the stepladder of racist ideas, on what we can call the wage of Black elitism. I may not be White, but at least I am not them niggers.

Racist Black elites thought about low-income Blacks the way racist non-Black people thought about Black people. We thought we had more than higher incomes. We thought we were higher people. We saw ourselves as the "Talented Tenth," as Du Bois named Black elites from the penthouse of his class racism in 1903. "The Negro race, like all races, is going to be saved by its exceptional men," Du Bois projected. "Was there ever a nation on God's fair earth civilized from the bottom upward? Never; it is, ever was, and ever will be from the top downward that culture filters."

I had come a long way by 2005. So had the Talented Tenth and the term "ghetto" in America's racial vocabulary. In the forty years since Clark's *Dark Ghetto,* dark had married ghetto in the chapel of inferiority and took her name as his own—the ghetto was now so definitively dark, to call it a dark ghetto would be redundant. Ghetto also became as much an adjective—ghetto culture, ghetto people—as a noun, loaded with racist ideas, unleashing all sorts of Black on Black crimes on poor Black communities.

IN MY NEW Philly home, I did not care what people thought about the poor Blacks in my neighborhood. Call them ghetto if you want. Run away if you want. I wanted to be there. To live the effects of racism firsthand!

I saw poor Blacks as the product of racism and not capitalism, largely because I thought I knew racism but knew I did not know capitalism. But it is impossible to know racism without understanding its intersection with capitalism. As Martin Luther King said in his critique of capitalism in 1967, "It means ultimately coming to see that the problem of racism, the problem of economic exploitation, and the problem of war are all tied together. These are the triple evils that are interrelated."

Capitalism emerged during what world-systems theorists term the "long sixteenth century," a cradling period that begins around 1450 with Portugal (and Spain) sailing into the unknown Atlantic. Prince Henry's Portugal birthed conjoined twins—capitalism and racism—when it initiated the transatlantic slave trade of African people. These newborns looked up with tender eyes to their ancient siblings of sexism, imperialism, ethnocentrism, and homophobia. The conjoined twins developed different personalities through the new class and racial formations of the modern world.

As the principal customers of Portuguese slave traders, first in their home country and then in their American colonies, Spain adopted and raised the toddlers among the genocides of Native Americans that laid the foundational seminaries and cemeteries on which Western Europe's Atlantic empire grew in the sixteenth century. Holland and France and England overtook each other as hegemons of the slave trade, raising the conjoined twins into their vigorous adolescence in the seventeenth and eighteenth centuries. The conjoined twins entered adulthood through Native and Black and Asian and White slavery and forced labor in the Americas, which powered industrial revolutions from Boston to London that financed still-greater empires in the eighteenth and nineteenth centuries. The hot and cold wars in the twentieth century over resources and markets, rights and powers, weakened the conjoined twins—but eventually they would grow stronger under the guidance of the United States, the European Union, China, and the satellite nations beholden to them, colonies in everything but name. The conjoined twins are again struggling to stay alive and thrive as their own offspring—inequality, war, and climate change—threaten to kill them, and all of us, off.

In the twenty-first century, persisting racial inequities in poverty, unemployment, and wealth show the lifework of the conjoined twins. The Black poverty rate in 2017 stood at 20 percent, nearly triple the White poverty rate. The Black unemployment rate has been at least twice as high as the White unemployment rate for the last fifty years. The wage gap between Blacks and Whites is the largest in forty years. The median net worth of White families is about ten times that of Black families. According to one forecast, White households are expected to own eighty-six times more wealth than Black households by 2020 and sixty-eight times more than Latinx households. The disparity stands to only get worse if racist housing policies, tax policies benefiting the rich, and mass incarceration continue unabated, according to forecasters. By 2053, the median wealth of Black households is expected to redline at $0, and Latinx households will redline two decades later.

The inequities wrought by racism and capitalism are not restricted to the United States. Africa's unprecedented capitalist growth over the past two decades has enriched foreign investors and a handful of Africans, while the number of people living in extreme poverty is growing in Sub-Saharan Africa. With extreme poverty falling rapidly elsewhere, forecasters project that nearly nine in ten extremely poor people will live in Sub-Saharan Africa by 2030. In Latin America, people of African descent remain disproportionately poor. The global gap between the richest (and Whitest) regions of the world and the poorest (and Blackest) regions of the world has tripled in size since the 1960s—at the same time as the global non-White middle class has grown.

Upward mobility is greater for White people, and downward mobility is greater for Black people. And equity is nonexistent on the race-class ladder in the United States. In the highest-income quintile, White median wealth is about $444,500, around $300,000 more than for upper-income Latinx and Blacks. Black middle-income households have less wealth than White middle-income households, whose homes are valued higher. White poverty is not as distressing as Black poverty. Poor Blacks are much more likely to live in neighborhoods where other families are poor, creating a poverty of resources and opportunities. Sociologists refer to this as the "double burden." Poor Blacks in metropolitan Chicago are ten times more likely than poor Whites to live in high-poverty areas. With Black poverty dense and White poverty scattered, Black poverty is visible and surrounds its victims; White poverty blends in.

Attributing these inequities solely to capitalism is as faulty as attributing them solely to racism. Believing these inequities will be eliminated through eliminating capitalism is as faulty as believing these inequities will be eliminated through eliminating racism. Rolling back racism in a capitalist nation can eliminate the inequities between the Black and White poor, middle-income Latinx and Asians, rich Whites and Natives. Antiracist policies in the 1960s and 1970s narrowed these inequities on some measures. But antiracist policies alone cannot eliminate the inequities between rich and poor Asians or between rich Whites and "White trash"—the inequities between race-classes. As racial disparities within the classes narrowed in recent decades, the economic inequities within the races have broadened, as have the class-racist ideas justifying those inequities.

Antiracist policies cannot eliminate class racism without anticapitalist policies. Anticapitalism cannot eliminate class racism without antiracism. Case in point is the persistent racism Afro-Cubans faced in socialist Cuba after revolutionaries eliminated capitalism there in 1959, as chronicled by historian Devyn Spence Benson. Revolutionaries demanded Afro-Cubans assimilate into an imagined post-racial Cuba—"Not Blacks, but Citizens"— built on White Cuban social norms and racist ideas after a three-year campaign against racism abruptly ended in 1961.

Socialist and communist spaces are not automatically antiracist. Some socialists and communists have pushed a segregationist or post-racial program in order not to alienate racist White workers. For example, delegates at the founding meeting of the Socialist Party of America (SPA) in 1901 refused to adopt an antilynching petition. Assimilationist leaders of some socialist and communist organizations have asked people of color to leave their racial identities and antiracist battle plans at the door, decrying "identity politics." Some of these socialists and communists may not be familiar with their ideological guide's writings on race. "The discovery of gold and silver in America," Karl Marx once wrote, "the extirpation, enslavement and entombment in mines of the aboriginal population, the beginning of the conquest and looting of the East Indies, the turning of Africa into a warren for the commercial hunting of black-skins, signalized the rosy dawn of the era of capitalist production." Marx recognized the birth of the conjoined twins.

In the 1920s, W.E.B. Du Bois started binge-reading Karl Marx. By the time the Great Depression depressed the Black poor worse than the White poor, and he saw in the New Deal the same old deal of government racism for Black workers, Du Bois conceived of an antiracist anticapitalism. Howard University economist Abram Harris, steeped in a post-racial Marxism that ignores the color line as stubbornly as any color-blind racist, pleaded with Du Bois to reconsider his intersecting of anticapitalism and antiracism. But the reality of what scholars now call racial capitalism—the singular name of the conjoined twins—made up Du Bois's mind.

"The lowest and most fatal degree" of Black workers' "suffering comes not from capitalists but from fellow white workers," Du Bois stated. "White labor . . . deprives the Negro of his right to vote, denies him education, denies him affiliation with trade unions, expels him from decent houses, and neighborhoods, and heaps upon him the public insults of open color discrimination." The United States has a White "working-class aristocracy," Du Bois constructed. "Instead of a horizontal division of classes, there was a vertical fissure, a complete separation of classes by race, cutting square across the economic layers." The vertical cutting knife? Racism, sharpened through the centuries. "This flat and incontrovertible fact, imported Russian Communism ignored, would not discuss."

But Du Bois discussed it. An antiracist anticapitalism could seal the horizontal class fissures and vertical race fissures—and, importantly, their intersections—with equalizing racial and economic policies. In 1948, he officially abandoned the idea of a vanguard Talented Tenth of elite Blacks and called for a "Guiding One Hundredth." Du Bois helped breed a new crop of antiracist anticapitalists before they were driven underground or into prison by the red scares of the 1950s, before resurfacing in the 1960s. They are resurfacing again in the twenty-first century in the wake of the Great Recession, the Occupy movement, the movement for Black Lives, and the campaigns of democratic socialists, recognizing "there is an inextricable link between racism and capitalism," to quote Princeton scholar Keeanga-Yamahtta Taylor. They are winning elections, rushing into anticapitalist organizations, and exposing the myths of capitalism.

I keep using the term "anticapitalist" as opposed to socialist or communist to include the people who publicly or privately question or loathe capitalism but do not identify as socialist or communist. I use "anticapitalist" because conservative defenders of capitalism regularly say their liberal and socialist opponents are against capitalism. They say efforts to provide a safety net for all people are "anticapitalist." They say attempts to prevent monopolies are "anticapitalist." They say efforts that strengthen weak unions and weaken exploitative owners are "anticapitalist." They say plans to normalize worker ownership and regulations protecting consumers, workers, and environments from big business are "anticapitalist." They say laws taxing the richest more than the middle class, redistributing pilfered wealth, and guaranteeing basic incomes are "anticapitalist." They say wars to end poverty are "anticapitalist." They say campaigns to remove the profit motive from essential life sectors like education, healthcare, utilities, mass media, and incarceration are "anticapitalist."

In doing so, these conservative defenders are defining capitalism. They define capitalism as the freedom to exploit people into economic ruin; the freedom to assassinate unions; the freedom to prey on unprotected consumers, workers, and environments; the freedom to value quarterly profits over climate change; the freedom to undermine small businesses and cushion corporations; the freedom from competition; the freedom not to pay taxes; the freedom to heave the tax burden onto the middle and lower classes; the freedom to commodify everything and everyone; the freedom to keep poor people poor and middle-income people struggling to stay middle income, and make rich people richer. The history of capitalism—of world warring, classing, slave trading, enslaving, colonizing, depressing wages, and dispossessing land and labor and resources and rights—bears out the conservative definition of capitalism.

Liberals who are "capitalist to the bone," as U.S. senator Elizabeth Warren identifies herself, present a different definition of capitalism. "I believe in markets and the benefits they can produce when they work," Warren said when asked what that identity meant to her. "I love the competition that comes with a market that has decent rules. . . . The problem is when the rules are not enforced, when the markets are not level playing fields, all that wealth is scraped in one direction," leading to deception and theft. "Theft is not capitalism," Warren said. She has proposed a series of regulations and reforms that her conservative opponents class as "anticapitalist." They say other countries that have these rules are not capitalist. Warren should be applauded for her efforts to establish and enforce rules that end the theft and level the play-ing field for, hopefully, all race-classes, not just the White middle class. But if Warren succeeds, then the new economic system will operate in a fundamentally different way than it has ever operated before in American history. Either the new economic system will not be capitalist or the old system it replaces was not capitalist. They cannot both be capitalist.

When Senator Warren and others define capitalism in this way—as markets and market rules and competition and benefits from winning—they are disentangling capitalism from theft and racism and sexism and imperialism. If that's their capitalism, I can see how they can remain capitalist to the bone. However, history does not affirm this definition of capitalism. Markets and market rules and competition and benefits from winning existed long be-fore the rise of capitalism in the modern world. What capitalism introduced to this mix was global theft, racially uneven playing fields, unidirectional wealth that rushes upward in unprecedented amounts. Since the dawn of racial capitalism, when were markets level playing fields? When could working people compete equally with capitalists? When could Black people compete equally with White people? When could African nations compete equally with European nations? When did the rules not generally benefit the wealthy and White nations? Humanity needs honest defini-tions of capitalism and racism based in the actual living history of the conjoined twins.

The top 1 percent now own around half of the world's wealth, up from 42.5 percent at the height of the Great Recession in 2008. The world's 3.5 billion poorest adults, comprising 70 per-cent of the world's working-age population, own 2.7 percent of global wealth. Most of these poor adults live in non-White countries that were subjected to centuries of slave trading and colonizing and resource dispossessing, which created the modern wealth of the West. The wealth extraction continues today via foreign companies that own or control key natural resources in the global south, taken through force with the threat of "economic sanctions" or granted by "elected" politicians. Racial capitalism makes countries like the Democratic Republic of the Congo one of the richest countries in the world belowground and one of the poorest countries in the world aboveground.

To love capitalism is to end up loving racism. To love racism is to end up loving capitalism. The conjoined twins are two sides of the same destructive body. The idea that capitalism is merely free markets, competition, free trade, supplying and demanding, and private ownership of the means of production operating for a profit is as whimsical and ahistorical as the White-supremacist idea that calling something racist is the primary form of racism. Popular definitions of capitalism, like popular racist ideas, do not live in historical or material reality. Capitalism is essentially racist; racism is essentially capitalist. They were birthed together from the same unnatural causes, and they shall one day die together from unnatural causes. Or racial capitalism will live into another epoch of theft and rapacious inequity, especially if activists naïvely fight the conjoined twins independently, as if they are not the same.

MY PARENTS WERE worried. I felt alive when I moved into this Black neighborhood. I felt I needed to live around Black people in order to study and uplift Black people. Not just any Black people: poor Black people. I considered poor Blacks to be the truest and most authentic representatives of Black people. I made urban poverty an entryway into the supposedly crime-riddled and impoverished house of authentic Blackness.

For Lerone Bennett Jr., the longtime executive editor of *Ebony* magazine, my identifying of poverty, hustling, criminality, sex, and gambling in the urban world as the most authentic Black world probably would have reminded him of the blaxploitation films of the late 1960s and early 1970s. The Black Power movement of the era, in shattering the White standard of assimilationist ideas, sent creative Black people on a mission to erect Black standards, a new Black aesthetic. Blaxploitation films arrived right on time, with Black casts, urban settings, and Black heroes and heroines: pimps, gangsters, prostitutes, and rapists.

Both of my parents saw *Shaft* (1971) and *Super Fly* (1972) upon their release. But their Christian theology, even in its liberational form, halted them from seeing *Sweet Sweetback's Baadasssss Song* in 1971. It was a movie about a male brothel worker who is brutalized by LAPD officers but then beats them up in retaliation, eludes a police manhunt in impoverished communities, uses his sexual prowess to secure aid from women, and reaches freedom in Mexico. "I made this film for the Black aesthetic," Melvin Van Peebles said. "White critics aren't used to that. The movie is Black life, unpandered."

I wanted to experience Black life, unpandered. I had moved to North Philadelphia in 2005 carrying dueling bags of Blackness: "Black is Beautiful" and "Black is Misery," to use the phrase Lerone Bennett Jr. tendered in his *Ebony* review of *Sweet Sweetback's Baadasssss Song*. Bennett blasted Van Peebles for his cinematic ode to the Black "cult of poverty," for imagining poverty "as the incubator of wisdom and soul," for "foolishly" identifying "the black aesthetic with empty bellies and big-bottomed prostitutes. . . . To romanticize the tears and the agony of the people," Bennett wrote, "is to play them cheap as human beings."

I thought I was so real, so Black, in choosing this apartment in this neighborhood. In truth, I was being racist, playing poor Blacks cheap as human beings. While others had fled from poor Blacks in racist fear of their dangerous inferiority, I was fleeing to poor Blacks in racist assurance of the superiority conferred by their danger, their superior authenticity. I was the Black gentrifier, a distinct creature from the White gentrifier. If the White gentrifier moves to the poor Black neighborhood to be a developer, the Black gentrifier is moving back to the poor Black neighborhood to be developed.

To be antiracist is to recognize neither poor Blacks nor elite Blacks as the truest representative of Black people. But at the time I believed culture filtered upward, that Black elites, in all our materialism, individualism, and assimilationism, needed to go to the "bottom" to be civilized. I understood poor Blacks as simultaneously the bottom and the foundation of Blackness. I wanted their authenticity to rub off on me, a spoiled—in both senses—middle-income Black man. Rap music made by people from "the bottom" was no longer enough to keep me stuck on the realness.

I was in full agreement with E. Franklin Frazier's *Black Bourgeoisie,* published in 1957. Situating White elites as the norm, Frazier dubbed Black elites as inferior: as quicker racial sellouts, as bigger conspicuous consumers, as more politically corrupt, as more exploitative, as more irrational for looking up to the very people oppressing them. This inverted class racism about inferior Black elites quickly became a religious belief, joining the religious belief about the Black masses being more pathological. In the bestselling *Beyond the Melting Pot,* written with Daniel Patrick Moynihan in 1963, sociologist Nathan Glazer argued that, unlike the other middle classes, "the Negro middle class contributes very little . . . to the solution of Negro social programs." Without any supporting data, Glazer positioned the Black bourgeoisie as inferior, in the scale of social responsibility, to other bourgeoisies. These racist ideas were wrong, of course—a decade earlier, Martin Luther King Jr. and a generation of elite Black youngsters from the Black bourgeoisie began the epic struggle for civil rights, economic justice, and desegregation. My generation of elite Black youngsters rushed into our own struggle—into Black studies, a Black space.

## CHAPTER 13

# SPACE

**SPACE RACISM:** A powerful collection of racist policies that lead to resource inequity between racialized spaces or the elimination of certain racialized spaces, which are substantiated by racist ideas about racialized spaces.

**SPACE ANTIRACISM:** A powerful collection of antiracist policies that lead to racial equity between integrated and protected racialized spaces, which are substantiated by antiracist ideas about racialized spaces.

W E CALLED OUR African American studies space a Black space—it was, after all, governed primarily by Black bodies, Black thoughts, Black cultures, and Black histories. Of course, the spaces at Temple University governed primarily by White bodies, White thoughts, White cultures, and White histories were not labeled White. They hid the Whiteness of their spaces behind the veil of color blindness.

The most prominent person in our Black space at Temple had been piercing this unspoken veil since 1970, when he first printed the *Journal of Black Studies*. Molefi Kete Asante, who in 1980 would publish the seminal work *Afrocentricity*, railed against assimilationist ideas and called for Afrocentric Black people. There were multiple ways of seeing the world, he argued. But too many Black people were "looking out" at the world from a European "center," which was taken as the only point from which to see the world—through European cultures masquerading as world cultures, European religions masquerading as world religions, European history masquerading as world history. Theories gleamed from European subjects masquerading as universal theories. "The rejection of European particularism as universal is the first stage of our coming intellectual struggle," Professor Asante wrote. In 1987, he established the nation's first African American studies doctoral program at Temple to wage the struggle, the program I entered twenty years later.

Asante's right-hand woman in our department was Professor Ama Mazama. A product of Guadeloupe and recipient of a doctorate in linguistics from La Sorbonne in Paris, Professor Mazama may have been more well-known outside the United States. Not minding, she enjoyed bolting the States to speak on her research on the Afrocentric paradigm, African religion, Caribbean culture and languages, and African American homeschooling. She loved African traditions deep in her soul. That same soul hated to see African people worshipping European traditions. "Negroes," she called them in disgust.

Professor Mazama spoke as softly as the African garb that draped her petite body. I remember her publicly debating an animated Maulana Karenga, the founder of Kwanzaa, with the same tranquility with which she spoke to her homeschooled children afterward. She taught me that the power of the spoken word is in the power of the word spoken.

Professor Mazama gave criticism the way she received it: unflappably. She almost welcomed ideological divergence from the people she held dear. We didn't agree on everything, but we shared a deep love of African people and scholarly combat. Professor Mazama was as intellectually confident, fearless, and clear as anyone I had ever met. I asked her to be my dissertation adviser and she obliged. I hoped at least a few of her intellectual qualities would rub off on me.

In my first course with Mazama, she lectured on Asante's contention that objectivity was really "collective subjectivity." She concluded, "It is impossible to be objective."

It was the sort of simple idea that shifted my view of the world immediately. It made so much sense to me as I recalled the subjective choices I'd made as an aspiring journalist and scholar. If objectivity was dead, though, I needed a replacement. I flung up my hand like an eighth-grader.

"Yes?"

"If we can't be objective, then what should we strive to do?" She stared at me as she gathered her words. Not a woman of many words, it did not take long.

"Just tell the truth. That's what we should strive to do. Tell the truth."

AFRICAN AMERICAN STUDIES took up part of the eighth floor of Gladfelter Hall at Temple University, which stoically faced its equally imposing twin, Anderson Hall. The two skyscrapers filled with middle-income White faculty and students loomed over North Philadelphia blocks teeming with low-income Black people. Temple's poorly paid security guards required anyone entering Gladfelter Hall or other campus buildings to show their university IDs to prevent those two worlds from meeting. Racist Whites saw danger in the "ghetto" walking on campus. They worried about safeguarding their White space inside North Philadelphia's Black space. But they could not understand why we worried about safeguarding our Black space inside Temple's White space. They branded Black studies a "ghetto," like my neighborhood in North Philadelphia, but insisted it was a ghetto of our making.

The defining character of Harlem's "dark ghetto," where Kenneth Clark lived and studied during the early 1960s, and of the North Philadelphia where I lived and studied four decades later was "creeping blight," according to Clark, "juvenile delinquency" and "widespread violence"—characteristics that exist in different forms in all racialized spaces. The idea of the dangerous Black neighborhood is the most dangerous racist idea. And it is powerfully misleading. For instance, people steer away from and stigmatize Black neighborhoods as crime-ridden streets where you might have your wallet stolen. But they aspire to move into up-scale White neighborhoods, home to white-collar criminals and "banksters," as Thom Hartmann calls them, who might steal your life savings. Americans lost trillions during the Great Recession, which was largely triggered by financial crimes of staggering enormity. Estimated losses from white-collar crimes are believed to be between $300 and $600 billion per year, according to the FBI. By comparison, near the height of violent crime in 1995, the FBI reported the combined costs of burglary and robbery to be $4 billion.

Racist Americans stigmatize entire Black neighborhoods as places of homicide and mortal violence but don't similarly con-nect White neighborhoods to the disproportionate number of White males who engage in mass shootings. And they don't even see the daily violence that unfolds on the highways that deliver mostly White suburbanites to their homes. In 1986, during the violent crack epidemic, 3,380 more Americans died from alcohol-related traffic deaths than from homicides. None of this is to say that White spaces or Black spaces are more or less violent—this isn't about creating a hierarchy. The point is that when we un-chain ourselves from the space racism that deracializes and nor-malizes and elevates elite White spaces, while doing the opposite to Black spaces, we will find good and bad, violence and nonvio-lence, in all spaces, no matter how poor or rich, Black or non-Black. No matter the effect of the conjoined twins.

Just as racist power racializes people, racist power racializes space. The ghetto. The inner city. The third world. A space is racialized when a racial group is known to either govern the space or make up the clear majority in the space. A Black space, for instance, is either a space publicly run by Black people or a space where Black people stand in the majority. Policies of space racism overresource White spaces and underresource non-White spaces. Ideas of space racism justify resource inequity through creating a racial hierarchy of space, lifting up White spaces as heaven, down-grading non-White spaces as hell. "We have a situation where we

have our inner cities, African Americans, Hispanics, are living in
hell, because it's so dangerous," candidate Donald Trump said
during a presidential debate in 2016. In an Oval Office meeting
in 2018 about Black and Latinx immigrants, President Trump
asked: "Why are we having all these people from shithole countries come here?"

AFTER EXITING THE elevator onto Gladfelter's eighth floor, no
one could miss the glassed-in classroom known as the fishbowl.
Inside the glass walls often sat, in a circle, a motley bunch of
mostly Black fish—many of whom had swum into Philadelphia
from historically Black colleges and universities and were still
soaked in school pride. One day before class, a Jackson State alum
had the audacity to announce the Sonic Boom as the best marching band in the land. He looked at me. I fell out laughing, a deep
and long and booming laugh that said everything I needed to say.
Almost all of us were boosting our school bands and academic
feats and homecomings and histories and alumni. Even Ali from
Fisk University. "There are more PhDs," Ali declared one day,
"walking around who went to Fisk for undergrad than any other
HBCU." We all knew Fisk used to be illustrious, but these days
small private HBCUs like Fisk were hemorrhaging students and
revenue and donations and respect. "This is 2006, not 1906!"
someone blurted. "All of Fisk's doctorates could easily fit in this
fishbowl," someone shouted. "What y'all got, two hundred students right now?"

Jokes aside, I respected Ali's pride in Fisk and all my classmates'
HBCU pride, no matter how outlandish they sometimes sounded.
I had no respect for those who hated their HBCUs. And no one
hated their HBCU more than the only other FAMU alum in our
graduate program.

Every time I lifted up FAMU's examples of Black excellence,
Nashay shot them down. She complained about the incompetence lurking on FAMU's campus the way Temple students complained about the dangers lurking off campus. One day, as we

awaited class in the fishbowl, I'd had enough. "Why you always dogging out FAMU?"

"Don't worry about it."

I pressed. She resisted. Finally, she opened.

"FAMU messed up my transcript!"

"What?" I asked, confused.

"I had them send my transcript and they messed it up. How can you have incompetent people working in the transcript office?"

She closed up. Class started, but I could not let it go. How could she use one horrible error from one person in one office to condemn the entire university—my university—as horrible? But I had said it all, heard it all before. I heard and heaped blame on HBCU administrators for the scarcity of resources. I heard Black students and faculty at historically White colleges and universities (HWCUs) say they could never go to HBCUs, those poorly run ghettos. I heard HBCU faculty and staff talk about escaping the dark ghettos and moving to HWCUs.

I heard my uncle say, like Dartmouth alum Aisha Tyler, that HBCUs do not represent "the real world." The argument: Black students are better served learning how to operate in a majority-White nation by attending a majority-White university. The reality: A large percentage of—perhaps most—Black Americans live in majority-Black neighborhoods, work in majority-Black sites of employment, organize in majority-Black associations, socialize in majority-Black spaces, attend majority-Black churches, and send their children to majority-Black schools. When people contend that Black spaces do not represent reality, they are speaking from the White worldview of Black people in the minority. They are conceptualizing the real American world as White. To be antiracist is to recognize there is no such thing as the "real world," only real worlds, multiple worldviews.

I heard people say, "Even the best black colleges and universities do not approach the standards of quality of respectable institutions," as economist Thomas Sowell wrote in 1974. Sowell's "description remains accurate," Jason Riley wrote in *The Wall*

*Street Journal* on September 28, 2010. Selective HBCUs lag behind "decent state schools like the University of Texas at Austin, never mind a Stanford or Yale."

Riley had pulled out the familiar weapon safeguarding space racism and menacing Black spaces: unfairly comparing Black spaces to substantially richer White spaces. The endowment of the richest HBCU, Howard, was five times less than UT Austin's endowment in 2016, never mind being thirty-six times less than the endowment of a Stanford or Yale. The racial wealth gap produces a giving gap. For public HBCUs, the giving gap extends to state-funding gaps, as racist policies steer more funds to HWCUs, like the current "performance based" state models.

Resources define a space, resources the conjoined twins divvy up. People make spaces from resources. Comparing spaces across race-classes is like matching fighters of different weight classes, which fighting sports consider unfair. Poor Black neighborhoods should be compared to equally poor White neighborhoods, not to considerably richer White neighborhoods. Small Black businesses should be compared to equally small White businesses, not to wealthy White corporations. Indeed, when researchers compare HBCUs to HWCUs of similar means and makeup, HBCUs tend to have higher Black graduation rates. Not to mention, Black HBCU graduates are, on average, more likely than their Black peers from HWCUs to be thriving financially, socially, and physically.

NASHAY FORCED ME to reckon with my own space racism, but I would learn there was more to her story.

A financial-aid officer had stolen thousands from her as an undergraduate student at a White university, but she still held that university in high regard. A botched transcript and she condemned her Black university. What hypocrisy. At the time, I could not be angry at her without being angrier at myself. How many times did I individualize the error in White spaces, blaming the individual and not the White space? How many times did I generalize the error in the Black space—in the Black church or at a Black gathering—and blame the Black space instead of the individual? How many times did I have a bad experience at a Black business and then walk away complaining about not the individuals involved but Black businesses as a whole?

Banks remain twice as likely to offer loans to White entrepreneurs than to Black entrepreneurs. Customers avoid Black businesses like they are the "ghetto," like the "White man's ice is colder," as antiracists have joked for years. I knew this then. But my dueling consciousness still led me to think like one young Black writer wrote in *Blavity* in 2017: "On an intellectual level, I know that Black people have been denied equal access to capital, training, and physical space. But does that inequitable treatment excuse bad service?" Does not good service, like every other commodity, typically cost more money? How can we acknowledge the clouds of racism over Black spaces and be shocked when it rains on our heads?

I felt Black was beautiful, but Black spaces were not? Nearly everything I am I owe to Black space. Black neighborhood. Black church. Black college. Black studies. I was like a plant devaluing the soil that made me.

THE HISTORY OF space racism is long. It is an American history that begins with Thomas Jefferson's solution to the "Negro problem." Civilize and emancipate the Negro. Send the Negro to Africa to "carry back to the country of their origin the seeds of civilization," as Jefferson proposed in a letter in 1811. But the Negro commonly wanted no part in returning and redeeming Africa "from ignorance and barbarism." We do not want to go to the "savage wilds of Africa," free Black Philadelphians resolved in 1817. Slaveholders were, meanwhile, decrying the savage wilds of free Blacks. A writer for the South's *De Bow's Review* searched around the world, through a series of articles in 1859 and 1860, for "a moral, happy, and voluntarily industrious community of free negroes," but concluded, "no such community exists upon the face of the earth."

On January 12, 1865, in the midst of the Civil War, General William T. Sherman and U.S. secretary of war Edwin M. Stanton met with twenty Black leaders in Savannah, Georgia. After their spokesman, Garrison Frazier, said they needed land to be free so "we could reap the fruit of our labor, take care of ourselves," Stanton asked if they would "rather live . . . scattered among the whites or in colonies by yourselves?"

"Live by ourselves," Frazier responded, "for there is a prejudice against us in the South that will take years to get over."

Four days later, German Sherman issued Special Field Order No. 15 to punish Confederate landowners and rid his army camps of runaways. Black people received an army mule and "not more than forty acres" on coastal plains of South Carolina and Georgia. "The sole and exclusive management of affairs will be left to the freed people themselves," Sherman ordered.

Horace Greeley, the most eminent newspaper editor of the day, thought Sherman's order deprived the Negroes "of the advantage of white teachers and neighbors, who would lead them to an understanding and enjoyment of that higher civilization of which hitherto they have been deprived as slaves." Freed Southern Blacks "like their fellows at the North" will be "aided by contact with white civilization," Greeley wrote in his *New-York Tribune* on January 30, 1865.

Black people were rejecting Greeley's integrationist strategy. By June 1865, roughly forty thousand Blacks had settled on four hundred thousand acres of land before Confederate landowners, aided by the new Johnson administration, started taking back "their" land.

The integrationist strategy—the placing of White and non-White bodies in the same spaces—is thought to cultivate away the barbarism of people of color and the racism of White people. The integrationist strategy expects Black bodies to heal in proximity to Whites who haven't yet stopped fighting them. After enduring slavery's violence, Frazier and his brethren had enough. They desired to separate, not from Whites but from White racism. Separation is not always segregation. The antiracist desire to separate from racists is different from the segregationist desire to separate from "inferior" Blacks.

Whenever Black people voluntarily gather among themselves, integrationists do not see spaces of Black solidarity created to separate Black people from racism. They see spaces of White hate. They do not see spaces of cultural solidarity, of solidarity against racism. They see spaces of segregation against White people. Integrationists do not see these spaces as the movement of Black people toward Black people. Integrationists think about them as a movement away from White people. They then equate that movement away from White people with the White segregationist movement away from Black people. Integrationists equate spaces for the survival of Black bodies with spaces for the survival of White supremacy.

When integrationists use segregation and separation interchangeably, they are using the vocabulary of Jim Crow. Segregationists blurred the lines between segregation and separation by projecting their policies as standing "on the platform of equal accommodations for each race but separate," to quote Atlanta newspaper editor Henry W. Grady in 1885. The U.S. Supreme Court sanctioned this spoken veil in the 1896 *Plessy v. Ferguson* decision. Separate but equal covered up the segregationist policies that diverted resources toward exclusively White spaces. In 1930, segregationist Alabama spent $37 for each White student, compared to $7 for each Black student; Georgia, $32 to $7; and South Carolina, $53 to $5. High school was unavailable for my maternal grandparents around this time in Georgia.

"Equal," thought to be the soft target of the "separate but equal" ruling, ended up being a formidable foe for civil-rights activists—it was nearly impossible to get equal resources for Black institutions. The NAACP Legal Defense Fund switched tactics to taking down "separate." Lawyers revived the old integrationist "assumption that the enforced separation of the two races stamps the colored race with a badge of inferiority," which Associate Justice Henry Billings Brown called a "fallacy" in his *Plessy v. Ferguson* decision.

In the landmark *Brown v. Board of Education* case in 1954, NAACP lawyer Thurgood Marshall attempted to prove the assumption using the new integrationist social science. Marshall asked psychologists Kenneth and Mamie Clark to repeat their famous doll tests for the case. Presented with dolls with different skin colors, the majority of Black children preferred White dolls, which the Clarks saw as proof of the negative psychological harm of segregation. White social scientists argued the harm could be permanent. The U.S. Supreme Court unanimously agreed. "To separate [colored children] from others of similar age and qualifications solely because of their race generates a feeling of inferiority as to their status in the community that may affect their hearts and minds in a way unlikely ever to be undone," Chief Justice Earl Warren wrote.

Justice Warren did not judge White schools to be having a detrimental effect upon White children. He wrote the "segregation of white and colored children in public schools has a detrimental effect upon the colored children." It retards their "education and mental development," Warren explained. "We conclude that, in the field of public education, the doctrine of 'separate but equal' has no place. Separate educational facilities are inherently unequal."

What really made the schools unequal were the dramatically unequal resources provided to them, not the mere fact of racial separation. The Supreme Court justices deciding both *Plessy* and *Brown* avowed the segregationist lie that the "Negro and white schools involved have been equalized, or are being equalized," to quote Justice Warren. By 1973, when the resource inequities between the public schools had become too obvious to deny, the Supreme Court ruled, in *San Antonio Independent School District v. Rodriguez,* that property-tax allocations yielding inequities in public schools do not violate the equal-protection clause of the U.S. Constitution.

. . .

THE 1973 SUPREME Court ruling reified the only solution emanating from the *Brown* decision in 1954: busing Black bodies from detrimental Black spaces to worthwhile White spaces. Since "there are adequate Negro schools and prepared instructors and instructions, then there is nothing different except the presence of white people," wrote an insulted Zora Neale Hurston in the *Orlando Sentinel* in 1955. Martin Luther King Jr. also privately disagreed. "I favor integration on buses and in all areas of public accommodation and travel. . . . I think integration in our public schools is different," King told two Black teachers in Montgomery, Alabama, in 1959. "White people view black people as inferior. . . . People with such a low view of the black race cannot be given free rein and put in charge of the intellectual care and development of our boys and girls."

King had a nightmare that came to pass. Non-White students fill most of the seats in today's public school classrooms but are taught by an 80 percent White teaching force, which often has, however unconsciously, lower expectations for non-White students. When Black and White teachers look at the same Black student, White teachers are about 40 percent less likely to believe the student will finish high school. Low-income Black students who have at least one Black teacher in elementary school are 29 percent less likely to drop out of school, 39 percent less likely among very low-income Black boys.

King's nightmare is a product of the dueling *Brown* decision. The court rightly undermined the legitimacy of segregated White spaces that hoard public resources, exclude all non-Whites, and are wholly dominated by White peoples and cultures. But the court also reinforced the legitimacy of integrated White spaces that hoard public resources, include some non-Whites, and are generally, though not wholly, dominated by White peoples and cultures. White majorities, White power, and White culture dominate both the segregated and the integrated, making both White. But the unspoken veil claims there is no such thing as integrated White spaces, or for that matter integrated Black spaces that are underresourced, include some non-Blacks, and are generally, though not wholly, dominated by Black peoples and cultures. The court ruled Black spaces, segregated or integrated, inherently unequal and inferior.

After *Brown,* the integrated White space came to define the ideal integrated space where inferior non-White bodies could be developed. The integrated Black space became a de facto segregated space where inferior Black bodies were left behind. Integration had turned into "a one-way street," a young Chicago lawyer observed in 1995. "The minority assimilated into the dominant culture, not the other way around," Barack Obama wrote. "Only white culture could be neutral and objective. Only white culture could be nonracial." Integration (into Whiteness) became racial progress.

"THE EXPERIENCE OF an integrated education made all the difference in the lives of black children," wrote Cal Berkeley professor David L. Kirp in *The New York Times* in 2016, speaking from the new low of integration's roller-coaster history. The percentage of Southern Black students attending integrated White schools jumped from zero in 1954 to 23 percent in 1969 to 44 percent in 1989 before falling back to 23 percent in 2011. The "academic-achievement gap" followed a similar roller coaster, closing with the integration of White schools, before opening back up, proving that "African-American students who attended integrated schools fared better academically than those left behind in segregated schools," Kirp argued. Standardized tests "proved" White students and White spaces were smarter. And yet, what if the scoring gap closed because, as Black students integrated White schools, more students received the same education and test prep?

Integrationists have resented the rise in what they call segregated schools. "Like many whites who grew up in the 1960s and

1970s, I had always thought the ultimate goal of better race relations was integration," wrote Manhattan Institute fellow Tamar
Jacoby in 1998. "The very word had a kind of magic to it," but
now "few of us talk about it anymore." We are not pursuing Martin Luther King's "color-blind dream" of "a more or less race-
neutral America."

The integrationist transformation of King as color-blind and
race-neutral erases the actual King. He did not live to integrate
Black spaces and people into White oblivion. If he did, then why
did he build low-income Atlanta apartments "using Negro workmen, Negro architects, Negro attorneys, and Negro financial institutions throughout," as he proudly reported in 1967? Why did
he urge Black people to stop being "ashamed of being Black," to
invest in their own spaces? The child of a Black neighborhood,
church, college, and organization lived to ensure equal access to
public accommodations and equal resources for all racialized
spaces, an antiracist strategy as culture-saving as his nonviolence
was body-saving.

Through lynching Black bodies, segregationists are, in the
end, more harmful to Black *bodies* than integrationists are.
Through lynching Black cultures, integrationists are, in the end,
more harmful to *Black* bodies than segregationists are. Think
about the logical conclusion of integrationist strategy: every race
being represented in every U.S. space according to their percentage in the national population. A Black (12.7 percent) person
would not see another until after seeing eight or so non-Blacks.
A Latinx (17.8 percent) person would not see another until after
seeing seven or so non-Latinx. An Asian (4.8 percent) person
would not see another until after seeing nineteen non-Asians. A
Native (0.9 percent) person would not see another until after seeing ninety-nine non-Natives. White (61.3 percent) Americans
would always see more White people around than non-White
people. They would gain everything, from the expansion of integrated White spaces to Whites gentrifying all the non-White institutions, associations, and neighborhoods. No more spatial

wombs for non-White cultures. Only White spatial wombs of assimilation. We would all become "only white men" with different "skins," to quote historian Kenneth Stampp in 1956.

Americans have seen the logical conclusion of segregationist strategy, from slavery to Jim Crow to mass incarceration and border walls. The logical conclusion of antiracist strategy is open and equal access to all public accommodations, open access to all integrated White spaces, integrated Middle Eastern spaces, integrated Black spaces, integrated Latinx spaces, integrated Native spaces, and integrated Asian spaces that are as equally resourced as they are culturally different. All these spaces adjoin civic spaces of political and economic and cultural power, from a House of Representatives to a school board to a newspaper editorial board where no race predominates, where shared antiracist power predominates. This is diversity, something integrationists value only in name.

Antiracist strategy fuses desegregation with a form of integration and racial solidarity. Desegregation: eliminating all barriers to all racialized spaces. To be antiracist is to support the voluntary integration of bodies attracted by cultural difference, a shared humanity. Integration: resources rather than bodies. To be an antiracist is to champion resource equity by challenging the racist policies that produce resource inequity. Racial solidarity: openly identifying, supporting, and protecting integrated racial spaces. To be antiracist is to equate and nurture difference among racial groups.

But antiracist strategy is beyond the integrationist conception that claims Black spaces could never be equal to White spaces, that believes Black spaces have a "detrimental effect upon" Black people, to quote Chief Justice Warren in *Brown*. My Black studies space was supposed to have a detrimental effect on me. Quite the opposite. My professors made sure of that, as did two Black students, answering questions I never thought to ask.

## CHAPTER 14

# GENDER

**GENDER RACISM:** A powerful collection of racist policies that lead to inequity between race-genders and are substantiated by racist ideas about race-genders.

**GENDER ANTIRACISM:** A powerful collection of antiracist policies that lead to equity between race-genders and are substantiated by anti-racist ideas about race-genders.

NO ONE OVERLOOKED the sheer size of her intellect, which was even more immediately apparent than her tall, full build and striking makeup. No one overlooked Kaila at all. She did not tuck away a single aspect of herself by the time I met her at Temple. No self-censoring. No closeting of her lesbian feminism in a Black space that could be antagonizing to lesbianism and feminism. No ambiguity for misinterpretation. All badass Joan Morgan "chickenhead" giving no fucks. All warrior poet giving all fucks, like her idol, Audre Lorde. Kaila was entirely herself, and her Laila Ali intellect wished for the world to voice a problem with what they saw.

Kaila had no problem telling you about yourself. Her legendary impersonations of African American studies students and faculty were as funny as they were accurate. I always wanted her to do an impersonation of me, but I was too scared and insecure to see what she saw.

Kaila held court with Yaba, whose roaring, full-bodied laughter often filled the room. Their back-and-forth jokes were as bad for victims as Venus and Serena Williams's matches were bad for tennis balls. When I sat down for a long talk—or, rather, to listen and learn—my mouth seemed to always be open, in laughter at their jokes or jaw-dropping wonder over their insights. They sat as the royal court of African American studies graduate students. Everyone feared or respected or battled them. I feared and respected them, too scared and awed to battle.

Yaba's irrepressible Blackness governed our Blacker-than-thou space. Blacker than thou not because of her Ghanaian features, her down-home New Orleans air, or her mixes of African garb and African American fashion. Not because she danced as comfortably to the beat of West Indian cultures as she did to her own. She seemed to have an encyclopedic knowledge of Black people: the most ethnically antiracist person in my new world. As up to date on Black American popular culture as African politics, as equipped to debate the intricacies of the rise of Beyoncé as she could the third rise of Black feminism, as comfortable explaining the origins of Haitian Creole as the conflicts between the Yoruba and Igbo of Nigeria. I always felt so ignorant around her.

I ARRIVED AT Temple as a racist, sexist homophobe. Not exactly friend material for these two women. But they saw the potential in me I did not see in myself.

My ideas of gender and sexuality reflected those of my parents. They did not raise me not to be a homophobe. They rarely talked about gay and lesbian people. Ideas often dance a cappella. Their silence erased queer existence as thoroughly as integrationists erased the reality of integrated White spaces.

On gender, Dad's perception of masculine strength did not derive from the perceived weakness of women. Maybe because Ma made no bones about her strength. She'd weight-lifted ever since I could remember. She carried heavy bags into the house, letting the three six-footers she lived with know that even at five foot three and 120 pounds, she was no physical slouch. Dad had always been more emotional and affectionate than Ma. Dad comforted my brother and me when we got hurt. Ma told us to suck it up, like the time I came in crying about breaking my wrist. She ordered me back outside to finish the basketball game.

Dad often joked at church about Ma being the CFO of the family. While other patriarchal men laughed, Dad was serious. She was. At other times, Dad's sexist ideas demanded he lead and Ma's sexist ideas submitted. She would call him the head of the household. He would accept the calling.

My parents did not strictly raise me to be a Black patriarch. I became a Black patriarch because my parents and the world around me did not strictly raise me to be a Black feminist. Neither my parents nor I came up in an age conducive to teaching Black feminism to a Black boy, if there ever was such an age. There seemed to be a low-level war being waged between the genders, maybe most clearly articulated in our popular culture. I was born the year of Alice Walker's *The Color Purple,* a seminal work of Black feminist art, but one that many Black male critics saw as a hit job on Black masculinity. I entered adolescence the year Black women were hitting theaters for a cathartic tour of Black male maltreatment, *Waiting to Exhale.* But the latest conflict had deeper roots, perhaps germinating in the summer of 1965, when the media got ahold of "The Negro Family: The Case for National Action," a government report written by President Johnson's assistant secretary of labor, Daniel Patrick Moynihan.

Nearly one-fourth of Black families were headed by women, twice the rate for White families, Moynihan warned, as the media swooned about the "broken" Black family. "The Negro community has been forced into a matriarchal structure which . . . imposes a crushing burden on the Negro male," producing a "tangle of pathology," Moynihan asserted. Moynihan called for national action to employ and empower Black men, who had been emasculated by discrimination and matriarchal Black women. "Keeping the Negro 'in his place' can be translated as keeping the Negro male in his place: The female was not a threat to anyone," Moynihan wrote.

"The reverberations" from the Moynihan report "were disastrous," historian Deborah Gray White once wrote. Racist patriarchs, from White social scientists to Black husbands, demanded the submission of Black women to uplift the race. A command in *Ebony* magazine became popular: The "immediate goal of the Negro woman today should be the establishment of a strong family unit in which the father is the dominant person." A decade later, Black patriarchs and White social scientists were still touting the idea that Black men had it worse than Black women. Racism had "clearly" and "largely focused" on the Black male, sociologist Charles Herbert Stember argued in his 1976 book, *Sexual Racism: The Emotional Barrier to an Integrated Society*. An America of integrated (White) spaces had not been achieved because at racism's core was the "sexual rejection of the racial minority, the conscious attempt on the part of the majority to prevent interracial cohabitation," he wrote. The White man's sexual jealousy of the Black man was the key.

For too many Black men, the Black Power movement that emerged after the Moynihan report became a struggle against White men for Black power over Black women. Dad witnessed this power struggle, after being raised by a single Black mother who never called him or his brother the head of the household, like other patriarchal single moms did. One day in 1969, Dad had been singing inside a storefront church. He stepped outside for air and confronted a Black Panther assaulting his girlfriend. On another day, in the summer of 1971, Dad and a girlfriend before Ma ventured up to the Harlem Temple of the Nation of Islam. The Nation had piqued Dad's interest. They were eating with one of the ministers. Dad's girlfriend said something. The minister smacked her and smacked from his mouth, "Women are not to speak in the presence of men." Dad sprang out of his chair and had to be restrained and strong-armed out of the temple.

In spite of everything, Dad and Ma could not help but join the interracial force policing the sexuality of young Black mothers. They were two of the millions of liberals and conservatives aghast at the growing percentage of Black children being born into single-parent households in the 1970s and 1980s—aghast even though my dad turned out just fine. The panic around the reported numbers of single-parent households was based on a host of faulty or untested premises: that two bad parents would be better than one good one, that the presence of an abusive Black father is better for the child than his absence, that having a second income for a child trumps all other factors, that all of the single parents were Black women, that none of these absent fathers were in prison or the grave, that Black mothers never hid the presence of Black fathers in their household to keep their welfare for the child.

In time for the midterm elections in 1994, political scientist Charles Murray made sure Americans knew the percentage of Black children born into single-parent households "has now reached 68 percent." Murray blamed the "welfare system." My parents and other liberals blamed sexual irresponsibility, a shameful disregard for the opportunities born of 1960s activism, pathologizing poverty, and a disconnect from the premarital abstinence of Christ. They were all wrong on so many levels. The increasing percentage of Black babies born into single-parent households was not due to single Black mothers having more children but to married Black women having fewer children over the course of the twentieth century. Ma could see that decline in her family. Ma's married paternal grandmother had sixteen children in the 1910s and 1920s. Ma's married mother had six children in the 1940s and 1950s. My mother had two children in the early 1980s—as did two of her three married sisters.

Ma and Dad and countless Americans were disconnected from racial reality and leapt to demonize this class of single mothers. Only Black feminists like Dorothy Roberts and Angela Davis defended them.

ON OTHER ISSUES, Ma sometimes put up a feminist defense. It was early August 1976, the Tuesday before the Saturday my parents were scheduled to wed. Running down the ceremony, Pastor Wilfred Quinby recited the Christian wedding vows for my parents. "Husbands, love your wives, and wives, obey your husbands."

"I'm not obeying him!" Ma interjected. "What!" Pastor Quinby said in shock, turning to look at my father. "What!" Dad said, turning to look at my mother.

"The only man I obeyed was my father, when I was a child," she nearly shouted, staring into Dad's wide eyes. "You are not my father and I'm not a child!"

The clock was ticking. Would Dad whip out Bible verses on women's submission and fight for the sexist idea? Would he crawl away and look for another woman, who would submit? Dad chose a different option: the only option that could have yielded their marriage of more than four decades. He slowly picked up his jaw, popped his eyes back in their sockets, and offered Ma an equitable solution.

"How about: Are you willing to submit one to another?" he asked.

Ma nodded. She liked the sound of "one to another," integrating the Christian concept of submission with feminist equity. My parents wrote their own wedding vows. Pastor Quinby married them as scheduled.


DAD SHOULD NOT have been shocked at Ma's resistance. For some time, Ma had been rethinking Christian sexism. After they wed, Ma attended "consciousness-raising conferences" for Christian women in Queens. What Kimberly Springer calls the "Black feminist movement" had finally burst through the sexist dams of Christian churches. Black feminists rejected the prevailing Black patriarchal idea that the primary activist role of Black women was submitting to their husbands and producing more Black babies for the "Black nation." Through groups like the Black Women's Alliance (1970) and the National Black Feminist Organization (1973), through Black women's caucuses in Black power and women's liberation groups, Black feminists fought sexism in

Black spaces and racism in women's spaces. They developed their own spaces, and a Black feminist consciousness for Black women's liberation, for the liberation of humanity.

Black queer activists, too, had been marginalized after they launched the gay-liberation movement through the Stonewall rebellion in Manhattan in 1969. Braving homophobia in Black spaces and racism in queer spaces, antiracist queer people formed their own spaces. Perhaps the most antiracist queer space of the era may have also been the most antiracist feminist space of the era. In the summer of 1974, a group of Boston Black women separated from the National Black Feminist Organization to form the Combahee River Collective, named for the Combahee River slave raid of 1863 led by Harriet Tubman. They revived the unadulterated freedom politics of General Tubman. In 1977, they shared their views, in a statement drafted by Barbara Smith, Demita Frazier, and Beverly Smith. The Combahee River Collective Statement embodied queer liberation, feminism, and antiracism, like perhaps no other public statement in American history. They did not want Black women to be viewed as inferior or superior to any other group. "To be recognized as human, levelly human, is enough.

"Our politics initially sprang from the shared belief that Black women are inherently valuable," they wrote. "No other ostensibly progressive movement has ever considered our specific oppression as a priority. . . . We realize that the only people who care enough about us to work consistently for our liberation are us." Maria Stewart, America's first feminist known to give a public address to a coed audience, considered and prioritized the specific oppression of Black women in her daring speeches in the early 1830s in Boston. So did Sojourner Truth and Frances Harper, before and after the Civil War. So did Ida B. Wells and Anna Julia Cooper, in the early 1900s. So did Frances Beal, who audaciously proclaimed in 1968, "the black woman in America can justly be described as a 'slave of a slave,'" the victim of the "double jeopardy" of racism and sexism. This position paper joined an anthology of pieces in 1970 by women like Nikki Giovanni, Audre Lorde, and a young

Mississippi prodigy named Alice Walker. Editor Toni Cade Bambara, a Rutgers literary scholar, ensured *The Black Woman* best reflected "the preoccupations of the contemporary Black woman in this country," including setting "the record straight on the matriarch and the evil Black bitch."

But 1991—the year Anita Hill accused U.S. Supreme Court nominee Clarence Thomas of sexual harassment—proved to be the pivotal year of Black feminist scholars. They constructed terminology that named the specific oppression facing Black women, which Black feminists from Maria Stewart to Anna Julia Cooper to Angela Davis had been identifying for more than a century. Behind the scenes of what Thomas mind-bogglingly called a "high-tech lynching" and Black feminists' frontline defense of Hill, Afro-Dutch scholar Philomena Essed worked on a project that would help define what was happening. She published her reflections on in-depth interviews she'd conducted with Black women in the United States and the Netherlands in *Understanding Everyday Racism*. "In discussing the experiences of Black women, is it sexism or is it racism?" Essed asked. "These two concepts narrowly intertwine and combine under certain conditions into one, hybrid phenomenon. Therefore, it is useful to speak of *gendered racism.*"

In 1991, UCLA critical race theorist Kimberlé Williams Crenshaw further explored this notion of "intersectionality." That year, she published "Mapping the Margins: Intersectionality, Identity Politics, and Violence Against Women of Color" in the *Stanford Law Review*, based on her address at the Third National Conference on Women of Color and the Law in 1990. "Feminist efforts to politicize experiences of women and antiracist efforts to politicize experiences of people of color have frequently proceeded as though the issues and experiences they each detail occur on mutually exclusive terrains," Crenshaw theorized. "Although racism and sexism readily intersect in the lives of real people, they seldom do in feminist and antiracist practices."

Racist (and sexist) power distinguishes race-genders, racial (or gender) groups at the intersection of race and gender. Women are a gender. Black people are a race. When we identify Black women, we are identifying a race-gender. A sexist policy produces inequities between women and men. A racist policy produces inequities between racial groups. When a policy produces inequities between race-genders, it is gendered racism, or gender racism for short.

To be antiracist is to reject not only the hierarchy of races but of race-genders. To be feminist is to reject not only the hierarchy of genders but of race-genders. To truly be antiracist is to be feminist. To truly be feminist is to be antiracist. To be antiracist (and feminist) is to level the different race-genders, is to root the inequities between the equal race-genders in the policies of gender racism.

Gender racism was behind the growing number of involuntary sterilizations of Black women by eugenicist physicians—two hundred thousand cases in 1970, rising to seven hundred thousand in 1980. Gender racism produced the current situation of Black women with some collegiate education making less than White women with only high school degrees; Black women having to earn advanced degrees before they earn more than White women with bachelor's degrees; and the median wealth of single White women being $42,000 compared to $100 for single Black women. Native women and Black women experience poverty at a higher rate than any other race-gender group. Black and Latinx women still earn the least, while White and Asian men earn the most. Black women are three to four times more likely to die from pregnancy-related causes than are White women. A Black woman with an advanced degree is more likely to lose her baby than a White woman with less than an eighth-grade education. Black women remain twice as likely to be incarcerated as White women.

Gender racism impacts White women and male groups of color, whether they see it or not. White women's resistance to Black feminism and intersectional theory has been self-destructive, preventing resisters from understanding their own oppression. The intersection of racism and sexism, in some cases, oppresses

White women. For example, sexist notions of "real women" as weak and racist notions of White women as the idealized woman intersect to produce the gender-racist idea that the pinnacle of womanhood is the weak White woman. This is the gender racism that caused millions of men and women to hate the strong White woman running for president in 2016, Hillary Clinton. Or to give another example, the opposite of the gender racism of the unvirtuous hypersexual Black woman is the virtuous asexual White woman, a racial construct that has constrained and controlled the White woman's sexuality (as it nakedly tainted the Black woman's sexuality as un-rape-able). White-male interest in lynching Black-male rapists of White women was as much about controlling the sexuality of White women as it was about controlling the sexuality of Black men. Racist White patriarchs were re-creating the slave era all over again, making it illicit for White women to cohabitate with Black men at the same time as racist White (and Black) men were raping Black women. And the slave era remains, amid the hollow cries of race pride drowning out the cries of the sexually assaulted. Gender racism is behind the thinking that when one defends White male abusers like Trump and Brett Kavanaugh one is defending White people; when one defends Black male abusers like Bill Cosby and R. Kelly one is defending Black people.

Male resistance to Black feminism and intersectional theory has been similarly self-destructive, preventing resisters from understanding our specific oppression. The intersection of racism and sexism, in some cases, oppresses men of color. Black men reinforce oppressive tropes by reinforcing certain sexist ideas. For example, sexist notions of "real men" as strong and racist notions of Black men as not really men intersect to produce the gender racism of the weak Black man, inferior to the pinnacle of manhood, the strong White man.

Sexist notions of men as more naturally dangerous than women (since women are considered naturally fragile, in need of protection) and racist notions of Black people as more dangerous than White people intersect to produce the gender racism of the hyperdangerous Black man, more dangerous than the White man, the Black woman, and (the pinnacle of innocent frailty) the White woman. No defense is stronger than the frail tears of innocent White womanhood. No prosecution is stronger than the case for inherently guilty Black manhood. These ideas of gender racism transform every innocent Black male into a criminal and every White female criminal into Casey Anthony, the White woman a Florida jury exonerated in 2011, against all evidence, for killing her three-year-old child. White women get away with murder and Black men spend years in prisons for wrongful convictions. After the imprisonment of Black men dropped 24 percent between 2000 and 2015, Black men were still nearly six times more likely than White men, twenty-five times more likely than Black women, and fifty times more likely than White women to be incarcerated. Black men raised in the top 1 percent by millionaires are as likely to be incarcerated as White men raised in households earning $36,000.

"CONTEMPORARY FEMINIST AND antiracist discourses have failed to consider intersectional identities such as women of color," Kimberlé Crenshaw wrote in 1991. All racial groups are a collection of intersectional identities differentiated by gender, sexuality, class, ethnicity, skin color, nationality, and culture, among a series of other identifiers. Black women first recognized their own intersectional identity. Black feminists first theorized the intersection of two forms of bigotry: sexism and racism. Intersectional theory now gives all of humanity the ability to understand the intersectional oppression of their identities, from poor Latinx to Black men to White women to Native lesbians to transgender Asians. A theory for Black women is a theory for humanity. No wonder Black feminists have been saying from the beginning that when humanity becomes serious about the freedom of Black women, humanity becomes serious about the freedom of humanity.

Intersectional Black identities are subjected to what Crenshaw described as the intersection of racism and other forms of bigotry, such as ethnocentrism, colorism, sexism, homophobia, and transphobia. My journey to being an antiracist first recognized the intersectionality of my ethnic racism, and then my bodily racism, and then my cultural racism, and then my color racism, and then my class racism, and, when I entered graduate school, my gender racism and queer racism.

## CHAPTER 15

# SEXUALITY

**QUEER RACISM:** A powerful collection of racist policies that lead to inequity between race-sexualities and are substantiated by racist ideas about race-sexualities.

**QUEER ANTIRACISM:** A powerful collection of antiracist policies that lead to equity between race-sexualities and are substantiated by antiracist ideas about race-sexualities.

RACIST (AND HOMOPHOBIC) power distinguishes race-sexualities, racial (or sexuality) groups at the intersection of race and sexuality. Homosexuals are a sexuality. Latinx people are a race. Latinx homosexuals are a race-sexuality. A homophobic policy produces inequities between heterosexuals and homosexuals. A racist policy produces inequities between racial groups. Queer racism produces inequities between race-sexualities. Queer racism produces a situation where 32 percent of children being raised by Black male same-sex couples live in poverty, compared to 14 percent of children being raised by White male same-sex couples, 13 percent of children raised by Black heterosexuals, and 7 percent of children raised by White heterosexuals. For children being raised by female same-sex couples who live in poverty, the racial disparity is nearly as wide. These children of Black queer couples are more likely to live in poverty because their parents are more likely than Black heterosexual and White queer couples to be poor.

Homophobia cannot be separated from racism. They've intersected for ages. British physician Havelock Ellis is known for popularizing the term "homosexual." In his first medical treatise on homosexuality, *Studies in the Psychology of Sex* (1897), he wrote about "the question of sex—with the racial questions that rest on it." He regarded homosexuality as a congenital physiological abnormality, just as he regarded criminality at the time. Ellis adored the father of criminology, Italian physician Cesare Lombroso, who claimed criminals are born, not bred, and that people of color are by nature criminals. In 1890, Ellis published a popular summary of Lombroso's writings.

Ellis spent many years defending against the criminalization of White homosexuality. Following racist scholars, Ellis used comparative anatomy of women's bodies to evidence the biological differences between the sexualities. "As regards the sexual organs it seems possible," Ellis wrote, "to speak more definitively of inverted women than of inverted men." At the time, racist physicians were contrasting the "bound together" clitoris of "Aryan American women" that "goes with higher civilization" and the "free" clitoris "in negresses" that goes with "highly domesticated animals." Homophobic physicians were supposing that "inverted" lesbians "will in practically every instance disclose an abnormally prominent clitoris," wrote New York City prison doctor Perry M. Lichtenstein. Racist ideas suggesting Black people are more hypersexual than White people and homophobic ideas suggesting queer people are more hypersexual than heterosexuals intersect to produce the queer racism of the most hypersexual race-sexuality, the Black queer. Their imagined biological stamp: the abnormally prominent clitoris, which "is particularly so in colored women," Lichtenstein added.

WECKEA WAS MY best friend at Temple. We were both brown-skinned with locs and hailed from prideful HBCUs. I usually befriended laid-back and calm people like him. He usually befriended daring and silly people like me. We were both curious by nature, but Weckea was as inquisitive a person as I had ever met. He wanted to know everything and damn near did. The only thing he seemed to love as much as a good idea was a good laugh. He was a few years older than me, and it did not take long for me to look up to him intellectually, in the way I looked up to Kaila and Yaba.

We arrived at Temple in the same cohort—Weckea, myself, and another student, Raena. We banded together.

On a rare day when Raena and I ate lunch together without Weckea, the two of us sat outside, near campus, probably delighting in the warm arrival of spring, probably in 2006. We both had food before us. First gossip and small talk and then, out of nowhere: "You know Weckea is gay, right." She barely looked up at me as she said it. Her eyes focused as she gobbled food.

"No, I didn't know that," I said, my voice breaking.

"Well, it's not a big deal he didn't tell you, right?"

"Right." I looked away. Cars honked. Peopled strolled by. An ambulance was coming. For me?

I glanced back at Raena, her chin tucked, eating. Wondering why she'd told me this. I did not see a friendly face of concern as I twitched in my chair. I saw a blankness, if not a face of satisfaction. Was she trying to break up my friendship with Weckea?

Neither of us had much to say after that. Mission accomplished on her part. Weckea's homosexuality made sense, as I thought about it. He had never spoken about dating a woman. When I asked, he deflected. I'd chalked it up to his extreme privacy. He would describe women as pretty or not so pretty but never in a sexual manner, which I chalked up to his conservatism. He was not so conservative after all.

I thought about Black gay men running around having unprotected sex all the time. But Weckea did not seem sex-crazed or reckless. I thought about this hypersexuality and recklessness causing so many Black gay men to contract HIV. I thought wrong. Black gay men are less likely to have condomless sex than White gay men. They are less likely to use drugs like poppers or crystal methamphetamine during sex, which heighten the risk of HIV infections.

I had been around gay Black men before, in FACES, a modeling troupe I'd joined at FAMU. But the gay Black men in the troupe (or, better yet, the ones I thought were gay) had what I thought of as a feminine streak to them: the way they moved, their makeup, the way they struggled to dap me up. They pinged my gaydar. Everything about my modeling troupe pinged the gaydar of my friends. My modeling ended up being the only thing my friends joked on more than my orange eyes. But they thought my orange eyes were "gay," too.

I assumed Black gay men performed femininity. I did not know that some gay men, like Weckea, perform masculinity and actually prefer gay men who perform femininity for partners. I did not know (and feminists like Kaila and Yaba were teaching me) about gender being an authentic performance; that the ways women and men traditionally act are not tied to their biology; that men can authentically perform femininity as effectively as women can authentically perform masculinity. Authentically, meaning they are not acting, as the transphobic idea assumes. They are being who they are, defying society's gender conventions. I learned this, once and for all, through my other close friendship at Temple, with a butch Black lesbian from Texas. I talked about women with Monica in the way I could not with Weckea. We were drawn to the same women. When we got to joking and relating our romantic experiences, my conversations with Monica did not sound too different from my conversations with my heterosexual male friends at FAMU.

MY MIND TURNED to introspection. Why had Weckea not told me? Why didn't he feel comfortable sharing his sexuality with me? Maybe he sensed my homophobia—in fact, he probably heard it in my rhetoric. He listened intently. He seemed to never forget anything.

In subsequent years, Weckea prided himself on showing off his "gaydar," pointing out to me closeted or down-low people at Temple. But Weckea was equally adept at identifying homophobia and taking the necessary precautions. He must have been protecting himself—and our early friendship—from my homophobia. Now I had a choice: my homophobia or my best friend. I could not have both for long. I chose Weckea and the beginning of our long friendship. I chose the beginning of the rest of my lifelong striving against the homophobia of my upbringing, a lifelong striving to be a queer antiracist.

Queer antiracism is equating all the race-sexualities, striving to eliminate the inequities between the race-sexualities. We cannot be antiracist if we are homophobic or transphobic. We must continue to "affirm that all Black lives matter," as the co-founder of Black Lives Matter, Opal Tometi, once said. All Black lives include those of poor transgender Black women, perhaps the most violated and oppressed of all the Black intersectional groups. The average U.S. life expectancy of a transgender woman of color is thirty-five years. The racial violence they face, the transphobia they face as they seek to live freely, is unfathomable. I started learning about their freedom fight from the personal stories of transgender activist Janet Mock. But I opened up to their fight on that day I opened to saving my friendship with Weckea.

I am a cisgendered Black heterosexual male—"cisgender" meaning my gender identity corresponds to my birth sex, in contrast to transgender people, whose gender identity does not correspond to their birth sex. To be queer antiracist is to understand the privileges of my cisgender, of my masculinity, of my heterosexuality, of their intersections. To be queer antiracist is to serve as an ally to transgender people, to intersex people, to women, to the non-gender-conforming, to homosexuals, to their intersections, meaning listening, learning, and being led by their equalizing ideas, by their equalizing policy campaigns, by their power struggle for equal opportunity. To be queer antiracist is to see that policies protecting Black transgender women are as critically important as policies protecting the political ascendancy of queer White males. To be queer antiracist is to see the new wave of both religious-freedom laws and voter-ID laws in Republican states as taking away the rights of queer people. To be queer antiracist is to see homophobia, racism, and queer racism—not the queer person, not the queer space—as the problem, as abnormal, as unnatural.

THEY SEEMED TO always be there—Yaba and Kaila—sitting around one of those tables near the entrance of Gladfelter Hall, sometimes with fellow doctoral students Danielle and Sekhmet. I usually caught these women on a smoke break or lunch break or dinner break from working together in Gladfelter's computer lab. They were finishing their doctorates in African American studies, nearing the end of a journey I was beginning at Temple.

Whenever Kaila and Yaba were seated there—whenever they were anywhere—their presence was unmistakable, memorable and unsettling and inspiring. I could go to war with them at my side. I learned from them that I am not a defender of Black people if I am not sharply defending Black women, if I am not sharply defending queer Blacks. The two of them exerted their influence on our department's events. When our department brought in speakers for a public event, they came. When graduate students shared their research at an event, they came. When there was an out-of-town Black studies conference, they came. When they came, let's just say they ensured that when patriarchal ideas arose, when homophobic ideas were put out there, when racist ideas came and intersected, they would come for those ideas like piranhas coming for their daily meal. I watched, stunned, in awe of their intellectual attacks. I call them attacks, but in truth they were defenses, defending Black womanhood and the humanity of queer Blacks. They were respectful and measured if the victimizer was respectful and measured with them. But I call them attacks because I felt personally attacked. They were attacking my gender racism about Black women, my queer racism about queer Blacks, my gender and queer racism about queer Black women.

I did not want to ever be their prey.

I binge-read every author they mentioned in their public exchanges and in their private exchanges with me. I gobbled up Audre Lorde, E. Patrick Johnson, bell hooks, Joan Morgan,

Dwight McBride, Patricia Hill Collins, and Kimberlé Crenshaw like my life depended on it. My life *did* depend on it. I wanted to overcome my gender racism, my queer racism. But I had to be willing to do for Black women and queer Blacks what I had been doing for Black men and Black heterosexuals, which meant first of all learning more—and then defending them like my heroes had.

They were the darkness that scared me. I wanted to run away whenever I came off the elevator, turned the corner, and spotted Yaba and Kaila, whenever I approached the building and they were there. They warmly tossed smiles and greetings as I walked by not fast enough, forcing me to awkwardly toss them back. Sometimes they stopped me in small talk. Over time, they let me join them in long talk, unnerving me the most. It is best to challenge ourselves by dragging ourselves before people who intimidate us with their brilliance and constructive criticism. I didn't think about that. I wanted to run away. They did not let me run away, and I am grateful now because of it.

These women were everything they were not supposed to be, in my patriarchal and homophobic mind. Queer people are run by sex, not ideas. Queer people are abnormal. Feminists hate men. Feminists want female supremacy. But these Black feminists obviously liked me, a male. They were as ideological as they were sexual as they were normal. They did not speak of women ruling men. They spoke of gender and queer equity and freedom and mutuality and complementarity and power. Their jokes and attacks knew no gender or sexuality. If anything, they were harder on women. They were harder on queer people like Raena. They saw through her long before Weckea and I did.

No one seemed to incite them more than "patriarchal women"—really, patriarchal White women standing behind racist White patriarchs. I can only imagine what they thought years later, watching Kayla Moore defend her husband, Alabama's U.S. Senate candidate Roy Moore, who had been accused of pedophilia and sexual assaults, who was asked on the campaign trail in 2017 when America was last great. "I think it was great at the time when families were united—even though we had slavery," he said. "Our families were strong, our country had direction." This was long before we had so many women publicly attacking the women saying #MeToo. Patriarchal women, as a term, made no sense to me back then, like the term "homophobic homosexuals." Only men can be patriarchal, can be sexist. Only heterosexuals can be homophobic. The radical Black queer feminism of those two women detached homophobic from heterosexual, detached sexist from men and feminist from women, in the way I later detached racist from White people and antiracist from Black people. They had a problem with homophobia, not with heterosexuals. They had a problem with patriarchy, not with men. Crucially, their going after all homophobes, no matter their sexual identity, showed me that homophobic ideas and policies and power were their fundamental problem. Crucially, their going after all patriarchs, no matter their gender identity, showed me that patriarchal ideas and policies and powers were their fundamental problem. They talked of queer people defending homophobia as powerfully as they talked about heterosexuals building a world for queer love. They talked of women defending sexism as powerfully as men building a feminist world. Maybe they had me in mind. Because they opened that feminist world to me where queer love is wedded to heterosexual love, in harmony. But this world scared me like they scared me. Opened by them, I learned, though—and eventually I wanted to help them create that new world.

I am forever grateful that the Black graduate-student discourse was ruled by queer Black feminists instead of by patriarchal Black male homophobes. They were my first role models of Black feminism, of queer antiracism, of antiracist feminism. They met my homophobic patriarchy and forced me to meet him, too. Their force forced me to check his ass, as desperate as I was to stay out of the way of their attacks, a desperation that transformed into a curiosity about Black feminism and queer theory itself, a curiosity that transformed into a desire to be a gender antiracist, to be a queer antiracist, to not fail Black people—all Black people.

# FAILURE

**ACTIVIST:** One who has a record of power or policy change.

THE TEMPLE UNIVERSITY classroom started filling. Bodies hugging. Smiles and small talk and catching up. It all annoyed me as I sat, stood, and then sat again at the professor's desk, hoping to begin our Black Student Union (BSU) meeting on time. It was early September 2007. We were laughing and chatting in Philly, but that day, in Louisiana, six teenage lives hung in the balance. We had devised a campaign to free them. I was prepared to present it in order to secure organizers to execute it. I hardly suspected I was bound to fail.

To understand why racism lives is to understand the history of antiracist failure—why people have failed to create antiracist societies. To understand the racial history of failure is to understand failed solutions and strategies. To understand failed solutions and strategies is to understand their cradles: failed racial ideologies.

Incorrect conceptions of race as a social construct (as opposed to a power construct), of racial history as a singular march of racial progress (as opposed to a duel of antiracist and racist progress), of the race problem as rooted in ignorance and hate (as opposed to powerful self-interest)—all come together to produce solutions bound to fail. Terms and sayings like "I'm not racist" and "race neutral" and "post-racial" and "color-blind" and "only one race, the human race" and "only racists speak about race" and "Black people can't be racist" and "White people are evil" are bound to fail in identifying and eliminating racist power and policy. Stratagems flouting intersectionality are bound to fail the most degraded racial groups. Civilizing programs will fail since all racial groups are already on the same cultural level. Behavioral-enrichment programs, like mentoring and educational programs, can help individuals but are bound to fail racial groups, which are held back by bad policies, not bad behavior. Healing symptoms instead of changing policies is bound to fail in healing society. Challenging the conjoined twins separately is bound to fail to address economic-racial inequity. Gentrifying integration is bound to fail non-White cultures. All of these ideas are bound to fail because they have consistently failed in the past. But for some reason, their failure doesn't seem to matter: They remain the most popular conceptions and strategies and solutions to combat racism, because they stem from the most popular racial ideologies.

These repetitive failures exact a toll. Racial history does not repeat harmlessly. Instead, its devastation multiplies when generation after generation repeats the same failed strategies and solutions and ideologies, rather than burying past failures in the caskets of past generations.

EARLY WHITE ABOLITIONISTS met regularly at a national convention, thinking the antislavery solution rested in continuing "our parental care" over free Blacks, as they stated in 1805. White abolitionists lorded over Black behavior as if on good Black "conduct must, in some measure, depend the liberation of their brethren," as their convention stated in 1804.

The White judge birthed the Black judge. "The further decrease of prejudice, and the amelioration of the condition of thousands of our brethren who are yet in bondage, greatly depend on our conduct," Samuel Cornish and John Russwurm wrote on March 16, 1827, in one of the opening editorials of *Freedom's Journal*, the first African American newspaper.

I grew up on this same failed strategy more than one hundred fifty years later. Generations of Black bodies have been raised by the judges of "uplift suasion." The judges strap the entire Black race on the Black body's back, shove the burdened Black body into White spaces, order the burdened Black body to always act in an upstanding manner to persuade away White racism, and punish poor Black conduct with sentences of shame for reinforcing racism, for bringing the race down. I felt the burden my whole Black life to be perfect before both White people and the Black people judging whether I am representing the race well. The judges never let me just be, be myself, be my imperfect self.

IT FELT COOL outside, sometime in the autumn of 2011. Sadiqa and I had been dating for months. I looked at this Spelman sister and Georgia peach as a future wife: smitten by her affability as much as her elegance, by her perceptiveness as much as her easygoing sense of humor; smitten by her love of Black people as much as her love of saving human lives as a physician. She, too, had been raised in a middle-income Black home by similarly aged parents who cut their teeth in the movement, who brushed her teeth in the movement. She, too, had been taught that her climb up the success ladder uplifted the race. She, too, tried to represent the race well.

We dined near the window at Buddakan, an Asian fusion restaurant in Old City, Philadelphia. On the opposite wall, a massive gold statue of Buddha sat on a tiny stage at almost table level, against a red background that faded into a black center. Eyes closed. Hands clasped. At peace. Not bothering anyone. Certainly not Sadiqa. But the statue attracted a middle-aged, brown-haired, overweight White guy. Clearly drunk, he climbed onto the tiny stage and started fondling Buddha before his laughing audience of drunk friends at a nearby table. I had learned a long time ago to tune out the antics of drunk White people doing things that could get a Black person arrested. Harmless White fun is Black lawlessness.

His loud laughs summoned Sadiqa's look. "Oh, my God!" she said quietly. "What is this guy doing?"

She turned back to her plate, took a bite, and looked up as she swallowed. "At least he's not Black."

I was taken aback but immediately recognized myself—my own thoughts—in Sadiqa's face.

"How would you feel if he was Black?" I asked her, and myself.

"I'd be really embarrassed," she said, speaking for me and for so many of us trapped on the plantation of uplift suasion. "Because we don't need anyone making us look bad."

"In front of White people?" I asked her.

"Yes. It makes them look down on us. Makes them more racist."

We thought on a false continuum, from more racist to less racist to not racist. We believed good Black behavior made White people "less racist," even when our experiences told us it usually did not. But that night, we thought about it together and shared a few critiques of uplift suasion for the first time.

Today, the few critiques would be many. We would critique paternalistic White abolitionists conjuring up uplift suasion. We'd argue against the assumption that poor Black conduct is responsible for White racist ideas, meaning White racist ideas about poor Black conduct are valid. We'd critique the White judge exonerating White people from the responsibility to rid themselves of their own racist ideas; upwardly mobile Black people deflecting responsibility for changing racist policy by imagining they are uplifting the race by uplifting themselves; the near impossibility of perfectly executing uplift suasion, since Black people are humanly imperfect. We'd notice that when racist Whites see Black people conducting themselves admirably in public, they see those Blacks as extraordinary, meaning not like those ordinarily inferior Black people. We'd remember what history teaches us: that when racist policy knocks Black people down, the judge orders them to uplift themselves, only to be cut down again by racist terror and policy.

Sadiqa and I left the restaurant, but we continued to talk about the uplift-suasion ideology that had been so deeply ingrained in us—to critique it, critique ourselves, and run away from it, toward freedom. All these years later, although the judges can catch us at any moment, I admire Sadiqa's freedom to be Sadiqa. I feel free to move in my imperfections. I represent only myself. If the judges draw conclusions about millions of Black people based on how I act, then they, not I, not Black people, have a problem. They are responsible for their racist ideas; I am not. I am responsible for my racist ideas; they are not. To be antiracist is to let me be me, be myself, be my imperfect self.

ABOLITIONIST WILLIAM LLOYD Garrison did not let the Black body be her imperfect self. "Have you not acquired the esteem, confidence and patronage of the whites, in proportion to your increase in knowledge and moral improvement?" Garrison asked a Black crowd not long after founding *The Liberator* in 1831. Uplift suasion fit his ideology that the best way to "accomplish the great work of national redemption" from slavery was "through the agency of moral power" and truth and reason. Garrison's belief in "moral suasion" and what we can call "educational suasion" also fit his personal upbringing by a pious Baptist mother, his professional upbringing by an editor who believed newspapers are for "instruction," his abolitionist upbringing by moral crusader Benjamin Lundy.

Moral and educational and uplift suasion failed miserably in stopping the astounding growth of slavery in the age of King Cotton before the Civil War. But success, apparently, does not matter when a strategy stems from an ideology. Moral and educational suasion focus on persuading White people, on appealing to their moral conscience through horror and their logical mind through education. But what if racist ideas make people illogical? What if persuading everyday White people is not persuading racist policymakers? What if racist policymakers know about the harmful outcomes of their policies? What if racist policymakers have neither morals nor conscience, let alone moral conscience, to paraphrase Malcolm X? What if no group in history has gained their freedom through appealing to the moral conscience of their oppressors, to paraphrase Assata Shakur? What if economic, political, or cultural self-interest drives racist policymakers, not hateful immorality, not ignorance?

"If I could save the Union without freeing any slave I would do it, and if I could save it by freeing all the slaves I would do that," President Abraham Lincoln wrote on August 20, 1862. "What I do about slavery, and the colored race, I do because I believe it helps to save the Union." On January 1, 1863, Lincoln signed the Emancipation Proclamation as a "necessary war measure." After winning the Civil War, racist Republicans (to distinguish from the less numerous antiracist Republicans) voted to establish the Freedmen's Bureau, reconstruct the South, and extend civil rights and voting privileges to create a loyal Southern Republican base and secure Black people in the South far away from northern Whites, who "want nothing to do with the negroes," as Illinois senator Lyman Trumbull, one of the laws' main sponsors, said.

The "White man's party," as Trumbull identified the Republican Party, grew "tired" of alienating their racist constituents by militarily defending the Negro from the racist terrorists who knocked Republicans out of Southern power by 1877. Republicans left Southern Blacks behind, turning their backs on the "outrages" of Jim Crow for nearly a century. "Expediency on selfish grounds, and not right with reference to the claims of our common humanity, has controlled our action," Garrison lamented in an address for the centennial of Independence Day, in 1876.

ON JUNE 26, 1934, W.E.B. Du Bois critically assessed the success of educational suasion, as Garrison had critically assessed moral suasion before him: "For many years it was the theory of most

Negro leaders . . . that white America did not know of or realize the continuing plight of the Negro." Du Bois spoke for himself, believing "the ultimate evil was stupidity" early in his career. "Accordingly, for the last two decades, we have striven by book and periodical, by speech and appeal, by various dramatic methods of agitation, to put the essential facts before the American people. Today there can be no doubt that Americans know the facts; and yet they remain for the most part indifferent and unmoved."

Gunnar Myrdal ignored Du Bois's 1934 call for Black people to focus on accruing power instead of persuading White people. The racism problem lay in the "astonishing ignorance" of White Americans, Myrdal advised in *An American Dilemma* in 1944. "There is no doubt, in the writer's opinion, that a great majority of white people in America would be prepared to give the Negro a substantially better deal if they knew the facts."

Popular history tells us that a great majority of White Americans did give the Negro a better deal—the desegregation rulings, Civil Rights Act (1964), and Voting Rights Act (1965)—when they learned the facts. "Gunnar Myrdal had been astonishingly prophetic," according to one captivating history of the civil-rights movement. Not entirely. As early as 1946, top State Department official Dean Acheson warned the Truman administration that the "existence of discrimination against minority groups in this country has an adverse effect on our relations" with decolonizing Asian and African and Latin American nations. The Truman administration repeatedly briefed the U.S. Supreme Court on these adverse effects during desegregation cases in the late 1940s and early 1950s, as historian Mary L. Dudziak documents. Not to mention the racist abuse African diplomats faced in the United States. In 1963, Secretary of State Dean Rusk warned Congress during the consideration of the Civil Rights Act that "in waging this world struggle we are seriously handicapped by racial or religious discrimination." Seventy-eight percent of White Americans agreed in a Harris Poll.

Racist power started civil-rights legislation out of self-interest.

Racist power stopped out of self-interest when enough African and Asian and Latin nations were inside the American sphere of influence, when a rebranded Jim Crow no longer adversely affected American foreign policy, when Black people started demanding and gaining what power rarely gives up: power. In 1967, Martin Luther King Jr. admitted, "We've had it wrong and mixed up in our country, and this has led Negro Americans in the past to seek their goals through love and moral suasion devoid of power." But our generation ignores King's words about the "problem of power, a confrontation between the forces of power demanding change and the forces of power dedicated to the preserving of the status quo." The same way King's generation ignored Du Bois's matured warning. The same way Du Bois's generation ignored Garrison's matured warnings. The problem of race has always been at its core the problem of power, not the problem of immorality or ignorance.

Moral and educational suasion breathes the assumption that racist minds must be changed before racist policy, ignoring history that says otherwise. Look at the soaring White support for desegregated schools and neighborhoods decades *after* the policies changed in the 1950s and 1960s. Look at the soaring White support for interracial marriage decades *after* the policy changed in 1967. Look at the soaring support for Obamacare *after* its passage in 2010. Racist policymakers drum up fear of antiracist policies through racist ideas, knowing if the policies are implemented, the fears they circulate will never come to pass. Once the fears do not come to pass, people will let down their guards as they enjoy the benefits. Once they clearly benefit, most Americans will support and become the defenders of the antiracist policies they once feared.

To fight for mental and moral changes *after* policy is changed means fighting alongside growing benefits and the dissipation of fears, making it possible for antiracist power to succeed. To fight for mental and moral change as a *prerequisite* for policy change is to fight against growing fears and apathy, making it almost impossible for antiracist power to succeed.

The original problem of racism has not been solved by suasion. Knowledge is only power if knowledge is put to the struggle for power. Changing minds is not a movement. Critiquing racism is not activism. Changing minds is not activism. An activist produces power and policy change, not mental change. If a person has no record of power or policy change, then that person is not an activist.

AS I WAITED to begin the BSU meeting, I had already grown alienated about mental change. I wanted to be an activist. I wanted to flee academia. I wanted to free the Jena 6.

On September 1, 2006, the day after Black students had hung out under the "White tree" at Jena High School, White students hung nooses from its branches. The school's superintendent only suspended the White perpetrators for the "prank," which did nothing to curb the subsequent racial violence against Black students in the small town of Jena, Louisiana. But days after Black students beat up a White student on December 4, 2006, the Jena 6 were arrested. Jesse Ray Beard was charged as a juvenile. Robert Bailey Jr., Mychal Bell, Carwin Jones, Bryant Purvis, and Theo Shaw were charged with attempted murder. "When you are convicted, I will seek the maximum penalty allowed by law," promised district attorney Reed Walters, meaning up to one hundred years in prison.

As I sat at the teacher's desk, I felt Mychal Bell's sentencing hearing on September 20 approaching like the butcher's cleaver. An all-White jury had already found him guilty of a lesser charge, aggravated second-degree battery, lining up his life to be cut by as much as twenty-two years.

A somber energy settled inside the classroom, like the darkness outside. Our goal, BSU officers told each other, was to free the Jena 6. But were we willing to do anything? Were we willing to risk our freedom for their freedom? Not if our primary purpose was making ourselves feel better. We formulate and populate and donate to cultural and behavioral and educational enrichment programs to make ourselves feel better, feeling they are helping racial groups, when they are only helping (or hurting) individuals, when only policy change helps groups.

We arrive at demonstrations excited, as if our favorite musician is playing on the speakers' stage. We convince ourselves we are doing something to solve the racial problem when we are really doing something to satisfy our feelings. We go home fulfilled, like we dined at our favorite restaurant. And this fulfillment is fleeting, like a drug high. The problems of inequity and injustice persist. They persistently make us feel bad and guilty. We persistently do something to make ourselves feel better as we convince ourselves we are making society better, as we never make society better.

What if instead of a feelings advocacy we had an outcome advocacy that put equitable outcomes before our guilt and anguish? What if we focused our human and fiscal resources on changing power and policy to actually make society, not just our feelings, better?


I COULD WAIT no longer. I cut off the talking and smiling and began presenting the 106 Campaign to free the Jena 6. I began with phase one: Mobilize at least 106 students on 106 campuses in the mid-Atlantic to rally locally by the end of September and fundraise for the Jena 6 legal defense fund. I presented phase two: Marshal those 106 students from 106 campuses into car caravans that would converge on Washington, D.C., on October 5, 2007.

I painted the picture. "Wonderfully long lines of dozens of cars packed with students on highways and byways driving toward the nation's capital from all directions, from Pennsylvania, Delaware, Maryland, Virginia, West Virginia, and North Carolina." I stared but did not look into the eyes of my audience. I looked at the beautiful picture forming from my lips. "Thousands of cars with signs in the window—'Free the Jena Six'—honking to drivers passing by, who'd honk loudly back in solidarity (or revulsion).

"Can you see it?" I asked excitedly a few times.

They could see it. For some, the ugly picture.

"Isn't that illegal, the car caravans?" one woman asked, obviously scared.

"What? No! People take car caravans all the time," I replied.

I spoke on, painting the beautiful, ugly picture. "When the car caravans arrived in D.C., they would park their cars in the middle of Constitution Avenue and join the informal march to the Department of Justice. Thousands of cars would be sitting-in on Constitution Avenue and surrounding streets as we presented our six demands of freedom to the Bush administration. When they came with the tow trucks, we would be ready to flatten truck tires. When police units started protecting the tow trucks, we would come with reinforcements of cars. When they blocked off Constitution Avenue, we would strike another street with our cars. When and if they barricaded all the downtown streets, we would wait them out and ride back into downtown Washington whenever they lifted the barricades. We would refuse to stop the sit-in of cars until the Bush administration leaned on the Louisiana governor to lean on Jena officials to drop the charges against the Jena Six."

"This is illegal. They will throw us in prison," someone rebutted with a look of fear.

I should have stopped but I continued my failure, hardly caring that the more I spoke, the more fear I spread—the more fear I spread, the more I alienated people from the 106 Campaign.

"Damn right we could go to prison!" I shot back, feeling like myself. "But I don't care! We're already in prison. That's what America means: prison."

I used the Malcolm X line out of context. But who cared about context when the shock and awe sounded so radical to my self-identified radical ears? When I lashed out at well-meaning people who showed the normal impulse of fear, who used the incorrect racial terminology, who asked the incorrect question—oh, did I think I was so radical. When my scorched-earth words sent attendees fleeing at BSU rallies and meetings, when my scorched-earth writings sent readers fleeing, oh, did I think I was so radical. When in fact, if all my words were doing was sounding radical, then those words were not radical at all. What if we measure the radicalism of speech by how radically it transforms open-minded people, by how the speech liberates the antiracist power within? What if we measure the conservatism of speech by how intensely it keeps people the same, keeps people enslaved by their racist ideas and fears, conserving their inequitable society? At a time when I thought I was the most radical, I was the most conservative. I was a failure. I failed to address the fears of my BSU peers.

Fear is kind of like race—a mirage. "Fear is not real. It is a product of our imagination," as a Will Smith character tells his son in one of my favorite movies, *After Earth*. "Do not misunderstand me, danger is very real, but fear is a choice."

We do not have to be fearless like Harriet Tubman to be antiracist. We have to be courageous to be antiracist. Courage is the strength to do what is right in the face of fear, as the anonymous philosopher tells us. I gain insight into what's right from antiracist ideas. I gain strength from fear. While many people are fearful of what could happen if they resist, I am fearful of what could happen if I don't resist. I am fearful of cowardice. Cowardice is the inability to amass the strength to do what is right in the face of fear. And racist power has been terrorizing cowardice into us for generations.

For segregationists like U.S. senator Ben "Pitchfork" Tillman, President Theodore Roosevelt crossed the color line when he dined with Booker T. Washington on October 16, 1901. "The action of President Roosevelt in entertaining that nigger will necessitate our killing a thousand niggers in the South before they will learn their place again." He was not joking.

On July 8, 1876, a young Tillman had joined the power-hungry White mob that murdered at least seven Black militiamen defending Black power in the Black town of Hamburg, South Carolina. All election year long, Tillman's Red Shirts had helped White supremacists violently snatch control of South Carolina. Tillman wore his involvement in the Hamburg Massacre as a badge of honor when he trooped on lynched heads into South Carolina's governorship in 1890 and the U.S. Senate in 1895. "The purpose of our visit to Hamburg was to strike terror," Tillman said at the Red Shirts reunion in 1909. As racist ideas intend to make us ignorant and hateful, racist terror intends to make us fear.

I WALKED OUT of that classroom building alone. I walked to the train station on the edge of campus, deciding on the long escalator down into the subway station that the BSU officers who voted down the 106 Campaign must be ignorant about racism, kind of like the White people supporting the Jena 6's incarceration. Deciding on the screeching train ride up to North Philadelphia that the "ultimate evil was ignorance" and "the ultimate good was education." Deciding as I lay flat on my couch and looked up at the ceiling mirror that a life of educational suasion would be more impactful than any other life I could choose.

I ran back down the lit path of educational suasion on the very night I failed to persuade my BSU peers. I failed at changing minds (let alone policy). But in all my enlightenment, I did not see myself as the failure. I saw my BSU peers as the failure. I did not look in the mirror at my "failure doctrine," the doctrine of failing to make change and deflecting fault.

When we fail to open the closed-minded consumers of racist ideas, we blame their closed-mindedness instead of our foolish decision to waste time reviving closed minds from the dead. When our vicious attacks on open-minded consumers of racist ideas fail to transform them, we blame their hate rather than our impatient and alienating hate of them. When people fail to consume our convoluted antiracist ideas, we blame their stupidity rather than our stupid lack of clarity. When we transform people and do not show them an avenue of support, we blame their lack of commitment rather than our lack of guidance. When the politician we supported does not change racist policy, we blame the intractability of racism rather than our support of the wrong politician. When we fail to gain support for a protest, we blame the fearful rather than our alienating presentation. When the protest fails, we blame racist power rather than our flawed protest. When our policy does not produce racial equity, we blame the people for not taking advantage of the new opportunity, not our flawed policy solution. The failure doctrine avoids the mirror of self-blame. The failure doctrine begets failure. The failure doctrine begets racism.

What if antiracists constantly self-critiqued our own ideas? What if we blamed our ideologies and methods, studied our ideologies and methods, refined our ideologies and methods again and again until they worked? When will we finally stop the insanity of doing the same thing repeatedly and expecting a different result? Self-critique allows change. Changing shows flexibility. Antiracist power must be flexible to match the flexibility of racist power, propelled only by the craving for power to shape policy in their inequitable interests. Racist power believes in by any means necessary. We, their challengers, typically do not, not even some of those inspired by Malcolm X. We care the most about the moral and ideological and financial purity of our ideologies and strategies and fundraising and leaders and organizations. We care less about bringing equitable results for people in dire straits, as we say we are purifying ourselves for the people in dire straits, as our purifying keeps the people in dire straits. As we critique the privilege and inaction of racist power, we show our privilege and inaction by critiquing every effective strategy, ultimately justifying our inaction on the comfortable seat of privilege. Anything but flexible, we are too often bound by ideologies that are bound by failed strategies of racial change.

What if we assessed the methods and leaders and organizations by their results of policy change and equity? What if strategies and policy solutions stemmed not from ideologies but from problems? What if antiracists were propelled only by the craving for power to shape policy in their equitable interests?

. . .

IN VOTING DOWN the 106 Campaign, the BSU officers crafted a different plan. They did something they did not fear. We loudly marched down North Broad Street and rallied on campus on September 20, 2007. That day, thousands of us thought we were protesting, when we were really demonstrating, from Philadelphia to Jena.

We use the terms "demonstration" and "protest" interchangeably, at our own peril, like we interchangeably use the terms "mobilizing" and "organizing." A protest is organizing people for a prolonged campaign that forces racist power to change a policy. A demonstration is mobilizing people momentarily to publicize a problem. Speakers and placards and posts at marches, rallies, petitions, and viral hashtags demonstrate the problem. Demonstrations are, not surprisingly, a favorite of suasionists. Demonstrations annoy power in the way children crying about something they will never get annoy parents. Unless power cannot economically or politically or professionally afford bad press—as power could not during the Cold War, as power cannot during election season, as power cannot close to bankruptcy—power typically ignores demonstrations.

The most effective demonstrations (like the most effective educational efforts) help people find the antiracist power within. The antiracist power within is the ability to view my own racism in the mirror of my past and present, view my own antiracism in the mirror of my future, view my own racial groups as equal to other racial groups, view the world of racial inequity as abnormal, view my own power to resist and overtake racist power and policy. The most effective demonstrations (like the most effective educational efforts) provide methods for people to give their antiracist power, to give their human and financial resources, channeling attendees and their funds into organizations and protests and power-seizing campaigns. The fundraising behind the scenes of the Jena 6 demonstrations secured better defense attorneys, who, by June 26, 2009, quietly got the charges reduced to simple battery, to guilty pleas, to no jail time for the accused.

As important as finding the antiracist power within and financial support, demonstrations can provide emotional support for ongoing protests. Nighttime rallies in the churches of Montgomery, Alabama, rocking with the courage-locking words of Martin Luther King Jr., sustained those courageous Black women who primarily boycotted the public buses and drained that revenue stream for the city throughout 1956.

The most effective protests create an environment whereby changing the racist policy becomes in power's self-interest, like desegregating businesses because the sit-ins are driving away customers, like increasing wages to restart production, like giving teachers raises to resume schooling, like passing a law to attract a well-organized force of donors or voters. But it is difficult to create that environment, since racist power makes laws that illegalize most protest threats. Organizing and protesting are much harder and more impactful than mobilizing and demonstrating. Seizing power is much harder than protesting power and demonstrating its excesses.

The demonstrations alone had little chance of freeing the Jena 6. A judge denied bail for one of the Jena 6 the day after the demonstrations. The news shocked and alienated some of my BSU peers from activism. After all, when we attend or organize demonstrations thinking they are protests, thinking they can change power and policy, and see no change happening, it is hard not to become cynical. It is hard not to think the Goliath of racism can never be defeated. It is hard to think of our strategies and solutions and ideologies and feelings as the true failures. It is hard to think we actually have all the tools for success.

## CHAPTER 17

# SUCCESS

FINANCE SCHOLAR BOYCE Watkins lectured on racism as a disease. I agonized over this conception. Not foundational enough, eternal enough, revolutionary enough on this eleventh evening of Black History Month in 2010. When the question-and-answer period arrived, I tossed up my arm from the back row, as Caridad smiled.

Caridad and I had been whispering for most of the lecture. For once, I felt confidence tingling in my head. Days before, Professor Asante had hooded me with my doctoral degree at Temple's commencement. The teen who hated school had finished graduate school in 2010, had committed himself to school for life.

Caridad was probably the one who ushered me to the lecture at SUNY Oneonta, our state college in the town of Oneonta, in upstate New York. Forgive me for calling Oneonta a town. Rural White people from surrounding areas labeled Oneonta "the city."

At Oneonta, Whiteness surrounded me like clouds from a plane's window, which didn't mean I found no White colleagues who were genial and caring. But it was Caridad, and all her

Puerto Rican feminism and antiracism, who took me by the arm when I arrived as a dissertation fellow in 2008 and brought me closer when I stayed in 2009.

We were bound to become as close as our chairs. I filled the Black history post left vacant by Caridad's husband of eighteen years, Ralph. Metastatic cancer had taken Ralph's Black body in 2007. She probably could not look at me without seeing me standing in Ralph's shoes.

Her husband lost his fight to cancer but Caridad's life as an Afro-Latinx woman had brought its own fights—for peace, to be still. But she was a fighter, tireless and durable, as antiracists must be to succeed.

SUCCESS. THE DARK road we fear. Where antiracist power and policy predominate. Where equal opportunities and thus outcomes exist between the equal groups. Where people blame policy, not people, for societal problems. Where nearly everyone has more than they have today. Where racist power lives on the margins, like antiracist power does today. Where antiracist ideas are our common sense, like racist ideas are today.

Neither failure nor success is written. The story of our generation will be based on what we are willing to do. Are we willing to endure the grueling fight against racist power and policy? Are we willing to transform the antiracist power we gather within us to antiracist power in our society?

Caridad was willing, which strengthened my will. Caridad understood that even as her students struggled with racist and gender-racist and queer-racist and class-racist ideas, they also had within them the capacity to learn and change. She did not free the antiracist power within them with ideological attacks. Her classes were more like firm hugs tailored to each student's experience, compelling self-reflection. She took her Black and Latinx students—who were fighting their own anti-African cultural conditioning—to Ghana each year, where they found themselves eagerly immersed in their African ancestry by the trip's end.

Meanwhile, I fought to survive at the intersections. The impulses of my bigoted past constantly threatened to take me back to the plantation of racist power. Caridad extended the arms of Kaila, Yaba, and Weckea around me, ensuring I did not revert to my old thinking when I left Temple.

"INSTEAD OF DESCRIBING racism as a disease, don't you think racism is more like an organ?" I asked the lecturer. "Isn't racism essential for America to function? Isn't the system of racism essential for America to live?"

All my leading questions did not bait Boyce Watkins into a defense of his disease conception. Too bad. I wanted to engage him. I was not much of an intellectual. I closed myself off to new ideas that did not *feel* good. Meaning I shopped for conceptions of racism that fit my ideology and self-identity.

Asking antiracists to change their perspective on racism can be as destabilizing as asking racists to change their perspective on the races. Antiracists can be as doctrinaire in their view of racism as racists can be in their view of not-racism. How can antiracists ask racists to open their minds and change when we are closed-minded and unwilling to change? I ignored my own hypocrisy, as people customarily do when it means giving up what they hold dear. Giving up my conception of racism meant giving up my view of the world and myself. I would not without a fight. I would lash out at anyone who "attacked" me with new ideas, unless I feared and respected them like I feared and respected Kaila and Yaba.

I DERIVED MY perspective on racism from a book I first read in graduate school. When both Hillary Clinton and Bernie Sanders spoke of "institutional racism" on the presidential campaign trail in 2016, when the activists who demonstrated at their events spoke of "institutional racism," they were using, whether they realized it or not, a formulation coined in 1967 by Black Power activist Kwame Toure and political scientist Charles Hamilton in *Black Power: The Politics of Liberation in America.*

"Racism is both overt and covert," Toure and Hamilton explained. "It takes two, closely related forms: individual whites acting against individual blacks, and acts by the total white community against the black community. We call these individual racism and institutional racism. The first consists of overt acts by individuals. . . . The second type is less overt, far more subtle, less identifiable in terms of *specific* individuals committing the acts." They distinguished, for example, the individual racism of "white terrorists" who bomb a Black church and kill Black children from the institutional racism of "when in that same city—Birmingham, Alabama—five hundred black babies die each year because of the lack of proper food, shelter and medical facilities."

It is, as I thought upon first read, the gloomy system keeping us down and dead. The system's acts are covert, just as the racist ideas of the people are implicit. I could not wrap my head around the system or precisely define it, but I knew the system was there, like the polluted air in our atmosphere, poisoning Black people to the benefit of White people.

But what if the atmosphere of racism has been polluting most White people, too? And what if racism has been working in the opposite way for a handful of Black individuals, who find the fresh air of wealth and power in racist atmospheres? Framing institutional racism as acts by the "total White community against the total Black community" accounts for the ways White people benefit from racist policies when compared to their racial peers. (White poor benefit more than Black poor. White women benefit more than Black women. White gays benefit more than Black gays.) But this framing of White people versus Black people does *not* take into account that all White people do not benefit equally from racism. For instance, it doesn't take into account how rich Whites benefit more from racist policies than White poor and middle-income people. It does not take into account that Black people are not harmed equally by racism or that some Black individuals exploit racism to boost their own wealth and power.

But I did not care. I thought I had it all figured out. I thought of racism as an inanimate, invisible, immortal system, not as a living, recognizable, mortal disease of cancer cells that we could identify and treat and kill. I considered the system as essential to the United States as the Constitution. At times, I thought White people covertly operated the system, fixed it to benefit the total White community at the expense of the total Black community.

The construct of covert institutional racism opens American eyes to racism and, ironically, closes them, too. Separating the overt individual from the covert institutional veils the specific policy choices that cause racial inequities, policies made by specific people. Covering up the specific policies and policymakers prevents us from identifying and replacing the specific policies and policymakers. We become unconscious to racist policymakers and policies as we lash out angrily at the abstract bogeyman of "the system."

The perpetrators behind the five hundred Black babies dying each year in Birmingham "because of the lack of proper food, shelter and medical facilities" were no less overt than the "white terrorists" who killed four Black girls in a Birmingham church in 1963. In the way investigators can figure out exactly who those church bombers were, investigators can figure out exactly what policies caused five hundred Black babies to die each year and exactly who put those policies in place. In the way people have learned to see racist abuse coming out of the mouths of individual racists, people can learn to see racial inequities emerging from racist policies. All forms of racism are overt if our antiracist eyes are open to seeing racist policy in racial inequity.

But we do not see. Our eyes have been closed by racist ideas and the unacknowledged bond between the institutional antiracist and the post-racialist. They bond on the idea that institutional racism is often unseen and unseeable. Because it is covert, the institutional antiracist says. Because it hardly exists, the post-racialist says.

A similar bond exists between implicit bias and post-racialism. They bond on the idea that racist ideas are buried in the mind.

Because they are implicit and unconscious, implicit bias says. Because they are dead, post-racialism says.

TOURE AND HAMILTON could not have foreseen how their concepts of overt and covert racism would be used by people across the ideological board to turn racism into something hidden and unknowable. Toure and Hamilton were understandably focused on distinguishing the individual from the institutional. They were reacting to the same moderate and liberal and assimilationist forces that all these years later still reduce racism to the individual acts of White Klansmen and Jim Crow politicians and Tea Party Republicans and N-word users and White nationalist shooters and Trumpian politicos. " 'Respectable' individuals can absolve themselves from individual blame: they would never plant a bomb in a church; they would never stone a black family," Toure and Hamilton wrote. "But they continue to support political officials and institutions that would and do perpetuate institutionally racist policies."

The term "institutionally racist policies" is more concrete than "institutional racism." The term "racist policies" is more concrete than "institutionally racist policies," since "institutional" and "policies" are redundant: Policies are institutional. But I still occasionally use the terms "institutional racism" and "systemic racism" and "structural racism" and "overt" and "covert." They are like my first language of racism. But when we realize old words do not exactly and clearly convey what we are trying to describe, we should turn to new words. I struggle to concretely explain what "institutional racism" means to the Middle Eastern small businessman, the Black service worker, the White teacher, the Latinx nurse, the Asian factory worker, and the Native store clerk who do not take the courses on racism, do not read the books on racism, do not go to the lectures on racism, do not watch the specials on racism, do not listen to the podcasts on racism, do not attend the rallies against racism.

I try to keep everyday people in mind when I use "racist policies" instead of "institutional racism."

Policymakers and policies make societies and institutions, not the other way around. The United States is a racist nation because its policymakers and policies have been racist from the beginning. The conviction that racist policymakers can be overtaken, and racist policies can be changed, and the racist minds of their victims can be changed, is disputed only by those invested in preserving racist policymakers, policies, and habits of thinking.

Racism has always been terminal *and* curable. Racism has always been recognizable and mortal.

THE RAIN FELL on his gray hooded sweatshirt. It was February 26, 2012, a boring Sunday evening. I looked forward to my first book, on Black student activism in the late 1960s, being published in two weeks. The hooded teen looked forward to enjoying the watermelon juice and Skittles he'd purchased from a nearby 7-Eleven. The seventeen-year-old was easygoing, laid-back, like his strut. He adored LeBron James, hip-hop, and *South Park,* and dreamed of one day piloting airplanes.

Over six feet tall and lanky, Trayvon Martin ambled back in the rain to the Retreat at Twin Lakes. His father, Tracy Martin, had been dating a woman who lived in the gated community in Sanford, a suburb of Orlando, Florida. Tracy had brought along his son to talk to him, to refocus his mind on attending college like his older brother. Trayvon had just been suspended for carrying a bag with a trace of marijuana at his Miami high school. While suburban White teenage boys partied and drank and drove and smoked and snorted and assaulted to a chorus of "boys will be boys," urban Black boys faced zero tolerance in a policed state.

Martin dodged puddles on his slow stroll home. He called his girlfriend. He talked and walked through the front gate (or took a shortcut) into the cluster of sandy-colored two-story townhouses. As in many neighborhoods during the Great Recession, investors had been buying foreclosed properties and renting them out. With renters came unfamiliar faces, transient faces, and racists who connected the presence of Black teenagers with the "rash" of seven burglaries in 2011. They promptly organized a neighborhood-watch group.

The watch-group organizer was born a year after me, to a White Vietnam veteran and a Peruvian immigrant. Raised not far from where my family moved to in Manassas, Virginia, George Zimmerman moved to Florida as I did, after graduating high school. His assault conviction and domestic-violence accusations altered his plans to be a police officer. But nothing altered his conviction that the Black body—and not his own—was the criminal in his midst.

Zimmerman decided to run an errand. He hopped in his truck, his licensed slim 9-millimeter handgun tucked in a holster in his waistband. He drove. He noticed a hooded Black teenager walking through the complex. He dialed 911. The Black body's presence, a crime. The historic crime of racist ideas.


I DID NOT plan for my second book to be a history of racist ideas, as Zimmerman zeroed in on what could have been any Black male body, as he zeroed in on the teenager President Obama thought "could have been my son." After my first book, on the Black Campus Movement, I planned to research the student origins of Black studies in the 1960s. Then I realized that Black students were demanding Black studies because they considered all the existing disciplines to be racist. That the liberal scholars dominating those disciplines were refusing to identify their assimilationist ideas as racist. That they were identifying as not-racist, like the segregationists they were calling racist. That Black students were calling them both racist, redefining racist ideas. I wanted to write a long history using Black students' redefinition of racist ideas. But the daunting task scared me, like Zimmerman's glare scared Martin.

Martin called a friend and told his friend he was being followed. He picked up the pace. "Hey, we've had some break-ins in my neighborhood," Zimmerman told the 911 dispatcher. "And there's a real suspicious guy. This guy looks like he's up to no good, or he's on drugs or something. . . . A dark hoodie, like a gray hoodie." He asked how long it would take for an officer to get there, because "these assholes, they always get away."

Martin ran. Zimmerman leapt out of his car in pursuit, gun at his waist, phone in hand. The dispatcher told him to stop. Zimmerman ended the call and caught up to Martin, a dozen or so minutes after 7:00 P.M. Only one person living knows exactly what happened next: Zimmerman, probably fighting to "apprehend" the "criminal." Martin probably fighting off the actual criminal for his life. Zimmerman squeezing the trigger and ending Martin's life. Claiming self-defense to save his own life. A jury agreeing, on July 13, 2013.

HEARTBROKEN, ALICIA GARZA typed "Black Lives Matter" into the mourning nights, into the Black caskets piling up before her as people shouted all those names from Trayvon Martin to Michael Brown to Sandra Bland to Korryn Gaines. The deaths and accusations and denials and demonstrations and deaths—it all gave me the strength each day to research for *Stamped from the Beginning.*

By the summer of 2012, I was finding and tagging every racist idea I could find from history. Racist ideas piled up before me like trash at a landfill. Tens of thousands of pages of Black people being trashed as natural or nurtured beasts, devils, animals, rapists, slaves, criminals, kids, predators, brutes, idiots, prostitutes, cheats, and dependents. More than five hundred years of toxic ideas on the Black body. Day after week, week after month, month after year, oftentimes twelve hours a day for three horrifically long years, I waded through this trash, consumed this trash, absorbed its toxicity, before I released a tiny portion of this trash onto the page.

All that trash, ironically, cleansed my mind if it did not cleanse my gut. While collecting this trash, I realized I had been unwittingly doing so my whole life. Some I had tossed away after facing myself in the mirror. Some trash remained. Like the dirty bags or traces of "them niggers" and "White people are devils" and "servile Asians" and "terrorist Middle Easterners" and "dangerous Black neighborhoods" and "weak Natives" and "angry Black women" and "invading Latinx" and "irresponsible Black mothers" and "deadbeat Black fathers." A mission to uncover and critique America's life of racist ideas turned into a mission to uncover and critique my life of racist ideas, which turned into a lifelong mission to be antiracist.

It happens for me in successive steps, these steps to be an antiracist.

I stop using the "I'm not a racist" or "I can't be racist" defense of denial.

I admit the definition of racist (someone who is supporting racist policies or expressing racist ideas).

I confess the racist policies I support and racist ideas I express.

I accept their source (my upbringing inside a nation making us racist).

I acknowledge the definition of antiracist (someone who is supporting antiracist policies or expressing antiracist ideas).

I struggle for antiracist power and policy in my spaces. (Seizing a policymaking position. Joining an antiracist organization or protest. Publicly donating my time or privately donating my funds to antiracist policymakers, organizations, and protests fixated on changing power and policy.)

I struggle to remain at the antiracist intersections where racism is mixed with other bigotries. (Eliminating racial distinctions in biology and behavior. Equalizing racial distinctions in ethnicities, bodies, cultures, colors, classes, spaces, genders, and sexualities.)

I struggle to think with antiracist ideas. (Seeing racist policy in racial inequity. Leveling group differences. Not being fooled into generalizing individual negativity. Not being fooled by misleading statistics or theories that blame people for racial inequity.)

Racist ideas fooled me nearly my whole life. I refused to allow them to continue making a fool out of me, a chump out of me, a slave out of me. I realized there is nothing wrong with any of the racial groups and everything wrong with individuals like me who think there is something wrong with any of the racial groups. It felt so good to cleanse my mind.

But I did not cleanse my body. I kept most of the toxic trash in my gut between 2012 and 2015. Did not talk about most of it. Tried to laugh it off. Did not address the pain of feeling the racist ideas butchering my Black body for centuries. But how could I worry about my body as I stared at police officers butchering the Black body almost every week on my cellphone? How could I worry about my body when racists blamed the dead, when the dead's loved ones cried and raged and numbed?

How could I worry about my suffering while Sadiqa suffered?

## CHAPTER 18

# SURVIVAL

ADIQA AND I rarely sat on the rounded cream sofa in our new home in Providence. But our nerves brought us into the living room on this day in late August 2013.

We'd moved in weeks before as newlyweds. We eloped and changed our last names together months before, in a picturesque affair captured in *Essence*'s "Bridal Bliss" column. Sadiqa's gold dress and red accessories and cowrie-shell adornments and regal aura sitting on her throne of a peninsula beach as the waves bowed under the colorful sunset were all so sublime.

Still high from the pictures, we were crashing down now. We held hands, waiting for the phone call from the radiologist who performed the ultrasound and biopsy. A week prior, Sadiqa told me about the lump. She did not think much of it, probably knowing that 93 percent of women diagnosed with breast cancer are over forty years old. She was thirty-four. But she obliged my requests to see a doctor that day. The phone rang. We jumped as if we were watching a horror flick. On speakerphone, the doctor said Sadiqa had invasive breast cancer.

Minutes later, we were upstairs. Sadiqa could not do it. I had to call and tell a mother who had lost a daughter that her living daughter had cancer. I stood in our guest room as her mother let out a wail, as Sadiqa wailed in our bedroom, as I wailed in my mind.

The wailing soon stopped, if the worry encircling and suffocating my wife did not. Sadiqa surveyed the fight ahead. Surgery to remove the lump. Chemotherapy to prevent a recurrence. Close monitoring to notice and treat a recurrence.

Sadiqa had time before surgery. We decided to freeze embryos in case the chemotherapy harmed her ovaries. The process dangerously overstimulated her ovaries, filling her abdomen with fluid, causing a blood clot. We slept in the hospital for a week as she recovered. All before her cancer fight.

The blood clot made doing surgery first too dangerous. Chemotherapy came first, which meant three months of watching and feeling her anguish. She was a foodie who couldn't really taste her food. She had to push through chronic fatigue to exercise. She'd just completed twelve years of medical training, but now instead of seeing patients, she'd become one herself. It was like training hard for a marathon and getting sick steps into the race. But she kept running: through chemotherapy, through three surgeries, through another year of less toxic chemotherapy. And she won.


I HAD TROUBLE separating Sadiqa's cancer from the racism I studied. The two consumed my life over the final months of 2013 and during the better part of 2014 and 2015. Months after Sadiqa survived stage-2 breast cancer, Ma was diagnosed with stage-1 breast cancer. She endured radiation and a lumpectomy in 2015. Those years were all about caretaking Sadiqa, helping Dad caretake Ma, and—when they were sleeping or enjoying company or desiring alone time—retreating from the pain of their cancer into the stack of racist ideas I'd collected.

Over time, the source of racist ideas became obvious, but I had trouble acknowledging it. The source did not fit my concep-

230 • HOW TO BE AN ANTIRACIST

tion of racism, my racial ideology, my racial identity. I became a college professor to educate away racist ideas, seeing ignorance as the source of racist ideas, seeing racist ideas as the source of racist policies, seeing mental change as the principal solution, seeing myself, an educator, as the primary solver.

Watching Sadiqa's courage to break down her body to rebuild her body inspired me to accept the source of racist ideas I found while researching their entire history—even though it upended my previous way of thinking. My research kept pointing me to the same answer: The source of racist ideas was not ignorance and hate, but self-interest.

The history of racist ideas is the history of powerful policy-makers erecting racist policies out of self-interest, then producing racist ideas to defend and rationalize the inequitable effects of their policies, while everyday people consume those racist ideas, which in turn sparks ignorance and hate. Treating ignorance and hate and expecting racism to shrink suddenly seemed like treating a cancer patient's symptoms and expecting the tumors to shrink. The body politic might feel better momentarily from the treatment—from trying to eradicate hate and ignorance—but as long as the underlying cause remains, the tumors grow, the symptoms return, and inequities spread like cancer cells, threatening the life of the body politic. Educational and moral suasion is not only a failed strategy. It is a suicidal strategy.


THIS MESSAGE OF focusing on policy change over mental change was written in my next book, *Stamped from the Beginning*. After the book came out in 2016, I took this message on the road from our new home at the University of Florida. I talked about racist policies leading to racist ideas, not the other way around, as we have commonly thought. I talked about eliminating racist policies if we ever hope to eliminate racist ideas. I talked and talked, unaware of my new hypocrisy, which readers and attendees picked up on. "What are *you* doing to change policy?" they kept asking me in public and private.

I started questioning myself. What am I doing to change policy? How can I genuinely urge people to focus on changing policy if I am not focused on changing policy? Once again, I had to confront and abandon a cherished idea.

I did not need to forsake antiracist research and education. I needed to forsake my orientation to antiracist research and education. I had to forsake the suasionist bred into me, of researching and educating for the sake of changing minds. I had to start researching and educating to change policy. The former strategy produces a public scholar. The latter produces public scholarship.

IN THE SUMMER of 2017, I moved to American University in the nation's capital to found and direct the Antiracist Research and Policy Center. My research in the history of racism and antiracism revealed that scholars, policy experts, journalists, and advocates had been crucial in successfully replacing racist policy with antiracist policy.

I envisioned building residential fellowship programs and bringing to Washington dream teams of scholars, policy experts, journalists, and advocates, who would be assisted by classrooms of students from the nation's most politically active student body. The teams would focus on the most critical and seemingly intractable racial inequities. They would investigate the racist policies causing racial inequity, innovate antiracist policy correctives, broadcast the research and policy correctives, and engage in campaigns of change that work with antiracist power in locales to institute and test those policy correctives before rolling them out nationally and internationally.

THESE TEAMS WOULD model some of the steps we can all take to eliminate racial inequity in our spaces.

*Admit racial inequity is a problem of bad policy, not bad people.*
*Identify racial inequity in all its intersections and manifestations.*

*Investigate and uncover the racist policies causing racial inequity.*

*Invent or find antiracist policy that can eliminate racial inequity.*

*Figure out who or what group has the power to institute antiracist policy.*

*Disseminate and educate about the uncovered racist policy and antiracist policy correctives.*

*Work with sympathetic antiracist policymakers to institute the antiracist policy.*

*Deploy antiracist power to compel or drive from power the unsympathetic racist policymakers in order to institute the antiracist policy.*

*Monitor closely to ensure the antiracist policy reduces and eliminates racial inequity.*

*When policies fail, do not blame the people. Start over and seek out new and more effective antiracist treatments until they work.*

*Monitor closely to prevent new racist policies from being instituted.*

On the September night I unveiled the vision of the Antiracism Center before my peers at American University, racist terror unveiled its vision, too. After my presentation, during my late-night class, an unidentified, middle-aged, hefty White male, dressed in construction gear, posted copies of Confederate flags with cotton balls inside several buildings. He posted them on the bulletin boards outside my classroom. The timing did not seem coincidental. I ignored my fears and pressed on during the final months of 2017. This wasn't the only thing I put out of my mind. I also ignored my weight loss and pressed on. It became annoying going in and out of bathrooms only to produce nothing, only to still feel like I needed to go minutes later. But I felt I had more important matters to worry about. After all, White nationalists were running and terrorizing the United States and their power was spreading across the Western world.

I did not have a rejuvenating break during Thanksgiving. I was bedridden. The throwing up started and stopped after the weekend. The bloody diarrhea did not. It all became worse. By Christmas, things had become acute. I obliged when Sadiqa urged me to get myself checked out.

Neither the nurse practitioner nor Sadiqa thought it was anything serious. I was thirty-five, about half the median age for the worst possibility, colon cancer. I did not exhibit any of the risk factors for colon cancer, since I exercised, rarely drank, never smoked, and had been a vegan since Sadiqa and I made the change to help prevent a recurrence of her cancer. We scheduled a precautionary colonoscopy for January 10, 2018.

I WAS GROGGY from the anesthesia early that morning. Cleaning out my colon had been an all-night affair. Sadiqa helped me put on my clothes in the small and dreary consultation room. No windows or striking colors or decorations, only pictures of the GI tract hanging on the walls. The Black woman doctor who'd performed the colonoscopy entered the room with a serious look on her face.

"I saw something abnormal," she said, sitting down. "I saw a mass in the sigmoid colon. It is large and friable, and it is bleeding." I looked at her in confusion, not knowing what she meant. Sadiqa looked at her in shock, knowing exactly what she meant.

She said she could not get her scope past the mass. It was obstructing the colon. "It is most likely cancerous," she said.

She paused as my confusion converted into shock. I checked out of myself. Sadiqa had to speak for me, really listen for me. The doctor told me to get blood work that day and get my body scanned the next day to confirm the cancer. I did not know what to think or feel. And so I did not feel or think anything other than shock.

At one point, several minutes later, perhaps as someone drained me of blood, I thought about Professor Mazama. About when I told her Sadiqa's diagnosis and asked, "Why her?"

"Why not her?" Professor Mazama responded.

*Why not me?*

I thought of Sadiqa and Ma and Dad's cancer fights. *Why not me?* They survived. *Why shouldn't I be the one to die?*

. . .

WE LEFT THE medical office in downtown Washington and headed for Busboys and Poets to meet Ma for breakfast. We sat down at the table. Ma had been waiting for a half hour. She asked why it took so long. I was still mute, looking down, up, away from anyone's eyes. Sadiqa told Ma about the mass. That it was probably cancer. "Okay, if it is, we will deal with it," Ma said. I looked up into her eyes, holding back tears. "We will deal with it," she said again. I knew she was serious. "Yes, we will," Sadiqa said, snatching my eyes. *Yes, we will,* I said to myself, absorbing their courage.

That night, I received more courage, when Sadiqa and I assumed we'd caught the cancer early. Probably stage 1 or 2. Perhaps 3. Not stage 4. About 88 percent of people diagnosed with stage-4 colon cancer die within five years.

The next day, they confirmed it. I had metastatic colon cancer. Stage 4. *Maybe we won't be able to deal with it.*

OUR WORLD IS suffering from metastatic cancer. Stage 4. Racism has spread to nearly every part of the body politic, intersecting with bigotry of all kinds, justifying all kinds of inequities by victim blaming; heightening exploitation and misplaced hate; spurring mass shootings, arms races, and demagogues who polarize nations; shutting down essential organs of democracy; and threatening the life of human society with nuclear war and climate change. In the United States, the metastatic cancer has been spreading, contracting, and threatening to kill the American body as it nearly did before its birth, as it nearly did during its Civil War. But how many people stare inside the body of their nations' racial inequities, their neighborhoods' racial inequities, their occupations' racial inequities, their institutions' racial inequities, and flatly deny that their policies are racist? They flatly deny that racial inequity is the signpost of racist policy. They flatly deny the racist policy as they use racist ideas to justify the racial inequity. They flatly deny the cancer of racism as the cancer cells spread and literally threaten their own lives and the lives of the people and spaces and places they hold dear. The popular conception of denial—like the popular strategy of suasion—is suicidal.

I HAD BEEN thinking all week about denial, before the diagnosis, after the diagnosis. I still could not separate racism and cancer. I sat in the waiting rooms, between medical meetings, tests, and procedures, writing an essay arguing that the heartbeat of racism is denial, the heartbeat of antiracism is confession. It appeared in *The New York Times* on Sunday, January 14, 2018, three days after my diagnosis. But my writing on the denial of racism did not stop me from denying the severity of my cancer. I could not confess I was likely to die.

I had been privately making sense of racism through cancer since Sadiqa's diagnosis. Except now I started making sense out of my cancer through my new conception of racism. Denying my ability to succeed in my cancer fight did not differ from those denying our ability to succeed in the antiracism fight. Denial is much easier than admission, than confession.

*I have cancer. The most serious stage. Cancer is likely to kill me. I can survive cancer against all odds.*

*My society has racism. The most serious stage. Racism is likely to kill my society. My society can survive racism against all odds.*

I prepared myself to fight. I looked past what could harm me in the fight to see all that could bring me joy if I survived. Dancing through life with my surviving and thriving partner. Watching my nearly two-year-old Black girl grow into a phenomenal woman. Growing myself into a better self through the love of my constructive family and friends and mentors I know and do not know. Engaging the open-minded readers of *Stamped from the Beginning*. Building the Antiracism Center into an intellectual factory of antiracist policy. Witnessing my beloved New York

Knicks finally win an NBA championship. Writing for *The Atlantic,* in the same pages as W.E.B. Du Bois. Finishing this book and sharing it with the world.

I looked at the antiracist progress coming in my lifetime, the antiracist society coming in my granddaughter's lifetime, our great-grandchildren refusing to return to the racist time when all the victims of all forms of bigotries that feed and are fed by racism had far less resources, far less of an opportunity to be one with their humanity, to be one with human difference, to be one with our shared humanity.

MY TREATMENT PLAN took shape like battle plans. Six months of chemotherapy. If my tumors shrank, the chance for surgery. The chance of removing the rest of the tumors. The chance at life if there was not a recurrence. A long shot. But a chance.

On Mondays, every three weeks, beginning in late January 2018, I received chemo injections and started taking two weeks of chemo pills. By Tuesdays, I already felt like I had been jumped by Smurf and his boys. Could barely climb out of bed. Could barely write this book. Could barely eat and drink. But I pushed myself to get out of bed, to write, to stay hydrated, because when I did not exercise my body and mind, when I did not consume enough protein and thoughts and fluids, I could feel the toxicity levels rising in my body, exacerbating all the symptoms.

To keep up with my normal life, I had to go outside into the bitter cold of winter, not merely to the gym but to meetings, to speaking engagements, to life. The chemo made me hypersensitive to cold. Thirty degrees outside felt like negative ten degrees inside me. Whenever I breathed in cold air, it hurt my lungs. Whenever I drank ice-cold fluids, it hurt my throat. Whenever I touched anything cold, it hurt my fingers.

Instead of wallowing in the chronic discomfort or asking the doctor to ease the chemo, I found ways to make myself more comfortable. Pain is usually essential to healing. When it comes to healing America of racism, we want to heal America without pain, but without pain, there is no progress.

MY TUMORS SHRANK enough for me to go on the surgical table by the end of the summer of 2018. Surgeons removed what was left and sewed me back together. Pathologists dissected what they took out and did not find any cancer cells. The six months of chemotherapy had obliterated, apparently, all the cancer. My doctors were as shocked as I had been when I was diagnosed. I had a good chance to land in the 12 percent of people who survived stage-4 colon cancer.

WE CAN SURVIVE metastatic racism. Forgive me. I cannot separate the two, and no longer try. What if humanity connected the two? Not just the number of people of all races who would not die each year from cancer if we launched a war against cancer instead of against bodies of color who kill us in far lesser numbers. Not just the better prevention and treatment options doctors would have if we diverted to cancer care and research a portion of the trillions of tax dollars we spend on cutting taxes for the rich, imprisoning people, bombing people, and putting troops in harm's way.

What if we treated racism in the way we treat cancer? What has historically been effective at combatting racism is analogous to what has been effective at combatting cancer. I am talking about the treatment methods that gave me a chance at life, that give millions of cancer fighters and survivors like me, like you, like our loved ones, a chance at life. The treatment methods that gave millions of our relatives and friends and idols who did not survive cancer a chance at a few more days, months, years of life. What if humans connected the treatment plans?

Saturate the body politic with the chemotherapy or immunotherapy of antiracist policies that shrink the tumors of racial inequities, that kill undetectable cancer cells. Remove any remaining racist policies, the way surgeons remove the tumors. Ensure there are clear margins, meaning no cancer cells of inequity left in the body politic, only the healthy cells of equity. Encourage the consumption of healthy foods for thought and the regular exercising of antiracist ideas, to reduce the likelihood of a recurrence. Monitor the body politic closely, especially where the tumors of racial inequity previously existed. Detect and treat a recurrence early, before it can grow and threaten the body politic.

But before we can treat, we must believe. Believe all is not lost for you and me and our society. Believe in the possibility that we can strive to be antiracist from this day forward. Believe in the possibility that we can transform our societies to be antiracist from this day forward. Racist power is not godly. Racist policies are not indestructible. Racial inequities are not inevitable. Racist ideas are not natural to the human mind.

Race and racism are power constructs of the modern world. For roughly two hundred thousand years, before race and racism were constructed in the fifteenth century, humans saw color but did not group the colors into continental races, did not commonly attach negative and positive characteristics to those colors and rank the races to justify racial inequity, to reinforce racist power and policy. Racism is not even six hundred years old. It's a cancer that we've caught early.

But racism is one of the fastest-spreading and most fatal cancers humanity has ever known. It is hard to find a place where its cancer cells are not dividing and multiplying. There is nothing I see in our world today, in our history, giving me hope that one day antiracists will win the fight, that one day the flag of antiracism will fly over a world of equity. What gives me hope is a simple truism. Once we lose hope, we are guaranteed to lose. But if we ignore the odds and fight to create an antiracist world, then we give humanity a chance to one day survive, a chance to live in communion, a chance to be forever free.

# ACKNOWLEDGMENTS

It was the people who kept asking the question that framed this book. People in audiences, in private conversations, in emails, on phone calls, on social media—the people urged me to write this book by asking again and again how they could be antiracist. I would like to first acknowledge and thank the people—the many people I know, and more I do not know—who trusted in me to deliver an answer.

I want to thank Ayesha Pande, my literary agent and friend, for encouraging the book idea when I relayed it to you in 2016. I am forever appreciative of your indelible confidence, support, and stewardship through this process from idea to book.

I would like to acknowledge Chris Jackson, my book editor, for your editorial wisdom and constructive vision. This book was quite difficult to wrap my head around and write—the chronological personal narrative interspersed with a series of connected chapter themes that build on each other like a stepladder to antiracism. And so I am filled with gratitude for your patience and clear-eyed conceptual tools that helped in this book's construction. And to the whole One World squad: thank you, especially you, Nicole. I must also acknowledge all the great folks in production, sales, marketing, and publicity at Random House, especially my fellow Eagle, Maria. I know how crucial you are in getting these pages into hands, and I can't thank you enough.

I could not have produced this book without the memories of its characters, especially my father, who has an almost perfect memory, and of course Ma, and Sadiqa, Kaila, Yaba, Clarence, and Weckea, another person whose memory is flawless. And so thank you. I could not have produced this book without the tremendous amount of scholarship and reporting on racism and antiracism. And so thank you to all those researchers and theorists and journalists of racism and antiracism.

I could not have produced this book without my health. And so thank you to all the medical providers who armed me during my cancer fight.

A horde of people throughout my life, knowingly and unknowingly, with good intentions and bad intentions, put up mirrors that forced me to self-reflect. I must thank all these people, many of whom are in this book. I want to express my gratitude to all those who assisted me during my journey through academia, from my professors, like Drs. Jackson, Asante, and Mazama, to my colleagues and mentors at colleges and universities where I was employed. I especially want to thank my colleagues at American University for your incredible support. There are too many people to name, but I want to acknowledge Sylvia, Mary, Teresa, Courtney, Fanta, Cheryl, Nancy, Camille, Peter, Christine, Jim, Jeff, Vicky, Eric, Max, Eric, Edwina, Theresa, Rebecca, Lily, Lisa, Kyle, Derrick, Keith, Kristie, Kelly, Rachel, Elizabeth, Alan, Jonathan, Gautham, Dan, and all my other colleagues in the Department of History and the School of International Service. I most especially would like to thank my friends and colleagues at the Antiracist Research and Policy Center, especially Christine, Christopher, Rachel, Amanda, Jordanna, Jessica, Derek, Garrett, Malini, and Kareem.

Thank you to all my friends and relatives, especially my brother, Akil, and my brother-in-law, Macharia. As you know, this book would have been impossible without you and your love. You know who you are. Thank you. Much love and respect.

Finally, I want to thank faith, my daughter, Imani. One day, you will learn how critical you were to the life of this book. And excuse me while I give another shout out to my rock, partner, and best friend, who has given so much to me and meant so much to me and humanity, Sadiqa.

# NOTES

## My Racist Introduction

8 **"Laziness is a trait in Blacks"** John R. O'Donnell, *Trumped!: The Inside Story of the Real Donald Trump—His Cunning Rise and Spectacular Fall* (New York: Simon & Schuster, 1991). O'Donnell is the former president of Trump Plaza Hotel and Casino in Atlantic City. In his memoir, he quoted Trump's criticism of a Black accountant. Here is the full quote. "Black guys counting my money! I hate it. The only kind of people I want counting my money are short guys that wear yarmulkes every day. . . . I think that the guy is lazy. And it's probably not his fault, because laziness is a trait in blacks. It really is, I believe that. It's not anything they can control." Trump at first denied he said this, but later told a *Playboy* reporter, "The stuff O'Donnell wrote about me is probably true." See Mark Bowden, "The Art of the Donald: The Trumpster Stages the Comeback of a Lifetime," *Playboy*, May 1997.

8 **as mostly criminals and rapists** " 'Drug Dealers, Criminals, Rapists': What Trump Thinks of Mexicans," BBC, August 31, 2016, available at www.bbc .com/news/av/world-us-canada-37230916/drug-dealers-criminals-rapists -what-trump-thinks-of-mexicans.

8 **"a total and complete shutdown of Muslims entering the United States"** This came from a Trump campaign statement released on December 7, 2015. For the statement in full, see " 'Preventing Muslim Immigration' Statement Disappears from Trump's Campaign Site," *USA Today*, May 8, 2017, available at www.usatoday.com/story/news/politics/onpolitics /2017/05/08/preventing-muslim-immigration-statement-disappears -donald-trump-campaign-site/101436780/.

8 **he routinely called his Black critics "stupid"** For a collection of his statements, see "Trump's Insults Toward Black Reporters, Candidates Echo 'Historic Playbooks' Used Against African Americans, Critics Say," *The Washington Post,* November 9, 2018, www.washingtonpost.com/politics/trumps-insults-toward-black-reporters-candidates-echo-historic-play books-used-against-african-americans/2018/11/09/74653438-e440-11e8-b759-3d88a5ce9e19_story.html.

8 **"all have AIDS"** See "Out of Chaos, Trump Reshapes Immigration," *The New York Times,* December 24, 2017.

8 **"very fine people"** See "Trump Defends White-Nationalist Protesters: 'Some Very Fine People on Both Sides,'" *The Atlantic,* August 15, 2017, available at www.theatlantic.com/politics/archive/2017/08/trump-defends-white-nationalist-protesters-some-very-fine-people-on-both-sides/537012/.

8 **"that you have ever interviewed"** See "Trump Says 'I'm Not a Racist' and Denies 'Shithole Countries' Remark," *The Washington Post,* January 14, 2018, available at www.washingtonpost.com/news/post-politics/wp/2018/01/14/trump-says-im-not-a-racist-and-denies-shithole-countries-remark/.

8 **"you've ever met"** See "Donald Trump: I'm 'the Least Racist Person,'" CNN, September 15, 2016, available at www.cnn.com/2016/09/15/politics/donald-trump-election-2016-racism/index.html.

8 **"you've ever encountered"** See "Donald Trump: 'I Am the Least Racist Person,'" *The Washington Post,* June 10, 2016, available at www.washingtonpost.com/politics/donald-trump-i-am-the-least-racist-person/2016/06/10/eac7874c-2f3a-11e6-9de3-6e6e7a14000c_story.html.

9 **Denial is the heartbeat of racism** For more on this idea, see Ibram X. Kendi, "The Heartbeat of Racism Is Denial," *The New York Times,* January 13, 2018, available at www.nytimes.com/2018/01/13/opinion/sunday/heartbeat-of-racism-denial.html.

9 **"'Racist' isn't a descriptive word"** For Richard Spencer's full quote, see "Who Is Richard Spencer?," *Flathead Beacon,* November 26, 2014, available at flatheadbeacon.com/2014/11/26/richard-spencer/.

10 **"Our Constitution is color-blind"** For Justice Harlan's full dissent, see "Separate but Equal," in *Great Decisions of the U.S. Supreme Court* (New York: Barnes & Noble Books, 2003), 46–58. For the specific quotes in this book, see 53.

## Chapter 1: Definitions

14 **Skinner was growing famous** For explanatory pieces on Skinner's life and influence and role in Urbana '70, see "The Unrepeatable Tom Skinner," *Christianity Today,* September 12, 1994, available at www.christianitytoday.com/ct/1994/september12/4ta011.html; and "A Prophet Out of Harlem,"

*Christianity Today,* September 16, 1996, available at www.christianitytoday
.com/ct/1996/september16/6ta036.html.

14 **third and fourth books** Tom Skinner, *How Black Is the Gospel?* (Philadelphia: Lippincott, 1970); and Tom Skinner, *Words of Revolution: A Call to
Involvement in the Real Revolution* (Grand Rapids, MI: Zondervan, 1970).

14 **"The Black Aesthetic"** For the lessons Addison Gayle shared in this course,
see his landmark book, *The Black Aesthetic* (Garden City, NY: Doubleday,
1971).

14 **Larry read** James Baldwin, *The Fire Next Time* (New York: Dial, 1963);
Richard Wright, *Native Son* (New York: Harper, 1940); Amiri Baraka
(LeRoi Jones), *Dutchman and the Slave: Two Plays* (New York: William Mor-
row, 1964); and Sam Greeley, *The Spook Who Sat by the Door* (New York:
Baron, 1969).

14 **Soul Liberation launched into their popular anthem** For a remembrance
of this evening with Soul Liberation playing and Tom Skinner preaching
that is consistent with my parents' memories, see Edward Gilbreath, *Reconciliation Blues: A Black Evangelical's Inside View of White Christianity* (Downers
Grove, IL: InterVarsity Press, 2006), 66–69.

15 **When the music ended, it was time: Tom Skinner** For the audio and text
of Tom Skinner's sermon at Urbana '70 entitled "Racism and World Evangelism," see urbana.org/message/us-racial-crisis-and-world-evangelism.

16 **saved into Black liberation theology** For a good book on the philosophy
of Black theology, see James H. Cone, *Risks of Faith: The Emergence of a Black
Theology of Liberation, 1968–1998* (Boston: Beacon Press, 2000).

16 **churchless church of the Black Power movement** For a good overview of
Black Power, see Peniel E. Joseph, *Waiting 'Til the Midnight Hour: A Narrative
History of Black Power in America* (New York: Henry Holt, 2007).

16 *Black Theology & Black Power* James H. Cone, *Black Theology & Black Power*
(New York: Seabury, 1969).

16 *A Black Theology of Liberation* James H. Cone, *A Black Theology of Liberation*
(Philadelphia: Lippincott, 1970).

18 **71 percent of White families lived in owner-occupied homes** These fig-
ures can be found in Matthew Desmond, "Housing," *Pathways: A Magazine
on Poverty, Inequality, and Social Policy,* Special Issue 2017, 16–17, available at
inequality.stanford.edu/publications/pathway/state-union-2017. This essay is
part of the Stanford Center on Poverty & Inequality's State of the Union
2017.

19 **"You do not take a person who"** For a full video of President Johnson's speech at Howard, see "Commencement Speech at Howard University, 6/4/65," The LBJ Library, available at www.youtube.com/watch?v=vcf
AuodA2x8.

19 **"In order to get beyond racism"** For his full dissent, see Harry Blackmun,
Dissenting Opinion, *Regents of the Univ. of Cal. v. Bakke, 1978,* C-SPAN

Landmark Cases, available at landmarkcases.c-span.org/Case/27/Regents
-Univ-Cal-v-Bakke.

20 **racist idea** See Ibram X. Kendi, *Stamped from the Beginning: The Definitive
History of Racist Ideas in America* (New York: Nation Books, 2016).

20 **"The blacks, whether originally a distinct race"** Thomas Jefferson, *Notes
on the State of Virginia* (Boston: Lilly and Wait, 1832), 150.

21 **Great Migration** For the best book on the Great Migration, see Isabel
Wilkerson, *The Warmth of Other Suns: The Epic Story of America's Great Migration* (New York: Vintage Books, 2011).

21 **non-White global south is being victimized** See "Climate Change Will
Hit Poor Countries Hardest, Study Shows," *The Guardian,* September 27,
2013, available at www.theguardian.com/global-development/2013/sep/27
/climate-change-poor-countries-ipcc.

21 **higher lead poisoning rates than Flint, Michigan** See "Reuters Finds
3,810 U.S. Areas with Lead Poisoning Double Flint's," Reuters, November 14, 2017, available at www.reuters.com/article/us-usa-lead-map/reuters
-finds-3810-u-s-areas-with-lead-poisoning-double-flints-idUSKBN1
DE1H2.

21 **Alzheimer's, a disease more prevalent among African Americans** For an
excellent essay on African Americans and Alzheimer's, see "African Americans Are More Likely Than Whites to Develop Alzheimer's. Why?," *The
Washington Post Magazine,* June 1, 2017, available at www.washingtonpost
.com/lifestyle/magazine/why-are-african-americans-so-much-more
-likely-than-whites-to-develop-alzheimers/2017/05/31/9bfbcccc-3132
-11e7-8674-437ddb6e813e_story.html.

22 **3.5 additional years over Black lives** For a summary of this data, see "Life
Expectancy Improves for Blacks, and the Racial Gap Is Closing, CDC Reports," *The Washington Post,* May 2, 2017, available at www.washingtonpost
.com/news/to-your-health/wp/2017/05/02/cdc-life-expectancy-up-for
-blacks-and-the-racial-gap-is-closing/.

22 **Black infants die at twice the rate of White infants** "Why America's
Black Mothers and Babies Are in a Life-or-Death Crisis," *The New York
Times Magazine,* April 11, 2018, available at www.nytimes.com/2018/04/11
/magazine/black-mothers-babies-death-maternal-mortality.html.

22 **African Americans are 25 percent more likely to die of cancer** For this
disparity and other disparities in this paragraph, see "Examples of Cancer
Health Disparities," National Cancer Institute, National Institutes of Health,
available at www.cancer.gov/about-nci/organization/crchd/about-health
-disparities/examples.

22 **Breast cancer disproportionately kills** "Breast Cancer Disparities: Black
Women More Likely Than White Women to Die from Breast Cancer in
the US," ABC News, October 16, 2018, available at abcnews.go.com/beta

-story-container/GMA/Wellness/breast-cancer-disparities-black-women
-white-women-die/story?id=58494016.

22 **Three million African Americans and four million Latinx secured health insurance** Namrata Uberoi, Kenneth Finegold, and Emily Gee, "Health Insurance Coverage and the Affordable Care Act, 2010–2016," ASPE Issue Brief, Department of Health & Human Services, March 3, 2016, available at aspe.hhs.gov/system/files/pdf/187551/ACA2010-2016.pdf.

22 **28.5 million Americans remained uninsured** "Since Obamacare Became Law, 20 Million More Americans Have Gained Health Insurance," *Fortune,* November 15, 2018, available at fortune.com/2018/11/15/obamacare -americans-with-health-insurance-uninsured/.

22 **Racist voting policy has evolved** For three recent studies on voter suppression, see Carol Anderson, *One Person, No Vote: How Voter Suppression Is Destroying Our Democracy* (New York: Bloomsbury, 2018); Allan J. Lichtman, *The Embattled Vote in America: From the Founding to the Present* (Cambridge, MA: Harvard University Press, 2018); and Ari Berman, *Give Us the Ballot: The Modern Struggle for Voting Rights in America* (New York: Farrar, Straus & Giroux, 2015).

22 **"target African Americans with almost surgical precision"** "The 'Smoking Gun' Proving North Carolina Republicans Tried to Disenfranchise Black Voters," *The Washington Post,* July 29, 2016, available at www.wash ingtonpost.com/news/wonk/wp/2016/07/29/the-smoking-gun-proving -north-carolina-republicans-tried-to-disenfranchise-black-voters/.

22 **Wisconsin's strict voter-ID law suppressed** "Wisconsin's Voter-ID Law Suppressed 200,000 Votes in 2016 (Trump Won by 22,748)," *The Nation,* May 9, 2017, available at www.thenation.com/article/wisconsins-voter-id -law-suppressed-200000-votes-trump-won-by-23000/.

23 **"We have all been programmed"** Audre Lorde, "Age, Race, Class, and Sex: Women Redefining Difference," in *Sister Outsider: Essays and Speeches* (Freedom, CA: Crossing Press, 1984), 115.

## Chapter 2: Dueling Consciousness

24 **"We must put drug abuse on the run"** Ronald Reagan, "Remarks on Signing Executive Order 12368, Concerning Federal Drug Abuse Policy Functions," in *Public Papers of the Presidents of the United States: Ronald Reagan, 1982* (Washington, DC: U.S. Government Printing Office, 1982), 813.

25 **American prison population to quadruple** See "Study Finds Big Increase in Black Men as Inmates Since 1980," *The New York Times,* August 28, 2002, available at www.nytimes.com/2002/08/28/us/study-finds-big-increase-in -black-men-as-inmates-since-1980.html.

25 **more people were incarcerated for drug crimes** Jonathan Rothwell, "Drug Offenders in American Prisons: The Critical Distinction Between

Stock and Flow," Brookings, November 25, 2015, available at www.brook
ings.edu/blog/social-mobility-memos/2015/11/25/drug-offenders-in
-american-prisons-the-critical-distinction-between-stock-and-flow/.

25 **White people are more likely than Black and Latinx people to sell
drugs** "Busted: The War on Drugs Remains as Racist as Ever, Statistics
Show," *Vice,* March 14, 2017, available at news.vice.com/en_ca/article
/7xwybd/the-war-on-drugs-remains-as-racist-as-ever-statistics-show.

25 **Nonviolent Black drug offenders remain in prisons** U.S. Department
of Justice, Bureau of Justice Statistics, *Compendium of Federal Justice Statistics,
2003,* 112 (Table 7.16) (2003), available at bjs.ojp.usdoj.gov/content/pub
/pdf/cfjs03.pdf.

25 **Black and Latinx people were still grossly overrepresented** "The Gap
Between the Number of Blacks and Whites in Prison Is Shrinking," Pew
Research Center, January 12, 2018, available at www.pewresearch.org/fact
-tank/2018/01/12/shrinking-gap-between-number-of-blacks-and-whites
-in-prison/.

25 **historian Elizabeth Hinton recounts** Elizabeth Hinton, *From the War on
Poverty to the War on Crime: The Making of Mass Incarceration in America* (Cambridge, MA: Harvard University Press, 2016).

25 **"the year when this country began a thorough"** Elizabeth Hinton, "Why
We Should Reconsider the War on Crime," *Time,* March 20, 2015, available
at time.com/3746059/war-on-crime-history/.

25 **Nixon announced his war on drugs in 1971** "President Nixon Declares
Drug Abuse 'Public Enemy Number One,'" Richard Nixon Foundation, June 17, 1971, available at www.youtube.com/watch?v=y8TGLLQ
lD9M.

25 **"We could arrest their leaders"** Dan Baum, "Legalize It All: How to Win
the War on Drugs," *Harper's,* April 2016, available at harpers.org/archive
/2016/04/legalize-it-all/.

26 **"the hard won gains of the civil rights movement"** James Forman Jr.,
*Locking Up Our Own: Crime and Punishment in Black America* (New York:
Farrar, Straus & Giroux, 2017), 126–27.

26 **"remedy . . . is not as simple"** Eleanor Holmes Norton, "Restoring the
Traditional Black Family," *The New York Times,* June 2, 1985.

27 **which were chopping the ladder** See "What Reagan Has Done to America," *Rolling Stone,* December 23, 1982, available at www.rollingstone.com
/culture/culture-news/what-reagan-has-done-to-america-79233/.

27 **The Reagan Revolution was just that** For a good overview of the racial
and economic effects of Reagan's policies, see Manning Marable, *Race, Reform, and Rebellion: The Second Reconstruction and Beyond in Black America,
1945–2006* (Jackson, MS: University Press of Mississippi, 2007).

28 **"It is a peculiar sensation, this double-consciousness"** W.E.B. Du Bois,
*The Souls of Black Folk* (New York: Penguin Books, 2018), 7.

29 **"relic of barbarism"** and **"the low social level of the mass of the race"** Ibid., 43.

29 **"Do Americans ever stop to reflect"** W.E.B. Du Bois, "The Talented Tenth," in *The Negro Problem: A Series of Articles by Representative American Negroes of To-Day* (New York: James Pott & Company, 1903). Full text of article available at teachingamericanhistory.org/library/document/the -talented-tenth/.

31 **Trump's descriptor for Latinx immigrants** See "Trump Ramps Up Rhetoric on Undocumented Immigrations: 'These Aren't People. These Are Animals,'" *USA Today*, May 16, 2018, available at www.usatoday.com /story/news/politics/2018/05/16/trump-immigrants-animals-mexico -democrats-sanctuary-cities/617252002/.

31 **"I am apt to suspect the negroes"** See Andrew Valls, "'A Lousy Empirical Scientist,' Reconsidering Hume's Racism," in *Race and Racism in Modern Philosophy*, ed. Andrew Valls (Ithaca, NY: Cornell University Press, 2005), 128–29.

32 **"It would be hazardous to affirm that"** Thomas Jefferson to Marquis de Chastellux, June 7, 1785, in The Avalon Project: Documents in Law, History and Diplomacy, available at avalon.law.yale.edu/18th_century/let27.asp.

32 **"history of the American Negro is the history of this strife"** Du Bois, *The Souls of Black Folk*, 7.

33 **"by white men for white men"** Senator Jefferson Davis, April 12, 1860, 37th Cong., 1st Sess., *Congressional Globe* 106, 1682.

33 **"become assimilated into American culture"** Gunnar Myrdal, *An American Dilemma: The Negro Problem and Modern Democracy* (New York: Harper, 1944), 929.

## Chapter 3: Power

35 **White New Yorkers were separating their children** For a few good books on what Whites in New York and across the nation were doing, see Matthew F. Delmont, *Why Busing Failed: Race, Media, and the National Resistance to School Desegregation* (Berkeley, CA: University of California Press, 2016); Jonathan Kozol, *The Shame of the Nation: The Restoration of Apartheid Schooling in America* (New York: Three Rivers Press, 2005); and Kevin M. Kruse, *White Flight: Atlanta and the Making of Modern Conservatism* (Princeton, NJ: Princeton University Press, 2007).

36 **Black parents did not mind paying** For some of the early research on this issue, see Diana T. Slaughter and Barbara Schneider, "Parental Goals and Black Student Achievement in Urban Private Elementary Schools: A Synopsis of Preliminary Research Findings," *The Journal of Intergroup Relations* 13:1 (Spring/August 1985), 24–33; and Diana T. Slaughter and Barbara Schneider, *Newcomers: Blacks in Private Schools* (Evanston, IL: Northwestern University School of Education, 1986).

39 **the first character in the history of racist power** Ibram X. Kendi, *Stamped from the Beginning: The Definitive History of Racist Ideas in America* (New York: Nation Books, 2016), 22–25.

39 **circumvent Islamic slave traders** For literature on this history, see Robert C. Davis, *Christian Slaves, Muslim Masters: White Slavery in the Mediterranean, the Barbary Coast, and Italy, 1500–1800* (New York: Palgrave Macmillan, 2003); Matt Lang, *Trans-Saharan Trade Routes* (New York: Cavendish, 2018); and John Wright, *The Trans-Saharan Slave Trade* (New York: Routledge, 2007).

39 **feared "black" hole of Cape Bojador** Martin Meredith, *The Fortunes of Africa: A 5000-Year History of Wealth, Greed, and Endeavor* (New York: PublicAffairs, 2014), 93–94; Gomes Eannes de Zurara, *The Chronicle of the Discovery and Conquest of Guinea* (London: Hakluyt Society, 1896).

40 **"Race . . . means descent"** See Aimar de Ranconnet and Jean Nicot, *Trésor de la langue française* (Paris: Picard, 1960).

40 *negros da terra* See Mieko Nishida, *Slavery & Identity: Ethnicity, Gender, and Race in Salvador, Brazil, 1808–1888* (Bloomington, IN: Indiana University Press, 2003), 13.

41 **"strong for work, the opposite of the natives"** David M. Traboulay, *Columbus and Las Casas: The Conquest and Christianization of America, 1492–1566* (Lanham, MD: University Press of America, 1994), 58.

41 **Linnaeus locked in the racial hierarchy** See Dorothy Roberts, *Fatal Invention: How Science, Politics, and Big Business Re-Create Race in the Twenty-First Century* (New York: New Press, 2011), 252–53.

42 **"to the great praise of his memory"** Zurara, *The Chronicle of the Discovery and Conquest of Guinea*, xii.

42 **"than from all the taxes levied on the entire kingdom"** Gabriel Tetzel and Václáv Sasek, *The Travels of Leo of Rozmital, 1465–1467*, translated by Malcolm Letts (London, 1957).

## Chapter 4: Biology

45 **Black students were four times more likely than White students to be suspended** See "Black Students More Likely to Be Suspended: U.S. Education Department," Reuters, June 7, 2016, available at www.reuters.com/article/us-usa-education-suspensions/black-students-more-likely-to-be-suspended-u-s-education-department-idUSKCN0YT1ZO.

45 **"microaggression," a term coined by eminent Harvard psychiatrist Chester Pierce** Chester Pierce, "Offensive Mechanism," in *The Black Seventies,* ed. Floyd B. Barbour (Boston, MA: Porter Sargent, 1970), 280.

46 **"brief, everyday exchanges that send denigrating messages"** Derald Wing Sue, *Microaggressions in Everyday Life: Race, Gender, and Sexual Orientation* (Hoboken, NJ: Wiley, 2010), 24.

49 "more natural physical ability" John Hoberman, *Darwin's Athletes: How Sport Has Damaged Black America and Preserved the Myth of Race* (New York: Houghton Mifflin Harcourt, 1997), 146.

49 "one drop of Negro blood makes a Negro" Thomas Dixon, *The Leopard's Spots: A Romance of the White Man's Burden, 1865–1900* (New York: Doubleday, 1902), 244.

49 "blacks have certain inherited abilities" Dinesh D'Souza, *The End of Racism: Principles for a Multiracial Society* (New York: Free Press, 1996), 440–41.

49 "large size of the negro's penis" William Lee Howard, "The Negro as a Distinct Ethnic Factor in Civilization," *Medicine* 9 (June 1903), 423–26.

50 "I've bounced this off a number of colleagues" See "Black Hypertension Theory Criticized: Doctor Says Slavery Conditions May Be Behind Problem," *Orlando Sentinel,* January 21, 1988, available at articles.orlandosentinel .com/1988-01-21/news/0010200256_1_grim-salt-hypertension.

50 "all his posteritie after him" See George Best, *A True Discourse of the Late Voyages of Discoverie* (London: Henry Bynneman, 1578).

51 released *Men Before Adam* Isaac de La Peyrère, *Men Before Adam* (London, 1656).

51 "race of Men, not derivable from Adam" Morgan Godwyn, *The Negro's and Indian's Advocate* (London, 1680), 15–16.

51 "each species has been independently created" Charles Darwin, *The Origin of Species* (New York: P. F. Collier, 1909), 24.

51 "second fate is often predicted for the negroes" Albion W. Small and George E. Vincent, *An Introduction to the Study of Society* (New York: American Book Company, 1894), 179.

52 "spread out a magnificent map" "Remarks Made by the President . . . on the Completion of the First Survey of the Entire Human Genome Project," The White House, Office of the Press Secretary, National Human Genome Research Institute, June 26, 2000, available at www.genome .gov/10001356/.

53 "planning the next phase of the human genome project" "For Genome Mappers, the Tricky Terrain of Race Requires Some Careful Navigating," *The New York Times,* July 20, 2001.

53 "People are born with ancestry" Dorothy Roberts, *Fatal Invention: How Science, Politics, and Big Business Re-Create Race in the Twenty-First Century* (New York: New Press, 2011), 63.

53 more genetic diversity between populations Ibid., 51–53.

54 "the mapping of the human genome concluded" Ken Ham, "There Is Only One Race—The Human Race," *The Cincinnati Enquirer,* September 4, 2017. Also see Ken Ham and A. Charles Ware, *One Race One Blood: A Biblical Answer to Racism* (Green Forest, AR: Master Books, 2010).

## Chapter 5: Ethnicity

57 **Korean storekeeper who killed fifteen-year-old Latasha Harlins** See Brenda Stevenson, *The Contested Murder of Latasha Harlins: Justice, Gender, and the Origins of the LA Riots* (New York: Oxford University Press, 2015).

57 **Haitian immigrant named Abner Louima** See "Twenty Years Later: The Police Assault on Abner Louima and What It Means," WNYC News, August 9, 2017, available at www.wnyc.org/story/twenty-years-later-look-back-nypd-assault-abner-louima-and-what-it-means-today/.

57 **forty-one bullets at the body of Amadou Diallo** See Beth Roy, *41 Shots . . . and Counting: What Amadou Diallo's Story Teaches Us About Policing, Race and Justice* (Syracuse, NY: Syracuse University Press, 2009).

58 **Congolese as "magnificent blacks"** Hugh Thomas, *The Slave Trade: The Story of the Atlantic Slave Trade, 1440–1870* (New York: Simon & Schuster, 2013), 399.

58 **from Senegambia "the best slaves"** Ibid.

58 **"the best and most faithful of our slaves"** Ibid., 400.

58 **nearly twice as much as captives from Angola** Ibid., 402.

59 **Angolans were traded more** Ibid., 401.

59 **captives hauled into Jamestown, Virginia, in August 1619** See James Horn, *1619: Jamestown and the Forging of American Democracy* (New York: Basic Books, 2018).

59 **"The Negroes from the Gold Coast, Popa, and Whydah"** Thomas, *The Slave Trade,* 401.

59 **"African chiefs were the ones waging war on each other"** See "Clinton Starts African Tour," BBC News, March 23, 1998, available at news.bbc.co.uk/2/hi/africa/68483.stm.

60 **Between 1980 and 2000, the Latinx immigrant population ballooned** See "Facts on U.S. Latinos, 2015: Statistical Portrait of Hispanics in the United States," Pew Research Center, September 18, 2017, available at www.pewhispanic.org/2017/09/18/facts-on-u-s-latinos/.

61 **As of 2015, Black immigrants accounted for 8.7** See "A Rising Share of the U.S. Black Population Is Foreign Born," Pew Research Center, April 9, 2015, available at www.pewsocialtrends.org/2015/04/09/a-rising-share-of-the-u-s-black-population-is-foreign-born/.

61 **West Indian immigrants tend to categorize African Americans** Mary C. Waters, *Black Identities: West Indian Immigrant Dreams and American Realities* (Cambridge, MA: Harvard University Press, 1999), 138.

61 **African Americans tended to categorize West Indians** Ibid., 69.

61 **1882 Chinese Restriction Act** For anti-Asian immigration violence and policies, see Beth Lew-Williams, *The Chinese Must Go: Violence, Exclusion,*

*and the Making of the Alien in America* (Cambridge, MA: Harvard University Press, 2018); and Erika Lee, *The Making of Asian America: A History* (New York: Simon & Schuster, 2015).

61  **"America must be kept American,"** President Calvin Coolidge said David Joseph Goldberg, *Discontented America: The United States in the 1920s* (Baltimore: Johns Hopkins University Press, 1999), 163.

61  **in the case of Mexican Americans, be forcibly repatriated** For literature on Mexican repatriations, see Francisco E. Balderrama and Raymond Rodríguez, *Decade of Betrayal: Mexican Repatriation in the 1930s* (Albuquerque, NM: University of Mexico Press, 2006); and "America's Forgotten History of Illegal Deportations," *The Atlantic,* March 6, 2017, available at www.the atlantic.com/politics/archive/2017/03/americas-brutal-forgotten-history -of-illegal-deportations/517971/.

61  **proclaimed Maine Representative Ira Hersey** See Benjamin B. Ringer, *We the People and Others: Duality and America's Treatment of Its Racial Minorities* (New York: Routledge, 1983), 801–2.

61  **"When the numbers reached about this high in 1924"** "The American People Are Angry Alright . . . at the Politicians," Steve Bannon interviews Jeff Sessions, SiriusXM, October 4, 2015, available at soundcloud.com /siriusxm-news-issues/the-american-people-are-angry.

62  **"We should have more people from places like Norway"** See "People on Twitter Tell Trump No One in Norway Wants to Come to His 'Shithole Country,'"* Huffington Post,* January 11, 2018, available at www.huffington post.com/entry/trump-shithole-countries-norway_us_5a58199ce4b0720 dc4c5b6dc.

62  **Anglo-Saxons discriminating against Irish Catholics and Jews** See Peter Gottschalk, *American Heretics: Catholics, Jews, Muslims and the History of Religious Intolerance* (New York: Palgrave Macmillan, 2013).

62  **Cuban immigrants being privileged over Mexican immigrants** See "Cuban Immigrants in the United States," Migration Policy Institute, November 9, 2017, available at www.migrationpolicy.org/article/cuban -immigrants-united-states.

62  **model-minority construction** See Ellen D. Wu, *The Color of Success: Asian Americans and the Origins of the Model Minority* (Princeton, NJ: Princeton University Press, 2014).

63  **"Five Civilized Tribes" of Native Americans** See Grant Foreman, *Indian Removal: The Emigration of the Five Civilized Tribes of Indians* (Norman, OK: University of Oklahoma Press, 1974).

65  **African Americans commonly degrading Africans as "barbaric"** For examples of these ideas, see Ibram X. Kendi, *Stamped from the Beginning: The Definitive History of Racist Ideas in America* (New York: Nation Books, 2016), 157, 200.

66 **calling West Indians in 1920s Harlem "monkey chasers"** See Marcy S. Sacks, *Before Harlem: The Black Experience in New York City Before World War I* (Philadelphia: University of Pennsylvania Press, 2006), 29.

66 **the median family income of African Americans** See "Chapter 1: Statistical Portrait of the U.S. Black Immigrant Population," Pew Research Center, April 9, 2015, available at www.pewsocialtrends.org/2015/04/09 /chapter-1-statistical-portrait-of-the-u-s-black-immigrant-population/.

66 **Black immigrants are more motivated, more hardworking** "Black Like Me," *The Economist,* May 11, 1996.

67 **Black immigrants . . . earn lower wages** "5 Fast Facts About Black Immigrants in the United States," Center for American Progress, December 20, 2012, available at www.americanprogress.org/issues/immigration /news/2012/12/20/48571/5-fast-facts-about-black-immigrants-in-the -united-states/.

67 **"immigrant self-selection"** Suzanne Model, *West Indian Immigrants: A Black Success Story?* (New York: Russell Sage, 2008), 56–59.

67 **the "migrant advantage"** Isabel Wilkerson, *The Warmth of Other Suns: The Epic Story of America's Great Migration* (New York: Vintage Books, 2011), 264–65.

67 **"West Indians are not a black success story"** Model, *West Indian Immigrants,* 3.

68 **Rosemary Traoré found in a study** Rosemary L. Traoré, "African Students in America: Reconstructing New Meanings of 'African American' in Urban Education," *Intercultural Education* 14:3 (2003), 244.

**Chapter 6: Body**

69 **the kids of working-class White families** For a good study on the transformation in New York City, see Walter Thabit, *How East New York Became a Ghetto* (New York: NYU Press, 2005).

70 **"Blacks must understand and acknowledge"** "Transcript of President Clinton's Speech on Race Relations," CNN, October 17, 1995, available at www .cnn.com/US/9510/megamarch/10-16/clinton/update/transcript.html.

70 **the Black body was as devilish as any people** John Smith, "Advertisements: Or, The Path-way to Experience to Erect a Planation," in *Capt. John Smith, Works, 1608–1631,* ed. Edward Arber (Birmingham, UK: E. Arber, 1884), 955.

70 **"make yourself infinitely Blacker than you are already"** See Cotton Mather, *A Good Master Well Served* (Boston: B. Green, and J. Allen, 1696).

70 **"the Cruel disposition of those Creatures"** Mary Miley Theobald, "Slave Conspiracies in Colonial Virginia," *Colonial Williamsburg,* Winter 2005–2006, available at www.history.org/foundation/journal/winter05-06 /conspiracy.cfm.

70 **federal "appropriations for protecting . . . against ruthless savages"** "A

Declaration of the Causes Which Impel the State of Texas to Secede from the Federal Union," Texas State Library and Archives Commission, February 2, 1861, available at www.tsl.texas.gov/ref/abouttx/secession/2feb1861.html.

70 **"The poor African has become a fiend"** Albert B. Hart, *The Southern South* (New York: D. Appleton, 1910), 93.

70 **"criminal display of the violence among minority groups"** Marvin E. Wolfgang and Franco Ferracuti, *The Subculture of Violence: Toward an Integrated Theory in Criminology* (New York: Routledge, 2001), 264.

71 **"The core criminal-justice population is the black underclass"** Heather Mac Donald, *The War on Cops: How the New Attack on Law and Order Makes Everyone Less Safe* (New York: Encounter Books, 2016), 233.

71 **Americans today see the Black body as larger** John Paul Wilson, Kurt Hugenberg, and Nicholas O. Rule, "Racial Bias in Judgments of Physical Size and Formidability: From Size to Threat," *Journal of Personality and Social Psychology* 113:1 (July 2017), 59–80, available at www.apa.org/pubs/journals/releases/psp-pspi0000092.pdf.

72 **I considered joining the Zulu Nation** I did not identify the Zulu Nation as a gang then; neither did its members. But I decided to add that term for clarity. Here is an article on the debate over the term as well as what the Zulu Nation was facing in the mid-1990s in NYC: "Hip-Hop Club (Gang?) Is Banned in the Bronx; Cultural Questions About Zulu Nation," *The New York Times,* October 4, 1995.

73 **in 2015, Black bodies accounted for at least 26 percent** See *The Washington Post* database on police shootings, available at www.washingtonpost.com/graphics/2018/national/police-shootings-2018/.

73 **Unarmed Black bodies** See "Fatal Police Shootings of Unarmed People Have Significantly Declined, Experts Say," *The Washington Post,* May 7, 2018, available at www.washingtonpost.com/investigations/fatal-police-shootings-of-unarmed-people-have-significantly-declined-experts-say/2018/05/03/d5eab374-4349-11e8-8569-26fda6b404c7_story.html.

74 **Republicans called those items "welfare for criminals"** Debate on 1994 Crime Bill, House Session, August 11, 1994, C-SPAN recording, available at www.c-span.org/video/?59442-1/house-session&start=12042.

74 **Twenty-six of the thirty-eight voting members** "Did Blacks Really Endorse the 1994 Crime Bill?," *The New York Times,* April 13, 2016, available at www.nytimes.com/2016/04/13/opinion/did-blacks-really-endorse-the-1994-crime-bill.html.

74 **their fear for my Black body—and of it** See James Forman Jr., *Locking Up Our Own: Crime and Punishment in Black America* (New York: Farrar, Straus & Giroux, 2017).

74 **"put politics and party above law and order"** "Crime Bill Is Signed with Flourish," *The Washington Post,* September 14, 1994, available at www.wash

ingtonpost.com/archive/politics/1994/09/14/crime-bill-is-signed-with
-flourish/650b1c2f-e306-4c00-9c6f-80bc9cc57e55/.

75 **John J. DiIulio Jr. warned of the "coming of the super-predators"** John
DiIulio, "The Coming of the Super-Predators," *The Weekly Standard,* November 27, 1995, available at www.weeklystandard.com/john-j-dilulio-jr
/the-coming-of-the-super-predators.

78 **In 1993, near the height of urban violent crime** "Urban, Suburban, and
Rural Victimization, 1993–98," Bureau of Justice Statistics Special Report,
National Crime Victimization Survey, U.S. Department of Justice, October
2000, available at www.bjs.gov/content/pub/pdf/usrv98.pdf.

78 **In 2016, for every thousand urban residents** "Criminal Victimization,
2016: Revised," Bureau of Justice Statistics, U.S. Department of Justice, October 2018, available at www.bjs.gov/content/pub/pdf/cv16.pdf.

78 **more than half of violent crimes from 2006 to 2010 went unreported**
"Report: More Than Half of Violent Crimes Went Unreported to Police
from 2006–2010," RTI International, August 13, 2012, available at www
.rti.org/news/report-more-half-violent-crimes-went-unreported-police
-2006-2010.

78 **more dangerous than "war zones"** "Donald Trump to African American
and Hispanic Voters: 'What Do You Have to Lose?,'" *The Washington Post,*
August 22, 2016, available at www.washingtonpost.com/news/post-politics
/wp/2016/08/22/donald-trump-to-african-american-and-hispanic-voters
-what-do-you-have-to-lose/.

79 **National Longitudinal Survey of Youth** Delbert S. Elliott, "Longitudinal
Research in Criminology: Promise and Practice," paper presented at the
NATO Conference on Cross-National Longitudinal Research on Criminal
Behavior, July 19–25, 1992, Frankfurt, Germany.

79 **the 2.5 percent decrease in unemployment between 1992 and 1997**
William Julius Wilson, *When Work Disappears: The World of the New Urban
Poor* (New York: Vintage Books, 1997), 22.

79 **Sociologist Karen F. Parker strongly linked the growth of Black-owned
businesses** "How Black-Owned Businesses Help Reduce Youth Violence,"
CityLab, March 16, 2015, available at www.citylab.com/life/2015/03/how
-black-owned-businesses-help-reduce-youth-violence/387847/.

79 **43 percent reduction in violent-crime arrests for Black youths** "Nearly
Half of Young Black Men in Chicago Out of Work, Out of School: Report,"
*Chicago Tribune,* January 25, 2016, available at www.chicagotribune.com
/ct-youth-unemployment-urban-league-0126-biz-20160124-story.html.

79 **Black neighborhoods do not all have similar levels** See "Neighborhoods
and Violent Crime," *Evidence Matters,* Summer 2016, available at www
.huduser.gov/portal/periodicals/em/summer16/highlight2.html.

80 **the highest rates of unemployment of any demographic group** For a
statistical graph, see fred.stlouisfed.org/series/LNS14000018.

## Chapter 7: Culture

82 **a term coined by psychologist Robert Williams in 1973** Robert L. Williams, *History of the Association of Black Psychologists: Profiles of Outstanding Black Psychologists* (Bloomington, IN: AuthorHouse, 2008), 80. Also see Robert L. Williams, *Ebonics: The True Language of Black Folks* (St. Louis: Institute of Black Studies, 1975).

82 **"the legitimacy and richness" of Ebonics as a language** "Oakland School Board Resolution on Ebonics (Original Version)," *Journal of English Linguistics* 26:2 (June 1998), 170–79.

83 **Jesse Jackson at first called it "an unacceptable surrender"** "Black English Is Not a Second Language, Jackson says," *The New York Times,* December 23, 1996.

83 **modern English had grown from Latin, Greek, and Germanic roots** See Albert C. Baugh and Thomas Cable, *A History of the English Language* (Upper Saddle River, NJ: Prentice Hall, 2002); and Tamara Marcus Green, *The Greek & Latin Roots of English* (Lanham, MD: Rowman & Littlefield, 2015).

83 **"In practically all its divergences"** Gunnar Myrdal, *An American Dilemma: The Negro Problem and Modern Democracy* (New York: Harper, 1944), 928.

84 **as President Theodore Roosevelt said in 1905** "At the Lincoln Dinner of the Republican Club, New York, February 13, 1905," in *A Compilation of the Messages and Speeches of Theodore Roosevelt, 1901–1905,* Volume 1, ed. Alfred Henry Lewis (New York: Bureau of National Literature and Art, 1906), 562.

84 **with those racist Americans who classed Africans as fundamentally imitative** As an example, see Lothrop Stoddard, *The Rising Tide of Color Against White World-Supremacy* (New York: Charles Scribner's Sons, 1921), 100–101.

84 **"This quality of imitation has been the grand preservative"** Alexander Crummell, "The Destined Superiority of the Negro," in *Civilization & Black Progress: Selected Writings of Alexander Crummell on the South* (Charlottesville, VA: University of Virginia Press, 1995), 51.

85 **Jason Riley . . . did not see us or our disciples** Jason L. Riley, *Please Stop Helping Us: How Liberals Make It Harder for Blacks to Succeed* (New York: Encounter Books, 2016), 51.

85 **"If blacks can close the civilization gap"** Dinesh D'Souza, *The End of Racism: Principles for a Multiracial Society* (New York: Free Press, 1996), 527.

86 **"outward physical manifestations of culture"** Linda James Myers, "The Deep Structure of Culture: Relevance of Traditional African Culture in Contemporary Life," in *Afrocentric Visions: Studies in Culture and Communication* (Thousand Oaks, CA: SAGE, 1998), 4.

86 **"North American negroes . . . in culture and language"** Franz Boas, *The Mind of Primitive Man* (New York: Macmillan, 1921), 127–28.

86 **"It is very difficult to find in the South today"** Robert Park, "The Conflict and Fusion of Cultures with Special Reference to the Negro," *Journal of Negro History* 4:2 (April 1919), 116.

86 **"Stripped of his cultural heritage"** E. Franklin Frazier, *The Negro Family in the United States* (Chicago: University of Chicago Press, 1939), 41.

86 **"the Negro is only an American, and nothing else"** Nathan Glazer and Daniel P. Moynihan, *Beyond the Melting Pot: The Negroes, Puerto Ricans, Jews, Italians, and Irish of New York City* (Cambridge, MA: MIT Press, 1963), 53.

86 **"we are not Africans,"** Bill Cosby told the NAACP "Bill Cosby's Famous 'Pound Cake' Speech, Annotated," *BuzzFeed,* July 9, 2015, available at www.buzzfeednews.com/article/adamserwer/bill-cosby-pound-for-pound.

86 **African cultures had been overwhelmed** See Boas, *The Mind of Primitive Man.*

86 **"the deep structure of culture"** See Wade Nobles, "Extended Self Rethinking the So-called Negro Self of Concept," in *Black Psychology* (2nd edition), ed. Reginald L. Jones (New York: Harper & Row, 1980).

87 **Western "outward" forms "while retaining inner [African] values"** Melville J. Herskovits, *The Myth of the Negro Past* (Boston: Beacon Press, 1990), 1, 298.

88 **Hip-hop has had the most sophisticated vocabulary** "Hip Hop Has the Largest Average Vocabulary Size Followed by Heavy Metal," *Musixmatch,* December 3, 2015, available at lab.musixmatch.com/vocabulary_genres/.

88 **"rap retards black success"** John H. McWhorter, "How Hip Hop Holds Blacks Back," *City Journal,* Summer 2003, available at www.city-journal.org/html/how-hip-hop-holds-blacks-back-12442.html.

88 **"You can't listen to all that language and filth"** See "Gunning for Gangstas," *People,* June 26, 1995, available at people.com/archive/gunning-for-gangstas-vol-43-no-25/.

89 **Nathan Glazer, who lamented the idea** Nathan Glazer, *We Are All Multiculturalists Now* (Cambridge, MA: Harvard University Press, 2003).

90 **"That every practice and sentiment is barbarous"** James Beattie, *An Essay on the Nature and Immutability of Truth, In Opposition to Sophistry and Scepticism* (Edinburgh: Denham & Dick, 1805), 308–11.

91 **"All cultures must be judged in relation to their own history"** Ashley Montagu, *Man's Most Dangerous Myth: The Fallacy of Race* (New York: Columbia University Press, 1945), 150.

## Chapter 8: Behavior

92 **"Did Martin Luther King successfully fight"** See "D.C. Residents Urged to Care, Join War on Guns," *The Washington Post,* January 14, 1995, available at www.washingtonpost.com/archive/local/1995/01/14/dc-residents-urged-to-care-join-war-on-guns/0b36f1f3-27ac-4685-8fb6-3eda372e93ac/.

93 **"You are costing everybody's freedom,"** Jesse Jackson told James For-

man Jr., *Locking Up Our Own: Crime and Punishment in Black America* (New York: Farrar, Straus & Giroux, 2017), 195.

93 **"It isn't racist for Whites to say"** "Transcript of President Clinton's Speech on Race Relations," CNN, October 17, 1995, available at www .cnn.com/US/9510/megamarch/10-16/clinton/update/transcript.html.

93 **Black people needed to stop playing "race cards"** Peter Collier and David Horowitz, eds., *The Race Card: White Guilt, Black Resentment, and the Assault on Truth and Justice* (Rocklin, CA: Prima, 1997).

94 **The same behavioral racism drove many of the Trump voters** See "Poll: Trump Supporters More Likely to View Black People as 'Violent' and 'Lazy,'" *Colorlines*, July 1, 2016, available at www.colorlines.com/articles /poll-trump-supporters-more-likely-view-black-people-violent-and-lazy; and "Research Finds That Racism, Sexism, and Status Fears Drove Trump Voters," *Pacific Standard,* April 24, 2018, available at psmag.com/news /research-finds-that-racism-sexism-and-status-fears-drove-trump-voters.

94 **"America's Black community . . . has turned America's major cities"** See "Homeland Security Official Resigns After Comments Linking Blacks to 'Laziness' and 'Promiscuity' Come to Light," *The Washington Post,* November 17, 2017, available at www.washingtonpost.com/news/powerpost /wp/2017/11/16/republican-appointee-resigns-from-the-dhs-after-past -comments-about-blacks-muslims-come-to-light/.

95 **"obvious for decades that the real culprit is black behavior"** Jason L. Riley, *Please Stop Helping Us: How Liberals Make It Harder for Blacks to Succeed* (New York: Encounter Books, 2016), 4.

95 **"had improved greatly in every respect"** See B. Ricardo Brown, *Until Darwin, Science, Human Variety and the Origins of Race* (New York: Routledge, 2015), 72.

96 **Freed Blacks "cut off from the spirit of White society"** Philip A. Bruce, *The Plantation Negro as a Freeman: Observations on His Character, Condition, and Prospects in Virginia* (New York: G. P. Putnam's Sons, 1889), 53, 129, 242.

96 **"All the vices which are charged upon the Negroes"** See Benjamin Rush, *An Address to the Inhabitants of the British Settlements in America, Upon Slave-Keeping* (Boston: John Boyles, 1773).

96 **Garrison stated that slavery degraded Black people** William Lloyd Garrison, "Preface," in Frederick Douglass, *Narrative of the Life of Frederick Douglass, an American Slave* (Boston: Anti-Slavery Office, 1849), vii.

96 **"the first and greatest step toward the settlement of the present friction between the races"** W.E.B. Du Bois, "The Conversation of Races," in *W.E.B. Du Bois: A Reader,* ed. David Levering Lewis (New York: Henry Holt, 1995), 20–27.

97 **Jim Crow historian's framing of slavery as a civilizing force** See Bruce, *The Plantation Negro as a Freeman.*

97 **Black "infighting," materialism, poor parenting, colorism, defeatism,**

**rage** See Joy DeGruy, *Post Traumatic Slave Syndrome: America's Legacy of Enduring Injury and Healing* (Portland: Joy DeGruy Publications, 2005).

97 **PTSD rates ranged from 13.5 to 30 percent** Miriam Reisman, "PTSD Treatment for Veterans: What's Working, What's New, and What's Next," *Pharmacy and Therapeutics* 41:10 (2016), 632–64.

98 **"There is not one personality trait of the Negro"** Abram Kardiner and Lionel Ovesey, *The Mark of Oppression: A Psychosocial Study of the American Negro* (New York: W. W. Norton, 1951), 81.

99 **The so-called Nation's Report Card told Americans the same story** For this data in the Nation's Report Card, see www.nationsreportcard.gov/.

99 **the lowest mean SAT scores of any racial group** "SAT Scores Drop," *Inside Higher Ed,* September 3, 2015, available at www.insidehighered.com /news/2015/09/03/sat-scores-drop-and-racial-gaps-remain-large.

100 **the U.S. test-prep and private tutoring industry** See "New SAT Paying Off for Test-Prep Industry," *Boston Globe,* March 5, 2016, available at www .bostonglobe.com/business/2016/03/04/new-sat-paying-off-for-test-prep -industry/blQeQKoSz1yAksN9N9463K/story.html.

101 **the so-called "attribution effect"** "Why We Don't Give Each Other a Break," *Psychology Today,* June 20, 2014, available at www.psychologytoday .com/us/blog/real-men-dont-write-blogs/201406/why-we-dont-give -each-other-break.

102 **"average intellectual standard of the negro race is some two grades below our own"** Sir Francis Galton, *Hereditary Genius: An Inquiry into Its Laws and Consequences* (New York: D. Appleton, 1870), 338.

102 **France's Alfred Binet and Theodore Simon succeeded in . . . 1905** See Margaret B. White and Alfred E. Hall, "An Overview of Intelligence Testing," *Educational Horizons* 58:4 (Summer 1980), 210–16.

102 **"enormously significant racial differences in general intelligence"** Lewis Madison Terman, *The Measurement of Intelligence* (New York: Houghton Mifflin, 1916), 92.

102 **Brigham presented the soldiers' racial scoring gap** See Carl C. Brigham, *A Study of American Intelligence* (Princeton, NJ: Princeton University Press, 1923).

102 **Physicist William Shockley and psychologist Arthur Jensen carried these eugenic ideas** See Stephen Jay Gould, *The Mismeasure of Man* (New York: W. W. Norton, 2006).

102 **genetic explanations . . . had largely been discredited** See Carl N. Degler, *In Search of Human Nature: The Decline and Revival of Darwinism in American Social Thought* (New York: Oxford University Press, 1992).

103 **"both genes and the environment have something to do with racial differences"** Richard J. Herrnstein and Charles Murray, *The Bell Curve: Intelligence and Class Structure in American Life* (New York: Simon & Schuster, 2010), 311.

103 **districts with a higher proportion of White students receive signifi-cantly more funding** "Studies Show Racial Bias in Pennsylvania School Funding," *The Times Herald,* April 15, 2017.

103 **The chronic underfunding of Black schools in Mississippi** "Lawsuit Al-leges Mississippi Deprives Black Children of Equal Educational Opportuni-ties," *ABA Journal,* May 23, 2017, available at www.abajournal.com/news /article/lawsuit_alleges_mississippi_deprives_black_children_of_equal_edu cational_op.

104 **"We must no longer be ashamed of being black"** Martin Luther King Jr., " 'Where Do We Go from Here?,' Address Delivered at the Eleventh Annual SCLC Convention," April 16, 1967, The Martin Luther King, Jr. Research and Education Institute, Stanford University, available at kinginsti tute.stanford.edu/king-papers/documents/where-do-we-go-here-address -delivered-eleventh-annual-sclc-convention.

106 **Florida A&M had outpaced Harvard** See "FAMU Ties Harvard in Re-cruitment of National Achievement Scholars," *Diverse: Issues in Higher Edu-cation,* February 1, 2001, available at diverseeducation.com/article/1139/.

**Chapter 9: Color**

107 **"the best college marching band in the country"** For a history, see Curtis Inabinett Jr., *The Legendary Florida A&M University Marching Band: The His-tory of "The Hundred"* (New York: Page Publishing, 2016).

109 **"white beauty repackaged with dark hair"** Margaret L. Hunter, *Race, Gender, and the Politics of Skin Tone* (New York: Routledge, 2013), 57.

109 **"colorism," a term coined by novelist Alice Walker** See Alice Walker, *In Search of Our Mothers' Gardens: Womanist Prose* (San Diego, CA: Harcourt Brace Jovanovich, 1983).

110 **relegate them to minority status** See "The US Will Become 'Minor-ity White' in 2045, Census Projects," Brookings, March 14, 2018, available at www.brookings.edu/blog/the-avenue/2018/03/14/the-us-will-become -minority-white-in-2045-census-projects/.

110 **the biracial key to racial harmony** See, for example, "What Biracial Peo-ple Know," *The New York Times,* March 4, 2017, available at www.nytimes .com/2017/03/04/opinion/sunday/what-biracial-people-know.html.

110 **"skin color paradox"** Jennifer L. Hochschild and Vesla Weaver, "The Skin Color Paradox and the American Racial Order," *Social Forces* 86:2 (Decem-ber 2007), 643–70.

110 **White children attribute positivity to lighter skin** "Study: White and Black Children Biased Toward Lighter Skin," CNN, May 14, 2010, available at www.cnn.com/2010/US/05/13/doll.study/.

110 **White people usually favor lighter-skinned politicians** Vesla M. Weaver, "The Electoral Consequences of Skin Color: The 'Hidden' Side of Race in Politics," *Political Behavior* 34:1 (March 2012), 159–92.

110 **disproportionately at risk of hypertension** Elizabeth A. Adams, Beth E. Kurtz-Costes, and Adam J. Hoffman, "Skin Tone Bias Among African Americans: Antecedents and Consequences Across the Life Span," *Developmental Review* 40 (2016), 109.

110 **significantly lower GPAs than Light students** Maxine S. Thompson and Steve McDonald, "Race, Skin Tone, and Educational Achievement," *Sociological Perspectives* 59:1 (2016), 91–111.

110 **racist Americans have higher expectations for Light students** Ebony O. McGree, "Colorism as a Salient Space for Understanding in Teacher Preparation," *Theory into Practice* 55:1 (2016), 69–79.

110 **remember educated Black men as Light-skinned** Avi Ben-Zeev, Tara C. Dennehy, Robin I. Goodrich, Branden S. Kolarik, and Mark W. Geisler, "When an 'Educated' Black Man Becomes Lighter in the Mind's Eye: Evidence for a Skin Tone Memory Bias," *SAGE Open* 4:1 (January 2014), 1–9.

111 **employers prefer Light Black men** Matthew S. Harrison, and Kecia M. Thomas, "The Hidden Prejudice in Selection: A Research Investigation on Skin Color Bias," *Journal of Applied Social Psychology* 39:1 (2009), 134–68.

111 **Dark Filipino men have lower income than their lighter peers** Lisa Kiang and David T. Takeuchi, "Phenotypic Bias and Ethnic Identity in Filipino Americans," *Social Science Quarterly* 90:2 (2009), 428–45.

111 **Dark immigrants to the United States . . . tend to have less wealth and income** Angela R. Dixon and Edward E. Telles, "Skin Color and Colorism: Global Research, Concepts, and Measurement," *Annual Review of Sociology* 43 (2017), 405–24.

111 **Light Latinx people receive higher wages** Maria Cristina Morales, "Ethnic-Controlled Economy or Segregation? Exploring Inequality in Latina/o Co-Ethnic Jobsites," *Sociological Forum* 24:3 (September 2009), 589–610.

111 **Dark Latinx people are more likely to be employed in ethnically homogeneous jobsites** Maria Cristina Morales, "The Ethnic Niche as an Economic Pathway for the Dark Skinned: Labor Market Incorporation of Latina/o Workers," *Hispanic Journal of Behavioral Sciences* 30:3 (August 2008), 280–98.

111 **Dark sons and Light daughters receive higher-quality** Antoinette M. Landor et al., "Exploring the Impact of Skin Tone on Family Dynamics and Race-Related Outcomes," *Journal of Family Psychology* 27:5 (2013), 817–26.

111 **Skin color influences perceptions of attractiveness** Mark E. Hill, "Skin Color and the Perception of Attractiveness Among African Americans: Does Gender Make a Difference?," *Social Psychology Quarterly* 65:1 (March 2002), 77–91.

111 **As skin tone lightens, levels of self-esteem among Black women rise** Adams, Kurtz-Costes, and Hoffman, "Skin Tone Bias Among African Americans," 107.

111 **Dark African Americans receive the harshest prison sentences** Jill Viglione, Lance Hannon, and Robert DeFina, "The Impact of Light Skin on Prison Time for Black Female Offenders," *The Social Science Journal* 48: (2011), 250–58.

111 **White male offenders with African facial features receive harsher sentences** Ryan D. King and Brian D. Johnson, "A Punishing Look: Skin Tone and Afrocentric Features in the Halls of Justice," *American Journal of Sociology* 122:1 (July 2016), 90–124.

111 **Dark female students are nearly twice as likely to be suspended** Lance Hannon, Robert DeFina, and Sarah Bruch, "The Relationship Between Skin Tone and School Suspension for African Americans," *Race and Social Problems* 5:4 (December 2013), 281–95.

112 **Even Dark gay men heard it** Donovan Thompson, "'I Don't Normally Date Dark-Skin Men': Colorism in the Black Gay Community," *Huffington Post,* April 9, 2014, available at www.huffingtonpost.com/entry/i-dont -normally-date-dark_b_5113166.html.

112 **"You're never Black enough"** "Colorism: Light-Skinned African-American Women Explain the Discrimination They Face," *Huffington Post,* January 13, 2014, available at www.huffingtonpost.com/entry/colorism -discrimination-iyanla-vanzant_n_4588825.html.

113 **their struggle to integrate with Dark people** "Light-Skinned Black Women on the Pain of Not Feeling 'Black Enough,'" *Huffington Post,* January 22, 2015, available at www.huffingtonpost.com/entry/light-girls-not -black-enough_n_6519488.html.

114 **"that the Negro's . . . do entertain as high thoughts"** Morgan Godwyn, *The Negro's and Indian's Advocate* (London, 1680), 21.

114 **African people must accept the "correct conception" of beauty** Johann Joachim Winckelmann, *History of the Art of Antiquity,* trans. Harry Francis Mallgrave (Los Angeles: Getty Research Institute, 2006), 192–95.

114 **slaveholders more often worked Light people in the house** William L. Andrews, *Slavery and Class in the American South: A Generation of Slave Narrative Testimony, 1840–1865* (New York: Oxford University Press, 2019), 102.

114 **"Ferocity and stupidity are characteristics of those tribes"** John Ramsay McCulloch, *A Dictionary, Geographical, Statistical, and Historical of the Various Countries, Places, and Principal Natural Objects in the World,* Volume 1 (London: Longman, Brown, Green, and Longmans, 1851), 33.

115 **Smith's racist light** See Samuel Stanhope Smith, *An Essay on the Causes of the Variety of Complexion and Figure in the Human Species* (New Brunswick, NJ: J. Simpson and Co, 1810).

115 **"a degenerate, unnatural offspring, doomed by nature to work out its own destruction"** J. C. Nott, "The Mulatto a Hybrid—Probable Extermination of the Two Races if the Whites and Blacks Are Allowed to Intermarry," *American Journal of Medical Sciences* 66 (July 1843), 255.

115 **private racist ideas, which typically described Light women as smarter** See Walter Johnson, *Soul by Soul: Life Inside the Antebellum Slave Market* (Cambridge, MA: Harvard University Press, 2001).

115 **Slaveholders paid much more for enslaved Light females** Ibid.

115 **White men cast these "yaller gals" and "Jezebels"** See Melissa Harris-Perry, *Sister Citizen: Shame, Stereotypes, and Black Women in America* (New Haven, CT: Yale University Press, 2011).

115 **"more likely to enlist themselves under the banners of the whites"** *A Refutation of the Calumnies Circulated Against the Southern and Western States Respecting the Institution and Existence of Slavery Among Them* (Charleston, SC: A. E. Miller, 1822), 84.

115 **Maybe Holland had the Brown Fellowship Society in mind** Thomas C. Holt, *Black over White: Negro Political Leadership in South Carolina During Reconstruction* (Urbana, IL: University of Illinois Press, 1977), 65–67.

116 **White and Light only barbershops** See Hayes Johnson, *Dusk at the Mountain* (Garden City, NY: Doubleday, 1963); and Chris Myers Asch and George Derek Musgrove, *Chocolate City: A History of Race and Democracy in the Nation's Capital* (Chapel Hill, NC: University of North Carolina Press, 2017).

116 **After slavery, Light people were wealthier** See Johnson, *Soul by Soul*.

116 **dozens of cities had "Blue Vein" societies** Willard B. Gatewood, *Aristocrats of Color: The Black Elite, 1880–1920* (Fayetteville, AR: University of Arkansas Press, 2000), 163.

116 **"not white enough to show blue veins"** Charles W. Chesnutt, "The Wife of His Youth," *The Atlantic Monthly*, July 1898, 55.

116 **Light people reproduced the paper-bag test, pencil test, door test, and comb test** Kathy Russell, Midge Wilson, and Ronald Hall, *The Color Complex: The Politics of Skin Color Among African Americans* (New York: Anchor Books, 1992), 27.

116 **Carroll considered the interracial intercourse** See Charles Carroll, *"The Negro a Beast"; Or, "In the Image of God"* (St. Louis: American Book and Bible House, 1900).

116 **framing Dark people as committing "more horrible crimes"** George T. Winston, "The Relation of the Whites to the Negroes," *Annals of the American Academy of Political and Social Science* 18 (July 1901), 108–9.

116 **biracial people were responsible for all Black achievements** Edward B. Reuter, *The Mulatto in the United States* (Boston: R. G. Badger, 1918).

117 **Marcus Garvey and his fast-growing Universal Negro Improvement Association** See Tony Martin, *Race First: The Ideological and Organizational Struggles of Marcus Garvey and the Universal Negro Improvement Association* (Dover, MA: Greenwood Press, 1976).

117 **"American Negroes recognize no color line in or out of the race"** W.E.B. Du Bois, "Marcus Garvey," *The Crisis*, January 1921.

117 **"If you're white, you're right"** Daryl Cumber Dance, ed., *From My People: 400 Years of African American Folklore* (New York: W. W. Norton, 2003), 484.

117 **his own "Talented Tenth" essay in 1903** See W.E.B. Du Bois, "The Talented Tenth," in *The Negro Problem: A Series of Articles by Representative American Negroes of Today* (New York: James Pott & Company, 1903), 31–76.

117 **the Dark masses needed "proper grooming"** See Charlotte Hawkins Brown, "Clipping," Charlotte Hawkins Brown Papers, Reel 2, Schlesinger Library, Radcliffe College, Cambridge, MA; and Constance Hill Mareena, *Lengthening Shadow of a Woman: A Biography of Charlotte Hawkins Brown* (Hicksville, NY: Exposition Press, 1977).

117 **John McWhorter's avowal of a post-racial America** John McWhorter, "Racism in American Is Over," *Forbes,* December 30, 2008, available at www .forbes.com/2008/12/30/end-of-racism-oped-cx_jm_1230mcwhorter .html#50939eb949f8.

117 **shied away from defending the dark and poor Scottsboro Boys** "Why the Communist Party Defended the Scottsboro Boys," *History Stories,* May 1, 2018, available at www.history.com/news/scottsboro-boys-naacp -communist-party.

117 **"unmixed" Negroes were "inferior, infinitely inferior now"** David Levering Lewis, *W.E.B. Du Bois: The Fight for Equality and the American Century, 1919–1963* (New York: Macmillan, 2000), 341.

117 **"Walter White is white"** W.E.B. Du Bois, "Segregation in the North," *The Crisis,* April 1934.

118 **"I had joined that multitude of Negro men and women in America"** Malcolm X recalled in Malcolm X and Alex Haley, *The Autobiography of Malcolm X* (New York: Random House, 2015), 64.

118 **Skin-lightening products received a boost** Ayana D. Byrd and Lori L. Tharps, *Hair Story: Untangling the Roots of Black Hair in America* (New York: St. Martin's Griffin, 2002), 44–47.

118 **Some Dark people took too much pride in Darkness** For example, see George Napper, *Blacker Than Thou: The Struggle for Campus Unity* (Grand Rapids, MI: Eerdmans, 1973).

118 **Light children were adopted first** Russell-Cole, Wilson, and Hall, *The Color Complex,* 37–39, 51–53, 90–91; Byrd and Tharps, *Hair Story,* 112.

118 **"The lighter the skin, the lighter the sentence"** Russell-Cole, Wilson, and Hall, *The Color Complex,* 38.

118 **Imus compared Rutgers's Dark basketball players** "Networks Condemn Remarks by Imus," *The New York Times,* April 7, 2007.

119 **casting call for the movie *Straight Outta Compton*** "The 'Straight Outta Compton' Casting Call Is So Offensive It Will Make Your Jaw Drop," *Huffington Post,* July 17, 2014, available at www.huffingtonpost.com/2014/07/17 /straight-out-of-compton-casting-call_n_5597010.html.

119 **Skin-bleaching products were raking in millions** "Lighter Shades of

Skin," *The Economist,* September 28, 2012, available at www.economist.com /baobab/2012/09/28/lighter-shades-of-skin.

119 **In India, "fairness" creams topped $200 million** "Telling India's Modern Women They Have Power, Even Over Their Skin Tone," *The New York Times,* May 30, 2007.

119 **70 percent of women in Nigeria; 35 percent in South Africa; 59 percent in Togo; and 40 percent in China, Malaysia, the Philippines, and South Korea** See "Mercury in Skin Lightening Products," News Ghana, June 13, 2012, available at www.newsghana.com.gh/mercury-in -skin-lightening-products/.

119 **the United States elected the "orange man"** See "NeNe Leakes Once Liked Donald Trump but Not 'This Orange Man Talking on TV,'" *Atlanta Journal-Constitution,* September 7, 2016.

119 **tanning bed every morning** "Omarosa Manigault Newman Says Trump Uses a Tanning Bed in the White House Every Morning," *People,* August 14, 2018, available at people.com/politics/omarosa-trump-daily -routine-tanning-bed-diet-coke-unhinged/.

119 **Survey shows that people consider tanned skin . . . more attractive** Cynthia M. Frisby, "'Shades of Beauty': Examining the Relationship of Skin Color to Perceptions of Physical Attractiveness," *Facial Plastic Surgery* 22:3 (August 2006), 175–79.

## Chapter 10: White

123 **Jeb Bush's termination of affirmative-action programs** "Jeb Bush Roils Florida on Affirmative Action," *The New York Times,* February 4, 2000, available at www.nytimes.com/2000/02/04/us/jeb-bush-roils-florida-on -affirmative-action.html.

123 **Al Gore's winning face flash on the screen** "The 2000 Elections: The Media; A Flawed Call Adds to High Drama," *The New York Times,* November 8, 2000, available at www.nytimes.com/2000/11/08/us/the-2000 -elections-the-media-a-flawed-call-adds-to-high-drama.html.

123 **a narrow lead in Florida of 1,784 votes** "Examining the Vote; How Bush Took Florida: Mining the Overseas Absentee Vote," *The New York Times,* July 15, 2001, available at www.nytimes.com/2001/07/15/us/examining -the-vote-how-bush-took-florida-mining-the-overseas-absentee-vote .html.

123 **stories of FAMU students and their families back home not being able to vote** For example, see "FAMU Students Protest Election Day Mishaps in Florida," *Diverse: Issues in Higher Education,* December 7, 2000, available at diverseeducation.com/article/1034/; and "Florida A&M Students Describe Republican Attack on Voting Rights," *World Socialist Web Site,* December 6, 2000, available at www.wsws.org/en/articles/2000/12/flor-d06.html.

124 **11 percent of registered voters but comprised 44 percent of the purge**

list Ari Berman, "How the 2000 Election in Florida Led to a New Wave of Voter Disenfranchisement," *The Nation,* July 28, 2015, available at www .thenation.com/article/how-the-2000-election-in-florida-led-to-a-new -wave-of-voter-disenfranchisement/.

124 **Palm Beach County** Henry E. Brady et al., "Law and Data: The Butterfly Ballot Episode," in *The Longest Night: Polemics and Perspectives on Election 2000,* eds. Arthur J. Jacobson and Michel Rosenfeld (Berkeley, CA: University of California Press, 2002), 51.

124 **Florida's highest percentage of Black voters and the highest spoilage rate** "1 Million Black Votes Didn't Count in the 2000 Presidential Election," *San Francisco Chronicle,* June 20, 2004, available at www.sfgate.com/opinion /article/1-million-black-votes-didn-t-count-in-the-2000-2747895.php.

124 **a *New York Times* statistical analysis** "Examining the Vote: The Patterns; Ballots Cast by Blacks and Older Voters Were Tossed in Far Greater Numbers," *The New York Times,* November 12, 2001.

124 **Ted Cruz served on Bush's legal team** Ari Berman, *Give Us the Ballot: The Modern Struggle for Voting Rights in America* (New York: Farrar, Straus & Giroux, 2015), 210.

124 **a silent march of two thousand students** See "FAMU Students Protest Election Day Mishaps in Florida" and "Florida A&M Students Describe Republican Attack on Voting Rights."

125 ***Message to the Blackman in America*** Elijah Muhammad, *Message to the Blackman in America* (Chicago: Muhammad Temple No. 2, 1965).

125 **According to the theology he espoused** For this story, I used the even clearer theology that Malcolm X espoused in his autobiography, as taught to him by Elijah Muhammad. Malcolm X and Alex Haley, *The Autobiography of Malcolm X* (New York: Random House, 2015), 190–94.

127 **"our unity as a people and the strength of our democracy"** "Gore: 'It Is Time for Me to Go,'" *The Guardian,* December 14, 2000, available at www .theguardian.com/world/2000/dec/14/uselections2000.usa14.

127 **"The white man is the devil"** Malcolm X and Haley, *The Autobiography of Malcolm X,* 184–85.

127 ***The Hate That Hate Produced*** See "The Hate That Hate Produced (1959): Malcom X First TV Appearance," available at www.youtube.com /watch?v=BsYWD2EqavQ.

128 **"Never have I witnessed such"** Malcolm X, "Letters from Abroad," in *Malcolm X Speaks: Selected Speeches and Statements,* ed. George Breitman (New York: Grove Press, 1990), 59.

128 **"You may be shocked by these words"** Ibid., 61.

128 **"I totally reject Elijah Muhammad's racist philosophy"** M. S. Handler, "Malcolm Rejects Racist Doctrine," *The New York Times,* October 4, 1964.

128 **as the resistance within White nations shows** See, for example, Sarah Jaffee, *Necessary Trouble: Americans in Revolt* (New York: Nation Books, 2016).

130 **identified anti-White discrimination as a serious problem** "Majority of White Americans Say They Believe Whites Face Discrimination," NPR, October 24, 2017, available at www.npr.org/2017/10/24/559604836 /majority-of-white-americans-think-theyre-discriminated-against.

130 **President Andrew Johnson reframed this antiracist bill** Andrew Johnson, "Veto of the Civil Rights Bill," March 27, 1866, in Teaching American History, available at teachingamericanhistory.org/library/document/veto -of-the-civil-rights-bill/.

130 **"hard-core racists of reverse discrimination"** Robert Bork, "The Unpersuasive Bakke Decision," *The Wall Street Journal,* July 21, 1978.

130 **Alicia Garza typed "Black Lives Matter" on Facebook** "Meet the Woman Who Coined #BlackLivesMatter," *USA Today,* March 4, 2015, available at www.usatoday.com/story/tech/2015/03/04/alicia-garza-black -lives-matter/24341593/.

130 **Giuliani called the movement "inherently racist"** "Rudy Giuliani: Black Lives Matter 'Inherently Racist,'" CNN, July 11, 2016, available at edition.cnn.com/2016/07/11/politics/rudy-giuliani-black-lives-matter -inherently-racist/index.html.

131 **these ground troops shelling out racist abuse** "Living While Black," CNN, December 28, 2018, available at www.cnn.com/2018/12/20/us /living-while-black-police-calls-trnd/index.html.

131 **bold black letters against a yellow background** "Where Does That Billboard Phrase, 'Anti-Racist Is a Code Word for Anti-White,' Come From? It's Not New," *The Birmingham News,* June 30, 2014, available at www .al.com/news/birmingham/index.ssf/2014/06/where_does_that_billboard _phra.html.

131 **Robert Whitaker, who ran for vice president** "Following the White Rabbit: Tim Murdock Sits Atop an Online Cult, Spreading Fears of 'White Genocide' That Have Fueled Violence and Terrorism," Southern Poverty Law Center, August 21, 2013, available at www.splcenter.org/fighting-hate /intelligence-report/2013/following-white-rabbit.

132 **43 percent of the people who gained lifesaving health insurance** "Who Gained Health Insurance Coverage Under the ACA, and Where Do They Live," Urban Institute, December 2016, available at www.urban.org/sites /default/files/publication/86761/2001041-who-gained-health-insurance -coverage-under-the-aca-and-where-do-they-live.pdf.

132 **destroyed the lives of more than forty million White people** "Research Starters: Worldwide Deaths in World War II," The National WWII Museum, available at www.nationalww2museum.org/students-teachers/student -resources/research-starters/research-starters-worldwide-deaths-world-war.

132 **more than five hundred thousand White American lives lost** "The Cost of War: Killer, Wounded, Captured, and Missing," American Battlefield Trust, available at www.battlefields.org/learn/articles/civil-war-casualties.

132 **a nuclear ideology that poses an existential threat to human existence** Ibram X. Kendi, "A House Still Divided," *The Atlantic,* October 2018.

133 **Diop's two-cradle theory** Cheikh Anta Diop, *The Cultural Unity of Negro Africa: The Domains of Patriarchy and of Matriarchy in Classical Antiquity* (Chicago: Third World Press, 1978).

133 **Bradley's version of the same** Michael Bradley, *The Iceman Inheritance: Prehistoric Sources of Western Man's Racism, Sexism and Aggression* (New York: Warner Books, 1978).

133 *The Isis Papers* Frances Cress Welsing, *The Isis Papers: The Keys to the Colors* (Chicago: Third World Press, 1991).

133 *The Rising Tide of Color Against White World-Supremacy* Lothrop Stoddard, *The Rising Tide of Color Against White World-Supremacy* (New York: Charles Scribner's Sons, 1921).

## Chapter 11: Black

137 **Chris Rock in his 1996 HBO special** See "Chris Rock—Bring the Pain," HBO, June 1, 1996, available at www.youtube.com/watch?v=coC4t7nCGPs.

138 **"the great truth that the negro is not equal to the white man"** Alexander H. Stephens, "Cornerstone Address, March 21, 1861," in *The Rebellion Record: A Diary of American Events with Documents, Narratives, Illustrative Incidents, Poetry, etc.,* Volume 1, ed. Frank Moore (New York: G. P. Putnam, 1862), 44–46.

139 **53 percent of Black people were surveyed** "Fewer Blacks in U.S. See Bias in Jobs, Income, and Housing," Gallup, July 19, 2013, available at news .gallup.com/poll/163580/fewer-blacks-bias-jobs-income-housing.aspx.

139 **59 percent of Black people expressed** "The Partisan Divide on Political Values Grows Even Wider: 4. Race, Immigration and Discrimination," Pew Research Center, October 5, 2017, available at www.people-press .org/2017/10/05/4-race-immigration-and-discrimination/.

140 **racist Whites dismissing antiracist policies and ideas as racist** It is most obvious through the attack on Black Power activists. See "Humphrey Backs N.A.A.C.P. in Fight on Black Racism," *The New York Times,* July 7, 1966.

140 **"Black people can't be racist"** Here is a typical argument: "Black People Cannot Be Racist, and Here's Why," *The University Star,* February 15, 2016, available at star.txstate.edu/2016/02/black-people-cannot-be-racist-and-heres -why/.

141 **154 African Americans** Ida A. Brudnick and Jennifer E. Manning, "African American Members of the United States Congress: 1870–2018," Congressional Research Service, updated December 28, 2018, available at www .senate.gov/CRSpubs/617f17bb-61e9-40bb-b301-50f48fd239fc.pdf.

141 **more than seven hundred Black judges on state courts** "National Database on Judicial Diversity in State Courts," American Bar Association, available at apps.americanbar.org/abanet/jd/display/national.cfm.

141 **more than two hundred Black judges on federal courts** "African American Judges on the Federal Courts," Federal Judicial Center, available at www.fjc.gov/history/judges/search/african-american.

141 **more than fifty-seven thousand Black police officers** "The New Racial Makeup of U.S. Police Departments, *Newsweek,* May 14, 2015, available at www.newsweek.com/racial-makeup-police-departments-331130.

141 **three thousand Black police chiefs, assistant chiefs, and commanders** "Blacks in Blue: African-American Cops React to Violence Towards and from Police," NBC News, July 11, 2016, available at www.nbcnews.com/news/nbcblk/blacks-blue-african-american-cops-react-violence-towards-police-n607141.

141 **more than forty thousand full-time Black faculty** "Table 315.20. Full-time Faculty in Degree-Granting Postsecondary Institutions, by Race/Ethnics, Sex, and Academic Rank: Fall 2013, Fall 2015, and Fall 2016," Digest of Education Statistics, National Center for Education Statistics, available at nces.ed.gov/programs/digest/d17/tables/dt17_315.20.asp.

141 **eleven Black billionaires and the 380,000 Black millionaire families** "The Black Billionaires 2018," *Forbes,* March 7, 2018, available at www.forbes.com/sites/mfonobongnsehe/2018/03/07/the-black-billionaires-2018/#19dd12935234; and "Black Millionaires Hardly Exist in America," *Newsmax,* October 4, 2017, available at www.newsmax.com/antoniomoore/black-millionaires-wealth-wealth-disparity/2017/10/04/id/817622/.

141 **sixteen Black CEOs** "The Number of Black CEOs at Fortune 500 Companies Is at Its Lowest Since 2002," *Fortune,* February 28, 2018, available at fortune.com/2018/02/28/black-history-month-black-ceos-fortune-500/.

142 **"When you control a man's thinking"** Carter G. Woodson, *The Miseducation of the Negro* (Mineola, NY: Dover, 2005), 55.

142 **Blackwell directed county boards** "GOPer Behind Ohio's Botched 2004 Election Eyes Senate Run," *Mother Jones,* April 21, 2011, available at www.motherjones.com/politics/2011/04/ken-blackwell-ohio-brown-senate/.

143 **174,000 potential votes walked away** "Was the 2004 Election Stolen?", *Common Dreams,* June 1, 2006, available at www.commondreams.org/views06/0601-34.htm.

143 **"Blackwell made Katherine Harris look like a cupcake"** Ibid.

143 **Trump officials had not forgotten Blackwell's state-of-the-art racist work** Ken Blackwell, "Time to Clean Up Our Elections," CNS News, July 17, 2017, available at www.cnsnews.com/commentary/ken-blackwell/time-clean-our-elections.

144 **"Negroes . . . leade a beastly kind of life"** Leo Africanus, trans. John Pory, and ed. Robert Brown, *The History and Description of Africa,* 3 volumes (London: Hakluyt Society, 1896), 130, 187–90.

145 **"but an act of Justice" Sambo says** Richard Ligon, *A True and Exact History of the Island of Barbadoes* (Indianapolis, IN: Hackett, 2011), 105–6.

145　authored the first known slave narrative James Albert, *A Narrative of the Most Remarkable Particulars in the Life of James Albert Ukawsaw Gronniosaw, an African Prince* (Leeds: Stanhope Press, 1811), 11, 12, 16, 25.

145　"to those waiting men who receive presents of old coats" For this quote and other details on the rebellion, see David M. Robertson, *Denmark Vesey: The Buried Story of America's Largest Slave Rebellion and the Man Who Led It* (New York: Alfred A. Knopf, 2009), 70.

146　By 1840, he'd acquired seven slaves of his own Ibid., 123.

146　"next to Mr. Booker T. Washington, the best American authority" "The Negro Arraigned," *The New York Times,* February 23, 1901. Also, for an excellent analysis of how William Hannibal Thomas fits in with discussions of Blackness at this time, see Khalil Gibran Muhammad, *The Condemnation of Blackness: Race, Crime, and the Making of Modern Urban America* (Cambridge, MA: Harvard University Press, 2010).

146　"intrinsically inferior type of humanity" William Hannibal Thomas, *The American Negro: What He Was, What He Is, and What He May Become* (New York: Negro Universities Press, 1901), 129, 134, 195.

146　Thomas's "list of negative qualities of Negroes seemed limitless" John David Smith, *Black Judas: William Hannibal Thomas and the American Negro* (Athens, GA: University of Georgia Press, 2000), 161–64, 177–78, 185–89.

146　But this "saving remnant" was set "apart from their white fellow-men" Thomas, *The American Negro*, xxiii, 69, 410.

147　"national assimilation" Ibid., 397–432.

147　stamped William Hannibal Thomas as the "Black Judas" See Smith, *Black Judas.*

147　Black officers were as abusive James Forman Jr., *Locking Up Our Own: Crime and Punishment in Black America* (New York: Farrar, Straus & Giroux, 2017), 107–8.

148　survey of nearly eight thousand sworn officers "Black and White Officers See Many Key Aspects of Policing Differently," Pew Research Center, January 12, 2017, available at www.pewresearch.org/fact-tank/2017/01/12/black-and-white-officers-see-many-key-aspects-of-policing-differently/.

148　The new crop of Black politicians, judges, police chiefs, and officers Forman Jr., *Locking Up Our Own,* 147.

148　"Black on Black crime has reached a critical level" John H. Johnson, "Publisher's Statement," *Ebony,* August 1979.

149　doubled the number of discrimination cases it dismissed See Manning Marable, *Race, Reform, and Rebellion: The Second Reconstruction and Black America, 1945–2006* (Jackson, MS: University Press of Mississippi, 2007), 196.

149　redirected billions of dollars in federal funds Ibid., 206–7.

## Chapter 12: Class

151 **two of the most dangerous neighborhoods in Philadelphia** And they are still being told this. See "These Are the 10 Worst Philadelphia Neighborhoods for 2019," *Road Snacks,* December 28, 2018, available at www.road snacks.net/worst-philadelphia-neighborhoods/.

151 **millions of Black people migrating from the South** For more on the migration and what happened to them when they arrived, see Isabel Wilkerson, *The Warmth of Other Suns: The Epic Story of America's Great Migration* (New York: Vintage Books, 2011); and Thomas J. Sugrue, *The Origins of the Urban Crisis: Race and Inequality in Postwar Detroit* (Princeton, NJ: Princeton University Press, 1996).

152 **"The dark ghetto is institutionalized pathology"** Kenneth B. Clark, *Dark Ghetto: Dilemmas of Social Power* (2nd edition) (Middletown, CT: Wesleyan University Press, 1989), 81.

152 **"the behavior of the African American underclass"** Dinesh D'Souza, *The End of Racism: Principles for a Multicultural Society* (New York: Free Press, 1996), 527.

153 **poor Whites as "White trash"** See Nancy Isenberg, *White Trash: The 400-Year Untold History of Class in America* (New York: Penguin Books, 2017).

154 **"We have got this tailspin of culture"** "Paul Ryan's Racist Comments Are a Slap in the Face to 10.5 Million Americans," *Mic,* March 13, 2014, available at mic.com/articles/85223/paul-ryan-s-racist-comments-are-a-slap-in-the-face-to-10-5-million-americans.

154 **"The evidence of this failure is all around us"** Kay Cole James, "Why We Must Be Bold on Welfare Reform," The Heritage Foundation, March 12, 2018, available at www.heritage.org/welfare/commentary/why-we-must-be-bold-welfare-reform.

155 **He positioned the Black poor as inferior** Clark, *Dark Ghetto,* xxix, xxxvi.

155 **Obama made a similar case** "Barack Obama's Speech on Race," *The New York Times,* March 18, 2008, available at www.nytimes.com/2008/03/18/us/politics/18text-obama.html.

155 **poor Blacks are more optimistic** See Carol Graham, *Happiness for All? Unequal Hopes and Lives in Pursuit of the American Dream* (Princeton, NJ: Princeton University Press, 2017).

155 **"wage" of Whiteness** W.E.B. Du Bois, *Black Reconstruction in America, 1860–1880* (New York: Simon & Schuster, 1999), 700. And also see David R. Roediger, *The Wages of Whiteness: Race and the Making of the American Working Class* (New York: Verso, 1991).

155 **as the "Talented Tenth"** See W.E.B. Du Bois, "The Talented Tenth," in *The Negro Problem: A Series of Articles by Representative American Negroes of Today* (New York: James Pott & Company, 1903).

156 **As Martin Luther King said in his critique of capitalism in 1967** Martin

Luther King Jr., " 'Where Do We Go from Here?,' Address Delivered at the Eleventh Annual SCLC Convention," April 16, 1967, The Martin Luther King, Jr. Research and Education Institute, Stanford University, available at kinginstitute.stanford.edu/king-papers/documents/where-do-we-go-here -address-delivered-eleventh-annual-sclc-convention.

156 **what world-systems theorists term the "long sixteenth century"** Immanuel Wallerstein, *The Modern World-System: Capitalist Agriculture and the Origins of the European World-Economy in the Sixteenth Century* (New York: Academic Press, 1974).

156 **Prince Henry's Portugal birthed conjoined twins** For histories of the conjoined origins of racism and capitalism, see Ibram X. Kendi, *Stamped from the Beginning: The Definitive History of Racist Ideas in America* (New York: Nation Books, 2016); Eric Williams, *Capitalism & Slavery* (Chapel Hill, NC: University of North Carolina Press, 1994); and Edward E. Baptist, *The Half Has Never Been Told: Slavery and the Making of American Capitalism* (New York: Basic Books, 2014).

157 **The Black poverty rate in 2017 stood at 20 percent** "Poverty Rate by Race/Ethnicity," Kaiser Family Foundation Database, available at www.kff .org/other/state-indicator/poverty-rate-by-raceethnicity/.

157 **The Black unemployment rate has been at least twice as high** "Black Unemployment Rate Is Consistently Twice That of Whites," Pew Research Center, August 21, 2013, available at www.pewresearch.org/fact -tank/2013/08/21/through-good-times-and-bad-black-unemployment-is -consistently-double-that-of-whites/.

157 **The wage gap** "Wage Gap Between Blacks and Whites Worst in Nearly 40 Years," CNN, September 20, 2016, available at money.cnn.com/2016 /09/20/news/economy/black-white-wage-gap/.

157 **median net worth of White families is about ten times that of Black families** "White Families Have Nearly 10 Times the Net Worth of Black Families. And the Gap Is Growing," *The Washington Post,* September 28, 2017, available at www.washingtonpost.com/news/wonk/wp /2017/09/28/black-and-hispanic-families-are-making-more-money-but -they-still-lag-far-behind-whites/.

157 **White households are expected to own eighty-six times more wealth than Black households by 2020** Dedrick Asante-Muhammad, Chuck Collins, Josh Hoxie, and Emanuel Nieves, "The Road to Zero Wealth: How the Racial Wealth Divide Is Hollowing Out America's Middle Class," Institute for Policy Studies, September 2017, available at ips-dc.org/wp -content/uploads/2017/09/The-Road-to-Zero-Wealth_FINAL.pdf.

158 **Africa's unprecedented capitalist growth over the last two decades** "Africa's Capitalist Revolution: Preserving Growth in a Time of Crisis," *Foreign Affairs,* July/August 2009, available at www.foreignaffairs.com/articles /africa/2009-07-01/africas-capitalist-revolution.

158 **nearly nine in ten extremely poor people will live in Sub-Saharan Africa by 2030** "The Number of Extremely Poor People Continues to Rise in Sub-Saharan Africa," The World Bank, September 19, 2018, available at blogs.worldbank.org/opendata/number-extremely-poor-people-continues-rise-sub-saharan-africa.

158 **In Latin America, people of African descent** "Behind the Numbers: Race and Ethnicity in Latin America," *Americas Quarterly,* Summer 2015, available at www.americasquarterly.org/content/behind-numbers-race-and-ethnicity-latin-america.

158 **The global gap between the richest (and Whitest) regions of the world and the poorest (and Blackest) regions of the world has tripled** "Global Inequality May Be Much Worse Than We Think," *The Guardian,* April 8, 2016, available at www.theguardian.com/global-development-professionals-network/2016/apr/08/global-inequality-may-be-much-worse-than-we-think.

158 **Upward mobility is greater for White people** Randall Akee, Maggie R. Jones, and Sonya R. Porter, National Bureau of Economic Research Working Paper No. 23733, August 2017, available at www.nber.org/papers/w23733.

158 **the highest-income quintile** "The Racial Wealth Divide Holds Back Black Earners at All Levels," *AlterNet,* April 3, 2018, available at www.alternet.org/2018/04/racial-wealth-divide-holds-back-black-earners/.

158 **Black middle-income households have less wealth** See "1 in 7 White Families Are Now Millionaires. For Black Families, It's 1 in 50," *The Washington Post,* October 3, 2017.

158 **White poverty is not as distressing as Black poverty** "Black Poverty Differs from White Poverty," *The Washington Post,* August 12, 2015, available at www.washingtonpost.com/news/wonk/wp/2015/08/12/black-poverty-differs-from-white-poverty/?utm_term=.6069bf66fb16.

158 **Antiracist policies in the 1960s and 1970s narrowed these inequities** "Equality Still Elusive 50 Years After Civil Rights Act," *USA Today,* January 19, 2014, available at www.usatoday.com/story/news/nation/2014/01/19/civil-rights-act-progress/4641967/.

158 **as chronicled by historian Devyn Spence Benson** Devyn Spence Benson, *Antiracism in Cuba: The Unfinished Revolution* (Chapel Hill, NC: University of North Carolina Press, 2016), 30–71.

159 **Socialist Party of America (SPA) in 1901 refused to adopt an anti-lynching petition** "Race and the U.S. Socialist Tradition," *Socialist Worker,* November 18, 2010, available at socialistworker.org/2010/11/18/race-and-us-socialist-tradition.

159 **"The discovery of gold and silver in America"** Karl Marx, *Capital: A Critique of Political Economy,* Volume 1, Part 2 (New York: Cosimo Classics, 2007), 823.

160 **pleaded with Du Bois to reconsider** David Levering Lewis, *W.E.B. Du Bois, 1919–1963: The Fight for Equality and the American Century* (New York: Macmillan, 2000), 309–10.

160 **what scholars now call racial capitalism** See Robin D. G. Kelley, "What Did Cedric Robinson Mean by Racial Capitalism," *Boston Review,* January 12, 2017, available at bostonreview.net/race/robin-d-g-kelley-what-did-cedric-robinson-mean-racial-capitalism.

160 **"The lowest and most fatal degree"** and **"working-class aristocracy"** Lewis, *W.E.B. Du Bois, 1919–1963,* 308–9.

160 **"Instead of a horizontal division of classes"** W.E.B. Du Bois, *Dusk of Dawn: An Essay Toward an Autobiography of a Race Concept* (Piscataway, NJ: Transaction Publishers, 1984), 205.

160 **called for a "Guiding One Hundredth"** See W.E.B. Du Bois, "The Talented Tenth: Memorial Address," in ed. David Levering Lewis, *W.E.B. Du Bois: A Reader* (New York: Henry Holt, 1995), 347–53.

160 **"inextricable link between racism and capitalism"** Keeanga-Yamahtta Taylor, "Race, Class and Marxism," *Socialist Worker,* January 4, 2011, available at socialistworker.org/2011/01/04/race-class-and-marxism.

161 **The history of capitalism** For an honest history of capitalism and the United States, see Howard Zinn, *A People's History of the United States, 1492–Present* (New York: HarperCollins, 1982).

161 **"capitalist to the bone"** "Elizabeth Warren's Theory of Capitalism," *The Atlantic,* August 28, 2018, available at www.theatlantic.com/politics/archive/2018/08/elizabeth-warrens-theory-of-capitalism/568573/.

162 **The top 1 percent now own around half** "Richest 1% Own Half the World's Wealth, Study Finds," *The Guardian,* November 14, 2017, available at www.theguardian.com/inequality/2017/nov/14/worlds-richest-wealth-credit-suisse.

164 **"I made this film for the black aesthetic,"** Lerone Bennet Jr., "The Emancipation Orgasm: Sweetback in Wonderland," *Ebony,* September 1971.

164 **Bennett blasted Van Peebles** Ibid.

165 **E. Franklin Frazier's *Black Bourgeoisie*** E. Franklin Frazier, *Black Bourgeoisie: The Rise of a New Middle Class* (New York: Free Press, 1957).

165 **"the Negro middle class contributes very little"** Nathan Glazer and Daniel Patrick Moynihan, *Beyond the Melting Pot,* 51–52.

165 **Martin Luther King Jr. and a generation of elite Black youngsters** Lewis, *W.E.B. Du Bois, 1919–1963,* 558.

## Chapter 13: Space

166 **seminal work *Afrocentricity*** Molefi Kete Asante, *Afrocentricity: The Theory of Social Change* (Buffalo, NY: Amulefi, 1980).

167 **"The rejection of European particularism"** See Molefi Kete Asante, *Afrocentricity* (Trenton, NJ: African World Press, 1988), 104.

167 **she enjoyed bolting the States to speak on her research** Ama Mazama and Garvey Musumunu, *African Americans and Homeschooling: Motivations, Opportunities, and Challenges* (New York: Routledge, 2015); Molefi Kete Asante and Ama Mazama, eds., *Encyclopedia of African Religion* (Thousand Oaks, CA: SAGE, 2009); and Ama Mazama, ed., *The Afrocentric Paradigm* (Trenton, NJ: Africa World Press, 2003).

168 **"creeping blight"** Kenneth B. Clark, *Dark Ghetto: Dilemmas of Social Power* (2nd edition) (Middletown, CT: Wesleyan University Press, 1989), 25, 87, 109.

169 **"banksters," as Thom Hartmann calls them** Thom Hartmann, "How to Take on the Banksters," *The Hartmann Report,* September 21, 2016, available at www.thomhartmann.com/blog/2016/09/how-take-banksters.

169 **Americans lost trillions during the Great Recession** "America Lost $10.2 Trillion in 2008," *Business Insider,* February 3, 2009, available at www.businessinsider.com/2009/2/america-lost-102-trillion-of-wealth-in-2008.

169 **Estimated losses from white-collar crimes** "White-Collar Crimes— Motivations and Triggers," *Forbes,* February 22, 2018, available at www.forbes.com/sites/roomykhan/2018/02/22/white-collar-crimes-motivations-and-triggers/#258d26351219.

169 **the combined costs of burglary and robbery** Patrick Colm Hogan, *The Culture of Conformism: Understanding Social Consent* (Durham, NC: Duke University Press, 2001), 15.

169 **3,380 more Americans died from alcohol-related traffic deaths** Ibram X. Kendi, *Stamped from the Beginning: The Definitive History of Racist Ideas in America* (New York: Nation Books, 2016), 437.

170 **"are living in hell"** "Trump at Debate: Minorities in Cities 'Are Living in Hell,'" *Politico,* September 26, 2016, available at www.politico.com/story/2016/09/trump-minorities-living-in-hell-228726.

170 **"from shithole countries"** "Trump Derides Protections for Immigrants from 'Shithole' Countries," *The Washington Post,* January 12, 2018.

171 **HBCUs do not represent "the real world"** "Hold Up: Aisha Tyler Thinks HBCUs Are Bad for Black Students?," BET, April 28, 2016, available at www.bet.com/celebrities/news/2016/04/28/aisha-tyler-slams-hbcus.html.

171 **"Even the best black colleges and universities do not"** Thomas Sowell, "The Plight of Black Students in America," *Daedalus* 103 (Spring 1974), 189.

171 **Sowell's "description remains accurate"** Jason L. Riley, "Black Colleges Need a New Mission," *The Wall Street Journal,* September 28, 2010, available at www.wsj.com/articles/SB10001424052748704654004575517822124077834.

172 **The endowment of the richest HBCU, Howard** See "HBCUs Struggle to Close the Endowment Gap," *Philanthropy News Digest,* July 19, 2017,

available at philanthropynewsdigest.org/news/hbcus-struggle-to-close-the
-endowment-gap.

172 **produces a giving gap** Ibid.

172 **like the current "performance based" state models** "Black Colleges Are
the Biggest Victims of States' Invasive New Funding Rules," *The Washington Post,* December 16, 2014, available at www.washingtonpost.com/post
everything/wp/2014/12/16/black-colleges-are-the-biggest-victims-of-states
-invasive-new-funding-rules/.

172 **HBCUs tend to have higher Black graduation rates** "How Are Black
Colleges Doing? Better Than You Think, Study Finds," *The Chronicle of
Higher Education,* April 13, 2018, available at www.chronicle.com/article
/How-Are-Black-Colleges-Doing-/243119.

172 **HBCU graduates are, on average, more likely** "Grades of Historically
Black Colleges Have Well-Being Edge," Gallup, October 27, 2015, available
at news.gallup.com/poll/186362/grads-historically-black-colleges-edge.aspx.

173 **Banks remain twice as likely to offer loans to White entrepreneurs**
"Study Documents Discrimination Against Black Entrepreneurs," NCRC,
November 17, 2017, available at ncrc.org/study-documents-discrimination
-black-entrepreneurs/; Sterling A. Bone et al., "Shaping Small Business
Lending Policy Through Matched-Paired Mystery Shopping," September 12, 2017, available at SSRN at papers.ssrn.com/sol3/papers.cfm?abstract
_id=3035972.

173 **Customers avoid Black businesses** For example, see "Jennifer L. Doleac
and Luke C. D. Stein, "The Visible Hand: Race and Online Market Outcomes," May 1, 2010, available at SSRN at papers.ssrn.com/sol3/papers
.cfm?abstract_id=1615149.

173 **"does that inequitable treatment excuse bad service?"** "Should Black
Owned Businesses Get a Hall Pass for Bad Service?", *Blavity,* 2017, available
at blavity.com/black-owned-businesses-get-pass-for-bad-service.

173 **"carry back to the country of their origin the seeds of civilization"**
Thomas Jefferson, "To Lynch, Monticello, January 21, 1811," in *The Writings of Thomas Jefferson,* Volume 9, 1807–1815, ed. Paul Leicester Ford (New
York: G. P. Putnam's Sons, 1898), 303.

173 **"savage wilds of Africa"** Claude Andrew Clegg III, *The Price of Liberty:
African Americans and the Making of Liberia* (Chapel Hill, NC: University of
North Carolina Press, 2009), 35.

173 **A writer for the South's** *De Bow's Review* **searched** "Free Negro Rule,"
*DeBow's Review* 3:4 (April 1860), 440.

174 **Sherman and U.S. secretary of war Edwin M. Stanton met** See *The War
of the Rebellion: A Compilation of the Official Records of the Union and Confederate Armies* (Washington, DC: U.S. Government Printing Office, 1895),
37–41.

174 **"will be left to the freed people themselves"** "Sherman's Special Field Orders, No. 15," in *The Empire State of the South: Georgia History in Documents and Essays*, ed. Christopher C. Meyers (Macon, GA: Mercer University Press, 2008), 174.

174 **Sherman's order deprived the Negroes** Horace Greeley, "Gen. Sherman and the Negroes," *New York Daily Tribune*, January 30, 1865.

175 **"on the platform of equal accommodations"** Henry W. Grady, "In Plain Black and White: A Reply to Mr. Cable," *Century Magazine* 29 (1885), 911.

175 **diverted resources toward exclusively White spaces** "Jim Crow's Schools," *American Educator*, Summer 2004, available at www.aft.org/periodical/american-educator/summer-2004/jim-crows-schools.

175 **"assumption that the enforced separation of the two races"** "Plessy v. Ferguson 163 U.S. 537 (1896)," in Abraham L. Davis and Barbara Luck Graham, *The Supreme Court, Race, and Civil Rights* (Thousand Oaks, CA: SAGE, 1995), 51.

176 **the majority of Black children preferred White dolls** For essays on their doll experiments, see Kenneth B. Clark and Mamie P. Clark, "The Development of Consciousness of Self and the Emergence of Racial Identification in Negro Preschool Children," *Journal of Social Psychology* 10:4 (1939), 591–99; and Kenneth B. Clark and Mamie P. Clark, "Racial Identification and Preference among Negro Children," in *Readings in Social Psychology*, ed. E. L. Hartley (New York: Holt, Rinehart & Winston, 1947); Kenneth B. Clark, *Prejudice and Your Child* (Middletown, CT: Wesleyan University Press, 1988).

176 **"To separate [colored children] from others"** "Brown v. Board of Education," LII Collection: U.S. Supreme Court Decisions, Cornell University Law School, available at www.law.cornell.edu/supremecourt/text/347/483.

176 *San Antonio Independent School District v. Rodriguez* See Paul A. Sracic, *San Antonio v. Rodriguez and the Pursuit of Equal Education: The Debate Over Discrimination and School Funding* (Lawrence, KS: University Press of Kansas, 2006).

177 **"there are adequate Negro schools and prepared instructors"** Zora Neale Hurston, "Court Order Can't Make Races Mix," *Orlando Sentinel*, August 11, 1955.

177 **"I think integration in our public schools is different"** "Deacon Robert Williams," in *Reflections on Our Pastor: Dr. Martin Luther King, Jr. at Dexter Avenue Baptist Church, 1954–1960*, eds. Wally G. Vaughn and Richard W. Wills (Dover, MA: The Majority Press, 1999), 129.

177 **an 80 percent White teaching force** "The Nation's Teaching Force Is Still Mostly White and Female," *Education Week*, August 15, 2017, available at www.edweek.org/ew/articles/2017/08/15/the-nations-teaching-force-is-still-mostly.html.

177 **40 percent less likely to believe the student will finish high school** Seth

Gershenson, Stephen B. Holt, and Nicholas W. Papageorge, "Who Believes in Me? The Effect of Student-Teacher Demographic Match on Teacher Expectations," *Economics of Education Review* 52 (June 2016), 209–24.

177 **Low-income Black students who have at least one Black teacher** "IZA DP No. 10630: The Long-Run Impacts of Same-Race Teachers," Institute of Labor Economics, March 2017, available at www.iza.org/publications /dp/10630.

178 **Integration had turned into "a one-way street"** Barack Obama, *Dreams from My Father: A Story of Race and Inheritance* (New York: Crown, 2007), 99–100.

178 **"The experience of an integrated education"** David L. Kirp, "Making Schools Work," *The New York Times*, May 19, 2012, available at www .nytimes.com/2012/05/20/opinion/sunday/integration-worked-why-have -we-rejected-it.html.

178 **The percentage of Southern Black students attending integrated White schools** "The Data Proves That School Segregation Is Getting Worse," *Vox*, March 5, 2018, available at www.vox.com/2018/3/5/17080218/school -segregation-getting-worse-data.

179 **"I had always thought the ultimate goal of better race relations was integration"** Tamar Jacoby, "What Became of Integration," *The Washington Post*, June 28, 1998.

179 **"using Negro workmen, Negro architects, Negro attorneys, and Negro financial institutions"** Martin Luther King, "'Where Do We Go from Here?,' Address Delivered at the Eleventh Annual SCLC Convention," April 16, 1967, The Martin Luther King, Jr. Research and Education Institute, Stanford University, available at kinginstitute.stanford.edu/king-papers /documents/where-do-we-go-here-address-delivered-eleventh-annual-sclc -convention.

180 **"only white men" with different "skins"** Kenneth M. Stampp, *The Peculiar Institution: Slavery in the Ante-bellum South* (New York: Alfred A. Knopf, 1967), vii.

## Chapter 14: Gender

183 **Alice Walker's *The Color Purple*** Alice Walker, *The Color Purple* (Boston: Harcourt, 1982).

183 **"The Negro Family: The Case for National Action"** Daniel P. Moynihan, *The Negro Family: The Case for National Action* (Washington, D.C.: U.S. Government Printing Office, 1965).

183 **"The reverberations" from the Moynihan report "were disastrous"** Deborah Gray White, *Too Heavy a Load: Black Women in Defense of Themselves, 1894–1994* (New York: W. W. Norton, 1999), 200.

184 **"immediate goal of the Negro woman today"** "For a Better Future," *Ebony*, August 1996.

184  **Racism had "clearly" and "largely focused" on the Black male** Charles Herbert Stember, *Sexual Racism: The Emotional Barrier to an Integrated Society* (New York: Elsevier, 1976), ix, 66.

184  **For too many Black men, the Black Power movement** See Eldridge Cleaver, *Soul on Ice* (New York: Dell, 1991).

185  **"has now reached 68 percent"** Charles Murray, "The Coming White Underclass," *The Wall Street Journal*, October 29, 1993.

185  **married Black women having fewer children** Angela Y. Davis, *Women, Culture & Politics* (New York: Vintage Books, 1990), 75–85; and "The Math on Black Out of Wedlock Births," *The Atlantic*, February 17, 2009, available at www.theatlantic.com/entertainment/archive/2009/02/the-math-on-black -out-of-wedlock-births/6738/.

185  **Only Black feminists like Dorothy Roberts** Dorothy Roberts, *Killing the Black Body: Race, Reproduction, and the Meaning of Liberty* (New York: Pantheon, 1997).

186  **Kimberly Springer calls the "Black feminist movement"** Kimberly Springer, *Living for the Revolution: Black Feminist Organizations, 1968–1980* (Durham, NC: Duke University Press, 2005).

187  **the Combahee River Collective (CRC)** See Keeanga-Yamahtta Taylor, ed., *How We Get Free: Black Feminism and the Combahee River Collective* (Chicago: Haymarket, 2017).

187  **"double jeopardy" of racism and sexism** Frances Beal, "Double Jeopardy: To Be Black and Female," in *The Black Woman: An Anthology*, ed. Toni Cade Bambara (New York: New American Library, 1970), 92.

188  **"preoccupations of the contemporary Black woman in this country"** and **"evil Black bitch"** Toni Morrison, "Preface," in *The Black Woman*, 11.

188  **"high-tech lynching"** See "How Racism and Sexism Shaped the Clarence Thomas/Anita Hill Hearing," *Vox*, April 16, 2016, available at www.vox .com/2016/4/16/11408576/anita-hill-clarence-thomas-confirmation.

188  **"In discussing the experiences of Black women"** Philomena Essed, *Understanding Everyday Racism: An Interdisciplinary Theory* (Newbury Park, CA: SAGE, 1991), 31.

188  **"Mapping the Margins"** Kimberlé Crenshaw, "Mapping the Margins: Intersectionality, Identity Politics, and Violence Against Women of Color," *Stanford Law Review* 43:6 (July 1991), 1242.

189  **involuntary sterilizations of Black women** Roberts, *Killing the Black Body*, 90–96.

189  **Black women with some collegiate education making less** See "Usual Weekly Earnings of Wage and Salary Workers, Fourth Quarter 2018," Bureau of Labor Statistics, U.S. Department of Labor, January 17, 2019, available at www.bls.gov/news.release/pdf/wkyeng.pdf.

189  **Black women having to earn advanced degrees before they earn more**

See "Usual Weekly Earnings of Wage and Salary Workers, Fourth Quarter 2018."

189 **median wealth of single White women being $42,000** "Lifting as We Climb: Women of Color, Wealth, and America's Future," Insight Center for Community Economic Development, Spring 2010, available at insightcced .org/old-site/uploads/CRWG/LiftingAsWeClimb-WomenWealth-Report -InsightCenter-Spring2010.pdf.

189 **Native women and Black women experience poverty at a higher rate** See "Black Women: Supporting Their Families—With Few Resources," *The Atlantic,* June 12, 2017, available at www.theatlantic.com/business/archive /2017/06/black-women-economy/530022/.

189 **Black and Latinx women still earn the least** "The Gender Wage Gap: 2017 Earnings Differences by Race and Ethnicity," Institute for Women's Policy Research, March 7, 2018, available at iwpr.org/publications/gender-wage -gap-2017-race-ethnicity/.

189 **Black women are three to four times more likely to die** "Why America's Black Mothers and Babies Are in a Life-or-Death Crisis," *The New York Times,* April 11, 2018, available at www.nytimes.com/2018/04/11/maga zine/black-mothers-babies-death-maternal-mortality.html.

189 **Black woman with an advanced degree is more likely to lose her baby** "6 Charts Showing Race Gaps Within the American Middle Class," Brookings, October 21, 2016, available at www.brookings.edu/blog/social -mobility-memos/2016/10/21/6-charts-showing-race-gaps-within-the -american-middle-class/.

189 **Black women remain twice as likely to be incarcerated** "A Mass Incarceration Mystery," The Marshall Project, December 15, 2017, available at www.themarshallproject.org/2017/12/15/a-mass-incarceration-mystery.

190 **as much about controlling the sexuality of White women** For a full study on the politics of women during the lynching era, see Crystal Nicole Feimster, *Southern Horrors: Women and the Politics of Rape and Lynching* (Cambridge, MA: Harvard University Press, 2009).

190 **were re-creating the slave era all over again** Rachel A. Feinstein, *When Rape Was Legal: The Untold History of Sexual Violence During Slavery* (New York: Routledge, 2018); and Daina Ramey Berry and Leslie M. Harris, eds., *Sexuality and Slavery: Reclaiming Intimate Histories in the Americas* (Athens, GA: University of Georgia Press, 2018).

191 **Casey Anthony, the White woman a Florida jury exonerated** "'What Really Happened?': The Casey Anthony Case 10 Years Later," CNN, June 30, 2018, available at www.cnn.com/2018/06/29/us/casey-anthony -10-years-later/index.html.

191 **the imprisonment of Black men dropped 24 percent** The Black male incarceration rate per 100,000 is 2,613, the White male rate is 457, the

Black female rate is 103, and the White female rate is 52, according to the Bureau of Justice Statistics, as shown in "A Mass Incarceration Mystery," The Marshall Project, December 15, 2017, available at www.themarshallproject .org/2017/12/15/a-mass-incarceration-mystery.

191 **Black men raised in the top 1 percent by millionaires** "Extensive Data Shows Punishing Reach of Racism for Black Boys," *The New York Times,* March 19, 2018, available at www.nytimes.com/interactive/2018/03/19 /upshot/race-class-white-and-black-men.html.

191 **"Contemporary feminist and antiracist discourses have failed to consider intersectional identities"** Crenshaw, "Mapping the Margins," 1242–43.

## Chapter 15: Sexuality

193 **32 percent of children being raised by Black male same-sex couples live in poverty** "LGBT Families of Color: Facts at a Glance," Movement Advancement Project, Family Equality Council, and Center for American Progress, January 2012, available at www.nbjc.org/sites/default/files/lgbt -families-of-color-facts-at-a-glance.pdf.

193 **their parents are more likely than Black heterosexual and White queer couples to be poor** See "Beyond Stereotypes: Poverty in the LGBT Community," *TIDES,* June 2012, available at williamsinstitute.law .ucla.edu/williams-in-the-news/beyond-stereotypes-poverty-in-the-lgbt -community/.

194 **"the question of sex"** Havelock Ellis, *Studies in the Psychology of Sex,* Volume 1 (London: Wilson and Macmillan, 1897), x.

194 **a popular summary of Lombroso's writings** Havelock Ellis, *The Criminal* (London: Walter Scott, 1890).

194 **"As regards the sexual organs it seems possible"** Havelock Ellis, *Studies in the Psychology of Sex,* Volume 2 (Philadelphia: F. A. Davis, 1933), 256.

194 **racist physicians were contrasting** Morris, "Is Evolution Trying to Do Away with the Clitoris?," Paper presented at the meeting of the American Association of Obstetricians and Gynecologists, St. Louis, September 21, 1892, available at archive.org/stream/39002086458651.med.yale.edu/39002 086458651_djvu.txt.

194 **"will in practically every instance disclose"** Perry M. Lichtenstein, "The 'Fairy' and the Lady Lover," *Medical Review of Reviews* 27 (1921), 372.

194 **which "is particularly so in colored women"** Ibid.

195 **Black gay men are less likely to have condomless sex and use drugs** "What's at the Roots of the Disproportionate HIV Rates for Black Men?," *Plus,* March 6, 2017, available at www.hivplusmag.com/stigma/2017/3/06 /whats-root-disproportionate-hiv-rates-their-queer-brothers.

197 **"affirm that all Black lives matter"** "Black Lives Matter Movement Awarded Sydney Peace Prize for Activism," NBC News, November 2,

2017, available at www.nbcnews.com/news/nbcblk/black-lives-matter
-movement-awarded-sydney-peace-prize-activism-n816846.

197 **U.S. life expectancy of a transgender woman of color** "It's Time for Trans
Lives to Truly Matter to Us All," *Advocate*, February 18, 2015, available at
www.advocate.com/commentary/2015/02/18/op-ed-its-time-trans-lives
-truly-matter-us-all.

197 **from the personal stories of transgender activist Janet Mock** See Janet
Mock, *Redefining Realness: My Path to Womanhood, Identity, Love & So Much
More* (New York: Simon & Schuster, 2015); Janet Mock, *Surpassing Cer-
tainty: What My Twenties Taught Me* (New York: Atria, 2017).

199 **watching Kayla Moore defend her husband** "Kayla Moore Emerges as
Her Husband's Fiercest and Most Vocal Defender," *The Washington Post*,
November 15, 2017, available at www.washingtonpost.com/politics/kayla
-moore-emerges-as-her-husbands-fiercest-and-most-vocal-defender/2017
/11/15/5c8b7d82-ca19-11e7-8321-481fd63f174d_story.html.

200 **"even though we had slavery"** "In Alabama, the Heart of Trump Country, Many Think He's Backing the Wrong Candidate in Senate Race," *Los
Angeles Times*, September 21, 2017, available at www.latimes.com/politics
/la-na-pol-alabama-senate-runoff-20170921-story.html.

## Chapter 16: Failure

202 **"our parental care"** and **Black "conduct must, in some measure"** See
David Scholfield and Edmund Haviland, "The Appeal of the American
Convention of Abolition Societies to Anti-Slavery Groups," *The Journal of
Negro History* 6:2 (April 1921), 221, 225.

202 **"The further decrease of prejudice"** "Raising Us in the Scale of Being,"
*Freedom's Journal*, March 16, 1827.

203 **the judges of "uplift suasion"** See Ibram X. Kendi, *Stamped from the Beginning: The Definitive History of Racist Ideas in America* (New York: Nation
Books, 2016), 124–25.

205 **"Have you not acquired the esteem"** William Lloyd Garrison, *An Address, Delivered before the Free People of Color, in Philadelphia* (Boston: S. Foster,
1831), 5–6.

205 **"accomplish the great work of national redemption"** " 'What we have
long predicted . . . has commenced its fulfillment,'" in *The Boisterous Sea of
Liberty: A Documentary History of American from Discovery Through the Civil
War*, eds. David Brion Davis and Steven Mintz (New York: Oxford University Press, 1998), 390.

205 **fit his personal upbringing** For a good biography of Garrison, see Henry
Mayer, *All on Fire: William Lloyd Garrison and the Abolition of Slavery* (New
York: W. W. Norton, 2008).

205 **astounding growth of slavery** Edward E. Baptist, *The Half Has Never Been*

*Told: Slavery and the Making of American Capitalism* (New York: Basic Books, 2016).

206 **"If I could save the Union without freeing any slave"** Abraham Lincoln, "To Horace Greeley," in *The Collected Works of Abraham Lincoln,* Volume 5, ed. Roy P. Basler (New Brunswick, NJ: Rutgers University Press, 1953), 388.

206 **"necessary war measure"** Abraham Lincoln's Emancipation Proclamation, January 1, 1863, American Battlefield Trust, available at www.battlefields.org /learn/primary-sources/abraham-lincolns-emancipation-proclamation.

206 **"want nothing to do with the negroes"** See Leonard P. Curry, *Blueprint for Modern America: Nonmilitary Legislation of the First Civil War Congress* (Nashville: Vanderbilt University Press, 1968), 79.

206 **The "White man's party"** See Francis P. Blair Jr., *The Destiny of the Races of this Continent* (Washington, DC, 1859), 30.

206 **militarily defending the Negro from the racist terrorists** For an excellent study of the decline of Reconstruction, see Eric Foner, *Reconstruction: America's Unfinished Revolution, 1863–1877* (New York: HarperCollins, 2011).

206 **"Expediency on selfish grounds"** Mayer, *All on Fire,* 617.

206 **"For many years it was the theory of most Negro leaders"** W.E.B. Du Bois, "A Negro Nation Within a Nation," in *W.E.B. Du Bois: A Reader,* ed. David Levering Lewis (New York: Henry Holt, 1995), 565.

207 **"astonishing ignorance"** Gunnar Myrdal, *An American Dilemma: The Negro Problem and Modern Democracy* (New York: Harper, 1944), 48.

207 **"There is no doubt, in the writer's opinion"** Ibid., 339.

207 **"Gunnar Myrdal had been astonishingly prophetic"** Gene Roberts and Hank Klibanoff, *The Race Beat: The Press, the Civil Rights Struggle, and the Awakening of the Nation* (New York: Vintage Books, 2007), 406. Aside from this assessment, this is a stunning work of journalism history.

207 **"discrimination against minority groups in this country has an adverse effect"** Mary L. Dudziak, *Cold War Civil Rights: Race and the Image of American Democracy* (Princeton, NJ: Princeton University Press, 2011), 100.

207 **"in waging this world struggle"** and **Seventy-eight percent of White Americans agreed** Ibid., 185–87.

208 **In 1967, Martin Luther King Jr. admitted** Martin Luther King, " 'Where Do We Go from Here?,' Address Delivered at the Eleventh Annual SCLC Convention," April 16, 1967, The Martin Luther King, Jr. Research and Education Institute, Stanford University, available at kinginstitute.stanford .edu/king-papers/documents/where-do-we-go-here-address-delivered -eleventh-annual-sclc-convention.

208 **Look at the soaring White support** Lawrence D. Bobo et al., "The *Real* Record on Racial Attitudes," in *Social Trends in American Life: Findings from the General Social Survey Since 1971,* ed. Peter V. Marsden (Princeton, NJ: Princeton University Press, 2012), 38–83.

208 **Look at the soaring support for Obamacare** "Support for 2010 Health Care Law Reaches New High," Pew Research Center, February 23, 2017, available at www.pewresearch.org/fact-tank/2017/02/23/support-for-2010 -health-care-law-reaches-new-high/.

209 **wanted to free the Jena 6** For a good interview that details the case, see "The Case of the Jena Six: Black High School Students Charged with Attempted Murder for Schoolyard Fight After Nooses Are Hung from Tree," *Democracy Now,* July 10, 2007, available at www.democracynow.org /2007/7/10/the_case_of_the_jena_six.

211 **used the Malcolm X line out of context** The full quote is, "When I was in prison, I read an article—don't be shocked when I say I was in prison. You're still in prison. That's what America means: prison." See Malcolm X, "Message to the Grassroots," December 10, 1963, available at blackpast .org/1963-malcolm-x-message-grassroots.

212 **"The action of President Roosevelt in entertaining that nigger"** Stephen Kantrowitz, *Ben Tillman & the Reconstruction of White Supremacy* (Chapel Hill, NC: University of North Carolina Press, 2000), 259.

212 **the Hamburg Massacre** Ibid., 64–71.

213 **"The purpose of our visit to Hamburg was to strike terror"** Benjamin R. Tillman, *The Struggles of 1876: How South Carolina Was Delivered from Carpet-bag and Negro Rule* (Anderson, SC, 1909), 24. Speech at the Red-Shirt Re-Union at Anderson, available at babel.hathitrust.org/cgi/pt ?id=mdp.39015079003128.

215 **That day, thousands of us thought we were protesting** See "Thousands Protest Arrests of 6 Blacks in Jena, La.," *The New York Times,* September 21, 2007, available at /www.nytimes.com/2007/09/21/us/21cnd-jena.html.

215 **quietly got the charges reduced to simple battery** "Plea Bargain Wraps Up 'Jena 6' Case," CBS News, June 26, 2009, available at www.cbsnews .com/news/plea-bargain-wraps-up-jena-6-case/.

216 **sustained those courageous Black women** For a fascinating firsthand account of the boycott, see Jo Ann Gibson Robinson, *The Montgomery Bus Boycott and the Women Who Started It: The Memoir of Jo Ann Gibson Robinson* (Knoxville, TN: University of Tennessee Press, 1987).

**Chapter 17: Success**

219 **Hillary Clinton and Bernie Sanders spoke of "institutional racism"** "Hillary: 'America's Long Struggle with Race Is Far from Finished,'" *The Hill,* September 23, 2015, available at thehill.com/blogs/ballot-box/ presidential-races/245881-hillary-americas-long-struggle-with-race-is-far -from; and "The Transcript of Bernie Sanders's Victory Speech," *The Washington Post,* February 10, 2016, available at www.washingtonpost.com/news /post-politics/wp/2016/02/10/the-transcript-of-bernie-sanderss-victory -speech/.

220 **"Racism is both overt and covert"** Kwame Toure and Charles V. Hamilton, *Black Power: The Politics of Liberation* (New York: Alfred A. Knopf, 2011), 4–5.

222 **" 'Respectable' individuals can absolve themselves"** Ibid., 5.

223 **The rain fell on his gray hooded sweatshirt** For perhaps the best overview of the Travyon Martin story, see *Rest in Power: The Trayvon Martin Story,* Paramount Network, available at www.paramountnetwork.com/shows/rest-in-power-the-trayvon-martin-story.

224 **on the Black Campus Movement** Ibram X. Kendi, *The Black Campus Movement: Black Studies and the Racial Reconstitution of Higher Education, 1965–1972* (New York: Palgrave, 2012).

225 **Zimmerman told the 911 dispatcher** "Transcript of George Zimmerman's Call to the Police," available at archive.org/stream/326700-full-transcript-zimmerman/326700-full-transcript-zimmerman_djvu.txt.

## Chapter 18: Survival

231 **produces public scholarship** For more on this concept of public scholarship, see Keisha N. Blain and Ibram X. Kendi, "How to Avoid a Post-Scholar America," *The Chronicle of Higher Education,* June 18, 2017.

232 **copies of Confederate flags with cotton balls inside several buildings** "Confederate Flags with Cotton Found on American University Campus," *The New York Times,* September 27, 2017, available at www.nytimes.com/2017/09/27/us/american-university-confederate.html.

234 **About 88 percent of people diagnosed with stage-4 colon cancer die within five years** "Survival Rates for Colorectal Cancer, by Stage," American Cancer Society, available at www.cancer.org/cancer/colon-rectal-cancer/detection-diagnosis-staging/survival-rates.html.

235 **that the heartbeat of racism is denial, the heartbeat of antiracism is confession** "The Heartbeat of Racism Is Denial," *The New York Times,* January 14, 2018.

237 **trillions of tax dollars we spend** "War on Terror Facts, Cost, and Timelines," *The Balance,* December 11, 2018, available at www.thebalance.com/war-on-terror-facts-costs-timeline-3306300.

# INDEX

# A grand new day

A YEAR *of* DAILY INSPIRATION

*and* ENCOURAGEMENT

THOMAS NELSON
*Since 1798*

NASHVILLE   DALLAS   MEXICO CITY   RIO DE JANEIRO   BEIJING

Published in Nashville, Tennessee, by Thomas Nelson. Thomas Nelson is a registered trademark of Thomas Nelson, Inc.

Manuscript compiled and prepared by Snapdragon Group℠ Tulsa, Oklahoma, USA.
Managing Editor: Darcie Clemen
Interior Design: Lori Lynch

Some material reprinted from previously published volumes may have been edited slightly from the original.

Thomas Nelson, Inc., titles may be purchased in bulk for educational, business, fund-raising, or sales promotional use. For information, please e-mail SpecialMarkets@ThomasNelson.com.

Excerpts from *If It's Not One Thing, It's Your Mother* and *If Your Can't Lose It, Decorate It!* by Anita Renfroe are used by permission of NavPress. © 2006 and 2007. All rights reserved. www.navpress.com

ISBN 978-1-4002-0230-0

*Printed in the United States of America*
09 10 11 12 QW 7

# FOREWORD

Have you ever noticed how frequently we think about winning? It's more than a thought; it's a feeling, and sometimes a deeply felt one. We cheer for our teams, our heroes, the candidates of our political choosing. Game shows bring out the competition in us. We like it when life goes "our" way. When my nieces and nephews were little, I spent a lot of time playing games with them. I cannot count the number of times (when it seemed like I might win and my little loved one might lose) that I'd hear those solemn words, "Mimi, can we start over?" Nobody likes to lose. When it happens . . . when mistakes are made or the news is bad, or our hearts are sad . . . we wonder if we could just start over. We want a new day.

Amazingly, that's the opportunity God gives us at every turn. He makes all things "new." "New" gives us fresh options; ones that offer possibility. A few years ago one of my sisters was seated in a rocking chair, and her two-year-old grandson raced across the room, dove through the air, and landed with his full body weight on her chest (he missed her lap only slightly but significantly nonetheless). Startled, she looked at him and said, "Oh, honey! You have to be careful. Grandma's old." Little Jackson turned to me sitting in the chair next to his Grandmother and said to her, "How about Mimi . . . is she new?"

New is fresh, novel, original, and grand, which is what God gives us every morning . . . a grand new day. The writer of Lamentations stated, "His mercies are new every morning." New opens up other potentialities—for starting over and perhaps even winning.

My friends, whose faithful lives you can follow day by day in this devotional collection, reveal with characteristic humor and candor the multiple ways they see God give them newness, fresh perspective, and joy for the journey of life. He gives it in abundance out of the generosity of his own heart, and as you'll see and learn from these friends, he has an unending supply of faithfulness. We get new choices every day with a fresh start. We receive, by his grace, a grand new day every twenty-four hours. Three hundred and sixty-five days every year of our lives. It creates possibility that whether we're young or old, rich or poor, married or single, happy or sad—every day is new. And so are we.

This morning I finished reading the manuscript for the book you now hold in your hands. I'm encouraged, enriched, and have gained new insight about life, love, and a relationship with God as I've peeked into the hearts, minds, and thoughts of women who've walked with God and found him faithful in both the soft and very hard places in life.

I'm grateful God gives us a fresh new day every twenty-four hours. And I'm grateful he gives us friends who remind us of that . . . every day.

—MARY GRAHAM, *Women of Faith President*

# A FORMULA FOR LAUGHTER

*When my anxious thoughts multiply within me,*
*your consolations delight my soul.*

—Psalm 94:19 NASB

I don't usually respond to formulas for this and that; they feel a bit too tidy. But I have developed one for cheerful thinking I'd like to toss your way for your consideration. To begin with, I love to laugh. I believe a giggle is always loitering about even in the most devastating of circumstances. I make a point of shuffling through the rubble in search of that giggle.

This isn't denial. I need to feel and express my pain. But I also need to find the light side—and there is *always* a light side! I've noticed that when I laugh about some minor part of a problem or controversy or worry the whole situation suddenly seems much less negative to me. After a good laugh, I can then rethink my circumstances. As a result, that which was threatening may now seem less threatening.

Paradoxically, after I've found the giggle, I am more ready to get serious (it's a more balanced seriousness) and consider the degree and the extent of my negative thinking. This is when negative thoughts have to be deleted and replaced with those that are realistically positive.

A transformed and renewed mind enables us to manifest an attitude of good cheer. Believe it, think it, and go for it! Don't let life get in your way.

—MARILYN MEBERG (*I'd Rather Be Laughing*)

# THE COUNSEL WITHIN

*Knowing what is right is like deep water in the heart;*
*a wise person draws from the well within.*

—Proverbs 20:5 MSG

God has put the counsel we need to hear and know within our own hearts. When he made us, he enabled us to store that wise counsel in a very deep, private place he created. It's like a deep river, running through our hearts in a place that's completely quiet and unique to each individual. When we get in touch with that, we find his counsel with a still heart and a waiting, open soul . . . without passion, desire, judgment, or opinions. It's pure and clean and from God. But how do we get in touch with that?

I believe that's where the listening heart comes into play. When a person listens, God-given counsel is drawn out of the heart of the one speaking. A person with a listening heart may ask a few pertinent questions, but for the most part he just waits and listens. He doesn't argue; he listens. He doesn't judge; he listens. He doesn't run ahead; he simply listens.

Therefore, if you want to be wise, listen with your heart—to others, to sounds, to words, to life itself. And in so doing, your heart will grow bigger, enabling you to be of more help to others in their needs.

—LUCI SWINDOLL (*Life! Celebrate It*)

# OUR BIG GOD

*I will meditate about your glory, splendor, majesty, and miracles.*
—Psalm 145:5 TLB

Some of us are slowly unfolding miracles, yet miracles nonethe-less. In God's timing and for his purposes, he has accomplished his work in me. And I'm grateful he continues the work. He knew I'd falter and question.

Someone once said, "Courage is fear that has said its prayer." That resonates within me. I do many things today not because I feel brave, but because I have prayed and God has answered and met me with his strength in my utter weakness.

I don't know what sends shudders down your spine, what threatens your security, what gnaws at your work, but my prayer is that my encouragement will bring you hope, even if it's just the size of a breadcrumb—enough for you to take the next liberating step. I've learned that life is exceedingly difficult and that God is amazingly big. He will reign over our greatest losses, rectify our worst failures, and remedy our deepest insecurities.

I don't understand all the ways of the Lord, but then I'm not supposed to. Faith carries us through life's unknowns and God's mysteries. But one day, one absolutely glorious day, I will "get it," and more importantly I'll see Jesus face to face. That irrepressible hope keeps me breathing deeply, walking faithfully, and singing triumphantly.

—PATSY CLAIRMONT (*I Grew Up Little*)

# FALLING FORWARD

*The LORD upholds all who are falling.*

—Psalm 145:14 NRSV

When I was a little girl, my father was just about the best daddy any daughter could have. (Still is.) He gave me a great picture of the heart of God by always coming the moment I called (or at least that's how I remember it). Therefore, I had a deep trust that my daddy always had my best interest at heart. One day, however, he tested this trust. I was up on a low roof and my dad was on the ground when he asked me to jump into his arms. I stood with my toes at the edge of the roof and could feel myself swaying. I was terrified. Then Daddy said, "Sandi, you're gonna fall either way. If you fall backwards, I can't help you. But if you fall forward, I'm going to be able to catch you."

That is exactly the picture I want you to hold in your mind if you are struggling in any area of your life. If you are wounded by circumstance or the betrayal of others, if you are in despair about your marriage or your children or your future, if you are being swayed by temptation, you probably feel like you are falling. Go ahead and fall, but fall into the arms of the one who can save you.

—SANDI PATTY (*Falling Forward*)

# YIELDING TO THE WIND

*Jesus answered, "The wind blows wherever it pleases. You hear its sound, but you cannot tell where it comes from or where it is going. So it is with everyone born of the Spirit."*

—John 3:8 NIV

Our ability to control often serves us well—in the ordering of our days, in our multitasking, in our dinner parties. On those occasions, we're not sailing. We just step into a motorboat and get it done. We openly take charge of things and happily run our little worlds. But when you are trusting God, you are sailing. Your hair is blown about but not your confidence. Your course is set, not by your own agenda, but by the wind of the Spirit. You have thrown the paddle of control overboard and in faith you have raised the sail to let God take you wherever he wants you to go.

Faith makes us certain of realities that we cannot see. I can't see the sun right now, but I can see the light. I can't see the wind, but I can feel it's there. I take one look up at the sail and there is no doubt. The storms will still come, the fear will still try to overtake me, but faith will sustain me. Faith—at first a gracious gift from God, it then becomes the muscle by which we can keep on trusting. No matter what happens, it is going to be okay.

—NICOLE JOHNSON (*Raising the Sail*)

# BECOMING MATURE

*Anyone who lives on milk, being still an infant, is not acquainted with the teaching about righteousness. But solid food is for the mature, who by constant use have trained themselves to distinguish good from evil.*

—*Hebrews 5:13–14* NIV

Why do so many of us stop short of the fullness God intends for each of us? I believe we get comfortable in our immaturity.

I watch birds out my office window all day while I work. I've noticed that when the weather gets rough and strong winds begin to blow, birds seek refuge. They don't protect themselves based on how they feel, whether they want to, or on what all the other birds are doing. Their "get out of danger" instinct tells them what to do, and they do it. But when the storm passes by, it doesn't take long for them to come out again—unscathed, undaunted, and grateful to be out foraging for food once more.

We humans, on the other hand, often foolishly decide to party in the middle of storms. We refuse to take shelter because we think we are smarter than those who say, "There is a storm coming." This lack of wisdom is the mark of immaturity. Remember, what the birds know to do by instinct, we know to do by wisdom. But wisdom by its very nature resides only in the hearts of the mature; that is, those who are in the process of finding their full potential.

—JAN SILVIOUS (*Big Girls Don't Whine*)

# CROOKED ARROWS

*If we are faithless, He remains faithful; He cannot deny Himself.*

—2 Timothy 2:13

"Life is tough but God is faithful" has become my motto. The Bible is full of stories of men and women who in the midst of personal failure and disappointment, even sin, discovered the faithfulness of God.

The psalmist David loved God, but he committed adultery and was responsible for sending a man to certain death. The apostle Peter was privileged to walk side by side with Jesus day after day. He saw the miracles, but when confronted, he claimed he'd never met Jesus.

Human history is an ongoing story of stumbling men and women and the constant grace and mercy of God. God hits straight shots with crooked arrows. It's all about him, never about us, never about the quality of the arrow. But we forget this.

These men left a light on for you and me. David's brokenness lit a candle in the dark. Peter's bruises gave me courage to walk on. This is the purpose of our lives. To learn to love God and to love one another. To let the light of Christ shine through the dark moments as well as in the glory days when everything is wonderful. He is faithful, even when we are not.

—SHEILA WALSH (*Life Is Tough But God Is Faithful*)

# BEES, BEES, AND MORE BEES

> *Be tenderhearted, be courteous; not returning evil for evil or*
> *reviling for reviling, but on the contrary blessing, knowing that*
> *you were called to this, that you may inherit a blessing.*
>
> —*1 Peter 3:8–9*

I'm fascinated by bumblebees and also by their cousins, the honeybees. In the darkness of the hive—and in the bright sunlight of the day—honeybees go about their work with a steadfast devotion that's hard to comprehend.

But there's something else about the honeybee besides its work that can teach us an important lesson. Did you know that when a honeybee stings someone, the sting is always fatal to the bee?

When I read that fact, I thought how it resembles what happens to us when we respond angrily and hurtfully to those who have wronged us. We can hurt them back. We can sting them with angry words and hurtful actions. But in the end, we probably do more damage to ourselves than we inflict upon them, especially when we consider whether or not our behavior was Christlike. What sadness we feel when we realize once again that we have failed to measure up. We bow our heads and ask the Savior to do for us what we've been unable to do for others: forgive us.

And once again he extends his honey-sweet gift of grace to us—and urges us to share it.

—THELMA WELLS (*Listen Up, Honey*)

# ALL GOOD THINGS TAKE TIME

*Water wears away stones.*

—Job 14:19 NIV

Where would you like to be in six months or a year? And how will you get there? Just as the ant picks up one grain of sand and moves it, then the next one, then the next one—and because of its long obedience in the same direction builds a city—one year from now, we will all be different. We don't get to stay the same, but we do get a choice in how we will have changed, whether it's for the better or not.

In your spiritual lives, too, as you "play the movie forward," where do you want to be in a year's time? If you want to be growing in your faith, closer to God and bold in your prayers, then day by day follow the example of the little ant and set your face in that direction by spending time in God's Word and in worship and prayer every day.

Everything that has value is worth intentional, daily commitment and obedience. I know that it's not easy, but just take the first step, then the next and the next, and before you know it you'll be much further down the road. Understand it can take time. All good things do. But that's okay, because the journey is worth it.

—SHEILA WALSH (*Get Off Your Knees and Pray*)

# MY TOP TEN LIST

*A good woman is hard to find . . . When she speaks she has
something worthwhile to say.*

—Proverbs 31:10, 26 MSG

Sleep researchers tell us that women have from 20 to 50 percent
higher incidence of insomnia than men. They say that this is due to
our fluctuating levels of estrogen. Women would tell you that this is
really because we are the only gender that truly has a grip on the
emotional complexities of life and once the lights go out our minds
zoom in like a laser pen on the most pressing issue de jour.

I made up this list during one of those sleepless nights. It's a
countdown a la *The David Letterman Show* of some things I probably should pass on to a younger generation . . .

10. Surround yourself with people who build you up.
9. Take care of your body.
8. You make your decisions—but then your decisions make you.
7. A chapter of Proverbs a day keeps the stupids away.
6. Keep your destiny in mind.
5. Pray about everything.
4. Never make important decisions when you are tired or hungry.
3. Take time to decide what is worth doing, then do it with your
   whole heart and with excellence.
2. Call home.
1. Love God.

—ANITA RENFROE (*If It's Not One Thing, It's Your Mother*)

# IT IS ENOUGH

*Those who wait on the L*ORD *shall renew their strength; they shall mount up with wings like eagles, they shall run and not be weary, they shall walk and not faint.*

—Isaiah 40:31

Eventually, we all have to live in circumstances that are different than we expected. That is the time we must understand that we have choices—the kind of choices we all need to make when our carefully developed life plan takes a U-turn or comes to a sudden halt. We must discover fresh hope and renewed courage when we would rather give up. We must willfully choose to make the future better. We must choose not to waste the sorrow. We must give hope to others in the middle of our brokenness and tears.

Because it is all we have to give, it is enough.

Perhaps you're feeling like folding up your cards. Making hope-filled choices may be the furthest thing from your mind right now. But I challenge you, as I have been challenged, to consider your life from some different angles. Are you willing to take the chance that your "new normal" might offer benefits you never expected? Perhaps even joy?

I can't promise easy answers. In fact, you might wind up with more questions than before. There will be frustration, hurt, and more bumps in the road. But your movement can be purpose-ful—in the direction of hope.

Take the risk. It is all we have. And it is enough.

—CAROL KENT (*A New Kind of Normal*)

# WE WERE BORN FOR THIS!

> *Your love, O LORD, reaches to the heavens, your faithfulness to the skies. . . . How priceless is your unfailing love!*
>
> —Psalm 36:5, 7 NIV

Since the beginning of time, humankind has puzzled over and considered the questions, *Why was I born? Why am I here? What is the purpose of life?* It's not unusual to hear those who are in the middle of emotional depression, personal heartache, financial calamity, or social disaster pondering whether their lives are meaningless and futile. Hardship can make us question whether our lives are actually serving a purpose.

The Scriptures tell us that God loved us before he flung the stars into place. He loved us even before he created us. In fact, he chose to create us so that he might make us the recipients of his never-ending, unfathomable love. We are it! God's best and his most loved! We don't even have to go to the playoffs. We've already won. We were born for this!

God did not create us to help around the earth. He did not create us to do what he can already do. He created us so that he might love us and have a relationship with us. Then, based on his love, we return that love, thus establishing a reciprocal relationship. We don't have to do anything to earn this relationship. God ordained it "even before he made the world."

—MARILYN MEBERG (*Love Me Never Leave Me*)

# SEARCHING FOR ANSWERS

*The entrance of Your words gives light; It gives understanding
to the simple.*
—Psalm 119:130

Several years ago, a dear friend gave me a thin, colorful little book
called *The Atlas of Experience* by Louise van Swaaji and Jean Klare.
It's based on the theory that human beings have always been
haunted by fundamental questions and searching for answers.
This book opens before the reader a sea of possibilities on which
we all travel. By means of its evocative maps and routes, one can
follow many passageways that lead to shorelines where our imagination, ideas, feelings, experience, and faith are enlarged.

That's the way life works. It's uncertain and has myriad ups
and downs. If we cannot or do not learn from these uncertainties,
we'll repeat patterns that keep us treading water. And if we get
stuck there, how will we find our sea legs? How will we become
adults?

As long as we are in the human condition, we'll have questions. You can count on it! A few of our questions will have easy
answers. Others will be difficult, taking time to work out. Some
will demand processing with counselors, friends, and God before
an answer will come. And some will never be solved this side of
heaven. We are not meant to know what to do. We simply have to
trust the one who is the keeper of our hearts.

—LUCI SWINDOLL (*Life! Celebrate It*)

# MESSY LOVE

> *If we walk in the light as He is in the light, we have fellowship with one another, and the blood of Jesus Christ His Son cleanses us from all sin. If we say that we have no sin, we deceive ourselves, and the truth is not in us. If we confess our sins, He is faithful and just to forgive us our sins and to cleanse us from all unrighteousness.*
>
> —1 John 1:7–9

Walking in the light means we are cleansed by the blood of Christ and able to have fellowship with other believers. We will be constantly cleansed, wrote John, if we confess our sins as they surface. When we hide our sins and cover our weaknesses, when we pretend to be Christian supermen, we live in denial—"the truth is not in us." We then become isolated from one another and from God. I think one of the greatest cancers of our day is loneliness, the way we hide our imperfections and doubts from one another. I think it's time to tell the truth.

My son, Christian, loves cupcakes. I frost them with a dark chocolate frosting. One day I was going out and had on a white cotton blouse and jeans. He saw me come into the kitchen, and he yelled "Mom!" and threw his arms around my neck and rubbed his grubby little face in my hair.

I thought, *This is how God invites us to come to him. Not to clean ourselves up, but to come and bury our face in the mane of the Lion of Judah. Come as we really are.*

Won't you come to your heavenly Father—just as you are!

—SHEILA WALSH (*Life Is Tough But God Is Faithful*)

# MERCY AND GRACE

> *The eternal God is your refuge, and underneath are the everlasting arms.*
>
> —Deuteronomy 33:27

God is everywhere, but I sometimes think he is especially near to the floor of our lives, when we mutter the most profound and heartfelt prayer that's ever been prayed by humans who are overwhelmed by brokenness or sorrow: "Please, help."

One of the most beautiful aspects of the story of the Prodigal Son in the Bible is that upon his return home, the son was given both mercy *and* grace. Well, you might be asking, what is the difference?

Mercy is not being punished as we deserve. It is being forgiven. The father met the son out on the road and did not chide or scold or dole out his punishment.

Grace is when you are given gift on top of gift that you don't deserve. Grace is the ring and the robe. Grace is the feast and the dancing and the party.

Grace is the Father's wholehearted embrace. Because the Father loves all his children without partiality, he equally offers mercy and grace to both the prodigal and also to his older brother, whose heart was filled with resentment over his brother's actions.

If you find yourself in need of help today, I have a boatload of comfort for you. Both God's mercy and his grace are yours for the asking.

—SANDI PATTY (*Falling Forward*)

# CHOOSING FAITH OVER FEAR

*"Do not be afraid . . . for I myself will help you," declares the*
*LORD, your Redeemer, the Holy One of Israel.*
—Isaiah 41:14 NIV

The nature of love is trust, even when it is betrayed. Trust is what brings us close. Fear, on the other hand, drives a wedge between us.

Fear is in the very fabric of life, because there is so much that we can't control. Maybe that's why "Do not fear!" is repeated in the Bible more than one hundred times. God is constantly telling us not to be afraid, because he knows we almost always are. And for good reasons. But it isn't fear that's the problem; it's what fear makes us do that concerns him. Somebody said, "Courage is just fear that has said its prayer." I'm saying mine every day.

One thing I've learned is that I'm not the person I want to be when I sit, trembling in the dark. I'm not the person I want to be when I'm swirling out of control in a cyclone of fear. What is going to happen now? What if . . . what if . . . what if . . . what if . . .

I don't want to live that way.

When I kneel by my bed and ask God to look after my loved ones and trust that he is doing so, I'm choosing faith over fear.

—NICOLE JOHNSON (*Raising the Sail*)

# IT IS DONE

*Jesus said, "All that the Father gives me will come to me, and whoever comes to me I will never drive away."*

—John 6:37 NIV

When Jesus Christ, God in human form, willingly hung on the cross to pay for every sin you and I ever committed or ever will commit, he made a bridge for us to get back to God. We are all sinners, separated from God (see Romans 3:23). So he did for us what we can never do for ourselves. We can never be religious enough or go to church enough or pray enough or give enough to perfectly keep God's law and therefore reach God. It is impossible.

Think about a speed limit. If the law says go twenty-five miles an hour and you go twenty-six miles an hour, even if you *meant* to go twenty-five miles an hour, you are guilty of breaking the law. No flexibility. That is the way the law operates. A mature woman knows she can't keep God's law perfectly, so she recognizes her need for a Savior and accepts the free gift of eternal life that comes through Jesus Christ. Once it is done, it is done. She stands firm no matter what wind blows. Once you have come to the Father, your life in him is a done deal. You can stand firm!

—JAN SILVIOUS (*Big Girls Don't Whine*)

# JESUS IS ENOUGH

*I am persuaded that neither death nor life, nor angels nor principalities, nor things present nor things to come, nor height nor depth, nor any other created thing, shall be able to separate us from the love of God.*

—Romans 8:38–39

No matter what kind of problem may land on our backs, all we finally have is Jesus, and he is worth it because he loves us.

Yes, we still have questions. Should we hesitate to ask them because we're supposed to have all the answers? Satan loves it when we are silent, afraid to ask the questions that can lead us to understanding.

Some of the greatest words Paul ever wrote start with questions: Can anything separate us from the love Christ has for us? Can troubles or problems or sufferings? If we have no food or clothes, if we are in danger, or even if death comes, can any of these things separate us from Christ's love?

Paul's answer is that nothing—*absolutely nothing*—in this entire world can separate us from the love of God that is in Christ Jesus our Lord.

Here is where we must start. Even in the darkest night, the most blinding pain, the most maddening frustration—when nothing makes sense anymore—we keep going because he alone is worth it all. Holding on is hard—it can seem impossible—but it is worth it because Jesus is worth it. No matter what happens, Jesus is enough.

—SHEILA WALSH (*Life Is Tough But God Is Faithful*)

# THE BRIGHT SIDE OF LIFE

*I am the LORD, your God ... Do not fear; I will help you.*
—Isaiah 41:13 NIV

I don't know of a person alive who has not, at one time or another, experienced bouts with depression. Sometimes it lasts a few hours or days, and it's simply unavoidable in this world. Other times it parks, settling in for a long visit.

Here are some suggestions for those times you find yourself sinking into depression:

> → *Change the way you talk to yourself.* Avoid negative talk. Employ affirmations—positive statements spoken in first-person singular, present tense. Example: "I like myself."
> → *Get it all out.* Find someone who is available to you, someone who can be objective and keep your confidence and talk out everything you feel with her.
> → *Take care of your physical health.* When we get depressed, we usually don't eat correctly, we eat too much, or not at all. Eating right and exercising can start you on your way to a healthier physical and emotional life.
> → *Get outside yourself.* When we have a lot of time on our hands to think, we'll think of the wrong thing. So stay busy. Focus on things larger than yourself.
> → *See a doctor.* If these things don't seem to work, you may need help breaking through to the bright side.

—THELMA WELLS (*Girl, Have I Got Good News for You*)

# MY REAL FRIEND

*Jesus said, "I have called you friends."*
—John 15:15

I can't begin to tell you how freeing it was when I first embraced Jesus Christ as my real Friend. For so long, he was simply a gigantic *idea* to me. Although I believed them to be true, the unfathomable images of Savior, Redeemer, and the ultimate sacrifice for mankind made God so big in my mind that what I knew of him didn't translate to what was going on in my everyday life. I had always been told of God's great love, and somewhere inside I believed it. But what completely melted my heart, what completely liberated me from choking insecurity, wasn't just the truth that Jesus loved me—but that Jesus *liked* me. He LIKED me! Exactly as I was.

Jesus had long been my Redeemer, but when I accepted him as my real Friend and began living like he was my Friend, my true healing began. I was ready to discover the truth of who I am without the masks, without the pretense, without the charade. Knowing and understanding Jesus as my Friend helped me see myself in a new light: the security I found in my relationship with him helped me open the door of possibility and see a glimpse of the person I could be.

—NATALIE GRANT (*The Real Me*)

# MOTHERS OF THE BIBLE

*The woman to be admired and praised is the woman who lives
in the Fear-of-God. Give her everything she deserves! Festoon
her life with praises!*

—Proverbs 31:30–31 MSG

If you have spent your adult life trying to live up to the mothering
standard set in the thirty-first chapter of Proverbs (and I know some
women do), you might as well just go ahead and take up permanent
residence in the I-Can't-Quite-Measure-Up Lane. We are left with
the impression that this sort of mother is the Approved Standard
Version—family centered, good business woman, great cook, generous, prepared, discreet, praiseworthy, wise, and beautiful.

This is precisely why I am so glad the Bible gives us pictures
of other kinds of mothers as well—like Eve, who made the monumental, mind-blowing, affects-everybody-forever mistake or
Rebekah, who schemed and connived to push her "favorite" son
ahead of his brother. She reminds us that it is a dangerous thing
to use maternal power for manipulation.

These moms reveal to us that mother-love is fierce and stubborn to a fault—even wrong-headed sometimes. We do right
things for wrong reasons and wrong things because we think
everyone needs our help. When you look at the moms in the Bible,
say a silent prayer of thanks that these women are included alongside the Oracle of Lemuel in Proverbs 31 to bring snapshots of
reality and spiritual caution cones to our journey.

—ANITA RENFROE (*If It's Not One Thing, It's Your Mother*)

# A NEW KIND OF NORMAL

*My soul melts away for sorrow; strengthen me
according to your word.*

—Psalm 119:28 NRSV

At some point, most of us will encounter a challenging situation that permanently alters the rest of our lives. It might be a knock at the door, a middle-of-the-night phone call, or a diagnosis from the doctor that changes the future as you envisioned it. It could be that your married child gets a divorce and you will no longer have opportunities to spend time with your grandchildren because they will have moved away with the other spouse. It may be that all of your friends are having babies and you've been told you will never be able to carry a child.

What you once thought of as "normal" will be adjusted to a new kind of normal. The question is: how will you respond? Will you close the blinds on communication with other people, focusing only on your personal pain and deep grief, or will you choose to live a meaningful and vibrant life, even it it's different from the life you always wanted? Will you make choices based on unshakable truth that will not only enhance the quality of your own life but also bring renewed hope and fresh courage to people in your sphere of influence?

Whatever you do, choose life. It's the first step in getting a foothold in your own new kind of normal.

—CAROL KENT (*A New Kind of Normal*)

# THE RIGHT STUFF

*When the kindness and love of God our Savior appeared, he
saved us, not because of righteous things we had done, but
because of his mercy. He saved us through the washing of
rebirth and renewal by the Holy Spirit.*

—*Titus 3:4–5* NIV

If there is any one thing I want to impress on you, it is for you to
know the amazing freedom—inside and out—that comes with
Christ's loving gift of salvation. My hope is that you know who you
really are, as God knows you. And that you understand his unconditional love that continues no matter what you find when you
delve into your innermost thoughts and feelings. In acknowledging and valuing his constant, unwavering love, you can find
freedom from the hard and hurtful experiences of life, and you can
get beyond even those old, painful wounds that refuse to heal.

God created you, and he has a plan for you, a plan that leads
to your divine destiny. He has put within you the "right stuff"
that can, if you choose to utilize it, enable you to defy defeat and
accomplish that destiny. He has equipped you to choose victory
when adversity strikes. Knowing you have what it takes, you're
freed from living in fear that bad "somethings" might happen to
you in the future. Something bad probably will happen, that's
just the way it is in life, but you'll get through it, and God will be
there to help you get through it.

—MARILYN MEBERG & LUCI SWINDOLL (*Free Inside and Out*)

# LISTEN UP!

*Love the LORD your God, listen to his voice, and hold fast to him. For the LORD is your life.*

—*Deuteronomy 30:20* NIV

There are two types of listening—listening with your head and listening with your heart. While I realize that people often listen and make decisions with both heart and head, in many ways it's impossible to separate them. I want to discuss them separately, however, because I so strongly feel unless we learn how to separate the two, we won't be able to make some decisions at all. Our evaluations will be too muddled.

When I was younger, that was often my dilemma. I simply couldn't decide between what my heart felt and what my mind thought, so I did nothing. I know a lot of people like that now. They operate out of involuntary inertia, unable to differentiate between knowledge and feelings. When we live between those two poles, it's very hard to make sound decisions.

Our primary goal as mature Christians, of course, is to find a happy medium between what our hearts tell us and what our heads tell us without compromising obedience. Nobody totally achieves that perfect balance, but the Holy Spirit can help us with our efforts. He comes alongside us and enables us to reach a conclusion we can live with.

—LUCI SWINDOLL (*Life! Celebrate It*)

# NEVER THIRST AGAIN

*Jesus answered her, "If you knew the gift of God and who it is that asks you for a drink, you would have asked him and he would have given you living water."*

—John 4:10 NIV

In the Bible we read about a woman drawing water from a well. But instead of simply filling her water vessel and heading back home as she had a thousand times before, she encountered a man sitting near the well who forever changed her life.

The man asked her for a drink. Sounds simple enough, right? But then he said that God could give her living water, and she would never thirst again. Now that statement gained her attention.

*Never thirst again.* Who wouldn't want that kind of water? Who wouldn't want the burden of daily responsibility lifted off her head . . . much less have the ache of her thirst relieved?

The Samaritan woman was searching for something that would quench her longing and perhaps fill her loneliness. No wonder Jesus' offer of living water captured her attention—and the empty cistern of her heart.

Jesus' offer to give us living water is as clear and pure now as it was that day at Jacob's well. He doesn't withhold his offer because we are empty, broken, or contaminated. In fact, he understands our condition, and he comes with the cleansing water of forgiveness, inviting us to drink and be forever refreshed.

Are you thirsty?

—PATSY CLAIRMONT (*All Cracked Up*)

# POP-UP PAIN

*As far as the east is from the west, so far has He removed our transgressions from us.*

—Psalm 103:12

Let's face it: there are some wrongs that we cannot make right. Once the feathers are out of the pillow, there is no way to get all those feathers back in. We simply have to grieve and accept the all-encompassing mercy and grace of our Father. Then we must ask for the forgiveness of others after we express our sorrow.

Though God forgives us right away, it may take many of the hurting, wounded human beings around us a lot longer to heal. They are all too human, as are we. Sometimes we still struggle with forgiving ourselves. We experience what I call "pop-up" pain—at times our hearts ache with the heaviness of what we did and the fallout that lingers.

When "pop-up" pain happens and I feel frozen in my failure, I just try to imagine my Father running down the road to meet me. I look in his eyes—brimming with acceptance—and remember that it isn't about my failures, it is about his love. It is about being God's beloved daughter, who is always welcome home. Then I dry my tears, lift my eyes toward heaven, and sing with all the gratitude my heart can hold the song he gave back to me.

—SANDI PATTY (*Falling Forward*)

# WHERE'S THE GOODNESS IN THAT?

*Jesus said, "I have come that they may have life, and that they may have it more abundantly."*

—John 10:10

I gave up. I surrendered. I let go. I stopped being in charge of my spiritual goodness, because I didn't have any spiritual goodness. I had worked for God and yet withheld my heart from him. I'd sought to please him, like a father who is hard to please, and missed that he was pleased with me. I tried to do so many things *for* God that I missed being *with* God. Where was the goodness in that? I discovered that the Christian life is not about trying harder. It is not about keeping it all together. It is about trusting in the one who can keep it all together. If we just roll up our sleeves and try harder, we are not walking with Jesus. If we can do it all ourselves, what do we need him for?

When I gave up, I felt a gentle stirring in my soul. He whispered to me, "Jesus came to give you life. Peace—real peace on the inside, from all of this climbing, striving, and worrying. Joy—unabashed delight in life, regardless of the circumstances. Love—foundational, unconditional, never-ending love." I didn't have to work for these things, I just had to surrender to them. I had to stop long enough to let them overtake me. Again and again.

—NICOLE JOHNSON (*Fresh-Brewed Life*)

# FAINTING GOATS

*My heart is glad, and my glory rejoices; my flesh also will rest in hope.*

—Psalm 16:9

I have a sister-in-law who raises fainting goats. What a contrast they are to the little leaping lambs! These goats are slightly nasty and not very pretty. They meander about foraging for food until they are startled by life in the goat yard and then they just up and faint! They can't stand to be startled, so they don't take time to rejoice. They just faint to get away from reality. They are programmed to avoid dealing with it!

Humanly speaking, they are like women who refuse to face the truth. They don't recognize that God is in control and in the situation that startled them. They just faint and go to La-la Land until the distress passes by. Of course, when they come to, the circumstances are still there. What good did their little escape do? The answer is none. Mature women know that no matter how much they might want to be like Scarlet O'Hara and deal with life's realities *tomorrow*, that is no way to live.

No matter your circumstances, rejoice and rejoice again, because God is the author and finisher of life. He is in the middle of everything you face, no matter what. That's worth knowing and holding on to.

—JAN SILVIOUS (*Big Girls Don't Whine*)

# LEANING ON HIS STAFF

*Even though I walk through the darkest valley, I fear no evil; for
you are with me; your rod and your staff—they comfort me.*
—Psalm 23:4 NRSV

As I look back down the path of my life, I see the care God took
every step of the way to draw me to his side. He spoke softly to
me through all the years, "I love you. I will walk beside you. You
can count on me."

When I think about the story of Job in the Bible, I would
never choose his life. I can't imagine the pain of losing all your
children, your home, your health, and yet there is something
about pain that repaints the picture of life. Of who we are, of who
God is. I've said it myself. I look at my life. I think of the things
I've suffered, but even though I would not have chosen this path,
I would not change a single day, a single step.

Why? Because I am now a different woman. It's one thing to
say that the Lord is my shepherd; it's quite something else to be
unable to walk one more step by yourself, to lean on that staff,
and to be held up.

I've heard the same thing expressed by so many of you who
share devastating losses but wouldn't go back because what you
have tasted of the love and grace of God in the midst of pain is
breathtaking. It's true!

—SHEILA WALSH (*Life Is Tough But God Is Faithful*)

## PRECIOUS IN HIS SIGHT

> *If you devote your heart to him . . . you will stand firm and*
> *without fear. You will be secure, because there is hope; you will*
> *look about you and take your rest in safety.*
> —Job 11:13, 15, 18 NIV

If you have suffered abuse at the hands of another, there is one thing you need to know. *Nobody was born to be abused.* When God created you, he intended for you to be safe and protected, not battered and bruised. In every incident of abuse, moral, ethical, and spiritual laws are being violated. God never intended for you to be mistreated. You are precious in his sight.

Here are some positive steps you can take out of the abyss of abuse:

→ *Know that Jesus loves you.* If you have received him as your personal Savior, then you are God's beloved child, bought with the highest price that has ever been paid. He longs to comfort you and let you feel his loving care.
→ *Don't be a victim.* As a woman of God, you can choose a different path. Give up the victim mentality because victims never win!
→ *Ask God for direction.* He can and will give you clarity about what to do.
→ *Keep the faith.* Sometimes you won't see him working . . . but thank him daily, listen carefully for his voice, and commit yourself to following his direction.

—THELMA WELLS *(Girl, Have I Got Good News for You)*

# THE REAL ME

*Those who look to him are radiant.*

—Psalm 34:5 NIV

I tried for so long to be perfect. I wanted so badly to look like those girls in my magazines that I harmed my health trying to find validation. But finally I found that the greatest sense of self came from finding my worth in God.

I'm not saying I no longer care how I look. I still love fashion. I find great satisfaction in adapting the latest trends to my personal style and wearing them modestly. I am always trying to find a new way to motivate myself to exercise, and I remind myself that taking care of my health is respecting the body God gave me. I love lip gloss, and I'm always looking for a new method to achieve that rosy complexion, so far be it from me to tell anyone not to wear makeup! But I've learned that if I want to have a true glow, I have to fix my focus on God, not on my makeup case.

As I looked to God, I found the key to my self-worth. As I uncovered the truth that Jesus really loves and accepts me, I was finally able to begin accepting myself. I discovered my sense of being. In short, when I found the real Jesus, I finally discovered the real me.

—NATALIE GRANT (*The Real Me*)

# OTHER MOTHERS

*Treat . . . older women as mothers, younger women as sisters,*
*with all purity.*
—1 Timothy 5:2

I'm old enough to recall when you could get in trouble every-where in your town by any female adult who felt motherly toward you. If someone caught you doing anything immoral, illegal, dis-respectful, or even questionable, they were not deterred by the fact that they did not share your particular strand of DNA. Wrong was wrong, and if you were wrong, they felt a social obligation to step in and mother you occasionally. That was the downside.

The upside was that you also had a cadre of women who would love, support, and encourage you in areas where your own mother did not have a background for input. This is the aspect of having Other Mothers that allows young women to excel and spread their wings beyond their own heritage. When women who are not bound to you by relational duty look into your life and tell you that you are gifted, you tend to listen to and believe them primarily *because* they aren't your mom.

You may be a woman who needs an Other Mother. You might be a woman with Other Mothering to give. Truth is, you're probably both. I hope you will seek out the Other Mothers you need and give Other Mothering liberally to the girls coming up the path behind you.

—ANITA RENFROE (*If It's Not One Thing, It's Your Mother*)

# PLEASE AND THANK YOU

*Everything is for your sake, so that grace, as it extends to more and more people, may increase thanksgiving, to the glory of God.*

—2 Corinthians 4:15 NRSV

Many of us grew up in homes where we were taught to say please and thank you. During those years, we were learning to be polite. However, as life weaves its tapestry of good times and bad times, we face new decisions. The words *thank you* can be difficult to internalize when life seems unfair and it appears that God is not answering our prayers for a desired outcome. Sometimes it's easier to choose withdrawal and denial over active participation in life.

When it seems as though everyone around us is experiencing the abundance of God's blessings while our situation continues to spiral downward, expressions of thanksgiving and praise can disappear from our vocabulary. Sometimes, while deep in our own pain, it's hard to express joy to others who are experiencing God's blessing and abundance. We try to be happy for them, but inside we wonder why our lives and family situations haven't turned out better?

Think about your own new kind of normal. Make a list of ten things you have to be thankful for in the middle of an unexpected or an unwanted change in your life. Practice praying through that list, verbalizing your thanks to God for any benefit, however small, of your unforeseen circumstances.

—CAROL KENT (*A New Kind of Normal*)

# HIS SPECIAL TREASURE

*GOD, your God, chose you out of all the people on Earth for himself as a cherished, personal treasure.*

—Deuteronomy 7:6 MSG

No one wants to be overlooked, ignored, or discounted in any way, but I don't believe there is anyone on earth who has not felt the sting of rejection. If rejections happen to us often enough, the inevitable assumption is that we aren't good enough, lovable enough, or smart enough to be included.

We generally assume our value is determined by what we *do*. If I do my job well, I may be promoted. If I do it poorly, I may be replaced or demoted. The same mentality is true with human relationships. If I'm pleasant, people will probably want to be around me. When I snarl and hiss I'll undoubtedly find myself without lunch partners. The earthly system is easily understood by all of us. Our performance is crucial to success as well as social acceptability.

The mind-blowing truth about the God of the universe is that he does not use the performance system. In the mind of Creator God, there is no questioning your value. You are chosen by him, and if that truth alone does not melt your socks, consider this: You are also viewed as his special treasure. You don't work toward it, earn it, or struggle to become good enough. Quite simply . . . you have been chosen.

—MARILYN MEBERG (*The Decision of a Lifetime*)

# LISTEN WITH YOUR HEART

*My dear friends, you should be quick to listen and slow to speak.*
—James 1:19 CEV

How can someone learn the fine art of listening with the heart? Let me suggest some ways.

First of all, make it a practice to listen to other people without your own agenda in mind. No matter what they say, pay attention to their words and keep your eyes on them as you drink in their sentences.

Second, don't interrupt—no matter how absurd their words, ideas, or stories may sound to you or how much you want to say something you think is vital.

Third, don't be afraid you'll forget your comment if you don't say it right now. Chances are, you won't. And if you do, your comment probably wasn't that important anyway.

And finally, don't offer an immediate solution. Many times, the key to listening with one's heart is the ability to simply hear what other people have to say without trying to help them solve anything.

People tend to share only when they feel accepted. The minute somebody judges us or tries to set us straight, we clam up because we want to be received, just as we are. The truth is most of us know down deep inside what to do in trying situations. It may take us awhile to get to it, but it's there . . . in our hearts.

—LUCI SWINDOLL (*Life! Celebrate It*)

# TURN THE LIGHT ON

*The LORD is my light and my salvation; whom shall I fear?*
—Psalm 27:1

"Fear has friends," I warn women when I address the topic of being afraid. When you emotionally surrender to one fear, you open the door to a myriad of others. I learned that the hard way, through my own experience. And I paid with years of my life. I'd like to offer you a shortcut.

When you are afraid, don't give in to fear—turn on the light!

→ *Turn on the light of God's Word.* "For God has not given us a spirit of fear, but of power and of love and of a sound mind" (2 Timothy 1:7).
→ *Turn on the light of faith.* And risk taking the next step out of your self-imposed limitations. What do you have to lose? Fear? Go for it.
→ *Turn on the light of your mind.* Believe what you can't see, which is that God holds you safely in his care no matter where you are and that he is unfolding his plan for your life. You can't travel outside his presence.
→ *Turn on the light of friendship.* Let others know when you are uneasy and then allow them to stand with you. It will comfort you, strengthen you, and keep you humble. We weren't meant to go this life alone.

—PATSY CLAIRMONT (*I Second That Emotion*)

# SURVIVING A CRISIS OF THE SOUL

> *[The LORD] heals the brokenhearted, and binds up their wounds.*
>
> —Psalm 147:3 NRSV

I have found that there are three things broken people need in order to survive a crisis of the soul.

First, you need people who will be "Jesus with skin on." A few "unshockable" saints who don't try to *see through you* but instead show up in work clothes with their spiritual sleeves rolled up to try to help *see you through.* They are the good Samaritans among us who don't lean back in an above-it-all posture, clicking their tongues, analyzing why you are lying facedown in the dirt. They simply bring bandages and try to get you where help can be found. They are the "safe people." And for a while, perhaps a long while, you'll need to put barriers up to protect yourself from "unsafe people."

Second, you need a "safe place," a physical space apart from the maddening crowd where you can have the space and time and nurturing environment that will help you to find your life's balance, your sanity, and your faith again.

Third, you need a "safe God." Not, mind you, a tame God. Not a watered-down version of God. But a great and powerful God who is as tender as a Shepherd is with his littlest lost lamb.

—SANDI PATTY (*Falling Forward*)

# BEYOND ALL TIME

*Jesus said, "Live out your God-created identity."*
—Matthew 5:48 MSG

*Who am I?* Have you ever lain awake at night asking that question? I take that back. Most women work too hard to miss sleep by lying awake at night, much less asking questions! So the questions probably come at other times. *Who am I?* Do you ever feel that you're faking your life? That you're living someone else's life, and you're not sure whose? You wonder how you got to this place of disguise. You want to give yourself to God, but what self are you going to give?

There is only one who can tell you this: the Lord himself. And he wants to tell you, he wants you to know your reason for being and to be led by it. But it is a secret he will entrust to you only when you ask, and then in his own way and his own time. He will whisper it to you not in the mad rush of your striving and your fierce determination to be someone, but rather when you are content to rest in him, to put yourself into his keeping, into his hands. Most delightfully of all, it is a secret he will tell you slowly and sweetly, when you are willing to spend time with him: time with him who is beyond all time.

—NICOLE JOHNSON (*Fresh-Brewed Life*)

# YOUR FAVORITE BAD FEELING

*Finally . . . whatever is true, whatever is noble, whatever
is right, whatever is pure, whatever is lovely, whatever is
admirable—if anything is excellent or praiseworthy—think
about such things.*

—*Philippians 4:8* NIV

If we can't control anything else in our lives, we can control what
we think about. But when we have been buffeted by a situation
that throws us, it is easy to abdicate our control and go to our
"favorite bad feeling." That's the feeling we went to as a child
because we learned that it helped us get what we wanted. Once
you are an adult, you will find that it is the first place your mind
rushes when there is something troubling on your mental radar
screen.

Some of us cry, some pout, some sleep, some eat chocolate,
some go shopping, some withdraw, and some slam doors, some
clean house, some sit and stare. You could probably fill in your
own favorite bad feeling. But you don't have to respond that way,
you can choose not to go there. Circumstances rarely change, but
how you feel about the circumstances can change dramatically.
How you feel is up to you, not to anyone else in your life.

Peace is the result of choosing to focus your mind on what is
true and honorable and right. When you choose to do that, it is
amazing how much peace will overtake your mind and heart.

—JAN SILVIOUS (*Big Girls Don't Whine*)

# HIDDEN PLACES

> *God has reconciled you by Christ's physical body through*
> *death to present you holy in his sight, without blemish and free*
> *from accusation.*

—Colossians 1:22 NIV

When guilt occupies the secret places in our lives, we can let it cripple us, or we can allow God to set us free.

I didn't understand it at the time, but my mind and emotions were really running on two different tracks when I was a teenager. Part of me was a fervent teen who wanted to serve God, and the other part was a frightened little girl who felt guilty.

I can see that part of my motivation was really wanting to serve God, but also driving me was the fact that I wanted to push myself harder than anybody else to prove to God that I was worthy of his love. My hidden places controlled my life, but I didn't realize it. I knew God, but I still needed a freeing touch from him. In many ways, I was like the searching people Jesus met as he walked the dusty roads of Palestine, individuals whose hidden places kept them trapped in lives they longed to change.

We all have a choice. When guilt occupies the secret places in our lives, we can let it cripple us or we can allow the painful, healing light of God's love to set us free.

—SHEILA WALSH (*Life Is Tough But God Is Faithful*)

# FINDING YOUR WAY THROUGH

*I forgive you all that you have done, says the Lord God.*
—*Ezekiel 16:63* TLB

We have all made poor, uninformed choices that we think are right at the time, because we are usually thinking about the immediate circumstances rather than the consequences. Living with the aftermath of an abortion is one of the cruelest and most daunting of poor choices to overcome. You may well suffer feelings of remorse, anger, guilt, shame, horror, and more. Actually, these are the same feelings we get when we commit any well-thought-out sin.

Here are some suggestions for seeing your way through and out of the pain and regret of abortion:

+ *Know that sin is sin.* There are no little sins, no big sins, just sin with a capital S. The good news is that God forgives sin, all of it! And he chooses never to remind us of it again.
+ *Know that God can make you whole again.* There is no sin so bad that God will not forgive it.
+ *Know that you must give it up to God.* Tell God how much you hurt and how sorry you are. Receive his forgiveness and then forgive yourself.
+ *Cling to God's love for you.* Your sin did not and does not stop God from loving you. He loves you with an everlasting love.

—THELMA WELLS (*Girl, Have I Got Good News for You*)

41

# THE HANDIWORK OF GOD

> *My frame was not hidden from You, when I was made in*
> *secret, and skillfully wrought in the lowest parts of the earth.*
> *Your eyes saw my substance, being yet unformed.*
>
> —Psalm 139:15–16

Your self-image is not this ethereal, theoretical thing that is hard to get your hands around. It is who and what you picture yourself to be. How you feel about you. Do you base how you feel about yourself on the expectations of others? Who do you think you are?

True self-worth is not based on what you feel about yourself or even on what others think about you. True self-esteem can only be based on how God sees you. You are only who God says you are.

And what exactly does he see when he looks at you?

God's definition of beauty is vastly different from the world's standard, so it may be easier to answer that question by first saying what he doesn't see. He doesn't see your flaws and failures. Remember, he doesn't make mistakes. He sees you as beautiful, and if you then view yourself as anything less, it's like you're saying to God, "Hey, maybe you need to get your eyes checked."

You are not a flawed creature, an accident in God's otherwise-perfect design. You are the beautiful handiwork of God, and he has a plan and a purpose for your life.

—NATALIE GRANT (*The Real Me*)

# MOMSENSE GEMS

*May the LORD give you increase, both you and your children.*
—Psalm 115:14 NRSV

The Mother Code of Wisdom is DNA encoded with Eve and is impossible to eradicate. Your own mother or some mother somewhere said these things to you and they were instantly placed into your memory bank for the exact moment when you would need them: when you became a mother yourself.

Here is but an introductory list of the Momsense Gems. Enjoy!

- → *Bundle Up.* This could mean she has already been out this morning and knows it's cold, saw the forecast and thinks it's cold, or is cold herself.
- → *Clean your plate.* Lots of children in Third World countries are starving.
- → *Eat your vegetables.* She doesn't know or care that lots of veggies fall under the category of "acquired taste" and have bizarre textures.
- → *Close your mouth and eat.* Any idea how you could eat without *opening* your mouth?
- → *Get that hair out of your eyes.* The eyes are the windows of the soul. She's trying to peer into your soul to learn "the truth" and the bangs are in the way.
- → *Don't use that tone of voice with me.* (Even less sense: don't look at me in that tone of voice.)

—ANITA RENFROE (*If It's Not One Thing, It's Your Mother*)

# EVEN MORE MOMSENSE GEMS

> *[God] gives children to the woman who has none and makes her a happy mother.*
>
> —Psalm 113:9 NCV

Even though your kids don't seem like they're listening to any of the fine advice you're offering them (free of charge, mind you), something kicks in around the age of twenty-one and all the Momsense you gave them finally crosses the waxy canal to find a resting place in their brains . . . where it lies dormant until they have children of their own. Do these sound familiar?

→ *Look at me when I'm talking to you.* I've read that if you are walking through your neighborhood and encounter a less-than-friendly dog, the absolute worst thing you can do is make eye contact with it. Mom knows.

→ *Shut that door. Were you born in a barn?* Seems like this is a question only your mom could answer.

→ *Is that what you're going to wear?* If you are seeking your mother's opinion on what you're wearing, forget about it. It just isn't the natural order of things.

→ *Do as I say, not as I do.* Every parent's hope and dream!

→ *Use your own judgment.* Translation: If you choose to do something other than the course I have advised you to take, I will *not* be responsible for the outcome. In other words—use *my* judgment!

—ANITA RENFROE (*If It's Not One Thing, It's Your Mother*)

# FELLOW STRUGGLERS

*In God, whose word I praise, in the LORD, whose word I praise—in God I trust; I will not be afraid. What can man do to me?*

—*Psalm 56:10–11* NIV

The "wounds" of being vulnerable mean some people will turn their backs on us, judge us, and criticize us in front of others. The cost can be high. However, the "healing" of being vulnerable means we no longer live in fear of having our secrets revealed. I am not advocating starting every conversation with our worst struggles. There are times and places when God leads us to speak up, but we need to be aware of when it is appropriate and whom it will impact. In the process of responding to the divine nudge of his voice, we discover amazing freedom and contagious joy.

Our openness, when fitting, makes us a magnet for the people around us who are longing for just one person in their lives to be "real," to listen to their story without raising an eyebrow, to let them weep without providing advice. Instead of being competitors who are trying to impress each other with how perfect we are, we become fellow strugglers who are attempting to live out our faith in an authentic way. Our carefully constructed facade melts away and is replaced with the genuine version of ourselves. Fear taunts, people will reject you. Faith says, allow God to use the broken places of your past to give hope to someone else.

—CAROL KENT (*A New Kind of Normal*)

# WE ARE THE CHOSEN

*I have chosen you and have not rejected you.*

—Isaiah 41:9 NIV

Few of us have any comprehension that we have value far greater than any masterpiece to be sold at a Sotheby's art auction. Most of us assume we're closer to being garage sale material—ordinary and not especially appealing. Why do you suppose it's so difficult to accept that divine opinion of ourselves? Why don't we just settle down and allow God to be what he wishes to be—our daily companion?

We've all probably experienced some sense of being thrown away—by divorce, by the rebellion of one of our kids, by a boss's disapproval, by a friend's rejection, by criticism from a parent . . . the list goes on.

We desperately want to hear the words "I love you." Those words are like drops of water on our parched and love-starved souls.

What's the answer to this common soul devastation? God! All of the Bible tells us we have been chosen, we are loved, and . . . we will never be thrown away by him.

What are we chosen for? We've been chosen for a relationship with him.

Why? Because we are his treasured masterpieces. A heavenly treasure is never thrown away; neither is it sold at a garage sale.

—MARILYN MEBERG (*The Decision of a Lifetime*)

# PICKY, PICKY, PICKY

*Don't be nitpickers; use your head—and heart!—to discern*
*what is right, to test what is authentically right.*

—John 7:24 MSG

Criticism is one of the hardest things to take and one of the easiest things to give. Unless we listen with our hearts we can find a hundred reasons to criticize other people—how they dress; what they drive; where they shop, travel, or go to church; their values, political beliefs, sexual or philosophical lifestyle; their thoughts on any given issue; their home, family life, husband, wife, children . . . right down to how they part their hair.

Jesus has a lot to say about being critical or judgmental. He is adamant about anyone passing judgment on another human being.

Jesus tells us not to be "picky, picky, picky." But we all are to some degree. Nitpickers find fault and criticism with everything they encounter, and they're a curse in the household of faith. They're maddening to the human race and *especially* to the body of Christ. Jesus is the only one qualified to judge, because he's the only one who sees our hearts and listens with his. Our judgment of another is no better than the information we have (or think we have), but Jesus knows us better than we know ourselves. He has the total picture.

—LUCI SWINDOLL (*Life! Celebrate It*)

# ROSE OF SHARON

*I am the rose of Sharon, and the lily of the valleys.*
—Song of Solomon 2:1

I'm impressed with the rose because of its fruitful existence. It begins as a bud, which has a beauty all its own; gracefully unfolds into velvet overlays; and then, with its last breath, when crushed, it leaves a heady fragrance and drips precious oil. OK, there is the thorn issue, but in the overall scope of flower life, the rose is the reigning queen.

As we consider the beauty and grace of the rose, we're not surprised to discover that Jesus is called the Rose of Sharon. He was born a bud of a babe in a manger; his beauty unfolded before others with each humble step he took; and in his last breaths on earth, with thorns pressed into his head, after being crushed by our sins, he shed precious drops of his blood and released a forever fragrance of love. In the overall scope of our life, Christ is our coming King.

That sacrifice, Christ's broken body, now calls us to receive the crushing blows of life as a way for his fragrance to be released through us. Our crushed and drooping lives become a holy potpourri. Take a shattered heart, mix with a crushed spirit, intermingle with Christ's oil of mercy, stir with his healing touch, and season with divine love. What a magnificent fragrance.

—PATSY CLAIRMONT (*All Cracked Up*)

# THE ARMS OF GOD

*Cast your cares on the LORD and he will sustain you; he will never let the righteous fall.*

—Psalm 55:22 NIV

Even though you may have been taught as a child that God is good and God is love, you may have a hard time grasping the truth of this when it comes to yourself personally. If your view of God is a condemning one (or even partially this way), I recommend that you immerse yourself in everything the Scriptures say about the love, mercy, grace, and forgiveness of God. Spend as long as it takes dwelling on these Scriptures until you recognize that you are God's beloved daughter and there is nothing you could do that could make him love you any more than he does right now. There is nothing you could do that would cause him to love you any less.

Once you have given yourself this triage of hope—soaking up the truth of God's love and revising your view of God—you will be well on your way to trusting him. You cannot possibly fall into the arms of a God you don't trust. If you hesitate to fall into the arms of God, there's a good chance you don't yet know the depth, the height, or the breadth of his deep, deep love for you. Fall in love with the one who waits to catch you up in his strong, gentle arms.

—SANDI PATTY (*Falling Forward*)

# NO OTHER LOVE

*There is no fear in love, for perfect love casts our fear.*
—1 John 4:18 NLT

We are loved passionately by God. And I don't know why. It is a mystery, and it must remain a mystery. To understand it is to dismiss it as we are prone to dismiss every other love in our lives. If we discovered that God loved us because we were smart, then we would try to do everything we could to be smarter so he would love us more. If we met someone smarter than we are, we would fall into despair. So I don't think God will ever let us know the reason that he loves us as passionately as he does. I don't have a clue why God loves me. But I believe in the core of my being that he does. So I surrender to it. I stop fighting it. I cease trying to figure it out. I collapse on it.

Nothing can take his love from us. I can say that of no other love. God pursues us, courts us, and woos us to remind us. His love changes every day; it either intensifies or my understanding of it grows. His love is all we have ever dreamed of. And his kiss, the most passionate we will ever know.

This love is why we were made.

—NICOLE JOHNSON (*Fresh-Brewed Life*)

# THE SIGNS OF A MATURE WOMAN

*He who has begun a good work in you will complete it until*
*the day of Jesus Christ.*

—*Philippians 1:6*

When a woman asks God to work in her heart and mind and learns to replace the old ways with mature thinking, she will notice an incredible difference in her life. Here are some ways to challenge your thinking as a mature woman in process. (It is always good to have a standard by which to check yourself.) Look for these signs in your life. A mature woman:

+ thinks things through to their natural conclusion. She can see not only the present but the future as well.
+ thinks about how her actions will affect others.
+ can see more than one side to any situation.
+ doesn't take things personally.
+ understands that life is never "all about me."
+ is a good, fair, and reasonable negotiator.
+ may like fairy tales, but she likes true stories, too, and she is well aware of the difference.
+ may tire, but she won't allow her fatigue to control her general attitude and demeanor.
+ knows what is best for her and is disciplined enough to go after it.

—JAN SILVIOUS (*Big Girls Don't Whine*)

51

# TRANSFORMING PRAYER

*My ears had heard of you before, but now my eyes have seen you.*
—Job 42:5 NCV

Does the actual act of prayer, of throwing ourselves on the mercy and grace of God, change us? I think one of the most powerful books in the Bible to support and perhaps answer that question is Job.

Job says (and this is my paraphrase): "God, I knew about you before, I knew of all the marvelous things you have done. But now that I have been in the ring with you for several rounds, I have a completely different kind of relationship with you and a new understanding of your greatness."

That's one of the many things I find interesting about Job's story. It's not the story of a treacherous man who encountered God and was converted by the experience. It's the story of a godly man who through tragedy and very bitter dialogue with God came to a whole new understanding of who God is. In other words, he wasn't a man who was changed from "bad" to "good." He was a man changed from "good" to "better"!

I long for that for each one of us. More specifically, I thirst for that in my own life—that my prayer life would become so vibrant, intense, and moment-by-moment I cannot help but be changed.

—SHEILA WALSH (*Get Off Your Knees and Pray*)

# WHAT'S THAT YOU SAY?

> *May Jesus himself and God our Father, who reached out*
> *in love and surprised you with gifts of unending help and*
> *confidence, put a fresh heart in you, invigorate your work,*
> *enliven your speech.*
>
> —2 Thessalonians 2:16–17 MSG

I've got good news: God is real, and he loves you and me like nobody's business! In fact, he loves us so much, he sent his only Son to earth to die for us. Can you believe it? Well, if you can, I've got even better news: Jesus is coming back to earth one of these days, and he's gonna take us believers to heaven to live with him forever. Did you get that? For-EV-uh!

What's that you say? You already knew that? Well, for heaven's sake, how can you just sit there reading? Don't you wanna jump up and dance like a honeybee and shout, "Hallelujah!" every time you think about it? Go ahead. Put the book down— just for a second, mind you! You come right back here as soon as you're finished—then lift up your hands and say, "Thank you, Lord! I praise you, Father! Glory to you, O God most high."

When I think that the one who created the universe—the one who hung the moon, ignited the sun, and flung the stars across the sky—also created me, I'm overwhelmed with wonder. When I realize the horrific sacrifice Jesus made for me, I'm moved to tears. And when I remember that there's a mansion waiting for me in heaven, I'm excited beyond words.

—THELMA WELLS (*The Buzz*)

# THE GET-ACQUAINTED SESSION

*The LORD used to speak to Moses face to face, as one speaks to a friend.*

—Exodus 33:11 NRSV

Sooner or later everyone experiences the reality that sometimes life is hard, pain is tangible, and hurt is genuine. But Jesus, who looks past the shell to the you inside, is interested in the details.

We all know people who constantly look at everything but us while we're talking to them, distracted instead of listening. Not Jesus. In fact, I believe if he were physically sitting in the room with me he would stop to hear my story, and while he listened, he would look me in the eye.

Maybe it makes you a little uncomfortable to picture yourself sitting alone with Jesus in a personal get-acquainted session. If so, you may feel inadequate, illegitimate, inferior, or imperfect, even though you've been told again and again that those aren't the feelings you were created to have. Maybe you know who Jesus is, but you don't know him. You have prayed until you are out of breath, yet you still feel empty and incomplete, so you stopped praying.

Try again. Talk to him. Ask him to become evident to you. And once you've asked him to authenticate himself, you must also be genuine with him. You have to be real.

—NATALIE GRANT (*The Real Me*)

# ANIMAL BABIES

*The wild animals honor me, the jackals and the owls, because I
provide water in the desert and streams in the wasteland.*

—Isaiah 43:20 NIV

If you watch Animal Planet you notice that, in the animal kingdom,
there are multiple mothering styles. You've got your marsupials
who carry their young in their pouches; the mares who let their
babies run alongside them and try to keep up. There are the mom
cats who evenly divide their time between giving their kitties milk
and giving them tongue baths. Mama ducks march in front and
expect their baby ducklings to waddle in line behind.

I found it fascinating that mama eagles anticipate their babies
leaving the nest even while they are building it. The mama eagle
adds sharp and jagged objects toward the bottom of the nest before
they line it with soft things so that as the baby eaglet gets larger and
starts wearing away the soft lining, it is met with things that make
the nest gradually more and more uncomfortable. This is so the
baby will *want* to leave. Perhaps this is why the eagle is our national
symbol—we admire the way they encourage their adolescents to
leave the nest. I'm just saying—something to think about!

Other little known mom facts: Polar bears sleep through
labor (I wonder what's in their epidurals!), and elephants give
birth to 200-pound "babies" (give that elephant mom whatever
the polar bear is having!).

—ANITA RENFROE (*If It's Not One Thing, It's Your Mother*)

# HE CHOSE US

*God has said, "I will never leave you nor forsake you."*
—Hebrews 13:5

Prior to the cross, Jesus endured hours of agonizing physical and emotional torture. Yet not once did he cry out. It was not until that culminating pain of separation from God that the heart of Jesus broke.

Jesus took upon Himself every sin, every pagan inclination, and all that is unholy in creation, and he died for it. For Jesus, the greatest hurt was the momentary abandonment from God, his Father. It happened because God, in his holiness, cannot look upon sin. When Jesus became the embodiment of sin, he was rejected. He was abandoned. He was ditched.

If you can identify with that feeling, you're not alone. But I've got great news for you. Jesus' separation from God—and ours—was bridged immediately the moment that sin-debt was paid. He was instantly restored to full correctedness with his Father. It's absolutely mind-boggling: we too are instantly awarded full family membership the moment we confess our sin and receive the forgiveness for which Jesus died.

That means we will never be abandoned by him. We will never be a throwaway from him. We will never be rejected by him. We'll never be ditched by him. We didn't get left by him. He chose us. He loves us and will never leave us.

—MARILYN MEBERG (*Love Me Never Leave Me*)

# STUDENTS OF LIFE

> *Jesus looked up at his disciples and said, "Do not judge, and*
> *you will not be judged; do not condemn, and you will not be*
> *condemned. Forgive, and you will be forgiven."*
>
> —Luke 6:37 NRSV

We're all looking for a place to be totally accepted just as we are, without criticism from others. We all want to be in a church body or group of friends or with a support team that will stand with us when we're facing an earth-shattering issue in our own lives. Especially if it's a private thing—struggling with homosexuality, going through a divorce, having an abortion, being involved in an affair, running from the law—any of those things qualify. And more. We all want somebody in our lives who won't pass judgment.

Nobody has answers to these dilemmas. We're all students of life with its confusing struggles. Let's try to be patient with each other, giving the benefit of the doubt and waiting for the Lord to work in the lives of those we love, while we give our prayerful support.

Remember these words written by George Washington Carver, a Negro slave in the 1800s: "How far you go in life depends on your being tender with the young, compassionate with the aged, sympathetic with the striving, and tolerant of the weak and the strong. Because someday in life you will have been all of these."

—LUCI SWINDOLL (*Life! Celebrate It*)

# LET'S LISTEN TO JAMES

*Consider it a sheer gift, friends, when tests and challenges come at you from all sides. You know that under pressure, your faith-life is forced into the open and shows its true colors.*

—*James 1:2–3* MSG

One of my favorite books is the book of James. I'm aware that some people aren't fond of James, because he talks a lot about works. But I love that the apostle James brings balance and accountability to the believer—and to me, because I need it! While I know God loves me no matter what I do, I also need to know that disobedience does interfere with my progress and growth. I'm certainly no theologian, but I know I'm often my biggest obstacle along the way.

So . . . come join me. Let's crack open the book and see what James has to say about hardship. He begins by saying, "Consider it a sheer gift, friends." Hardship is a gift? Well, I don't want it under my Christmas tree! It's just natural to bolt and run when life tightens up. I guess that's why James had to tell us to sit tight and be thankful. Even though this is a tall order from James, it's also full of hope. When I understand that pain, loss, and difficulty have a purpose, a work to do within me, I can learn to see meaning in my suffering. I'm grateful James reminds me of it. I don't know how God does it; I'm just grateful he does.

—PATSY CLAIRMONT (*All Cracked Up*)

# STEP INTO THE RIVER

*When the priests got to the Jordan and their feet touched the*
*water at the edge (the Jordan overflows its banks throughout*
*the harvest), the flow of water stopped.*

—Joshua 3:15–16 MSG

Sometimes, even when we realize we are beautiful, free, and beloved children of God, we continue to play the victim. I found it was tempting to stay mentally stuck on one sad page of my life and never fall forward into freedom. Don't make that mistake.

I urge you to consider making a choice, right now, today, to get well. Even if all you can pray right now is, "God, help me be willing to be *willing*"—it's a beginning, that important first step.

One of the songs we're working on for my next CD is called "Step into Joy," and it's about deciding whether you are going to stay on the sidelines and whine, "Why doesn't joy ever come to me?" or step right into it. I love the story in Joshua 3 where God instructed the Israelites to cross the river Jordan. That river was roaring! But God promised he'd make a way. And as soon as the priests who carried the ark reached the Jordan and their feet touched the water's edge, the water from upstream stopped flowing. Did you catch that? They actually had to step into the river *before* God parted the waters. God blesses our baby steps of faith.

—SANDI PATTY (*Falling Forward*)

# HOLES IN MY SOUL

*He satisfies the longing soul, and fills the hungry soul with goodness.*

—Psalm 107:9

Coming face-to-face with the fact that there are empty places in our lives that haven't been filled. Yearnings. Wanting more than we have: more love, more enjoyment, more passion, more hope, more rest. The hope of finding something that will satisfy the rumbling we feel in the stomach of our souls.

Our yearnings, longings, cravings, and hopes are telling us something: there isn't enough love, peace, hope, friendship, and intimacy on this earth to completely satisfy us. We will always want more.

This feels like a no-win situation. Are longings one big cosmic setup for frustration? Perhaps, if we view them as something to be overcome or eradicated. If we spend more time trying to get them "filled up." But if we lean in close, and put our ears to the chest of our soul and listen to our longings—they can teach us to understand God and ourselves in a way that would not happen if we were permitted to have everything we longed for.

The holes in us are actually *supposed* to be there. The holes are the things that make us who we are. The holes are the places God has reserved in us for himself! The longings identify our real hunger. A hunger that drives us to him to be satisfied.

—NICOLE JOHNSON (*Fresh-Brewed Life*)

# THE SECRET

*I have learned the secret of being content in any and every*
*situation.*

—*Philippians 4:11 NIV*

I know a secret! What secret is that? It's the same secret the apostle Paul spoke about in the book of Philippians. Contentment with the life you have been given is a choice.

Your true value is not about whom you married or didn't marry. It is not about how good you are at what you do. It is really just about one thing: What is your relationship to God? Have you made the decision to allow him to call the shots? Have you decided to listen to him and let him comfort your soul? Have you given up your perceptions of how you think life should be? Have you accepted the fact that your life is in his hands, and that he will enable you to do everything you need to do? Can you face each day with the confidence that you can do all things through Christ?

If so, my friend you are living with joy and contentment the life you have been given. What a difference it makes when you give in and give up! You reach the point of living life with nothing to prove and nothing to lose. You can choose contentment and accept the sweet comfort of Christ's presence and provision for every step of the way.

—JAN SILVIOUS (*Big Girls Don't Whine*)

# GOD'S THOUGHTS

*Your thoughts—how rare, how beautiful! God, I'll never comprehend them! I couldn't even begin to count them—any more than I could count the sand of the sea.*

—Psalm 139:17–18 MSG

Did you know that the God of the universe, the sovereign ruler over all the earth is thinking about you? Our president has the people of the United States of America on his mind on a daily basis. Occasionally, some are granted the privilege of a personal meeting and a few exchanged words; then, it is time to move on. He probably doesn't go to sleep each night thinking of everyone he met that day, never mind the millions he has never met.

But God our Father is thinking about us every day, and his thoughts are one hundred percent accurate. He doesn't think we are smarter or less able than we are. He doesn't think we are as godly as the image we try to present at times or dismiss us as hopeless wretches when that is how we feel. God knows all that is true and loves us totally.

God always sees us as beautiful and amazing; it is we who change as the world around us changes. Our challenge is to keep the image of the woman God sees more prominent than the image of the woman we see with our human eyes. The new hat that God offers for our wardrobe represents putting on his truth every time we look in our human mirror.

—SHEILA WALSH (*I'm Not Wonder Woman*)

# SINGING AND DANCING

*Give thanks to the LORD! Call upon His name; make known*
*His deeds among the peoples! Sing to Him, sing psalms to*
*Him; talk of all His wondrous works!*

—*1 Chronicles 16:8–9*

Do you remember that old, traditional song that says, "If you're happy and you know it, then your life will surely show it"? That should be a theme song for Christians everywhere because we know Jesus.

We're admonished to praise God in good times and bad, to praise him with everything we have, to honor him with singing and dancing. We're to clap our hands, stomp our feet, and shout hurrah so we show the world the joy we find in the Lord. Except for the few people we may scare off by our wild exaltations, that kind of joy is contagious. It's infectious. It's impossible to resist. Even God himself is drawn to us when we praise him with all our being—and then he joins in the praises himself!

To be honest, that's almost too much for my poor little mind to grasp. But I know with all my heart that when I sing praises to God, something is happening in heaven, because my spirit gets relief, my emotions change from negative to positive, my mind feels inspired to think more wisely, my heart is guarded from the pain I might otherwise experience, my physical body relaxes, and I'm drawn into his presence knowing his loving arms are wrapped around me.

—THELMA WELLS (*Listen Up, Honey*)

# WHO AM I?

> *"Before I formed you in the womb I knew you, before you were*
> *born I set you apart," says the* LORD.
>
> —*Jeremiah 1:5* NIV

If all we do is look at our outer shell, we're not all that unique. For example, there are many people who look like me: blonde, medium-length hair; petite; blue eyes. Actually, I think I have really pretty eyes. They are as blue as the Caribbean Sea. The depth of their color reminds me of the true depth that is inside me.

Writing that felt funny, but it also felt good. Why are we so timid to point out the things we like about ourselves? I've always spent my time listing those things about me that I don't like. But it sure feels good to recognize those things about my shell that I do like.

But who I am isn't the color of my eyes. I am the one peering out of them. I am the one who is hiding inside this skin of mine. And who is that, exactly? Well, I'm still figuring that out. I don't know if there is one answer or several. I am not the woman I was five years ago, and hopefully I am not the woman I will be five years from now. I am evolving, changing, becoming. It's not so much who I am but that I am a work in progress, striving to become more like the one who made me.

—NATALIE GRANT (*The Real Me*)

# A HANGING TAG

*God looked over all that he had made, and it was excellent in every way.*

—Genesis 1:31 *TLB*

They say that the average size woman in America is a size 14. The funny side of me wants to ask, "So who wants to be below average?" and the more reasonable side of me asks, "If you are healthy and active, what difference does the number on the tag of your pants make?" But let's face it: When it comes to our bodies, circumnavigating all the messages we receive in our culture is not for the faint of heart.

I will never forget a comment I heard from a fashion designer several years ago. He said that the fashion industry is all about the clothes, not the people wearing the clothes, and the best way to highlight the clothes is to drape them over a "human hanger" rather than an actual person whose curves would interrupt the lines of the design.

I bought a blouse the other day. It was hand beaded, striking, beautiful (and on sale!) But I was as taken by the message on the hanging tag as I was with the blouse. It reads: "I am your special garment. I am unique and often hand-woven, hand-beaded, hand-printed, and hand-painted. My defects are part of my beauty!" If only we came with such a tag!

—ANITA RENFROE (*If You Can't Lose It, Decorate It!*)

# GOD'S DIVINE MASTER PLAN

*The wise mind will know the time and the way.*
—*Ecclesiastes 8:5 NRSV*

To what degree do facts determine your decisions? Frankly, I tend to be a "fly-by-the-seat-of-the-pants" type of decision maker. I like to know the facts, but sometimes there's simply too much information.

I think it is wise to be a fact gatherer and make well-informed decisions based on those facts. The truth is, though, some experiences come into our lives whether or not we have the facts.

For those times when our knowledge of the facts does not seem to influence the circumstances in which we find ourselves, it is important to remember there is a divine master plan. The master plan that is based upon God's love for his creation provides peace in the midst of turmoil, faith in the midst of uncertainty, and joy in spite of loss.

It is encouraging to know we're not alone as we make our decisions in life. We have the freedom of personal choice, but we also have the promise of God's participation. We are not robots responding to divine directional switches. The way our decisions are made reflects our human uniqueness. But the existence of a divine master plan where our decisions are honored or perhaps even altered reminds us we all have the promise of a divine partnership.

—MARILYN MEBERG (*The Decision of a Lifetime*)

# WORDS THAT STING

*When you talk, do not say harmful things, but say what people need—words that will help others become stronger.*

—*Ephesians 4:29* NCV

When you think about the relationships in your life—friends and acquaintances, family members, co-workers, or fellow students—is there anybody who has hurt you by what they've said? Their words might have been an offhanded comment or a momentary attack. Their words might have been just an aside, but they stung deeply and left you reeling.

I want to suggest six principles that often help me when I'd rather react or attack instead of listening to the one who makes me feel chided. Although the pain may not go away immediately (or maybe ever), the effort to apply helpful actions will see you through and keep you from giving up on that other individual.

1. *Let the person finish talking before you say anything.* Sometimes all the other person wants is to make her point known.
2. *State back to the person what you think she said.* We can easily misunderstand what's been communicated, so try to repeat to the other person.
3. *Own what you believe to be true about her words.*
4. *Thank her for being honest with you.*
5. *Try not to personalize what is not your problem.*
6. *Pray with the person to whom you have been listening.*

—LUCI SWINDOLL (*Life! Celebrate It*)

# THE FILTERS OF KINDNESS

*Who can find a virtuous woman: for her price is far above*
*rubies. . . . She openeth her mouth with wisdom; and in her*
*tongue is the law of kindness.*

—Proverbs 31:10, 26 *KJV*

What coils your rubber bands into a flaming missile? Tele-marketers? Taxes? Teenagers? Tardiness? Traffic?

I remember a male stranger being infuriated because he thought my friend and I shouldn't have eased into his lane of traffic, even though he wasn't close and we had scads of room. The guy sped up and then went bonkers as he tried repeatedly to force us off the highway. Then he pulled in front of us and slammed on his brakes.

More times than I would like to admit, I've emotionally slammed on the brakes of my frustration in front of a loved one. But I've learned it can take a lifetime to correct that kind of tire-screeching approach. It leaves skid marks on people's spirits, and they become self-protective and look for the nearest exit.

Scripture guides us toward more dignified resolutions, ones that leave all of us intact. When we put our words through the filters of kindness, anger won't have a chance to exact a greater price from everyone involved. If our motive is to reconcile differences and not to offend our offender or to prove her wrong, then we will have a heart resolve that leaves us feeling settled and holds the potential for restoration of the relationship.

—PATSY CLAIRMONT (*I Second That Emotion*)

# SURVIVAL TIPS
*(Extra help for the early days following a crisis)*

> *Whatever things were written before were written for our*
> *learning, that we through the patience and comfort of the*
> *Scriptures might have hope.*

—Romans 15:4

You might feel like you are losing your memory or going crazy. Don't worry—this is normal. Just go with it!

Keep your tasks for each day small and short. Make lists. This will clear your mind just a bit and unburden your overtaxed brain. Write each one down and check them off—even if your list says, "Get up. Get dressed. Cry. Dry tears. Eat. Nap. Cry. Get undressed. Pray for the day to end. Sleep."

Have a good cry if you need to, whenever you can. Tears are a language God understands, and they clear your body of built-up toxins.

Laugh as soon as you possibly can, even if it is dark humor. Laughter releases tension and perks up your whole internal system. You'll know you will live through your crisis the minute you can laugh.

You may feel like you need to be demoted to life's slow class. You probably won't be able to read a lot, and the Bible may seem daunting. Be gentle with yourself. Meditate on one or two comforting Scriptures or quotes. Talk to God as if he were your friend, and tell him everything without fear. He can take it.

—SANDI PATTY (*Falling Forward*)

# MORE SURVIVAL TIPS
*(Extra help for the early days following a crisis)*

> *Pursue righteousness, godliness, faith, love, patience, gentleness.*
> —1 Timothy 6:11

Remind yourself that if you've survived thus far, you'll make it around the bend and be stronger than ever before. You are probably already starting to grasp one of the gifts of having been in crisis. You get the gift of perspective—it is very clear now what matters and what doesn't.

Visualize yourself in the arms of Jesus. Let him hold you and remind you that you are his beloved child. Your picture is still on his refrigerator.

Breathe in, breathe out, put one foot in front of the other. Some of these early days are simply about endurance, holding on, and letting time do its work. You will feel better. You will survive.

Hold your loved ones close, especially if they are able to express their love in kind and helpful ways.

If none of the above works for you, you might do what I did—go to a batting cage! I would spend about fifteen minutes trying to hit the stuffing out of a baseball. Every time I would swing, I would really get into it, sometimes even imagining that I was hitting the problems right out of my life. It worked for me!

—SANDI PATTY (*Falling Forward*)

# THIRSTY FOR GOD

*He satisfies the thirsty soul and fills the hungry soul with good.*

—*Psalm 107:9* TLB

Saint Augustine said that our souls will never find their rest until they find it in God. *He* is the treasure. Our longings will point the way to him every single time. Each longing in my life that I have discovered, or that has discovered me, drives me to confront a truth that I might not have confronted otherwise: I need God. I am thirsty for God. Desperately thirsty. In every area of my life. I was made by him and for him, and apart from him, I will not be satisfied. My desires for things to fill me and make me whole bear witness to the one who will fill me ultimately. My longing to be known reveals to me the existence of a greater knowing by the one who created me. My hunger for heaven gently sings to me a haunting lullaby that reminds me why we will never feel fully at home here.

It is easy to miss this. Listen closely to your longings.

God is the only one big enough to hold our longings. He created them, and when we bring them to him, we have finally found the right place.

—NICOLE JOHNSON (*Fresh-Brewed Life*)

# SHE "GOT IT"!

> *It was Christ who gave some to be apostles, some to be prophets,*
> *some to be evangelists, and some to be pastors and teachers, to*
> *prepare God's people for works of service, so that the body of*
> *Christ may . . . become mature, attaining to the whole measure*
> *of the fullness of Christ.*
>
> —*Ephesians 4:11–13 NIV*

Hannah Whitall Smith, author of *The Christian's Secret of a Happy Life,* was a woman of profound influence in her time as well as today. But she didn't become that woman of influence naturally or overnight. She was born into a prosperous family who practiced a barren religion that left her with no answers. When she and her husband, Robert Pearsall Smith, came to Jesus Christ, she found a new source of hope. But even then, everything was not wonderful. She struggled with her longing for some physical evidence that she truly knew Jesus. Life wasn't what Hannah thought it would be.

But at that point, Hannah came to believe, even in her pursuit of certainty, that *faith* was the stabilizing message of Scripture. She chose to take God at his word. She chose to recognize that he was always with her. She chose to believe that he is a loving Father. These choices enabled her to grasp the life for which God had created her.

Hannah Whitall Smith "got it," and as a result, enabled others to "get it" as well. Despite the challenges of her circumstances, she chose to become a mature, fully-committed woman of God.

—JAN SILVIOUS (*Big Girls Don't Whine*)

# TIME WITH THE FATHER

*Draw near to God, and he will draw near to you.*

—James 4:8 NRSV

I truly believe that one of the most important lessons I am learning at the moment is the call to spend some alone time with God in the midst of the rush of my life. Christ knew that his times were in the Father's hands. He knew that he was about to walk through the darkest night a human being would ever experience, and it was in his times of quiet communion with his Father that he received the grace and strength for what was to come. He made a place in his inner closet to sit with his Father and be still.

Think about your life for a moment. Are you anxious about anything? What are the thoughts that typically run through your head as you rush from thing to thing? When was the last time you found a quiet spot to sit and do nothing but enjoy being there (without falling asleep!)? Are you facing a dark and difficult time in your life?

It isn't enough to simply remove activity from your life. You must replace it with something better. You are invited to fill the void with the intentional habits of a strong, peaceful woman. You can live in this world with its constant change and threats, from within and without, and know his perfect peace.

—SHEILA WALSH (*I'm Not Wonder Woman*)

# TURNING TROUBLES INTO JOY

*May the Lord continually bless you with heaven's blessings as
well as with human joys.*

—Psalm 128:5 *TLB*

Sister, did you know that hard times and messy relationships can
help you appreciate your blessings? Most people who know me
today will tell you I am a happy, joyful person, but I've known
some hard, hard times.

Granny Harrell raised me in a humble back-alley apartment,
but it was a palace compared with the place my young, disabled
mother lived. When I visited her in the small tent she had set up
on a vacant lot, we slept together on a narrow cot.

Hard times, for sure.

I've endured a broken heart, an empty bank account, and a
serious health problem more times than I care to remember. But
all those messes in my past—and those I may face in my future—
just serve as the dark canvas that makes the bright happiness of
my life today all the more noticeable, all the more precious.

But Jesus has already helped me turn my troubles into joy so
that today my life is full and happy—and I'm still living here on
old planet Earth. Just imagine what kind of happiness he has in
store for me when I move on to that grand family gathering up in
heaven.

—THELMA WELLS (*Listen Up, Honey*)

# EAGERLY CHOSEN

*The LORD said: "Before I formed you in the womb I knew y*
*before you were born I sanctified you."*
—Jeremiah 1:5

We are chosen. We are set apart. We are meant to live big,
lives full of joy—unafraid, loved supremely by the one who c
ated us. And God didn't choose us because he thinks we
always going to win. In fact, he chose us knowing that we may b
clumsy, self-conscious, ashamed, too quick to give our opinion
dreadful at listening, full of pride, shy, too smart for our own
good, or possessing a host of other characteristics that are
deemed by the world as the traits of a loser. God knows us intimately, in all our imperfections, and he loves us beyond measure.
That truth—rooted deeply in our hearts, coloring every thought
that runs through our minds—is more than enough to see us
through the game.

When was the last time you were eagerly chosen, picked out
of the crowd, or given recognition? Do you remember what that
felt like? Were you surprised, or did you see it coming? How did
the people around you react? What would your life look like
today if you truly believed what God says about you—that you
were chosen, even before you were born? Understanding who
you really are will change your life.

—NATALIE GRANT (*The Real Me*)

# DIVINE DESIGN

*I will spend time thinking about your miracles.*

—Psalm 145:5 NIrV

Even though some companies are trying to balance out the messaging, it's hard to hear over the roar of the fashion industry at large. We get mixed messages from the media to "love" and take care of our bodies, yet most of us feel as if our bodies have betrayed us through some cruel metabolic joke, hormonal upheavals, and the effects of time and gravity. No wonder it's such a struggle to move from lamenting our bodies to accepting them. Learning to *celebrate* our bodies is an even taller order.

Your body is a miracle; you know that, right? The fact that you have the organs and systems to keep everything running and cleaned out and oxygenated and balanced is nothing short of Divine Design. If you were to segment out just one minute of your existence, a mere sixty seconds, and have a biologist break down for you what happens in that single moment of respiration and cell rejuvenation alone, you would kiss your own toes (if you could reach them) and bless your very busy body for all it takes to keep you going from breath to breath. Because God has created you so uniquely and intricately, you are "Designer" no matter what label you wear on your clothes.

—ANITA RENFROE (*If You Can't Lose It, Decorate It!*)

# A HOPE AND A FUTURE

> "I know the plans I have for you," declares the LORD, "plans to
> prosper you and not to harm you, plans to give you hope and
> a future."
>
> —*Jeremiah 29:11* NIV

In spite of our best-laid plans, we all experience being broadsided
by the unexpected and the unwanted. To what degree does the
divine master plan figure into our experiences? In fact, what is a
divine master plan?

The Bible clearly states that God does, indeed, have a plan for
each of us. We are not creatures wandering haphazardly from point
A to point B. We are told that his plan is designed to give us a future
and a hope. The degree to which we can mess up the divine master
plan with poor choices or disobedience is a matter of some debate.
But I do know this about the divine master plan: God created the
plan to show his love for us, not his judgment of our mistakes. His
plan offers forgiveness when we need it, encouragement when we
feel weak, and clarity when we don't see clearly.

If you've ever thought you have blown it too badly for God to
love you, forgive you, or make anything out of your life, remember: Not only are you a divine treasure, you are one for whom
God has a plan—a plan that will give you a future and a hope.

—MARILYN MEBERG (*The Decision of a Lifetime*)

# STARTING POINTS

*Your beginnings will seem humble, so prosperous will your future be.*

—Job 8:7 NIV

Do you travel? I do! A lot! And there are certain things I have to take on every trip. I've learned first to work on the knowns—cosmetics, underwear, medications, pajamas, and night-light (I never travel without a night-light). Then I move to clothes, shoes, and accessories, depending on the season, engagement, and destination. It finally comes down to a science. Starting with what I know (in any dilemma) is helpful and will ultimately get the job done.

Starting points of any endeavor can be debilitating. We don't want to start something because it seems too hard, too involved, and too much work. Whether it's writing a term paper, building a house, saving money, losing weight, or packing for a trip, we don't know where to begin—so we don't.

Life's highway is littered with people who had good intentions but never punched the start button. I know a few people like this, and their questions are always the same: "How did you do that?" "How do you always finish projects?" "How did you plan that far-fetched vacation to that out-of-the-way spot?" The answer to each of these is the same—*start*. Nobody has the key to the outcome, but we all have the key to possibility. Open the door and walk through it.

—LUCI SWINDOLL (*Life! Celebrate It*)

# WHAT IS HOPE?

*Lord, what do I look for? My hope is in you.*
—Psalm 39:7 NIV

I wonder if it's possible to fully describe hope or how it feels. I know hope feels bigger than my ability to hold it inside without becoming airborne. It activates fresh shipments of blood, energy, and gratefulness that seem to surge with holy force. Hope seems light like a wisp of down on a soft breeze; it's sparkling clean like a new sky after a spring rain. Hope is a baby's coo, a toddler's first step, a prodigal's return.

Wait . . . oh, now I'm getting it: hope is an infinity pool that has no boundaries. It can't be limited to a word, a phrase, a dissertation, or even a heavily-volumed library. Hope is eternal and, therefore, beyond us to define. Yet sometimes I see hope in a life, and when it's there you can spot it, even if you can't touch it or taste it, because hope is palpable.

Hope is definitely an inside job. While we can't pump it up, we know it when it arrives. It fills the air with honeysuckle and fresh water. Hope shows us a better way, a higher path, a different perspective. Hope reconfigures hearts. Redirects energies. We not only pursue hope as a lifeline, but also hope pursues us. It is the essence of Christ.

—PATSY CLAIRMONT (*I Second That Emotion*)

# PARTNERSHIP WITH GOD

*Jesus said, "Get up, take your bedroll, start walking." The man
was healed on the spot. He picked up his bedroll and walked
off.*
—John 5:8–9 MSG

If you've ever had a garden of any kind, you know that God is the
one who does the miracle in making the seed grow. However,
you also know that you had to get out of your bed, plant the
seed, water it, and weed it. Growing fruits, veggies, or flowers is
a partnership between the gardener and the Creator.

The same is true for recovering from any trauma or crisis in
your life. It has to be a partnership between you and God. God
will bless, guide, lead, and heal. But you have to seek out the help.
You have to dial the number of a recommended counselor. You
have to read books that will help retrain your brain. You have to
have a "come to Jesus" moment every day. When the man at the
pool of Bethesda assured Jesus he wanted to get well, Jesus said,
"Get up! Pick up your mat and walk" (John 5:8). He asked the
man to *do something* to prove his desire was sincere.

What I have learned is that lasting change means to conscientiously make three joyful choices: the choice *to reveal,* the
choice *to heal,* and the choice *to be real.* (And isn't it just too cute
how they all rhyme?)

—SANDI PATTY (*Falling Forward*)

# HE GIVES US HOPE

*We have this hope as an anchor for the soul, firm and secure.*
—*Hebrews 6:19* NIV

God gives us some powerful promises to live by. We are not without hope. He has given us his word that one day we will live in a better place than here. A place where our longings will be met. First Corinthians 13, verse 9, reminds us that "for now we only know in part. We love in part, we speak truth in part." Everything is in part. Can you remember when you were a child? You loved as a child loves, simple and free. It was good, but it wasn't even close to what it would be. And remember when you grew older? You loved as an adult, passionate and committed. But one day—one glorious day—we will love as God loves.

Right now, it's like looking in one of those mirrors that isn't glass. It's really difficult to see anything. You get an image, but there's no definition. However, one day we will see him face-to-face—his glorious face to our less-than-we-want-it-to-be face. Right now we can only see a dim reflection, but one day we will look into his eyes—the eyes that have seen from the foundation of the world.

—NICOLE JOHNSON (*Fresh-Brewed Life*)

# WITH ME IN THE FUTURE

*Continue to reverence the Lord all the time, for surely you have
a wonderful future ahead of you.*

—Proverbs 23:18 *TLB*

As I look back over the seasons of my life, I feel as if I have spent
so many years thinking about what it would be like when . . .
What will life be like when I get married? What will it be like
when I have children? What will life be like when I have an
empty nest? What will it be like when I'm a grandmother? Now I
know the answers to all those questions. What life will be like
then has been revealed, but only in the past few years have I
stopped thinking about the future and what it will be like. I finally
have learned a great truth: when each season comes, it will be
what it will be. There is an appointed time for every event yet to
occur, and God will be with me in the future just as he has been
alongside me all the way, every step, for every event and for
every feeling, good or bad.

We have today, my friend. That's it. We have the joy of yesterday's memories and the delight of future anticipation, but we
have no tangible reality except today. This day is yours. This is
your time to do, to be, to accomplish, to fulfill your reason for
living.

—JAN SILVIOUS (*Smart Girls Think Twice*)

# OH, TO BE FREE

*The LORD sets prisoners free.*
—Psalm 146:7 NIV

The ability to dream and to believe God's dream for our lives requires a liberty of soul and spirit. Although our circumstances may be confining, our spirits do not have to be confined. Internally, we can be free!

I wonder what comes to your mind when you reflect on the word *freedom*. Perhaps your first thoughts are of happy memories, going off to college, or driving your first car. You may think of external freedom, of someone released from prison or hostages liberated. As world events are piped into our homes every day, you may think of images from overseas. I will never forget the pictures of high school girls in Afghanistan who were able to take off their traditional burkas after the liberation of Kabul. Their smiling faces told a story of what it felt like to finally be free to expose their faces to the sunlight.

The freedom that we are looking at here, however, is not simply external freedom. What we are pursuing, by God's grace, is the internal liberty that comes from Christ alone. Freedom is not the absence of bars but the presence of Christ. It is not a changing of our circumstances but a changing of our hearts.

—SHEILA WALSH (*God Has a Dream for Your Life*)

# MY MEMORY LIFELINE

*Oh, how I love all you've revealed; I reverently ponder it all the day long.*

—Psalm 119:97 MSG

Before I head out to remind others what God has done for us, I always want to know what God, our Creator, has said to us. So I study his Word. I read the Bible and soak up the teaching in it. I immerse myself in the Scriptures and fill my head with its promises and teachings so that whenever I'm confronted with a challenging situation, a difficult choice, a personal setback, I can find in my memory a lifeline of scriptural guidance and encouragement that will help me take the next step.

This practice began for me when I was a child. I memorized two of the most treasured passages in the Bible: the Lord's Prayer (found in Matthew 6:9–13) and the Twenty-third Psalm.

My beloved great-grandmother taught me to pull those passages from my memory and recite them in stressful situations to find both peace and strength. I've followed her advice all my life. I've hurriedly whispered those words to myself in no telling how many far-flung airports, hospital waiting rooms, conference arenas, business offices, hotel rooms, and government offices. And every time I recite them, I can feel my worry easing, my blood pressure dropping, my muscles relaxing. The experience teaches me again and again the truth and power of God's Word.

—THELMA WELLS (*The Buzz*)

# INSIDE AND OUT

*Great is our Lord, and mighty in power; His understanding is infinite.*
—Psalm 147:5

If God sees me as priceless, as a treasure, as one worthy of sacrificing his only Son for, how can I believe less of myself? To believe myself unlovable, unreachable, or unacceptable is to believe that God made a mistake. And God does not make mistakes. His understanding is infinite.

Anyone capable of mistakes would be finite, not infinite. God is not like me. I make mistakes and misjudgments. I change my mind and say things I don't mean. I have destructive thoughts at times. Not God. His works are wonderful, and he thinks about me a lot (see Psalm 40:5)! In fact, as unimaginable as it might seem, God thinks so much about me, and about you, that his thoughts are too many to number.

I belong.

I am accepted.

I am loved.

I am alive.

To say these words and believe them to be true is absolutely mind-blowing. In the midst of my struggles with self-acceptance, I came to understand that God really knows me—inside and out. He knows when I'm faking, and he knows when I'm being real with him. He desires the real me. And he wants nothing more from me than that.

—NATALIE GRANT (*The Real Me*)

# YOU CAN'T TAKE IT WITH YOU

*Jesus said to them, "Watch out! Be on your guard against all kinds of greed; a man's life does not consist in the abundance of his possessions."*

—Luke 12:15 NIV

Jesus spoke more about money, wealth, the problems associated with money (usually from having so much that you forget the source of the wealth), how to give it (cheerfully) and save it (like the ants), and how to make more in your endeavors (by investing rather than hoarding) than he did about the existence of heaven or hell.

I think this is incredibly interesting of Jesus to camp on the subject matter that reveals our true feelings about God's provision, his sovereignty, the abilities he's gifted us with by which we make a living, the virtue of generosity, and what makes life worth living. So what does money represent for you? Security? Stability? The ability to provide for your family? Power? A hedge against hard times?

Whether you are barely getting by, just getting along, starting to get ahead, or getting rich, you can view your financial status in a way where "getting" is not the primary goal of your life. You can't take it with you, but you can do a lot of good with what you're entrusted with while you're here. Your money or your life, indeed. If time is money, and time is life, you can literally exchange one for the other. Choose carefully.

—ANITA RENFROE (*If You Can't Lose It, Decorate It!*)

# THE BIBLE TELLS US SO

*All Scripture is God-breathed and is useful for teaching, rebuking, correcting and training in righteousness.*

—2 Timothy 3:16 NIV

The Bible tells us who God is and also much of what he thinks. I realize some of you reading this may be skeptics who don't believe the Bible. The reality is, I can't prove the Bible to be true. There are, however, many convincing reasons to believe it to be true. To cite a few, isn't it interesting that this Book has inspired the highest level of moral living known to humankind? And this Book speaks of a Christ who is admired and quoted even by skeptics?

Consider this: the Bible is made up of sixty-six books that evolved over a period of fifteen centuries. It was written in three different languages by forty different human authors ranging from kings to fishermen. All those authors with centuries between their writings are in total agreement as they describe who God is and what his purpose is.

How does one account for that total unity of theme and message? Quite simply, it's because God wrote the Book! He has a message he wants his people to hear, so he stated it over and over through different biblical writers down through the centuries. That message has never changed: God loves his people and wants a personal relationship with them.

—MARILYN MEBERG (*The Decision of a Lifetime*)

# TELLING THE TRUTH

*He who speaks truth declares righteousness.*
—Proverbs 12:17

The book *Telling the Truth: The Gospel as Tragedy, Comedy, and Fairy Tale* by Frederick Buechner has a wonderful story about how the role of the pastor—or anyone—is to stand in the pulpit and simply tell the truth. If you don't tell the truth, everyone in the building knows you're lying.

I discovered that in my own life. I spent so many years in ministry trying to be inspirational, trying to show what it would look like if someone sold out to God. Now I know that my apparent perfection left a gulf between me and other people. My open brokenness was the first bridge that allowed people to cross over and come to me.

Admitting our need for help to quit being victims or abusers or addicts or hypocrites can free us and the generations to come. I want to live with real people. And I want to be real too.

Perhaps some of us walk with a limp. Perhaps we will always have scars. The one we follow has carried his scars for a long time, and he longs for us to show him ours so he can heal them. And he longs for us to reach out to one another as servants and fellow travelers on this treacherous journey called life.

—SHEILA WALSH (*Life Is Tough But God Is Faithful*)

# START WITH WHAT YOU KNOW

*To him who by the power at work within us is able to*
*accomplish abundantly far more than all we can ask or*
*imagine.*

—*Ephesians 3:20* NRSV

I live in the first and only house I have ever built and, I'm sure, ever will. It's a once-in-a-lifetime project. When I started, I knew zero about buying a lot and building a house on it. But I punched start, and my desires began to move down the track. I started with what I knew—I called a realtor, hired a builder, began making drawings of what I wanted, sent e-mails, asked questions, and kept going. I started doing what I knew and when we start there, the unknowns begin to clear up little by little.

We will never get anywhere unless we start. If we begin with a feeling or an urge to do something we've never done before, and if we have the confidence and freedom to believe it can be done, then somehow the difficulties attached to it begin to lose their scary power of intimidation. By trusting in God and believing all things are possible with him, doors to the unknown begin to open; and in time, a sense of certainty sets in. Now the house is finished. I love it, live in it, and have learned from it numerous lessons about God's keeping his word and giving me abundantly more than I could have ever asked or thought.

—LUCI SWINDOLL (*Life! Celebrate It*)

# STOCKING THE PANTRY

*The LORD guides the humble in what is right and teaches them his way.*
—Psalm 25:9 NIV

Food, what an emotional magnet! It's a lifetime challenge—well, not for everyone. Some folks actually manage it just fine. Then there's me. Therapists say eating is one of our earliest nurturing memories, and therefore many of us try to comfort ourselves with food. One remedy is to keep our emotional and spiritual pantries stocked with healthy, nutritious items like these:

→ *Dignity*—I have found dignity comes as we embrace our heritage in Christ and as we choose to do what is ours to do.

→ *Discernment*—While this is a gift, it also is worked into our hearts as we learn from our mistakes and seek God's counsel.

→ *Intelligence*—This is showcased as we apply God's Word to our own hearts before we offer it to others and when we think before we speak or react.

→ *Self-control*—This means placing balanced boundaries on our choices and our habits.

→ *Preparedness*—This means having on hand items such as the wine of God's spirit, the humble heart of a lamb, and the fruit of righteousness.

→ *Fortitude*—This involves internal resolve for whatever arises regardless of the difficulty level.

—PATSY CLAIRMONT (*I Second That Emotion*)

# REVEALING YOURSELF

*The Lord is fair in everything he does, and full of kindness. He is close to all who call on him sincerely.*

—*Psalm 145:17–18* TLB

The first thing we have to do in order to reclaim joy is to be willing to be vulnerable—an open book, warts and all, before God and at least one other person (a counselor or trusted friend). There's a story in the Bible about a woman who had some kind of disease that involved bleeding, and for twelve years she had consulted every healer imaginable. No one had been able to help her. When she heard Jesus was coming to town, she must have known he was her last hope. But he was surrounded by crowds, and in the crush of people, she could not get his attention. She barely managed to simply touch the edge of his garment—and she was healed! Not only that, but Jesus stopped in his tracks, having felt some power go out of him, and asked that whoever had touched him would *reveal* herself or himself. The woman was rewarded for her choice to *reveal herself.*

So many women are walking around with tumors of secrets, cancerous emotions, or broken spirits that have mended the wrong way because they weren't tended to in a healthy way. The first step to healing is to reveal your deepest hurts and struggles to God and then to one other safe person.

—SANDI PATTY (*Falling Forward*)

# EMBRACING YOUR BEAUTY

*God has made everything beautiful in its time.*

—Ecclesiastes 3:11 NIV

For some women, beauty has been the enemy. Beauty, or the perceived lack of it, has been the cause of painful rejections, missed promotions, struggles in marriage, or even self-hatred. Given the challenge, let alone the opportunity, to embrace beauty seems about as dumb as trying to spit into the wind. But the more we dismiss beauty as belonging to others, the more we reject opportunities to nurture our spirits.

We must embrace our beauty because beauty is part of who God created us to be. We are mind, body, and soul. Each of these elements possesses beauty in its own right and deserves to be embraced. That embracing transforms us to live our lives in a whole and healthy, honoring-to-God way.

Are we seeking to embrace beauty so that the world will accept us? No. Beauty needs to be redeemed unto the Lord. Do we embrace beauty so we can look as if we have it all together spiritually? No. Beauty is embraced because we don't have it all together, and we are trusting God in a more radical way than ever before to make something beautiful out of our surrendered lives.

—NICOLE JOHNSON (*Fresh-Brewed Life*)

# PERFECT TIMING

*As for me, I trust in You, O LORD; I say, "You are my God."*
*My times are in Your hand.*

—Psalm 31:14–15

Do you have trouble resting in the fact that God is in control and that he knows the times and seasons in your life? Think twice before you are tempted to worry or force life to move at your pace. God moves according to his sovereignty, not according to our timetable, and peace will come only when you learn to trust his timing in every area of your life.

Resist the urge to constantly ask questions like, "When is Mr. Right going to come along?" or "When will I get the promotion I deserve?" or "What will happen if my biological clock runs out before I get pregnant?" When you grasp the truth that when he moves it will be according to his perfect plan, it makes a huge difference.

God is the God of all times, and to know him is to know faithfulness itself. He has the big picture in mind, and he knows the plans he has for you. Your times are safe in his hand. There is no need to be anxious about when God is going to answer your prayer or move on your behalf. You can relax in the certainty that his ways and his timing are perfect.

—JAN SILVIOUS (*Smart Girls Think Twice*)

# THE TRUTH ABOUT DOUBT

*Be merciful to those who doubt.*

—Jude 22 NIV

*Why did you do this, God?*

*Is this just one more thing that you are asking me to experience so I can better understand others when they suffer? If it is, I quit!*

*If I had your power, I would never let those I love suffer!*

*I can't do this, Lord!*

I realize these prayers might be disturbing to some who have never believed it appropriate to question God. But I'm not relating my story for sensationalism; at that time in my life, that's where I found myself: at a moment of mistrust in God.

Be truthful—haven't you ever felt the same way? Have you ever been desperate to regain control when your life has taken a drastic and unexpected turn? I imagine so. After all, our world is imperfect.

But God understands and allows our doubt. Why? Because if we use it productively in our relationship with God, it changes us.

Yes, there is something to Satan's allegation that when Job's life was going smoothly, it was relatively easy for him to maintain a grateful attitude toward God. What Satan didn't realize, though, is that when we humans dig deep into our souls and pour out our hearts, even in bitterness, God is there and we come to know him more deeply than ever before.

—SHEILA WALSH (*Get Off Your Knees and Pray*)

# JOY YET TO COME

*[God] will yet fill your mouth with laughter and your lips with shouts of joy.*

—Job 8:21 NIV

Everybody's had some kind of bad stuff in her life; I sure have. And nobody's saying we're supposed to laugh every time another punch finds its mark. The important thing is to remember, during those times of weeping and mourning, the promise that God "will yet fill your mouth with laughter and your lips with shouts of joy." Whisper it to yourself when you find yourself at trouble's doorstep: "God will yet fill my mouth with laughter and my lips with shouts of joy." Let that promise of joy-yet-to-come be your strength during the hard times.

The more you practice this attitude, the more powerful it is and the faster it pops into your mind when you're confronted with difficulties. During my own trials, and I've certainly had my share, I've learned to reach into my innermost human computer and pull out scriptural data that can help me remember what God has done for me in the past and what he has promised to do for me in the future. I can document the trials he has pulled me through, and, reviewing that history, I can anticipate where he might be taking me, even in the middle of trouble.

—THELMA WELLS (*The Buzz*)

# PAGEANT LOGIC

*Embracing what God does for you is the best thing you can do for him.*

—Romans 12:2 MSG

Sometimes we think life is a pageant and we have to win in at least one category, so we apply the Pageant Logic: If you're not so good-looking, surely you could win the talent portion. If you're not talented, maybe you're congenial. Some are not talented but smart—others are not smart or talented, but have amazing beauty, sometimes only on the inside.

The truth is that we are all gifted in our own right, and it is a spiritual tenet that we are to have a sane evaluation of our gifts and intelligence. Overestimate and we stumble into pride. Underestimate and we cheat ourselves out of opportunities because we fail to see ourselves in that role. Only we can rightly value the gifts God has placed inside us and use them to honor him.

There are a couple of universal truths that apply no matter what your education, your IQ or your list of talents. Choose every day for the rest of your life to focus on what you *do* have. Value your intelligence. Own your mental real estate. Celebrate your areas of expertise and revel in your unique talents. You aren't competing in a pageant or proving your IQ on a piece of paper. Just be your best at whatever God has intentionally made you to be.

—ANITA RENFROE (*If You Can't Lose It, Decorate It!*)

# WHO IS GOD?

*The LORD is gracious and compassionate, slow to anger and rich in love.*

—Psalm 145:8 NIV

This is just a sample of what the Bible has to say about God:

1. ***God was before everything everywhere.*** "Before the mountains were created, before you made the earth and the world, you are God, without beginning or end." (Psalm 90:2).
2. ***God is the Creator of all things.*** "By the word of the LORD were the heavens made, their starry host by the breath of his mouth" (Psalm 33:6 NIV). "It is I who made the earth and created mankind upon it" (Isaiah 45:12 NIV).
3. ***God's nature is love.*** "The LORD is loving toward all he has made" (Psalm 145:13 NIV). "The LORD is good and his love endures forever." (Psalm 100:5 NIV).

If we choose to believe that God has always been, that he is the Creator of all that is, and that his nature is love, we can stop making up our own versions of God. But we can't stop here in our formulations because there is more we need to know about him. It is astounding to realize that two thousand years ago, in accordance with the divine master plan, God sent his son Jesus to this earth! This world-altering event changed the assumptions and images of God forever.

—MARILYN MEBERG (*The Decision of a Lifetime*)

# DESIRE TO FORGIVE

*Be kind to one another, tender-hearted, forgiving each other,*
*just as God in Christ also has forgiven you.*

—*Ephesians 4:32* NASB

About a year ago, I got an e-mail from someone who had attended a Women of Faith conference in Hartford, Connecticut. She confessed when she came that weekend, she'd been very burdened by a relationship that had gone awry many years before, but she couldn't forgive the person who had wronged her.

She wrote something like, "You spoke about being hurt by a friend of yours for twenty-five years because she had told a lie about you. I couldn't believe it! I sat there, stunned. It's like I was hearing you say, "Listen to me. You don't have to live like this any longer. You can find hope if you want to. Start with a desire to forgive, and you can." Amazingly, when I heard you, it was the first time in years I wanted to do something to put an end to my rotten attitude. Thank you."

Forgiveness doesn't come by osmosis. And it's not easy. It begins in our will and moves through our body as we take steps to change things. It's humbling to forgive those who hurt us because there's something in us that wants them to suffer. But those feelings rob us of all the freedom that's possible to enjoy through Christ. And freedom won't come until we *start with forgiveness*.

—LUCI SWINDOLL (*Life! Celebrate It*)

# AVOIDING THE DUMPS

*Jesus said, "Do not let your hearts be troubled. Trust in God;
trust also in me."*

—John 14:1 NIV

Have you noticed individuals with certain temperaments just have
an innate spring in their steps, a jiggle to their wiggle, a throttle on
their waddle, no matter what befalls them? Still other personality
types are given to bouts of melancholy.

Here are some of the ways I've found to help me not take the
escalator down into the dumps every time things don't go my way:

- → *Our wills are powerful.* We can choose how we behave.
  We don't have to be a victim to our emotions, nor should
  others have to be.
- → *We don't have to wear our sadness like this year's fashion
  statement.* We can deliberately don kindness and
  compassion for others.
- → *Enlist a prayer partner.*
- → *Monitor the types of stimuli around you.* Don't work
  yourself into a mood by what you view or listen to.
- → *Relax—not everything we think needs to be formed into
  words.* Remember, the Tower of Babel didn't stand.
  Conserve your energy, preserve your friendships . . . shh.

—PATSY CLAIRMONT (*I Second That Emotion*)

# BETTER OR BITTER?

*Why are you cast down, O my soul? And why are you*
*disquieted within me? Hope in God; For I shall yet praise*
*Him, the help of my countenance and my God.*
—Psalm 43:5

What is the difference between those who become more alive and beautiful and get *better* after crisis or loss and those who grow old, ugly, and *bitter?* I think those who get better have learned the secret of gleaning the lessons from their losses. They do not waste their pain.

Those who grow bitter seem to have an especially hard time openly asking God to teach them something of eternity, particularly after they either have experienced a major loss or have fouled up in some way. They may no longer trust God because he didn't protect them from their pain. They might even be afraid that God will point his finger at them, saying they don't deserve his help, that they are not worthy of healing. So they deflect and reject and play the blame game and never allow God to enter into the most secret part of their hearts and lovingly heal what is wrong and forgive what has been done.

People who get better, on the other hand, allow God into the center of their situations, *expecting* healing. They ask God not only to walk with them through the pain, but to redeem their sorrow so that their future can be better.

—SANDI PATTY (*Falling Forward*)

# YOU ARE BEAUTIFUL

*Charm is deceptive, and beauty is fleeting; but a woman who fears the LORD is to be praised.*

—*Proverbs 31:30* NIV

There is no beauty in makeup. Expensive clothes will not make you beautiful. The secret lies in being an alive, awake woman with something to offer the world. Namely, yourself. Beauty is less about your face and more about your smile. Less about the shape of your eyebrows, more about the light in your eyes. Less about the length of your legs, more about the bounce in your step. Real beauty is being a viable, vital human being. As you participate in your life with a warm smile and a generous spirit, you are beautiful.

Living your life will bring out the beauty in you because it is uncovering you. It is revealing more of the authentic you that is beautiful. Because life is a living, breathing work of art, you are a painting as you go. Be a masterpiece. Drink in life. Laugh too loud. Compliment others constantly.

Cultivate beauty all around you. Plant a garden. Embrace beauty wherever you find it—in the fall leaves, in the spring flowers. This will help you embrace it in yourself. When you appreciate a sunset or your child's clay candlestick or a beautiful piece of music, you are saying yes to beauty. You are saying yes to God.

—NICOLE JOHNSON (*Fresh-Brewed Life*)

# A WAY WITH WORDS

*Let everything you say be good and helpful, so that your words*
*will be an encouragement to those who hear them.*

—*Ephesians 4:29* NLT

You and I make an impact on other people by what we say. We can offer them life-infused words or we can throw death darts at them. We can purpose to bless them or curse them simply by our choice of words.

My hairstylist, Rodney, has a gracious way of giving words of affirmation to the women who visit his salon. He speaks kind words of encouragement and offers a listening ear to weary women who sit in his chair. He is a focused listener who truly hears his clients' words, and he often writes cards of kindness, sympathy, and support to those who are going through a difficult time. When you sit in Rodney's chair, you have his undivided attention; he doesn't get distracted by chatting with other people in the shop. His job is to beautify hair, but he draws on the power of words to beautify hearts and uplift spirits as well.

Compliments breathe amazing life into a woman's soul. When someone says that she loves your outfit, comments that your jewelry is beautiful, or asks "What's that great perfume you're wearing?" she has offered you words of life. You hold your head up a little higher because someone has noticed something special about you. When it happens to me, I appreciate it so much.

—JAN SILVIOUS (*Smart Girls Think Twice*)

# THE MOVIE OF YOUR LIFE

*This then is how we know that we belong to the truth, and how we set our hearts at rest in his presence whenever our hearts condemn us. For God is greater than our hearts, and he knows everything.*

—1 John 3:19–20 NIV

One of my dearest friends in this world, author and speaker Ney Bailey, once said to me, "Imagine that a movie was made of your life. Nothing was left out. Everything that you have ever thought or said or done was displayed on the big screen for anyone to see. How would you feel?"

My initial response was that I would be ashamed. It is one thing to take refuge in the absence of what I might consider to be "huge" sins, but to have all my secret thoughts and feelings revealed would be terrifying. The truth is that we all hide part of who we can be when left to our own humanity. Then Ney said, "God has seen your movie, and he loves you anyway." Let's stop for a moment and let that sink deep into our hearts and souls.

The God of the universe, the one who holds the stars and the moon in place, knows everything about us and loves us with unprecedented abandon. He knows the good, the bad, and the ugly. He knows the things we are proud of and the things we hide. He knows it all, and he invites us to come just as we are and live the dream he has for each of us.

—SHEILA WALSH (*God Has a Dream for Your Life*)

## ALL ATWITTER

*Restore to me the joy of your salvation, and sustain in me a
willing spirit.*

—Psalm 51:12 NRSV

I have always admired the honeybee. It faces never-ending toil
each day. Either it works tirelessly in the total darkness of the
hive, tending the young, building perfectly hexagonal cells (with
a slight downward tilt so the honey doesn't run out), grooming
the queen, serving on guard duty, or providing climate control by
fanning its wings or huddling with other bees in a trembling
clump for warmth—or it flies back and forth over great distances
in the heat of the day, constantly carrying heavy loads of pollen
and nectar between the blossoms and the hive.

Despite all this hard work the honeybee just seems to exude
a joyfully enthusiastic attitude. When it discovers a new source
of food, it zips back to the hive, all atwitter, and then, buzzing
with excitement, it does that special honeybee dance that tells
the other bees just where the banquet can be found.

That's how I feel when the joy of the Lord fills my heart to
overflowing. I work hard too, just like the honeybee. But that
godly gift of joy just sets me all atwitter, and without any conscious effort, it bubbles up out of me in the form of laughter.
Then I can't wait to tell all those around me where they can find
the banquet of God's goodness too.

—THELMA WELLS (*The Buzz*)

# TRUE FRIENDSHIP

*Some friends play at friendship, but a true friend sticks closer than one's nearest kin.*

—*Proverbs 18:24* NRSV

The truth is that true friendship = risk. That's the only thing about relationships that is absolutely certain. Whenever you extend yourself in relationship, you extend yourself in risk. For those who don't handle risk well, the prospect of relationship is always difficult. You are sharing a degree of intimacy and information that you must now entrust to another's ability to keep a confidence. But alongside these risks is the possibility for rich emotional rewards that only camaraderie and shared life experience can afford.

Intimacy with a true friend requires a higher level of commitment from those of us who are followers of Jesus. Because there is a spiritual element that permeates our friendship, we take on spiritual responsibilities: honesty, accountability, and a commitment to pray for her. There is something about praying for a friend that draws you closer, and the intimate knowledge you have of her life allows you to pray in a way that other people cannot. It is so comforting to know that a friend who is walking the same spiritual journey as you can "have your back" in prayer for your life and your needs. It is also a privilege to provide spiritual intercession on behalf of your friend.

—ANITA RENFROE (*If You Can't Lose It, Decorate It!*)

# PART OF THE FAMILY

*You should behave . . . like God's very own children, adopted
into his family—calling him "Father, dear Father."*

—*Romans 8:15* NLT

Do you realize what those words mean? You, dear one, were up
for adoption, and God the Father chose you to be in his family.
God the Father chose you to be his child. What a sweet truth to
realize that you are a chosen, deeply valued treasure to the God
of the universe. He wants to adopt you! But unlike most adoptions, you have a choice in deciding whether you want to be
adopted.

Let's assume wisdom guides your choice and you decide you
want to be adopted. What do you do? What do you say? How do
you close the deal? Let me suggest you simply tell the Father,
through Jesus, you want to be in the family. Tell him you agree to
the terms of adoption: confession of sin and then believing in
and receiving Jesus as Savior. Simply pray, "Lord Jesus, I want to
be adopted into the family of God. Thank You for choosing me.
Thank You, Jesus, for dying for all my sin. I believe in You, and I
receive You as my Savior."

If this prayer expresses the desire of your heart and you have
agreed to the terms for your adoption, you, dear one, have just
made the decision of a lifetime!

—MARILYN MEBERG (*The Decision of a Lifetime*)

# A GRATEFUL HEART

*Let the word of Christ dwell in you richly as you teach and admonish one another with all wisdom, and as you sing psalms, hymns and spiritual songs with gratitude in your hearts to God.*

—*Colossians 3:16 NIV*

When something doesn't go my way or come down the pike the way I want it to, I tend to gripe. It can be any number of things that irritate me—delayed flights, being put on hold, or having to wait in line. Traffic jams. Interruptions. People who don't keep their word. You name it! (You have your own list, don't you?)

At times like these when I'm tempted to gripe, I have to start talking to myself. And when I come to my senses, this is what I say: "Luci, if you can't be content in this moment of inconvenience, be content that it's not worse. Shut up and count your blessings."

But there are times I can't pull myself out of that morass until I *start with a grateful heart.* Our constant attitude should be gratitude. But it seems to be the rarest of virtues. God has given us thousands of reasons to celebrate life every day, even in the worst of times, if we just open our eyes, live in the moment, take in the beauty, and see the possibilities. It's been said, "The worst moment for the atheist is when he feels grateful and has no one to thank."

—LUCI SWINDOLL (*Life! Celebrate It*)

# BREATHING SPACE

*Return to your rest, O my soul, for the LORD has dealt*
*bountifully with you.*
—Psalm 116:7

We all need breathing space from our routines, relatives, and other relationships. But here's my biggest struggle: how to get away from me. I often get on my own nerves. When I start to gripe at myself, I sometimes head for the beauty parlor, maybe because it's such a girly thing to do. Of course I enjoy the personal attention and usually the results. Besides, it gives me a mini breathing space.

I think every woman should have a lost-in-space place. It needs to be something you do and somewhere you go that not only pleases your senses but also results in satisfaction. What a reprieve for our emotions to have something to look forward to in the midst of the hustle and bustle, even if it's just to take a few moments to flip through the pages of a home magazine or to sink into the wonder of a well-woven tale. After a few pages of walking around in someone else's fiction, our reality seems easier to face. After a good read I seem to breathe easier. Last week to unplug I went for my first professional facial, which had to have been invented by angels on a sabbatical. It was heavenly.

—PATSY CLAIRMONT (*I Second That Emotion*)

# SOMETHING TO BE GRATEFUL FOR

*He who cherishes understanding prospers.*

—*Proverbs 19:8* NIV

The Bible is full of examples of people who gleaned understanding from their pain. The apostle Paul, for example, "caught" the lessons of gratitude, particularly in his letter to the Philippians. He asked God to help him see his bleak circumstances with an attitude of thankfulness, and soon the very chains that held him bound in prison became something to be grateful for.

At this season of Paul's life, he had learned the lessons of a grateful spirit so well that the book of Philippians is overflowing with the word *joy*—despite his circumstances being less than ideal, to say the least. (Most of us would consider being chained to a Roman guard 24/7 to be something of an inconvenience.) Paul shares at the end of the book that he has learned the secret of contentment so that he can live just as happily in riches or in poverty, in prison or free—and in fact, he actually spends a bit of time discussing whether it would be better to live or to die. Now that's a free man! He saw that all circumstances carry with them some lessons that lift us closer to God if we allow the Lord to use them for our good.

—SANDI PATTY (*Falling Forward*)

# THE WAY YOU LOOK

> GOD *judges persons differently than humans do. Men and*
> *women look at the face; GOD looks at the heart.*
>
> —1 Samuel 16:7 MSG

It is so easy to believe that God is silent on the subject of beauty. Maybe it is because the church is silent, or maybe it's because we have to be so still to hear what God is saying. Either way, so many women simply think God is not saying anything about how they feel about themselves. Here is the simple truth: God loves you passionately and intensely, and that love has nothing to do with the way you look. It isn't affected one ounce by the size of your blue jeans or the way your nose slopes up or how much dental work you've had done. It isn't lessened by wearing the wrong dress to a party or having no skill in applying makeup or by hating exercise. God simply loves you as you are.

But before we just gloss over that and go right on to the next thing, let me ask a hard question. Have you let that truth into your soul? I mean, really let it in? God is the one who has never criticized you or belittled you or made fun of your appearance in any way. He is the one who formed you, and said afterward, "This is good."

—NICOLE JOHNSON (*Fresh-Brewed Life*)

# WISE WORDS

*The speech of the upright rescues them.*
—Proverbs 12:6 NIV

Have you mastered the art of talking to others and to yourself in kind, helpful ways? Our words are what we use to communicate from the inside out. They tell volumes about the health of our thoughts because we only can verbalize what has passed through our brains.

A dear friend of mine told me, "I think I've been whining, and I don't believe I want to keep that up." I listened as she listed all of the bounty in her life, and then she said, "But I think I've gotten in a habit of complaining about what I have to do, and I've realized I wouldn't have it any other way. There are women all over the world who would love to have the life that I live." I smiled at my friend's wise words. She remembered that the words we speak influence the quality of the life we live. She, like you and like me, has been richly blessed, and she doesn't want to lose sight of that.

The ability to speak gives us power in our own lives and in the lives of others. With that power comes great responsibility. What we say is heard not only by others, but also by the God who loves us and who has given us all that we have.

—JAN SILVIOUS (*Smart Girls Think Twice*)

# GOD LOVES YOU! YES, YOU!

*Blessed be the LORD, for he has wondrously shown his steadfast love to me.*

—Psalm 31:21 NRSV

If I had to give you my life's message in one sentence, it would be this: as you are, right now, God loves you; and that will never change.

God loves you not because of who you are or what you have done but because of who he is. Your behavior does not impact the heart and character of God. You might think that on good days, God is proud of you; and in your not-so-attractive moments, he loves you less. But that is applying human logic to the heart of God, and it will always come up short. There is life-changing truth in the message of these three little words:

God loves you.

*You!*

Not just the woman whose kids learn their Bible verses while yours struggle to remember their names. Not just the woman who has been happily married for many years while you are still waiting for a husband. Not just the woman who is pregnant one more time while you weep with empty arms.

God is crazy about you.

When we grasp this truth, really get it as deep as the marrow in our bones, it changes everything. Now we have a place to build our dreams again.

—SHEILA WALSH (*God Has a Dream for Your Life*)

# A MOTHER'S LAUGHTER

*God has made me laugh, and all who hear will laugh with me.*

—*Genesis 21:6*

Laughter must be pretty important to God or he wouldn't have spent so much time talking about it. Depending on which version of the Bible you're studying, the word *laughter* appears about forty times. One of my favorite laughter verses is part of the Old Testament story of Abraham and his wife, Sarah, who gave birth when Abraham was one hundred years old and Sarah herself was well past her childbearing years. When their son Isaac was miraculously born, Sarah commented that she couldn't stop laughing about the situation and everyone who heard about it would be laughing too.

Frankly, I don't know too many women today who would think it was funny to have a new baby in their old age. Having a hundred-year-old husband to care for would be hard enough, let alone an infant too! But God had promised Abraham and Sarah a family, and when that promise was fulfilled, Sarah laughed with delight. I'm guessing that joy-filled attitude worked like a daily dose of vitamins, keeping Sarah going so that she could be a good mother to her son and a loving wife to her husband despite their increasing age. She knew the wisdom of a merry heart.

—THELMA WELLS (*The Buzz*)

## FOLLOW YOUR BLISS

*My heart took delight in all my work, and this was the reward for all my labor.*

—Ecclesiastes 2:10 NIV

I saw Anderson Cooper (of CNN) give an interview recently, and in it he responded to a question regarding the best advice his mother (Gloria Vanderbilt) ever gave him. He responded that she advised him to follow his bliss and the money would come. He had a dream to be a reporter and he now anchors each weeknight with his own news show. I don't know what your "bliss" might be, but I urge you to find a calling in life and attach it to your work.

Whether you have a job and wish you didn't, or don't have one and wish you did, or if you wish you had different people to work with or report to, the dailyness of your workplace can become a mental drag if you don't choose to see it as a place of purpose and mission. The Bible gives us clear principles regarding whatever labor we undertake. Read Colossians 3:23, Luke 9:62, Romans 13:1, Matthew 7:12.

These scriptural principles allow us to see that we are working for more than a paycheck, that we are committed to endurance and excellence in any undertaking, and that our Real Boss doesn't inhabit the corner office, but has it all in his hands.

—ANITA RENFROE (*If You Can't Lose It, Decorate It!*)

# NEW WAYS OF LIVING

*Do you not know that your body is a temple of the Holy Spirit within you, which you have from God, and that you are not your own?*

—I Corinthians 6:19 NRSV

Did you know that the Holy Spirit lives in you? The moment you said yes to Jesus, the Holy Spirit entered your interior world, which motivates and guides your exterior world. The Holy Spirit literally lives in you and, in so doing, wants to teach you new ways of living.

Many people have misconceptions about who the Holy Spirit is and how he operates. Possibly you, too, have wondered who he is, how he operates, and what it means to have him living within you.

The answer to the question of who he is, is simple: He is God. However, while the answer is simple, understanding it is not so simple. The Holy Spirit is the third part of the Trinity. The Trinity is composed of three divine entities: God the Father, Jesus the Son, and the Holy Spirit. All those entities have separate roles, but *all* are God.

We must recognize that much of God is a mystery and often beyond our comprehension. But here's what is clear: The Holy Spirit of God is your personal power pack. As you continue your Christian walk, it's fantastic to know that living within you is this Spirit who means to give you the power to begin new ways of living.

—MARILYN MEBERG (*Assurance for a Lifetime*)

# DOING WHAT IS EXPEDIENT

*The prudent are crowned with knowledge.*
—Proverbs 14:18

Do you have trouble doing those things in life that are practical, prudent, or suitable for the moment? The doing of them may not be long-term, but they have the best immediate end in view. They're the methods we employ along life's way to make life work better and easier for us. These little temporary enterprises are born out of our desire to achieve a particular goal.

When I was in my twenties and thirties, I had four jobs. All but the first job (I worked for Mobil Oil Corporation as a draftsman-artist) were jobs of expediency. They were short-term with an end view in mind. My reason for all those jobs, obviously, was to have more income for personal goals I had set for myself during that time. Now my financial needs have changed, and I don't have the energy to do any more than I'm doing. But they served a very important purpose back then.

I do other things now for expediency's sake. I can think of twenty things I do every day, week, and month that enable me to reach my goals. But five years from now, I may do none of them. They serve their purpose now, and now is where I live and have to get the job done. You get my point!

—LUCI SWINDOLL (*Life! Celebrate It*)

# FRESH OXYGEN

> *Two are better than one, because they have a good reward for*
> *their toil. For if they fall, one will lift up the other.*
>
> —*Ecclesiastes 4:9–10* NRSV

Sometimes what I need most is to plug into others. My girlfriends are a lifeline. Yes, they can contribute to some of my emotional knots, but more often than not they resuscitate me.

Here are some of the ways I've received fresh oxygen from my friends:

+ *Friends help us think.* They often bring a different perspective that opens up a new view.
+ *Friends help us hear our inconsistencies and pinpoint blind spots.* I'm not suggesting that's fun, but it's valuable.
+ *Friends help pull us out of small spaces.* Even when they share their struggles, it can give our fears wings as we realize that we're not alone in our emotional complexities.
+ *Friends rally when the winds of hardship bluster across our paths.*
+ *Friends believe in us.* They applaud our gifts, and they celebrate our good fortune.
+ *Friends aren't perfect and may not be forever.* My caution would be not to expect more of a friend than she can give. My expectations have been too high at times, and that only leads to disappointment, ill will, and exhaustion.

—PATSY CLAIRMONT (*I Second That Emotion*)

# PETER, PETER!

*The Lord said, "Simon, Simon! Indeed, Satan has asked for*
*you, that he may sift you as wheat. But I have prayed for you,*
*that your faith should not fail."*

—Luke 22:31–32

In the book of Luke, there's a story about Simon Peter's journey from being a brand-new disciple—full of vigor and self-assurance—through the valley of disappointing himself and the one he loves most. But through this realization of his fallenness and a deeper understanding of the love and mercy of his best friend, Jesus, Peter emerges shabbier but more beautifully real. Before Peter's denial of Christ, right before the crucifixion, Jesus warned him that the enemy "has asked to sift you as wheat." He also assured Peter that he had already been praying for him. What does sifting mean? In biblical days, it meant the wheat was put through a sieve to separate the grain from the chaff.

In Peter's case, what was sifted out of him was overconfidence and pride. Peter went on to become a great leader in the early church. And like other great leaders, he realized that he was totally dependent on God to do his job. He developed the qualities of empathy, integrity, trust, and a realness of heart, and the early Christians came to trust him. Like some other Christ-followers I know, Peter had some of his fur rubbed off. He'd been sifted and humbled and become more compassionate, more genuine and more authentic.

—SANDI PATTY (*Falling Forward*)

# NO APOLOGIES

*Don't be concerned about the outward beauty that depends
on fancy hairstyles, expensive jewelry, or beautiful clothes. You
should be known for the beauty that comes from within.*

—*1 Peter 3:3–4 NLT*

If you have given up on your outward appearance out of fear or
self-rejection, now is a great time to begin healing. A special fragrance or a new pair of shoes can show your soul an act of
kindness. Clothes don't define you; they reveal you. Makeup isn't
meant to cover anything up; it is intended to help you look as
alive as you feel. Start allowing the living, breathing, feeling you
to encounter the world in an authentic way, with no apologies!

There is freedom from the tyranny of beauty. I am embracing
it. If you could see me, you would laugh out loud. I'm sitting at
my computer with wet hair in two-day-old clothes. Not a pretty
sight. But we live by faith, not by sight. I feel beautiful. Right now.
Because I am alive and awake and participating in my life. I am
loved and cherished, and I love and cherish others. I am embracing my beauty as I am. For years my mother told me I was
beautiful, but I didn't believe her. She told me that beauty wasn't
about what I looked like. Today I am at the best place of my life
to choose to believe her. And paint my toenails.

—NICOLE JOHNSON (*Fresh-Brewed Life*)

# DREAMS AND EXPECTATIONS

*My soul, wait silently for God alone, for my expectation is from Him.*

—Psalm 62:5

Have you noticed? We tend to enter adulthood with great expectations. Young girls do a lot of dreaming about what their lives will be when they grow up: Of course, dreams and reality don't always run on parallel tracks. One of the best lessons I have learned in my journey is this: what might have been does not exist, so don't even go there! It saves so much torment and expended energy when we refuse to ponder the "if onlys" and stick to reality.

Is your life different from how you once dreamed it would be? Perhaps you are making the best of relating to a difficult and defiant child you expected to be cuddly and compliant. Or you may be holding the household together while your husband travels constantly and you both endure the lonely nights. Maybe you're single while your heart longs for a mate, caring for a parent who has forgotten who you are, or dealing with debilitating illness yourself?

Much as we may wish our situations were different, we have what we have, and a wonderful serenity comes in accepting each person and each situation as God's plan for us. Amy Carmichael, missionary to India for fifty years, said it best: "In acceptance lies peace."

—JAN SILVIOUS (*Smart Girls Think Twice*)

# LIVES THROWN WIDE OPEN

> *Love is patient and kind. Love is not jealous, it does not brag,*
> *and it is not proud. Love is not rude, is not selfish, and does not*
> *get upset with others. Love does not count up wrongs that have*
> *been done.*

—1 Corinthians 13:4–5 NCV

I think that very little disturbs our peace and crushes our dreams more than the area of our relationships. We thrive when they are good and healthy, but when they're permeated with conflict and pain, we suffer. We either strike out like a wounded animal or withdraw inside our shells. But God wants us to live lives thrown wide open to his love and abandoned to his care. He calls us to love others with a generous heart.

How on earth is that possible? There is no earthly way to love like this. We are simply not wired to be that selfless. But I have discovered that in Christ there is another path offered to us. On this path, we choose to love simply because we are loved by God. We are not threatened, because God is in control. We are not defensive, because we have nothing to defend. We are not arrogant, for we are teachable. We are not bitter, because we forgive. We are not blown around by the whims of those surrounding us, because we have determined to hold on to what is true no matter what appears to be true. We are not easily offended, because we extend grace. We choose to see beauty in absolutely everyone.

—SHEILA WALSH (*God Has a Dream for Your Life*)

# LAUGH ANYWAY

*Rejoice in the Lord always. Again I will say, rejoice!*
—Philippians 4:4

Occasionally we may feel overwhelmed by anger, bitterness, or sorrow, but those harsh emotions cannot extinguish the true, God-given joy that was placed in our heart by the Holy Spirit the moment we accepted Jesus as Lord and Savior. It may be temporarily overshadowed by raging hormones and hostile feelings, but when we regain control and begin to think about God's goodness and love, the joy re-exerts itself, and before we know it, our negative emotions have evaporated as once again our mouth is filled with laughter and our lips with shouts of joy. Our facial expressions change. Our aggressive body language stands down. Our demeanor sweetens. God's joy is powerful. Even in the most stressful situations, if we allow it to work within us, we find a way to follow the instructions of the apostle Paul and rejoice!

Joy and laughter are God-given gifts that help us live less stressful, more productive lives. When you have nothing to laugh about, laugh anyway; soon you'll feel the healing power of joy and laughter bringing new energy and life to your weary, frustrating day. In the words of C. S. Lewis, "Joy is the serious business of heaven."

—THELMA WELLS (*The Buzz*)

# THE GIFT OF AGE

*Even to your old age and gray hairs I am he, I am he who will sustain you. I have made you and I will carry you.*

—Isaiah 46:4 NIV

What does your age really represent? Days and nights spent living your life, coming through a myriad of experiences that sometimes seem mind-numbingly monotonous, only to be interrupted by life-altering surprises and unforeseen tragedies. Your age reflects years of (hopefully) collected wisdom.

Your age also represents mounds of memories. You've exchanged some of the energy of youth for them, but the higher the number on your birthday card, the more wealth you have in your little treasure trove of reminiscences.

In our culture, age is viewed as some kind of disease that, if we just keep treating it, might be defeated or go away altogether. Like we can somehow push back the edges of mortality. The only thing we're pushing back is the edges of our acceptance of the gifts of time and the physical limitations that make the interior gifts more precious.

So you've got a year or two on your friends. So you've got a wrinkle or two. So your hair is changing color and your body is giving you fits. No matter. Age is a gift from the hand of God. Any measure of health to enjoy your age is a gift from God. The memories you've made along the way are precious and priceless. Thank God for every year he's given you.

—ANITA RENFROE (*If You Can't Lose It, Decorate It!*)

# OVERCOMING THE WORLD

> *The Holy Spirit helps us in our distress. For we don't even*
> *know what we should pray for, nor how we should pray. But*
> *the Holy Spirit prays for us with groanings that cannot be*
> *expressed in words.*
>
> —Romans 8:26 NLT

As believers, we have a wonderful freedom to access the power of the very Spirit who lives within us. When we encounter problems involving marriage, kids, our finances, relatives—anything—the Holy Spirit "helps us in our distress." We are not alone. He knows, he cares, and he is there. Our prayers ignite his power to meet our needs.

You may be wishing your problems were as simple as impatience, health, or decision making. Some of you are anguishing over issues of alcoholism, drug addiction, pornography, or promiscuity. How can the inner presence of the Holy Spirit help you deal with those huge challenges? Let me point you to a fantastically encouraging statement Jesus made; it's recorded in John 16:33: "Here on earth you will have many trials and sorrows. But take heart, because I have overcome the world."

What did he mean? The world is full of many evils. Among them are the various addictions and unhealthy habits that shackle the human spirit. But Jesus said he had overcome all the evil in the world. Jesus is an overcomer. And he lives within you. So you, too, are an overcomer.

—MARILYN MEBERG (*Assurance for a Lifetime*)

# MAKING YOUR LIFE WORK

*These commands are a lamp, this teaching is a light, and the corrections of discipline are the way to life.*

—Proverbs 6:23 NIV

Everything has a shelf life, my friends. Every cause has not only an effect but a means to be accomplished. That's called being expedient. When we think like that, we get a lot done; and slowly, slowly, our goals are realized. For some of us it will mean hiring a nanny or baby-sitter, having a secretary, using a maid service to clean our houses, or engaging an assistant to keep us on track.

My computer has a funny little quirk: it won't start unless I punch the start button twice. It's been that way since the first day it was up and running. I've had tech people work on it, and it still has the quirk. So I accept it as part of its idiosyncrasies. I've learned what it takes to get the thing started, and that's what I do. It's as simple as that.

Some of our lives are the same way. We have a hard time getting off the start line. I'm suggesting you do what it takes to make your life work. Study your habits and patterns. See what's best for you. Keep pressing ahead, and punch whatever buttons will get you up and running. Once you learn that and keep doing it, many of your battles will be over.

—LUCI SWINDOLL (*Life! Celebrate It*)

# JUST IMAGINE!

*There shall be no night there: They need no lamp nor light of the sun, for the Lord God gives them light.*

—Revelation 22:5

Getting up in the wee hours to experience the first rays of light conquering darkness heartens me. I watch the ebony melt from the sky and drizzle behind the distant stand of trees, and my senses awaken. Those first morning moments when the sun seems to ignite a horizon of hope—a new dawn, a new day, a new beginning—who doesn't need that?

Yesterday can't be altered, tomorrow can't be predicted, and today can't be controlled any more than I can adjust the sun's path. While that could make us feel helpless, I find a deep comfort in the knowledge that the one who placed the sun on its course has lit a distinct path for us. The path is filled with purpose and with the potential for interior prosperity: "You will show me the path of life" (Psalm 16:11).

While on earth, we will encounter both darkness and light, but that will not always be so. A day will come when Christ in all his glory and light will fill every shaded nook and every shadowed cranny, and darkness will be no more. Nothing will be as we now know it, and earth and God's people will experience full redemption. Imagine that. Just imagine!

—PATSY CLAIRMONT (*I Second That Emotion*)

# THE PARTY OF FRIENDSHIP

*A friend loves you all the time.*
—Proverbs 17:17 NCV

Getting an invitation to anything is a special occasion. Whether it comes in a phone call, a letter, an e-mail, or smoke signals, the message is, "Your presence is requested." The excitement is undeniable. An invitation piques our curiosity and starts us imagining wonderful things. It doesn't really matter if it's Cinderella at the ball, a dinner at the White House, or Tuesday morning coffee with your neighbor. We love being invited. Even if we can't attend, it feels good to have been invited.

Every friendship arises out of some kind of invitation. Inviting is active. Inviting says, "I was thinking about you, and I am requesting your presence." Inviting says, "I have made time for you and me to celebrate." Inviting makes a hopeful promise of good times.

To the party of friendship, you must bring a gift. You've been invited, remember? "Your presence is requested." It would be far easier to bring a kitchen gadget. C. S. Lewis cautions us that we may act kindly, correctly, justly . . . and yet withhold the giving of ourselves, which is love. To offer a vulnerable nugget of your soul that has been mined from a deep, sometimes dark, place is more valuable than gold to your friend.

—NICOLE JOHNSON (*Fresh-Brewed Life*)

# LEAVING A LEGACY

*A good life gets passed on to the grandchildren.*
—Proverbs 13:22 MSG

Are you leaving a legacy that will give your children and grandchildren—all those who look up to you—wings to fly? Have your children (no matter what their age) seen evidence that you love, honor, respect, talk to, and rely on the Lord for all you are?

I plan to leave five Bibles with my markings, thoughts, prayers, and notes. I want each of my five grandchildren to know that their grandmother knew the Lord and took notes on what he said! I want them to think about the things they do and who they are because they remember that their grandmother prayed for them and believed in God's plans for them.

I also want them to know they are and were always loved very much. My seven-year-old granddaughter Rachel has had her eye on a starfish paper weight on my desk since she was about three. She has held it in her little girl hands with wonder and asked if she could have it when she got married. I assured her that she could, and now I keep it in a special place where she can admire it until then. It is valueless in terms of money, but it's a treasure in her brown eyes. It says her grandmother loves her. It's all about leaving a legacy.

—JAN SILVIOUS (*Smart Girls Think Twice*)

# GOD'S DAUGHTER

*I will be your God through all your lifetime, yes, even when your hair is white with age.*

—Isaiah 46:4 *TLB*

Do you know in the deepest place in your heart that you are loved? I pray you do. And I pray that you understand that God never takes his eyes off you, that you are not alone. I pray that you will grasp hold of the truth that because you are God's daughter, his princess, anything is possible.

I believe with all my heart that God has a dream for your life that is far greater than any you could dream for yourself. When God looks at you, he sees a woman whom he passionately loves. That love compelled him to give his Son to redeem you from the nightmare of a life spent apart from him. No matter whether any of your smaller dreams are realized on this earth, God has an amazing dream for your life that nothing and no one can touch. God's dream for you outweighs every other dream in your life.

And remember, each one of us is given only one life. Your days on earth are not a dress rehearsal so that you can come back and try again. Every life counts. Your life counts. Heaven is watching to see what you will do with the life you have been given.

—SHEILA WALSH (*God Has a Dream for Your Life*)

# PUTTING SOME HALLELUJAH IN THE HUMDRUM

*The LORD will fulfill his purpose for me; your love, O LORD, endures forever.*

—Psalm 138:8 NIV

Isn't God good? Isn't it amazing how, while we're in the midst of what may seem like ho-hum, ordinary, everyday routines and careers, we're actually living out pieces of the puzzle that will eventually create the big picture God has planned for our lives? The important thing to remember, while we're trudging along through every ordinary day, is to make ourselves available and open to God. Start every day with the request, "Dear Father, please fulfill your purpose for me; your love, O Lord, endures forever—do not abandon the works of your hands. Put me to use in your service, Lord, wherever that service might be today."

I get e-mail messages and letters from people who are desperately looking for their purpose in life, people who feel unfulfilled, people wondering why they were born, people asking, "Is this all there is to life, just getting up in the morning, going to work, coming home, doing the chores, eating, sleeping, watching television, and starting all over again with the same routine the next day?" I tell them they need an attitude adjustment. They need to realize that their daily routine is connected with their purpose in life. It's how we fulfill our purpose daily.

—THELMA WELLS (*The Buzz*)

# MAKE SURE YOU DANCE

*I've decided that there's nothing better to do than go ahead*
*and have a good time and get the most we can out of life.*
—Ecclesiastes 3:12 msg

Life—your life—is The Party to which you're invited. You can choose to stay away (denial), show up but choose not to dance (acceptance), or show up and dance 'til you break the strap on your shoes (celebrate). The latter means refusing to sit out a number. Dancing to every song, be it a slow dance, boogie, Macarena, electric slide, line dance, tango, salsa, dirge, or swing. At different times in your life they'll play them all. Dance them all, and don't worry about the steps; they'll come to you.

Pay attention to what you say to God. Even if you don't consider yourself particularly eloquent in your prayer times, you still talk to him. What are you saying when you turn your internal thoughts heavenward? Are you telling him how appreciative you are for your very breath? For your life? You know, not the one you thought you were signing up for, but the one you're in, with all its raging, glorious imperfection. It's yours. And no matter what you're saying to God about it, regardless of where you are in gaining expertise at decorating your reality, God is listening to you. He is loving and accepting you. All of heaven is pulling for you to move past acceptance to celebration, one dance step at a time.

—ANITA RENFROE (*If You Can't Lose It, Decorate It!*)

# TRUST IN ACTION

*One who trusts in the LORD is secure.*

—Proverbs 29:25 NRSV

Do you know what it means to our Father and to Jesus our Savior when you choose to trust him in everything? I love the truth that we can give back to the one who has given everything for us by trusting in his love. It is of course a totally win-win situation, since the one we are being asked to trust is one hundred percent trustworthy, and as we continue to walk with him, we understand that more and more. It's not that we won't ever be tested but rather that testing plus trust is love. A time of testing can paralyze us, but when we mix it with trust, we move out in love.

There is no greater gift we can give God than our trust, and there is nothing more liberating than to do that in prayer. We are invited to bring our lives, our families, our hopes, and our dreams and lay them as a gift before our Father, believing he can be trusted with everything we treasure most. Prayer is the place where we take our hands off our lives—it is trust in action.

Your heavenly Father waits with open arms to hold your treasures. There is no safer place in heaven or on earth.

—SHEILA WALSH (*Get Off Your Knees and Pray*)

# THE SOLITARY HEART

*O give thanks to the LORD, for he is good; for his steadfast love endures forever.*

—Psalm 107:1 NRSV

For those of you out there who live alone, I can tell you from experience that it's important to have a grateful heart about living by yourself. And in many ways, each one of us is essentially alone. We "exist within our own unique epidermal envelope as a separate thing," Thomas Wolfe once wrote. But that can be a wonderful thing.

Living alone has taught me not only to tolerate solitude but revel in it. I've learned to confront my fears and become comfortable with my inner self. In fact, solitude isn't a luxury but a requirement for me now. It gives me good mental health. When I'm alone, I process life's experiences, think through choices, replenish my energy, and face myself without other distractions. Sometimes that's pleasant; sometimes it's not. But it's never without value.

The German psychologist Erich Fromm believes our ability to love others is predicated upon whether or not we can enjoy time alone. He says if we're not comfortable with our own company, we'll never be able to love anybody else out of desire rather than need. That's an enormous thought! A heart of gratitude leads us down many avenues that enhance personal growth and teach us to celebrate life just as it is, without balloons, streamers, confetti, and horns blowing.

—LUCI SWINDOLL (*Life! Celebrate It*)

# OH YES YOU ARE!

*As each one has received a gift, minister it to one another, as good stewards of the manifold grace of God.*

—1 Peter 4:10

I love that God gave us imagination. He knew we would need it to see beyond where we are to what might be. Certainly the dark enemy longs to corrupt the bright light of imagination; so we must put boundaries on where we allow our thoughts to go. Yet we must not ignore the gift of thinking beyond ourselves because that's how we explore creativity and hope.

When imagination is used to explore art, it can be enlightening. We tend to be boxy in our perspectives, but art can help us to take a leap into a bigger world. I believe in the emotionally healing value of creative endeavors. If you're one of those who say as I once did, "I'm not artistic," may I say unequivocally, "Oh, yes you are." Give yourself a chance to explore your creativity; risk making mistakes to find your undiscovered artist.

You may not ever be lauded in an art museum, but your "brush strokes" might take place in the kitchen. Your soufflés may become fine enough to frame; your roast, a tender masterpiece of culinary genius. Perhaps you are a talented musician, jewelry designer, poet, tender caregiver, teacher, photographer, seamstress, hairdresser, inspired letter writer, or decorator. The list is limitless when it comes to all the ways art can be expressed.

—PATSY CLAIRMONT (*I Second That Emotion*)

# THE UNLIKELY FIVE

*Fear not; you will no longer live in shame. Don't be afraid;
there is no more disgrace for you. You will no longer remember
the shame of your youth.*

—Isaiah 54:4 NLT

Each of the women listed in the book of Matthew in the genealogy
of Jesus could probably be nominated as least likely to show up in
the Messiah's royal line. Five out of five women listed came with
*issues.* Rahab was a prostitute. Tamar seduced her father-in-law.
Bathsheba committed adultery. Ruth was a Gentile, considered a
pagan and an outsider. Then there was Mary, who was just a young,
common peasant girl. A nobody. Just another pregnant teenager.

Rarely were women ever mentioned in lineages. Yet God
seemed to have made a special place in his heart for these
Unlikely Five. I wonder if each woman represents, perhaps, the
things that generally hold women back from being used greatly
of God. In this list we have sexual sins (many of them probably
stemming from early sexual abuse); we have someone who feels
like a newcomer or outsider to Christianity; and we have a gal
who comes from humble means and probably considers herself
much too young and insignificant to become anything special.
The thing is the New Testament writers did not remember these
women for their sins of perceived flaws but rather for the goodness God birthed through them during their time on earth.

I love that! God uses broken men and women.

—SANDI PATTY (*Falling Forward*)

# FRIENDSHIP IS FRESH WATER

*These God-chosen lives all around—what splendid friends they make!*
—Psalm 16:3 MSG

Looking for reasons to celebrate, I uncover gratitude. I realize how much I have to be thankful for. Spending time with my friends allows me to stay in that place of gratitude a little while longer. Celebrating birthdays, victories, answered prayers, and accomplishments lets me savor them before I move on to something else. Throwing a party, even if it's just a cup of coffee shared, is good for the soul.

I am a better wife when I celebrate my friendships. In addition, I am a more contented person when I celebrate my friendships. I become a better friend. It puts a spring in my step, a smile on my lips, and gives me a much lighter heart. I can be by myself, five hundred miles from any of my friends, and something one of them has said will cause me to laugh out loud.

I have exponentially more joy in my life because of them. I bring more joy to my marriage and to my family because of them. Friendship fills a deep well within me with fresh water. When I celebrate my friendships, it's like dropping a huge rock into the well. It splashes that water everywhere, on everyone else in my life.

—NICOLE JOHNSON (*Fresh-Brewed Life*)

# EXPRESSING GENEROSITY

*A generous person will be enriched.*

—*Proverbs 11:25* NRSV

Generosity and kindness aren't meant to be held in reserve for big storms or hard times. Generous living is an art to be practiced, a lifestyle that springs naturally from understanding that God really owns everything, and we are merely conduits through whom he delivers his blessings.

If we're paying attention, we'll notice examples of generosity—and opportunities to express it—all around us. And generosity isn't limited to money. A short note of encouragement, a basket of muffins, a flower left on someone's desk or doorstep, a surprise phone call, or a kind word in passing are all small generosities anyone can give. You don't have to have a lot, just the desire to share your time or skills or whatever God has blessed you with. Sometimes we forget all the tangible ways we can express God's love unless we've been in similar need ourselves. Providing a meal for a family whose mother is sick, volunteering to care for a friend's children while she goes to the grocery store, visiting someone who is confined in assisted living, offering a ride to someone who can't drive—all of these are physical offerings that require only your time, energy, and the willingness to be involved in someone else's life.

—JAN SILVIOUS (*Smart Girls Think Twice*)

# GOD HONORED HERE

*You were bought at a price; therefore glorify God in your body
and in your spirit, which are God's.*

—1 Corinthians 6:20

If I could hang a sign around my neck to indicate that I am a
believer, I'd want it to read: God Honored Here. I have realized for
years, however, that when I am consumed by how I look and what
diet I am on or off, "God Honored Here" would not be an accurate
statement. More than the waste of money, I regret the time I have
wasted in self-punishing cycles. Instead of having on internal running shoes that would take me to a healthy place of honoring God
with my body, I kept going in self-defeating circles.

I knew that one of the big issues for me is how I look to others, and I wanted to be free from that compulsion. As I prayed for
God to help me find victory to live free from these endless cycles,
one phrase kept coming to me over and over again: a long obedience in the same direction, which is also the title of a book by
Eugene Peterson that I read many years ago. This phrase captures
the heart of what it actually looks like to put on your running
shoes and honor God every day in your body.

—SHEILA WALSH (*I'm Not Wonder Woman*)

# FIRST CHURCH

*We look inside, and what we see is that anyone united with the*
*Messiah gets a fresh start, is created new. The old life is gone; a*
*new life burgeons! Look at it!*

—2 Corinthians 5:17 MSG

First United Methodist Church in Oklahoma City, where I was born, is more than one hundred years old. Called "First Church" by its members, it stands across the street from the national memorial marking the site where the Murrah Federal Building was bombed on April 19, 1995.

The violent explosion that killed 168 people caused smaller losses as well. When the front walls of the grand old church collapsed, the beautiful old stained-glass windows were shattered.

Almost before the dust settled, volunteers and church members lovingly collected the fragile shards of glass from the heaped-up rubble of the collapsed walls. Over the next five years, they carefully put those pieces back together in totally new creations. Today, wonderful new stained-glass windows glow on the building's reconstructed façade.

The windows at First church are especially meaningful for people like me, and for families who feel like their lives have gotten all cracked up and glued back together—who know what it's like to be broken and end up in a totally new creation. We are living out the powerful truth of the inscription on one of the windows: *The Lord takes broken pieces and by His love makes us whole.*

—SANDI PATTY (*Life in the Blender*)

# STONE-COLD WORDS

*God's judgment is right, and as a result you will be counted worthy of the kingdom of God.*

—2 Thessalonians 1:5 NIV

Have you ever trembled and told a friend something you've done terribly wrong, and then, emotionally hunched over, waited for their stone-cold words of judgment to hit you? But instead you heard the flat thud of grace as their rock hit the ground.

Throwing rocks will never make us more loving. As we clutch and throw our rocks, we reveal our pettiness and our inability to change our own lives. Only when we drop our rocks and choose to love do we become more loving.

So the next time someone trembles in fear and tells you something you really didn't want to know, or you see your sin in someone else's life, or your loved one is braced to feel your stone-cold words, you'll know what to do. Loosen your grip, and listen for the flat thud of grace as you choose love over judgment.

The only one who has the right to throw a rock is the one who has never done any wrong—ever. There has been only one, and only that one can pick up the rock.

And he did. Jesus became the Rock and took care of our wrong for all time. He still stands between our accusers and us. He still lifts our heads and sets us on the path to freedom.

—NICOLE JOHNSON (*Dramatic Encounters with God*)

# LIKE AN EAGLE

*God loved the world so much that he gave his one and only Son so that whoever believes in him may not be lost, but have eternal life. God did not send his Son into the world to judge the world guilty, but to save the world through him.*

—*John 3:16–17* NCV

When God dealt with the children of Israel, he protected them like an eagle caring for his young. Because we also are "a people for God's own possession" (1 Peter 2:9 NCV), part of his chosen because of our belief in Jesus (Ephesians 2:11–16), he hovers over us with the same concern.

He watches and when we are big enough to leave the nest, he stirs it up, forcing us to get out and fly. But he is always ready to catch us on his strong feathers if our weak little wings should fail.

You may be saying, "Well, how can I know that he loves me? I don't always feel it." I understand, but when we recall what he has done for you and me, there is no rational explanation but love. And besides, he not only has said he loves us but he also has shown us.

God sent his Son, Jesus, to let us know that he loves us, just as he showed Israel in so many ways that they were loved and that he could be trusted. He never stops being the Supreme Ruler of the universe, and he never gives up his role as the great Lover of our souls.

—JAN SILVIOUS (*Smart Girls Think Twice*)

# FIX YOUR EYES

*Let us run with endurance the race that is set before us, looking
unto Jesus, the author and finisher of our faith.*

—Hebrews 12:1–2

If you are like me, you have been familiar with the phrase "Fix
your eyes on Jesus" for some time, but you may wonder what it
means, what it looks like. When I was a teenager I was stumped
by Christ's command to pick up my cross every day and follow
him. I had no idea how to do that. Did it mean that I should carve
up the breakfast table and drag it around the neighborhood? As
I studied and prayed, I became convinced that it means that
every time my will crossed God's will, I dragged my will back in
line with his. It means doing the things that I know are good and
true, whether I feel like it or not. It means setting my face and
heart toward heaven just as Jesus did. But what about "Fix your
eyes on Jesus"?

I believe that phrase means that we study how Jesus lived,
how he loved, and follow his example. When we find ourselves in
a difficult place, we do what he did: we turn to our Father.

Faith is not wishful thinking or theatrics. Faith is born in us
as we fix our eyes on Jesus and as we recognize the fingerprints of
God the Father all over our lives.

—SHEILA WALSH (*Extraordinary Faith*)

# DIVINE APPOINTMENTS

*The human mind may devise many plans, but it is the purpose of the LORD that will be established.*

—Proverbs 19:21 NRSV

When you look at everyday life as a gift from God and as your gift to him—and as one little piece of the puzzle of purpose that God has planned for you from the beginning of the universe—then each day can be an exciting occasion for discovering the divine appointments God has for you.

I don't know what I'd do if I couldn't look forward to something exciting each day. Now, I'm not talking about drama-queen excitement but about activities that keep the spark in my life. I wake up with Jesus on my mind and spend some quiet time either in the bedroom, the bathroom, or the kitchen praising God. You know, we women can do a lot of things at one time! So sometimes I'm praying and preparing my day's agenda at the same time. And as I prepare, I become filled with anticipation, thinking about the people and events God is going to bring into my life that day.

I pray, "Father, open the doors I need to walk through today. Put people in my way that I need to talk to, and show me what you want me to do. The results I see in the people I speak to are amazing. It is as if I have found my God-given purpose.

—THELMA WELLS (*The Buzz*)

143

# OUT OF NOWHERE

*I am the Lord your God ... and I have put my words in your*
*mouth and hidden you safely in my hand.*

—Isaiah 51:15–16 NLT

Whether they surface frequently or rarely, we all have strong feelings that impact us, causing tears to spring up unexpectedly, sending grief sweeping over us "out of nowhere," or pushing us to behave in specific ways. By studying these feelings and by remembering back to the events and issues that sparked them, we gain understanding that helps us cope.

As we acknowledge the damage inflicted on the crucial bonds our hearts innately crave, we also seek desperately to give meaning to our experiences, no matter how grievous the damage. The fact is, the human psyche can withstand almost any assault if we can find purpose in our lives in spite of that assault.

Our supreme purpose and meaning in life are to know, believe, and trust that we are loved by the God who does not "do" throwaways. That knowledge—understanding we are loved and valued by our Creator even more than we can comprehend—makes productive lives possible for all of us.

And here's the most important thing to understand: whether we are abandoned intentionally or due to uncontrollable circumstances, we are the intentional creation of the Lord Almighty. We are hidden safely in his hand because that's where he chooses for us to be, and that's where we *will* forever be.

—MARILYN MEBERG (*Love Me Never Leave Me*)

# THE ENERGY GIVER

*[God] gives power to the weak, and to those who have no might He increases strength.*

—Isaiah 40:29

The dictionary defines *energy* as the vigorous exertion of power. It has to do with effort, strength, potency, and might. Who has all these attributes? The Lord!

Scripture tells us that God not only has his own power and strength, but he's given that same power to us. He enables us to have energy when we tap into his. David says to God in Psalm 31:4, "You are my strength." And again in Psalm 27:1, "The LORD is the strength of my life; of whom shall I be afraid?" What great verses! What comforting verses! God gives us all the energy we need.

When I'm exhausted and fall into bed at night, I often think I'll never get up the next morning because I'm utterly played out. Or when I have no more strength to take care of a need or do the things that have been assigned to me, I have to force myself to remember my strength comes from God, not from inside me. There's a vast difference.

So, remember—strength doesn't come from exercise; strength comes from waiting on God. Tomorrow is another day, and God energizes us for it . . . no matter our age. Every day that I get older, his strength brings more comfort.

—LUCI SWINDOLL (*Life! Celebrate It*)

# NOW THAT'S ART

*Who endowed the heart with wisdom or gave understanding to the mind?*

—Job 38:36 NIV

We have been made in God's image (from which the word *imagination* derives), and no one outdoes God's artistic flair, which is why people copy his art all the time. From a forsythia bush bursting with blooms, to a bowl of green apples, to clear vases of white tulips, they all drip with his creative involvement.

I just came in from my after-dinner walk, and I was delighted to view the beginning of God's Spring Collection. Daffodils, pansies, and even a deep-purple hyacinth greeted me. Now that's art. Art inspires, and inspiration beckons us to join in the creative process in all we do.

Color is paramount to art, and the wonderful thing about color is it can be splashed across all of life's offerings: our attitudes, our speech, our clothing, our gift giving, and our emotional lives.

Why are we so moved by a crimson sunset, an ocher-dappled masterpiece, and a fistful of fuchsia peonies? Have you ever become misty over a glorious musical arrangement, a stunning sunrise, or a stirring dramatic performance?

We are hardwired to respond emotionally to the wonder of art. I believe God has given us many elements in this life that help to heal us, inspire us, and remind us of our Creator, as well as enlarge our interior worlds.

—PATSY CLAIRMONT (*I Second That Emotion*)

# OUR LIFE AND OUR BREATH

*Get down on your knees before the Master; it's the only way you'll get on your feet.*

—James 4:10 MSG

There is no greater gift that we are given on this earth, after our salvation, than the open line we have directly to the heart of God. Sometimes, all we want to do is kneel. Other times we want to lay on our faces and call on the name of Jesus. There are moments when we want to stand with our faces toward the warmth of the sun or battle against the driving rain as we share our hearts with him. Prayer is our life, our very breath. Share everything you love and everything that troubles you with him. Sing, cry, scream, laugh, dance, and rejoice always, knowing you are in his presence, loved and received.

This doesn't mean every prayer will be answered as we might hope it would, but there is a day coming when this detour will end and we will be home free. Until that day we have our Father who loves us, our Savior who died for us, and the Holy Spirit who intercedes for us when we don't know what to say. And we have each other. When we give our lives to him, we can experience a life where we get off our knees, lift our hands in the air, and pray until we see him face to face.

—SHEILA WALSH (*Get Off Your Knees and Pray*)

# WAYS TO CELEBRATE FRIENDSHIP

*Love one another with mutual affection; outdo one another in showing honor.*

—Romans 12:10 NRSV

+ *Celebrate your spiritual birthday, or someone else's.* Go on a picnic, have a party, or just have a big slice of cake in honor of "rebirth." Celebrate being found by God!

+ *Request the honor of someone's presence.* Practice inviting. Invite your daughter to join you on an errand that you normally do by yourself. Write an invitation to a friend to meet you for a cup of coffee or tea or lemonade, and give her a book, just because. Invite someone to attend church or Bible study with you, and bring cookies.

+ *Plan an extravagant, expensive, special day with a close friend.* Think of as many fun things as possible to squeeze into one day. Give your friend a copy of the expensive day you planned—then do something inexpensive together.

+ *The goal is not to form an exclusive circle of celebration among your friends.* The goal is to celebrate life. To say yes to being more loving, more caring, and more gracious. The choice to celebrate is about us, not about the other person. Like a rock dropped into a well, when celebration begins in your friendships, it will have a ripple effect and touch every area of your life.

—NICOLE JOHNSON (*Fresh-Brewed Life*)

# WHO IS YOUR HIGHER POWER?

> *Do you not know? Have you not heard? The LORD is the*
> *everlasting God, the Creator of the ends of the earth. He will*
> *not grow tired or weary, and his understanding no one can*
> *fathom. He gives strength to the weary and increases the power*
> *of the weak.*
>
> —Isaiah 40:28–29 NIV

I have heard dear, dear people say, "Oh, I believe in a Higher Power." I want to say, "If you really know the God who created the universe, he would be more than a Higher Power to you. He would be the God of your very life."

When you know that you know that God is who he says he is, you'll be infused with strength to walk through situations you never dreamed you'd be able to endure. When you know God and trust him for whatever you need, you can relax and rely on his strength to be your strength and his peace to be your peace.

I recently bumped into a good friend at the grocery store. This woman has faced many tough trials, including chronic illness and financial reversals, but she has a strong trust in the Lord. As we chatted, she said, "I guess I should be worried about this latest mess, but I'm not! I trusted God a long time ago, and he's always come through, so what good would it do to worry now?" Great point! She knows he is all-powerful, all-knowing, and all-loving, so she's decided to trust what she knows and see what he does. After all, he is the Highest Power, and he is her life.

—JAN SILVIOUS (*Smart Girls Think Twice*)

# ROCK-SOLID CONVICTION

*Faith is the confidence that what we hope for will actually happen; it gives us assurance about things we cannot see.*

—*Hebrews 11:1* NLT

I asked the young Vietnamese girl who does my nails what the word *faith* meant to her. At first she was unsure what I was asking. I told her that I was aware that the girls in the salon prepared a bowl of fruit and set it in front of a small effigy of Buddha. She said they did that for protection and out of respect, for good luck. I asked her if she talked to Buddha, and she gave me one of her big smiles and said something I have heard from her many times: "Miss Sheila, you crazy!"

When we study faith in the biblical context, it has both an active and a passive sense. In an active sense, faith is our loyalty and devotion to God; in a passive sense, our resting confidence in God, in his Word, and in his promises.

Faith is not just what we believe, our doctrine or denominational creed but also and more importantly, a rock-solid conviction that what we believe and whom we believe in are worth staking our lives on; they are real and living.

Christian faith is more than wishful thinking; it is a certainty, a constant assurance based on God's track record in our lives and the lives of the faithful through the generations.

—SHEILA WALSH (*Extraordinary Faith*)

# CONNOISSEUR OF SUNSETS

*Don't burn out; keep yourselves fueled and aflame. Be alert*
*servants of the Master, cheerfully expectant. Don't quit in hard*
*times; pray all the harder.*

—Romans 12:11–12 MSG

Think about this. How can we know what it means to really trust someone if we'd never been betrayed? How can we appreciate God's amazing gift of grace if we'd never had to ask his forgiveness for making some kind of horrendous, hurtful, and hopelessly stupid mistake?

I know a woman who has gone through some rough times. Honey, I'm talkin' really rough times. Yet her faith is strong, and her attitude is joyful. One of her small pleasures is watching the sun go down in the evening. She calls herself a connoisseur of sunsets, and she has made this observation: a sunset—and a life—are richer, deeper, and more vibrant when there are clouds.

A sun that sets cleanly, without clouds, turns the sky a soft, pretty pink. That kind of sunset is OK but nothing special. In contrast, when there's a messy sky with patches of dark clouds hovering over the horizon to reflect back the full, glorious colors of the sunset, then the sky is streaked with a magnificent spectrum of incredible hues: deep purple, hot pink, velvety gray, flashing crimson, vivid violet, and dozens of other colors. That kind of sunset takes your breath away.

—THELMA WELLS (*Listen Up, Honey*)

# YOUR CALLING IN LIFE

*We love Him because He first loved us.*
—1 John 4:19

Some of you may be wondering about your personal calling in life. Being married or not being married can indeed be a calling. So can having children or having no children, working outside the home or being a full-time mom, traveling on a job or staying in an office, working out of your home or being president of something, sewing drapes, cooking at the school cafeteria, finding a cure for cancer, or creating a better meat thermometer. Dare I say, your calling in life lies not in *what* you do but in *who* you are?

Remember this. Scripture says God created us for the express purpose of giving himself the joy of loving us. In being loved, we return that love. That is who we are: persons loved by God. When we return his love, we do it in a spirit of response that produces service to him. That is what our relationship with him is all about. If we do things for God because we are trying to pay him back, we miss the point of the relationship. We are not asked to *earn* the relationship; we are asked to *receive* the relationship.

So what is the call for each of our lives? To receive God's love and return God's love. We can experience that in everything we do.

—MARILYN MEBERG (*Love Me Never Leave Me*)

# THE TRUTH ABOUT TIME

*There is a time for everything, and a season for every activity under heaven.*

—*Ecclesiastes 3:1* NIV

Time is my highest priority right now. I never have enough of it. And the truth is, I'll never have enough time because it's all up to God, and he views time differently than I do.

My time has to do with *duration,* a measurable period when something occurs. I don't have enough "duration" during the day. I lack the continuum for everything I want or need to do to actually get it done. It's that simple. But God's timing is in terms of *division;* He operates moment by moment or through seasons or a lifetime or a dispensation. His time is not measurable, because He's eternal and earthly time is temporal.

The reason this is important is because when I look at my life from a human viewpoint, I run out of time. But when I look at it from a spiritual viewpoint, I see that God is in charge of everything; I'm not! Therefore, I will accomplish whatever comes my way even though it may not be written into the schedule of my daily planner.

Realistically speaking, then, I do have enough time. I have all the time God wants me to have and can spend it any way I like. I just need God's help to learn to spend it better.

—LUCI SWINDOLL (*Life! Celebrate It*)

# ART EXPRESSIONS

*Think about the things that are good and worthy of praise.*
*Think about the things that are true and honorable and right*
*and pure and beautiful and respected.*

—*Philippians 4:8* NCV

Do you have a favorite artist? What about a favorite classical piece? What flowers thrill your senses? When was the last time you walked through the woods? Have you handpicked a bouquet lately? Or attended a play, ballet, or read a classic? Have you in recent months walked on a beach, skipped rocks on a lake, or photographed a child or a pet?

Sometimes unplugging from our routines and losing ourselves in life's art is the most healing thing we can do for our stretched-out emotions. That's why therapists use handcrafts in recovery programs, doctors recommend vacations, and folks escape to tents, cabins, mountains, boats, and camps with sketchpads, Bibles, cameras, and journals tucked into their backpacks. We seem to instinctively understand that we need art expressions.

We just know if we sit on a pier with a fishing line in the water we might snag a little sanity. Or if we sleep under the stars, we'll air out our musty minds. Or if we float across a rhythmic bay, we'll step back on land calmer and better prepared to handle the tidal waves of obligations on our desks. I personally love to get lost in a museum for a morning and then reflect on what I saw with a friend over blueberry muffins and hot tea.

—PATSY CLAIRMONT (*I Second That Emotion*)

# WHO ARE YOU—REALLY?

*Your hands have made me and fashioned me.*

—Job 10:8

Do you know who you really are? Do you really?

I know this may sound like a radical concept to some of you, but the more I've soaked myself in the truth of God's Word, the more I believe I know who I really am. God has the kindest and most amazingly brilliant methods of affirming who we are to him.

Well, just in case you aren't completely sure who you really are, consider this wonderful list of verses as a daily reminder of what God thinks when he thinks of you—which is, by the way, constantly. Let them lift you up and open your heart to see your true identity.

1. I am God's daughter. (John 1:12)
2. I'm a friend of Christ. (John 15:15)
3. I'm God's coworker. (1 Corinthians 3:9)
4. I'm God's workmanship. (Ephesians 2:10)
5. I can't be separated from the love of God. (Romans 8:35–39)
6. I am free. (John 8:31–32)
7. I am forgiven. (Romans 8:1–2)
8. I can do all things through Christ. (Philippians 4:13)
9. I have been blessed with every spiritual blessing. (Ephesians 1:3)
10. I have Christ's mind. (Philippians 2:5–7)

—SANDI PATTY (*Falling Forward*)

# DISCOVERING YOUR PASSION

*Jesus said, "Love the Lord God with all your passion and
prayer and intelligence and energy."*
—Mark 12:30 MSG

I have a friend who says, "The deepest question of our lives is not
'If you died tonight, do you know where you would spend eternity?' That's a good question, and one that must be settled, but
the deeper question is 'If you wake up tomorrow, do you know
how you will spend the rest of your life?'" A lot of us aren't afraid
of dying. We're afraid of living. We don't know what we are living
for. We know that Jesus will be there for us when we die, if we
have a relationship with him, but we don't understand what kind
of life he is calling us to today.

There is something that God is calling you to do. You know
it. You've always known it. You may not know exactly what it is,
or what shape it will ultimately take, but it is unique to you and it
is why you were put here on this earth. I don't think this passion
is just handed to us like a gift. I think it is revealed in us over time
like an excavation. Everything extra gets chiseled away.

Uncovering God's purpose for your life and following it will
lead you to the greatest satisfaction there is.

—NICOLE JOHNSON (*Fresh-Brewed Life*)

# BE QUIET AND LISTEN

*Be still, and know that I am God; I will be exalted among the nations, I will be exalted in the earth.*

—*Psalm 46:10* NIV

Taking time to listen to God and to discern what he's calling us to do is a discipline we all can embrace. Sometimes in our great need to be heard we forget that listening allows God to be heard. I believe I've learned more in the silence, listening to him, than I've ever learned as I prayed and begged him for answers. At times I wasn't even asking the right questions, but when I quieted my mind and listened, really listened, I heard what I needed to hear.

Contemplative listening is a rich experience for those willing to make time to be still in God's presence. Set aside ten minutes and just be quiet. Turn off the music, the phone, and the television. Be quiet and invite God to speak to you in your spirit. As you grow comfortable with the silence and learn to hear God's voice, I think you'll want to set aside longer periods of time in which you deliberately listen for his counsel.

When I actually get quiet and listen, I find that God usually has something to tell me about myself. Sometimes when I think I have things all figured out, he reminds me that his ways are not my ways and his thoughts are far better than my best ideas.

—JAN SILVIOUS (*Smart Girls Think Twice*)

# WHEN THINGS DON'T MAKE SENSE

*Jesus said to him, "Have you believed because you have seen me? Blessed are those who have not seen and yet have come to believe."*

—John 20:29 NRSV

If you are like me, you want life to be more black and white than grey. I like things to make sense to me. I want to be able to understand what God is doing, but that's not always the case. Sometimes the plans we have made, the hopes and dreams we carry, fall apart at our feet. Are you in that place now? Do you wonder if God has abandoned you, or if you have missed God somewhere along the path?

It is the loneliest place on earth as a believer to feel as if God has left you or to live with the taunting voice that says you have blown it and missed God's best for your life. I pray that each of us will receive a clearer picture of what it means to walk by faith, no matter what sight tells us. Perhaps that is the whole point of faith: that we follow God faithfully when nothing makes sense anymore.

I've faced some of those dark days when things didn't make sense. Surprisingly, they made me take a much deeper look at faith than I had ever done. Is that where you find yourself? Cling to your faith—don't give up! God is faithful!

—SHEILA WALSH (*Extraordinary Faith*)

# A RECIPE FOR LIFE

*You have made known to me the paths of life; you will fill me with joy in your presence.*

—Acts 2:28

The messy mixture of sunshine and sorrow, happiness and heartache, triumph and tragedy, rest and toil is not the easiest recipe for a full, vibrant life. But it *is* the recipe. We need to be able to look back on our past and appreciate our successes and our failures. We need to recognize God's presence beside us every step of the way, leading us through the good times, guiding us through the hard times, and carrying us through those times when we can't make it on our own.

Don't hold back from living an active, outwardly focused life because you're afraid you might make a mess of things. Don't sit home alone in your immaculate house and worry that a guest might carry in a particle of dust. Remember that you are dust! Sure, dust can be disturbing when it's just dust. But add a few other ingredients, and dust can become so much more: a road leading you to others, a sculpture that inspires, a shelter when you need rest, a source of children's laughter when they're playing in the mud.

Go out there and make some messes. Let the living water of our Lord Jesus Christ flow into your dusty soul, then have fun stirring up some marvelous spiritual mud pies. Celebrate the blessings of your messy life!

—THELMA WELLS (*Listen Up, Honey*)

# EXPECTATIONS

*"My thoughts are not your thoughts, nor are your ways My
ways," says the LORD.*

—Isaiah 55:8

We all have expectations of God. For one thing, most of us think
it makes sense to be rewarded for good behavior. We expect God
thinks that too. When we're good, doing all the "right things," we
expect God to notice and protect us as well as reward us. When
he does not always do that, we may be tempted to grumble, but
we won't grumble loudly or noticeably because that would not be
the right thing to do. We wait, though. We wait for our reward.

I've needed to abandon my expectations of God. I know all
that great scripture about God's ways not being my ways, but it's
hard for me to swallow the fact that he does not always seem fair.
(I know. I'll never get a reward for talk like that.)

Now I too know what I didn't know then. By abandoning my
expectation of God and realizing I can't coerce his mystery into a
predictable formula based upon the merit system, I free up more
space in my mind for his ways. And because his ways are not my
ways, I have to choose to let him be God and rest in his invitation
to trust him. I don't always do that well, but I know it is the only
path to peace.

—MARILYN MEBERG (*Love Me Never Leave Me*)

# RENEWED DAY BY DAY

> *Outwardly we are wasting away, yet inwardly we are being renewed day by day.*
>
> —*2 Corinthians 4:16* NIV

Scripture teaches us to number our days and to apply our hearts unto wisdom. It also says even though we're "wasting away" on the outside, we are being renewed inwardly day by day. Those two verses say a lot about the aging process. It's a lifelong journey that has neither a clear beginning nor clear ending. But there are signs along the way that one's body is changing. We see our hair turning gray. Wrinkles show up in our faces as they become seasoned and worn with time. We do things more slowly and deliberately. These are the signs of the outside wasting away.

But it's the inside that's being renewed daily. And *that's* what we want to concentrate on. This is the secret of happy aging. Although obvious signs of physical changes are known to all of us, life's journey takes us beyond the obvious. It reaches inside and teaches us lessons we can only learn with our mind, spirit, and heart. The outward appearance becomes secondary to a far more endearing beauty and strength. The physical appearance of youth may be gone, but the capacity to love, experience, enjoy, share, and create grow even stronger. Therefore, these are the areas we must learn to stop and ponder.

—LUCI SWINDOLL (*Life! Celebrate It*)

# AN ART TOUR

*He has made everything beautiful in its time.*
—*Ecclesiastes 3:11*

Have you ever stepped inside a painting? In your imagination, I mean. It's wonderful to find a painting you love and then to study it. Sit, observe it, and then ask yourself what you like about it: the subject matter, the color palette, the artist's style? Then mentally enter the picture and try to imagine what the artist was thinking, what time of day you think the picture was painted, where the light source originates, what the people in it are doing, how you think they feel (tired, bored, joyful, in love). And before you leave the museum, visit the gift store and buy postcard-size pictures of your favorite paintings to refer to later.

Then, when you get home from your art tour, expand your experience by researching the artists you most appreciated. Just Google the artist's name and learn who inspired him or her and what struggles the artist faced. You might want to check online for Mary Cassatt, Pierre-Auguste Renoir, George Seurat, or Thomas Eakins. Or you may prefer Ansel Adams's black-and-white photography or the sculptures of Michelangelo or Gianlorenzo Bernini, and then there always are those who become ardent Pablo Picasso fans. Find your interests and explore them. Not only will you broaden your mind, but also just think how impressed your friends will be.

—PATSY CLAIRMONT (*I Second That Emotion*)

# GOD-WIRED FOR FELLOWSHIP

*Love the family of believers.*

—1 Peter 2:17 NRSV

Women need women friends, even if they have a great marriage. The rub can happen when we, for a variety of reasons—pride, shame, mental exhaustion, independent personality—tend to think, *All I need is God and no one else.* In essence we hibernate, acting like monks without a monastery.

But cloistering ourselves away from others isn't the way of true spiritual healing. God is there to fill our God-voids for sure, but he created human beings to fill our need for human connection. In Eden, God gave Adam a human helpmate right after declaring, "It is not good that man should be alone." God did not create us to thrive without each other, so never assume that you are somehow weak if you feel you cannot make it alone, just you and God. You weren't created to do life by yourself. Most of us tend to get a little crazy when we are alone for too long: introspective or edgy or sad. Our physical bodies are wired to push us toward the cure—being with supportive people.

I encourage you to proactively seek out women who like to do (or talk about) the same things you enjoy. Do it on a regular basis until your comfort level with them increases.

—SANDI PATTY (*Falling Forward*)

# EMBRACE YOUR LIFE

*Celebrate God all day, every day. I mean, revel in him!*
—*Philippians 4:4* MSG

Do you realize that the quality of each day is determined by one thing—your attitude toward it? Don't miss the life that is right in front of you. If you don't think enough meaning exists in your life, create it. Don't just run errands; use the opportunity to meditate. Pray for the businesses in your community you have to visit. Your bank and your dry cleaners both could use your prayers. You are on God's agenda now. He has given you meaning and purpose; splash in it. Don't just eat a quick bite; "dine instead." Even if it's peanut butter and jelly by yourself. Take it outside, savor the taste, enjoy the moment, breathe in the beauty. Look for the extraordinary in the ordinary.

In your drive to work or to take care of chores, think of all the things you pass, yet don't notice every day. Someone crying in the car next to you, the sunrise, a cornfield bringing forth first-fruits, the new shrubs in the neighbor's yard. Opportunities to minister, chances to have your breath taken away by beauty, a great idea for a new business.

Celebrate the significance and wonder of life. Don't wait until it hits you over the head. It's already there; waiting for you to embrace it.

—NICOLE JOHNSON (*Fresh-Brewed Life*)

# KNOWING GOD

*The people who know their God shall be strong, and carry out great exploits.*

—Daniel 11:32

When you know God—really know his character based on his Word, his past actions, and his promised intentions toward his people—you will be a strong, smart, settled woman of God.

In fact, what you know and believe about God is the foundation for every decision you'll make. You may have a good head on your shoulders and certainly you draw on your intelligence and common sense for guidance. But if you're truly smart, you'll recognize that all wisdom originates with and is given by God.

For all of our experience, logic, theories, and intelligence, there remains so very much we don't know and can't know as limited, finite human beings. Just about the time we figure out one situation, we're confronted with fresh questions from another direction. The best we can do when the answers aren't clear is to go with what we do know and rest in the fact that what we don't know is somehow wrapped up in the mystery of the God we trust. We can rely on him to show us ways we could never devise ourselves and answers we could never conceive on our own.

Thank God, we know who he is and who we are not.

—JAN SILVIOUS (*Smart Girls Think Twice*)

# START WHERE YOU ARE

*The Lord said, "If you have faith as a mustard seed, you can say to this mulberry tree, 'Be pulled up by the roots and be planted in the sea,' and it would obey you."*

—Luke 17:6

Perhaps as you look at your own life, you feel as if you have no faith at all. I think of Mary Graham's words that faith is not about our mustering up huge reserves of mountain-moving power but about leaning on Christ, trusting our Father, and taking one more step. We start with what we have. We bring the tiniest seed of faith that God has placed in our spirits, and God honors that faith. If we spend our time looking at the mountain, we will be overwhelmed, so we nurture the seed that God has planted in us.

I received a letter from a woman who wanted to talk to her neighbor about Jesus but felt overwhelmed at the thought of leading another to faith. I asked her, "What seems doable to you?"

"I could invite her in for coffee," she suggested.

"That's a great beginning," I said.

After that she wrote and told me that she believed she could invite her neighbor to a concert at her church. Then when the neighbor responded warmly to that, she invited her to a Sunday service. A few weeks later, the neighbor gave her life to Christ.

My point is, start where you are and leave the rest up to God. Just take the first step.

—SHEILA WALSH (*Extraordinary Faith*)

# SECOND CHANCES

*Because of the LORD's great love we are not consumed, for his compassions never fail. They are new every morning; great is your faithfulness.*

—Lamentations 3:22–23 NIV

I'm so grateful for every second chance God has granted me. The way I see it, if we can manage to live through a failure, then it's not a failure; it's the first step in a valuable learning experience. God has such a marvelous way of selecting those of us who seem the unlikeliest to succeed or are the most miserable misfits and using us for his glory.

The apostle Paul's story is told in the New Testament. Over the last two thousand years, his letters to the early churches have become blueprints for generations of Christians, showing us how we're to live our lives and serve our Savior. But before Paul became one of the most passionate of Christ's followers, he was their greatest persecutor, devising every way imaginable to torture and kill them.

Then Jesus touched his life, and Paul came to understand that we serve a gracious God who blesses us with second chances.

Jesus has unlimited patience to forgive us for being stupid. Or mean. Or thoughtless. Or hurtful. When we confess our failures and ask him to forgive us, he does so gladly. And then he loves to see us use our second chances to correct our mistakes and get back on the Christlike path.

—THELMA WELLS (*Listen Up, Honey*)

## OUR MYSTERIOUS GOD

*Trust the Lord with all your heart, and don't depend on your own understanding.*

—*Proverbs 3:5* NCV

I've never liked secrets unless I'm in on them. God has not let me in on some things he knows, plans, and, in love, means to accomplish for my good. There is an odd sort of comfort to that in spite of my wanting to know his secrets that pertain to me. I'm invited to rest in his mystery and in his love.

So then, how am I to live in harmony and peace with a God who holds secrets and whose mystery I'll never fully understand? I must first realize this truth. I'm not meant to understand it all. If I did, trust would not be necessary. Understanding would be all I need, but trust is what God needs.

Trust comes to me when I remember what God says about his love for me. Trust also comes as I recognize that his love provides a promise about my circumstances that don't always change when I want them to. His purpose for me is that I love and trust him in all things. His purpose for me is that I stay in constant touch with him through prayer, no matter what I'm asking for. His invitation is always, "Come unto me, . . . and I will give you rest" (Matthew 11:28 KJV).

—MARILYN MEBERG (*Love Me Never Leave Me*)

# THE JOYS OF JOURNALING

*Reflect on what I am saying, for the Lord will give you insight into all this.*

—2 Timothy 2:7 NIV

I counted my journals today. There are fifty-four. Some are travel journals from different trips and excursions through the years, but most are daily journals in which I've recorded activities, thoughts, ponderings, and concerns. By writing them, I've wanted to leave a trace that I've crossed life's threshold and hopefully made a difference in someone else's life.

There are numerous times I've reread those journals and thought about the moment this or that was written. I've pondered stories of my past. I've cried over pictures of those I loved who are no longer with me here on earth. I've laughed over antics by which my friends made me happy. I've read scriptures that meant something very meaningful to me at a particular time. I've remembered how I felt in an embarrassing moment or time of deep sadness. I've spent *hours* reflecting in those pages—tracing the route that a particular memory first took through my senses—and I'm richer for it.

I could talk all day about the benefits of keeping a journal, but that may not work for you. Primarily, I'm suggesting you think back, remember, be still and thoughtful about where you've come from, what you've come through, and why it's important.

—LUCI SWINDOLL (*Life! Celebrate It*)

# RELEASING THE IMAGINATION

*So God created man in His own image; in the image of God He
created him; male and female He created them ... Then God
saw everything that He had made, and indeed it was very good.*
—Genesis 1:27, 31

What turns the crank on your imagination? Perhaps stimulating
conversations do. I've found intentional chat sessions helpful to
stretch my mind in problem solving. That's a healing form of art, for
sure. When someone helps me to see beyond my stuck place, it
paints my world with perspective. Maybe you're a songwriter. What
a holy exercise. And oh, how it pleases the Lord when we sing to
him. Perhaps you prefer to twirl your imagination wheel by teaching.
We all applaud those who impart life-giving information with zeal.

Here's an idea: sign up for a class just outside your comfort
zone. Maybe a cooking class, book club, stained-glass demonstration, writing seminar, or pottery or dulcimer lesson. Some of these
only require an evening but could enhance and expand your creative repertoire and surprise you with your untapped potential.

Artistic endeavors can be therapeutic to our uptight bundle of
emotions and crucial for our mental health. If you're already over-
obligated, please don't join a class. Instead, take a nap. Really. Then,
when you are well rested, figure out what you can do to thin your
uptight must-do list to make sane space for art. It will make you
more ingenious, fun, textured, and more satisfied with your trek here
on this wondrous, spinning kaleidoscope called God's green earth.

—PATSY CLAIRMONT (*I Second That Emotion*)

# TRUST MUST BE GIVEN

*Those who are attentive to a matter will prosper, and happy are those who trust in the LORD.*

—Proverbs 16:20 NRSV

Trust is like faith. You cannot see it; you just do it. It must be given. Here are some other words from the thesaurus for *trust*: confidence, belief, credence. To trust is to "depend on, rely on, bank on, build on, count on." You cannot trust without moving out of your head. You cannot depend on someone or build on something with mere knowledge. The soul must be part of the equation. The words call us to action, not inspection. The word *on* is significant as well. You can't merely rely. You can't depend by yourself. You can't build in air. There is a requirement of someone or something else that moves us out of ourselves.

We can know, yet not do. We can gather facts, and give nothing in return. We can observe all day long without ever caring. But we do not trust if we don't care. We do not give to something if we don't trust it. And if we say we trust the truth, and yet do nothing with it, it reveals we have not trusted it at all. Trust requires something of us. Trust holds the feet of knowledge to the fire of action.

—NICOLE JOHNSON (*Fresh-Brewed Life*)

# FELLOW SOJOURNERS

*Therefore comfort each other and edify one another, ju*
*you also are doing.*

—1 Thessalonians 5:11

After a crisis, or the beginning of recovery or a major
it is especially vital to begin creating a network of mu
portive sojourners. Even Jesus, in his darkest mo
Gethsemane's garden, confessed the need to have h
nearby. If God's Son needed friends during his hour of
would be silly to say that we don't.

What holds us back from reaching out and connecti
of rejection, perhaps. Or the thought that our dilemma o
so unique that there will be no one out there who w
understand or care. We know others are busy with full li
assume they do not have time for us.

But what I've discovered is that, in general, quite the
site is true. Most people are "God-wired" deep within to v
help others who are in pain in any way they can, especially
who have traversed a path similar to yours. Follow up o
leads you come across until you find someone whose thi
healing has been quenched and is now delighted to hold
hand and show you where she found the living water.

—SANDI PATTY (*Falling For*

# DEEP ASPIRATIONS

> Jesus replied, "The seed cast on good earth is the person who
> hears and takes in the News, and then produces a harvest
> beyond his wildest dreams."
>
> —Matthew 13:23 MSG

Let's talk for a moment about holding onto your dreams. The
word *dream* can be defined as a "wild fancy or hope." It can also
be defined as a "reverie, a trance, or a state of abstraction." The
Webster definition I am using is that a dream is "a deep aspiration." I'm also using the word in relation to God's plans for our
lives; He has deep aspirations for us, which I often refer to as his
dreams for us. God knows what he's doing when he places his
desire in our hearts to do what he has ordained for us from the
beginning of time.

People's experience with personal dreams is as varied as the
people themselves. No one's dream history is the same as another's,
and yet we all know what it is to have dream yearnings. I think
the very existence of those yearnings ties into God's personal
dreams for our lives. He placed within us an awareness of certain
preferences and in the awareness of those preferences we can
find our dreams and motivations. In other words, he places the
dreams, and we live them out. When we do, there is internal
peace.

—MARILYN MEBERG (*Love Me Never Leave Me*)

# THE PARADOXES OF FAITH

*Jesus said, "If you try to hang on to your life, you will lose it. But if you give up your life for my sake and for the sake of the Good News, you will save it."*

—*Mark 8:35* NLT

It was a beautiful Indian summer day, and I was sitting in the back of a church I had never attended before. As I listened to the old traditional hymns washing over me, I felt I was healing from my dark night of depression. The pastor said, "Some of you in here feel as if you are dead inside. Christ is here in all his resurrection power. If you will simply call on him, he will reach into that place and pull you out."

Quickly, I ran up the aisle and lay flat on my face in front of the altar. It was the first time I had gone to God empty-handed. Before I'd always gone with a new book or a new record or a new something I'd done to make God love me. I felt like I came as a filthy, broken, bedraggled orphan. "There's not a thing in the world I can do to make you love me," I said to God, "but I also realize there's not a thing in the world I can do to stop you from loving me." I felt such peace.

Christ reached down that day and gathered me to his heart. It's one of those great paradoxes of faith—you give up control and yet you feel so free.

—SHEILA WALSH (*Life Is Tough But God Is Faithful*)

# LEARNING TO TRUST

*Whoever trusts in the LORD shall be safe.*
—Proverbs 29:25

As Christians, we are the beloved of God. We can stake our claim on that promised land. We can choose to trust it and allow it to change us, or we can mistrust it. Not trusting it doesn't make it any less true. It simply makes it untrue for us. It keeps us locked out of the freedom of experiencing God's embrace. It's like being invited to a party and mistrusting the invitation. The party is going on with or without us. Should we choose not to attend, we are the ones who lose.

Understanding who we are in Christ intellectually will not change us unless we *trust* that identity in the core of our being. We are completely and totally loved and embraced in the arms of God. Allowing that relationship to transform us is the key.

Does trusting God come easily to you? Or do you struggle? Giving yourself in relationship to God affords you the opportunity to enter into a relationship with a spiritual foundation to build on and with someone who will never fail you. Once you've learned to trust him, you can better trust others.

—NICOLE JOHNSON (*Fresh-Brewed Life*)

# CHANGING YOUR ATTITUDE

*Let your minds and hearts be made new.*
—Ephesians 4:23 NLV

If you're one who, like me, tends to get impatient when you're forced to wait and wait and wait, consider changing your *maditude* to *gratitude*. Instead of fretting about the time you're wasting and all the things you have to do, take advantage of the break you've been given.

Close your eyes and pray, "Thank you, Lord, for giving me this time to rest. I'm overwhelmed with all the things I have to do, and I know I don't have time for all of them. Help me to shift my focus away from those long lists of have-to-dos and want-to-dos. Please plant a little sweet-pea flower of peace in my mind right now, and help me imagine it slowly sprouting and flowering, entwining my weary spirit like a fragrant vine growing up the trellis by the porch swing. Put me there now, Lord; help me see myself relaxing in that old porch swing on a cool summer's evening, enjoying the beautiful blessing of your creation surrounding me. Thank you, Lord. I praise you, Lord. Amen."

If you're not a porch-swing kind of person, ask Jesus to give you an image of your own favorite relaxing place where you can mentally and physically take a break and step back from the hustle and bustle of the world.

—THELMA WELLS (*Listen Up, Honey*)

# IT WILL RISE AGAIN!

> *I know, LORD, that our lives are not our own. We are not able*
> *to plan our own course.*
> —*Jeremiah 10:23* NLT

What happens when we're not obedient to God's original dream for our lives? What happens when we choose a direction other than the one that fulfills God's dream—when we abandon the dream and try to comfort ourselves in pursuit of something else? Does that mean God also abandons his dream for us?

The question reminds me of the old quip about how to make God laugh: tell him your plans. One of my favorite things about God is that he is stronger than I am, smarter than I am, and cares more about everything and everyone than I do. That means nothing, including my misguided determination to follow my own plans or my willful disobedience to do his will, is going to derail God's plan.

It *will* rise again because God will always prevail.

There again is the mystery of God: He does allow us to do stupid things, but just as the good shepherd goes after one lost sheep, God goes after us. He has a dream for our lives; that dream will prevail because he does.

If you're not following God's plan for your life, change course! If you've abandoned your dream, reclaim it. God is in the business of turning ashes into beauty.

—MARILYN MEBERG (*Love Me Never Leave Me*)

# COMPASSION POURED OUT

*If there is any consolation in Christ, if any comfort of love, if any*
*fellowship of the Spirit, if any affection and mercy, fulfill my joy*
*by being like-minded, having the same love, being of one accord,*
*of one mind.*

—*Philippians 2:1–2*

The desperate plight of two young prostitutes I'd seen on the *Geraldo*
*Show* so touched my heart that I decided to talk about them during a
concert. Midway through, however, I was so overcome with emotion
that I got down on my knees, right there and began to pray.

When I looked up, the whole front of the church was filled with
people who had come forward to kneel or fall flat on their faces. I
could hear people asking God to forgive them for their apathy and
unconcern. I ended the evening with a song and prayer, but that
didn't end the evening at all. God was there, speaking to people.

A Vietnam veteran was bitter and angry because he'd come
home and found people who didn't seem to care. But he found
Jesus that night and was able to forgive.

A little eight-year-old girl said to me, "I love the Lord. My mom's
not a Christian; will you pray with me?" So I joined hands with her
and her little friend, and the three of us prayed for her mother.

Young couples having trouble with their marriages came forward to talk. One person after another reached out to communicate
with God—and to be honest and real, totally open to him. Now
that's a concert!

—SHEILA WALSH (*Life Is Tough But God Is Faithful*)

# ANYONE FOR DESSERT?

*You show me the path of life. In your presence there is fullness*
*of joy; in your right hand are pleasures forevermore.*
—Psalm 16:11 NRSV

Pleasure has many forms: beauty, laughter, solace, companionship, solitude, love. Even giftedness. It can be playful, sensual, enriching, or frivolous. Even worshipful. Sometimes when I'm praying, I thank the Lord for the pleasure of his company. I love knowing he is with me, that he cares about me and he makes my heart feel grateful, content, and full. All of those thoughts bring me pleasure, and I want him to know that from my heart. I want to tell him.

What is your most pleasant feeling? Mine is relief. I love that feeling more than any other. When I'm hungry, eating brings relief. When I'm tired, sleep gives relief. When I'm lonely, companionship gives relief. When I'm standing in a long line wearing bad shoes, even an inadequate place to sit feels wonderful. Anything uncomfortable that finds relief gives the feeling of pleasure. And nothing on this earth is more wonderful than something that relieves my soul. This is what I'm talking about. Someone has said, "Work is the meat of life; pleasure is the dessert." Pleasure is a wonderful, delightful, enjoyable feeling, and I believe we should stop for it in life. It makes our time on this earth sweeter and easier to bear.

—LUCI SWINDOLL (*Life! Celebrate It*)

# TRUST'S SILVER LINING

*Those who trust in the LORD are like Mount Zion, which
cannot be shaken but endures forever.*

—Psalm 125:1 NIV

Everyone has a story of how trust was broken and why he or she
can't trust. Not trusting comes naturally. Actually trusting came
first, and then sadly we learned to distrust. Once we distrust, it is
hard to go back to trusting again. But the path of enriching our
relationships is a way of trust.

But what about people who aren't trustworthy? Are we supposed to trust even when we might get hurt? What if someone
has let us down? How can we trust that person, and should we?
When we distrust we hurt ourselves. If we trust someone and
that person lets us down, were we wrong for trusting? Or was
that person wrong for letting us down? Just because we trusted
someone doesn't make us foolish. If anything, we can be proud
of the fact that we trusted.

It's much like that with love. When we love someone who
doesn't love us, are we fools? Or are we better people for having
loved, even if that love wasn't returned? When we learn to trust
others, we are changed in the process. We trust because of what
it does for us, not because of what it does for the other person.

—NICOLE JOHNSON (*Fresh-Brewed Life*)

# PARTNERING WITH GOD

> *To him who by the power at work within us is able to*
> *accomplish abundantly far more than all we can ask or*
> *imagine, to him be glory in the church and in Christ Jesus to all*
> *generations, forever and ever.*

—*Ephesians 3:20–21* NRSV

One of the most gracious ways God receives our love is to make us partners with him in doing those things that make the world a better place. We already know God could get things done without us, but he wants us to be a part of everything he does. God places dreams and plans within us as motivators to accomplish his already conceived dream plan. So we do together what he could do alone.

When Jesus established his earthly ministry, he chose twelve disciples to partner with him. They not only had a relationship with Jesus, they ultimately spread the news that he was the Son of God. When they didn't understand his miracles, Jesus explained them. When they didn't get the meaning of his parables, Jesus taught them. He also taught them how to love and how to live in the divine reciprocity of give-and-take. All that helped them later to establish the Christian church after the resurrection of Jesus and his return to heaven.

God's concept of partnering is a tremendous relief to us because we realize it is not we who are fully responsible for the results of our efforts to serve. Our internal engine is powered by him—not just by ourselves. We serve and work together.

—MARILYN MEBERG (*Love Me Never Leave Me*)

# BAPTIZED IN LOVE

> *The LORD is near to those who have a broken heart, and saves such as have a contrite spirit.*
>
> —Psalm 34:18

I was walking through the mall the other evening, flipping through the pages of a new book I had just purchased. I became so interested I almost walked into the tiny wheelchair of a little girl who couldn't have been more than four years old. My heart ached as I looked down at that little child, and I thought, *Lord, how I wish I had the faith of a mustard seed to look into the eyes of this little girl and say, "In the Name of Jesus Christ of Nazareth, rise up and walk!"*

I long to see God's power and glory strewn across people's lives rather than the wreckage and chaos that is so often there. I do believe with all my heart that a new Christian leadership has emerged during the last decade. I believe they are people who have been baptized in love, people who have had their hearts broken.

You can tell when you're in the company of those who have been through deep water. They have been through the very valley of the shadow of death, but they have walked every step of the way holding on to Jesus' hand. And they have emerged on the other side with a brighter light, a more tender heart, and a loving, outstretched hand for others.

—SHEILA WALSH (*Life Is Tough But God Is Faithful*)

# POST IT!

*Thy word have I hid in mine heart, that I might not sin against thee.*

—*Psalm 119:11* KJV

In Deuteronomy the Lord instructed the Israelites regarding how they were to respond to God's counsel: "And these words which I command you today shall be in your heart; you shall teach them diligently to your children, and shall talk of them when you sit in your house, when you walk by the way, when you lie down, and when you rise up. You shall bind them as a sign on your hand, and they shall be as frontlets between your eyes. You shall write them on the doorposts of your house and on your gates" (Deuteronomy 6:6–9).

If I condensed those verses down for someone, I would suggest that person place God's Word like memos, first inside, then outside of herself. Memorize it. Study it. Sing it. Rehearse it. Teach it. It will do her well, and it will secure her people. (You got people? I got people, people I want to know his Word.)

Psalm 119 is a good starting place for Post-Its. Select your favorite verses and write them in your journal, pen them in calligraphy and frame them for your walls, tape them to your mirror, magnetize them to your fridge, and most importantly walk in the light they will add to your path.

—PATSY CLAIRMONT (*I Second That Emotion*)

# NO SMALL TEST

*The LORD is the true God, he is the living God, and an everlasting king.*

—*Jeremiah 10:10 KJV*

I always feel like I want to stand up and cheer when I read Matthew 16, where Jesus asks the disciples, "Who do you say I am?" Simon Peter, apparently with hardly a thought, steps right up and answers boldly, "You are the Christ, the Son of the living God" (verses 15–16).

Peter got this one right—and it was no small test. Upon this answer, Jesus told Peter two amazing things. First, this truth had been revealed to Peter directly from God himself—it wasn't just earthly wisdom, it was truth that came straight from the Holy Spirit. Second, Jesus said that based on this confession, Peter would be the rock upon which he would build his church. Peter's answer to the question revealed Christ's true identity, and believers ever since have been making the same confession of faith.

The truth of Christ's identity and the truth of who God really is are the truths that outweigh everything else. When you are struggling to revive your life after a tough time, you can fall forward into the truth of who God is. Who *we are* becomes less important in the face of *who God is.*

—SANDI PATTY (*Falling Forward*)

# FANNING THE FLAME OF HOPE

*The LORD is good to those who hope in him, to those who seek him.*

—Lamentations 3:25 NCV

Hope is not a positive mental attitude. I have hope but I'm not always positive. There is no way to conquer despair with happy thoughts. Hope has real strength, but not strength of its own. The power of hope comes from the truth it hopes in; no matter what the outcome, I can have life, because the loving, merciful God of the universe is good and he is looking after me. So if I fan the flame of hope every day, I win.

Now I can smile, a lot. Living with real hope is like discovering a savings account that was started for me before I was born. It frees me to laugh more and make jokes about things—even painful circumstances. Hope also allows me to cry my eyes out when I need to.

No one who fights with her hope in the Lord never loses the last round. No matter what you may be facing, today is only one chapter, not the complete book of your life. No adverse circumstance can claim your spirit.

Rest assured, when the battle that is raging is over, your life will still be with the one in whom you've put your hope. Can you imagine his hand in yours, raising it in victory?

—NICOLE JOHNSON (*Stepping into the Ring*)

# FINDING REAL PEACE

*Christ Himself is our peace.*
—*Ephesians 2:14* NCV

Some say they have experienced a peace that passes all understanding, but the peace of most is constantly being disrupted by negative thoughts, bad news, frightening medical reports, lack of financial stability, wayward children, unfaithful spouses, conditional love, quarrels and fights, crime, wars and rumors of wars, changes in circumstances—the list goes on into next week.

There is no way to avoid some of life's scary situations. God doesn't guarantee that the storms will go around us. Rather, he promises to be in control of every storm. Understanding that with your heart, not just your head, makes the difference. Remember:

> ✦ ***Peace is a direct by-product of faith in Christ.*** You will not find peace in anything at all, except faith in the peace giver. He promises to make a way for you to regain peace in the midst of tribulation.
> ✦ ***Live in the present.*** A lot of worries are about "what ifs." Choose to focus on how he's providing for you right now.
> ✦ ***Meditate on God's promises.*** Take all your requests to him with a thankful heart and leave them there.

When God promises peace, Sister, he means peace! Take him at his word!

—THELMA WELLS (*Girl, Have I Got Good News for You*)

# NEVER MEANS NEVER

*Be strong and of good courage, do not fear nor be afraid of them; for the Lord your God, He is the One who goes with you. He will never leave you nor forsake you.*

—Deuteronomy 31:6

When we find ourselves in the greatest places of testing, the Lord tells us over and over and over and over and over: "I will be there!" When I face new trials, I look back at God's track record in my life, and God's faithfulness increases my faith. When he says, "I will never leave you, *never* means never!"

As you look at your life today, my prayer is that you will take some time and write out for yourself what God's track record is with you. Consider:

* When did you come to faith, or have you yet?
* What do you trust about God today that you may not have trusted him for some time ago?
* Can you look back and see God's hand at work now in situations where you could not see it before?
* Do you love God today more than you did a year ago?
* Do you believe he loves you?

I believe that God's love for us is overwhelming and his faithfulness unending. Whatever you are facing right now, be it the worst of times or the best, remember you are loved by a God who spared nothing of himself to show his faithfulness.

—SHEILA WALSH (*Extraordinary Faith*)

# OUR "IN THE BEGINNING" RELATIVES

*I bow my knees before the Father, from whom every family in
heaven and on earth takes its name.*

—Ephesians 3:14–15 NRSV

The Bible is the best family album going. It's all about our family
tree, our "in-the-beginning" relatives. For example, I know for
sure I'm related to Moses. He started off his life as a basket case,
for heaven's sake; of course we're kin!

But quite honestly I've been a Jonah as well. Like him I ran
away and got in over my head. And I've certainly known a number of folks who would have relished the idea of throwing me
overboard.

The Word is part of our heritage so that we might see that
since Eden we've been in need of a Savior. God gives us his family, which deepens our connection with each other. Without fail
when I study the Scriptures I find snapshots of myself in those
who came before me. I have Eve tendencies and hide when I'm
afraid, I have been a Naomi bitter with heartbreak, I have been an
impetuous Peter with more words than sense . . . and I've been a
Paul encountering Christ and experiencing a changed life.

Reading Scripture will help us to get a grip on our genealogy.
Once we're adopted into God's family, we, like Ruth, can say,
"Your people shall be my people" (Ruth 1:16).

—PATSY CLAIRMONT (*I Second That Emotion*)

# THE SKY'S THE LIMIT

*I praise you, for I am fearfully and wonderfully made.*
*Wonderful are your works; that I know very well.*

—Psalm 139:14 NRSV

If you respond to the fact of God loving you as the reason you were born, the sky's the limit in how you conduct your life. God's love gives you purpose; it gives you a great depth of meaning. You then partner with him as you experience that meaning and how it is to be communicated.

Meaning for life comes when you realize God made you because he wanted to. First John 4:10 states, "It is not that we loved God, but that he loved us." God made the first move; you choose whether to make the next one.

I hope you see the profound love principle at work that prompted God to create you. Psalm 139 describes how carefully He watches over the processes that knit you together in your mother's womb. We are not mass produced. We are one-of-a-kind creations over whom God always has a loving and watchful eye. He calls us by name. He knows how many hairs are on our heads. He knows when we stand up and when we sit down. He is never indifferent to any hurt, challenge, or joy we experience in life. His ear is ever inclined toward our voice when we call out to him.

—MARILYN MEBERG (*Love Me and Never Leave Me*)

# MY HEART IS NEVER OLD

*Rejoice that your names are written in heaven.*

—Luke 10:20 NIV

Everything has a shelf life. There will come a day when my life will end as I know it. Do I have a will or a living trust? Are the bills paid? Do I owe anybody money? Have I done the best I could? All these are little "housekeeping" duties. As sure as night will come, so will my death. Am I ready for that?

I know for a fact where I will go when I die, and I believe God's Word on that subject is absolutely true. Nevertheless, I do wonder about some things. Will anything about death hurt? Will I go right into the throne room with Jesus? Will I see people right away who have gone before? What age will I be when I get there?

I don't know any of those things for sure, and I'm curious about them. But I do know I'm going to heaven, and I'm ready.

In short, I'd like to live forever. And I will—not on this earth, of course, but in heaven. Until then, I want to be looking for new possibilities, trying new things, and enjoying new friends, ideas, and accomplishments. No matter how many years I live on this earth, my heart will never be old.

—LUCI SWINDOLL (*Life! Celebrate It*)

# TAKING HOLD OF SALVATION

*I will greatly rejoice in the LORD, my soul shall be joyful in my God; for he hath clothed me with the garments of salvation, he hath covered me with the robe of righteousness.*

—Isaiah 61:10 KJV

For many years, I was controlled by the hidden places in my life. I thought I was suffering alone, but over the years I've learned that my story is not unique. Many people have secret places where they hide and lick their wounds. They choose to live a life of denial and doubt rather than be honest with themselves. Sometimes they are unaware of what they're hiding, or why.

For so many of us, it takes years to come face-to-face with the fears that lurk in our past. We bury them so deeply because we are convinced that if they were released they would overwhelm us. We don't allow ourselves to think about them even for a moment, but their long shadows cast a dark cloud over our minds nonetheless.

The Greek word for salvation means "to save, to heal, to make complete." That is what happens at the cross. The Father is committed to shining his light into the darkest corners where fear and sorrow lurk and bringing peace.

I was able to walk away from the past, reveal those hidden places. With God's help I was able to focus on what God was going to do with my future. I allowed his love to set me free. You can be free too, my friend.

—SHEILA WALSH (*Life Is Tough But God Is Faithful*)

# WHAT MATTERS

*Jesus Christ is the atoning sacrifice for our sins, and not only for ours but also for the sins of the whole world.*

—1 John 2:2 NIV

Sometimes when I'm having trouble accepting my own failures and foibles, I am helped by focusing on some of the "I am" statements of Jesus in the book of John. I find comfort in knowing that all my "I am" statements ("I am a failure"; "I am unworthy"; "I am a loser"; "I am tired") are insignificant. What matters is what Jesus says *he* is.

- ✣ He is the Bread of Life, and if I come to him, I will not be hungry (6:35).
- ✣ He's the Light of the World, and with him I'll never be in darkness (8:12).
- ✣ He is the Gate, and if I enter through him, I'll be saved (10:9).
- ✣ He is the Good Shepherd who laid down his life for me, one of his sheep (10:11).
- ✣ He is the Resurrection and the Life, and if I believe in him, I will never die (11:25).
- ✣ He is the Way and the Truth and the Life, and through him I will get to the Father (14:6).
- ✣ He is the Vine and I am a branch, and if I remain in him, I will bear much fruit (15:5).

Now I ask you, is that some amazing truth or what?

—SANDI PATTY (*Falling Forward*)

# THE HEART OF A PRINCESS

*Jesus said, "Do not fear, little flock, for it is your Father's good pleasure to give you the kingdom."*

—Luke 12:32

It wouldn't be so hard to have the heart of a princess if we lived in a fairy-tale world. The birds would wake us in the morning, we would have beautiful clothes laid out for us every day, a song would always be on our lips, and our good fairy godmother would be there to make certain our dreams always came true.

And in the real world it wouldn't be so hard to give up hope instead of struggling day after day to keep our dreams alive, because in this not-so-fairy-tale world, life is hard.

Just when it seems we must settle for one of the two extremes, faith shows us another way. It illuminates a new place—an invisible kingdom that can only be seen with the eyes of the heart. It's a place where our glimpses of the goodness of fairy tales can fit into a different view of reality. And it's where the realities of the so-called real world are framed in a way that lightens the darkness and removes the cynicism.

In the invisible kingdom we'll discover that the unseen dreams to come are bigger and more powerful than the small ones we've held so tightly in the past. We'll get new dreams—full of the kind of hope that is far stronger than despair.

—NICOLE JOHNSON (*Keeping a Princess Heart*)

# SUCCESS AS MOTHERS

*Train children in the right way, and when old, they will not stray.*

—Proverbs 22:6 NRSV

How we mothers pine for our children to be perfect! We want the best for them so much that we grieve when they're not doing what we want, how we want. We all want our children to be the epitome of all that stands for good so that people can see they are wonderful and can count us successful as mothers.

The truth is that none of us are perfect moms. All of us have made some mistakes while raising our children. I certainly did. But we must accept that the decisions they make when they are old enough to decide for themselves are their decisions. So how can we cope? Here are some suggestions:

+ ***Remember, we're all in process.*** You taught your children principles about how to live, but they will almost surely have to test those principles for themselves. Just like us, they will be able to learn some things only by making mistakes.

+ ***Never stop loving and praying.*** You can't do much about your children's choices when they are grown, but you can accept them, love them, and pray for them.

+ ***Let go.*** Remind yourself daily that God himself is their parent for eternity, and it is only through his grace and by his power that they can live holy lives.

—THELMA WELLS (*Girl, Have I Got Good News for You*)

# THE BACK OF THE TAPESTRY

*The Lord is my helper; I will not be afraid. Jesus Christ is the same yesterday and today and forever.*

—Hebrews 13:6, 8 NIV

When the world asks if there is any hope, we can say, "Absolutely!" If you happen to be questioning this, I'd like to tell you about an illustration Corrie ten Boom used on many occasions. As she spoke, she would hold up the wrong side of a tapestry for her audience to see.

"Isn't this beautiful?" she would ask.

As the people looked at the back of the tapestry, all they could see were threads crossed at odd intervals, knotted in places, looking clumsy and disjointed. It was, to be blunt, ugly.

The audience would stare back at Corrie, not knowing how to respond to her question. Corrie would be silent for a few moments, and then she would say as if in a moment of great insight, "Oh! Yes, of course. You can't see the tapestry from my perspective." Then she would turn the piece of cloth around to show the front, and there would be a picture of a beautiful crown!

At times, life makes no sense. It seems disjointed, distorted, and ugly. But if we surrender our little view of life for God's much grander portrait, we will always be able to hold our eternal hope in Jesus Christ.

—SHEILA WALSH (*Life Is Tough But God Is Faithful*)

# THE REASON YOU WERE BORN

*The LORD your God goes with you; he will never leave you nor forsake you.*

—Deuteronomy 31:6 NIV

We have all had our hearts broken by someone who did not choose us, or by someone who rejected our offer to love that would have brought the fulfillment of a relationship. Some of us have even said under our breath. "It's your loss. I would have been good for you. We could have had a great life together, but . . . oh, well."

God never says, "Oh, well." He is relentless in his love pursuit of us while at the same time honoring our right to say, "No. I'm not interested."

How blessed we are that, in the cocooning security of God's choice to love us, we also have his promise to *never* abandon us. He will not desert us; He will never choose against us. No human being in our lives can make such a declaration of steadfast love. Only God can; only God does. Let's remember yet again Isaiah 41:9, which promises, "I have chosen you and will not throw you away."

My prayer for you is that you choose to accept the very reason for which you were born and that you rest in your place of one whom God will never abandon . . . never throw away.

—MARILYN MEBERG (*Love Me Never Leave Me*)

# SINGING THE SONG IN YOUR HEART

*Each one should use whatever gift he has received to serve others, faithfully administering God's grace in its various forms.*

—1 Peter 4:10 NIV

Being creative is to find your own voice inside yourself, to identify your own ideas and aspirations. It means singing the song that's in your heart, to your own melody. You're the only one who can hear it, because it's coming to you from God. If you look at this song with your intellect, it goes away because it doesn't respond to your mind; it responds to your heart.

Consider Henri Matisse, the famous French artist who painted in oils. When he was an old man, he became very ill and was confined to a wheelchair or his bed. He was too weak to hold a pen or brush, so he took a pair of scissors and cut out designs and life forms. He created a new way of thinking and looking at art and life. He sang the song that was inside him and found a new, creative voice.

I have a framed print of a cut-out by Henri Matisse on my living room wall; I bought it at the National Gallery of Art in Washington, D.C. It's a great reminder to me that life is still flowing through my veins, and I must continually stop to create what I hear inside my heart.

—LUCI SWINDOLL (*Life! Celebrate It*)

# GOD'S FRIEND

*Jesus said, "I no longer call you servants, because a servant does not know his master's business. Instead, I have called you friends, for everything that I learned from my Father I have made known to you."*

—John 15:15 NIV

You remember the story of Job, don't you? As this incredible Bible story unfolds, we see that there is more between this man and God than an employer-employee relationship. He was God's servant, true, but he was also God's friend. Throughout his entire ordeal, Job's reactions prove that he did not serve God for what he could get out of him but for what he could give to him from the very core of his being. Job did not serve God out of fear or duty. He served God out of love, and so it should be between friends.

At times it is easy for us to get caught up in Christian "service." We can become members of every committee and attend every prayer group. Wherever there is a job to be done in the church, we will be there. We may run ourselves ragged doing things for God and lose him in the midst of it all.

Serving God is important, even vital, but it should never come ahead of realizing that he is first of all our Friend, and without his friendship, life is an empty treadmill. Christianity is not an employer-employee contract; it is a relationship between a loving heavenly Father and his children.

—SHEILA WALSH (*Life Is Tough But God Is Faithful*)

# THE ROAD TO EMMAUS

*The same day two of them [disciples of Jesus] were walking to
the village Emmaus . . . . They were deep in conversation, going
over all these things that had happened. In the middle of their
talk and questions, Jesus came up and walked along with them.
But they were not able to recognize who he was.*

—Luke 24:13–16 MSG

As we continue on our journeys, each of us on an individual path,
my prayer is that we will recognize Jesus when he comes to walk
alongside us. Unlike his disciples who were trudging along on the
road to Emmaus but didn't know the resurrected Jesus was traveling with them, may we listen studiously and take notes as he
explains to us some of life's complexities. He does that for us
through his Word, his Spirit, his people, and his creation.

Along our way we mustn't allow our sorrows to disable us, but
instead we must filter them through God's plan and mercies, which
will add depth to our heart's content. God made us gals emotionally
wealthy, giving us the potential to be prosperous in our dispositions
and intuitions. We all have regrets, but we must learn to receive
what Christ offers freely: forgiveness. And we must realize that Jesus
redeems our failures for his divine purposes.

Expect life to be joyful and rugged. Let's be wise enough to lean
into what comes our way. If God has allowed it, it comes with purposes we may not understand . . . yet. Follow the narrow road; it leads
to the widest joy. Along the way, enjoy your rich emotional design.

—PATSY CLAIRMONT (*I Second That Emotion*)

# SHIFTING MY FOCUS

*In him we have redemption through his blood, the forgiveness*
*of sins, in accordance with the riches of God's grace that he*
*lavished on us with all wisdom and understanding.*

—Ephesians 1:7–8 NIV

I'm not ashamed to tell you that there was a time when I was desperately in need of forgiveness. As my accountability group walked me through the long months of restitution and restoration, I asked forgiveness from God and from each individual who had been hurt by my actions. By the time my restoration process was declared finished, I was assured that I'd been fully forgiven.

But I still had two problems: (1) I didn't *feel* forgiven, and (2) I still had to deal with the consequences, which kept my weaknesses right in front of my face.

Then one day it dawned on me that my focus was blocking my ability to forgive myself. I was focusing on my junk—my lack of worthiness to receive forgiveness. And in doing so, I was actually ignoring God's beautiful gift of his Son. I needed to shift my focus to Christ on the cross. Like the song says, "Turn your eyes upon Jesus, look full in his wonderful face."

If you struggle with forgiving yourself or someone else, remember that Jesus died for all of us equally. As you focus on the beauty of his redemptive sacrifice, your heart wells with gratitude. Paralyzing guilt or energy-sapping grudges flee "in the light of his glory and grace."

—SANDI PATTY (*Falling Forward*)

# WITH THANKSGIVING

*Do not worry about anything, but in everything by prayer
and supplication with thanksgiving let your requests be made
known to God.*

—Philippians 4:6 NRSV

In 1991 I spent some time with Ruth Graham in her lovely mountain home in North Carolina. On that evening, I asked Ruth how she handled the tough days as a young wife and mother. How did she respond when she was, at times, pushed into an unsolicited spotlight? Her answer was simple yet profound.

"Worship and worry cannot exist at the same time in the same heart," she said. "They are mutually exclusive."

Ruth then told me about a time when she awoke in the middle of the night, concerned about one of her children. Unable to sleep, she got out of bed and picked up her Bible. Ruth soon realized that the missing ingredient in her heart at that time was thanksgiving, so she began to thank God for this son, for his life, for the joy he had brought to their home. Her burden lifted.

We can pray and make our requests known to God, but we have to trust that God will answer our prayers. Thanksgiving helps us do that. When we pray with thanksgiving, we are saying we believe he will answer us and provide for our needs or for the needs of those we love—and we will be happy with his provision.

—SHEILA WALSH (*Life Is Tough But God Is Faithful*)

# FAIRY TALES

*May the God of hope fill you with all joy and peace in believing,*
*that you may abound in hope by the power of the Holy Spirit.*

—Romans 15:13

Long before I knew the stories were called fairy tales, I loved them. It would be years before I understood how fairy tales are different from other stories, but in my earliest memories, my heart soared when I heard the words "Once upon a time . . ."

Fairy tales are still very precious to me, but for far deeper reasons. Many of the tales provide direct glimpses into the way the world should have gone, delightfully confirming a deep suspicion that life should be different.

Fairy tales are like a pair of glasses—not the rose-colored kind that make everything look wonderful, but the kind that bring reality into focus. Like good bifocals, they help us discern the way the world really is up close, without losing the bigger picture of the way the world was intended to be.

The world of fairy tales sharply reveals that what we see around us is not all there is. There is more, much more. Fairy tales suggest and give glimpses of a very different, invisible kingdom—a world that lives between the illusions of the perfect and the real worlds. Fairy tales offer hope. And hope, like nothing else in the world, inspires us and motivates us to keep going.

—NICOLE JOHNSON (*Keeping a Princess Heart*)

# HEALTH CHALLENGED

*Beloved, I pray that all may go well with you and that you may be in good health, just as it is well with your soul.*

—3 John 2 NRSV

I talk to a lot of people with illnesses every week. If that's where you are, you aren't alone. Sometimes when our health declines and things don't seem to be working out for us, our faith begins to waver. We question God and his promises to us. We think God doesn't care about us and has abandoned us.

Here are some suggestions for hanging on to your faith when your health is challenged:

> → *Believe that God has a plan.* I believe that God has a plan for each of our lives. Maybe it is part of his master plan for you to go through this period of failing health. Keep your trust in your Creator.
> → *Do your part.* You can choose to take a positive approach to your health challenge by caring for your body wisely. Avoid health risks, and do what you can do to be healthy.
> → *Trust in God's healing power.* Our loving God cares about our well-being. He wants us as healthy as we can be. He heals today, just as he did generations ago. Put your faith in him alone. And even if he does not heal you the way you want him to, continue to trust him.

—THELMA WELLS (*Girl, Have I Got Good News for You*)

# LET GO AND LET GOD

*I can do everything through him who gives me strength.*
—*Philippians 4:13 NIV*

The love of God is the key to trusting him enough to let him "do it." Do what? Everything! Absolutely everything. The joy of responding to God's love for us comes in the partnership he offers us in overcoming our difficulties. We are not alone in them. He partners with us by providing the wisdom and strength—and even abstinence from those life issues that threaten to derail us. In our love for him, in our trust of him, we receive from him all we are not. This is what it means to "let him do it." He invites us to climb off the treadmill of self-effort and rule keeping.

Letting God "do it" is not a passive action. We partner with him. He has the power; we do not. We recognize his power, and in our powerlessness we pray, "Jesus, help me!"

That he *will* help us is a given. God plays the major role while we rest in who he is and what he has done and in the knowledge that we were, are, and will always be the focus of his love. And that powerful love is what brings us from death to life.

—MARILYN MEBERG (*Assurance for a Lifetime*)

# I'VE GOT QUESTIONS

*You have preserved me because I was honest; you have
admitted me forever to your presence.*

—Psalm 41:12 TLB

Questioning God sounds blasphemous to some people. They
might say, "How dare you? Who do you think you are, that you
can come before God and question him?" But I don't think being
honest with God is blasphemous at all. I believe God wants us to
be honest because he wants a real relationship with us, not something plastic or halfhearted.

I sometimes ask myself how it must feel to be God and love
people with a passion so great that you would give your only Son
to hang on a cross. How must it feel to know that that kind of love
is the very essence of your being, and yet day after day you can
see that your children are hurting, but they never open up. They
are never honest.

I believe God much prefers to have his children come before
him and say, "God, this makes no sense to me. I hurt so badly. I
just don't understand. I don't think I'll ever understand, but,
God, I love and trust you, and I rest in the fact that you know
how I feel. You've been there. I can't understand what is happening to me, but help me to glorify you through it all."

—SHEILA WALSH (*Life Is Tough But God Is Faithful*)

# FINDING YOUR *QUERENCIA*

> *Those who hope in the LORD will renew their strength. They*
> *will soar on wings like eagles; they will run and not grow*
> *weary, they will walk and not be faint.*

—Isaiah 40:31 NIV

My grandmother refused to get buried under the load of care she had as a mother, a wife, a church member, a grandmother, and a human being. Every one of those callings has problems attached to it. So how did she do it? She had her own *querencia.* (It sounds like the word *Corinthian*, only with "ah" on the end.) In Spanish, this word means a favorite and frequent place of rest.

We human beings have an undefined place of peace that God offers to us. By shifting the weight of tough stuff off our shoulders onto God's, we find that place to relax. It's still a jungle out there, but we unconsciously find that quiet place—our *querencia*—where we stop grinding out life's maddening pace for a few minutes. This spot is inside us, and God makes it available so we can pause and catch our breath. Laugh. Sing. Think. Pray. Everyday rhythms and patterns of life keep going, but we're not going with them. We're listening to the beat of a different drum.

Find your own *querencia*—and go there. If you are overwhelmed by a problem that seems impossible to solve, don't! Shift the weight of your problems to God, and the rest of your life and your family will be the richer for it.

—LUCI SWINDOLL (*Life! Celebrate It*)

# TRUDGE OR HIGH-STEP

*Since we live by the Spirit, let us keep in step with the Spirit.*
—Galatians 5:25 NIV

The Bible speaks of footwear, but even more of our walk. Genesis mentions Adam and Eve's barefoot walk with the Lord in the cool of the evening. The Bible closes with the dramatic account of John's vision of the Son of Man in which his feet are like fine brass. Scripture reminds us of the importance of where we walk, how we walk, and with whom we walk.

Life is so textured, full of nubs like a bolt of tweed fabric, interesting and unpredictable. We are walking down a delightful path when, without warning, we find ourselves on a path we never would have chosen. Then our choice becomes whether we will trudge or high-step our way to the finish line.

Loss opens a walkway to what really matters in life. It presses us to see and feel in ways we hadn't previously considered. And while loss doesn't seem like a friend, it often brings refining touches to our character. It can hone compassion toward others, it can move us beyond fear, it can help us to determine a clear-cut path, and it can deepen our dependence on God.

My tendency is to pull on track shoes and sprint in the opposite direction of loss. But I am learning ever so slowly to lean into it and lift my heels.

—PATSY CLAIRMONT (*All Cracked Up*)

# THE TRUST FALL

*The LORD upholds all who fall, and raises up all who are bowed down.*

—Psalm 145:14

Have you ever been in a corporate or retreat situation where you had to take part in "trust-building exercises"? Sometimes you're led blindfolded by someone and you have to trust they won't bash you into a wall or send you tumbling down a flight of stairs. I don't know about you, but I just hate those things, because trusting someone else means giving up control.

But sometimes I need a visual picture, to help make over-used phrases like "Just trust in God" come to life. One of the most common of those dreaded corporate team-building exercises is called the Trust Fall. So when I have no idea *how* to trust God in a given situation, I think of myself climbing up on a ladder to get in position to fall, with God's strong and mighty presence waiting below. And then I mentally do the Trust Fall into his arms.

When I have to perform onstage and I'm beyond tired, and I really just want, with all my aching bones and heart, to go home and put on a robe and fuzzy slippers and sleep for a week, I pray, "Lord, you know I'm out of gas. I'm going to do the Trust Fall into your arms right now." And then I simply let go. He never fails me.

—SANDI PATTY (*Falling Forward*)

# CHOOSING TO FORGIVE

*Jesus said, "Our Father in heaven . . . forgive us our debts, as
we forgive our debtors."*
—Matthew 6:9, 12

I once had a friend who lied about me to my two closest friends,
and I could not defend myself without betraying the trust of
someone dear to me. I spent many sleepless nights and wept
many bitter tears, feeling helpless and betrayed. But in the midst
of it all, I was faced with Christ's command to forgive so that my
heavenly Father would forgive me.

When we refuse to forgive, we are setting ourselves up as a
judge and demanding that others be perfect—something we
can't do. God will judge and demand perfection of us when we
judge others.

When we forgive, we see through other people's behavior to
their need. We recognize their guilt and at the same time see our
own. We realize that we won't find justice in this world—it
doesn't live here. So we give up the fruitless, heartbreaking search
for it, and we give mercy to those who have wounded us.

In my case, I asked God to bless the girl who had wronged
me. I asked him to pull her close to his heart, believing that she
had to be pretty miserable herself to lie about someone. I remembered my own need and was finally able to choose to forgive.

—SHEILA WALSH (*Life Is Tough But God Is Faithful*)

# A SIMPLE ACT OF LOVE

*Live a life of love, just as Christ loved us and gave himself up*
*for us as a fragrant offering and sacrifice to God.*
—*Ephesians 5:2 NIV*

The deepest identity and worth that my heart longs for will never be found in human applause. Although it feels good most of the time, it is far too short-lived. The deepest satisfaction of my heart is found in the faith to work and build and love for a greater purpose than my own.

When I see an unselfish, simple act of love, I am deeply moved. I am left speechless by the silent sacrifices love makes without ever drawing attention to itself. Often my hardened heart is reduced to liquid when I see a daughter wiping the drawn mouth of her parent or a wife sitting by the bedside reading to a husband who can no longer see, or a friend helping a co-worker in a wheelchair get situated into an airplane seat. Through my tears, I want to stand and applaud the beauty of their sacrifice. It is a building in progress and it encourages me to keep going. Some people might be looking around to see who is watching them, or complaining about the task at hand, or even doing nothing instead of giving selflessly. I am fully convinced that invisibility is love's most beautiful costume, given only to its choicest of servants when they are really serious about serving.

—NICOLE JOHNSON (*The Invisible Woman*)

# SLEEP ON IT

*Do not forsake wisdom, and she will protect you; love her, and she will watch over you.*

—*Proverbs 4:6* NIV

I have wonderful memories of my Granny, who raised me. Growing up, we'd talk and laugh as we worked in the kitchen together. She would tell me Bible stories, and I would tell her *everything*.

As I got older and moved into adolescence and my teenage years, she wouldn't agree with some of the things I told her, but I knew I could always tell her whatever was on my mind, and she would listen.

If I told her something she didn't like, she might get very quiet. Looking back I'm sure that in her quietness she was praying for wisdom on how to deal with me. She was more than sixty years old while she was rearing me, and I'm sure it was quite a culture shock to have a child in the household again after all the years since she had reared her two sons.

Sometimes when I would pour out a problem to Granny, she would say, "Sleep on the problem, child, and it'll be better in the morning." This lesson may seem trite, but Granny said it, and I've proved it to be true many times.

Granny taught me not to make snap decisions when emotions are high and pressures are great, "Sleep on it, baby," she would tell me.

—THELMA WELLS (*Listen Up, Honey*)

211

# REMEMBERING

*A book of remembrance was written before Him for those who fear the LORD and who meditate on His name.*

—Malachi 3:16

I am convinced that one of life's most easily accessible sources of cheer is to remember some of the off-the-wall, crazy things that happen to us. It doesn't have to be a Big Moment, just something zany and fun. Sometimes those memories are bittersweet as we recall an out-of-the-ordinary moment with a loved one who is now gone. But those times nevertheless provide cheer because that was the emotion felt when the experience occurred. That original cheerful feeling will always remain attached to that memory.

Pleasant memories can give us an immediate cheer-producing mind switch. We don't have to wait until we're seventy to do it! Those memories can be as recent as this morning or as distant as thirty years ago. All that matters is that the quirky memory cheers you.

Incidentally, the whole "remembering" thing is a biblical concept. God was continually urging his people to remember what he had done for them as a means of encouragement. He wanted them to remember that he was their rock and their redeemer.

For us believers, remembering starts out by recalling God is the source of our cheer. From that foundational position, we can move into the human realm and remember those experiences that were cheer producing.

—MARILYN MEBERG *(I'd Rather Be Laughing)*

# THE CRUCIBLE OF DOUBT

*What if some did not believe? Will their unbelief make the*
*faithfulness of God without effect? Certainly not!*

—Romans 3:3–4

I find that those who walked with God in the Old Testament seem far more honest than some of us today. The psalmist David, for example, was brutally honest with God. The prophets poured out their hearts to God; Job railed against God. Those who were able to bring their doubts and fears, however raw, into the presence of God, and who truly wrestled with their faith, found a faith that could withstand anything.

The apostle Peter was pretty sure that whatever Jesus needed, he was the man for the job. But as he faced the greatest failure of his life, he was about to be transformed . . . into a man of faith.

Doubts unexpressed isolate us and drive us from the heart of God. God's heart is big enough to carry whatever burden you are bearing.

Do you doubt that God loves you?

Do you doubt that he cares?

Do you doubt that he will see you through any and every circumstance?

Do you doubt that he even exists and that faith is real?

I encourage you to bring your doubts to him. He can be trusted with your questions.

—SHEILA WALSH (*Extraordinary Faith*)

# IT CAME TO PASS

*The darkness is passing away and the true light is already shining.*

—1 John 1:8 NCV

If shifting the weight and clearing your head fail to provide a measure of relief, then remember this: whatever difficulty you're facing today has only come to pass. You know how great literature as well as Scripture often reads, "And it *came to pass* . . ."? That's what I'm talking about. Whatever your burden at the moment, you can be sure that it, too, will pass. One day, it will be no more!

The word *pass* is a wonderful word. In my dictionary, it has twelve different meanings. And while each is interesting, and most of us have used the word in all its meanings at one time or another, it's the first definition to which I refer here: "to proceed; to go away; to depart."

Whatever burden you're facing at the moment *will* depart. It's just a matter of time. It came to pass, and it will. But it's between those two moving targets—*came* and *pass*—that we need to look for humor, isn't it?

When we accept the inevitability of trials and suffering and their mandate for living fully wherever we are and whatever we're doing, a great part of the battle has already been won by someone much stronger and braver than we.

—LUCI SWINDOLL (*Life! Celebrate It*)

# A PICTURE OF COURAGE

*Lord, you are my shield, my wonderful God who gives me courage.*
—*Psalm 3:3* NCV

Don't you just love great stories of courage? There's nothing better than grabbing a bowl of popcorn and sitting down to watch a movie about brave people standing up to evil and winning. When the Narnia movie came out, based on C. S. Lewis's classic book *The Lion, the Witch and the Wardrobe,* our family got a chance to enjoy a "good versus evil" battle.

Like wishy-washy Edmund at the beginning of the movie, I've never thought of myself as a particularly courageous person. I don't jump out of airplanes, and I'm not going to climb Mount Everest. I don't even like spiders! Bravery? That's for other people, right?

Wrong.

With the amount of courage it has taken to get through the trials of the last dozen years . . . well, some days I wished all I had to do was *just* climb Mount Everest. All the times my heart threatened to wilt under the strain of holding my head up high; all the times I wanted to give up and hide out in my bedroom forever; all the times I nearly cowered under all the lies the enemy was trying to feed me—these were moments that required me to suck it up, get a backbone, grab on to God's strength, and be a picture of courage.

—SANDI PATTY (*Falling Forward*)

# CLOAKED IN HUMILITY

*As God's chosen people, holy and dearly loved, clothe yourselves with compassion, kindness, humility, gentleness and patience.*

—Colossians 3:12 NIV

Everyone—and I include myself—wants to be a servant until we're treated like one. I want to look like a servant, but not have to suffer. And if I have to suffer, I would like to be exalted for my servanthood. I have no idea how many years Mother Teresa worked invisibly in the streets of Calcutta before anyone ever knew her name, but I'm certain it was decades. When she came to renown ironically her name was not the one that mattered. She walked among the poor, cloaked in humility, completely disguised as Jesus. Disappearing among the poorest of the poor, she made them visible with her quiet, strong love.

It is possible that the opposite of love is not hate or even apathy, but showy, self-serving acts. Talking or writing about how much you love, demanding your right to be loved, or being loud and brassy about the way other people don't love will never reveal love's truest essence. The greatest demonstrations of human love in history stand in direct opposition to such circus acts, in the way they are freely and quietly given. They humble us all, and by their power they change the world.

—NICOLE JOHNSON (*The Invisible Woman*)

# TWO OPTIONS

*We walk by faith, not by sight.*
—2 Corinthians 5:7

I used to think that I had just two options in my life:

1) I could live with full abandon and passion, pour out my life and heart to God and to others, take risks, and give generously of heart and spirit. If I did that, I set myself up for disappointment and loss, for heartache and rejection.
2) I could live cautiously, care about others but not too much, love what I do but not too much, give what I have but hold back some reserve. If I did this I would feel safe; not so alive, but safe.

For years I chose option 2, and I think part of me despised that. As believers we are not called to live safe, small lives. We are called to live as Christ lived, to love as he loves.

But here is the dilemma: we can live that way only by faith!

If we do not trust that God is good—that he is in control all the time, no matter what is going on; that whatever we pour out in his name, he will pour back and more into our spirits—we live lesser lives. We know intrinsically that we were created for more!

—SHEILA WALSH (*Extraordinary Faith*)

# SPEAKING OF WORMS

*Let the wise also hear and gain in learning, and the discerning
acquire skill.*

—*Proverbs 1:5 NRSV*

Someone told me an interesting story about a minister who
wanted to impart some wisdom to his congregation. To illustrate
his point, he dropped four worms into four separate jars. The first
worm was put into a jar of alcohol. The second worm was put into
a jar of cigarette smoke. The third worm was put into a jar of chocolate syrup. The fourth worm was put into a jar of good, clean soil.

At the conclusion of his sermon, the minister showed his
congregation the results: the worm in alcohol was dead, the
worm in cigarette smoke was dead, and the worm in chocolate
syrup was dead. But the worm he had placed in good, clean soil
was still alive.

"So," the minister asked, "what can we learn from this lesson?"

A little old woman in the back raised her hand and said, "As
long as you drink, smoke, and eat chocolate, you won't have
worms?"

Listen up, honey. As long as you listen to the gentle and quiet
voice of God whispering into your heart, you can bottle up those
worms of worry and know that the King of kings will guide you
with wisdom and love through whatever lies ahead. Connect
with him. Feel his presence in your life.

—THELMA WELLS (*Listen Up, Honey*)

# AT OUR WITS' END

*God's love will continue forever.*

—*Psalm 52:1* NCV

I have some good news: when our backs are against the wall—when we cry out to the Lord—he is there. God is always at our wits' end. How do we know? Because God is wherever we are. His promise is to never, ever leave us. Wherever we may wander, in foolishness or fear, God stays with us and brings us out of our distresses, because his love for us endures forever.

So what's the problem? Why can't we simply settle into the biblical drumbeat message that God's love endures forever? I believe the problem lies in the contrast between what we believe and what we think. In our hearts we believe that God's love endures forever, but in our heads we sometimes think in a way that creates roadblocks to faith. This faulty thinking leads to shaky faith. Then that shaky faith puts our backs against the wall. It keeps us at our wits' end.

God wants you to have a faith that is practical and within your grasp. His intent is to meet you where you are in your faith need and to lovingly show you what it means when he tells you he will bring you out of your distresses.

—MARILYN MEBERG (*God at Your Wits' End*)

# NOTHING GIVES HOPE LIKE LAUGHTER

*A merry heart does good, like a medicine.*
—Proverbs 17:22

I love being around people who seem to have nonsense in their veins. They're the ones who erase tension in business meetings, liven up a schoolroom or office discussion, and relieve boredom wherever they go. If you have someone like that in your life, you need to stop right now and thank God, because that person is a beautiful gift straight from heaven. Anne Lamott says, "Nothing gives hope like laughter. It moisturizes the soul." The difficulties of life break down into manageable sizes. It's a "momentary anesthesia of the heart," to quote French philosopher Henri Bergson.

Interestingly, research shows that laughter itself serves no biological purpose. It's a reflex action, sometimes called a "luxury reflex," unrelated to humanity's struggle for survival. Yet the emotional service it provides can't begin to be measured. According to the Bible, laughter is good medicine—and we've all experienced a healthy dose of that medicine when we didn't even know we were sick. Laughter lifts our spirit and drops the fever. Somehow, it opens the windows to our soul, letting in light and fresh air. A friend of mine used to say, "Laughter is kind of like changing my baby's diaper—it doesn't solve any problems permanently, but it certainly makes things more enjoyable at the moment."

—LUCI SWINDOLL (*Life! Celebrate It*)

# WHAT ABOUT HOPE?

*Be strong and take heart, all you who hope in the LORD.*
—Psalm 31:24 NIV

According to the apostle Paul, three things will continue forever: faith, hope, and love. Paul makes it clear that the greatest of these is love, and we all agree. But what of the other two?

We know faith is crucial. Without faith it is impossible to please God or to hang on when life is tough. Doubt can creep in so easily, and the only answer is to remember that Jesus is worth it all.

But what about hope? In our haste to be sure we have faith and love, do we sometimes fail to give hope its proper due? Without hope, life is a sorry game, played without enthusiasm or joy.

As our society marches into the twenty-first century, people wonder what our real chances are. Is there any hope?

Those are legitimate questions, and I believe that only Christians have the legitimate answers. When our dreams seem to go sour or remain unfulfilled, hopelessness can dominate our lives—or we can hold on with open hands, knowing that we have hope because God is faithful.

—SHEILA WALSH (*Life Is Tough But God Is Faithful*)

# HOPE IS A DIAMOND

*No one whose hope is in you will ever be put to shame.*

—Psalm 25:3 NIV

Hope, that glorious light at the end of the tunnel, is a multi-faceted, brilliant dimension of life. If you've ever experienced hope or observed it in another person, you know that it's indescribable yet undeniable.

But hope often is unearthed in the dark mines of hospital wards, funeral parlors, senior homes, rehab centers, prison cells, abuse centers, counselors' offices, every arena of life. Hope can seem elusive and outside of our price range when, in fact, it's available to pauper and prince alike, thanks to Jesus.

I wish I could wear my hope as a pendant so all who see it might be drawn to my dazzling Christ. But isn't that what happens when we live out our faith in spite of hardships and opposition? What looks impossible suddenly glistens with hope, and others come to observe and ask questions.

Ever notice how a dark velvet backdrop enhances a diamond's qualities? So, too, does hope shine on a backdrop of pain, failure, and loss. Like Corrie ten Boom's life, which included a death camp, or Mother Teresa's, which included the poverty and sicknesses of India. Their diamond-studded lives continue to glitter and refract Christ's hope. What unlikely candidates they must have appeared to be. Yet that's what hope is—the unlikely, even the impossible, becoming the absolute.

—PATSY CLAIRMONT (*All Cracked Up*)

# A HEART OF THANKFULNESS

*In everything give thanks; for this is the will of God in Christ Jesus for you.*

—*1 Thessalonians 5:18*

A five-year-old girl was asked to say the blessing at Thanksgiving dinner. She began by thanking God for all her friends, naming them one by one. Then she thanked God for Mommy, Daddy, Brother, Sister, Grandma, Grandpa, and all her aunts and uncles. Finally, she gave thanks for the turkey, the dressing, the fruit salad, the cranberry sauce, the pies, the cakes. Then she paused. After a long silence, the young girl looked up at her mother and asked, "If I thank God for the broccoli, won't he know I'm lying?"

Have you ever felt that way? We know we're supposed to cultivate a heart of thankfulness. But let's be honest: there's a bunch of broccoli in our lives that is really hard to give thanks for.

Amazingly enough, by cultivating thankfulness for God's work in me as I try to glean the lessons of loss, I've even come to be thankful for the trials I've experienced. I know that through them God has made me into the person I am today, a new and hopefully improved version, full of much more grace and love. Being thankful for everything—intentionally nurturing a heart of gratitude—is a way to bolster your faith on a daily basis. And (broccoli notwithstanding) I guarantee it will keep you in a better mood.

—SANDI PATTY (*Falling Forward*)

# HE TAKES NO NOTICE

*Honor God by accepting each other, as Christ has accepted you.*

—Romans 15:7 CEV

The Christian life is full of challenges. For example, following God command to accept others as he has freely accepted us is a great goal toward which to strive, but if the truth were known, not one of us is able to fully comply. Most of us even have trouble accepting ourselves. We know too much. We see others and ourselves in the light of reality, and sometimes we tend to step back from that reality. It isn't always to our liking; it isn't always a pretty picture.

That's why God's love for us is difficult to grasp. He knows what we know. In fact, he knows even more. Yet there it is: his unconditional love. It's interesting he does not circle around us to keep from encountering our weaknesses and imperfections. Why? Because once they are confessed and forgiven he takes no notice of them. Scripture says he does not even remember them.

Can you imagine greater freedom for our guilt-prone souls than to fully realize he does not remember our sins? And, in turn, can you imagine the gift we give others when we extend that kind of unconditional, fully accepting love to them—despite their flaws?

—MARILYN MEBERG & LUCI SWINDOLL (*Free Inside and Out*)

# THE BLESSED RAINBOW

*God said: "I set My rainbow in the cloud . . . and I will*
*remember My covenant which is between Me and you and*
*every living creature of all flesh; the waters shall never again*
*become a flood to destroy all flesh.*
—Genesis 9:13, 15

Doesn't seeing a rainbow flood you with rest, awe, and amazement? While some people understand the scientific reason behind rainbows, I've always found those explanations real yawners. I like to think of rainbows as a signal that God is present and cares. They're symbols of rest for the weary, broken, and disheartened.

A few months ago, as I was driving home from the airport after a tiring trip, I glanced out the window and saw a double rainbow. It was vividly colored, almost neon, and so close. For a minute I thought about rushing over for those pots of gold. But then I remembered that rainbows *are* pots of gold, shining with God's love. And that's priceless.

But my amazement must have been small compared to what Noah must have felt when he saw the first rainbow. After all that work corralling the animals, feeding them, and cleaning up their mess, Noah was probably moaning, "I can't take it anymore, Lord." Then the skies cleared, and he knew that finally he and his family could disembark and let the animals loose. Ah what a relief, especially when he looked up and saw the symbol of God's enduring promise of rest—the rainbow!

—PATSY CLAIRMONT (*All Cracked Up*)

# THREE KINDS OF PRAYER

*Pray in the Spirit on all occasions with all kinds of prayers and requests. With this in mind, be alert and always keep on praying for all the saints.*

—Ephesians 6:18 NIV

If the muddy path you've traveled has kept you from praying as much as you'd like (or at all), I want to encourage you to start talking to God again. Even just a few words a day. It gets easier, I promise.

I read once that there are three kinds of prayer we can practice, based on the example of Jesus when he walked this earth. First, there's praying without ceasing, which is our ongoing silent conversation with God throughout our days. Next, there's our "set aside" time each day for focused prayer, when we do nothing but converse with God, whether or not we choose to use words. Finally, there are the longer periods of prayer and meditation—a day or more maybe once a year—when we get away from family and responsibilities to spend extended time with God.

Now, my purpose in telling you this is not to give you more rules to follow or to persuade you to be legalistic about prayer! I simply find it helpful to conceptualize prayer in these three ways because it gives us options and allows for our varying personalities, schedules, and seasons of life. Whatever works best for you—start there. Personally, I tend to pray continually throughout my day, because I am always singing to God!

—SANDI PATTY (*Falling Forward*)

# WHEN THE CHIPS ARE DOWN

*When times are good, be happy; but when times are bad,
consider: God has made the one as well as the other.*

—*Ecclesiastes 7:14* NIV

How do you react to life's unpleasant circumstances? Do you
look for ways to find happiness and joy or do you just give in . . .
give up, and join the ranks of the "if-anything-bad-can-happen-it-
will-happen-to-me" people? Granted, every dilemma doesn't have
a humorous side, but I believe more do than we realize.

Here are a few principles that have helped me thrive through
disappointments, turning around a difficult circumstance. Remember these when the chips are down:

- Realize most problems are inconveniences, not
  catastrophes.
- Don't take yourself too seriously, and stop being so literal.
- Count your blessings instead of your blunders.
- Take everything as a compliment.
- Enjoy your freedom because Christ has set you free.
- Look for the funny side of everything even if it's teensy-
  weensy.
- Don't sweat the small stuff.
- Do something fun just for yourself that makes you laugh.

—LUCI SWINDOLL (*Life! Celebrate It*)

# GOD'S MYSTERIOUS WAYS

*"My thoughts are not your thoughts, neither are your ways my ways," declares the LORD.*

—Isaiah 55:8 NIV

At every conference I hear someone say, "I am so grateful that you share your experience with depression. It gives me hope. The fact that you still take your little blue pill makes me feel that I'm not alone, and that I don't have to be ashamed."

I don't always understand why God works as he does, why he heals one and not another, why he delivers one and not another, but I do believe that he is good all the time. Our faith is tested in many ways. Sometimes we are immersed in a situation that seems hopeless, and we wonder, God, are you there? Sometimes he delivers us from a situation in such a miraculous way that we know it had to be God; sometimes he calls us to walk with a limp, following the one who was wounded for us.

I don't know what you have walked through or what pain you have known. I don't know where you find yourself at this moment, but I encourage you to invite Christ into the midst of your struggles and heartache. Offer your scars to the one who is scarred for you. The very wounds that seemed that they might break you will be used by God to strengthen you and to give strength to others.

—SHEILA WALSH (*Extraordinary Faith*)

# SHARING THE JOY

*Jesus said, "Let your light so shine before men, that they see your good works and glorify your Father in heaven."*
—*Matthew 5:16*

Did you know that we can inspire others to praise God simply by our actions and example, by the way we love and praise and serve the Lord? It's true—and what a privilege it is!

Praising God soothes us and glorifies him. As I have increased my practice of praise, I have become more content, more confident, and more joyful in my everyday life. I'm able to relax more easily, knowing the glorious, all-powerful, majestic God who created the universe cares about me, watches over me, and is preparing a place for me. And that part about his exulting over me—well, that still seems too good to be true!

And what do you know? My relaxed and joyful state is much more appealing to my family and the people who have to work with me. As they've seen the continual praise I live, they've caught the contagious attitude it brings. Ask them, and I think they'll tell you that the atmosphere of my home and office is infused with the fragrance of joy.

Are you inspiring people to praise God and share the joy that comes from it? Let your light shine—before your neighbors, your friends, your loved ones.

—THELMA WELLS (*Listen Up, Honey*)

# BELIEF AND FAITH

*May your unfailing love rest upon us, O LORD, even as we put our hope in you.*

—Psalm 33:22 NIV

I can't impress on you enough how important it is to have an accurate understanding of God. When great difficulties beset us—when a child dies, a job is lost, a marriage fails, or some other calamity occurs—we long for reassurance that his love for us will not fail as well. We want assurance that God is actively working for good in our lives.

But when we have faulty thinking (a misunderstanding of who God is) we think we need a tangible, visible sign that his promises are true. And when there's no visible, emotional, or tangible evidence of his working things out in our lives, answering our prayers the way we want him to and within the time frame we want him to—we may sink into the dirt of discouragement.

To get past this pit of faulty thinking, we need to understand the difference between *belief* and *faith*. Though similar, the two have an important difference. The dictionary defines *belief* as "mental acceptance of or conviction in the truth or actuality of something." In contrast, faith goes beyond mental acceptance. *Faith* is believing what we can't see, what is not tangible, and in some cases, does not make sense.

Do you have faulty thinking? Move from belief to faith in God's enduring love.

—MARILYN MEBERG (*God at Your Wits' End*)

# WHEN GOD LAUGHS

*If we please God, he will make us wise, understanding, and happy.*
—Ecclesiastes 2:26 CEV

When we know God personally and have invited his Son, Jesus Christ, into our hearts as our Savior, we learn we can laugh in God's presence and he laughs with us. It may not be recorded in Scripture with clear definition, but I know full well that God has created us to be happy and full of joy.

When I think of laughing with God, I refer to those ways he communicates with us where we're comfortable settling into his presence. When we do things to please him, bring honor to him, share his grace with others, and exercise the gifts he's given us, I picture God laughing. I believe when we reflect who he is, he laughs. He's happy.

Here's an illustration of what I mean. When I was growing up, my family talked a lot about the Bible. We memorized scriptures, asked each other what we thought different verses meant, and kept little books and/or cards with different scriptures on them that we were trying to learn by heart and use in our lives. So tell me, when we learn of him and talk about what he likes and who he is and why he cares, are we not bringing him joy? Is it not conceivable that he is laughing in delight? I think so!

—LUCI SWINDOLL (*Life! Celebrate It*)

# QUIETLY PERSEVERING

*You must hold on, so you can do what God wants and receive what he has promised.*

—Hebrews 10:36 NCV

The Bible provides us with good examples of folks who patiently persevered, working in the background until they were called center stage to strut their stuff. Why, Moses was so far offstage, it took a burning bush to get him to move in the right direction. Joseph was thrown in prison. He used that time to prepare for God's call. David was out in the field watching the sheep and learning how to take on lions, tigers, and bears when Samuel came calling to anoint David king.

Gideon was threshing wheat on his farm when an angel popped in for a little visit and an assignment to lead the Israelite army. James and John were fishing when Jesus called them to fish for men.

Moses, David, Gideon, James, and John all remind us that we should go about the business God has appointed for us today—whether that's tossing out our chipped china saucers, puzzling over a long-lost process (like remembering how to cook), or tending the garden.

The Lord is perfectly capable of finding us wherever we are and calling us forward for his service. It's his choice; ours is to persevere—preferably quietly—and to make sure we're fit to serve the King.

—PATSY CLAIRMONT (*All Cracked Up*)

# OTHER SIDES OF THE DIAMOND

*My flesh and my heart may fail, but God is the strength of my heart and my portion forever.*

—Psalm 73:26 NIV

Have you experienced a shift in your faith since there was a trauma, failure, or crisis in your life? That's not uncommon—life crisis can precipitate faith crisis. God hasn't changed. The Bible hasn't changed. But your faith in God and the way you read Scripture may have changed.

Think of God as a multisided diamond. Perhaps before you stumbled and fell, you saw only one or two sides of the diamond of who God is. Maybe you felt you were able to be a pretty good girl, spiritually speaking, and you were keen on the justice of God, on obedience. Maybe you loved the black-and-white, practical qualities of the epistles of Paul.

But in your broken state, perhaps you, like legions before you, found your comfort smack in the middle of the book of Psalms, or even that tragic book of Job, where all manner of emotions are aired and soothed. At this point, God is probably balancing you out, and you'll find yourself hungry to look at the other sides of God's diamond: mercy, grace, and compassion are now all-compelling.

Don't be overly alarmed if your faith feels a bit shaken up. You've probably not lost your faith at all! You are just searching for the other sides of the diamond that is God.

—SANDI PATTY (*Falling Forward*)

# GOD IS LISTENING

*When you call upon me and come and pray to me, I will hear you.*
—Jeremiah 29:12 NRSV

Perhaps you're thinking, prayer has never been easy for me. I stink at it! You feel like what you say to him is insincere, unsure. Or you question whether he even really cares to hear from you. Or you're so overwhelmed you don't even want to talk to him.

It isn't. He does. He still wants you to.

God hears all our prayers, the good and the bad. He is big enough to handle our honest questions and our doubts and even our anger.

God receives our prayers—the thankful ones and the not-so-thankful ones, the eloquent ones and the less-than-perfect ones. He accepts not only our joyful prayers and self-confident prayers, but the prayers we offer when we're not certain of things—or when we're not sure we really want the answer. He accepts our anguished questioning when we experience trauma or loss. He even accepts the prayers that beg him to rain down disaster on someone who has wounded us (although he may not answer them). He accepts all our prayers because they acknowledge we believe he is in control. When we're happy, when we're angry, when we're hurting to the point that words are lost and all we can offer is a cry for help—he is still there.

God is listening.

—SHEILA WALSH (*Get Off Your Knees and Pray*)

# CONQUERING FINANCES

*My God will meet all your needs according to his glorious riches in Christ Jesus.*

—Philippians 4:19 NIV

If you are experiencing financial difficulties, I know how you feel. My husband and I took a terrible financial tumble in the 1980s. The whole economy in Texas went down with the bank failures. I lost 85 percent of my gross income—within six weeks. My husband's small business was adversely affected, and we found all our enterprises floundering at the same time. We're back on our feet now, and we've learned a few things that might help you:

→ *Be honest with your creditors.* We wrote all our creditors and informed them of our circumstances. We were even nice to the bill collectors. When we treated them with dignity, we usually got the same treatment in return.

→ *Live on a cash-only basis.* It's that simple—if you don't have the cash, don't get the product.

→ *Ask God to be your CEO.* We focused on the one we belonged to and what we really wanted out of life. We laid all our plans and agendas and dreams at God's feet and asked Him to take over.

→ *Remember God is for you.* Ask him to help you be a wise steward over the resources he has given you, and for favor with your creditors.

—THELMA WELLS (*Girl, Have I Got Good News for You*)

# THIS WHOLE NOTION OF FORGIVENESS

*Be gentle and ready to forgive; never hold grudges. Remember,*
*the Lord forgave you, so you must forgive others.*

—*Colossians 3:13* TLB

Asking forgiveness or finding within ourselves the capacity to forgive others is a real cheer squelcher. As a Christian, the only way you could have missed hearing that we have to forgive is if you were somehow mistakenly left on a rock in Eden eating custard-filled chocolate eclairs by a fern-shrouded waterfall. To make the subject even more unpalatable, we have to forgive people who don't deserve it.

Sometimes the subject of forgiveness seems just plain dumb. Why forgive when someone has lied to us, cheated us, maligned us, abused us, or deceived us? Forgiveness for those persons simply goes against our emotional and logical sense of justice. Our more civilized selves know not to put sharp tacks on their driveway or send birthday cakes laced with arsenic. Though we might experience short-term pleasure in imagining such retribution, most of us refrain from taking overt retaliatory action. Perhaps we even congratulate ourselves for such restraint and smugly think that such control in itself is virtuous.

The part that is *not* dumb about forgiving people who have wounded us is that forgiving those who have wronged us restores our sense of balance and allows us to "be of good cheer."

—MARILYN MEBERG (*I'd Rather Be Laughing*)

# THE LAST LAUGH ON EARTH

*...us be glad and rejoice before God; may they be happy and joyful.*

—*Psalm 68:3* NIV

It's the nature of what I do, but people often ask me if I think God laughs. They also sometimes ask, "Is God funny?" or, "Is there anything about God that's funny?" My answer is always "Yes." There are a lot of things that make me think God has a sense of humor. Maybe it's my quirky sense of humor, but when I think of some of the animals he's made (been to a zoo lately?) I know he laughs. Or situations that are so weird, nobody could put all the parts together but God. Even answers to prayer are hilarious sometimes. I think he laughs often.

Personally, I think the last laugh on earth will come from God. It will sound "like the laughter of the universe," as Dante said in his allegory *The Divine Comedy*. When the Easter story is completed, the risen Christ will come to earth again and take us with him to heaven. Scripture says, "We'll be walking on air!" (1 Thessalonians 4:18 MSG).

And God himself will have the last laugh. The entire universe will be proclaiming the love of God in Christ Jesus—and then we'll all laugh together, celebrating our risen and reigning Lord.

—LUCI SWINDOLL (*Life! Celebrate It*)

# WINGED VICTORY

> *Thanks be to God, who gives us the victory through our Lord*
> *Jesus Christ.*
>
> —1 Corinthians 15:57

My favorite statue is a marble sculpture of a Greek goddess, discovered in 1863. It's best known as Winged Victory or Nike. What draws me to this figure is her name, Victory, and her elegant grace in spite of significant damage. The sculpture has lost her head—literally. Draped in marble, the folds of her garments fall like rare silk. Her outstretched wings appear luminous and ready for flight.

Victory originally was designed for the bow of a ship, proclaiming its triumphant fleet. She is believed to have had outstretched arms with an extended trumpet that she used to blow a victory song. Victory is just over ten feet of marble splendor. Her broken beauty is simultaneously strong and fragile. Her remains are a picture of defiance against the odds and of beauty, not only in spite of hardship, but also because of it.

What I love most about this statue is its ability to inspire. When I'm functioning "headless," Victory reminds me that my heart can carry me through. When I'm feeling helpless to assist others, as if my hands were encased, I'm reminded that I can rely on God's supernatural work. It's OK if I'm damaged by life's adversities; I can still stand strong because the Lord makes his strength known in our weakness.

—PATSY CLAIRMONT (*All Cracked Up*)

# REVIVE YOUR FAITH

*Those who are right with God will live by faith.*
—*Habakkuk 2:4 NIrV*

You've experienced a crisis in your life—one of your own making. We all do from time to time. Now you are desperate to revive your faith. Here are some things to remember:

→ *Experience the freedom that comes with understanding that forgiveness is about God's grace, not about your mess.* Focus on that, and you'll make great strides.
→ *Cultivate the habit of the Trust Fall (letting go and letting yourself fall into God's arms) whenever a crisis comes, large or small.*
→ *Remember there is a time to deal with your crisis.* This involves the cultivation of old-fashioned courage.
→ *Be grateful to God, in any and all circumstances.* Realize that you can be thankful for the lessons gleaned from loss, even though you cannot thank God for the bad things that happen.
→ *Strike up a conversation with God again.* That can be daunting, especially after guilt or hurt, so go slowly. Your first prayer may be, "Hello, up there. It's me again." It's a start!

Stay proactive in your spiritual journey. The rewards are simply out of this world.

—SANDI PATTY (*Falling Forward*)

# NOW THAT I'M FIFTY!

> *Though our outward man is perishing, yet the inward man is being renewed day by day.*
>
> —2 Corinthians 4:16

Now that I'm fifty, change in every arena of life has become an ongoing reality.

My eyesight has deteriorated to the shifting terrain of bifocals. At my last eye test, when the optometrist covered my left eye, I could only read the first two lines on the chart. When he covered my right eye, I couldn't see the wall!

I am definitely getting shorter. To remedy this, I have two clear choices: wear higher heels or have all my pants altered.

I need my roots retouched every three weeks now instead of every six. When I suggested going back to my natural color, my hair stylist said I no longer have one.

But in the midst of all these unsettling changes, I am discovering profound and simple gifts. I've learned I have good friends—friends I can count on. We laugh at all the petty indignities of aging and cry together when life takes one of us through a dark night.

I am changing in my understanding of my spiritual life too. I am more inclined to listen for God's voice than to present to him a list of requests. I have a quiet confidence that no matter what seems to be true, God is always in control.

—SHEILA WALSH (*Get Off Your Knees and Pray*)

# THAT CRAZY BOSS

> *I urge, then, first of all, that requests, prayers, intercession and*
> *thanksgiving be made for everyone—for kings and all those*
> *in authority, that we may live peaceful and quiet lives in all*
> *godliness and holiness.*
>
> 1 Timothy 2:1–2 NIV

So you say you are dealing with a crazy boss, and you are just at your wits' end? Let me share with you a few things I've learned through the years that might help you out with your difficult boss:

- ❖ ***Take the initiative.*** Write out a set of goals and objectives for yourself that are in line with your company's objectives. Then ask for a meeting to discuss them. Document your performance throughout the year, and occasionally ask your boss how you are doing and what you can do to help the department succeed.
- ❖ ***Create positive visibility.*** Take an honest look at yourself, and see what kind of visibility you're earning. If it's not appealing to you, change it for the better.
- ❖ ***Understand your boss.*** Take time to notice what motivates your boss. Ask God to give you wisdom, and take you out of the picture so that you can surrender the whole deal to him.
- ❖ ***Look for another job.*** After you've gotten yourself in line with God's plan for your current situation and things still don't work out, trust God to provide another one.

—THELMA WELLS (*Girl, Have I Got Good News for You*)

# TWO DIFFERENT MATTERS

> *Wisdom is a tree of life to those who embrace her; happy are those who hold her tightly.*
>
> —Proverbs 3:18 NLT

Forgiveness is often a tough topic—even tougher because we sometimes harbor certain misconceptions. We need God's wisdom as we strive to embrace it.

Misconception Number One: If you forgive someone, you have to "get back together" with that person? Not true! That very thought could send us racing to the airport for a one-way ticket to Antarctica. We need to mentally separate the act of forgiveness and the act of reuniting. They are not the same. We can forgive our offender and still plan never to see that person again. Forgiving the offender does not change the offender . . . it changes you.

Misconception Number Two: Forgiving someone's offense against you excuses that person's behavior. Forgiving does not excuse or condone . . . it simply forgives. The behavior remains the same: unacceptable, immoral, or even life-threatening.

Misconception Number Three: Forgiving means forgetting the pain that individual inflicted on you. The concept of "forgive and forget" is something only God can do. We can't come anywhere near forgetting.

Don't let these misconceptions deprive you of the healing effects of forgiving those who have wounded you. It's the first step to reclaiming your laugh, your smile, and your merry heart.

—MARILYN MEBERG (*I'd Rather Be Laughing*)

# LOVING THROUGH THE PAIN

*Love covers over all wrongs.*
—*Proverbs 10:12* NIV

I don't believe unforgiveness and love can live in the same heart at the same time. And I also don't believe love comes to the person who has been offended until he or she forgives the offender. It might take weeks, months, even years. And it may never happen. The hurt is too deep, too hard to overcome, and too raw to find common ground. I've been there, so I know. What did it take for me to learn to love through the pain?

Let me try to list some principles I've learned.

+ *Work out in your own mind exactly what's wrong.* Identify the problem; call it what it is and take it apart piece by piece. Admit where you were wrong and where the other person was wrong.
+ *Start talking to God about it.* Be very, very honest about what hurts and why. Stay at this task until you feel God's direction on how to change things.
+ *Be brave and courageous.* Contact the offender in your calmest manner and trust God to help you find creative ways to make things right.
+ *Don't back down from your commitment to get rid of the feelings of hurt and pain.* Love with all your heart, and never stop loving.

—LUCI SWINDOLL (*Life! Celebrate It*)

# LET IT RAIN

*The rain fell, the floods came, and the winds blew and beat on that house, but it did not fall, because it had been founded on rock.*

—Matthew 7:25 NRSV

Texas isn't the only place that knows how to throw a storm. From sea to shining sea, tempests are to be expected in our weather patterns and in our lives. Try as you might, you can't find a picture-perfect weather spot in the world.

But do we want to? No clouds and no rain translate to no green terrain. Why, our gardens would be stubble, our trees stumps, flowers dried-up seeds, and our wells dust. Makes one want to sing, "Let it rain, let it rain, let it rain."

Clouds are typecast according to how far off the ground they are—high level, midlevel, and low level. Depending on their height, they are composed of water droplets, ice crystals, ice particles, or snow. The moisture content in the clouds, when touched by the light of the evening sun, creates the magnificent array of colors in a sunset.

That's true of our lives as well. Clouds will blow through our neighborhoods, whether we live in Texas or Michigan. Some will be fair-weather friends, while others will pummel us with the hail of hardships and swirls of sorrow. While we may have to step through the cleanup, we know the Son will once again fill our skies with color.

—PATSY CLAIRMONT (*All Cracked Up*)

# I SURRENDER ALL

*There's an opportune time to do things, a right time for*
*everything on the earth: . . . A right time to hold on and*
*another to let go.*

—*Ecclesiastes 3:1, 6* MSG

It is interesting how often surrendering to God is precipitated by hitting a wall in our attempts to orchestrate our own lives. Surrender is sincerely saying to God, "Lord, I'm out of energy. Have your way in this area of my life. I am choosing to let go of my expectations about how it turns out. I need to stop striving and I need to rest! I am giving this to you—please take over."

Though the hymn says, "I surrender *all*"—it is nearly impossible to surrender every part of yourself and your life at one time. It's more like a lifelong journey of small surrenders as circumstances present themselves. I've found that when I practice the small surrenders, the bigger ones come quicker, with less hanging on. The more I let go of my cherished delusions of having control over my life, the easier it is for me to surrender. The good news is that peace enters when the struggle for control is over. Freedom arrives when the last bit of self-sufficiency departs.

In order to turn the corner to freedom, I had to learn this lesson the excruciatingly hard way. I had to relinquish my right to everything, my expectation of anything. I had to say, "Whatever, Lord," and really mean it.

—SANDI PATTY (*Falling Forward*)

# STOP AND LISTEN

*Jesus said, "My sheep listen to my voice; I know them, and they follow me."*
—John 10:27 NIV

You say you have questions? That's okay. My plea to you even in the midst of the questions is simple: talk to God and take time to listen. No matter how "vertically challenged" we may believe ourselves to be, God is listening and talking to us all the time. We only need to learn to stop and listen.

We are living in difficult times. War and terrorism are no longer a million miles away from home. Cancer and heart disease are waging an unprecedented battle against younger and younger people. The financial "golden days" of the 1980s are long gone. People worry if they will have enough savings to help their children through college or if they themselves will have enough to retire on. The bottom line is, life is hard.

God knows all about it. And more than that, right in the center of the tornado of our lives, he offers a quiet place, a shelter where he waits with open arms and an open heart to embrace any of us who will come. Whether you are young or old, full of hope or full of fear, angry or excited, bitter or grateful, this remains my conviction: God is listening.

—SHEILA WALSH (*Get Off Your Knees and Pray*)

# ONE HAND IN HEAVEN

*Precious in the sight of the LORD is the death of His saints.*
—*Psalm 116:15*

If you've lost a loved one, then you know first hand just how devastating it can be. If you haven't yet lost someone close to you, you can be certain that day will come. None of us live forever on this earth. When it happens, you understand how fragile life really is, and you also know that in some ways, you will never really "get over it." We can learn to savor the happy times however and benefit from things we learned during the difficult times.

Here are some suggestions that I hope will help you deal with the loss of someone you love:

- → *Don't bottle up your grief.* The more we can express ourselves, the faster we can heal. Talk to someone you trust, and set those emotions free.
- → *Remember, death is not the end.* None of us wants our loved ones to leave this earth, but when they do, I know without a doubt that their entrance into heaven will be the grandest entrance ever.
- → *Look forward to the future.* One day you will be with your loved ones and never without them again. In eternity, nothing will be bad. It'll all be glorious. Your loved ones' spirits are still with you now, but one day they themselves will be with you again.

—THELMA WELLS (*Girl, Have I Got Good News for You*)

# LOVING ARMS OF THE FATHER

> *[The Lord] will feed his flock like a shepherd. He will carry the lambs in his arms, holding them close to his heart. He will gently lead the mother sheep with their young.*
>
> —Isaiah 40:11 NLT

What is your need right now? Let's suppose it is to overcome a difficult situation such as making it through the pain and anxiety of divorce. You need to be convinced that God is for you and not against you. Perhaps you need the strength and wisdom to deal with your kids, who have turned their backs on God and on the family. You must be certain that God cares even more for your children than you do. If your need has to do with the devastation that comes from a cancer diagnosis or some other debilitating disease, you have to know that God's love for you will never leave you as you begin to walk a path you never expected to make your way down. His love guarantees you won't walk it alone.

God is gently, lovingly, calling your name and inviting you to venture toward him, inviting you not to be afraid. Crawl into the loving arms of your Father, and let him rock you until you find quietness and peace. With the renewed confidence that you are loved, you will be able to find ways to deal with your circumstances and find reasons to have a heart full of cheer.

—MARILYN MEBERG (*I'd Rather Be Laughing*)

# THANKS FOR THE LESSONS

*We also glory in tribulations, knowing that tribulation*
*produces perseverance; and perseverance, character; and*
*character, hope.*

—Romans 5:3–4

How do you handle crazy-making dilemmas like these? You're treated unfairly by "the system." Somebody gets a promotion, and you don't. Somebody gets selected for a team, and you don't. What do you do then?

For me . . . I talk to myself first. I tell myself it's not fair and I don't like it. (I'm a big fan of "fair." But, if I'm honest, I have to admit that life itself isn't fair; and as long as I'm in this life, it ain't ever gonna be fair. *So face that first, Lucille, and move on.*) I do my best to get beyond it. And getting beyond something takes commitment. I think it also takes wanting to be an adult. Wanting maturity. God's going to do his best to bring us all to maturity, but we can help a bit by shutting up and getting out of his way.

I've come to realize that those disappointments, those situations in life that we feel aren't fair can be great teachers. There's no amount of money that could pay for the lessons learned while I was struggling, and there's no amount I would take in place of the learning. They've taught me to be careful and prayerful and to thank God for his lessons every day.

—LUCI SWINDOLL (*Life! Celebrate It*)

# CREATING A MASTERPIECE

*This is what the Sovereign LORD says, "I will give them an
undivided heart and put a new spirit in them; I will remove
from them their heart of stone and give them a heart of flesh."*

—Ezekiel 11:19 NIV

Imagine you have invested a great deal of time and creativity into
a piece of art. You think it's coming along nicely, and then you
concentrate on a feature of the face or on the arm. As you set mallet
to hammer, you pound into a flaw—and the whole upper corner
of the marble crumbles onto the floor. That's what happened to
Michelangelo as he worked on his masterpiece *Madonna and Child*.
Since Michelangelo had hand-cut the marble block himself, he
must have felt like pounding the mallet into his own head.

Sometimes it feels like someone is swinging a mallet our way!
But then we turn around and see that it's our loving Lord at work.
He carefully selects his material and sets to work, chiseling and
shaping us into his image.

Yet, like Michelangelo, God is dealing with flawed stone.
Sometimes we crack and drop off chunks under the hands of the
Artist. So what does he do? Toss out our rocklike souls? No, he
works around our hard heads and stony hearts to make us into
something remarkable. Like Michelangelo, God knows how to
make the best of the material at hand and manages to create something out of so little.

—PATSY CLAIRMONT (*All Cracked Up*)

# EXTRAORDINARY LOVE

*We saw it, we heard it, and now we're telling you so you can experience it along with us, this experience of communion with the Father and his Son, Jesus Christ.*

—1 John 1:3 MSG

What a wonderfully amazing gift God has given us: freedom that comes from knowing and loving our authentic self, freedom that takes us beyond our past hurts and still-bleeding wounds, and freedom from the fear of what lies in the future. Such a gift of extraordinary love is really too good to keep solely for our exclusive use, don't you think?

As believers, we know we're loved by a compassionate God, and we're taught by his Word to love ourselves as Christ loves us, unconditionally. We may have behaviors that require determined work in order to be changed, but we are to love ourselves despite our shortcomings because that's how Christ loves us.

Once we accept and understand the extraordinary love Jesus has poured out on us through the gift of salvation, we're ready to take the next step: sharing that same unconditional love with others. Are you ready to open your heart and your lips and tell others what He has done for you?

—MARILYN MEBERG & LUCI SWINDOLL (*Free Inside and Out*)

# A CLEAN HEART

*Create in me a clean heart, O God, and put a new and right*
*spirit within me.*

—Psalm 51:10 NRSV

What exactly is a "clean heart"?

As women, our hormones lead us on a lively dance for most of our lives. So what do we do on those days when we don't feel very holy or sometimes even sane? Does God hear our prayers when our emotions are taking us on a roller coaster ride? What if we want to have a clean heart, but we're having trouble with it? What if we believe we have a clean heart, but there is some little seed of unforgiveness buried deep inside us we've forgotten about? Are we only responsible for the sins we remember or for every little offense we've committed in our lifetime?

When it is our earnest desire to be clean, God sees that—whether we can remember every detail of our lives or not. Yes, he wants us to come before him with a pure heart, but he also tells us that he hears our honest petitions.

We can't keep worrying about how clean the corners of our soul are. If we get caught up in that whirlpool of self-loathing and doubt, we're only headed down. But if we come before the God who makes all things new, believing in faith that he knows our true hearts, we are certain to be uplifted.

—SHEILA WALSH (*Get Off Your Knees and Pray*)

# FORGIVING THE UNFORGIVEABLE

*Jesus said, "Whenever you stand praying, if you have anything against anyone, forgive him, that your Father in heaven may also forgive you your trespasses."*

—Mark 11:25

There have been pains in my soul that hurt so deeply that I never thought I could be healed, let alone forgive the people who harmed me. If you feel that way, you know what I mean. The good news is that God is big enough to reach down into our hearts and take care of those jumbo hurts that we may think are hopeless.

Here are a few suggestions that might help you as you work with God's help to forgive the unforgiveable hurts in your life:

→ *Forgiveness is for you.* More often than not, the person you are not forgiving is unconcerned or unaware of your feelings. Who have you hurt by not forgiving? Yourself.
→ *You can't forgive in your own power.* Forgiving is too hard for us to do by ourselves. Only the Spirit within us is holy enough to replace the poison of bitterness with the balm of forgiveness.
→ *Let God judge.* One of the reasons we hold on so tightly to anger and bitterness is that we're afraid those who've hurt us will "get away with it" if we let go. Let God decide how the people who've hurt you should be judged so you can heal and change your focus. Life is short.

—THELMA WELLS (*Girl, Have I Got Good News for You*)

253

# CAN YOU IMAGINE!

*"Cheer up, don't be afraid. For the Lord your God has arrived to live among you. He is a mighty Savior. He will give you victory. He will rejoice over you in great gladness; he will love you and not accuse you." Is that a joyous choir I hear? No, it is the Lord himself exulting over you in happy song.*

—*Zephaniah 3:16–18* TLB

Can you imagine that God's delight in us is so genuine, so spontaneous, so spirited that he exults over us by singing happy songs? Can you imagine that he not only lives among us (within us) and promises to give us victory, but also that he rejoices over us in great gladness? Who in your lifetime—past, present, or future—has ever been or will ever be so utterly in love with you?

Only God! Plain, simple, profound. That realization is enough to cause me to look up, up, up, and topple over with cheer-inducing, heartfelt gratitude. It's wonderful to know that no matter what or whom I meet on the road, I can be of good cheer. How? Why? It is because Jesus lives within me, and he is an overcomer. And because of his indwelling presence, so too am I.

So come on! Grab your robe and join the joyous choir. There's a lot more living, loving, and laughing to do. Sure, there's plenty of stuff in this world to steal your joy. But remember, you have Jesus. You have a choice. You can choose cheer over fear. And after all is said and done, wouldn't you rather be laughing?

—MARILYN MEBERG (*I'd Rather Be Laughing*)

# THE SECRETS OF FRIENDSHIP

*Those who love a pure heart and are gracious in speech will have the king as a friend.*

—Proverbs 22:11 NRSV

I'm often asked if I have a formula for maintaining rich, meaningful relationships.

Honestly, there's no formula because every relationship is different. But for me there are two major qualifiers for having friends and being a good friend to somebody else.

*First, hold people loosely in your heart.* I used to be very hurt when people didn't do things my way or when they chose to be with somebody else. I pouted. I was rude to the one who hurt me. But when I got sick enough of acting that way, I brought God into the problem and asked him to help me grow up. He taught me to release my will and my grip on those who really meant something to me. There's nothing like being free, and that's one of the main ingredients in a meaningful friendship—to be free and let the other person be free.

*Second, a rich relationship has to have an investment from both persons.* Friendships don't grow rich unless you make deposits: you spend time together, you connect with each other, and you change things around to give balance where it's needed. You constantly have to study the input of that account to see what it needs. I promise you, if you take care of the relationship, it will grow.

—LUCI SWINDOLL (*Life! Celebrate It*)

255

# DIRECTIONALLY MUDDLED

*I will instruct you and teach you in the way you should go; I will guide you with My eye.*

—Psalm 32:8

I've spent a lifetime directionally muddled. But logistically challenged or not, we are all travelers. Life forces us to hit the road in search of doctors, banks, dry cleaners, groceries, and many other things. My husband, Les, and I divide our time between Texas and Michigan, which means for me, a non-mapper, that I seldom know where I am, much less where the bank is in relationship to our home. So sweet Les, in an attempt to simplify my perpetual lostness, chose the bank directly across the street from our subdivision. No missing piece there—out the driveway, into the bank. Now, if only life were that simple!

Thank heavens for Jesus, who offers to walk with us wherever we are. He promises to guide our steps and light our path. Jesus is there for us if, like Zacchaeus, we are out on a limb. He's there for us if, like Eve, we've taken the wrong path. He's there for us if we are wandering aimlessly or high-stepping with certainty.

Jesus never loses sight of us, even when we're feeling hopelessly lost. He holds all our puzzle pieces. What looks broken to us is whole to him, because he is the beginning and the end of all things.

—PATSY CLAIRMONT (*All Cracked Up*)

# BELOVED PILGRIM

*When pride comes, then comes disgrace; but wisdom is with the humble.*

—Proverbs 11:2 NRSV

You might be amazed at how freeing it is to lose your reputation. Devastating, yes. I have to admit, it has been one of the most painful experiences of my life. But I'll tell you what—it has freed me from worrying that I might lose my reputation! Been there, lost that, and I'm still breathing. When you survive what you once thought would be an insurmountable loss, you realize that you and God can face just about anything together. I have found that being real, being yourself, is a lot more attractive to others than trying to impress them anyway.

It has forced me to rely not on my own reputation but on God's. It's been made painfully clear that I am not perfect—but *he* is. I can't atone for my sins—but *he* did. God is the only credential we need, and that frees us from worrying about our own lack of certifications, diplomas, and degrees.

To find ultimate freedom, you begin to let who you really are inside shine to the outside world. The world becomes a sort of "come as you are" party—where you are happy to show up just as plain old you: a beloved pilgrim, very much in progress.

—SANDI PATTY (*Falling Forward*)

# BETTER BOYS AND GIRLS

*The LORD has heard my supplication; the LORD accepts my prayer.*

—Psalm 6:9 NRSV

Both of my grandfathers died before I was born. But my mom tells a story about her father that I think is hilarious.

From what I understand, my grandfather was a hardworking man with a simple faith. At mealtimes, his standard grace was: "For what we are about to receive, may the Lord make us truly thankful." But on one particular occasion when they were having guests for lunch after church, my nana asked him to embellish the usual blessing a bit.

He must have forgotten her request, because he started out as he always did: "For what we are about to receive, may the Lord make us truly thankful."

There was a noticeable pause before he added, "And make me a good boy, amen!"

Now, at this point my granddad must have been in his sixties—but I guess that's the only other prayer he could remember from his childhood. I am so sorry I wasn't there. I would have fallen off my chair in hysterics, high-fiving my granddad on the way down!

My nana wanted my granddad to come up with a few more impressive words, but I am convinced that the words we use are of less interest to God than the intent of our hearts. God hears our heart no matter the words we use. Just by being in God's presence, we become "better" boys and girls.

—SHEILA WALSH (*Get Off Your Knees and Pray*)

# MOVING ON

*If anyone is in Christ, there is a new creation: everything old has passed away; see, everything has become new!*

—2 Corinthians 5:17 NRSV

If you have been through the pain of a divorce, you can be certain you aren't alone. Many marriages fail these days for a variety of reasons. No matter what the reason you find yourself divorced, you should know this is not the end of the story. It never is for a child of God!

Consider these suggestions for making your way through the fog of divorce:

→ *Let go of guilt.* Beating yourself up because of your choice to get a divorce is like crying over spilled milk. When it's spilled, it needs to be wiped up. You made a choice, good or bad; now you need to wipe up the mess and move on with your life.

→ *Stay open.* It would be tempting to shut down all your emotions and isolate yourself, but I urge you to keep your heart open, rebuke negative thoughts in the name of Jesus, and meditate on God's Word.

→ *Fall in love with Jesus.* There is life after divorce. What better way to spend your intimate time than with the Creator of love and life, God through his Son, Jesus? Now, go on about your life, living free in Jesus.

—THELMA WELLS (*Girl, Have I Got Good News for You*)

# FOUND WORTHY

> *Come now, let us argue it out, says the LORD: though your sins are like scarlet, they shall be like snow; though they are red like crimson, they shall become like wool.*
>
> —Isaiah 1:18 NRSV

God's heart is always tuned to the needs of his creation. Our cries for help are always heard. In addition to that good news, there's no sin he cannot or will not forgive. There are no good deeds we must first perform in order to be good enough for salvation. The thief who hung next to Jesus on the cross brought nothing to him but his splattered record of sin. And yet, the second he asked, he was granted forgiveness. He was immediately deemed worthy to join Jesus in paradise.

What motivates Jesus' selection of those who are imperfect? What motivates Jesus to put aside his own agony and focus on the request of a man who was scum before he met Jesus on the cross? The answer reverberates and fills the entire universe; it is the love of God for those whom he created to receive that love.

If we persist in thinking there's just something about us that God does not cotton to, we would have to rewrite the Bible to prove it! There is instead just something about us he is crazy about! To think otherwise is faulty thinking. To think otherwise is to have no faith in the Word of God, which tells us just how strong his love is for us.

—MARILYN MEBERG (*God at Your Wits' End*)

# AN ATTITUDE OF JOY

*I will greatly rejoice in the LORD, my soul shall be joyful in my God.*
—Isaiah 61:10

My life is not full of joy every minute, but it's true that joy is my most natural posture. I had a happy childhood, and that no doubt makes a big difference in the way I am today. In addition, I've trained myself to look for the bright side of things. I'm rarely around negative people, and if I am, I don't make camp there.

Joy is not only a marvelous gift from God; it's a command (Philippians 4:4 says, "Rejoice!"). Joy is also a learned behavior. If you're generous with other people, they will be generous with you, and that alone will bring you unspeakable joy. Joy starts inside yourself. You can't expect to get it from somebody else first.

Although I experience abundant joy in life, laugh heartily and often, and appreciate humor at every turn, my temperament poses certain challenges: when I tire, I get cranky. When things are out of order, I can be stubbornly controlling. When I find myself at the mercy of another's plans or schedule, I can be very frustrated. In that sense, joy does not always come naturally to me . . . it's an attitude I choose and try very hard to maintain.

—LUCI SWINDOLL (*Life! Celebrate It*)

# THE RISEN SAVIOR

*They said to one another, "Did not our heart burn within us while He talked with us on the road, and while He opened the Scriptures to us?"*

—Luke 24:32

Long ago and far away, two men traveled by foot on a dusty road. As they walked, they were deep in conversation about someone they knew, a teacher. They had heard of him in the conversations of others in the villages, and as time went on, more and more stories of him were exchanged among the townspeople. Finally, these men were drawn into his company and followed his teachings.

But this day, the men spoke of his shocking crucifixion. He had left behind a handful of stories, promises, and unanswered questions. Their expectations were dashed. Great mystery surrounded this teacher as they spoke of his intentions and his resulting death. It was said he died of a broken heart—a heart broken for humankind.

They wondered aloud about him. They had many stories—and what stories they were! What did it all mean?

A thousand thoughts whirled through their minds as they chattered on. In fact, they were so caught up in their questions that they hardly noticed that the Answer had joined them on their journey. Until he spoke . . . and their hearts burned within them. What man is this? They took a second look. Then their eyes were opened. It was Jesus, the risen Savior.

—PATSY CLAIRMONT (*All Cracked Up*)

# TESTING GOD

*Fear not, for I am with you.*
—Isaiah 43:5

During a particularly tough time in my life, I asked myself a difficult, life-changing question. Is the God I have been following since I was eleven years old big enough to handle my questions, fear, and anger? I needed to know.

So I tested him. I questioned his will. And every time I expressed to him my fear and weakness, he was there with me. At first I didn't want to acknowledge his presence, as if by doing so I was saying I accepted what was going on. In some strange way it was almost as if I thought my protests would keep the pain away.

But even though I continued to struggle, I was deeply aware of God's comfort and understanding. And in time, I opened my heart to what he was speaking to me. And slowly but surely, as the weeks passed, I found a strength I hadn't had before. It was nothing to do with me. I didn't see myself as any stronger than I was before. In fact, quite the opposite. I became aware that God was right beside me and that when I fell down, he would pick me up. He imparted his own strength to me.

—SHEILA WALSH (*Get Off Your Knees and Pray*)

# TOO MUCH TO DO

*To everything there is a season, a time for every purpose under heaven.*

—Ecclesiastes 3:1

Are you the kind of person who tries to meet everyone's expectations? It can't be done, you know. And that's what you have to come to terms with in order to change your life for the better.

Here are some suggestions to help you when you have too much to do and too little time:

> → *Ask for what you need.* Why not call a family meeting and gently, with kindness, tell the family how you feel about needing more help at home? You may even ask them what chores they would prefer . . . if everyone pitches in and helps, it will not be hard on any one person.
> → *Practice setting boundaries.* Consider Jesus' example: He certainly laid down his life for people on a daily basis; but he also pulled away from the crowds in order to pray and spend time alone. He didn't always give people what they wanted when they wanted it.
> → *Let God set your priorities.* My daily prayer is, "Lord, open the doors I need to walk through today. Close the doors I don't. Get people out of my way that I don't need to talk to today, and put those in my path that I do. And, Lord, please don't let me waste your time!"

—THELMA WELLS (*Girl, Have I Got Good News for You*)

# FAITH IS NOT BLIND

*Jesus said, "So, you believe because you've seen with your own eyes. Even better blessings are in store for those who believe without seeing."*

—John 20:29 MSG

Many people seem inclined to consider faith a more or less blind system of belief while others just can't quite fall for it. It seems too hard to do, blindly believing without any evidence. The Danish philosopher Kierkegaard referred to the need for a "leap of faith" to enter into a realm of spirituality.

But thinking that faith is a hard, complicated concept that must be blindly accepted is faulty thinking, because viewing faith as "blind" totally misses the scriptural teaching of what faith is. When the Bible describes blindness, it is an image representing people who have chosen sin as a way of living. They walk in darkness. The plan of God is to call people out of the darkness. Faith cannot be blind, because faith is authored by he who leads us to the light.

The word *faith* means "trust." To trust God is not an act of blind, unreasonable belief, because God proves himself to be utterly trustworthy at all times. Christianity is not based on myths or made-up stories. It is based on the testimony of those who witnessed jaw-dropping evidence that God sent his Son, Jesus, to this earth. Our faith is not blind. It is based on facts we can trust, facts that inspire faith.

—MARILYN MEBERG (*God at Your Wits' End*)

# DOUBTS AND FEARS

*Let us hold fast the confession of our hope without wavering,*
*for He who promised is faithful.*

—*Hebrews 10:23*

By nature, I'm not prone to doubt and fear. I really, really, really try to believe what God says and trust him to come through with the goods. When he says I don't have to be afraid, I try hard to believe that and go on. When he says he will always be with me, I know he will. When he promises to provide for my needs, I look to him to do that. In short . . . when I take God at his word, I don't have many doubts or fears.

The key to all this is learning to trust God in every little nook and cranny of your day. Life works when we trust, and the love comes because we feel blessed in that trust. We love the one who keeps his word.

Commit your way to the Lord, and see where he takes you. When you hit a bump in the road, ask yourself, "What could God be teaching me in this?" Remember, even when you are struggling, he is not making a mistake with your life. You don't have to live with doubt and fear. Let God help you turn your fear to fearlessness and your doubt to miracle-working faith!

—LUCI SWINDOLL (*Life! Celebrate It*)

# SO SAY THE JOYOLOGISTS

*When the righteous see God in action they'll laugh, they'll sing, they'll laugh and sing for joy.*

—*Psalm 68:3* MSG

According to some joyologists (uh-huh, *joyologists*—those given to the promotion of joy), you can lose weight if you guffaw daily. So does this mean we can titter till our tummies tuck? Or better yet, chortle till the cellulite runs smooth? I'm afraid I'd have to be permanently hysterical to accomplish that task.

Can't you see it now? A world emphasis on belly laughing, with people lining up single file around the block, waiting to slip into a joy booth so they can laugh off lunch. Or employers offering health incentives for workers who snicker heartily. Have you ever wondered why God designed us with the ability to laugh and cry? I guess he knew we would need to do both as a way to pour off emotional excess; otherwise, we might blow a gasket.

I've heard it said that hearty laughter sends fresh shipments of oxygen to the brain, which causes it to loosen up. Hmm, if it can loosen up my brain, then maybe, just maybe, the joyologists are right, and it could loosen up my jeans. That would be great. Then I wouldn't have to unsnap them to eat, sit, travel, and breathe. I'd much rather chuckle myself fit than deny myself indulgences, but I have this nagging feeling I may need to do both.

—PATSY CLAIRMONT (*All Cracked Up*)

# UNPACK THOSE BAGS

*Praise be to the LORD, to God our Savior, who daily bears our burdens.*

—*Psalm 68:19* NIV

I wonder how many of us are weighed down by the stuff we drag around, day after day. Baggage is inevitable; who among us can walk through life without picking up some shame or fears or insecurities, right? The question is, why do we persist in hanging on to these things, jealously guarding our junk as though it's worth keeping?

Scripture reminds us to cast our cares on our Father, but even though we have God's open invitation to unpack our heavy bags, we seem to find that very hard to do. We'd rather cart the weight around than take God up on his offer.

I have asked people why they don't just surrender their burdens to God in prayer. Here are a few of their answers:

- ✦ I don't have time to pray.
- ✦ I'm too tired to pray.
- ✦ I start all right, but then I get distracted.
- ✦ To be honest, I'm not sure God is listening.

I empathize with those concerns, yet I am convinced it would revolutionize our lives if we were better able to understand that prayer is a gift, rather than a chore. Something to look forward to, rather than something we're graded on. It's not about how well we pray, but about who is listening to our prayers.

—SHEILA WALSH (*Get Off Your Knees and Pray*)

# BECOMING LIKE JESUS

*We know that all things work together for good to those who*
*love God, to those who are called according to His purpose.*

—Romans 8:28

Why does God help us up again and again when we stumble and
fall? To help us become more like his Son, Jesus! That point was
reinforced when I heard my pastor teach from a powerful chapter
in Romans. He began by reading Romans 8:28, another one of
those beloved passages we all repeat when we need to encourage
ourselves in not-too-good situations.

But my pastor said that we often fail to read verse 29, which
has as much or maybe more significance than verse 28. Here's
how it reads in The Living Bible paraphrase: *From the very begin-*
*ning God decided that those who came to him—and all along he*
*knew who would—should become like his Son, so that his Son would*
*be the First, with many brothers.*

The key words in this passage are "become like his Son."
How can we do that? Only by surrendering our lives to his Son's
perfect will for us and fully realizing that whatever God allows in
his children's lives is for one purpose: to draw us closer to his
Son. He wants to build our confidence in his Son to the extent
that we depend on him for everything.

—THELMA WELLS (*The Buzz*)

# SATISFYING THE MIND

*This is my prayer: that your love may abound more and more
in knowledge and depth of insight, so that you may be able to
discern what is best and may be pure and blameless until the
day of Christ.*

—*Philippians 1:9–10* NIV

Faith is not a mindless leap into the unknown that's too hard for
us to fathom. Faith enables reason to go beyond its human limitations. But faith is not a simple result of reason; it is reason
submitting to the truth of Scripture, which is saturated with and
enlivened by the Holy Spirit of God. There are mysteries of faith
that lie beyond my human understanding, but I believe them
because they are rooted in the strength of God's Word. I don't
pretend to understand the mystery of his ways, but Scripture
describes God in ways that satisfy my mind.

Reason is a gift of God. It speaks to that God-placed center
within us all that recognizes truth. We choose to believe that
truth. We choose to embrace that truth. And we choose to live by
faith, which is trustworthy.

I am not advocating an academic or sterile approach to our
faith, but I am thrilled that it can stand up to scrutiny. Faith produces in us responses that go far beyond our scrutiny once our
scrutiny is satisfied.

—MARILYN MEBERG (*God at Your Wits' End*)

# THE DINNER PARTY

*God, who gets invited to dinner at your place? How do we get on your guest list?*

—Psalm 15:1 MSG

We all want to sit at God's dining table. We long to have fellowship and fun with him. We want to see how he sets the table and who else is there and find out what will be the topics of conversation. And here's the great part—in Psalm 15, he tells us what it takes to get on that list. He says, "Walk straight, act right, tell the truth. Don't hurt your friend, don't blame your neighbor; despise the despicable. Keep your word even when it costs you, make an honest living, never take a bribe" (vv. 2–5).

That list is perfect because there's not one thing about how the person has to be dressed or what she must weigh, or whether she has money or is educated or famous. There's nothing about looks or beauty or ability. It's all—*all!*—about character. It's about the inside of the person. And who doesn't want to be with people like that? This is what we want in a dinner guest. It's what God requires in order to be on his guest list. And you can bet your bottom dollar if you value these attributes as well, you'll be right at the top of everybody's list.

—LUCI SWINDOLL (*Life! Celebrate It*)

# THE FINE ART OF SPINNING

*Be constantly renewed in the spirit of your mind [having a
fresh mental and spiritual attitude].*

—*Ephesians 4:23* AMP

Did you know that you can tell if an egg is raw or hard-cooked by
spinning it? If the egg spins like a top, it's hard-cooked, but if it
wobbles like a Weeble, it's raw. Try it.

Spinning people is far riskier. If they're raw, well, who knows
what they might do? They could break open and slobber all over
you. I hate when that happens. And if they're hard-cooked, all I
can say is watch out when they run out of spin.

I personally am a conundrum—both hard and delicate
(sounds better than "raw"). Perhaps that's true of most of us. We
have our ornery times and our fragile moments. I become very
Weeble-like when my nerves are frayed and my coping mecha-
nisms are stretched rubber-band thin. Whereas, if I'm full of my
agenda and pressed for time when you twirl into my space and
set me in a spin, I can be hard-boiled. My shell thickens, and the
color of my yolk fades.

A yolk's color depends on the hen's diet. Similarly, I find that
if I've had a regular diet from the Scriptures, I'm not only brighter
but I also handle an unexpected spin with greater finesse.

Lesson? Don't let your Weeble wobble. When life throws
you into a spin, enjoy the ride!

—PATSY CLAIRMONT (*All Cracked Up*)

# TOO TIRED TO PRAY

*Jesus came to the disciples and found them sleeping, and said to Peter, "What? Could you not watch with Me one hour?"*
—Matthew 26:36–41

In the Garden of Gethsemane, as Jesus agonized over his coming crucifixion, he found Peter sleeping. Peter loved Jesus and was devoted to him, but he was clothed in human flesh like you and me. I'm sure he agonized when Jesus woke him that night. Imagine how Peter felt when he saw Jesus' tear-stained face and realized he had fallen asleep instead of obediently watching and praying.

Scripture explains that there is a war between our spirit and our flesh, between wanting to do more and wanting to take five before doing it. Of course, we often bring it upon ourselves by doing too much. The apostle Paul describes this battle between spirit and flesh in Romans 7. He writes, "Why don't I do the thing I want to do but instead do the thing I don't want to do?" (verse 15, my paraphrase). I'm sure Paul knew that when we relegate prayer to the bottom of our priority list, we won't have enough energy left to do more than mutter a few familiar phrases before we call it a day.

So we have to consciously work toward increasing our strength for prayer. I encourage you to fight the "I'm too tired to pray" blahs.

—SHEILA WALSH (*Get Off Your Knees and Pray*)

# THE PAGES OF YOUR LIFE

*Our steps are made firm by the LORD, when he delights in our
way; though we stumble, we shall not fall headlong, for the
LORD holds us by the hand.*

—Psalm 37:23–24 NRSV

As God's children, our lives unfold daily like pages in a book.
Each circumstance is a different chapter. Each page is a new
opportunity to live out God's plan for us. God's will is upon us in
the hurt and the sorrow and in the joy and the peace.

As I turn the pages of my life, I see chapters I could never
have completed on my own. It was the sovereign hand of God
that caused those chapters to be written. He was working things
out for me before the foundation of the world, before my mama
and daddy even knew each other. He caused me to be raised in a
godly home by my God-fearing great-grandparents. He caused
me to overcome great obstacles and be blessed with the resources
to finish college. He caused me to learn about his healing power
when I was a very young woman. He opened career doors for me
that I did not even know existed. He provided for me when I
didn't have a dime. Glory! We need to trust God and obey him.
That's the only way to gain the total benefits of his providence,
and it's the best way for his purpose to be fulfilled through us.

—THELMA WELLS (*The Buzz*)

# WHO IS YOUR FAITH CENTER?

*Let us run with perseverance the race that is set before us,*
*looking to Jesus the pioneer and perfecter of our faith.*

—Hebrews 12:1–2 NRSV

My mom was the faith person in our family. Both my father and I would seek out the encouragement of her gentle but unwavering faith. Early in life my thought about faith was that some have it and some don't, and I believed I fell into the "don't have it" category. For that reason I wanted always to be near my mom's faith center.

Do you recognize the faulty thinking in that? Somehow I felt I had to find a "faith person" to help me with my challenges because I wasn't sufficiently faith-endowed. There is nowhere in Scripture that says God has a faith camp where some of his children "have it" and some don't—that thinking is totally unscriptural. But I'll have to admit this thinking still seeps into my soul from time to time and says, *You need to find someone to believe for you, Marilyn. . . . Your faith is shaky. It's too small.*

We must remind ourselves of a very basic truth. Our faith source is Jesus. He is the author of my faith. He is the giver of my faith. I am not. My mother was not. Any other person is not. Jesus gave me faith when I received him into my heart and life. That faith is totally, personally my Jesus-given faith.

—MARILYN MEBERG (*God at Your Wits' End*)

# LOVING YOURSELF

*We love because he first loved us.*
—1 John 4:19 NIV

God's desire is for you to love yourself and accept yourself just as you are. He doesn't want you to go through life trying to fake it because you wish you were somebody else. He puts stock in character rather than playing charades. No one I know is able to maintain perfect behavior patterns all the time. The apostle Paul was right when he said that which we don't want to do we find ourselves doing and that which we want to do, we so often don't (see Romans 7:19). That's why being yourself is "the hardest battle that any human being can fight and never stop fighting." But it's a battle you can win, just like so many others already have.

Let me suggest ten areas I work on when I get bogged down and forget to love myself as God commanded me to:

+ Be content with what you have.
+ Stop comparing.
+ Count your blessings.
+ Quit personalizing every comment.
+ Maintain a servant spirit.
+ Do the unexpected for a loved one.
+ Keep a heart of gratitude.
+ Don't be negative.
+ Respect yourself.
+ Take God at his word.

—LUCI SWINDOLL (*Life! Celebrate It*)

# TRUE VIEW

*Let me live whole and holy, soul and body so I can always walk with my head held high.*

—Psalm 119:80 MSG

Do you ever wonder where your self-esteem resides? Which body part houses it? Does it bunk in your heart? Or lease a room in your mind? Perhaps it's a vagabond or a multi-tasker and divvies up its locales. Or perhaps it's sharing a room with emotions.

I have no idea where my self-esteem lives, but I do know it's alive. Some days, it lags behind what I know to be true; while other days, it inspires me to do cartwheels.

I guess what we should ask ourselves is whether we need to replace the mirror on our self-worth so we can capture a true view of who we are. While I believe we can spend too much time on myopic examinations, I also think we can spend too little effort embracing our value. Before we realize it, that delicate balance slips a notch, which leaves us off kilter. That puts us in as much trouble as viewing ourselves through a fractured mirror, which suggests we are irreparable.

Life comes with distortions—proof the enemy has a strategy, which includes diminishing our view of ourselves so we don't live fully or joyously. Christ has come to heal the network of cracks in our self-esteem, that we might view him more clearly and therefore see our own worth.

—PATSY CLAIRMONT (*All Cracked Up*)

# ALONE WITH GOD

*Devote yourselves to prayer, being watchful and thankful.*
—*Colossians 4:2* NIV

It's easy to get so caught up in the physical challenges of our days that we forget the very real spiritual battle that rages on around us. We have an enemy who would love to keep us so distracted and busy that we forget to focus on what really matters: our relationship with our Father.

Jesus knew this and he purposely pulled away, not only from the crowds, but even from his friends, to be able to be alone with his Father. He obviously craved that time to restore himself.

Of course, not all of us are refreshed by being alone the way Jesus was. Each of us has a unique, God-given personality that affects how easily we're distracted and by what, what helps us refocus and what doesn't. What matters is finding a place where you know you can block out other distractions and enjoy being with the Father, who longs to spend time with you.

Even more important is making the commitment to fight our human tendency toward distraction. Sometimes I will take a notebook and write down twenty things that I love about being God's daughter. I can only imagine that our specific declarations of love to God are precious to him.

—SHEILA WALSH (*Get Off Your Knees and Pray*)

# GOD'S PLAN FOR MY LIFE

*This is the will of God, your sanctification.*
—I Thessalonians 4:3

Just as God's providence is upon us, his will is in us, doing the work of sanctification. Sanctification is the grace of God shaping us according to the will of God. As we are sanctified, the Holy Spirit gives us the willingness to grow in holiness and submission, and as we grow this way, we take on the image of Christ and become separated from the world's systems.

This transformation requires a daily act of submission and servanthood, in which we die to self and live for Christ. The will of God working in us says that we want to do the will of the Savior; we want him to be the Lord of our lives. We want him to be in charge of our every decision, our every action.

It takes faith to accept that God's providence is upon us and God's will is in us. We must have confidence in things we cannot see. How often do I have to remind myself that I can't look at things the way they appear but the way God's Word says they will be? I must trust that God is working in the supernatural to carry out his plan for my life. I can do that because I know God keeps his promises.

—THELMA WELLS (*The Buzz*)

# CHOOSING TO BELIEVE

*Without faith it is impossible to please God, because anyone who comes to him must believe that he exists and that he rewards those who earnestly seek him.*

—Hebrews 11:6 NIV

What about faith? What does it require? Faith requires choosing: choosing to believe. For example, I choose to believe the evidence I see of God in his creation. I can't deny that creative power came from somewhere. In addition, I believe Jesus, God's Son, was with him in the beginning and created everything there is.

I also choose to believe the Word of God, and when I am at my wits' end I crawl into its pages so my spirit can be enlivened, strengthened, and enabled to believe beyond what I see. The Bible is my faith object. It is crucial to my spiritual balance and my understanding of the degree to which God loves me. It teaches me about faith.

Faith is not as complicated as I have sometimes made it. It is not hard. Quite simply, faith is a gift, and this gift is mine for the taking. It is not a gift I work to be worthy of or can work to achieve. As is true of any gift, I reach out for it. I accept it from the hand of God my Father. My part in all this is to believe in the giver of the gift and then in the gift itself. I trust. I believe. I receive Jesus as Savior. Faith initiates that process.

—MARILYN MEBERG (*God at Your Wits' End*)

# DOORS OF POTENTIAL

*Jesus said, "I came so they can have real and eternal life, more and better life than they ever dreamed of."*
—John 10:10 MSG

This year I'll be seventy. I look at the word *seventy* and it doesn't seem possible. Have I really lived that long? Where did all those years go? The reflection in the mirror answers the question to the whereabouts of some of them, but only my heart can tell me whether or not I have lived well. And it's very important to me to live well. God wants us all to live fully . . . and well. It is part of his dream for us.

We have no idea what lies ahead or how God will open doors of potentiality when we consciously choose to get out of the ruts we're in and start moving down new paths about which we can be excited—even passionate. Some think being adventuresome means taking a trip around the world, bungee jumping, or walking into a lion's cage at the zoo. Not at all. It's an attitude, not a behavior. It's daring to be curious about the unknown, to dream big dreams, to live outside prescribed boxes, to take risks, and above all, daring to investigate the way we live until we discover the deepest treasured purpose of why we are here.

—LUCI SWINDOLL (*I Married Adventure*)

# GOD'S AMAZING ARTWORK

*[Christ] is the image of the invisible God, the firstborn over all creation. For by Him all things were created that are in heaven and that are on earth, visible and invisible . . . All things were created through Him and for Him.*

*—Colossians 1:15–16*

We live in a broken world in which many things are askew; so it's no wonder we forget all the lovely things God has written his signature on, starting with the heavens and the earth.

Perhaps because children live so close to the earth, they often are the messengers that remind us of a frog's throaty croak or a cricket's high-pitched chirp or a katydid's tattletale song. Kids are the ones who affirm the dandelion's beauty, a stick's usefulness, and a pebble's colors.

When was the last time you stared into the dazzling pattern of the stars? Or gathered a fistful of lilies of the valley or crammed a jar full of hydrangeas or arranged a vase of peonies? When did you sit at the water's edge and lean in to hear its song? Has it been too long since you sifted sand through your toes or traced the lines on a beautiful shell that you discovered? Who was the last child you introduced to a tadpole? Or helped to catch a turtle?

Creation is bursting with discoveries. A billowing cloud, a sun pattern on a patch of pumpkins, or a bulging garden all comfort us. I guess the Lord knew we would need these undeniable reminders of his presence on earth.

—PATSY CLAIRMONT (*All Cracked Up*)

# THE DISCIPLINE OF PRAYER

*Never stop praying.*

—1 Thessalonians 5:17 CEV

Sometimes we find it difficult to pray because we're not sure God is listening to us. That's what a man—he looked to be in his forties, successful, married with children—once said to me. When I asked him why he thought God might not be listening, he said he could see no evidence of God having heard him. He told me he has been in the church most of his life but recently has found himself wondering if anything he believed was actually true. To be honest, he's not alone. I hear similar concerns in many e-mails and letters I receive.

I think one of our greatest challenges in prayer is feeling God's presence. We live in a sensory age where we are bombarded by ads for quick fixes and miracle drugs. The discipline of prayer offers no easy solutions for the wounds and worries of life, and it often goes without physical sensation. It's therefore tempting to believe prayer isn't worth the time.

But prayer isn't supposed to offer a simple solution. It's meant to be a place to take our concerns and lay them at Jesus' feet. When we approach our petitions in that way, they become not just a time to test God's response but an opportunity to release the cares of our lives.

—SHEILA WALSH (*Get Off Your Knees and Pray*)

# THROUGH CHRIST

*I can do all things through Christ who strengthens me.*

—*Philippians 4:13*

I am a confident person, I know I'm good at what I do, and I believe I can do just about anything I set my mind to. But I also need to remember something else as I'm tearin' out the door on my way to conquer some new challenge. I need to remember the two most important words in the Scripture above: "through Christ."

It's Christ who gives me the strength to do the things that really matter, to endure whatever challenges he sets before me, and to persevere when the hard times come. When I discern God's will in a situation, when I feel him leading me to take on a task or accept a challenge, then I pray for strength to endure what's to come, and set out confidently, knowing I'll get the job done. I like to say that the will of God will never take me where the strength and power and grace of God cannot keep me.

I've had to cope with some pretty hard stuff during my life. But you know what happens when God repeatedly gives you strength to survive overwhelming difficulties? You learn that when the next difficulty comes, he'll give you strength again to persevere. See it proven true a few times, and you start believing it!

—THELMA WELLS (*The Buzz*)

# MORE GOOD NEWS ABOUT FAITH

> "If your faith were only the size of a mustard seed," Jesus answered, "it would be large enough to uproot that mulberry tree over there and send it hurtling into the sea! Your command would bring immediate results!"
>
> —Luke 17:6 TLB

Want some good news about faith? If you feed it, it grows! We don't need to continue thinking we are feeble and weak in our faith. Jesus talked about the mustard plant, an annual plant with very small seeds. It grows to a considerable size in Palestine. Jesus' listeners were well acquainted with the mustard plant and its tiny seeds.

When his disciples told Jesus they needed more faith and asked how they could get it, Jesus said, "Believe." Then he walked away.

With all due respect, I don't find that a very satisfying answer.

I would like it if Jesus spelled out how to get more faith in an easy formula that I could slip into my purse. When I am feeling feeble, I could pull out the list . . . mutter over it . . . find the problem . . . and then fix it. But the whole thing about our spiritual walk is that it is not defined by formulas.

My job is to remember I can choose to believe because it was God who authored my faith—enabled my faith in the first place. "I believe, Lord; help my unbelief." In other words, "Help me grow." And just look what can happen if my faith is no bigger than a mustard seed!

—MARILYN MEBERG (*God at Your Wits' End*)

# THE ADVENTURESOME SPIRIT

*The way you tell me to live is always right; help me understand it so I can live to the fullest.*

—Psalm 119:144 MSG

It seems like there is something electrifying about individuals with adventuresome spirits. They see life through a different lens. They don't wait on the sidelines. They don't keep saying, "If only . . ." or "Why me?" They don't battle against unusual circumstances or departures from the norm. It's as if they operate from a whole different voltage or current. They almost emit electricity because nothing about them is dull or uninteresting or unplugged.

A life of adventure is ours for the taking, whether we're seven or seventy—whether we throw a paper route, take care of an aging parent, study for a degree, work around the clock, stay at home to raise our children, or circle the globe in the service of our Creator. I'm convinced that the whole world is better when we, as individuals, capture and savor each moment as the gift that it is, embrace the challenge or joy of it, marry it (if you will), and thereby transform it with the magic of creative possibility. Life, for the most part, is what we make it. We have been given a responsibility to live it fully, joyfully, completely, and richly, in whatever span of time God grants us on this earth.

—LUCI SWINDOLL (*I Married Adventure*)

# FLOOD DAMAGE

*"I will restore health to you and heal you of your wounds," says the* LORD.

*—Jeremiah 30:17*

After Hurricane Katrina blasted the Gulf Coast, officials warned that it would take a lot of time, money, and cooperation to restore people's lives to anything resembling normal. New Orleans experienced not only damage caused by rain and wind but also from cracks in the levies, which caused severe flooding.

At one time, my life was awash with emotional whirlpools, I felt hopeless. I didn't want to pray. . . . I felt like my power lines were down and fear rampaged its windy way through my life, leaving a swath of instability. I could feel my life cracking apart—my emotions were erratic, my relationships were troubling, I was flooded with regret, and my future was dim.

That is, until I committed to rolling up my sleeves and doing the hard work of recovery. That meant I had to begin hauling away the debris of anger and fear, repairing the wind-damaged roof of my mind, and become willing to receive outside assistance from wise counselors.

Waiting for all the broken pieces of a life to be reworked is neither fast nor easy, but the end result is transformation. Nothing is more satisfying than to see God's light peering through. It changes everything.

—PATSY CLAIRMONT (*All Cracked Up*)

# A DOOR IN THE WALL

*Cast all your anxiety on him because he cares for you.*

—1 Peter 5:7 NIV

Yes, it is hard to pray. It's much easier to spend our free time flopping down and turning on the television than following the example of Christ and pulling away from the noise and distractions for alone time with our Father. Every believer has experienced the difficulties of an intentional prayer life. But when we persist in seeing prayer as a challenge—as a wall between us and God—and walk away in defeat, we walk away carrying the same burdens we arrived with.

Instead of walking away unsatisfied, see if you can imagine that there's a door in that wall, like the wonderful wardrobe that took Lucy into Narnia in C. S. Lewis's *The Lion, the Witch and the Wardrobe*. Prayer is our escape from this world. Prayer is not a chore or something we'll be tested on at the end of each week. It's our time to crawl into our Father's embrace and lay our cares upon him. It's only when we are able to quiet the noises outside and within that we remember all his amazing promises to us. Prayer is not something that belongs on our to-do list, but rather on our to-live list.

—SHEILA WALSH (*Get Off Your Knees and Pray*)

# HEAVENLY PALACES

*Jesus said, "These things I have spoken to you, that in Me you may have peace. In the world you will have tribulation; but be of good cheer, I have overcome the world."*

—John 16:33

Saying that we can do all things through Christ doesn't mean we can suddenly perform impossible physical feats. Don't try to stop a train by standing on the tracks! What the apostle Paul was saying to the Philippians in this bit of encouragement was that in Christ we can *endure* all things. We can get through hard times. We can persevere against great odds, because Christ gives us the strength to "keep on keepin' on." We can handle the hard times on earth because we know we're not here to stay; we're just passing through on our way to heaven. The bad times are gonna end, and the good times will begin—if not on earth, then in heaven!

When I read John 16:33, I always get a little surge of joy when I come to that word "but." The first part of that verse seems pretty heavy; then when I see that word *but*, I know something good's coming on the other side of that word! Jesus said we're gonna hit hard times during our time here on earth; tribulations are inevitable. But we're gonna make it. Jesus has already overcome the world and has prepared mansions for us in heaven. Just think! Our heavenly palaces are already there, just waiting for us.

—THELMA WELLS (*The Buzz*)

# HELP, GOD

*Faith comes by hearing, and hearing by the word of God.*
—Romans 10:17

The apostle Paul said that faith comes from hearing the Word of God. The Bible is our faith object. Our faith grows as we study it.

Scripture reassures us, "No one who trusts God like this—heart and soul—will ever regret it. Everyone who calls, 'Help, God!' gets help." I am blown away by the fantastic encouragement these words from Scripture provide. Forgive me, but I'm going to throw out a formula I see in Romans, chapter 10:

* You say the words "Help, God."
* You trust him to help you.
* You remember you're not doing anything, just calling out to God and trusting him to do it for you.

Does this sound too easy? Too passive? Too laid back in my hammock and munching Milk Duds while God works? It is not passive at all, in that God not only invites our participation as he builds our faith lives, he requires it. You try lying back in your hammock, and he'll tip you out of it. You are in a loving partnership, but he's in charge. You first say the words, then you trust him with your growth, and he takes over. But he takes you with him.

—MARILYN MEBERG (*God at Your Wits' End*)

# BRINGING THE WORLD DOWN TO SIZE

*Jesus said, "Anything is possible if a person believes."*
—Mark 9:23 NLT

One of my most treasured possessions is a big, elaborate world globe. Sometimes I just twirl it and think about the cultures spinning across my mind's eye. When something earth shattering happens on the other side of the world, and I read about it in the newspaper or see it happen on TV, I go over to the globe and find that very spot. If I'm reading a book about a particular place in the ocean or on a mountain peak, I check it out on my globe. I like knowing what country borders on another, where the oceans meet, what's on the equator. I'm a nut for all that stuff.

Even though the world is huge, there's something personal and intimate about it when it's right in front of me, in a round ball, with all the countries and oceans delineated. Everything seems accessible, within reach. No borders or boundaries or impasses. I love that. Anything is possible.

This outlook gives us the capacity to dream big, dare to try new things, and believe we can overcome detours and obstacles that get in our way or hold us back. If the world isn't such an ominous, scary place, then we are more inclined to reach out to others and give our hearts to them.

—LUCI SWINDOLL (*I Married Adventure*)

# JIGGLE WITH JOY

> *You have let me experience the joys of life and the exquisite*
> *pleasures of your own eternal presence.*
>
> —Psalm 16:11 TLB

On my birthday last year, a friend sent me a duck. Yep, a duck. He's short and squat, which seemed a tad too personal, but my perception changed when I squeezed his wing. He began to sing and dance, and I began to laugh aloud. He was the cutest bundle of yellow, wrapped up in a song. His toe tapped, his wings flapped, and his shoulders (do ducks have shoulders?) gyrated to the song "Singin' in the Rain." He was touting a yellow slicker hat atop his fuzzy head and a green-and-white striped bow around his chubby neck. I'm crazy about this perky bundle of fun because he never fails to make me jiggle with joy.

Ever notice how a good giggle renews your energy and refreshes your attitude? I think that's why comical folks are so popular. Humor makes everyone's life a little easier.

My friend Marilyn, when feeling unheard in a group, will walk to the nearest wall and begin talking to it. It cracks me up every time. I've taken to imitating Marilyn. I just release my verbal offering on a nearby door, empty chair, or painting on the wall. Even if no one in my group notices, it makes me chuckle. Of course, be prepared to receive odd stares from passersby.

—PATSY CLAIRMONT (*All Cracked Up*)

# OUR FATHER

*Jesus said, "You should pray like this: Our Father in heaven,*
*help us to honor your name."*
—Matthew 6:9 CEV

If you ask me, one of the reasons it is important for us to talk to God is that prayer implies trust. It's our way of saying to God:

> → I believe you are in control.
> → I believe you love me.
> → I believe you make everything work out for good no matter how things may appear.

The first words of the prayer Jesus taught his followers were, "Our Father." The picture is a very intimate one—an invitation to come as a child and curl up on your father's lap and tell him all about it.

I've heard Donald Miller speak of the way believers often approach God as if he were their boss, apologizing for being late or not quite "on task." He reminded us of Christ's welcome to pray to "Our Father" and asked, "When was the last time you curled up in your boss's arms and shared your heart?"

Avoiding the obvious bad jokes, Miller's point is clear. We are invited into a relationship of absolute trust and draw close to our Father's heart. The more time we spend in God's presence, the more our trust grows even when things don't go as we planned.

—SHEILA WALSH (*Get Off Your Knees and Pray*)

# EMBRACE THE JOURNEY

*Do not neglect to do good and to share what you have, for such sacrifices are pleasing to God.*

—*Hebrews 13.16* NRSV

God has put the world on my heart—he's put it on all our hearts. His desire is that we would go into it—in whatever way we can. He has a gift for the entire world and it is in us, his people.

Every person is a combination of many factors woven together from the joys and sorrows of life. We're also the product of our choices. We're the result of what was or was not done for or to us by our parents, siblings, associates, and friends. The journey we're on is planned and watched over by a loving God who wants us to treasure the gift of being alive and who sets us free to participate in our own destiny. Embracing that journey— whatever it is for each of us, wherever it takes us—is imperative to capturing the spirit of adventure.

When we realize our lives are to be given away, everything about our outlook changes and grows. God takes our youth and gives us in exchange his truth. We see and do things differently as a result. We think beyond our own borders. The world becomes accessible through the power of God's Spirit and love. We capture each moment, embrace the journey, and go forward.

—LUCI SWINDOLL (*I Married Adventure*)

# STAYING AFLOAT

*Be of good courage, and God shall strengthen your heart, all ye that hope in the LORD.*
—Psalm 31:24 KJV

Hope can float a boat. And that's great news for those of us who have been at the helms of our lives for more than a half century. Wind in our faces, hands on the wheel, eyes on the horizon, we've learned to appreciate any gusts that fill our sails and keep us seaborne.

Mom's life had spanned many years, and I knew her time to leave was near. But no matter how securely we batten down our emotional hatches, no matter how storm-savvy we might be, no matter how many warnings we receive, nothing prepares us for the tsunami of the death of a parent. The vacancy it leaves in our lives howls like straight-line winds.

Yet I found solace in the life preserver of hope, that irrepressible buoy that keeps us afloat. I had hope that this generational waterspout within me would lose intensity, hope that my churning emotions would eventually even out, and hope that Mom's charted course to her "home in Glory" lay ahead for me as well. Until I step onto that shore, I choose to lift anchor and reenter the thrill of the open seas, to risk the exploration of uncharted waters (even if it means getting in over my head), knowing that the final destination will be worth the sometimes-upending voyage.

—PATSY CLAIRMONT (*All Cracked Up*)

# WHAT'S LOVE GOT TO DO WITH IT?

*I love those who love me, and those who seek me diligently will find me.*

—Proverbs 8:17

When I was twenty-five years old, British pop star Cliff Richard produced an album for me using his band members. One of Cliff's guitar players was a shy, sweet man named Terry Britton. Terry was also a songwriter, and one day he played a little bit of a song he had just written. I'm sure Terry had no way of knowing when he sat down with his trusty guitar that this song—"What's Love Got to Do with It?"—would be recorded by Tina Turner and go straight to number one on the Billboard charts.

As I think about the title of that song and our question on the relevancy of prayer, it would seem clear to me that love has everything to do with it. Prayer is a way for us to experience love—and not just us showing our love for God, but receiving love from God!

God longs to share his heart with us. He is not looking for perfect little robots to follow directions but people who will share his love. I think it's very difficult for us to embrace the love of God because we have never been loved that way before. That's because all human love—even the best—is conditional and impacted by our behavior or changing circumstances. But God's love is not.

—SHEILA WALSH (*Get Off Your Knees and Pray*)

# WHISPER THE LIFELINE NAME

*We do not know what we should pray for as we ought, but the Spirit Himself makes intercession for us with groanings which cannot be uttered.*

—Romans 8:26

In one of his New Testament letters the apostle Paul assured the Romans (and us today) that "the Holy Spirit helps us in our distress." Then he went on to say that the Holy Spirit helps us even when we don't know exactly what kind of help we need or when our needs are so great we can't even express them in words.

Sometimes we feel so low—we're hurting so badly or we're grieving so hard or we're feeling so lost—that we want desperately to feel the Lord's presence in our lives, but we just don't have the words to express the depths of our despair. Sometimes all we can do is whisper again and again that lifeline name of "Jesus . . . Jesus . . . Jesus." That's when the Holy Spirit steps in and intercedes for us in "groanings that cannot be expressed in words." The Message interprets the verse this way: "If we don't know how or what to pray, it doesn't matter. He does our praying in and for us, making prayer out of our wordless sighs, our aching groans."

Hallelujah! God speaks our language even if it's one of "wordless sighs" and "aching groans."

—THELMA WELLS (*The Buzz*)

# QUESTIONS FOR GOD

*Grace and peace be multiplied unto you through the
knowledge of God, and of Jesus our Lord.*

—2 Peter 1:2 KJV

Max Lucado refers to the AIDS epidemic in Africa as the worst
global disaster since the days of Noah. One wonders about God
in such a disaster. We read accounts of the Holocaust, the Killing
Fields of Cambodia, and the torture chambers in the Middle East.
We see television coverage of hurricanes, floods, and earthquakes
where thousands lose their lives, and we wonder about God.

As C. S. Lewis watched his wife suffer during her terminal
illness, he said, "Not that I am in danger of ceasing to believe in
God. The real danger is of coming to believe such dreadful things
about him. The conclusion I dread is not 'So, there's no God after
all'; but 'So this is what God's really like.'"

Feeling abandoned by God is soul shattering. It raises the
question of whether or not God truly is involved with his creation. Is that involvement motivated by the overwhelming love
and compassion we were led to believe characterize his attitude
toward us? Why do our experiences sometimes not coincide
with that image? Why does he allow suffering?

Sooner or later in life our circumstances will force us to ask
these questions. Admittedly, much about God will remain a
mystery, but we can seek knowledge where it may be found.

—MARILYN MEBERG (*God at Your Wits' End*)

# FULLY ALIVE

*Your life is a journey that you must travel with a deep consciousness of God.*

—1 Peter 1:18 MSG

Moments come and go so fast, but they are what make up the whole of life. Little bitty moments here and there. They turn into hours and days and weeks—ultimately an entire lifetime. When I consciously think about that, it makes me want to slow down. Sometimes I can't slow down. I don't have the time to go slowly. But I can capture a moment in a postcard or photograph. Then, years later it all comes back to me as a sweet gift to myself.

Life is short and everything is irrevocable. No matter what we do to lengthen the moment, we can't. No matter how eager we are to shorten uncomfortable events, that can't be done either. If we don't learn to live fully in the present, much of life passes us by, lost in the cobwebs of time forever. The passage of time can't be retrieved except in our memory banks. That's why we must be all there at any given moment. Even during the times that are frightening or difficult.

Everything has a purpose, and if we don't want to miss that purpose and the adventure along the way, then we must be conscious, alert, curious, open-hearted. When we capture the moment we're in, we're fully alive.

—LUCI SWINDOLL (*I Married Adventure*)

# THE COLORS OF HOPE

> *It came to pass in the process of time that Hannah conceived and bore a son, and called his name Samuel, saying, "Because I have asked for him from the LORD."*
>
> —1 Samuel 1:20

Hope is a type of kaleidoscope. Through its lens, we can believe the impossible and *see* what might be. Hope's hues are rainbow in promise, bringing rays of light into once dark corners. When I think of the colors of hope, I think of Hannah . . .

Hannah was heartsick because she couldn't have a baby. She stopped eating and cried continually. Yet she never gave up hope. She continued to pray. A priest named Eli observed Hannah at the altar and spoke to her. When she explained her anguish, Eli blessed her and sent her on her way.

After that encounter, something shifted inside Hannah. Someone spun the wheel of her heart, for we are told color returned to her cheeks, she ate, and her face was no longer sad. We don't know how long it was before Hannah gave birth. Over the years, Hannah must have found the waiting cruel. But after her prayers and her breakthrough moment with Eli, it appears that she was liberated and at peace.

Eventually, Hannah gave birth to the prophet Samuel and a house full of others. She marveled at what God had done. It was as if she were looking through a kaleidoscope. All the things that had seemed so splintered now refracted dazzling light.

—PATSY CLAIRMONT (*All Cracked Up*)

# JESUS KNEW . . .

*Jesus said, "Father, if it is Your will, take this cup away from Me; nevertheless not My will, but Yours, be done."*

—Luke 22:42

Jesus, our Savior was fully man, and he suffered during his crucifixion just as a man would (although without sinning). Jesus knew that he was about to walk into the greatest inferno ever faced by one in human flesh and that this was the plan from the beginning of time to redeem fallen humanity. He knew that his Father would allow him to drink from the cup of his wrath and not deliver him.

Jesus prayed but he *knew* his Father would say no. He also knew that even when God was telling him no, he was still with him. His prayer is left as a gift for us, a light in the darkest night.

Why does God sometimes say no to our prayers? As I'm sure you realize, I don't have the answer to that question. No one does. But what we do have is the knowledge that when we keep praying—when we move beyond "Why?" to "Be with me, Lord"—we begin to learn more about our faith and our strength in our Father. Confronting God with our why becomes being with God in our need. He is there when we need him—always. He might not answer our prayers as we would like, but he will be there to hold us through the trials.

—SHEILA WALSH (*Get Off Your Knees and Pray*)

# OUR GREAT HIGH PRIEST

*Seeing then that we have a great High Priest who has passed through the heavens, Jesus the Son of God, let us hold fast our confession. For we do not have a High Priest who cannot sympathize with our weaknesses, but was in all points tempted as we are, yet without sin.*

—Hebrews 4:14–15

Just as the Holy Spirit translates our moans and groans and intercedes with us before God, so he also interprets, or helps us understand, God's will for our lives, convicting us when we do wrong, comforting us when we are sad, guiding us in what we should do. The Holy Spirit moves into our heart the instant we accept Jesus as our personal Lord and Savior, God's always-on-call gift to us and intercessor for us.

Jesus also hears the unspoken cries of our hearts and intercedes for us with the Father. He understands what we're going through because he came to earth as a human being and endured the same trials and temptations we face today. That's why Hebrews 4:16 assures us, "Let us therefore come boldly to the throne of grace, that we may obtain mercy, and find grace to help in time of need."

Girl, it's time to shout hallelujah! Think of it this way: God not only hears our prayers directly, but we also have these two holy intercessors, Jesus and the Holy Spirit, translating our prayers into the language of heaven and whispering them into God's ear. Well, it just doesn't get any better than that!

—THELMA WELLS (*The Buzz*)

# SAVORING EACH MOMENT

*God deals out joy in the present, the now.*
—*Ecclesiastes 5:20* MSG

Perhaps you remember the *New Yorker* cartoon in which two monks in robes and shaved heads are sitting side by side, cross-legged on the floor. The younger one, with a quizzical look on his face, is facing the older who is saying: "Nothing happens next. This is it."

That's exactly what it means to live in the here and now. We aren't waiting for something else to occur, we aren't distracted by anything around us, and we aren't trying to escape mentally to another time. We are "mindfully awake." Paying attention. Savoring the moment for all it's worth. We are fully alive!

I feel this when I'm engaged in rich, meaningful conversation with an interesting person. Questions are enticing, listening is acute, and eye contact is direct. I also experience this feeling when I'm alone . . . in an art museum or lost in a good book. When I'm all there—or rather, all here!—I never want the moment to end. It's as though I can actually hear my heart beat—my very own heart, which sustains the life I'm living. I'm breathing. I'm feeling myself breathe . . . in and out, in and out. It's wonderful. It's this moment. It's the "it" to which the wise old monk referred.

—LUCI SWINDOLL (*I Married Adventure*)

# CELEBRATING THE GIGGLE PHRASE

*If one has the gift of encouraging others, he should encourage.*
—Romans 12:8 NCV

A friend gave me a magnet for my refrigerator that reads, "There's only one more shopping day until tomorrow."

That made me giggle aloud. I love giggle gifts because a dose of laughter is a gift in and of itself. The magnet business seems to be soaring these days, and I think it's because the makers have discovered the marketability of a good giggle-phrase.

What day couldn't use a hearty chuckle? If I can laugh aloud, I don't even mind that my eyes narrow to slits, leaving me discombobulated.

Have you ever wanted to make your own magnets? I have. Here are the possibilities:

*Menopause: a target for heat-seeking devices*
*Need a facelift? Try smiling!*
*Hormones: emotional chiggers*
*Trifocals: triple ripple*

Well, you can sure tell my age. But since I can't change the modifications or the complications that come with maturing, let me toss back my head and chortle.

How long has it been since you laughed yourself sane? Today, go in search of a giggle—you won't be sorry, no matter your age. And remember to give some giggles to others along the way.

—PATSY CLAIRMONT (*All Cracked Up*)

# GO TELL PETER

*Jesus said to them, "Do not be afraid. Go and tell My brethren to go to Galilee, and there they will see Me."*
—Matthew 28:10

God's Word is full of stories of those who messed up and were forgiven by God and restored to a place of far greater joy and purpose. I think especially of the apostle Peter. This rough and tough fisherman who was devoted to Christ took quite a fall when he heard the words, "I don't know this man!" tumble from his own lips. I am sure he beat himself up over the next few brutal hours and days as Jesus was crucified and placed in a tomb.

On that glorious Easter morning, the women encountered an angel guarding an empty tomb. The angel told them to go tell Jesus' disciples—and Peter—that they would see him in Galilee. There was to be no doubt that Peter should know that he was welcomed.

Have you messed up? Perhaps you are ashamed to even face what you have done. It may have been something that caused harm not just to you but to others. If so, have the faith to remember that with God all things can be made new. Your past is just that. But your future in him is limitless. All God looks for is a desire to begin moving in the right direction, and he will be there to embrace you.

—SHEILA WALSH (*Get Off Your Knees and Pray*)

# LET US PRAY

*Pray without ceasing.*
—I Thessalonians 5:17

Someone has said that "prayer is the heart's sincere desire unspoken and unexpressed." While God hears our unspoken thoughts, there are many times when we are able to—and need to—express prayer in words, either alone or shared openly with others.

We can pray "secret" prayers of words that we send up silently to God. I like to close my eyes and look at Jesus in my mind's eye. There is a sense of comfort and intimacy that sweeps over me when I see him in my spirit.

Family prayer is another form of personal, intimate communication with our Creator. The other kinds of prayer—group prayer and public prayer—happen every Sunday in my church.

It doesn't matter so much what kind of prayer you're praying as that you are praying. I used to think that when Paul told us to pray without ceasing he was asking for the impossible because I knew we couldn't walk around all the time mumbling prayers. Then I realized he meant for us to have a constant attitude of prayer. It's sort of like having radar that's locked on to God's signal so we're in constant "communication" everywhere we go, even while we're doing other things. So now I can confidently say that I do "pray without ceasing."

—THELMA WELLS (*The Buzz*)

# BANDING TOGETHER IN PRAYER

*Where two or three have gathered together in My name, I am there in their midst.*

—*Matthew 18:20* NASB

I want to say how vital, even crucial, I believe it to be for us to band together with other believers in prayer. We are his children. We unite our hearts as a faith family, bringing our heart cries to him. Jesus modeled for us the role of group prayer support as he implored the disciples to help bear his burden and pray for him as he entered the Garden of Gethsemane.

The early church met regularly to pray together and to experience the growth of each person's faith in the company of one another. For us to bear one another's burdens requires sharing, requesting prayer support, and allowing ourselves to be vulnerable in each other's presence. In these ways we build one another up and further the work of the church. There's power in corporate prayer.

Paul reminds us in Ephesians 6:18 (MSG), "Pray hard and long. Pray for your brothers and sisters. Keep your eyes open. Keep each other's spirits up so that no one falls behind or drops out." There is no doubt we need to pray together, and by the same token, there is no doubt that when we are alone, we need to believe God hears us as clearly as he hears the giants of the faith.

—MARILYN MEBERG (*God at Your Wits' End*)

# SNAP THE WHIP

*Discipline isn't much fun. It always feels like it's going against the grain. Later, of course, it pays off handsomely, for it's the well-trained who find themselves mature in their relationship with God.*

—Hebrews 12:11 MSG

One of my favorite paintings is a lineup of boys playing a game called Snap the Whip outside a one-room, red schoolhouse. Using vivid colors, Artist Homer Winslow beautifully captured the barefoot boys, and the lush summer day. But I also like that the painting is filled with contrasts and relationships. You feel the tension as two lads have fallen, while the others remain upright. The boys are playing, yet you are aware their schoolwork awaits them.

My pleasure in the painting isn't because I like the game. That's for sure. My mom knew how to play Snap the Whip too. Did I say, "play"? Mom was a no-nonsense lady. On occasion, she would send me out to bring her a switch, which she applied to my lower legs. And talk about snapping the whip!

Then there are times that God "snaps the whip."

God's loving design is to guide us onto a higher path. It's always for our good. I like that a lot. Guidance that's dispensed for our betterment gives us a sense of security. It helps me not to resist what God is doing in my life, and it reassures me that my difficulties have not launched me outside of his care, even when I feel I've fallen headlong into my muddled circumstances.

—PATSY CLAIRMONT (*All Cracked Up*)

# THROUGH THE STORM

*Be merciful to me, O God, be merciful to me, for in you my soul*
*takes refuge; in the shadow of your wings I will take refuge,*
*until the destroying storms pass by.*

—Psalm 57:1 NRSV

As I was driving home from the studio one day, a storm began to build. The sky became a strange shade of deep red I had never seen before. Thunder rumbled overhead, and lightning slashed across the sky as if someone had taken a blade to rip the heavens to shreds. Rain battered my car and traffic slowed to a crawl.

Finally, I pulled over and stopped my car. I felt so abandoned. The storm seemed to me a physical representation of my spiritual turmoil: nothing made sense to me anymore. I even wondered if I had caused the storm because somehow God was angry with me. I felt as if I had lost my way—or as if God had lost me.

That afternoon I called my mom, and told her what was going on with me. She encouraged me to take a long look back down this road I have traveled with God. "Has he ever left you before?" she asked.

I knew that he never had. But this time it felt different.

"Sheila," she said, "no matter where you are or what is happening with you, God has promised that he will never leave you. And he can't lie."

Is there a storm in your heart? Let my mom's wise words see you through!

—SHEILA WALSH (*Get Off Your Knees and Pray*)

309

# A SPOON FULL OF HONEY

*To Him who is able to do exceedingly abundantly above all*
*that we ask or think, according to the power that works in us.*
—*Ephesians 3:20*

Did you know that there is power in prayer, and there is blessing? Whether our prayer follows Jesus' perfect model and includes all the elements of full communication with God, or whether it's an emergency SOS—"Oh, Jesus! Help me!"—prayer is our heart's sincere desire to communicate with our Creator. Imagine this: The one who holds the universe in his hands also invites us to talk to him anytime we want and tell him whatever we want. Remember, we're told to "pray without ceasing." Gladly accepting the invitation, we hand over our burdens into his keeping.

It's wonderful to know that we can pray by lifting our hearts and hands and voices to heaven while taking others along with us—or we can pray without saying a word, knowing that even our thoughts and the groanings of our spirit are lifted up to God by his Son, our intercessor. Thank you, Almighty God! You are able to do exceedingly abundantly over and above anything I can imagine. Whoooooeeeee! That's a spoonful of honey! I'm getting happy about this. Watch me: I'm going to dance and praise his name. Come on, baby, join me! Glory! Hallelujah! Praise the Lord! Amen!

—THELMA WELLS (*The Buzz*)

# GOD'S SOVEREIGN HAND

*The Sovereign LORD has given me an instructed tongue, to
know the word that sustains the weary.*
—Isaiah 50:4 NIV

God is sovereign, and he has a sovereign design for each of our
lives. But knowing, believing, and having faith in God's sovereign
design does not necessarily mean we like the design. We may
actually hate the design.

Do we dare tell God we aren't crazy about his plan? Of
course. He already knows our feelings anyway. He knew what we
would be feeling long before we had the experience that produced those feelings. He knows the beginning from the end,
including our emotions. So go ahead and boldly tell him what he
already knows. And don't worry, he will receive your emotions.

How do I know? The Bible tells me he knows that humans
"are as frail as breath" (Isaiah 2:22). It also tells me, "All humanity
finds shelter in the shadow of your wings" (Psalm 36:7).

A part of experiencing his shelter is trusting the one who
provides that shelter. We can settle into the comfort of that shel-
tering promise. We can trust him and have faith in his character
of love that a higher good is in the making and that one day, we
will look back and say, "Ah, yes . . . God's hand was in that."

—MARILYN MEBERG (*God at Your Wits' End*)

# GOD'S SOUL-TRANSFORMING LESSONS

> *Whoever catches a glimpse of the revealed counsel of God—*
> *the free life!—even out of the corner of his eye, and sticks with*
> *it, is no distracted scatterbrain but a man or woman of action.*
> *That person will find delight and affirmation.*
>
> —James 1:25 MSG

The soul in each of us is imprisoned until it is set free by Jesus Christ. We all have shells around us, protecting us from being eaten alive by the pain of life. And when those shells break, we believe we are at grave risk of being hurt, depressed, or even dying on the spot. To prevent this pain and loss, we guard ourselves by retreating deeper and deeper into the shell, being available only to what is pleasant, predictable, and safe.

But every person I've ever known who really had something to give has been burst open by the explosive force of God's soul-transforming lessons. They have each been willing to be vulnerable to the truth about themselves, to admit selfishness and behavior patterns that are maddening to other people and destructive to their own souls.

If we aspire to pay complete attention to the present, then we must stay connected to our individual centers, and at the same time get out of our own ways. Living fully in the present starts deep inside as we allow the self-protective shell to break open so the liberating grace of God can flow in to heal and renew and establish genuine meaning in our lives.

—LUCI SWINDOLL (*I Married Adventure*)

# ALWAYS WITH ME

*I am not alone because the Father is with me.*
—*John 16:32* NRSV

I saw a drama play out on a National Geographic special. A father bird ushering his son to the edge of a broken cliff for his first flight, which just happened to be a thousand-foot drop to the ocean below. The father stayed at his baby's side as he teetered to the edge; and when the baby toppled forth into the air, his dad went with him.

The father stayed close for the plummeting ride down until they both sliced into the water, safely bobbing to and fro on the churning sea. It was amazing. I wondered if that little bird knew his father had been with him all the way down, ready to swoop under him if he spun out of control. The baby was always safe; but his descending perspective was probably very different as he frantically beat his little wings.

Ever feel that way? I have. But as my history with the Lord has accumulated into a growing faith, I realize he is with me, ever so close, even as I thrash about in my littleness and my frailty. I'm learning that I can trust his presence, and that realization buoys my spirit, whether I'm on the edge of the ledge, floundering in problems as vast as the sky, or in my splashdown to the valley below.

—PATSY CLAIRMONT (*All Cracked Up*)

## LETTING GO

*Whenever you stand praying, forgive, if you have anything against anyone, so that your Father who is in heaven may also forgive you your transgressions.*

—*Mark 11:25* NASB

In my life, one of the greatest rocks to climb over has been when I am unwilling to forgive. I'm sure I'm not alone in that burden. It's hard to admit we've done wrong and say we're sorry. But often it's even harder to forgive. We sometimes thrive on self-righteousness—knowing we've been wronged and wanting to hold that hurt against another indefinitely instead of letting it go.

To my mind the most amazing declaration from the cross is when Jesus cried out, "Father, forgive them, for they do not know what they are doing" (Luke 23:34). Jesus asked God to forgive his torturers while he was still in physical and spiritual agony, not after he had risen from the dead. He prayed that prayer of forgiveness in the midst of the storm, not when the sun began to remind the earth there are better days ahead. Can you imagine how difficult that must have been?

Forgiveness is hard. It is even more difficult when the person who wronged us is not sorry in the least. But when I listen to Christ's words recorded in Matthew's gospel, it's clear to me that if I want to live freely and lightly, then I need to study how Jesus lived.

—SHEILA WALSH (*Get Off Your Knees and Pray*)

# KEEP YOUR HOPES UP!

*This I call to mind and therefore I have hope: Because of the
LORD's great love we are not consumed, for his compassions
never fail. They are new every morning; great is your faithfulness.*
—Lamentations 3:21–23 NIV

I love that word *hope*. It's a term that brings sunshine into the
darkest closet, a promise that brings courage and faith to the
hardest situation. It's found in the place where we would least
expect it. If you don't believe me, just look where our beautiful
focus verse for this chapter is found. Girl, it's in the book of
Lamentations! If you're like me, you're wondering, What's an
uplifting, full-of-promise verse like that doing in a book full of
laments? But that's the wonderful thing about hope. It pops out
in impossible circumstances and sprouts from the worst and
rockiest soil. Hope is that pinprick of light that leads us out of
the darkest tunnel of despair.

One of the things my great-grandmother told me again and
again as I was growing up was, "Keep your hopes up, girl!" I
always tried to do what Granny told me to do, so I've kept my
hopes up through some very difficult situations in my life.

There's an Arabian proverb that says, "He who has hope has
everything," and for Christians that is the absolute, no-frills,
barebones truth. Because you know what? Our hope is Jesus!
And when you have Jesus, baby, you have everything you'll ever
need to hang on through the hard times.

—THELMA WELLS (*The Buzz*)

# THERE IS NO GREATER POWER

*With God's power working in us, God can do much, much more than anything we can ask or imagine.*

—Ephesians 3:20 NCV

Have you ever wondered what hand God has in the calamities in your life? I did and yet, it seemed blasphemous to ever think of God that way. My assumption was that calamities originated with Satan's efforts to overthrow my soul's peace, joy, and equilibrium. And of course that is Satan's resolve, but now I know God fits in there in ways I had refused to think about.

The God I know and love came to earth to heal and restore. He was compassionate and wept over death, and he ultimately conquered it by dying on the cross. How could anyone possibly assume God would choose suffering for us? The truth I've come to embrace is that God is indeed compassionate, loving, and kind. And yet I need to recognize another dimension of God; he is the sovereign initiator. There is no greater power.

Knowing this frees me to simply say, "Lord, let me rest in this experience even though I may not want it, like it, or understand it. You know what you intend to accomplish; you have the big picture, and I don't. Thank you that I don't have to figure out, *Where did this come from and why?* It came from you in one way or another, and I choose to trust you in it."

—MARILYN MEBERG (*God at Your Wits' End*)

# CAPTURING EACH MOMENT

*The Spirit of God has made me, and the breath of the
Almighty gives me life.*

—Job 33:4

Are you the kind of person who is curious about life, saying
"yes!" to its strange and unusual possibilities? God gave us life
and vitality and a sense of wonder, and an enormous capacity to
flourish emotionally, personally, and spiritually.

The most interesting people I know drink in life and savor
every drop—the sweet and the sour. The good and the bad. The
planned and the unplanned. And isn't that what God intends?
When Jesus modeled humanity for you and me to see, he was
out there—everywhere! He took risks. He embraced life and
responded to everyone and everything, the tender and the
tumultuous. His capacity for life was without measure. And, we
are designed like him. I don't want to miss anything he has in
store for me, even if the path he takes me on winds through some
pretty rough terrain. Right in the midst of what seems to me to
be a detour from the map, I'm often gifted with something precious and unforgettable.

Capturing the moment is a choice, a way of life. It requires
us to wake up, live life, and be present—here, there, and everywhere. Sometimes that's scary; sometimes it's exhilarating.
Always, it's an adventure I keep learning to welcome with a full
and grateful heart.

—LUCI SWINDOLL (*I Married Adventure*)

# LESSONS LEARNED IN THE LOWLAND

*Blessed are those whose strength is in you ... As they pass
through the Valley of Baca, they make it a place of springs; the
autumn rains also cover it with pools. They go from strength to
strength, till each appears before God in Zion.*

—Psalm 84:5–7 NIV

Do you remember when the disciples left the valley and joined
Jesus on the Mount of Transfiguration? They experienced such a
rush of joy that they wanted to stay there. Who wouldn't! But
Jesus let them know they had to go back down, down, down to
the people and the problems—because that's where our faith is
forged. The valleys are littered with lessons; the wise lean in and
learn.

The sights are spectacular from the rocky pinnacles, and we
get a great overview of the orchards, but I also want to hold the
pear in my hand and taste its sweet offering. That happens in the
lowlands. From the peaks, we see the lakes; but in the valley, we
can explore the water's refreshing depths. From the crest, we see
the canopy of trees; but in the valley, we can sit in the cool shade
and listen as the wind sings through the branches.

We live the majority of our lives in the lowland; yet, if we
look close enough, we'll find fruit, catch breezes, and hear music
as we learn lessons along the way. For me, that makes the jolts of
valley life more bearable and, at times, downright joyful.

—PATSY CLAIRMONT (*All Cracked Up*)

# HE IS WITH YOU

*[God] is not far from each one of us.*
—*Acts 17:27* NRSV

As I have told my son countless times, forgiveness is God's gift to help us live in a world that is not fair. More important, though, is the lesson: the more we allow our anger to fade, the more we center ourselves on forgiveness and God, the more opportunity we have to feel his presence and response to our petition. The boulder of bitterness and resentment rolls from our path, and once again we're in communion with God and his will.

There's no doubt this is a difficult topic. The reasons for God's seeming distance from us are many, and we've all felt that separation at one time or another. But no matter what, we need to remember this: God is sovereign.

One of the greatest lessons I took from a dark moment in my life is that God is always there, no matter how we feel. There will be times in our lives that illness or depression, insecurity or doubt, the enemy of our souls or the enemy that we can be to ourselves will make us doubt God is listening. Our feelings, however, do not change the facts and do not alter the character of God. He is with you! Hold on to that truth!

—SHEILA WALSH (*Get Off Your Knees and Pray*)

# PERSONAL PEACE

> *Do not be anxious about anything, but in everything, by prayer*
> *and petition, with thanksgiving, present your requests to God.*
> *And the peace of God, which transcends all understanding, will*
> *guard your hearts and your minds in Christ Jesus.*

—Philippians 4:6–7 NIV

I want to focus on what we all want most as we near the end of each day: peace.

Of course we want peace all the time in all places—global peace, political peace, civil peace. But even more importantly, we long for personal peace. That's the kind of peace that lets us rest easy at night, even when the world around us is anything but peaceful. It's an amazing thing, this kind of peace; in fact it "surpasses all understanding."

Surely that's the kind of personal peace we all long for: trusting, childlike peace, a mentality in which we feel totally protected. Fortunately, it's the kind of peace God offers us when we make our requests known to him. As adults, we don't get to sleep through the crises that affect us, but we can call upon God's great power and mercy to give us confident, incomprehensible peace in the midst of a life storm, whether it's a minor shower of inconvenience or a whirlwind of devastating loss. In that state of inner peace we're able to connect more securely to God's guidance and protection so that we can endure, and even be levelheaded leaders, as we ride out the storm.

—THELMA WELLS (*The Buzz*)

# FINISHED AT THE CROSS

*Yes, I have loved you with an everlasting love.*
—*Jeremiah 31:3*

When I'm hurting, I don't want someone explaining the *why* to me. I want to know God truly loves me. Is his heart truly one of love and compassion in spite of how it appears? Paul described Jesus as "the image of the invisible God" (Colossians 1:15 NIV). The writer of Hebrews referred to Jesus as the "exact representation" of God's being (1:3 NIV). When Jesus wept at the tomb of Lazarus . . . so did God. When Jesus invited the children to come to him . . . that was God. The touch of Jesus restored sight, healed bodies, and renewed physical life . . . and that was also the touch of God.

Our faith is encouraged by knowing that the compassionate acts of Jesus were the compassionate acts of God. He sits with us in our pain and refuses to leave us. He turns his ear toward our cries and listens until we're spent. Jesus hung on a cross for our sins and said, "It is finished!" (John 19:30). What started in the Garden was finished at the cross. The price was paid, the death sentence lifted.

What motivates such intense attention? Love. The love of God. The love of God demonstrated through the earthly ministrations of Jesus, God's Son.

—MARILYN MEBERG (*God at Your Wits' End*)

# CAPTURING THE LIGHT

*How precious is Your lovingkindness, O God! . . . with You is
the fountain of life; in Your light we see light.*

—Psalm 36:7, 9

Living in the light is one of the most difficult tasks we have. It means getting out of the way so there is no shadow blocking the source. When we read or write or engage in hobbies or reach out to others, why do we do that? What do we hope to gain? I think it's to be illuminated . . . enlightened . . . or we hope to give off illumination of some kind. That's what light is: illumination—whether emotional, financial, mental, physical, or spiritual. To capture the light available to us is one more aspect of divining the spirit of adventure. The more light we live in, the more we grow and change.

God reminds us to quit holding things too tightly—whether an event, a viewpoint, a desire, a particular time in life, or a person we thoroughly enjoy. He urges us to stop struggling, resisting, coercing, or manipulating for what we want. When we simply do what he asks, no matter how hard it seems, and we keep our focus on the Light of the world, an amazing brightness comes, all within the embrace of his love.

—LUCI SWINDOLL (*I Married Adventure*)

# EXPECT DELAYS

*My soul waits for the Lord more than those who watch for the*
*morning—yes, more than those who watch for the morning.*
—Psalm 130:6

When the gentleman put up his hand to stop me from going through security at the airport, I complied. I already had stripped off my shoes, jacket, and purse to be scanned. Finally, the man waved me through and then immediately began wanding me. The wand sounded like a loaded Geiger counter that had just struck pay dirt as he whisked it around my chubby anatomy. The woman on the scanner then pointed out that my purse and carry-on needed to be searched.

I bet the Israelites never anticipated that it would take forty years to reach the Promised Land. Talk about delays. Enemies, rebellion, war, sickness . . . there was always something slowing them down and delaying their arrival.

What looked like sheer inconvenience and man-made barriers actually had been orchestrated by the hand of God. He knew the exact moment they would reach their destination. Delays were as much in his plan as manna and quails.

I remind myself of that when a flight is canceled, a mistake is made, an order is lost, a doctor's report is delayed, or a request is misunderstood. We don't know, but God might be protecting us with these delays. They may be God's way of helping us realize our need for trust, patience, adaptability, and relinquishment.

—PATSY CLAIRMONT (*All Cracked Up*)

# WHO'S THE BOSS?

*Let the favor of the Lord our God be upon us, and prosper for us the work of our hands—O prosper the work of our hands!*

—Psalm 90:17 NRSV

Can you imagine what an impact it would have on the world if everyone who follows Christ would wake up each morning and thank God for the gifts he or she has been given and ask for opportunities that day to use them for his glory?

I'm not saying this is always easy. The trouble is that some gifts receive immediate praise and recognition, and others don't. We must keep in mind who we're working for. If we're dependent on the approval of others, life will be very discouraging. But if we wait only on the Lord, his love will uplift us no matter what. To God, there are no small jobs or menial tasks. He sees all the late-night laundry and lunches packed. He sees the extra work your boss never credits you for. He sees it all.

As far as I am concerned, I work for God. He is my boss, and he is my King. So whether I am writing a book, recording a CD, speaking to thousands of women, or sitting in the carpool lane waiting to pick up my child, it doesn't matter. No one thing that I am called to do is more important than another; all that matters is my heart.

—SHEILA WALSH (*Get Off Your Knees and Pray*)

# PERFECT PEACE

*You will keep him in perfect peace, whose mind is stayed on*
*You, because he trusts in You.*

—Isaiah 26:3

The precious gift of peace from our gracious and loving God can soothe and comfort us in the midst of the harshest, most trying situations. It doesn't necessarily fix things; in fact things might just go on ahead and get worse! But God's peace can help you survive the dark times.

When I've had problems in relationships, when I was refused admission to a school simply because of the color of my skin, I knew peace—because I knew Jesus. I had asked him to be Lord of my life when I was four years old, and I knew exactly what I was doing. Granny had created an environment for me that set the stage for my spiritual development. She reared me in a praying household, a churchgoing household, a household that did not doubt the ways of God, and as I filled my mind with him, he has kept me in perfect peace.

I've noticed too that peace can be contagious. One person who demonstrates peace during a hopeless or heated situation can reverse the direction of an escalating trial. One person who is filled with God's peace can bring hope to a friend who's drowning in despair or ease the anxiety of a room full of worriers. What a wonderful thing peace is!

—THELMA WELLS (*The Buzz*)

# CHOOSE LIFE

*To choose life is to love the LORD your God, obey him, and stay close to him. He is your life.*

—Deuteronomy 30:20 NCV

From the beginning of recorded time God has committed himself to loving his people. He will continue loving his people until we all gather in that place called "eternity" where all tears will be wiped away, all pain will be eliminated, and all anguishing memories will be forgotten.

In the meantime, how do we cope with the problems pain presents to our faith? How do we maintain faith when suffering wrenches it from our feeble grasp? I go back to one of the freedoms given to me at creation: I choose.

I can choose to turn away from God in bitterness, despair, and disbelief, or I can choose life. What does it mean to choose life? It means to believe God's love for me is a dependable fact and in that love to find sustaining encouragement. It means I choose to live in the mystery of what I may not understand but feel buoyed by faith in the midst of that mystery. It means taking God's promises and believing they were written for me.

In choosing life, I choose to believe the enormous implications of those promises when I'm at my wits' end. What will you choose? Will you believe and depend on God's love for you?

—MARILYN MEBERG (*God at Your Wits' End*)

# WHAT TURNS YOUR CRANK?

*We all have different gifts, each of which came because of the grace God gave us.*

—Romans 12:6 NCV

In the formative years of my childhood, my parents were the human factors that provided the nourishment I needed to begin growing. They put me on a playing field where the game of life began. With their teachings as a springboard, I started making decisions that caused me to be the person I am today, for good or bad.

As I branched out and began seeing patterns form, traveling revealed an adventuresome side of my temperament. I went here, did this, saw that, and felt thus and so. My friend Mary says, "People do what makes sense to them," and it's true. We all have to determine what makes sense to us and do it, whether or not it seems logical to anyone else. We don't live fully until we do this for ourselves. Some of the things that make sense to me are art, music, photography, literature, and theater. These are the considerations in life that turn my crank, make me think, and fill my heart with appreciation and wonder. They are vehicles that transport me into the light that illuminates and enriches my journey.

What are the things that transport you into the light? What makes sense to you? If you don't yet know, it may be time to look around you and discover what turns your crank!

—LUCI SWINDOLL (*I Married Adventure*)

# EMBRACING THE GOOD

*Endure hardship as a good soldier of Jesus Christ. Consider what
I say, and may the Lord give you understanding in all things.*
—2 Timothy 2:3, 7

It isn't natural to look for good in bad. It's far more human, when
bad rears its ugly head, to gaze upon it stymied. But when we
believe that God designs and redesigns all things for our good,
even when the intent of others is for our demise, it allows us to let
them off the hook and look up. Our task is to detect and embrace
the good, which means we will have to be alert and discerning if
we are to benefit from the windbreaker of gratitude.

I'm not thankful when my heart is broken, yet I'm grateful
that through internal ruptures comes a deeper compassion for
others who grieve. I had no idea how unaware and indifferent I
was toward the agony of others until I suffered through a season
of intense winds and came out of that time with enhanced sensitivity. It wasn't that I hadn't cared about others; I just didn't have
a clue what their struggles were costing them until hardships
exacted a high price from me.

Someone once said, "We can only know joy to the degree we
have known pain." Hardships have the potential of carving out
greater space for God's grace within us. And grace helps us to live
with life's inequities without the disabling residuals of anger, bitterness, and disillusionment.

—PATSY CLAIRMONT (*All Cracked Up*)

# CELEBRATING CHRIST IN OTHERS

*It is God who is at work in you, enabling you both to will and
to work for his good pleasure.*

—*Philippians 2:13* NRSV

If the whole point of our lives is to become more like Christ and
be a conduit for the love of God, then we will each be given different paths to take—which may or may not correlate to our
prayers. Some paths seem more attractive than others, but no
one really knows the burdens another carries. What I am convinced of is that God loves his children. I don't know why he
answers one person's prayers one way and another person's differently, only that he has a reason for it.

One of the ways we can measure whether we are at peace in
the love of God is by asking ourselves whether we are able to
celebrate Christ shining through another's life—whether we can
recognize God's wisdom as he lovingly hand-packs each life himself. Because only when we can do that—when we can accept his
hand working differently in your life as opposed to mine, answering each prayer in his own time and understanding—can we
truly be at peace with God. Believing that God is not listening to
us dampens our relationship with him. But taking joy in living
out his plan for us—that's freeing!

—SHEILA WALSH (*Get Off Your Knees and Pray*)

# SHE KNEW

*She said, "If only I may touch His clothes, I shall be made well."*
—Mark 5:28

It's true that sometimes when we need him most we feel far away from God—hurting, alone, forgotten, trampled down by a crowd of problems. Maybe at that point we've given up on ever feeling close to him again. Maybe we feel dirty and unfit, covered with worldly dust that robs us of courage and weakens our faith.

Well, girlfriend, let me tell you: when you find yourself in that kind of ordeal, remember the woman who reached out through the mob to touch the hem of Jesus' cloak. There may have been something in her that wanted to think he had passed her by or forgotten her or turned his back on her. Ah, but she *knew* better. She knew that even if she didn't feel close to Jesus, even if she couldn't look him in the eye and talk to him face to face, *he* still knew she was there. So she came up behind him and flung out her arm through the raucous crowd, knowing, *If I only touch his cloak, I will be healed.*

And she did. And she was.

How thankful I am that she knew what she knew—and that her story has been handed down to me two thousand years later.

—THELMA WELLS (*What These Girls Knew*)

# A LITTLE LESS IMPERFECT

*The God of all grace, who hath called us unto his eternal glory by Christ Jesus, after that ye have suffered a while, make you perfect, stablish, strengthen, settle you.*

—1 Peter 5:10 KJV

Have you ever thought life might be easier if you could be someone else altogether? Here's one woman's fantasy for her own identity change: she'd like to be a bear. Her reasons?

- → If you are a bear you get to hibernate; you do nothing but sleep for six months.
- → Before you hibernate, you must eat huge amounts of food—the more calories the better.
- → The children (cubs) are born while you are sleeping and are the size of walnuts.
- → As a mama bear, you swat anyone who bothers your cubs. Swatting is socially acceptable behavior.
- → Your mate expects you to wake up growling and have hairy legs and excess body fat.

Life is not perfect. We know that, but the longing for perfection has always been with us. Why? We were created for perfection. We live hoping for what we've never known, somehow knowing one day it will be ours. The good news is, perfection is on its way. One day all evil will be banished, taking with it all that is not perfect.

—MARILYN MEBERG (*God at Your Wits' End*)

# GOD'S TRUTH

*We should no longer be children, tossed to and fro and carried about with every wind of doctrine, by the trickery of men, in the cunning craftiness of deceitful plotting, but, speaking the truth in love, may grow up in all things into Him who is the Head—Christ.*

—Ephesians 4:14–15

I don't know about you, but I don't always get God's truth exactly right, and sometimes I'm way off, but I do believe a great part of my adventure in living is nourished at the well of having built my foundation on solid doctrinal truth.

In his letter to the Ephesians, Paul says that being grounded in the truth makes us strong adults who know the ropes. We can't be pushed around. Because we know that Christ is our leader, we don't ever have to waver in our beliefs. We are secure in him.

In my lifetime, I've seen thousands of fads come and go, philosophies of life change like the weather, political systems overturned in revolutions. Nothing stays steady. Except God! The essence of his being is always the same: yesterday, today, and forever. We can trust him and his Word.

Is your life anchored in the truth? If not, it's never too late to build a foundation for your life based on God's Word. Ask the Holy Spirit to teach you, and make yourself a student of the Bible. When you bank your life on God's truth and "grow up into him who is the Head," you will be stable, secure, and immovable in your faith.

—LUCI SWINDOLL (*I Married Adventure*)

# THE BEGINNING OF THE CONVERSATION

*Jesus said, "My sheep listen to my voice; I know them, and they follow me."*

—John 10:27 NCV

In my twenties and thirties, I was surrounded by people who seemed to hear from God on a remarkably frequent level. Almost every week, people reported that God was showing up and giving them specific directions. But those kinds of experiences never happened to me. I worried that somehow I was missing God—that everyone else had a better listening ear than I did. Perhaps I was destined to hear from God secondhand.

What about you? What do you rely on when you want to hear from God on a specific issue or a general direction? Do you sit and wait, hoping you'll find direction in a book or through someone else? Or do you take time to pray and meditate on God's Word?

Yes, that's right. I'm saying that prayer is sometimes just the beginning of the conversation. Sometimes we need more. It takes an intentional choice to carve out time in our overfull schedules to listen to the voice of God. Perhaps we have lived such busy lives for so long that we have forgotten how, or perhaps we have never learned to listen for God in that way. But Jesus assured us that when we look past all the books and speakers and seek to commune with him, we will know his voice.

—SHEILA WALSH (*Get Off Your Knees and Pray*)

# ADVANCING THROUGH ADVERSITY

*Don't be afraid, don't waver. March out boldly tomorrow—*
*God is with you.*

—2 Chronicles 20:17 MSG

When things don't work out the way we plan . . . when we're handed loss while we're hoping for luck . . . when our rewarding work suddenly collapses into rubble . . . when someone or something we love is taken from us . . . the light goes out of our lives. We're lost, not understanding why calamity has swept through our lives and dumped us in some dark place far from hope. We think of what we had planned and what has happened instead, and our hearts break open with cries and questions. *Why, Lord? Why me? Why now? Why this? Why my child* or *my husband* or *my loved one?*

When hardships hit, when our heart breaks, of course we grieve for what we've lost. But in our sadness, let's resolve to learn through our grief. Let's ask God what he's trying to teach us through the difficult experience.

Sometimes the answer is immediately clear. Sometimes we may not realize until weeks or even years later what God was teaching us in our time of trial. We may not know until we get to heaven and can ask God face to face. Meanwhile, we need to let our heartache send us into God's loving embrace, knowing that he *will* make a way.

—THELMA WELLS (*What These Girls Knew*)

# FINDING OUR HOME IN GOD

*Jesus answered him, "Those who love me will keep my word, and my Father will love them, and we will come to them and make our home with them."*

—John 14:23 NRSV

There is a homelessness of the self we impose upon ourselves when we don't realize it is God who is our home. We know believers anticipate a mansion in heaven, but here on earth God is also our home.

It is he who provides the comforts of home. These comforts are the security of being adored—nurtured and comforted, approved of and cherished—as he walks our human path with us. I believe many of us are afraid to cry out because we think to do so would alienate us from God. The result of that faulty thinking is that we don't go home, where honesty is rewarded and faith is increased. We stay in a homeless state, perhaps toughing it out on a park bench somewhere. What we need to do is cry out in the comfort of home.

Home is that interior place in our spirits where God speaks words of encouragement to us. It's where he soothes our tattered souls and promises comfort. Home is that place where I can be real . . . where I can be honest . . . where I dare to say what I feel. Come home, dear friend, you will find him there.

—MARILYN MEBERG (*God at Your Wits' End*)

# COMPLETE IN HIM

*May the God of peace . . . make you complete in everything good so that you may do his will, working that which is pleasing in his sight, through Jesus Christ.*

—Hebrews 13:20, 21 NRSV

It's not so easy to balance between your head and your heart? Have you noticed? I sure have! How *do* we establish ourselves firmly in the unshakable foundation of truth and at the same time feel things deeply? The integration of what we think with how we feel affords a rich, authentic spiritual life and ensures meaningful connections with others. But where do we find the formula? Is there one?

As simplistic as it sounds, we find it in relationship to God. He created us—will, intellect, and emotions. Scripture says we are complete in him. By nature, I'm more cerebral than emotional. I have friends who are just the opposite. And I've known folks with wills like steel, but they don't necessarily think straight or care. But none of us can create within ourselves that harmonious blend that echoes the essential ground of our being in Christ. Only our Maker can synthesize us and make us whole.

When we find our center, when our identity is in him, when the core of our being revolves around him, we're not just academic (as I tend to be) or emotional (like Eeyore in Winnie-the-Pooh) or willful (like a two-year-old I once knew). We're whole, because he's made us so.

—LUCI SWINDOLL (*I Married Adventure*)

# GOD'S STILL, SMALL VOICE

*I will instruct you (says the Lord) and guide you along the best pathway for your life; I will advise you and watch your progress.*

—*Psalm 32:8 TLB*

You only have to watch the news or read a newspaper to be aware of the evil that is rampant in our world. We hear stories of those who are called to be servants to God's people and then are arrested for misappropriating funds or embezzlement. Perhaps you are discouraged by the times you live in and wonder how you can hear God's voice in the midst of all the evil in this world. God looks for those who still have hearts open to him and gives them ears to hear his voice.

Do you recognize moments when God has been speaking in your life? Perhaps you have felt a prompting to do something, go somewhere, stop for coffee somewhere you wouldn't normally go, speak to a stranger and only in retrospect can you see the hand of God. There might have been someone there who just needed a word of encouragement or you might have seen a book that answers something you've been asking God about. You may be surprised to realize how often these things occur in your life. We have a Father who loves to talk with his children, so listen for his still, small voice.

—SHEILA WALSH (*Get Off Your Knees and Pray*)

# ACCENTUATE THE POSITIVE

*To You, O LORD, I lift up my soul. O my God, I trust in You.*
—*Psalm 25:1–2*

Girl, do you talk to yourself? Do you ask yourself questions? Do you answer those questions? If you do, you're in good company. Most people who talk to themselves are not crazy; they're at least talking to someone intelligent for a change. So, it's fine to talk to yourself if you're saying the right things.

I believe in affirmations. An affirmation is a positive statement spoken in first-person singular, present tense, as if it had already happened. Here are some affirmations. Repeat them after me:

"I like myself."

"Things work out well for me."

"I am attractive and charming."

"I am blessed. I am healthy. I am appreciated."

"I enjoy rest and relaxation."

"I like people."

"I am successful and I am progressing in my career."

"I love my family."

"I have wonderful friends."

"I cherish the gift of life."

"I have all the money I need to do whatever I want."

Now, stop laughing. If you keep saying it and working toward it, you'll make room in your life for God to make it all come true.

—THELMA WELLS (*Girl Have I Got Good News for You*)

# DOUBTING YOUR DOUBTS

*Lord, when doubts fill my mind, when my heart is in turmoil,
quiet me and give me renewed hope and cheer.*

—Psalm 94:19 TLB

Doubt may be a difficult topic for you. I'd like to make a few suggestions that may contribute to your "renewed hope and cheer."

+ Be assured that you do not lose your heavenly citizenship when you doubt.
+ Make a conscious decision about your doubt: do you will to believe? If so, you will need the Author of your belief to help you.
+ Read the Gospel of John over and over and over again. (It has the greatest number of Jesus quotes.)
+ Get involved in a Bible study where you will not receive gasps and groans when you honestly share your doubts.
+ Keep a prayer journal. Write your prayers to God. Then read your prayers out loud to him.
+ Go to church. Jesus went to church, and I can't imagine how he kept from being bored. After all, he knew more than anyone there! But he went to worship.

Our challenge is to love him for what we do see and trust him for what we cannot see. Our doubts may occasionally persist, but they do not have to dictate our behavior.

—MARILYN MEBERG (*God at Your Wits' End*)

# OUR ADVOCATE

> *Humble yourselves under the mighty hand of God, that He*
> *may exalt you in due time, casting all your care upon Him, for*
> *He cares for you.*
> —1 Peter 5:6–7

There is no escaping the undeniable fact that we need an advocate to go before us as well as run with us. Someone who will fight our battles and cheer us on. Someone who will renew us and strengthen us for the next task. This person is the Savior, Jesus Christ, God and man in one person forever. This hypostatic unity of undiminished deity and true humanity enables him to know my need, receive my burden, heal my wound, and send me on my way with his blessing and power. Not only that, but it enables me to experience his love, forgiveness, and solace because he knows my longing heart so intimately.

At the moment we cast our anxiety on our heavenly Father, believing he'll listen, understand, care, and act on our behalf, our burden is lifted. Believing he truly cares is worth a fortune in hope, victory, and spiritual rest. And knowing he is able to respond to our need is a comfort beyond all measure. I know he can do anything, and I feel safe and carefully tended, knowing he will accomplish what concerns me. These precious truths are in my head, and they've become priceless treasures buried deeply in my heart.

—LUCI SWINDOLL (*I Married Adventure*)

# USING WISDOM

*I am continually with You; You hold me by my right hand. You will guide me with Your counsel.*

*Psalm 73:23–24*

We don't live in the days of Samuel or Moses—the days when God spoke only through prophets or kings. We live in a time when God speaks to each of his children through his Word and through the Holy Spirit and through wise counsel. Whenever I have found myself in a place of wanting to hear God's voice before I move in one direction or another, I ask myself several questions:

- → Does anything in this situation go against the revealed Word of God?
- → Do I feel a great urgency and stress to do something right away? When I feel a compulsion to move quickly, I wait. God is a God of order and peace.
- → Do those whom I respect and trust sense God's presence in this situation too? There will be times when God will ask us to step outside of what others understand, but it has been my experience that those situations are rare.

If we can follow these three guidelines, our lives will be much simpler and more fulfilled. God loves to talk to his children, so ask for ears to hear and a heart to know his voice.

—SHEILA WALSH (*Get Off Your Knees and Pray*)

# SEARCHING FOR CLUES

*You who seek God, your hearts shall live.*

*—Psalm 69:32*

The "searching for clues" mentality undoubtedly characterizes many of us as we puzzle through Scripture in an effort to find God's truth, especially when we're spending wits'-end time with our backs against the wall.

For example, we tend to think there's no possible place for humor as we cry out to God and wait for him to deliver us. But that's faulty thinking. In fact, humor can be a great source of strength and encouragement during our wits'-end wall-waiting time. It helped me see how our search for God's sovereign will and his purpose in our trip to the wall can be a benefit in itself, inspiring us to find hidden rewards in the experiences we've been called to endure. Those rewards—or that deliverance—may be different from the way we imagined them. And one of those hidden treasures we find during our search might be the gift of humor God may have left for us in unexpected places . . . even places like that wits'-end wall.

The Bible frequently speaks of searching and of the reward to those who seek spiritual truth found only in God. Let me encourage you to begin looking for hidden treasure.

—MARILYN MEBERG (*God at Your Wits' End*)

# GIVING FREELY

*Remember this: Whoever sows sparingly will also reap sparingly, and whoever sows generously will also reap generously.*

—2 Corinthians 9:6 NIV

One of the greatest adventures available to us as God's children is trusting our Father with respect to our finances, our time, and our energy. Giving from our wealth—no matter how small or large—is not even a gamble, although we're dealing with the great unknown because of our own limited vision. But God has promised to meet our needs, and he won't go back on his promise.

Giving freely of the resources he has given me has become downright enjoyable. I figure if he can turn water into wine, he can provide riches out of nowhere. He's got the goods to do it! I could recount story after story of his surprises to me in terms of replenishing my well of money, time, and energy. His bounteous goodness constantly rains on my parade.

I also find in the matter of giving that the greater the trust, the wider the blessing. And the wider the blessing, the sweeter the joy. I couldn't have made those statements forty years ago, or maybe even twenty, when I wasn't as free in my spirit as I am now. But I've learned from personal experience that God keeps his word and continually gives out of a well that never runs dry.

—LUCI SWINDOLL (*I Married Adventure*)

# EMBRACING GOD'S WILL

*I cry to God Most High, to God who fulfills his purpose for me.*
—Psalm 57:2 NRSV

I celebrate the fact that God accepts us in all of our humanity. We are allowed to ask questions, to be sad when we don't get the answers we long for, to grieve over losses no matter how insignificant they may seem to others. Yet, as I think about the requests I myself have made to God through the years and the stories I have heard from others, I see one big problem: when we take what we want and try to twist God's arm to answer us, we shift from worshippers to spoiled children. That is not the heart Jesus displayed while he walked in human flesh. When Jesus prayed in the Garden of Gethsemane, the pattern he modeled in agony and tears was this:

> + Total honesty and vulnerability.
> + Total surrender to God's plan.

Jesus lived every moment of his life with an awareness of what mattered. He knew that the purpose of this life we are gifted with is to bring honor and glory to God, not to make life easy or comfortable for us. He knows how hard it is at times to embrace God's will, but he urges us to reach out and grasp hold of whatever will bring glory to his Father.

I want to live like that!

—SHEILA WALSH (*Get Off Your Knees and Pray*)

# GOD'S DELIVERANCE

*They cry to the LORD in their trouble, and He brings them out*
*of their distresses.*
—Psalm 107:28

Scripture tells us when we "cry out" to God, he delivers us from our "distresses." What we do not know is how or when he delivers. We assume, as well as hope, his deliverance means a change in our circumstances. We want to see that deliverance!

As much as we would like to see a change of circumstances as evidence that God is delivering us from our distresses, often our circumstances do not change. Then how can God promise he will deliver us from our distresses? Is there a little clause somewhere that we missed? Is it written in invisible ink?

I believe God always delivers us from our distresses just as he promised, but sometimes that deliverance is within our hearts, where the pain of our circumstances has shredded our interior being. God meets us at the shredding place. His deliverance may be simply to give us comfort in that place. His deliverance may be a lifting of our heads . . . of our spirits . . . and an assurance that he is there with us. His deliverance may be giving us the knowledge that we will have his strength to endure even though our circumstances may not change.

—MARILYN MEBERG (*God at Your Wits' End*)

# YOUR SINS ARE FORGIVEN

*I write to you, little children, because your sins are forgiven you for His name's sake.*

—1 John 2:12

One of the most liberating truths we find in Scripture is that bad things happening to us are not God's punishment for sin. Isaiah 13:11—"I will punish the world for its evil, and the wicked for their iniquity"—was written for those who never sought forgiveness from the God who freely forgives and thoroughly cleanses us from the stain of our sins. He tenderly says to us, "My child, your sins are forgiven for my name's sake!"

We need always to keep in mind the distinction between the consequences of sin and punishment for sin. Punishment for sin, which is death, has already taken place. That occurred at the cross. But the consequences of our sins may go on for a lifetime. Those consequences may be felt in our daily lives. For example, drugs, alcohol, or sexual addictions leave their mark upon our bodies as well as upon our psyches. But the good news is, whatever was the sin that held us in its grip is forgiven. We can look at the consequences as reminders of God's grace and love for us. He is not holding that sin against us but is encouraging us to move on with our lives and enjoy the grace of his forgiveness.

—MARILYN MEBERG (*God at Your Wits' End*)

# TURNING POINTS WE ALL FACE

*Give yourselves completely to God. Stand against the devil, and the devil will run from you. Come near to God, and God will come near to you.*

—James 4:7–8 NCV

When life doesn't make sense anymore, we can give up, or we can remember who Jesus really is and that, no matter how dark it gets, he is worth it all.

When low self-esteem and doubt paralyze us, we can give up and accept these clouded images of ourselves, or we can remember who we are in Christ.

When guilt occupies the secret places in our lives, we can let it cripple us, or we can open our hearts and allow God to set us free.

When the heat of problems and pain burns into our very souls, we can crawl away and hide when it gets too hot, or we can choose to be living sacrifices who stay on the altar for his sake.

Christian service is a poor substitute for Jesus himself. We must ask, "Do I want to run myself ragged doing things for God, or do I want the best part—being his friend and knowing him face-to-face?"

When this complex, plastic world tries to squeeze us into a designer mold, we can let pride take over, or we can shake free to live the simple truth of the gospel with humility.

—SHEILA WALSH (*Life Is Tough But God Is Faithful*)

347

# MORE TURNING POINTS WE ALL FACE

*Obey God because you are his children; don't slip back into
your old ways.*

—1 Peter 1:14 TLB

When God seems far away and our prayers bounce off the ceiling,
we can give in to despair, or we can keep holding on to heaven in
simple trust. Hold on, my friend, hold on!

When we feel weak and overcome, we can wallow in self-pity,
or we can choose to reach out and help one another. You really
aren't the only one going through a tough time.

When life is tough, we can give up, or we can come before the
Lord with our problem—and wait patiently for his answer. It is
always worth the wait.

When the needy cross our path, we can choose to show selfish indifference, or we can take our eyes off our own needs and
follow the example Jesus set by loving the unlovely.

When our dreams seem to go sour or remain unfulfilled, hopelessness can dominate our lives—or we can hold on with open
hands, knowing that we have hope because God is faithful.

When we face our choices, large or small, we can settle for
lukewarm, diluted faith—or we can seek the real thing, because
we know that one life does make a difference now and through all
eternity.

—SHEILA WALSH (*Life Is Tough But God Is Faithful*)

## GOD'S PURPOSES

*The human mind plans the way, but the LORD directs the steps.*
—*Proverbs 16:9* NRSV

I want a reason to get up in the morning. When I ask God for a sense of personal destiny, and then listen carefully, I get a sense of direction. Not always, and not always immediately, but I rely on God's promise to consistently guide me toward fulfilling the purpose for which he created me.

I know that nothing any of us experiences is pointless or useless. The good, the bad, the ugly, even the things we think will kill us—God uses it all, and he devises our destiny out of the stuff in our trash. He sifts it out, shows us the value, and then uses us to help others because of it.

When we look at the desires of our hearts in light of reality, we know none of them is achievable all the time. They're changeable, like the weather. Some days we're content; others we're not. There are places in the world we feel completely at home, others less so. There are even days when we wonder if we have a purpose at all, and the uncertainty lingers for a while. But our desires give shape and substance to our unique essences. And when we pray out of the depth of those desires, our faith is strengthened and our fellowship with the Lord is sweeter.

—LUCI SWINDOLL (*I Married Adventure*)

# IT WORKS EVERY TIME

*You never saw him, yet you love him. You still don't see him,
yet you trust him—with laughter and singing.*

—1 Peter 1:8 MSG

I've been to the wall of adversity. I've wondered about God's promise to deliver, and I've tried to seek out answers to the dilemmas I've faced. In the wall-waiting, searching time, I've learned something very valuable about how to do that waiting. It's a method that joins forces with my will to believe God is working on my behalf and affirms the fact that God is sharing the wall with me. (Remember, he is wherever we are. If we're at the wall, he is too.) The method? Humor. It works every time.

Laughter serves a greater purpose than just distracting us from our misery as we do our time at the wall. It's good medicine. We now know laughter releases the brain's natural painkillers, endorphins, which can be fifty times more powerful than morphine. Laughter not only reduces pain, it lowers blood pressure and relaxes the skeletal frame. A good laugh may drive us to our knees simply because the skeletal frame can no longer hold us up. (Some prefer that to prayer.)

Many of my experiences have taught me the value of using humor during wits'-end times. In fact, laughter often precedes trust. When I laugh, I am in essence saying to God, "I trust you, even though I'm not sure what you're doing."

—MARILYN MEBERG (*God at Your Wits' End*)

# ASKING THE RIGHT QUESTIONS

*Teach me to do your will, for you are my God. Let your good
spirit lead me on a level path.*

—Psalm 143:10 NRSV

If you can, imagine for a moment that before Jesus left this earth
he commissioned you to represent him (which he did!). So,
when you come to the Father with your prayer requests you are
representing the person of Jesus, coming in his authority. I
believe that if we carried that awareness with us, it would impact
how we pray and what we ask for.

That notwithstanding, can we ask God for anything if our
faith is strong enough? Well, yes. But is that really the right question? It's not so much about our level of faith as what we put our
faith in. Are we asking for the right things? Are we seeking God's
will in the situation? And are we comfortable with his response
if things don't end up the way we wanted?

I hope so. It's not always easy. But we have a guide. When
you meditate on the life of Christ you see how often he pulled
away from the crowd to be alone with his Father. He lived every
moment of his time on earth as a representative of the heart of
God. Looking at that and longing to be like Jesus are changing
the way I pray—as I hope it will change yours.

—SHEILA WALSH (*Get Off Your Knees and Pray*)

# THE SEEDS OF POSSIBILITY

*Jesus replied, "I tell you the truth, if you have faith as small as a mustard seed, you can say to this mountain, 'Move from here to there' and it will move. Nothing will be impossible for you."*
—Matthew 17:20 NIV

It has been said that sixty-five thousand thoughts float through our minds each day. Every one of those thoughts has the seed of possibility in it. We choose with our will what we'll do with that thought. Will we stay stuck in "If only . . ." or "Why me?"—or will we open our minds to "What if?" and "Why not?"

Asking the right questions keeps us open-minded and open-hearted to what was and is and might be in the years to come. They send us on our way into all sorts of journeys in search of adventure.

Being a spiritual sojourner, now seems like a good time to pause and look back. I want to assess where I've come from and where I'm going—I want to ask myself what things I'd do the same, might do differently, or regret I never did at all.

Want to come with me? I invite you to make your own list as we go along. We'll both see how the possibilities never end. We can do all things through Christ. His is the hand that launches us; his Spirit propels us. The voyage doesn't get any better than that.

—LUCI SWINDOLL (*I Married Adventure*)

# PART OF THE SALVATION PACKAGE

*Think of yourself with sober judgment, in accordance with the measure of faith God has given you.*

—Romans 12:3 NIV

Another crucial clue for understanding our lives with God is to realize that faith is his gift to us. We can't scrunch it into existence. We received that gift when we received him into our hearts and lives for salvation. With salvation came faith to believe. Without faith, we would not have it in our hearts to receive Jesus in the first place. In our natural selves, we would be indifferent to the spiritual light, which is Jesus. Why? The sinner prefers darkness. So no one who knows Christ can say, "I have no faith." Faith is part of the salvation package.

Do you fear that your faith is too poor or weak? Remember this, all faith, no matter how poor or weak, serves as our conduit . . . our contact to the source of our faith, who is Christ Jesus, who is not small or feeble.

Our faith depends on our choices. We can will in our spirits to grow, develop, and mature in that God-given faith by eating the "food" found in Scripture. Everything we need for healthy faith-growth is in the Bible. We may eat all we can hold and not gain weight. If you supplement with chocolate . . . that's your choice.

—MARILYN MEBERG (*God at Your Wits' End*)

# GOD IS SOVEREIGN

*To You, O LORD, I lift up my soul. O my God, in You I trust.*
—Psalm 25:1–2 *NASB*

As I look at my life today, I believe God is sovereign all the time, not just some of the time. Nothing—absolutely nothing—that comes into your life or my life is a surprise to him. Everything has to pass through his merciful hands. Now, much of the time we don't see it coming, so it knocks us over. But even in that prone place, as we are reeling from what just happened, we can say thank you.

I am not suggesting we just up and move into a place of denial, as if nothing happened. Not at all! What I am saying is that even in some of life's most painful moments deep in my spirit, I thank God. I thank him because he knew it was coming and has provided everything I need to get through it. The saying goes that we're either victims in this world or we are not. If Christ had not come and taken all the sin and hatred on himself, we would be without hope. But he did come and he did die and he did rise from the dead, so we are not victims! We are beloved children of God Almighty, the Sovereign King of heaven and earth.

—SHEILA WALSH (*Get Off Your Knees and Pray*)

# REGRETS ARE REVERSIBLE

*The desires of the diligent are fully satisfied.*

—Proverbs 13:4 NIV

A few years ago I was enjoying casual conversation with friends and asked if they could identify their greatest regret in life. After thinking a long while, one friend said, "I wish I would have taken a really good writing class." The rest of us looked at her for a few seconds then roared with laughter. After the initial shock, she joined us. It struck us all so funny because it certainly wasn't too late for her to take that really good writing class. If that is her greatest regret in life, she is one child of fortune.

The truth is that many of life's regrets are reversible. Sometimes what we wish we'd done when we were younger or in different circumstances, we can still pursue. And even mistakes that loom in our history like savage beasts don't have to define us or devour us.

When we start believing anything's possible, regrets turn into challenges, defeats into lessons learned, and heartache into magnanimity. It's all in our outlook—the lens through which we choose to view life. Besides, if we had it all to do over, how do we know we wouldn't do it the same way again? Better to live fully in today and place our hope in the future God has planned for us.

—LUCI SWINDOLL (*I Married Adventure*)

# GOD RULES

*This is what the Sovereign LORD, the Holy One of Israel, says:*
*"In repentance and rest is your salvation, in quietness and trust*
*is your strength."*

—Isaiah 30:15 NIV

God is sovereign—not just a little bit sovereign, but utterly and completely sovereign. He controls everything. Not just some things . . . *everything*. Plain and simple: he rules.

There is a settled peace deep within my soul as I realize I am not in charge of my life. I'm responsible to that life, but I don't have the power to orchestrate the events in my life any more than I have the power to make the moon appear twice every month instead of once. What I can do is enter into a partnership with God about my life.

In that partnership, I know I'm to daily seek his guidance and wisdom. I also know I'm to conscientiously live my days according to the practical principles he has laid out for me in Scripture.

God's sovereignty will always hold levels of mystery for me, but that mystery actually feeds my peace. Why? Because I have faith in him. He has a good track record. I like it that he knows more than I do. I also like his style. He's creative, has a flair, and does the unexpected. But coupled with that drama and flair are his tender love and regard for me.

—MARILYN MEBERG (*God at Your Wits' End*)

# JOURNALING YOUR GRATITUDE

*Let them thank the LORD for his steadfast love, for his*
*wonderful works to humankind. And let them offer*
*thanksgiving sacrifices, and tell of his deeds with songs of joy.*

—Psalm 107:21–22 NRSV

I don't know what your life is like today, whether you would say you are in the best days or the most difficult days—or perhaps, like me, a mixture of both. I want to suggest that you start keeping a gratitude journal. This is not a prayer journal, which is obviously a great thing to do and something that can greatly enrich your prayer life. Rather, this is just to write down all the things you are grateful for. Our prayer journals reflect our requests, but our gratitude journals can contain how God has answered our prayers or simply be a gateway to wonder and worship. I find it very helpful to use my gratitude journal in prayer. It gives me a written account of the faithfulness and goodness of God.

You might think if you add one more thing to your to-do list, it will push you over the edge and you'll be calling me for the number to the wee place with locks on the windows! Relax, this is not a major undertaking. Just keep any kind of journal by the bed, and each night jot down three things you are grateful for. It's just a way to refocus away from all the stuff that isn't working and thank God for what is.

—SHEILA WALSH (*Get Off Your Knees and Pray*)

# THE BEST ADVENTURE OF ALL

*Your ears shall hear a word behind you, saying, "This is the way, walk in it," whenever you turn to the right hand or whenever you turn to the left.*

—Isaiah 30:21

I can say with confidence that the Lord has led me every step of the way into a life of adventures worth remembering and celebrating. Through the years he's opened door after door of possibility. Some of those doors I've walked through, others I haven't. Now, at seventy, so many of my dreams have come true. I've followed the road map, and although I can't see very far ahead, I feel certain I'm going in the right direction.

The most important thing for each of us is to embrace and celebrate life for what it is. Being alive is a gift, and we will never exhaust all the adventures or possibilities that are ours because Jesus Christ has provided an inexhaustible legacy for us, established before the foundation of the world. Every day he opens new doors for us to walk through. He gives us a new way of looking at old problems. He challenges us to take him at his word as we consider how to resolve different dilemmas. He assures us of his constant presence. And here's the best adventure of all—he lives in us! We can go anywhere and do anything, because the one who leads us never fails.

—LUCI SWINDOLL (*I Married Adventure*)

# FAITH THINKING

*Jesus said to Thomas, "Reach your finger here, and look at My hands; and reach your hand here, and put it into My side. Do not be unbelieving, but believing."*

—John 20:27

Remember Thomas? He's the most famous doubter on record—a disciple of Jesus who saw miracles only Jesus could do. But in spite of all he had seen that should have translated from belief to faith, after the Crucifixion, Thomas lost his faith. Why? What he saw did not make sense. Jesus died on a cross. Thomas was doing some faulty thinking that eroded his faith.

We all need encouragement to raise the level of our faith from seeing to trusting. But we must remember that the author of our faith is Jesus. He meets us at our level of need, just as he did Thomas.

When you and I are at rock bottom, when our backs are against the wall in a wits'-end experience, Jesus will meet us there. Faulty thinking would be to think our faith development is our job and we had better get on the ball! Faith thinking is trusting God to give us what we can't produce apart from him.

My prayer is that we all will avoid faulty thinking and shaky faith, that we will always choose to joyfully live out our days of prosperity and trust his sovereign design for our days of adversity.

—MARILYN MEBERG (*God at Your Wits' End*)

# SIMPLE TRUST

*Steadfast love surrounds those who trust in the LORD.*
—*Psalm 32:10* NRSV

In my life, I have been challenged to take an honest look at how much I trust God.

We live in the visible world. Even though I believe the invisible world, the kingdom of God, is far more real, the visible world is what we see and deal with every day. When we are faced with bills we can't pay or a diagnosis we did not expect, it's hard to remember God is in control and can be trusted all the time. We live in a world where we are barraged with messages about how to take care of our health, our family, and our future. But although it is obviously wise to use common sense and responsibility, our lives ultimately rest in God's hands. Doctors can make well-educated guesses, but God is the one who has numbered the hairs on our head and knows how long our race is. Financial planners can offer good advice, but only God knows what tomorrow brings.

Isn't that great news? He has promised to lead us and guide us, and he is the one who invites us to come to him in simple trust. As I've heard Max Lucado say, "You have never lived an unloved moment in your life."

—SHEILA WALSH (*Get Off Your Knees and Pray*)

# ACCEPTED: AS IS!

*He made us accepted in the Beloved.*

—*Ephesians 1:6*

I'm a girl who likes to go to the mall. OK, I love to go to the mall. I go to the mall a lot. I love a good bargain, but I'm not typically the type who scours the sale racks trying to find the perfect buy. I don't have the patience for that. There are times, however, when the ideal item crosses my path. I instantly fall in love with it . . . but then I see there's something wrong with it—a missing button, a broken zipper, or a seam that's starting to come apart. But usually when I find those flaws, I'm happy, not sad, because that's an instant discount, one I'm all too happy to take advantage of. So I purchase the item, get my discount, and say, "Thank you very much." Often the salesperson writes on the tag, "Sold as is, no return."

That is how Jesus accepts us. AS IS. Broken, cracked, tattered, and in all of our ordinariness, he receives us with a no-return policy. He never gives up on us, and he will never give us back. He looks at me with my freckles, my large pores, and my even larger sins, and says, "You are wonderfully and beautifully made."

—NATALIE GRANT (*The Real Me*)

# AMAZING GRACE

> *Being justified by faith, we have peace with God through our Lord*
> *Jesus Christ: By whom also we have access by faith into this grace*
> *wherein we stand, and rejoice in hope of the glory of God.*
>
> —*Romans 5:1–2* KJV

As Christians, the grace of God is ours. The grace of God differs from the grace afforded by people simply because people *sometimes* come through and sometimes they don't. The giving of human grace may depend on temperament, circumstances, or level of personal generosity. God, however, is constant and totally committed to giving grace to his people. His grace is not dependent upon his temperament, circumstances, or level of personal generosity. The bestowing of grace is a part of God's divine intent and passionate love. Next to your salvation experience, grace is the most important facet of God's love.

Many Christians feel they need to do things for God as a way of earning his grace and love. Those people believe they need to be better and better Christians so God will be glad his Son died for them. But that is not how grace/love operates. *It's a gift.* Not a solitary thing we do (none of our "works") will make us good enough for his grace. Jesus already made us good enough. God's love (grace) declares us worthy even though we are not. Human grace may not find us worthy, but God's grace never wavers.

—MARILYN MEBERG (*Assurance for a Lifetime*)

# WHY NOT?

*God, make a fresh start in me, shape a Genesis week from the chaos of my life.*
—Psalm 51:10 MSG

Crisis is often just the invitation we need to cross the threshold into a new adventure. Crisis can give you the courage to try things you've never tried before. Perhaps the pride that once held you back has been thoroughly sifted out of you. Postcrisis people, particularly those who are determined to let the crisis make them better instead of bitter, find themselves no longer protesting, "Oh, I could never do that." Instead, they greet invitations into adventure with a hearty "Why not?"

Here is a profound bit of wisdom. Allow your past, even your worst failures, into your present only as part of the experience that led up to the person you are today. But do not let one experience determine who you will be tomorrow.

It's been said that there is the life you learn from and then the life you live. Many of us can relate to this concept. Take whatever lessons you can possibly glean from your past—especially from your sorrows, your losses, and your failures. Scoop up this backpack of wisdom so you can peek into it now and then for its profound lessons. Finally you can begin hiking toward your new life and new mountaintops.

—SANDI PATTY (*Falling Forward*)

# LIFE IS ALL CRACKED UP

*The LORD is close to the brokenhearted and saves those who are crushed in spirit.*

—Psalm 34:18 NIV

I don't know who spun the dial on my internal compass, but I'm not laughing. I just came from the mall, where I misplaced my car in the parking lot; and then, after finding it, I immediately got lost, detouring through three strip malls before careening (not purposely) onto the correct road headed for home. No, there are no strip malls on the way to my house. And no, the mall is not in another town. And yes, I had been there many times.

What I've learned thus far in life (besides never travel alone) is that my internal compass isn't the only thing broken. We also have obvious fissures of the heart, like fractured relationships, weakening moral fiber, and religious disillusionment. That's where our Redeemer comes in. We need someone who can fix broken hearts, adjust our perspective, and even give us a reason to laugh.

God sent Jesus as a Redeemer to do just that—to redeem the shards of our lives and create a stained-glass perspective. When we realize we're broken and acknowledge Jesus as our Redeemer, then the crushing blows of life do not destroy us. Instead we live with hope, we dance more often, we laugh more deeply, and we are not taken by surprise by the fact that life is all cracked up.

—PATSY CLAIRMONT (*All Cracked Up*)

# COMPASSION IS LOVE AND GRACE

*Never walk away from someone who deserves help; your hand is God's hand for that person.*

—*Proverbs 3:28* MSG

The ultimate meaning of compassion is love and grace. When we grasp what God's love and grace have done for us, we cannot help but show compassion to others.

I think it's important to remember that Jesus told the story of the Good Samaritan in answer to the lawyer's question, "Who is my neighbor?" This simple story, which almost every Christian knows by heart, surely shows that we may find ourselves in situations where we need compassion, but we might not always get it. Those whom we think will offer it do not, and when compassion does appear, it comes from unlikely neighbors, indeed.

We westernized Christians are in grave danger of staying within the comfortable confines of our own lives, failing to have compassion for others, and simply sitting at home to struggle with our own failures and temptations.

Fortunately, many have learned a vital secret to keeping on when life is tough. That secret is compassion. When you reach out to others in the name of Jesus, you have to take your eyes off yourself. It is then that you suddenly realize you don't have to hold on at all. Because you are so close to Jesus, he has you in the hollow of his hand.

—SHEILA WALSH (*Life Is Tough But God Is Faithful*)

# OUR ULTIMATE TOMORROW

*Jesus said, "In My Father's house are many mansions; if it were
not so, I would have told you. I go to prepare a place for you.
And if I go and prepare a place for you, I will come again and
receive you to Myself; that where I am, you will be also."*

*—John 14:2–3*

My daddy's favorite Bible verse was 1 Corinthians 2:9, "No eye
has seen, no ear has heard, no mind has conceived what God has
prepared for those who love him." He quoted it many times to me,
wrote it in letters, and jotted it on gift cards. It makes me wonder
if he, too, wondered what was in the distance, over life's horizon.
Now he knows, of course, since he's been in the presence of the
Lord over twenty years. He knows, even as he is known.

Gratefully, my own ultimate tomorrow is a given as well.
When I put my faith in Jesus Christ as my Savior, I sealed my
destiny. The finished work of Christ and his promise about what
is to come assures me I'll spend eternity with him. God has made
it clear in his Word that someday he will come get me and take
me to live with him forever.

Frankly, I love the fact that God has a plan for the future, for
every tomorrow of my life on earth and beyond. Even though I
can't figure it all out, he's got it wired. This reassures me that I'm
loved and safe. God knows our course and he knows us. He loves
us. He provides. He plans ahead.

—LUCI SWINDOLL (*I Married Adventure*)

NOTES

# NOTES

NOTES

# THE NATURE OF MAN

# The Nature of Man

## A SOCIAL PSYCHOLOGICAL PERSPECTIVE

*The Third John G. Finch Symposium on
Psychology and Religion*

### RICHARD L. GORSUCH
*Associate Professor
Institute of Behavioral Research
Texas Christian University*

*and*

### H. NEWTON MALONY
*Associate Professor of Psychology
Graduate School of Psychology
Fuller Theological Seminary*

CHARLES C THOMAS · PUBLISHER
*Springfield · Illinois · U.S.A.*

*Published and Distributed Throughout the World by*
CHARLES C THOMAS • PUBLISHER
Bannerstone House
301-327 East Lawrence Avenue, Springfield, Illinois, U.S.A.

© *1976,* by CHARLES C THOMAS • PUBLISHER
ISBN 0-398-03327-7
Library of Congress Catalog Card Number: 74-22022

*With THOMAS BOOKS careful attention is given to all details of
manufacturing and design. It is the Publisher's desire to present books that
are satisfactory as to their physical qualities and artistic possibilities and
appropriate for their particular use. THOMAS BOOKS will be true to those
laws of quality that assure a good name and good will.*

*Printed in the United States of America*
*R-1*

**Library of Congress Cataloging in Publication Data**

John G. Finch Symposium on Psychology and Religion, 3d,
  Fuller Theological Seminary, 1973.
  The nature of man.

  Bibliography: p.
  Includes index.
  1. Social psychology—Addresses, essays, lectures. 2. Social ethics—Addresses,
essays, lectures. 3. Man (Theology). 4. Philosophical anthropology. I. Gorsuch,
Richard L., ed. II. Malony, H. Newton, ed. III. Title.
HM251.J475 1973     301.1     74-22022
ISBN 0-398-03327-7

# PARTICIPANTS

RICHARD L. GORSUCH, Ph.D., *Associate Professor, Institute of Behavioral Research, Texas Christian University*

H. NEWTON MALONY, Ph.D., *Associate Professor of Psychology, Graduate School of Psychology, Fuller Theological Seminary.*

RALPH D. WINTER, Ph.D., *Professor of the Historical Development of the Christian Movement, School of World Mission, Fuller Theological Seminary*

PAUL K. JEWETT, Ph.D., *Professor of Systematic Theology, Fuller Theological Seminary*

DOUGLAS R. MATTHEWS, Ph.D. *Candidate, Graduate School of Psychology, Fuller Theological Seminary*

HENRY B. VENEMA, Ph.D. *Candidate, Graduate School of Psychology, Fuller Theological Seminary*

# PREFACE

THE NATURE OF MAN has been of perennial interest to laymen and scholars alike. During the twentieth century, the social sciences have become self-conscious. Social psychology, as a separate discipline, has made distinct contributions to our understanding of such diverse concerns as conformity, leadership, social attraction, group processes and motivation. It is altogether fitting that the implications of these conclusions for our understanding of the nature of man should be detailed. Gorsuch has done this.

He has related the data of social psychology to ethics, to moral decision making, to individual differences and to the state of man's existence. Further, he has suggested some implications for the study of theology and for the life of the church.

Several of us have responded to his proposals. The disciplines of anthropology and theology as well as psychology are represented in these reactions.

Gorsuch's essays were the addresses of the third John G. Finch Symposium in Psychology and Religion delivered at Fuller Theological Seminary in January, 1973.

One is always indebted to his secretary and I am no exception. Marsha Lucas performed a monumental task in shepherding the project to fruition. I am grateful to her. Further, I am especially grateful to the Trustees of Fuller Theological Seminary and Lee Edward Travis, Dean of the Graduate School of Psychology, for their continued undergirding of these endeavors.

It is our hope and trust that these ideas will be stimulating and contributory to the continuing dialogue among the disciplines of theology, anthropology and psychology. We feel these concerns will have wide appeal to all students of the relationship between the social sciences and the Christian faith.

H. Newton Malony

# CONTENTS

# THE NATURE OF MAN

## CHAPTER I

# Introduction*

RICHARD L. GORSUCH

THE QUESTION OF THE NATURE of man is an ancient and noble one which has been pursued philosophically and theologically. Determining the nature of man and exploring the implications of that analysis forms a considerable portion of classical writers such as Plato. The nature of man is also a central topic within the Bible and the general Judaeo-Christian heritage. The tradition continues with current works such as those by Comfort (1966), Doniger† (1962), and Radhakrishnan and Raju (1960).

The question of the nature of man has also been approached by generalizing from the physical sciences. The results of science have been used to build a model of man which follows the scientific and technological marvels of the writer's era. The clock was a scientific marvel whose ability to function autonomously for extended periods of time impressed a culture in which the only other machinery depended on the direct activity of animals, wind, or water for its "life." The mechanistic clock was then used

*The author, **Richard L. Gorsuch**, was Kennedy Associate Professor of Psychology at the John F. Kennedy Center for Research in Education and Human Development at George Peabody College, and gratefully acknowledges the gracious support of the Joseph P. Kennedy Jr. Foundation. Many useful comments were made on an earlier draft of these lectures by William L. Wallace and Martha K. Key, to whom the author is indebted. The work of Betty Howard in preparing the initial manuscript is gratefully acknowledged.

The title and text refer to the discussion under its traditional name, the Nature of Man. The term man was used for its ability to inform the audience that the lectures relate to the traditional area but was without sexist intent. The author explored other terms, but they were also sexist—such as hum*a*nity —or extremely awkward. Suggestions are welcome.

†While the title of Doniger's volume refers to psychology, only one of the twenty-three contributors is a psychologist. The contributions are not based on social science data and therefore it is an example of the "arm-chair" approach to man.

3

as a model for a mechanistic man in a mechanistic universe, made by "that great clock maker in the sky" who could then go off to other activities. The same tendency to build a model of man based upon the obvious achievements of the sciences has continued. In the contemporary age, the amazing capabilities of the computer have suggested an information processing model of man complete with internal and external storage, feedback loops and interacting systems.

While the computer image of man is a definite advance over the clock image, no generalization from the physical sciences can provide a complete understanding of the nature of man. In particular, man's self activating nature, his continuing curiosity, and his constant desire to analyze and understand are not natural characteristics of a computer, but must be programmed into the computer by outside forces. Since a model of man based either upon the clock or the computer is an attempt to generalize from an inanimate area to man, it is no surprise to find the models being only analogies. To understand the nature of man, it seems most appropriate to turn to the study of man himself as found in the social sciences.

## A SOCIAL PSYCHOLOGICAL PERSPECTIVE

Disciplines such as anthropology, archaeology, history, psychology and sociology all have their role to play in a contemporary understanding of man. While it would be desirable to integrate these disciplines into a total picture of man, a total integration is beyond the capabilities of any single person and outside the scope of the present task. Instead, I shall examine the question of the nature of man from a psychological perspective. The psychological perspective used will be primarily concerned with those areas of psychology which study people per se. Social psychology will be the principal area within psychology that will be utilized, but topics from other areas of psychology will be included where appropriate.

By focusing the discussion on a social psychological perspective, many vital and distinctive characteristics of man will be ignored. For example, mankind's upright posture, the opposition of thumb and fingers, language, the power of faith, mental abnormalities, and the tendency to build and change cultures are some of the important characteristics of man which are not discussed here. Ignoring such vital characteristics is not to imply that they are less than crucial, but they are relinquished to keep the discussion within definable bounds.

In the social psychological literature, the question of human nature has seldom been directly examined. Early psychologists found that all too often such discussions would be misinterpreted as explaining *why* a behavior occurred rather than describing *what* behavior occurred. When a particular behavior was observed, it was "explained" by stating that it was "just human nature," and the search for the causes of that behavior ceased.

In the present discussion, the question of the nature of man is seen as a descriptive task rather than an explanatory one. It will, hopefully, provide an understanding of the characteristics of mankind. While identifying man's characteristics has implications for his future behavior, the nature of man cannot be viewed as an explanation of why or how human nature came to be like it is nor of how long the characteristics shall continue to describe man. A psychological view of human nature simply provides a "snapshot" of what characterizes man at that moment in history.

In discussing man from a social psychological perspective, the points made will generally be developed from points well established within the scientific literature of psychology. Consequently, no attempt will be made to document in detail the scientific basis of the psychological statements but, instead, only illustrative references and samples will be given of the supporting literature. Where the conclusions are less well established or less well known, more detailed references will be given or the concepts will be phrased in a speculative mode.

The implications of the conclusions about human nature will be discussed for areas such as theology and philosophy. It would be presumptious to suggest that a psychologist could answer theological or philosophical questions and my comments should not be taken as an attempt to do so. But I do feel that each discipline needs to probe surrounding areas and raise questions at those points where the discipline's data appear relevant to the questions of other disciplines. This I shall attempt to do with the hope that those in the other disciplines will also be interested in cross-disciplinary dialogue. The spirit of the present lectures is exemplified by Wickler's (1972) *The Sexual Code: The Social Behavior of Animals and Men.* In response to the Pope's statement in the *Humanae Vitae,* wherein the major purpose of sexual behavior was said to be procreation, Wickler examined the role of sex across several species. His data showing that sex serves major functions not directly related to procreation provide an empirical basis for the examination of the issues raised in *Humanae Vitae.* The present work will, hopefully, be another contribution to interdisciplinary dialogue on the nature of man, although it will be a more general discussion than Wickler's and not directed to examining the assumptions of any one theological position.

## MAN'S CONSISTENT PSYCHOLOGICAL NATURE: ETHICAL MAN AS AN EXAMPLE

To discuss the nature of mankind requires that man have a set of psychological characteristics which are relatively constant across cultures. The assumption of a constant nature is more tentative when working from psychology than when examining the physiological or sociological nature of man. In physiology, it is widely known that major physiological characteristics are constant across the varieties of mankind. In sociology, a heavy stress has been placed upon sampling of people from relatively large populations so the generality of the conclusions is immediately known. But in psychology, explicit sampling from defined populations has seldom occurred and most research is based on people who are relatively accessible, principally college students. Psychology can be of value in the present discussion only if mankind's nature is sufficiently constant so that we can generalize from college students and other North Americans to most people.

It does not appear that a constant psychological human nature can be assumed as obvious since writers in the present era have been impressed with the fact that man is historical. Any individual lives during a certain era in a particular cultural context, and the historical conditions under which he lives have a generally acknowledged influence upon his characteristics. In the present discussion, the problem of changes in the nature of mankind across history will not be a concern since the discussion is based upon research conducted with people of the present era, that is, *we are only concerned with the nature of contemporary man.* But an evaluation is necessary to determine if a high degree of cross-cultural generality might be expected in areas of cultural importance. As Sherif and Sherif (1969, pp. 316-331) document, the culture of which a person is a part does influence his concepts and behaviors.

Since it would be impossible to examine the cross-cultural generality of the many areas necessary for a social psychological understanding of human nature, the current discussion of cross-cultural constancy is limited to the ethical nature of man. Social psychology covers most of human relationships, many of which would warrant separate discussion for a complete coverage of the topic. Not only is complete coverage beyond the scope of the present task, cross-cultural data does not exist for many areas since empirical social psychology has been a North American phenomena. But some cross-cultural data is available in the area of values and how man processes those values to reach decisions.

Ethics and morality is a crucial area for evaluating if contemporary man has the same characteristics regardless of his culture since ethical values are often assumed to be inconsistent across contemporary cultures. The variations in the number of wives and political systems, not to mention the changes in student activism across recent decades, suggest that values are indeed culturally specific. But if values are culturally relative, then we could not assume that man is sufficiently the same to identify basic characteristics on the basis of those who have participated in psychological research.

## Cross-cultural Consistency of Ethical Reasoning

A sufficient body of literature studying values cross-culturally now exists to suggest an answer to the question of whether the ethical nature of man is relatively constant across cultures. In this research, psychologists have found it worthwhile to distinguish between the process used in moral reasoning and the contents which are utilized in the reasoning process. Roughly speaking, process refers to *how* a person thinks in ethical situations while content refers to *what* he thinks with.

As a simple illustration of process, consider how a person might respond to a story where the main character is tempted to cheat another person. When asked whether the main character should or should not cheat, different individuals respond in different ways. Some use a limited thought process which focuses only on the probability of being caught. If that probability is quite high, then their answer is that the principal character should refrain from cheating. If the probability of being caught is low, then they hold that the principal character would cheat the other person. Others, however, do not take into account the probability of being caught in answering the question. Instead, their thought processes focus on the question of whether or not a "good person" would engage in the behavior. The decision is then based upon their norms defining a "good person" rather than the characteristics of the situation. It is apparent that the approach to an ethical dilemma differs considerably between these two types of individuals, and they are therefore said to have different processes of moral reasoning.

The content that a person could use in his reasoning processes consists of his values and norms. To continue the illustration, a person tempted to cheat could feel either that to cheat is to be a "bad person" or that cheating is alright so long as you don't cheat your friends and do share the spoils. The values and norms, that is, the content, differ in these two cases although both are concerned with social approval.

Although little research has been conducted, process and content appear to interact in decision making. When faced with a moral dilemma, the person's thought processes select that content which is used to reach the decision. The person who uses a limited thought process will examine only the immediate characteristics of the situation and his broader principles and values will not be seen as relevant. The person who uses more abstract thought processes will consider the values and norms of his group as more relevant than the immediate characteristics of the situation. Therefore the same norms will be used in differing ways to differing degrees according to the person's thought processes.

Research exists (Gorsuch & Barnes, 1973) to support the contention that conclusions about the processes and contents of ethical reasoning need not be the same in cross-cultural research. It could be that only process oriented conclusions are culturally invariant, only content conclusions are invariant, both are invarient or neither is culturally invariant. Therefore the question of the cross-cultural generalizability of man's ethical nature needs to be examined separately for the processes by which decisions are made and the content involved in making value laden decisions.

Kohlberg (1968, 1969) has been able to identify several types of moral reasoning processes in his analyses; those analyses have extended across several technologically advanced and emerging societies. Kohlberg's suggestion is that the process (which he calls structure) may be relatively constant across cultures whereas content may be culturally specific. If this is true, then the ethical nature of man can be discussed in terms of the process of moral reasoning, although discussing the nature of ethical man on the basis of content would require further evaluation.

Most of the studies suggest that the processes used in ethical reasoning are similar across cultures. In Figure I-1., typical results from empirical research on the process of moral reasoning in rural U.S.A. boys (Turiel, 1969) is plotted along with data from a study we conducted in rural Iran (Shamsavari, 1973). The figure has combined Kohlberg's six stages into three levels. The

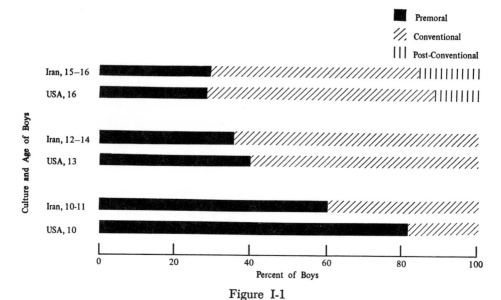

Figure I-1

first level consists of premoral thinking, which is that type of thinking where the sole concern is the immediate sanctions in the situation. The second level, conventional morality, consists of those individuals whose principle concern is whether the proposed behavior agrees with that which is commonly accepted as the right course of action among his friends or in his culture. The third level, post-conventional thinking, is identified by the respondent basing his rationale for a course of action on highly internalized standards that could be recommended regardless of the culture.

The research studies show that the same types of moral reasoning are identified across the cultures, that they appear in the same developmental order from children to adults, and that the modal level of adults in almost all cultures is that of conventional ethical reasoning. In Figure I-1., it can be seen that the younger boys show more pre-conventional thinking than older boys, and that conventional thinking occurs late in adolescence in both cultures. Similar results have occurred in almost every culture studied. While boys in some cultures do lag behind those in the U.S.A., the data suggest that they will ultimately use the conventionally moral thought processes as do most American adults. The difference is one of the speed with which they go through the levels rather than any difference in the process of thinking. Therefore it is apparent that the nature of ethical reasoning is similar regardless of the culture under study. One can talk about the nature of man's ethical reasoning processes, rather than being restricted to a discussion of different processes in different cultures.

### Cross-cultural Consistency of Ethical Content

Is it also legitimate to assume that the content of man's ethical reasoning has some generality across cultures? In two of our studies, we have collected information relevant to that question (Gorsuch, 1971; Gorsuch & Barnes, 1973). The first study was concerned with differences in subculture values in Nashville, Tennessee. The respondents were Black and White children from the lower and middle socioeconomic classes. Each child was asked a series of questions designed to probe the content of the social norms he saw in his environment. All of the children's responses were disguised and mixed so that the coders did not know either the social class or race of the respondent. Categories were developed from the responses to represent the values expressed in the answers. This procedure allowed for a value to occur solely within, for example, the lower class Black males which might not occur in any other subcultural group. The second study utilized the same procedures but the respondents were Caribs of British Honduras. The children were from obviously more primitive conditions than that of the U.S.A., often living in thatched roof huts in villages accessible only by dugout canoe.

Despite the fact that careful procedures were established so that each subgroup could have its own value content, almost all the value categories occurred in all groups. For example, 84 percent of the Carib responses fell into the same categories used by middle class, White U.S.A. girls. The percent of responses falling into each category were also remarkably similar. While differences did occur, these differences seemed minor compared to the similarities. In these studies, it does seem possible to identify a subset of value contents which are cross-culturally invariant. Such common children's values include academic achievement, physical appearance and development, good manners, diligence, obedience and being kind.

The two studies of value content were, however, with children. It may be that a part of the common developmental task of mankind is to pass through a stage where one is socialized to those values that allow him to fit into any society. In later years, particularly adolescence, values may diverge as the person is introduced to the values of his own particular subculture. Kohn (1969) studied the differences in values of middle and working class mothers. While his emphasis was upon the statistically significant differences between classes—and most people who reference him quote only these differences—Kohn notes that "it must be repeated that the class differences are variations on a common theme, most of the highest rated values reflecting respect for the rights of others" (Kohn, 1969, p. 21).

Kohn's implication that subcultural value differences are, on an absolute basis, not as large as might be commonly expected is supported in other lines of research. For example, Tomeh (1971) had Middle Eastern and U.S.A. college students rate a number of behaviors as to "how wrong" they were. His conclusions are similar to those from a number of other studies using such questionnaire procedures: "An important finding of this study is the great similarity of many moral codes." Again differences were noted, but the differences appeared to be variations on a common theme. Behaviors such as kidnapping, bribery, perjury, unjust dealings with weak nations, robbing, lying and cheating on income tax reports are universally condemned although they are condemed somewhat more stringently by the Mid-Easterners than by American college students.

Using the same questionnaire as Tomeh, Gorsuch and Smith (1972) examined the values of college students in 1969 and compared them with data reported on the values of college students in 1939, 1949, and 1958. Since the 1969 college student was at the end of an activist era wherein there appeared to be a definite shift towards more liberal moral standards, the differences between these students and the earlier students are relevant to our current discussion. A typical finding is given in Figure I-2. where the data showing the shifts in three of the eight areas investigated are presented. The shifts are shown for females since they appeared to have slightly greater changes than did the males, although the general trends of the results were virtually identical. It can be seen that there was no apparent change in students' negative ratings of misrepresenting oneself for personal gain. There was a slight change in the rating of sexual

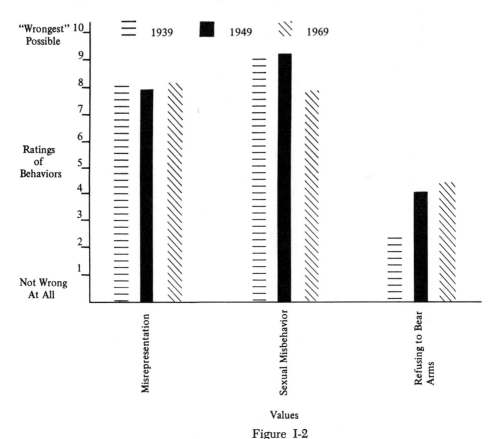

Values

Figure I-2

misbehavior. Whereas the earlier college students had rated it as almost as wrong as it could possibly be, the 1969 students rated it as only severely wrong. They certainly do not approach the score of zero which would be "not wrong at all." In response to the question of refusing to bear arms in a war deemed unjust, the students generally considered it moderately, but not severely, wrong during all eras. Despite current misconceptions, only the 1939 sample considered resisting service in the armed forces as less wrong than the other samples.

As in the previous analyses of value content, it is possible to find some statistically significant differences across the years in college student values. However, these differences are slight compared to those which arise from the act which is being judged as right or wrong. Students of all eras basically agree that misrepresenting oneself for personal gain at the expense of others is extremely wrong as are such acts of sex outside of marriage. They also agree that refusing to bear arms in a war one deems unjust is wrong, but not nearly as wrong as many other behaviors. These relative rank orders are the same as those generally found in other cultures although, as Tomeh mentioned, there is a tendency for U.S.A. respondents to be more lenient in their judgments. It certainly does not appear that the values of college students have changed radically in the years during which social psychological research has been conducted.*

### Conclusions on the Cultural Relativity of Man's Ethical Nature

Before one draws the conclusion that both ethical processes and contents are sufficiently stable to examine the question of the ethical nature of man, the reasons for the existence of theories stressing the cultural relativity of values need to be noted. The widespread belief in cultural relativity appears to be a function of two phenomena. On the one hand, that which is different is most striking to us and is therefore most noticeable. The minor

---

*College students have changed more radically in other ways. For example, recent Peabody freshmen are considerably more anxious and more cynical than were the students of ten to fifteen years ago (Wrightsman, 1972a).

differences which do exist are then the focus of discussion and the major cross-cultural similarities are ignored.

The second reason theorists have been impressed with the cultural relativity of values is because values have been judged from individual behaviors which *are* culturally relative. Individual behaviors are a function of the interaction between a person's evaluation of the situation and his value processes and contents. Given a wide range of situations, people with identical value processes and contents will behave in many different ways. For example, even when the same values are held in the areas of sex and respect for women, one society may be strictly monogamous whereas another society may allow several wives per husband because the latter society finds itself with a large number of women relative to the number of men. It is therefore necessary to ignore behaviors per se and to examine the process used and the values which the behavior is maximizing to draw conclusions about the cultural relativity of ethical man.

Despite the expectations from the known cultural differences of man, it does appear that common ethical thinking processes and common values exist cross-culturally. Since the area of ethics and values would appear to be an area as sensitive to a person's culture as any other area critical to the study of the nature of man, it does appear that current psychology can speak to basic issues of the nature of contemporary man. While cultural differences do exist, these are variations upon a common theme; it is the common theme of mankind that is the subject of these lectures.

## CHAPTER II

# Man and Finitude

RICHARD L. GORSUCH

THE ONE ESSENTIAL CHARACTERISTIC of man that any study of human nature must take into account is man's finiteness. As a finite creature, he experiences only a limited part of reality for a limited time. When he encounters a new experience that requires him to judge which course of action to take, he cannot base a decision upon all the factors which should be taken into account. To consider all factors would require man to have infinite judgmental capabilities, a characteristic no finite creature can have. Without a consideration of all the factors, a decision is prone to error. Therefore, a basic characteristic of the nature of man is his fallible judgment.

### FINITUDE AND HUMAN JUDGMENT

The fact that man makes errors needs no documentation by psychology. It is readily apparent in almost any set of lay or scholarly analyses. Our analyses of ethical reasoning processes and content suggested that scholars who stressed the cultural relativity of man's ethical nature have communicated only a limited part of that nature, which is to say that some decisions previously reached in this area are inconsistent with the more extensive data now available. But to imply that the decisions may have been inaccurate is not to necessarily say that the judgments in question have been poorer than they are in most scholarly areas. It may be that poor judgment is as typical of mankind as is good judgment. An understanding of how man's finiteness limits the accuracy of his judgments is a prerequisite to the tasks of any scholarly area, including a study by people of their own basic characteristics.

16

## Man's Finite Ability to Comprehend

One simple reason for man's poor judgment is the limited information upon which he often bases his decisions. Without sufficient information, any decision is subject to error. Psychological theories of the nature of man have, for example, often been based upon the scholar's own experiences with other people in his personal life and in the clinic. Despite the fact that the scholar experiences only a finite subsegment of the human race during a finite period, he assumes he can generalize to all mankind without systematic checks on the quality of that generalization. Freud's conclusions on the Oedipus complex may, for example, have been perfectly true for Jews with psychological problems who lived in victorian Vienna of the early twentieth century, but the extent to which they would also apply to a commune-raised American of 1990 is unknown. In a similar manner, the rejection of religious people who engage in speaking-in-tongues by someone who has nothing other than hearsay knowledge of the phenomena is suspect because of a lack of in-depth information.

But even if an individual has a wide range of experiences, there is no guarantee that the information in those experiences will actually be absorbed. The amount of information a person absorbs from a given experience is very small. This can be illustrated by showing a short film of an accident and asking the viewers to report what they saw. In the analysis by Marquis, Oskamp, and Marshall (quoted by Wrightsman, 1972), the amount of information reported after viewing a short film was no more than 20 percent of the information they could have gained from the film. Without systematic procedures to guarantee that all the relevant information is actually brought to bear on the decision, judgments reached by people will be far from perfect.

Even when the appropriate information is available for an accurate decision, the judgment reached may not be appropriate because the information may not be comprehended at an appropriate level. Man's limited comprehension is particularly notable when comparing a child with an adult. As Piaget first pointed out, ten year old children are able to work with concrete propositions but are unable to utilize formal operations in their thought processes. This means that a child of ten can understand simple arithmetic or "do's and don'ts" but cannot possibly integrate information in the same manner that a college student might in a course in abstract algebra or that would be required to apply the agape principle across a wide range of situations.

The ability of the child to process ethical problems is also noticeably less than that of the adult (Kohlberg, 1968, 1969; Turiel, 1969). When a child is presented with an argument which requires a more mature reasoning process than that which he is currently using, he is unable to reproduce the process. In attempting to reproduce the argument, he simplifies it down to his own level of thinking. Therefore, the conclusions reached by a child at a lower level of moral thinking cannot replicate those of an adult at a more mature level of thinking even if they both have the same data.

The analysis of the differences between children and adults points out that a person at a lower level of reasoning cannot be expected to understand a higher level of reasoning. To understand the possible limits of adult thinking, the analysis can be extrapolated by postulating a hypothetical being whose judgmental powers are a level or two higher than man's level of reasoning, just as an adult's reasoning is at a higher level than a child's. When an adult heard the reasoning of the hypothetical creature, he might reject or accept the conclusion but he would not be able to understand it. But man's lack of comprehension due to his finitude would not prevent the hypothetical being's judgment from being better than man's. Therefore no man should be surprised if he cannot comprehend part of the infinite universe or the decisions of God. Man should only be surprised if any of his equally finite brothers speaks as if he were capable of understanding God and the infinite.

Improper conclusions reached because an individual fails to comprehend the information at hand is a dangerous situation because that individual seldom realizes that a poor judgment has been reached. The child who reproduces a higher thinking process by restating it according to his own more primitive processes actually feels that he has reproduced the heart of the argument. *Since a person's judgments will often be faulty even with the best of information, and since he still feels they are correct, it is apparent that any conclusion reached by any finite individual should be viewed skeptically.*

### The Accuracy of Man's Finite Judgments

Recognizing that man's judgmental powers are finite is only the beginning of the analysis, for man may not realize the degree to which his judgments are limited. While it would be possible for man to restrict his judgments to those situations where even his finite powers are adequate, the evidence suggests that this is not always the case. It may not be necessary to go so far as Karl Barth and deny the possibility of theological knowledge by man, but it does appear apparent that many people have more confidence in their ability to reach decisions than is warranted by the data.

The accuracy of man's judgmental powers can be analyzed in a simple situation, such as determining who should be admitted to graduate school. To evaluate potential students, a graduate department has a committee rate the applicants as to their potential for scholarly endeavors. These ratings should, hopefully, be relatively good predictors of student success in graduate school. The graduate departments seem to think so and they assume that the quality of the prediction from individual ratings is much better than that which would be obtained by a simple mathematical formula involving such elements as undergraduate grade point average and scores from the Graduate Record Exam. So far, psychologists have been unable to find data to document this assumption. Dawes (1972) summarizes several studies where the ratings by individuals have been compared with sophisticated statistical procedures and goes on in his study to use a very simple statistical procedure. He found that even the simple statistical procedure does better than almost all of the individuals who attempt this task. An occasional person does about as well as the simple mathematical procedure for selecting graduate students, but no one does much better. And yet man's confidence in his own judgmental processes are such that faculties continue to waste time making decisions that could be made at least as well by a statistical clerk.

The fact that people's judgments are not as accurate as they suppose is not limited to graduate faculties. Research on the general accuracy of man's judgment about other people suggests that the degree of accurate perception is not great. A typical example of the problems involved in the accuracy of interpersonal perception is given in Crow and Hammond (1957). One of their conclusions was that interpersonal perception is highly influenced by response sets, that is, the respondents in the study based their ratings primarily on the stereotypes that they had for man in general and not on the characteristics of the person being rated. The respondent's view of the nature of mankind therefore contaminated his judgments of other people, even though most people feel that their judgments of others are relatively good.

These illustrations from judgments made about others underscore the point that human judgment is finite to a degree not comprehended by the average person. Since judgments about the nature of mankind have generally been made on the same basis as judgments about other people, it is apparent that some of the conclusions about mankind may also reflect the scholar's stereotypes more than the scholar's subject matter.

### Accuracy of Judgment: Man's Personal Involvement

One major factor limiting a scholar or layman's judgments is his personal involvement in the situation. For proper judgments to be made, man must be able to step outside his motivational involvements. But at this point man's finite nature again limits him, and he is unable to transcend himself sufficiently to make judgments without his own perspectives interfering.

Even very simple tasks show that mankind is unable to transcend himself in reaching judgments. In a series of studies discussed by Sherif and Sherif (1969, pp. 340-344), Sherif and his associates have investigated how people judge single sentence statements. The task was a relatively simple one. Each person was asked to sort a set of sentences about blacks by placing each statement on an eleven point scale. One end of the scale was to be used for those items which were pro-Black, the other end for those items which were anti-Black, and the points in-between for sentences that were neither completely pro-Black nor anti-Black.

How the items were actually placed varied as a function of the judge's personal involvement with racial issues, as can be seen in Figure II-1. The extreme items, A-5 and A-6, were seen by all judges as anti- and pro-Negro, respectively. The middle items, B-1 and A-16 in Figure II-1, were judged differently by the three sets of judges. Some judges were relatively uninvolved and were neither strong pro- nor anti-Black; they scattered sentences B-1 and A-16 almost equally across the eleven point scale. But the judges who were pro-Black placed the middle items, B-1

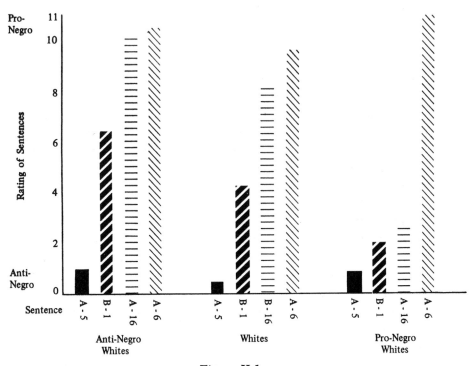

Figure II-1

and A-16, in the anti-Black section; those who were anti-Black placed the same middle sentences in the pro-Black section. The judgments reached by the personally involved judges therefore followed the principle "if it isn't for us, it must be against us," and saw relatively neutral items as being against their own positions. This phenomena will come as no surprise to those who have been in the middle of a church feud; the moderate runs a real danger of being rejected by people at both of the extremes.

The major advantage the personally involved individual might have in reaching a decision involves his more extensive command of information on the topic. If this is so, the personally involved individual naturally has a greater opportunity to arrive at a better conclusion *if* his personal involvement does not cause him to selectively ignore part of the available information. But if the same information is available to all—which we shall generally assume to be true throughout this discussion—then the nonpersonally involved individual will be the better judge since there is no need for him to transcend his desires.

The effects of one's own position on his decision are hard to avoid, even for professionals who have the possibility of collecting the same amount of information. In Sullivan's (1971) study of psychiatric judgments on whether a person was qualified to return to combat duty, it was found that the decision was a definite function of the psychiatrist's orientation towards military life and combat. Psychiatrists who thought that winning the war was important saw more men as fit for combat than did those who were less favorably disposed towards military activities.

The effect of a person's expectations and values on his judgments means a woman may be less qualified to judge whether an abortion is the best course of action than a man who has the same information. Or the person who believes that God has a message for him may be the person least qualified to judge what the message might be. Likewise, those who feel strongly that events recorded in the New Testament are "only allegories" may be those least qualified to engage in demythologizing activities to test that hypothesis.

The seriousness of judgmental distortions from personal involvements can be reduced by following appropriate procedures. The primary procedure is to establish an objective decision rule which can be applied by another individual who does not have a strong personal involvement in the area. The appropriate data are then passed to this individual who applies the decision rule. The person doing the judging should not know any extraneous information which could unduly influence his decision. In medical research, objectivity in evaluating the effects from a new drug is increased by the "double-blind" procedure. Half of the patients are given a new drug and half are given a placebo which has no physiological effect. The patients' reactions to the drug are then recorded by the attending physician. However, the personal involvement of either the physician or the patient could produce a noticeable difference between the reports of the effectiveness of the drug and the placebo. Therefore the doctor engaged in such research has another individual determine which patients are going to receive the drug so that the impact of the personal involvement of the doctor and patient will not influence their estimates of the drug's effects.

Society needs more uninvolved judges to help reflect on the proper course of action to be followed in almost every situation. Those directly related to a situation, which includes both policy makers and administrators, are generally those whose decisions are most likely to be distorted by their personal involvement. However, individuals who have less personal involvement but equal amounts of information are more likely to come to accurate decisions. This suggests that there is a definite role in society for scholars such as theological ethicists who stand outside of society's institutions, provided that they spend considerable time gathering information.

But the ethicist is also human and may have such deep personal commitments that his judgment is also limited. I believe that a study of history would show that ministers, for example, have often reached different conclusions about bombing cities in different wars depending upon their own political stand and the political stand of the enemy. When the enemy is a fascist dictatorship, then it is easy for a minister with liberal political views to argue that fighting that dictatorship is a worthwhile task despite the cost in innocent lives. On the other hand, a minister with conservative political views will find it easy to argue that a communist dictatorship should be fought despite the cost in innocent lives. Most ministers' views on most wars appear to be primarily a function of their political stand rather than an objective analysis of the ethics involved.

To reduce the influence of personal involvement, an analysis probably would be required where objective criteria would be systematically applied to other historical situations to determine if the procedures achieve their goals despite personal involvements. The procedures that were found to be trustworthy would then be applied blindly to the present situation by an individual who did not know he was judging the present situation. The resulting evaluation would be relatively free of distortions from personal involvement.

### Accuracy of Judgment: the Finiteness of the Situation

Since finite man has limited capabilities for comprehending and processing the data necessary for accurate judgments, one corollary is that his judgments decrease in accuracy as the situation transcends his finite capabilities. When the situation is also finite, i.e. concrete and well defined, then man's judgments will be more accurate than when the situation is more abstract and involves the integration of many factors. This principal is, as is true of most of the others being discussed here, obvious in extreme cases. (Sherif and Sherif (1969, pp. 51-60) provide research examples of where the reactions to abstract stimuli are determined by miscellaneous factors.)

But the importance of the principle is not obvious when cases are not so extreme. In one study, we were asked to analyze materials from seminary students who were working in a Chicago ghetto during a summer. Each student had kept a log of his experiences which was passed on to us. The logs were not concrete but neither were they highly abstract. It would seem relatively simple to read these logs and make decisions on how they were adapting to and benefiting by their experience. It was, however, virtually impossible. When we established several scales and had several raters go through the materials, we found major disagreements between the raters. What one person saw happening in one situation was entirely different from the way another individual interpreted the same events. Since each rater's interpretation seemed logical, we would not have known the impossibility of our task unless we had checked the results by empirical methods.

The effect of the abstractness of the situation on the judgment reached can be illustrated by another example.* Asking anyone to define Fuller Theological Seminary as a concrete physical entity is asking a question to which most would give reasonably accurate answers. They would agree as to the location of the Seminary, its size, and so forth. But asking the meaning of Fuller Theological Seminary as a theological community serving God is asking an abstract question to which many answers would be given, and for which it is next to impossible to know what the right answer would be or if one even exists.

If the task is not sufficiently finite, then all accuracy of judgment may vanish even though the judges may not realize that is so. The Rorschach, better known as the ink blot test, produces responses which are almost as abstract in meaning as the ink blots themselves. Holtzman and Sells (1954) asked some of the nation's best Rorschach interpreters to separate out the flyers who had been grounded for psychiatric reasons from flyers who were known to be well adjusted. The Rorschach experts were unable to do so at above chance level. This is unfortunate, since many psychologists still believe that their judgments based upon the Rorschach will produce better than chance classification in just such situations. Mankind does not realize that the situation needs to be very finite indeed before his judgment is adequate. If the situation is not obviously concrete and well structured, then any judgments will need to be validated with other data before they can be considered anything but speculative.

---

*Personal experiences—whether in life, clinic, or lab—are not proofs of any principle since they are too open to the problems of human judgment, particularly personal involvement. The role of personal experiences is that of suggesting hypotheses and of illustrating principles established on more rigorous grounds.

### Finite Judgments About Finite Judgments

The previous discussion has underlined the fact that man's finitude means he often errs in his judgments. The fact that his judgment is better when the situation is finite has been noted along with situations where his judgment departs from perfection, as when he is personally involved. The problem is further complicated since man's judgments *about* his judgments are at least as fallible as the judgments themselves.

Finite man's judgments about the quality of his judgments may even be more fallible than the initial judgments. This is suggested by the two confounding influences upon judgments that were noted earlier. First, a person is personally involved in the evaluations of his judgments because society uses the success of a person's judgment as a criterion for rewarding and punishing him. A minister may be relieved of his duties because he erred by recommending building a new educational plant when it was not needed; it is easier for him to blame a change in the cultural climate than it is to accept it as a personal error.

The second reason that judgments about judgments are usually difficult to make is that they are often more abstract than the original judgments. Since we have already noted that the accuracy of judgments decreases as the situation becomes less concrete, judgments about judgments will generally be more inaccurate than the original judgment.

Since man has difficulty in separating out good judgments from bad judgments, he often does not realize he is making sense in a situation where it is not possible for him to come to an accurate conclusion. The propensity of man to integrate meaningless data is found in a study of personality test interpretation (Forer, 1949). A group of college students were given a personality test and their scores on the test were, they thought, passed back to them. Actually, the results from the personality test which were returned to the students were identical for each student and unrelated to any of their responses. Instead, they were the same type of statement that a fortune teller might make. Each student was then asked his opinion of how well the personality data integrated with his own view of himself. With only a few exceptions, they all felt that the description given them was extremely good.

The ability to make sense out of nonsense—and the inability to recognize that it is happening—is not restricted to undergraduates. Armstrong and Soelberg (1968) factor analyzed meaningless data with randomly assigned labels. They found the results were easily interpreted by most psychologists, a conclusion with which I concurred on looking at the results. A further example is in a recent analysis of data we collected about peer group effects on children's values. That analysis showed that the values of lower class black males had been more affected by their peers than had the values of other children. An interpretation of the data readily came to mind. However, on checking further, the significant effect was found to be the result of an extra number accidentally punched in one card before the data analysis was conducted.

In my years of processing data, I have seen several judgments based on incorrect analyses. In every case, the psychologist involved was able to interpret the data quite well until the error was uncovered, and then he was able to interpret the corrected analysis equally well. I fully expect that any graduate student who is qualified to become a psychologist will be able to develop a reasonable interpretation of random labels assigned to meaningless data; from my seminary experiences, I expect most theologians would be able to pass such a test readily if the labels were theological instead of psychological.

If the data is nonsense, then the pattern being interpreted will not repeat itself, that is, a pattern found in one set of data will not appear in another set of data. Therefore the scientist reduces the possibility of making sense out of nonsense by collecting a new set of data to test his earlier interpretation.

The problem of making sense out of nonsense may be critical for Biblical form criticism since that area has only one set of data and therefore cannot confirm interpretations by new data. Finding patterns in any data is to be expected by chance. It is therefore likely that some Biblical scholars are coming to conclusions that could only be reached if they had special revelations from God.

For examples, II Corinthians has been subdivided into a series of "original epistles." The subdivision often hinges upon the style and pattern of comments Paul makes in one section of the letter versus the style and pattern of comments that he makes in another. To make such decisions requires that the data have a high degree of accuracy. This is only true if Paul was an unusually careful and consistent letter writer. If he was only an average to above average letter writer, then he would have occasionally misphrased his statement, returned to earlier arguments after going on a tangent, and so forth. In addition, he was dictating to a scribe. When the scribe got behind in dictation, he might, as many secretaries do, write the gist of what Paul had said but with a few of his own words and phrases. This would produce definite changes in style and explain, for example, why six words appear in II Corinthians 6:14-7:1 that are not found elsewhere in Paul's writings.

Biblical scholars who wish to hinge interpretations on a few critical verses must recognize that the chances are extremely good that they are making sense out of nonsense. They should expect no other scholar to take them seriously until they have shown that they can accurately analyze, for example, present day letters pastors have written to churches. Until scholars do so, there is no reason for anyone to believe that they are engaged in any endeavor other than making sense out of nonsense.

Biblical scholars may be fortunate in that it is difficult to prove that they are making sense out of nonsense; other scholars have not been so fortunate since their fields have advanced to the point to where it is apparent that they have been making sense out of nonsense. For centuries, astronomers saw canals on Mars. Since the close-up photographs of Mars show no canals, it appears that they were interpreting random distortions in their view of Mars. As noted previously, psychologists interpreted Rorschachs for years before learning that the data are unrelated to the main task for which the Rorschach was recommended.

Making sense out of nonsense appears to be another case of assuming mankind's judgmental powers are more infinite than what they actually are. As would be expected from the discussion above, accurate judgments about judgments are likely only if concrete information on the quality of a person's judgments are available and if the person judging that quality is not personally involved in the outcome.

### Conclusion

The general conclusion is that man's finitude limits his judgment, and that the limits are greatest where the data are abstract and where the judge is personally involved, i.e. in areas such as theology. Since man evaluates his own judgments, he often does not know when his judgment is faulty. The impact of man's finitude on his judgments suggests that an apologetic by a believer for the infinite nature of an infinite god can seldom be taken seriously. The highly abstract nature of the topic suggests that the chances are extremely slim that any valid judgments could be made in the area. Indeed, based upon the ability of man to reach valid decisions, it could be argued that theology needs to be restricted to the analysis of religious experiences and Biblical content. The development of theological systems would be a questionable enterprise because it is impossible not to be personally involved and because of the highly abstract nature of the analysis.

### FINITE MAN IN AN INFINITE UNIVERSE

Man is finite and therefore has limited judgmental powers, but it is obvious that the world in which man lives requires that he make complex decisions regardless of his ability to do so. Man cannot decide to ignore the environmental effects of the use of pesticides simply because he cannot understand all of the aspects of their use. Neither can man afford to remain undecided about the existence of Christ, for not making a decision is as influential in what he believes and how he lives as is deciding to accept Jesus as Christ. Man's existential situation does not allow him the luxury of being agnostic, for no decision often means a different course is followed than if a choice had been made.

Man is involved in such existential predicaments not only in the area of theology but in all areas of life as well. Science is only now beginning to understand how deeply it is influenced by its own world view, a view which is needed because scientists confront decisions which cannot be made on the basis of their data.

## SCIENTIFIC PARADIGMS AND THEOLOGICAL WORLD VIEWS AS AIDS FOR FINITE MAN*

Kuhn (1962) has provided an interesting analysis of the function of scientific theory as an aid for a finite man in a world too complex for him to fully comprehend. He stresses that the usual view of the scientific construct being proposed, tested by data, and accepted or rejected on the base of that data is not correct. Instead, a set of constructs is better conceived of as a "paradigm" for research rather than a theory to be tested. A paradigm integrates the same data as a theory but its constructs have uses and functions which are independent of the truth value of the paradigm and which often determine when the paradigm is accepted or rejected.

A prime purpose of a scientific paradigm is to organize the data so that it can be absorbed by a finite mind. For that reason, a theory integrates the major verified conclusions in the area as simply as possible. This simple integration is then used as a communication device and to simplify the phenomena so scientists can understand it.

In order to integrate "the major verified conclusions," it is necessary to develop a decision rule to separate important from unimportant data. Therefore a second purpose of a paradigm is to identify that which is relevant. But since what is relevant is defined by the paradigm, the nature of the data shifts as the paradigms and theories shift. For example, the original chemical studies of carbon dioxide did not show two elements of oxygen for every element of carbon. Instead, the ratio of carbon to

*The ease with which a person generates judgments outside his area of competence can be illustrated by the development of these lectures. I spent six hours outlining why man utilizes world views before the realization came that I was far exceeding the psychological knowledge currently available. Without data from history, psychology, or some other discipline to act as a corrective, there was no guarantee that the constructs I was building had any relationship to reality.

oxygen varied widely, and would be 1.47 to one in one study and 2.4 to one in another. It was only after the ratio theory became accepted as a general paradigm that the chemical litera- ture started carrying values such as two to one. Even today, experiments carefully done seldom give the value of two to one exactly, an experience to which most students who have taken a chemistry lab will testify. But with the introduction of the paradigm, the data were reorganized and experiments which do not give the "proper result" are no longer reported.

Not only does a paradigm serve to select and integrate existing data, it is also an aid for deciding what research to pursue. A finite scientist confronted with an infinite universe must select both the problems to be examined and how to attack them. Such a selection process requires a prior view of what the relevant variables are and how they might relate. A paradigm provides a perspective for the scientist which allows him to make necessary decisions in spite of his finitude.

Scientific paradigms have interesting parallels to religious world views and the task of theology, but differ since they are not as abstract. A close reading of Kuhn shows that paradigms bear a striking resemblance to Hare's (1955) "bliks" and Hick's (1966) "total interpretations." All are concerned with abstract integrations of mankind's past experiences to help him relate meaningfully to his present and future experiences. However, philosophical and theological world views are more abstract than a scientific paradigm since they have the task of integrating both the scientific paradigms and religious experience. Not only is this a more difficult task because more elements are involved, it is more difficult because it is more abstract than scientific data. As an integration becomes more abstract, it is, of course, more diffi- cult to reach valid judgments.

Although the development of a world view seems critical for most people, and no world view is complete without an examina- tion of man's role in it, psychologists have yet to analyze the role of world views or scientific paradigms for behavior. In the little research that has been done, few relationships have been found between a person's attitude towards people and how they respond in actual situations (Wrightsman, 1972a). However, the major differences between behavioristic psychologists such as Skinner and the humanistic psychology movements appear to be in their world views, which suggests that these broader constructs influence how man conducts his science.

## Judging Paradigms and World Views

Because man must make decisions even though he is unsure of his judgments, scientists appear to need to choose among paradigms and men appear to need to choose among world views. Since judgment is faulty in these matters, alternative paradigms and world views are usually available. With competing positions and man's finite judgmental powers, how is man to decide among the possibilities so as to maximize the number of elements in his own world view which are correct or useful?

Deciding among several scientific paradigms is partially a function of their truth value, as Kuhn pointed out. A paradigm will generally be challenged when a body of experience gathers which is not easily integrated into that paradigm. The scientific paradigm is therefore highly dependent upon and open to data. In this manner, scientists explicitly recognize that the paradigm itself may be faulty and seek to correct it by procedures which, from our previous analysis of the problems of human judgment, have a reasonable likelihood of leading to improved judgments.

In discussing theological world views, the usual criteria suggested are consistency, coherency and simplicity (e.g. Yandell, 1971, p. 220), and it appears that, unlike science, a major theological emphasis is on consistency. For example, paradoxes in a philosophical or theological system are generally deemed sufficient evidence to seriously question that system. However, paradoxes are not unusual in scientific theories and are a matter for less concern. Everyone knows that a theory constructed by finite man can be neither complete nor perfect, and a paradox stands as testimony to that fact.

The tolerance of paradox within scientific theories is consistent with the emphasis in science that the paradigm be relevant to the data. Paradoxes arise because two sets of data are examined in slightly different ways and lead to two different conclusions. In keeping the paradox within the theory and openly recognizing it, the scientific paradigm remains true to its data at the cost of consistency.

On the basis of the implications of man's finitude for human judgment, it would seem that theology needs to be reoriented. Criteria such as consistency and simplicity should be less important than the ability of theology to organize relevant experience for mankind. Such an emphasis would require further discussion of the exact subject matter of theology. Some may wish to hold it only to Biblical analysis, but such a move would restrict its ability to organize contemporary religious and non-religious life. It would seem that all of God's interactions with man, including contemporary religious experience, should be part of the data for a theological world view.

Perhaps the psychology of religion could provide some of the necessary data for new theological analyses. Indeed, I suspect that theologians could readily construct a list of psychological questions that should be asked, particularly questions concerning how well different religious views integrate and direct life in the contemporary world. Such interdisciplinary endeavors should prove most interesting, but would require that all concerned explicitly recognize the finitude of human judgment. Such a recognition would demand a readiness to revise ancient and contemporary traditions.

The reasons for adding a psychological perspective to discussions about the nature of man are now more apparent. The nature of man is an abstract problem and one with which scholars can be assumed to be personally involved. Therefore the concepts about man must also fall under the restriction on man's judgmental powers. Since it seems apparent that concepts of man are necessary as part of a person's world view, philosophers and theologians will continue to analyze human nature. But since these scholars are also finite, their judgments need the continuing corrective that can be provided by the science of psychology. Cooperating together, psychologists, theologians and philosophers may be able to help finite man live in an infinite universe.

## CHAPTER III

# Man and Man

RICHARD L. GORSUCH

## THE INFLUENCE OF MAN ON MAN

TO SAY THAT MAN is a social creature is, technically, to say nothing new since "no man is an island" and other such phrases are common. Therefore a discussion of the nature of man would be incomplete without considering his social characteristics. Since the importance of man's social relationships can be assumed, the question is not whether others are important in a person's life but the magnitude of that importance. It may well be that the concept of man as a part of society is so trite that its meaning is forgotten and the pervasiveness of its effect is overlooked.

### Social Influences on Decisions

The importance of a person's being part of a group can be readily seen through the analysis of all types of decisions. The most likely time for a group effect on decisions is when the situation is abstract and complex. In such situations, a person may not trust his own judgment but may rely more extensively on the judgments of others. In more concrete situations, the social influences should be minimal.

Asch (1951) conducted a set of classical studies which showed the impact of groups on clear-cut decisions. In these studies, each participant was asked to match the length of a given line with one of three unequal lines. The drawings were sufficiently clear so that only a few people would have a problem in reaching the correct judgment. But when the other members of a group were instructed to publicly announce an obviously wrong match, one-third of the subjects selected the line the group said was right instead of the correct line. That is, the group influence distorted some people's decision even in a concrete situation.

Perhaps another effect was even more important in Asch's research: the conforming individuals appeared convinced that their publicly stated erroneous choice was correct. Other research (Tuddenham and McBride, 1959) also found that conformers often saw themselves as *not* conforming to the group. These studies suggest that *man cannot trust his own judgment about the extent of group influence upon his decisions for he will underestimate his dependence upon others.*

The rate of conformity to a group increases as the situation becomes more ambiguous. While the initial conformity rate is one-third, the number of conformers increases as the unequal lines become closer in length. If a variety of types of judgment are made, it appears almost everyone conforms to the group decision part of the time.

The above experiments were in a psychological laboratory but the impact of group pressure in decisions and behavior occurs outside the laboratory as well. In real life, people are involved in varying degrees in groups around them and their decisions reflect it. If a critical activity develops where the individual needs to decide whether he will participate in it, his decision will be principally a function of his group's decision. If they are in favor of the activity, then he will tend to participate. If they are not in favor of the activity and do not participate themselves, then the individual is less likely to participate as well. Only if the individual is a social isolate, i.e. not a member of any group concerned with the particular issue, does he appear to make the decision solely on the ground of his own needs.

Real life group effects are illustrated in a study of an apartment complex by Festinger, Schachter, and Back (1950). They identified several types of individuals in an apartment complex, such as group members who had a network of friendships within the apartments and social isolates who had only lived there a short time. The participation of each type of individual in the tenants' organization, which made decisions for the entire apartment complex, was evaluated. The social isolates decided whether or not to participate on the basis of how long they expected to remain in the apartment complex but the length of time group members expected to remain was unrelated to their participation. Those who were a part of groups which favored active participation in the tenants' organization participated. Those whose friends did not favor the organization tended not to participate. It is interesting to note that the friendships appeared to be primarily a function of who lived close to each other and were, therefore, relatively accidental in nature. The social isolates were those whose living quarters tended to cut them off from the other people in the apartment complex. Since the groups were not formed on the basis of beliefs and values but rather on accidental physical arrangements, the effects on participation in the tenants' organization appear to be a result of norms developed within the group rather than a function of associating only with people with the same views. The people, therefore, functioned as members of groups and not independently.

The fact that man continually makes his decisions in at least an implicit group context can be further illustrated by the work of Latané and Darley (1970). Their research shows that the direction and the extent of an implicit group effect is not always predictable nor is it always desirable. Their studies were concerned with identifying the conditions under which a person in obvious trouble is helped by a bystander. Fortunately, helping others in trouble is an almost universal human value. If an individual knows that another person is in serious need of help and is relying on him, that individual invariably helps the other person. But what if the person needing help is in a group setting? If that is the case, the influences on the bystander's decision become more complex.

Latané and Darley set up an experiment where one person was obviously in need but where either the bystander was the only one who could know of the person's need or where the bystander was one of several who could know of the need. Table III-I summarizes the results. Whereas the helping rates were high

TABLE 3.1.   PERCENT OF PEOPLE RECEIVING HELP AS A FUNCTION OF THE NUMBER OF BYSTANDERS

| Experiment | One Bystander | Several Bystanders |
|---|---|---|
| Reporting Smoke | 75% | 38% |
| Helping injured woman | 70% | 40% |
| Reporting person having seizure | 100% | 62% |

(Adapted from Latené & Darley, 1970)

when the bystander thought he was the only one who knew of the situation, the helping rate was considerably less when several bystanders were there who could help. Indeed, the chances are often less than 50-50 that a person having a serious problem would be helped if there were several people around; it seems that each person assumes that someone else in the group will take the leadership in offering the needed help. The influence of others on a bystander's decision may therefore be undesirable to a person who is in serious need of help. It is this type of social influence that stresses both the importance of man's social nature and the need for an informed theological ethics which is aware of the pervasiveness of social influence.

The social effect may also be such as to encourage a deviant response, and that effect may often be stronger than any personal norms the individual brings to the situation. After extensive and thorough investigations of deceitful behavior by children in real life situations where they did not know they were being observed, Hartshorne and May (1928) found little support for the impact of personal norms on behavior. Instead, they concluded that the only important determinant of children's deciding to cheat was the nature of their social group. If the classroom climate, as formed by both the teacher and children, encouraged deceitful behavior, then children chose to cheat. If the climate discouraged deceitful behavior, then decisions for honesty were made. Hartshorne and May also concluded that behavior oriented toward

helping others (Hartshorne, May and Maller, 1929) was a function of social influence and not personal norms. To the extent
that group norms determine a person's decisions, it is impossible
to speak of an individual's values or norms; it is only possible to
speak of the values and norms of the group of which he is
a part.

### Social Influences on Personal Norms

Even if personal norms do play a minor part in behavior,
those norms themselves are a function of group effects. Using
children in the same setting as Hartshorne and May, we have
found that children absorb norms differentially according to their
peer groups. Figure III-1 shows the effects of the child's peer
group upon his norm development. The lines give the scores for
children who scored below the teacher on a values scale. The
graph shows most children to be considerably lower than the
teacher in September, but closer to her after a one-semester experience in her classroom. This change is expected from a social-
psychological perspective. Experience in a social setting dominated by one individual will tend to shift the other participant's
values and norms towards that of the dominant individual.

Children who maintained their own normative system were

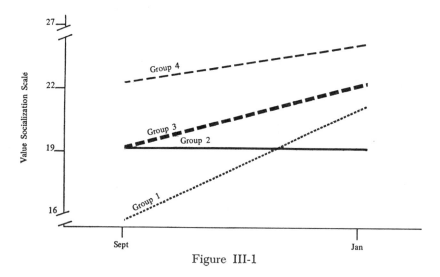

Figure III-1

only able to hold to their values because they received other social support. The mean values for these children are also plotted in Figure III-1 as Group 2. Although they had essentially the same initial scores as did some of the other children, they did not change over the semester. The reason they did not change is that their playmates had norms deviating from the teacher and provided social support for the child's deviant values. Therefore, the degree to which a person accepts or does not accept a new value is also a function of his social environment. He does not accept the value on the basis of an independent decision, but accepts the values for which he has social support.

The groups which influence a child's values are often formed independently of the child's values. While the reason for the children of Figure III-1 choosing the peer group that they did is not known, further analysis did show that the group choice was almost unrelated to the child's values. Therefore, one can not say the children deliberately selected a group which would encourage and maintain their own values. Instead, they seem to have picked their associates on other grounds, such as availability. The children were probably unaware that their choice of playmates also had long term effects on their value development.

The effects of a person's network of associates on his attitudes and values have been well documented for older people as well as children. In several studies (e.g. Newcomb, et al., 1967; Siegel and Siegel, 1957) college students have been followed for several years to identify how and when their values change. It appears that the major conclusions of these studies can be summarized in terms of the effects by the peer group. College students shift their values towards those groups of which they are a member, just like a chameleon changes its colors to fit its environment. College students are not, it must be remembered, individuals who are in a state of normlessness or who are necessarily searching for identity; they are simply people going to college who happened to room with or associate with a few other students. The students seem unaware that their values are shifting to match the group of which they are a member.

It can be argued that college students change values rapidly because they really have no values; however, commitment to a strong value system, such as occurs among religious people, does not free a person from the effect of the group. Festinger, Riecken and Schachter (1956) report an interesting analysis of people committed to a religious value system. The people were members of a sect which believed the city in which they lived was going to be destroyed by a flood, but that they would be saved before the flood occurred. The strength of the belief system is shown by the fact that they continued with their plans even though the newspapers discovered the group and gave them adverse coverage. Naturally, the major disaster they predicted did not occur.

The response of individual members of the sect to the nonfulfillment of their beliefs was a function of the group they were with during a crucial period. When the flood did not appear, those who had not joined the others to await the predicted flood did not have social support during the critical period immediately following the predicted time of the disaster and lost all their beliefs in the religious system. Those who were waiting together for the occurrence of the flood quickly made a shift in their ideology through a "new revelation." They were able to maintain their belief system with only a minor shift because of the social support they provided for each other. However, those who remained together appeared to need more social support for their beliefs than they could provide for each other. To gain that support, they became highly evangelistic and attempted to convert others to their position. Inasmuch as they convinced others of the validity of their position, they then received further social support for their beliefs.

The major impact of an individual's social relationships upon his values and behavior suggests that ethics need to be viewed as a group function. The division between individual and social ethics is artificial since the nature of man allows little but social ethics. The only distinction within the area of ethics that can be made is between the social ethics of small groups and the social ethics of a large group such as a society. Discussing individuals who face an ethical dilemma alone, which is the usual case studied in ethics, is to consider a creature not known to exist. Instead, an individual who is in a true moral dilemma will be interacting with other people, and those interactions will be crucial to his decision. In the rare case where the decision is made in solitude, the average person will make his decision on the basis of how he thinks the significant others in his life would make the decision.

In concluding that personal norms play a minor role compared to the group norms, the social psychologist is not basing his analysis upon what people feel they are doing, but upon what they are actually doing. Ethics as normally practiced may well describe what an individual feels is happening but that, of course, is not important if what he actually does is a function of other variables. A valid and non-trivial ethics needs to examine the variables affecting a decision and help the person come to terms with the actual influences upon him, especially the social influences.

## Man's Need for Social Support

With man so intimately involved with his fellow man, one would expect serious conditions to be noted if research on individuals cut off from their social support could be conducted. This would be a critical test for evaluating whether mankind is truly a social creature or whether he happens to have accidentally fallen into a social way of life. Because of the difficulties in conducting appropriate research, no clear evidence exists on what happens when man's social supports are removed. In every known society, men always choose to associate with one another and to maintain systems of social support. Therefore, it is not possible to observe mankind existing under long term conditions of no social support.

A few situations have been observed where people had less social support than is normally the case. For example, some children are placed in nursing homes at an early age. Either because these homes have insufficient personnel due to a lack of funds or because they feel that babies do not need the social contacts which others might desire, situations have occurred where only the physical needs of the child have been met. In those cases, the children are definitely handicapped in their further development (e.g. Goldfarb, 1943; Bowlby, 1952). Indeed, the death rate in such institutions is often considerably higher than in institutions where the babies have someone to fondle and handle them.

While the effects of institutions on babies may be simply due to the lack of stimulation, the experimental results with monkeys suggest that the future social relations of children without early social contact may be seriously impaired (Harlow, 1962). Monkeys who had only their physical needs taken care of but who were cut off from others of their kind were unable to form adequate sexual relationships in adulthood. Therefore, monkeys as a species would not survive unless baby monkeys have extensive interpersonal contact. While not wishing to equate mankind with monkeykind, we have no evidence to suggest that man would be able to form the meaningful social relationships necessary to continue the race if he were cut off from early social contact.

On a more subjective basis, other evidence suggests that being cut off from social support is a damaging factor in a person's life. A person who travels abroad has some culture shock when he enters a new society due to the strangeness of their customs. However, he quickly associates with others of his kind or makes friendships within that society, and thus regains his social support. When returning to his home country, the culture shock seems to be greater than that experienced when entering a foreign culture. I would suggest that this occurs because the individual comes back to a setting where his friends and associates have moved in different directions than he has. He therefore lacks the social support he expects until he reestablishes his old friendships, a process which takes time. For this reason, returning prisoners of war as well as Baptist Journeymen coming out of the mission field seem to have more problems with their own goals and identity than their associates who were not POW's or in the mission field.

## Conclusion

The fact that people are deeply intertwined with each other

has not been as widely recognized as it should be. The mystical, existentialist and fundamentalist traditions are faulty to the degree to which they feel that man can believe for himself. While it is obviously true that each man must die for himself, few men ever believe for themselves. Individualistic traditions probably need to give expanded treatment to the community of faith. The social nature of man also suggests that understanding the general culture of the first century and the nature of the early church is critical to a proper understanding of the New Testament.

The shift in emphasis from man to men may become crucial for salvation theories. Instead of asking how one man comes into the faith, the discussions need to be concerned with how families, groups of friends, co-workers, or students living in a common dorm on a college campus are converted.

The social nature of mankind is a construct needing thorough exploration by anyone who would seek to understand the human species. Indeed, it may be that one should not talk of the nature of *man*, but, instead, should talk of the nature of *men*.

## MAN'S INHUMANE TREATMENT OF MAN

Having established that people are intimately interwoven and dependent upon each other, the nature of man's treatment of his fellows can be explored. Is mankind such that people respect and help others? Or do men characteristically seek to take advantage of others for their personal profit?

If the question of whether men are humane toward their fellows is evaluated solely on the basis of mankind's behavior, the question is not open to debate. Given man's history of wars, it is apparent that man can be and often is inhumane to man. The fact that the individual man can be equally brutal is proven by each news report as well as by the national crime statistics. Man certainly treats his fellow man inhumanely on many occasions.

A complete analysis needs to look beyond human behavior to human intentions. Given man's finite judgment, it is likely that some of man's inhumane behavior towards his fellows arises from his errors. If that is the only source of man's evil, then it is unnecessary to call him inhumane except as a further amplification of the meaning of his finitude. On the other hand, it does appear that some of man's inhumane acts arise from a conscious, deliberate attempt to injure others. If this is the case, then labels such as "evil" and "inhumane" are necessary for a complete description of mankind.

Since the current discussion is focused on the psychological nature of man, the term evil is used as a psychological rather than a theological category. To say that man is evil means that man's treatment of his fellow man increases the amount of injustice and injury in the world. Such a decision is independent of the theological problem which defines man as evil because he willfully disobeys God. But since Christian doctrine holds that ethical behavior is intrinsic to obeying God, the psychological analysis may provide data for the theological analysis.

Like many basic questions, determining if man is inhumane in his social relations depends on how the terms are defined. Due to the abstractness of the question, objective decision rules for deciding when a label is to be applied are first required before a psychologist can approach the problem. When objective definitions are given, the next step is to define a threshold level for using terms such as humane, inhumane, good and bad. For example, would we be willing to describe mankind as good if only 20 percent of his intentions towards others fell within the definitional limits of the term? Would we be willing to describe him as good if 50 percent of his intentions fell within the definitional limits? Or would we require that 85, 95, or 100 percent of his intentions be good? It is apparent that different scholars will choose different percentage points for using a term even as they will use different definitions for the terms.

I am approaching the topic as a psychologist and can therefore leave the final decision of whether man is inhumane in his social relations to the philosophers and theologians. The psychologist's task is, instead, to assemble and analyze evidence which might be used once the definitions and the threshold levels for use of the terms have been established within the appropriate discipline.

### Finite Judgments as a Source of Man's Inhumanity

Some of the major incidents of man's inhumane treatment of man are a function of finite judgment as described in the first lecture. Since man's judgments are often wrong, disastrous results can occur.

As already noted, Latané and Darley (1970) have investigated a situation where poor judgment causes problems. Stimulated by the incident in New York where thirty people watched a man take an half an hour to kill Kitty Geneviese, Latané and Darley investigated the conditions under which a bystander helps a person in trouble. The researchers found that society's norms are for one person to help another and that almost everyone follows the norms to the best of his ability. But man's limited abilities to properly evaluate situations cause many people to go unhelped.

The reason why a person in need is ignored is primarily a function of poor judgment on the part of the bystanders. The first judgment which must be made is whether or not the person actually needs help. Despite what seems to be an obvious situation, many people pass by unaware that something unusual is happening. If the bystander does correctly evaluate the situation, then another judgment must be made. The bystander must decide what role he is to play, if any, in helping the person in need. If others are around, most bystanders assume, incorrectly, that someone else is or will shortly respond to the person's need, or that the group will take appropriate action. Since all the bystanders assume someone else will lead, the likelihood of the person receiving help is small. One is therefore wrong to criticize others for not being concerned about individuals in need; the problem lies in a failure to judge correctly the need and is complicated by failures to judge correctly one's own responsibility in that situation.

### Inhumanity and Moral Immaturity

The problem of man's being a source of acts injurious to others is complicated by the fact that some people are morally immature. Because their development has failed, they do not make ethical decisions and treat others justly. Therefore moral immaturity may be a direct cause of inhumane treatment.

In this discussion, the term immaturity is not used to indirectly introduce a specific set of values; immaturity is defined empirically by examining differences between children and adults. If the ethical decisions reached by adults are systematically different from those reached by children, then we define those reached by adults as more mature than those of children. An adult who is still functioning at the children's level is labelled immature.

Growth curves by which immature people can be identified do exist within, for example, the area of moral reasoning processes. In our discussion of the cultural relativity of reasoning processes, we presented Figure I-1. which showed the types of processes used by children at different age levels in two different cultures. In Figure I-1. it was apparent that the older children more typically reasoned in a different way than the younger children.

On the basis of the evidence available (e.g. Turiel, 1969), the less mature reasoning process would be considered amoral or immoral while the more mature method of reasoning would be considered moral or good. The older adolescent and adult takes into account the norms of his society and the basic principles which are represented by those norms. Such norms are usually codified in the legal systems. The child or the immature adult, however, does not yet abstract and systematize ethical principles; he only responds on the basis of his short term gain in the situation. The individual using immature thought processes does not yet have the skills to make decisions which would maximize the good for other people as well as for himself. Inasmuch as adults still use immature modes of thought, their decisions will not be concerned with possible injury to others.

Other such growth curves can also be plotted which show differences in man's treatment of man as a function of maturity. After interviewing English children of several different ages, Bull (1969) was able to score each child for the degree to which he stressed the intrinsic value of life. This value is one which can be considered essential if man's treatment of other men is actually good. The percentage of children who did place a definite stress on the value of life is plotted in Figure III-2. The figure shows that the older children tend to be more concerned about the value of life than are the younger children. Therefore, the value of life shows a growth curve and one can identify immature adults as those whose concept of life is more like a child's than like an adult's.

Inasmuch as ethically immature people are in positions of responsibility, then their amoral decisions will create many problems for others, problems which could be interpreted as evidence for the evil nature of mankind. If one appraises only acts, then the observable behavior of the ethically immature individual will be a strong argument for such constructs as original sin, every man's need for salvation and redemption, and the generally evil nature of man. A judgment of man's nature based upon the apparent intentions of immature people would also support this argument. When talking to a person who uses immature reasoning processes, one is impressed with his concern for his own gain, i.e. his selfishness. And the immature person who has not yet

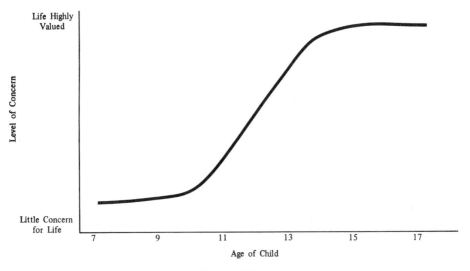

Figure III-2

developed a sense of values will also be seen as having bad intentions. Such data would then support a negative view of mankind.

Evidence for man's inhumane treatment of man which arises from immaturity raises an interesting question: Should we judge man by what some men are, by what men usually are, or by what man can be? If we judge man by what some men are, then serious attention must be given to the immature individual and the decision may be that man is inherently bad. On the other hand, if only those who are mature are examined, the picture shifts. The conclusion would probably be that mankind is basically good. In all likelihood, some of the differences among classical philosophers and theologians on the question of the goodness of man probably arises from their different views of immature adults.

## Is Man Naturally Aggressive?

Still undiscussed is the question of whether mature adults consciously make decisions with the primary intent of injuring other people, i.e. whether man is naturally aggressive. For those who answer "yes," man cannot be considered to be inherently prone to treat his fellows humanely since he has natural aggressive tendencies which override his good impulses. For those who answer "no," man's nature is considered to have a tendency towards being good to his fellow man. Does, then, evidence exist for the view that man is inherently aggressive?

The evidence is certainly strong that aggression can be a learned characteristic. Parents, for example, often learn to be aggressive. A parent of an infant quickly learns that he can control the child extremely well through shouting, hitting, and other acts normally interpreted as aggressive. Fortunately, parents usually distinguish between aggression appropriate towards a young child who "needs" such treatment and others for whom such treatment would be inappropriate. But distinguishing conditions where mild aggression may be appropriate does not always occur, and many instances of child beating have resulted because the parent learned all too well that aggression can work.

Just as a parent learns that aggression against children can be useful, a child growing up can observe that aggression pays for his parents. Learning of aggression may also come from the child's successful experiences of dominating other children. Learning principles underlying such aggression have been long known (e.g. Bandura and Walters, 1963). The learning principles apply equally well to all species; even the gentle dove can be taught to be aggressive by simple Skinnarian procedures.

Johnson (1972) has admirably reviewed the area of aggression and agrees that aggression is often learned. He also points out that virtually all species find patterns of attack biologically adaptive and often necessary to their survival. Such attacks are directed not only at potential prey but also at members of their own species to a degree not commonly recognized.

According to Johnson's review, little evidence exists, outside wars, that people are inherently more aggressive towards their own kind than other animals are. For example, the noble lion will fight other lions even to the death. One male was observed to kill another male who was defending a lioness and a zebra carcass. Cannibalistic murder by lions has also been observed (Johnson, 1972, p. 19). In lower species, such as fish, cannibalism is rampant. There is no evidence that man is necessarily more aggressive than most of the other creatures on earth, for whom the term "depraved" is seldom used.

### Intergroup Conflict

A distinctive feature of man's aggression is that it often occurs between groups of people. Tribes fight tribes and nations make war on nations. Wars are a particularly impressive form of aggression because of their size and because of the cold, detached way in which they are conducted. Our analysis of man's aggressiveness towards man is incomplete without considering such aggression between groups as evidence against the goodness of man's nature.

The causes of conflict between groups has been illuminated by a series of studies conducted by the Sherifs (cf. Sherif and Sherif, 1969, chapter eleven for a summary of their research) which showed that aggression between groups is a by-product of competitive goals. They used boys' camps for their research and varied the camp activities. In some activities cabins of boys could attain the goal only if the other cabins did not also attain the goal. A typical example would be a baseball game or tug-of-war where a very desirable prize was given to the winning cabin. When the competitive games were the prominent camp activity, the good sportsmanship initially shown by the boys began to evaporate. As the competition continued, the good sportsmanship was replaced by name-calling, fighting, and night time raids by one cabin upon another. These boys were no longer playing; they meant business. The situation rapidly became so serious that the experiment was called off and several days were spent reducing the hostility and aggression among the boys. Other experiments were carefully conducted to explore the conditions under which aggression occurred and under which it was reduced.

Sherifs found the principle determining aggression between groups to be simple: If a highly desired goal is attainable by only one of the groups, then aggression is encouraged. If a highly desirable goal requires all groups to cooperate for anyone to obtain it, then hostility decreases and intergroup friendships increase. Aggression, then, arose solely as the means of obtaining a desirable end when no other means was available.

From the perspective of the research by the Sherifs, aggression is the result of man's striving for intrinsically good goals which happen to exclude other men achieving the same goals. When obtaining the goal, others are harmed as a byproduct of seeking the goal. When several groups are competing for the same goal, the groups will eventually conflict with each other. Since intergroup conflicts usually take place under ambiguous circumstances, a group can see its own acts of aggression as justified on the basis of the other group's past acts, which they can argue were aggressive towards them.

Further justification for attaining the goal for one's own group at another group's expense would come from those with premoral reasoning processes; premoral people would want their group to obtain the goals and would ignore what happened to the other people. Those with a conventionally oriented reasoning process would be inclined to go along with the immature reasoning at this point because (a) their norms come from the group of which the immature are a part and because (b) helping their friends is deemed to be a worthy cause in conventional thought processes. It is for these reasons that one nation finds it moral to kill 10,000 of the enemy in order to save 5,000 of their own people.

Socially unacceptable behavior as a means to socially desirable goals was also observed by the Sherifs (1964) in their research on adolescent groups. From the reports of observers in the groups, the Sherifs were able to analyze the conditions under which adolescent deviancy and crimes tended to occur. The general findings were that the adolescents sought the same goals as everyone in society but were blocked in achieving the goals. The only means they had open to achieving the goals were those which society deemed undesirable. The undesirable means were, however, less undesirable to the adolescents than not obtaining the goals, and so they performed anti-social acts.

The general conclusions from analyses of man's inhumanity is that man has no drives or goals which can only be satisfied at the expense of others. Instead, the drives and goals a person seeks may cause evil because he has no means of obtaining the goals without harming others. Our general results would suggest that there are three major causes of observed inhumane treatment of man by his fellow man: Man's tendency toward judgmental errors, his failure to approach problems with a mature ethical reasoning process, and the environmental situations which place him in competition with his fellow man to achieve the same goals.

## Social Conformity: The Magnification of Man's Good and Evil

The evil that man does as a function of his finite judgment, his lack of ethical maturity, and the effects of competition are magnified by man's social nature. Relying upon others for norms and behavior, people will follow bad norms as well as good. Once an unjust norm has been established, the group conformity effect tends to magnify and stabilize that injustice.

The extent to which people do conform to potentially harmful norms established by others is illustrated by Milgram's (1965) research on obedience. He asked a series of college students, business men, and other people to participate in his research studies. These people were requested to act as a "helper" in an experimental setting. The people who participated thought they were being asked to work for the experimenter but they were actually the focus of the research. The participant's task was to punish a "pupil" whenever the pupil failed to make a proper response. Unknown to the people who were participating, the pupils were actually confederates of the experimenter who had been carefully trained to put on an appropriate act.

As a pupil went through his materials, he made numerous mistakes. Whenever he made a mistake, the person participating was instructed to give the pupil an electrical shock. (In actuality, no shock was given but the pupil acted as if he had been shocked.) As a pupil continued to make mistakes, the experimenter continued to instruct the "helper" to turn up the voltage and give the pupil still another shock. In extreme cases, the experimenter was having the participant turn the voltage up into an area clearly labeled as dangerous. The pupil, in turn, acted as if the shocks were dangerous by screaming, crying, begging them to stop, and fighting to break loose of the apparatus. The experimenter kept telling the participant to give the learner a still stronger shock. From the reaction of the people who participated in this study, it was apparent that they did feel they were giving dangerous shocks to the pupil.

In a situation where a person thinks he is harming another person, how far will he go simply to conform to somebody's instructions? When Milgram's experiment was described to psychiatrists, they judged that less than one percent of the participants would give the highest shock possible to the learner. In actuality, almost two-thirds of the participants obeyed the experimenter's commands fully and gave the pupil the highest shock possible, a finding which occurred regardless of whether or not college students were used in the study.* This research suggests that people do injure others by following another person's fallible judgments.

Social conformity effects will magnify bad or evil decisions by a person who is in a position of power and influence. They will also magnify good decisions equally well. For example, in the research by Hartshorne and May (1928, 1929), social conformity effects were found which supported honest and helpful behavior. *There is no current reason to hypothesize that social conformity effects are only negative in their results. Social conformity is influential in protecting the rights and lives of many people.*

## Conclusion

The analysis just given provides further data for deciding whether man is basically humane in his treatment of his fellow man. While the final decision lies outside the realm of psychology, the present analysis does suggest that it is hard to justify the view that man is naturally depraved in his relationships with others if the judgment is based on mature intentions rather than behavior. It also suggests that man is capable of both good and evil acts, and often performs more evil than he intends because of his finite nature.

*Perhaps as serious as man's intentions is his corruptibility.* It appears that a person's development can be easily disrupted so that conventional moral reasoning processes are beyond his grasp as an adult. Man can also be directly taught to enjoy hurting others. Even if he is not directly taught to be aggressive, he may easily become so if he is a member of a group in a competitive situation. Despite man's intentions and possibilities, he is often inhumane to his fellows—and he can come to enjoy it.

---

*The difference between the psychiatrist's judgments and actual results illustrates the conclusions of the first lecture: Human judgment is fallible. It shows that unanimity among experts does not necessarily mean the judgment is better. All judgments need as many validity checks as possible.

## SOCIAL SYSTEMS TO INCREASE
## THE GOOD AMONG MEN

The extent of social influence in the life of man suggests that man's inhumane treatment of man can only be countered through the social system. For example, in a study of three ethnic subcultures within one community, Jessor, *et al.* (1968) found the Indians to be in a particularly disadvantageous situation. Their situation gave them few legitimate means to obtain the same goals as others in the community and the destruction of their culture meant that the social networks provided few social controls to limit deviancy. The result was a high rate of problems such as alcoholism. Regardless of whether these people are to be blamed for their situation, it is apparent that their children have little chance to maximize whatever good exists within human nature unless the social situation of which they are a part is changed. Men are too influenced by their group to have much hope for their being righteous unless they are part of a righteous subculture.

Constructing better social situations will become increasingly possible as social psychological principles become utilized. Presently, social support systems are influenced by decisions made in ambiguous, abstract situations with little or no feedback on the results of the decisions. Social psychological research can reduce the abstractness of some decisions by providing relevant, explicit information. Applying social psychological research techniques within an institutional setting can also enable administrators to evaluate the positive effects of their decisions as well as alerting them to potentially harmful side effects.

But using social psychological research as a basis for maximizing the good in man does not mean that social institutions can be remade to remove all evil from the world. People are central to social situations, and people will continue to have finite judgmental powers for the foreseeable future. Given the high probability of human error, institutions will always make many mistakes. Even so, mankind cannot do without institutions, for they are his means of shaping the groups which provide him with his social supports.

Religious institutions will be the focus of the present discussion since the Church has the ideology and possibility of building a social system that will increase good among men. As Lenski (1963) has shown, religious institutions already are reasonably influential in our society. Their effect is sufficiently large so that a simple definition of social-religious group membership was found to be almost as predictive of behavior as social class.

Can institutions be changed to increase their effect? It appears so, since Stern (1971) has noted that some colleges have been able to change their characteristics even without changing their membership. The results of the changes reconfirm our evaluation that the social networks generated by institutions are powerful determinants of human behavior.

### Encouraging Positive Human Relations

Within a social support system, practices can be established to encourage the participants to show a greater concern for others. Rosenhan (1969) summarizes research derived principles which can be used for this purpose. In particular, the research supports the concept of witnessing, or, as it is called by psychologists, modeling. Individuals who see others perform acts of concern are more likely to exhibit such behavior themselves. This is a widely confirmed finding which helps to explain why people give to UGF, participate in a civil rights demonstration, and so forth.

However, the witnessing in psychological studies is not of the persuasive type nor is the person who observes the model placed under any pressure to conform. Instead, the results occur when the model is obviously behaving to fulfill *his* values, rather than witnessing to convince others of his own goodness or to convert others to his position. The person who observes the model must also feel free to behave as he sees fit or else any results from the modeling will be short-lived.

Since one of the handicaps for living a moral life can be an inability to reason through moral dilemmas in a mature manner, the research on changing levels of moral judgment is also relevant to the activities of religious institutions. The principal element in developing more mature reasoning processes is, in addition to a minimum level of cognitive maturity, appropriate opportunities to hear others discuss moral dilemmas and to try out one's own reasoning powers (Turiel, 1969). Such opportunities are often provided in one of the more effective of many religious organizations: the youth group. In youth groups, young people often discuss the moral and ethical problems faced by people like themselves and faced by the country. The free-wheeling discussion allows the adult advisors to interject their opinions occasionally and also allows the more immature youth to hear and benefit from the judgment of the more mature youth. The youth group thus aids in the moral development of its members, as well as providing them with a religious social support system. This may be one reason why congregations often grow through their youth activities.

Recommendations based upon the effects of models in developing concern for others and of discussion in the improvement of moral reasoning are positive and non-coercive. In this respect, the recommendations seem similar to the practices of most social support systems. Although the phrase "group sanctions" is often used and occasional examples of group pressures may occur, it appears that most social support systems are almost exclusively positive in their approach, i.e. they reward individuals for conformity and do not punish nonconformity (Sherif and Sherif, 1964). Punishment and coercion are effective, but only on a short term basis where the individual has no choice as to whether or not he participates. Since a person can usually pick his social groups, the response to punishment and coercion is to find a more positive group atmosphere. An effective Christian organization must therefore be based upon love and forgiveness rather than upon legalism and hell-fire.

## Building a Religious Social Support System

Most religious social support systems are not sufficiently strong and close-knit to maximize the positive effects of the social group, as Lenski (1963) has found. Instead, the religious institution involves only a part of the interpersonal networks in the community that can be identified with that religious tradition.

Churches could be considerably improved as social support systems.

The research shows that a strong group develops when the membership has a common goal which can only be obtained by cooperation, a condition which is often met in Christian groups. Part of the historical success of the Christian faith has arisen from its emphasis upon noncompetitive goals that all could achieve together. For example, "being saved" does not exclude anyone else from being saved and the ideology stresses helping others, particularly with their salvation. An evangelistic thrust forms a common goal in which an entire group can participate so long as they are surrounded by a reasonable number of nonbelievers. Inasmuch as the members of the group accept a task such as evangelism or social service as a common goal, then the goal can form an unifying force to turn that group into a significant social support system for its members.

Potential participants in a Christian support system may not be sufficiently concerned about salvation for that to be a unifying goal. Classically, evangelistic theology has begun by stressing the personal, hedonistic goal of "going to heaven" to the potential member. If the recipient of the message is convinced of the validity of the supernatural theology, then such an approach can be quite productive. Even the ethically immature person can readily understand and grasp such arguments. However, many people are not sufficiently convinced of supernaturalistic theology for salvation in heaven to be meaningful. For such individuals, other goals will need to be used to involve them in religious groups.

As noted earlier in both the case of children who accidentally selected peers with values like their own and in research on changes in values during college, it seems that the typical person selects his friends and groups without much regard for the values they hold. Rather, interpersonal associations are developed more accidentally. The accidental basis of most groups allows a religious organization to reach those who do not have the theological understanding necessary to make constructs such as salvation and brotherly love meaningful.

Our analysis of the social nature of mankind suggests that the individual being brought into the religious group should not be considered an individual if he is to be changed. Most people already have social support systems and will maintain most of those social support systems even though they are involved in a religious organization. The non-religious social support will often effectively counteract the religious social support so that the person remains essentially unchanged.

Only as the religious bonds begin systematically replacing the prior social support system can a major effect be expected on a particular individual. The religious institution needs to be sure that the social support provided by the individual's family, friends, co-workers and neighbors is compatible with the more formal religious group. Inasmuch as one or more of the person's social support systems provides him with support for nonreligious norms, nonreligious alternatives will remain a live possibility for him.

Replacing normal social support systems might, in part, take place through parochial school systems. Tentative evidence suggests that such schools have long term effects when they are paired with a family situation which is also religious, i.e. when the social support systems are mutually supportive (Greeley and Gockel, 1971). Religious school systems could also be used to resocialize parents to provide effective social support for the developing faith of their children.

The effects of an interlocking social support system on behavior can be considerable. Spivak (quoted by Walters and Bradley, 1971) found that a Catholic physician's behavior adhered to Catholic norms when he was trained at a Catholic institution, was actively involved in the Catholic Church, and practiced at a Catholic hospital. Involving people in a series of religious social support systems allows the religious norms greater opportunities to affect the individual.

## Maintaining a Religious Social Support System

By establishing a strong interlocking social network, a religious institution can have a powerful impact upon its participants, but it has a constant problem of keeping the social support systems of the membership within the religious body. Whenever there is contact with the rest of society through members living beside nonmembers, working with non-Christians, and children attending school with nonreligious children, the carefully built Christian social support system will break down over time. Historically, this appears to have happened to most religious bodies. They were originally effective because the initial converts were totally involved. Over time, the descendants of the initial converts mixed more and more into society and lost a considerable part of their distinctiveness. Too great a reliance upon interacting with the society leads to de-Christianization of the membership, a point many liberal groups seem not to realize. Therefore, a religious group needs to give considerable thought to how it is going to insulate people from society once it has effectively involved them in its group.

An effective procedure for maintaining an exclusive social support system is to limit all possible interactions with the greater society. This procedure has been followed by groups such as the Amish with reasonable success. They live in their own area, conduct their own schools, and work only among themselves. Only carefully chosen leaders are allowed to interact with society at large. By using unique modes of transportation and clothing, even the leaders are insulated from the effects of the society since the society instantly recognizes them as members of the religious group and expects them to conform to their religious norms.

But to physically limit contact with the larger society would be self-defeating for most Christian bodies. Most theologies consider the church's primary goal to be helping others to develop a Christian perspective on life and to become more concerned for their fellow man. Cutting themselves off from society means that they can influence only those already in the fellowship.

Partial substitutes for physical insulation can be developed by relying on labeling effects. As the members of a religious body come to be known for some unique behaviors, the society will come to expect this behavior and reward individual members for following the norms of the religious group. The labeling will, however, cut the religious group off from those members of the larger society whom they are interested in reaching.

Social psychological principles suggest there may be other and possibly better procedures for maintaining a religious social support system while still interacting with the society at large. The first such principle is based on a distinction between reference groups and membership groups. The latter, membership groups, are those social networks in which a person participates on a day by day basis. Reference groups are the groups which he uses to support his norms for beliefs, values and behavior. While membership and reference groups are identical for many people, it is often possible and useful to distinguish them so that a person's norms come from a group with which he may have only occasional contact.

In Christian theology, constructs such as "a people of God" have utilized the reference group principle to emphasize the distinctiveness of the religious group from society. By the special label, the institution helps the membership use the institution's norms as their referent so that they can be in society while maintaining religious norms.

Another principle for helping people be "in the world but not of it" derives from experiments on conformity such as those that were discussed earlier. Conformity research has consistently found that the group pressure effects are reduced if the individual has even limited social support for his nonacceptance of the group norms. Although a person will often conform to a group of three or four others when he is the lone dissident, he will conform less if he has only one other person to support his position. This effect occurs with larger groups as well.

Social support for Christian beliefs and behaviors by members of a religious group can be provided in the greater society by both assuring that the religious membership knows each other and by emphasizing the need for mutual support when they are in the society. Two people from the same congregation working at the same place of employment can, if they are both concerned about their religious norms, help each other resist the group conformity effects that will always be present in a work setting.

To be effective, the religious organization would need to work explicitly and directly with such pairs and small groups as they go out into the society. The explicit use of pairs of religious people—as when Jesus sent out the disciples two by two—may be difficult if the religious doctrine and practices stress the individual person making his own decisions and his own witness, but it is nevertheless necessary.

### Growth as a Problem for a Religious Support System

Religious groups which do involve their members in religious social systems and norms may have problems from a high growth rate. The problem with a high growth rate is at least two-fold. First, larger groups form less effective support systems than do smaller groups. As the group increases in size, the diffusion of responsibility occurs along the same lines as it occurred in the case of bystanders in emergencies: The individuals are less involved and less active. As Moberg (1971) notes, research on congregations shows an inverse relationship between the congregation's size and almost any measure of participation. Insomuch as people do not participate in a social support system, the social support system cannot help them.

Another problem with a high growth rate is that most individuals do not exchange all their social support systems for religious ones upon admission into the religious body. The full change takes time, often years. Inasmuch as the growth rate is high, the congregation will come to have a large number of "partially involved" members. Since these individuals have significant nonreligious social support systems, they will adhere to only part of the norms of the total organization. The social support that they provide for others may complement a few of the religious norms and will dilute the effect of the religious leadership on the other norms. Eventually, the dilution may be such that the original religious norms are no longer effective. At that point the religious leadership may need to leave the institution they founded and start all over again.

Despite the deterioration that often occurs in religious bodies as they grow, the leadership seldom breaks off to form a purer group. The reason is that religious leaders are also human and require social support systems. As the religious institution grows, the leaders receive their social support from the changing religious support system. While the social network may continue to include many with a firm commitment to the norms on which the organization was originally established, others who become involved will have a primary commitment to the institution. The norms of the original leadership's social support system will therefore increasingly stress the survival of the institution. The best course is, therefore, to establish sufficient feedback systems so that the dilution and shift of norms is identified before it affects the leadership as well as the average members.

## Conclusion

From a social psychological perspective, the principles seem sufficiently well established that institutions could make major improvements in their procedures and have a significantly greater effect for the good of man if we knew how to reshape the institutions. By building a strong unified group, providing explicit norms, and psychologically separating the members sufficiently from society so that they can be sent back into society as witnesses, conditions can be created where most individuals will follow the set of norms established for them. No one currently seems to have extensive empirical data on reshaping institutions to increase their positive effects upon their members.

In our analysis of the nature of mankind, our current description is of a man whose destiny is determined by the social support system established by a religious institution. The institution determines what he is going to be like and carefully uses social psychological principles to develop and preserve his characteristics. The goals of the institution are therefore served.

But few would hold that man is made for the institution alone, even a religious institution. We would rather hold that the institution is made to serve man. So how can man break free of his social support system and determine his own destiny? This is a topic we shall consider in the next lecture.

CHAPTER IV

# Man and Destiny

RICHARD L. GORSUCH

IN THE PREVIOUS LECTURES, mankind has been found to be finite in his judgmental powers and highly influenced by the others around him. Man could be characterized as stumbling half-blind along life's path while being shoved this way and that by the crowd of half-blind others stumbling along the same path. Mankind's control over his own destiny would seem to be out of his hands.

While the first two lectures did stress the limits and the influences upon man, ways in which man could overcome those limits were occasionally suggested. Comments were made on how the finiteness of human judgment could be offset and on how man could build his own social support systems to help him become what he wanted to become. Implicit in these discussions was an expectation that man could have a voice in his own destiny.

A view of man is incomplete until it incorporates the fact that man is a creature constantly striving to take his destiny into his own hands. He wills, seeks, and desires. A whole view of the nature of man needs to evaluate the degree to which man is able to transcend his finite judgment and his social nature so that he can be said to influence his own destiny. The question now becomes one of asking whether human nature is such that man can indeed play a significant role in shaping his own destiny.

## FREE WILL, DETERMINISM AND PSYCHOLOGY

Similar to the question of whether man can shape his own destiny is the continuing debate between the advocate of determinism and the proponent of free will. The determinist believes that man is predestined or completely determined, and therefore lacks control over his behavior and destiny. Deterministic views appear to be based upon a person's awareness of the influences shaping his behavior or of feeling that he has been chosen by God whereas others seem not to have been so chosen. The deterministic view has grown in favor partly because of the obvious gains of science, an endeavor which most people view as completely deterministic.

The free will position also has its advocates. They usually appeal to the phenomenological experience of choice which each individual has and to which he must respond. Their view is supported by theological considerations which reject the notion that God would arbitrarily reward some and punish others. They further maintain that an assumption of free will is necessary to make responsibility meaningful.

From the present perspective, the question of determinism vs. free will is probably a bad one. It is abstract, has terms which are difficult to define, and there appears to be no way to solve the problem by appeal to any type of data. From the conclusions reached in the first lecture on the finitude of human judgment, it is a typical question for which any human answer, regardless of the unanimity of agreement, would have a low probability of being correct.

The difficulty in answering the determinism-free will question is reflected in the fact that both deterministic and free will answers have major problems. If the determinism position were to be true, then, as Kant and James have pointed out, mankind could never know that it is true. Any person's position on the question of free will vs. determinism will be controlled by causes which are not necessarily related to the answer. Even if all but one person advocated a free will position, the last remaining determinist could still hold that their conviction was a function of that which caused their behavior. There would be no way to falsify or refute his claim.

A major problem in the free will position is the definition of free will. Does it mean that man responds at random? Or does it mean that man responds in keeping with his long term goals and choices which are, in turn, provided by his social support system? Most free will advocates want to avoid both of these options, but the meaning of free will is then unclear. An additional definitional problem centers on how free a person must be to be called free. No one can argue that man is 100 percent free since the evidence, some of which was mentioned in the first two lectures, clearly shows that many factors do influence man's behavior.

Despite the problems with either view, advocates of determinism or free will may argue for their position because they feel their view is necessary for men to live a worthwhile life. The free will advocate holds that responsibility is a meaningless term without free will, and the man who is not responsible will give in to his baser drives; certainly, the argument that one is a product of his environment has been used to excuse irresponsible behaviors. The determinist, on the other hand, often claims that determinism frees one from the immobilizing anxieties of choice, and it is true that the anxieties contingent upon choice can inhibit desirable behavior.

There is no reason to doubt either argument for the effects of these positions on behavior for they are not mutually exclusive. The impact of feelings of responsibility could be important for different people at different times than the impact of the feelings of being determined. As noted in the first lecture, such paradoxes are not uncommon when finite man seeks to integrate his experiences of an infinite universe.*

---

*The positions probably arose because they both represented a distinct aspect of man's experience. Those who prefer a deterministic position are probably reasoning from those human experiences where man is obviously limited, coerced, and forced into a particular mode of action. They also look at the numerous experiences where the "coercion" is by extremely attractive rewards which make the recipient quite pleased that he was the object of the deterministic ploy. The advocate of free will, on the other hand, is probably reasoning from those existential situations where people experience the pains of choice and where people do feel that they have an opportunity to influence their own destiny. From my vantage point, both positions represent some of man's experiences and therefore are true in representing those particular experiences. But given the problems of human judgment in abstract matters, a firm decision that either free will or determinism is universally true is inappropriate. Rather, the two views need to be held in a dynamic tension so that we can be reminded that man does look somewhat different from different perspectives.

Despite commonly held views, complete determinism is not the only position within which a viable, empirical psychology can exist; psychology can function equally well within a model which also contains a free will component. All a particular psychological investigator needs to assume is that there is at least one more determinant of the behavior under investigation than what has been previously found. So long as one more determinant still remains undiscovered, the scientific enterprise can continue.

Psychologists have often been ingenious in surmounting the deterministic-free will question. A popular psychological technique is to ask people questions, often inquiring what they would do in a wide range of situations. These responses are then used to predict the individual's behavior in some of those situations. Note that the firm free will advocate can carry out this research with no qualms whatsoever. In his question, he is asking for the decisions that people have made on a free will basis. He then uses each person's free will choice in his research to predict the person's behavior, i.e. to predict whether or not they carry out the free will choice. Such a research study would violate a free will paradigm only if being free is defined as responding randomly. In contemporary social psychology, asking a person what he intends to do has been dignified as "investigating behavioral intentions" (e.g. Fishbein, 1967).

While it is impossible for empirical data to falsify either the deterministic or free will position, it is interesting to examine the question in light of current psychological knowledge. For example, Schwartz (1968) investigated the impact of individual feelings of responsibility on behavior. The individuals involved in the study were undergraduates who lived in distinct residential groups. Each member of each group rated the behavior of the group members who were in the study. Schwartz found that a person's norms and values were related to his behavior if and only if the individual saw himself as responsible. If the individual did not feel he was responsible, then his norms were unrelated to his behavior. The research tends to support the free will position on the effects of beliefs in responsibility.

Psychological research has found man to be only somewhat

predictable. The usual research study — whether in the laboratory or in real life situations — finds that some variables can be used to predict man's behavior. But the level of prediction is not high except in rare situations which are concerned with a limited range of behavior. It may well be, as determinists argue, that this is solely due to our ignorance and lack of research sophistication. But it is also possible that mankind may not be predictable on an individual basis; he may be predictable only in terms of group behavior, just as has been found for molecules of gases.

Since psychology does not require one to assume either complete determinism or complete free will, we will be able to leave the question to the philosophers and theologians and proceed with examining ways in which man transcends some of the limits of human nature that have been pointed out in the last two lectures. Whether or not such transcendence is a result of the forces controlling a particular individual or a result of his free decision is a question we need not answer at this time.

## HUMAN JUDGMENT AND DESTINY

For man to take his destiny into his own hands, it would be helpful if he could increase the accuracy of the decisions which he makes. Inasmuch as his decisions are inadequate, the results of his efforts will be unrelated to his intentions. While this does not necessarily mean that he will be controlled by outside forces, it increases the likelihood that outside forces will dominate his behavior. The only way in which the impact of outside forces can be reduced is by making proper decisions about how such forces can be shaped to fit man's decisions.

The procedures for increasing the quality of human judgment are relatively simple, and several were mentioned in the first lecture. All procedures begin with a conviction of the finitude of human judgment. While this is simple conceptually, it appears to be more difficult in actuality. It is socially undesirable in our culture for anyone to admit that they may be finite and therefore fallible. This applies not only to persons who hold positions of power, such as presidents, congressmen and business executives, but to anyone who is making decisions, including psychologists, theologians and ministers. We all must recognize that our judgments are more likely wrong than right. If people do recognize that their decisions may err, then there should be a greater reliance on techniques designed to provide information to determine and improve the quality of the decision.

The information necessary to make long term decisions about man's proper destiny will be increased in accuracy as a function of increasing the comprehensiveness of the information. If decisions are made only on one person's experiences, then the data base is narrow and any destiny chosen will be equally narrow. If the decisions are made only on the basis of one culture's experiences, then the concepts of man's proper destiny may be seriously challenged by contact with another culture or by a new set of experiences.

The quality of man's long term goals can be expected to increase as his goals are based upon the experiences of many cultures, vicariously gathered. From the viewpoint of the finitude of human knowledge, the gaining of vicarious experiences is one of the major values of historical and Biblical studies. By understanding the destiny of man as conceptualized in radically different cultures, a conceptualization can be built to match both that culture and present day culture. Such a view should be more widely useful and more valid in the sense of generating less historically conditioned goals.

Unfortunately, psychologists have little research information about the impact of historical and Biblical study upon man's world views, and even less on how such knowledge influences his choice of a destiny. It is not known, for example, whether or not a study of history actually increases the quality of the decisions made by congressmen concerned with the destiny of the country, or by theologians concerned with the destiny of "God's people." Therefore, the notion that studying other cultures influences man's understanding and control of his destiny is still an unproven hope.

Knowledge of psychological principles may provide another basis by which human judgments can be improved so that man can shape his destiny. It could be hypothesized that more extensive knowledge of the power a person's social support system has over his beliefs and values would allow man to select between social systems which are in keeping with man's own goals. This hypothesis can be tested in the same manner as any other psychological hypothesis. For example, Luchins (1957) found that one person's judgment of another is based more upon the initial information he gains than upon later information which he obtains. However, when people were warned of this potential bias, the primacy effect decreased.

But the Luchin's studies are only one example of the research which *could* be conducted on the impact of psychological knowledge on man's behavior. Few studies of this topic have actually been conducted. However, our knowledge of how man can shape his own destiny will never be complete until the question of how psychological knowledge might enable man to use the principles in his own behalf is investigated.

## SOCIAL TRANSCENDENCE AND DESTINY

Man's achieving of his own destiny is limited by his conformity to his social setting, since beliefs, values and behavior can be viewed as a function of his group norms. As long as man conforms extensively to the group, his destiny will be a function of the group. Man needs to partially transcend the group before he can be said to shape his own destiny.

The impact of the social system is perhaps more crucial than man's limited judgmental powers because the social influence is so pervasive. It affects the information which a person uses in his decisions, the norms guiding the decisions, and the manner in which the decisions are carried out. Even if his judgmental powers were infinite, the strong effects of the social support system might prevent an individual person from determining his own destiny. The social effect is also more important than man's limited judgments because man has generated many information storage systems, feedback systems and other judgmentally oriented processes which increase the validity of his decisions. But man has yet to consciously establish procedures to help him break free from the social support system so that he can determine his own destiny.

The effect of man's social nature has been found to vary widely from one individual to another in the conformity research. Some people are highly susceptible to group norms whereas others are relatively insusceptible. Even in complex, abstract situations, there are individuals who maintain their own norms and do not conform to others. In Milgrim's (1965) studies on obedience, the majority did conform and deliver what they thought to be a potentially dangerous shock to another individual solely because the experimenter told them to. However, one third of the individuals involved in this study refused to conform when it appeared that the other individual might be seriously harmed. It would therefore seem crucial to examine the nature of nonconformity to understand the characteristics of people who appear to transcend the impact of their social environment.

### Social Transcendence as a Function of Value Commitment

A crucial variable in transcending the group appears to be the degree of commitment to one's own values. Without a solid commitment, the individual has no standards to apply to the decisions he must reach, and so he relies upon the norms of the group of which he is a part. If strong value commitment exists, then the person's need for socially defined norms is not as great.

Bowers (1968) reports interesting data on the role of the personal norms of college students in resisting the group's effects. He asked students from ten different colleges to indicate their approval or disapproval of several behaviors and whether they had engaged in that particular behavior themselves. An examination of the data at each college showed distinct differences in the normative climates. Bowers was therefore able to evaluate the behavior of people as a function of the degree to which they disapproved of the behavior and as a function of the normative climates.

Bowers' results are shown in Figure IV-1. Of those who strongly disapproved of a particular behavior, no more than ten percent ever participated in the behavior. But of those who did not disapprove of the behavior, the percentage participating varied from a high of seventy-five percent when two-thirds of

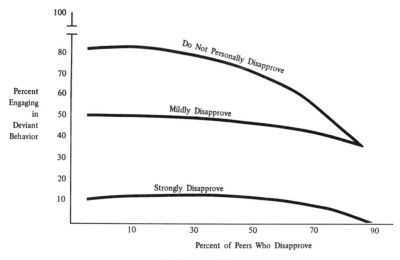

Figure IV-1

his fellow students did not disapprove of the behavior, to a low of twenty-seven percent when the normative climate of the college was one of strong disapproval. *Therefore, those who were deeply committed to a value tended to live by that value whereas those who were not deeply committed behaved in accordance with the normative climate around them.*

A similar interaction between personal values and the situation was found among lawyers. Carlin (1966) distinguished between situational pressures, including group norms, and the degree of the lawyers' internalized concern with ethics. As one would expect, there was little violation of ethical norms when there was no pressure towards violation; in this circumstance, the ethical and unethical all behaved the same. But when the pressures were to violate the ethical norms, then those with a strong concern for ethics seldom recommended unethical behavior while those who had a low concern for ethics usually recommended unethical behavior. The lawyers, then, who had an internalized set of values seemed to shape their own behavior, whereas those without definite values let the situation decide for them.

Understanding the relationship between deep commitment

and group norms may be further clarified by examining the relationship between prejudice and religious commitment.* For several centuries, white superiority has been one norm of the American social system. Racist norms could be expected to be held by all those who are not sufficiently committed to make a value judgment independently of society's norms. Only those with a definite value commitment would be sufficiently independent of group norms to possibly see the injustice of racism.

In a similar manner, being a church member has also been a part of the American tradition and it would be expected that those following society's norms would be casual members of religious organizations. But they would be neither highly religious nor nonreligious since both of those positions are not part of the central American tradition. Only a person who evaluated religion independently of society's norms would therefore be able to take religion seriously. Those making an independent decision would be more likely to be either strongly religious or strongly nonreligious, and stand in contrast to the uncommitted, casually religious person.

What then would be the relationship between religion and prejudice? Since those who have a strong religious commitment would have evolved a value system more independent of society's norms, they would not be as likely to have relied upon society for their racial constructs. Hence, they would, on the average, be less prejudiced than would those who relied upon society's racist norms. In like manner, the atheist would have selected values more independently of society's norms and would also tend to reject racism. The uncommitted individuals would be those most likely to accept unquestioningly all elements of the American way of life, including prejudice and religious membership.

Research on the relationship between religion and prejudice is consistent with this hypothesis (e.g. Allen and Spilka, 1967;

---

*In this discussion, "religious" is used in its more structured sense and is not synonymous with a person's conscious or unconscious response to questions of the ultimate, to existential anxiety, and so forth. It is therefore meaningful to speak of no religious commitment, a casual religious commitment, and a deep religious commitment.

Dittes, 1971). Figure IV-2 shows that those who are most prejudiced are those who have moderate religious commitments whereas those who are least prejudiced are either strongly religious or not religious at all. This graph is the same for most definitions of religiosity. For example, the same effect is found if church participation is plotted against degree of prejudice or if the degree to which a person values religion for its own sake is plotted against prejudice. This finding is one of the most widely substantiated results in social psychology (Gorsuch and Aleshire, 1974).

The conclusion from these studies is that an individual begins to transcend the group when he has an internalized normative system. It is a lack of clear personal values that leads to man being so heavily influenced by the people around him.

## Social Transcendence as a Function of Reasoning Processes

The research noted above has been concerned with a person's

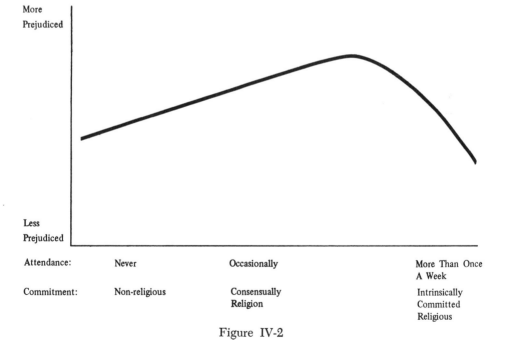

Figure IV-2

commitment to a particular set of values. Another body of psychological literature has not been concerned with the particular goals a person is committed to but, instead, with the reasoning processes a person uses in reaching those goals. This literature provides further information on how one can transcend the norms of the group.

Numerous investigators have broken down the moral reasoning process into a number of stages (summarized by Kohlberg, p. 375 ff, 1969); these stages can be grouped into three levels. In the earlier lectures, we have already referred to these levels as exemplified in Kohlberg's research. The first level was that of immature or *premoral* thinking processes where the person's concern is solely with the short term personal benefits of a particular course of action.

The second level of moral reasoning consists of thinking which is based upon generalized group norms, and is referred to as *conventional* moral reasoning. At this level, the person's commitments are to the norms of his group, either as expressed through the characteristics which everyone accepts as "nice" or by appeal to the codified principles or laws of a society, a religious body, or other group. The conventionally moral appear to be those who are committed to a course of action solely because of the norms of the social groups of which they are members.

The third level is referred to as *post-conventional* thinking. Individuals utilizing this reasoning process have come to see the relativism inherent in basing one's set of values on his membership group. Their response to the obvious cultural relativity of behaviors and mores is to look for the underlying principles which can guide all human behavior. Some, using this thought process, turn to principles of social utility and social contract whereas others adopt principles such as justice and love.

Individuals who habitually use post-conventional moral reasoning do appear to function more independently of the social setting than do the conventionalists. In the Milgram studies, where most people conformed to the directions to give another person what they thought to be a dangerous shock, some people refused to participate (Kohlberg, 1969, p. 395f) that is, those who used post-conventional reasoning processes seldom conformed. The post-conventional people were able to determine their own course of action rather than letting the environment determine it for them. These are the people whom we would expect to be shaping their own destinies.

While these three levels can be conceptually distinguished, identifying whether or not a person is at the conventional or post-conventional level of reasoning is more difficult than it sounds. For example, in my course on ethical and moral development, the students studied the moral development stages for a week or so. I then played a tape of an interview with a youth and asked them to identify the stage of thinking. None of the thirty or so students correctly identified the stage of the boy. Instead, they all saw the boy's level of moral judgment as being higher than did trained scorers (Barnes, Gorsuch and Kohlberg). Observation suggests that almost all conventional people see themselves as being post-conventional. The lack of self knowledge arises because the normative influences of our social support systems are pervasive and subtle. Conventional people seldom realize that their norms and values are almost exclusively a function of the people with whom they associate.

The difficulties in judging who uses what level of moral reasoning are confounded because everyone's behavior may be superficially alike. The conventionalist often acts from a sense of commitment in what appears to be a true and dedicated manner. His functioning is a result of his involvement in a social group which may not be physically present but which gives him vital social support for his commitments (see discussion of reference groups in the second lecture). For this reason, he may be the lone dissenter in another group and fight for "his" values in a manner not unlike that of the post-conventional person. And since the premoral individual is concerned solely with himself, he too will tend to function independently of the group and will often reject its norms because they do not match his own hedonistic desires. The judgments of individuals who use premoral reasoning processes may be readily confused with individuals whose judgments arise from a post-conventional reasoning process.

Both pre-conventional and post-conventional people can be observed operating outside the norms given by groups of which they are a part, but can they both be considered to be shaping their own destinies? It appears that an answer can only be given from a definitional basis. If shaping one's own destiny includes anyone who works for his own goals, then both those who use premoral and those who use post-conventional reasoning would be considered the same. If, however, shaping one's own destiny means persistently following a course of action to achieve a long term, abstract goal, the premoral people do not shape their own destinies. Instead, the premoral thinkers work to satisfy their own needs and desires within the normative structure of groups which they encounter. So long as they know what the norms of the groups are, they will abide by them in public so as to be able to use the group for their own hedonistic goals. The post-conventional thinker will, however, follow the group norms only when they are not in violation of his more basic values. In this sense, the post-conventionalist can be said to be more concerned with his destiny.

## Conclusion

The above discussion has shown that a person transcends the group norms by being deeply committed to a personal value and by using post-conventional thought processes. When these conditions are met, the evidence suggests that the person will be more able to resist group pressures. When an individual is not committed to a value relevant to the choice he faces or when he does not use post-conventional thought processes, then the norms which guide his decisions will be a direct function of his social support system.*

---

*In addition to the highly committed person who uses post-conventional moral thought processes, psychologists have investigated another type of individual who, in a sense, shapes his own destiny. He is generally referred to as a *creative person* (Berelson and Steiner, 1964, pp. 226-235). One of the prime characteristics of a creative person is that he is not bound by social constraints or authority. Rather, he strikes out on his own and therefore develops novel approaches.

(continued)

It should be noted that the socially transcendent person is more capable of transcending group influences but that his transcendence is not infinite. A person's social setting provides him with his basic guidelines for living, with his norms for noncritical areas, and sets limits on how he can pursue his destiny.

A person's social transcendence is especially limited if the individual is forced to be part of a group where the norms do not allow for his values or reasoning processes to operate. Every group has pressures it can exert upon any individual which will prevent him from achieving his goals. At times those influences may be as extreme as concentration camps and martyrdom, but this is the exception rather than the rule. In most cases, the group seems able to force the individual to regress to a more conventional view of life by simple reinforcements. Psychology knows little about this process.

## THE DEVELOPMENT OF SOCIALLY TRANSCENDENT PEOPLE

The people who are able to transcend their social support systems by being deeply committed to values or by post-conven-

---

(continued from facing page)

It appears that a creative person looks for problem situations in which to be involved. On the basis of the principles developed above regarding change in levels of moral thinking, we would expect heavy involvement in problem situations to lead to an improvement in judgmental processes. Consequently, it would not be surprising if the creative person was also found to be the more ethically mature and value committed individual who shapes his own destiny.

Because the creative person is more independent, it does not automatically follow that the creative person is synonymous with one who creates his own destiny. Porpoises can be trained to be creative simply by rewarding them with a fresh fish every time they do something which they have not done before. Such creativity is as much a function of the environment as is any other act which they are taught to perform. In like manner, the person who is creative simply because he enjoys novel ideas or who is creative because he does not like any one group is not necessarily a person who shapes his own destiny. A person who enjoys novel ideas allows the problems he confronts to shape his behavior and a person who rejects the group is bound by the obverse of the group.

It is only the individual who is creative within a purpose who would be considered to be shaping his own destiny. To work creatively for one's own goals probably requires the characteristics described above in terms of value commitment and post-conventional thinking, and not just creativity.

tional thought processes are few. The research on religion and prejudice indicates that only those individuals who participate more than once a week in religious affairs could be considered to be truly committed to religious values. Those who attend, on the average, only two or three religious affairs during a month are probably only involved because the norms of their subculture suggest that religion is a "good thing." The casually religious are far more numerous than those participating more than once a week. Similarly, most college students have been found to use conventional reasoning processes. Only 10 to 20 percent of college students use post-conventional thinking processes (Haan, Smith, and Block, 1968; S. McFarland, personal communication). *Since the overwhelming majority of mankind is oriented toward their group's norms, they cannot be considered shapers of their own destinies.*

Perhaps the number of people who are deeply committed and use post-conventional thought processes could be increased if appropriate knowledge were available. There is nothing in the characteristics of the socially transcendent person that suggests their number is innately limited. But for their number to increase, should this be desired, it will be necessary for conditions to be deliberately established which would foster their development. Such conditions can be established only upon the knowledge of how people come to use post-conventional thought processes or come to be deeply committed to values.

## Value Commitment

Basic knowledge on the initial development of values comes from the social learning theorists. These theorists suggest that values develop because they are rewarded by people with whom an individual associates. The values would also be developed as a result of observing the successes and failures of other people who did or did not hold to those values. Social learning theory analysis is probably adequate in so far as one is concerned with relatively low levels of commitment which depend upon continuing support from the normative system. Whether or not social learning theory principles are sufficient to explain a person's continuing dedication to a value not currently rewarded by the group is not yet clear.

A basic principle underlying many of the social psychological theories of values and attitudes is the consistency of one's cognitive constructs. In these theories, it is suggested that one reshapes his beliefs and values if he finds major inconsistencies within them or between them and his behavior. For example, Rokeach (1971) found that he was able to make major shifts in college students' values by using a cognitive consistency approach. First he had the students rank in order a number of values. The eighteen values included constructs such as world peace, beauty, salvation, equality, freedom, and national security. Rokeach then informed the students of a study where those who rated freedom high also rated equality down in the middle of the list. He then commented upon the inconsistency between these two positions, for how can those who value freedom say that some should be enslaved by being treated as unequal? When the students were tested later, those who had previously rated freedom high and equality low now rated equality as more important. Rokeach also found that those individuals who altered their ratings changed some of their overt behaviors towards others. The cognitive consistency theorists suggest that the changes occurred because these students had an opportunity to compare their values, found that their value systems were not what they had thought that they were, and could not tolerate the inconsistencies. One would suspect that Rokeach's argument for rating equality higher would have been as or more powerful for religiously committed college students if the discussion had juxtaposed rating personal salvation high and equality low with the standards of Christian brotherhood.

For a person to maintain a deep commitment to a set of values, he not only must be committed to values but he must also be acquainted with the arguments against his position. The research (e.g. McGuire, 1962) suggests that prior contact with other value systems may be crucial for resisting counter-arguments. The person who has a set of values but has never heard reasons for rejecting those values will be easily swayed when he first encounters those arguments. But the individual who has previously encountered arguments against his values in a context where problems with the counter-arguments are emphasized, is less likely to change his position. Therefore one prerequisite for a person being sufficiently committed to a value so that he can transcend temporary normative effects is a wide range of experiences with other value systems.

Note that the need for knowing other value systems as a prerequisite to maintaining one's own values is diametrically opposed to those who feel that the best way to keep someone's values pure is to keep them in ignorance of other systems. Allowing individuals to be exposed to only one value position will keep them functioning within that value system so long as all the person's social support systems support the value. However, when the person becomes involved in a social support system with alternative values, it will then be found that most people have not become committed to the prior group's values. People who have lived only within a restricted normative setting will shift rapidly as their membership groups shift. In this sense, their destiny will be in the hands of others.

## Post-Conventional Reasoning Processes

Some information is available on how people progress through the lower levels to reach post-conventional thought processes. First, it is apparent that children think by premoral processes. Conventional thinking only occurs after the child develops cognitive powers which enable him to abstract principles of behavior, i.e. after puberty. In addition to needing the ability to abstract principles, it is also necessary that the individual be surrounded by a stimulating environment which confronts him with choices that can only be decided on the basis of abstract principles.

Turiel (1969) has pursued a program of research which shows the impact of stimulation on the development of more mature thought processes. His procedure is simple. He presents a moral dilemma as a topic for group discussion. During the discussion, he makes sure that arguments are discussed at a slightly higher level than that at which the children currently think. Those children who are exposed to higher levels of thinking find the limitations within their own thought processes and move towards the more mature thought processes.

It is important to note that exposure to more mature thinking is not made through a preaching or indoctrination approach. Rather, it occurs in the ordinary give-and-take of discussions centering on difficult problems where it is obvious that neither a person nor an authority has the correct answer. The child then sees the limits of premoral thought processes and adopts the more mature, conventional thought processes.

The current thinking is that an individual moves from conventional modes of thought to post-conventional thinking processes by the same method, that is, his thought processes develop when he is confronted by a moral dilemma for which there is no ready answer and for which conventional modes of thought are inadequate. For example, having based his life's decisions upon an authority, a person finds that other people rely on different authorities and that there is no final authority by which he can decide which authority is best. The conventional thinker is forced to either increase the consistency of his social support system so that he only hears of one authority, or to look for principles and values which will transcend any human group.

The only study that does report evidence on the background of post-conventional thinking is supportive of the concept that post-conventional reasoning processes are developed by stimulating environments (Haan, Smith, and Block, 1968). When people who use different levels of moral reasoning look back on how their parents treated them, several major differences stand out. The adults who still use premoral thinking appear to have been raised under inconsistent conditions where no principles were apparent in their environment. Therefore, the premoralists never learned to use principles and could not develop their own. Those using conventional thinking appear to have been raised according to the recommendations of the behavior modification school of learning. Each child was confronted with a definite set of norms and he was rewarded when he adopted those norms.

The social support system for the child was consistent so the child could abstract norms from the groups of which he was a member, but the emphasis was on conformity. The college students who used post-conventional moral reasoning appear to have had a more conflicted environment. While there was sufficient consistency so that principles and values could be learned, there were also occasional clashes of value systems. When the clash came, the maturing individual was forced to choose for himself which side he was on, and probably learned that he could stand up against the group without an ultimate disaster occurring. He, therefore, found that he had to think through and become committed to his own value system, and not simply to adopt that given him by others.

### Religious Social Support Systems: Help or Hindrance?

The distinction between holding values because they are the norms of one's group, on the one hand, and being truly committed to values by post-conventional modes of thought, on the other hand, produces some interesting questions for the work of the church. As noted in the last lecture, religious bodies can be designed as social support systems which will encourage participants to believe and live like the followers of God. To do so requires a fairly consistent social environment which rewards and encourages such beliefs and behaviors. The outcome of such an environment would be rewarding to the clergy involved since they would have strong programs with many participants.

Since the religiously uninvolved person generally has no religious values, he must be involved in religious groups on the basis of his nonreligious desires and needs, such as friendship, to give him a basis for religious values. When the individual is involved in a group with consistent values, he will begin to take on those values simply because he is involved with those people. This allows him the opportunity to begin integrating the values into his own thought processes. Consequently, the church needs to build the social support systems discussed in detail in the last lecture. It is only as people become involved in the types of social support systems described previously that there is an opportunity for them to make a decision which would involve a strong religious commitment.

One danger is that religious social support systems can be built which would be only conventionalistic and enslave people rather than free them. The members would be locked into beliefs, values, and behaviors because they have been taught to heed the norms of the religious group. These individuals would not be free to shape their own destinies and cannot be said to freely believe or to value.

It is apparent that the church must go beyond social support systems to develop deeper belief and value commitments. While psychologists have insufficient information on how this occurs to provide the same depth of background analysis that was provided for building an environment which would lead to consensual commitment, the church must be aware of the need to go beyond conventionalistic social support systems.

The aforementioned data suggest that a person moves from conventionalism to post-conventionalism by being made to see the limits of his conventional reasoning processes. The arguments against conventional positions and the norms of other groups need to be presented to each person. The church must develop settings where the person can avoid neither challenge nor the need to develop his own response. If a "canned" response is given him, then that response will be adopted as simply another group belief or norm and the conventionalism will be maintained. The challenges to develop more mature thought processes and deeper commitments should be directed towards those who have integrated the norms of the group at the conventional level to prevent regression to premoral thought processes. Social support systems should only be challenged when the person is mature enough to withstand the pressures of the other groups in his environment if the goals of the church are to be achieved. To carry out such a program effectively would probably require careful analysis on an individual by individual basis rather than "preaching sermons to shake people up." If the challenge to conventional thinking is given to those who are not ready to receive it, they will probably regress back to a precommitted, premoral level.

## THE IMPACT OF THE SOCIALLY TRANSCENDENT PERSON

The post-conventional person committed to a set of values is still human and therefore a social creature. He continues to be a part of groups for he also must rely on and interact with others. He can transcend the group, but such transcendence is primarily limited to the area in which he has firm commitments.

### Leadership and Social Support Systems

In his social involvements, the post-conventional committed person often desires to exert influence over the groups of which he is a member. By doing so, he would be able to remake his social support systems so that they could aid him in living his values. This raises a question of how a post-conventional person might be able to exert leadership within conventional social settings.

The question of the impact of a committed person is part of the larger question of how each member influences the norms of a group. While the group forms part of the social support system for an individual and thereby influences him, he is also part of the social support system of the other members of the group and influences them. Only as the total process is understood can the role of the committed person in the process be understood.

Group norms develop from joint interaction over an extended period of time among the group members. The norms are not dictated by any one individual and seldom develop from negotiations between a few members on a particular occasion, but, instead, arise from an ongoing group process to which each member contributes as the norms evolve. Such an ongoing process is referred to as transactional.

In the transactional process, it is recognized that each individual's contribution is integrated into the others' contributions during the process of developing group norms. Sherif (Sherif, 1936; Sherif and Sherif, 1969, Chapter 10) used a simple experimental setting to show this fact. When people are placed in a dark room and a single spot of light is shown, they have no empirical guidelines by which to determine how far and in what direction the light moves. As they report the movement of the light, one person may initially estimate that it moves a centimeter or so whereas another might estimate that it moves several centimeters. As a group observes the light together, they begin to establish group norms, i.e. they integrate their views to establish certain limits within which they see the light moving. Typical results of one group's development of norms over three sessions are shown in Figure IV-3, where the convergence of norms over time can be observed. The norm building process is one in which each individual contributes; since a transaction is taking place, the contributions may not be equal and the results need not be a simple average of the group. If one person has stronger norms, he will probably play a disproportionate role in establishing the norms of the group. In Figure IV-3, it is apparent that the norm was established by two of the three members and the third member shifted to that norm.

The fact that group norms are established by transaction

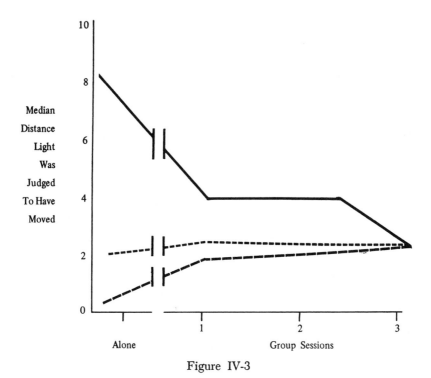

Figure IV-3

among the group members indicates that even conventional men jointly influence their destiny. The transaction producing group norms exists in virtually all groups whether the members are committed or uncommitted, premoral, conventional or post-conventional. The group norms shape the direction in which people, and particularly conventionalists, move.

While the transactional production of group norms is a topic of great importance, social psychology is not as knowledgeable in the area as might be desired. We are forced to leave the pursual of the transactional development of group norms to future endeavors of psychologists and sociologists.

What social psychologists have studied is the influence exerted by individual members upon the group norms. The most important determinant of a person's influence in a group appears to be the degree to which he is seen as enabling the group to reach their common goal. If he has special knowledge or skills which are needed by the group, then the group will be easily swayed in the direction of his opinion. When a new problem arises, the group turns first to those who have been most successful in aiding the group in the past. Those individuals who have been influential on many occasions are virtually always consulted.

It is also true that if the individual begins interfering with the achievement of the group goals instead of aiding them, the group will turn from his past informal leadership and seek new leadership that is more oriented towards the group goals. As a result, only a limited amount of leadership can be exerted in new and significant directions within a group at any particular time. If a person attempts to influence the group in such a way that he interferes with the goals of most of the group members, the group will ignore the leadership he is attempting to exert.

Another aspect of leadership widely acknowledged by social psychologists is that two types of leaders exist. One type of leader, referred to as an instrumental leader, is oriented towards the tasks of the group. This leader shapes and influences the group in its striving to obtain the mutually agreed on goals. The other type of leadership is concerned not so much with the group achieving its goals but with the maintenance of the group itself, and can be referred to as process leadership. The emphasis of the process oriented leader is on interpersonal events. If people are disturbed, for example, he is quick to smooth over the problems in the interest of group unity. (In religious terminology, the former type of leadership could be referred to as prophetic and the latter as pastoral.)

In both religious and nonreligious groups, the instrumental and process leaders may be two people or both leadership functions may be occasionally fulfilled by one person, but both functions are important in a social system. When a clergyman or other leader is of the instrumental type, the process leadership of the religious body needs to be strong to prevent divisions from occurring. If the clergyman is a process leader, then the congregation must supply its own instrumental leadership if it is to achieve goals in addition to having "good fellowship."

If an individual wishes to shape his destiny by influencing the groups of which he is a part, he will need to be sensitive to both the instrumental and process leadership functions within the group. I wish that I could provide suggestions on how this might occur, but at this point the social psychological literature does not proceed beyond the level reached by many astute observers of groups in action. It appears to be another area to which social psychologists need to devote further attention.

### When is the Shaping of Social Systems Manipulation?

Regardless of how a person comes to the knowledge necessary to deliberately shape a group, a leader can influence social norms so that the social system then supports his goals at the possible expense of the other group members. By building a supportive social system, the individual will be able to influence his own destiny. But the social support system an individual builds for himself is also a social support for the others who are involved; the norms of the group will influence all the members of that group. Therefore when a committed person shifts norms to influence his own destiny, he is shaping the destiny of the other group members as well. The others in the social support system need not be aware that their own beliefs, values, and behavior are being altered.

The influence of a person who seeks his own destiny upon those involved in his social support system could be considered manipulative since the others in the social support system are not as free to choose their own destinies. Exerting such influence is obviously manipulative if the destiny the leader seeks for himself is concerned only with his personal needs and wants. Such manipulation occurs when a premoral individual uses others for his own ends without regard for the long-term effects upon them.

The social support system devised by several people who all use post-conventional thought processes and are deeply committed to values is seldom viewed as manipulative since it usually maximizes no one person's destiny at the expense of somebody else's. Instead, the group processes lead to a transaction among the members so that a common destiny is negotiated. In such a situation, each post-conventional, committed individual is a leader in the sense of influencing the group norms, but he utilizes no hidden powers, no mass delusions and does not hypnotize anyone else into agreeing with him. In this case, manipulation does not seem to be an issue.

Between the case of the premoral manipulator and the post-conventional transactor lies a grey area involving consensually committed conventionalists. It is particularly crucial because most individuals depend upon their social support system for their beliefs, values and norms and are not truly committed to anything. Inasmuch as a person who shapes his own destiny influences groups containing conventional people, is he manipulating them?

The problem becomes more complex when it is recognized that, for the foreseeable future, it will not be possible to shift all conventionally oriented people to becoming post-conventional thinkers committed to their values, and who thus can influence their own destiny. This fact was implicitly recognized in the second lecture where the building of religious social support systems to increase concern for other people was the focus of the discussion.

To argue that the deliberate use of psychological principles underlying man's social nature to improve the lives and practices of conventionalist thinkers is manipulative would ignore the basic social character of man's nature. As long as man remains a social creature, each will continually influence others regardless of the label placed on the influence. The basic question is not whether he is controlled, but how man controls or is controlled by social influences.

If man is aware of the principles of social influences, then it may be possible for a person to use those principles to shape his own destiny. If man remains unaware of how social influences work, they will still operate just the same, but man will have less control over them. In this sense, not deliberating building a designed social support system leaves man enslaved to accidental groups and accidental norms.

The need for man to recognize the influences upon him and take charge of them is a common theme among psychologists who are socially concerned. Even the determinist Skinner (1971) attacks traditional concepts only so that he can replace them with other concepts. The concepts Skinner recommends explicitly focus on forces which shape man so that those forces can be used to improve the quality of human life. Psychologists who advocate a less deterministic position also recognize that there are influences at work upon man which limit his freedom. From both perspectives man can only determine his own destiny insofar as he takes charge of those influences.

### DESTINY, HUMAN NATURE, AND THE FUTURE

When man takes charge of the influences which shape his beliefs, values, and behavior, the nature of man may change. At the present time, psychologists do not know the extent to which contemporary human nature — the focus of these lectures — is a function of the basic social environment in which all men currently exist. If the social environment were drastically altered, changes in man's more superficial characteristics may well occur.

Little is known about how current changes being introduced into man's social environment might affect the social nature of man. For this reason, there are definite dangers in man's attempts to improve his social environment unless considerable experimental work is carried out in advance. For example, the past several decades have seen a shift in the size of schools, as administrators have become convinced that having a few large schools is less expensive than having several smaller schools. The individuals working in the schools generally approve of such shifts since the principal of a large school has more prestige in our society than the principal of a small school. But the social environment of a large school is different from that of a small school. As Barker and Gump (1964) show, most of the social effects in large schools do not appear as positive for children's total development as are the social effects in small schools. For example, in the large schools the students are seldom involved in activities where they have any responsibility to others. Without practice in taking responsibility where others are involved, it is not likely that these young people will be prepared for responsible positions in the society after they graduate from the public schools.

Another example of the problems in reshaping social environments without adequate knowledge of their effects on man is provided by current welfare programs. The welfare programs were begun to overcome a definite problem, but, as is generally known, the results have been to build a social support system for poverty. Children raised within the welfare social support system have a difficult time transcending that system and hence have a high likelihood of being welfare recipients themselves. The results should not be surprising since the shifts in school size and the welfare program began without empirical information and feedback. In those conditions, as was discussed in the first lecture, finite human judgment is likely to be poor.

Human judgments producing engineered social environments, including religious social support systems, will only be improved as appropriate research is carried out. Unfortunately, religious institutions have shown little inclination to seriously pursue experimental social psychology. Without such efforts, religious groups may one day awake to find themselves losing what little influence they have to groups with a higher social psychological awareness.

Basic changes in human nature are possible through designed

genetic change (Sinscheimer, 1969; Munsinger, 1972). The extent to which basic changes in human nature can occur as a result of genetic alteration is currently unknown, but the present indications are that man may be able to remake his basic nature in significant ways. For example, the alteration of genetic structures of man's intellectual capacities may slightly reduce the finitude of his human judgment.

The potential for error through genetic mistakes is at least as great as the potential for error through misshaping social environments. Inasmuch as the geneticists look only at the immediate direct effects of their changes, the results may look quite good. But the effects upon social structures of even minor changes in the hereditary nature of man may be unpredictable and great. Genetically altering the nature of man is another area where the finiteness of human judgment needs to be emphasized so major errors can be avoided.

Whether the changes in man result from altering his genetic structure or changing his social environment, man needs to evaluate the desirability of the effects on his destiny which arise from the changes. The individuals who provide such evaluations need, on the basis of our discussions of finite human judgment, to be as personally uninvolved as possible. It would also be helpful if some degree of cultural transcendence was involved so that the judgments would not be limited by one culture's norms. At this point, the theologian may be helpful as a public ethicist (Seller, 1970). Since the theologian is not involved in genetic or social psychological research, not likely to be a direct recipient of the treatments, and is grounded in a tradition which extends across several cultures, he would seem to be an appropriate individual for reflecting on decisions which could reshape man.

Theological reflection upon ethical problems in medicine and other areas is already occuring, but as a response to the demands of other professions rather than as a part of man's shaping his own destiny. Hopefully, the view of man's destiny developed by theologians and philosophers would exert pressure on appropriate sciences and policy makers to produce the necessary principles and procedures to help men reach towards a worthwhile, self-determined destiny.

For some theologians to start demanding that science produce what is needed for man would require shifts in their style. No longer could the theologian remain abstracted from and ignorant of data-oriented disciplines such as social psychology; some knowledge of those disciplines would be necessary for him to carry out his task. With such knowledge, philosophers and theologians could reflect on the possibilities open to man and how best to achieve them as well as the areas where more research is needed. Cooperation between disciplines such as theology and psychology could produce an informed shift in man's practices and, perhaps, even in his nature. By informed action, man may yet shape his own destiny.

## CHAPTER V

# A Response To
# Doctor Richard Gorsuch

**PAUL K. JEWETT**

SINCE LANGUAGE is the incarnation of our thought, we can communicate with one another only as the terms employed have, for all parties concerned, at least a modicum of common meaning. At this elementary level of understanding, I have found the John Finch Symposium Lectures for 1973 quite unexceptionable and would commend Gorsuch for a stimulating presentation which, though scholarly, is yet accessible in its major themes to the uninitiated. Of course a theologian, like myself, seeking to understand a psychologist, has to adjust to terminology not characteristic of his own discipline. For example, when Gorsuch speaks of the church as a "religious social support system," or describes the person who acts from ethical conviction as employing "post-conventional reasoning processes," the theologian must attune his ears to terminology he is not accustomed to using.

There are one or two places in the lectures, however, where I have problems of understanding which seem to involve more than the use of language in a specialized way unfamiliar in theological usage. A case in point is found in the opening lecture in which Gorsuch speaks of man and finitude. Theologians have used the word finitude in the sense of "limitation" and have spoken of man as finite in that he always finds himself shut up in a specific space in which he exists for a limited span of time. This is true whether one thinks of the individual or of the race as a whole; man the species and all men as individuals are finite. With this meaning of finiteness, Gorsuch seems to agree, for he begins the discussion by observing that man as a finite creature "experiences only a limited part of reality for a limited time."

As the discussion unfolds, however, other terms are employed, which, for me, obscure the argument. For example, finitude seems to merge with the factor of personal involvement. When whites who are racists judge propositions to be pro-Black which non-racists regard as neutral or anti-Black, this is said to be an illustration of the way in which man's finite nature limits him. The theologian would deplore the bias of the white racists as perverse, but he would hardly look upon such bias as an instance of the limitations of human finitude. Finitude is an attribute of our nature as creatures; racial bias is a perversion of our nature as sinners. These are quite different concepts for the Christian theologian. A further instance of the use of the concept finitude in a way that is obscure to me concerns the question of whether a woman is less qualified than a man to judge of the merits of abortion. This seems hardly to be a matter of finitude. Men are just as finite as women by any definition of the term that the theologian understands.

On page 24 and following, the concept of finitude merges with the concept of the concrete. "When the situation is also finite, that is, concrete and well defined, then man's judgments will be more accurate than when the situation is more abstract and involves the integration of many factors." For theologians, the abstract is, indeed, set over against the concrete, but not the finite. That is abstract which does not deal with some particular object or thing. The pure sciences are more abstract than the applied sciences. Both are equally finite, however. Gorsuch suggests that the more concrete the situation, the more accurate are human judgments. But could not one say the reverse? What could be more accurate—and more abstract—than the logic of Aristotle or the geometry of Euclid? When a high school student follows Euclid in providing that the interior angles of a triangle are equal to two right angles, his proof is very accurate and highly abstract, since there are no real triangles having such a shape.

The second lecture, entitled "Man and Man" raises the ethical question of right and wrong, good and bad, moral and immoral behavior. Though not always agreeing on what acts are good or bad, theologians and ethicists have always used these terms to describe human behavior as measuring up to a standard or coming short of a standard. In the course of Gorsuch's discussion, this definition of the terms is sometimes made imprecise by juxtaposing the question of morality with that of maturity. This he does, evidently, in order to approach the question of morality "empirically," as he says. Since the ethical judgments of children are different from those made by adults, we may, he observes, call the former immature, the latter mature.

Now it is true that ethical principles cannot be formulated wholly apart from any consideration of the empirical situation—as the debate over situation ethics illustrates—but this is quite another question from immature vs. mature judgments. Maturity is a matter of growth, development, completion, perfection, as when one speaks of a mature plan or deliberation. But this implies nothing to the theological ethicist as to whether the deliberation is moral or immoral, good or bad. The advice of Ahithopel to Absalom that he should choose a band of men and pursue David immediately was surely a mature deliberation (See II Samuel 17:1-3). But it was an evil counsel for all its maturity, since it would have meant the death of God's anointed king, which was indeed Ahithopel's design and intent. By the same token, Lincoln's decision to emancipate the slaves was a mature deliberation on the part of the President; and it was a good deliberation, since slavery is an affront to the divine image in man. So far as maturity and immaturity are concerned, Christian ethicists would say that the more mature a decision the more it is either good or bad; the less mature, the less it is either good or bad. The decisions of children are less susceptible of ethical analysis than the decisions of adults just because children are immature as persons. All of this is simply to say that for the theologian ethics is not an empirical science; its concern is normative, not descriptive.

Beside these occasional problems in understanding exactly what Gorsuch means by certain terms, I am also puzzled by some of the observations he makes about theology and the theological enterprise. Probably these matters would have been clarified by elaboration on his part and one can appreciate his diffidence touching questions not directly in his field of specialty. Perhaps in his rejoinder he will be able to provide such elaboration.

I have in mind the following: On page 29 he expresses little enthusiasm for the making of theological systems. "The development of theological systems would be a questionable enterprise because it is impossible not to be personally involved, and because of the highly abstract nature of the analysis." However, since man's existential predicament does not afford him the luxury of indecision, he needs a world view. Gorsuch therefore sees the development of "theological world views" as an aid to finite man.

I gather from this that the development of theological systems for Gorsuch means the same as the development of theological world views. It would also appear that this questionable yet necessary activity of the theologian is not a matter of reflecting on the various affirmations of the Christian faith with a view to an orderly exposition of the teaching of the church. Rather, it is a matter of framing world views, *Weltanschauungen,* from a theological perspective. This has been attempted, to be sure, especially by St. Thomas Aquinas. Protestant theologians, following the lead of John Calvin, have been rather less ambitious however, leaving such system building to the philosophers of religion. In fact, the most influential theologians of this century, taking their cue from Soren Kierkegaard, the Danish philosopher who struggled valiantly to save Christianity from being swallowed up by Hegel's system, have eschewed all world views as the overweening dream of *Geist.* When asked about his "system," Barth was wont to say that it consisted of two affirmations: God is in heaven and man is on earth. Brunner went even further and indicated the building of world views as the manifestation of the fall into sin at the intellectual level.*

I wonder, then, if Gorsuch really believes that "theological world views" could be framed that would aid finite man. Perhaps he speaks this way because for him there is no essential difference between philosophy and theology, between the system of Plotinus and the thought of Augustine after he left Neo-Platonism and became a Christian theologian.

I suspect Gorsuch would see little difference ultimately between philosophy and theology since he observes ". . . paradoxes in a philosophical or theological system are generally sufficient evidence to seriously question that system. However, paradoxes are not unusual in scientific theories and are not a matter of great concern." The reverse is true so far as my own understanding of theology and science is concerned. It is quite correct that philosophical systems have striven for consistency and coherence. In this Gorsuch cannot be gain-said. One has only to recall Kant's essay on radical evil (*Hang zum Bösen*), ignored by his followers as absurd, to have an illustration of the philosophic concern with coherence. The natural sciences also have, like philosophy, endeavored to eliminate the paradox. Such endeavor is reflected in the celebrated meeting at Copenhagen of the world's leading physicists when confronted with the paradox of Heisenberg's principle of indeterminacy, or the endless debates about the paradoxes of relativity among cosmologists and astronomers. The slowing down of the clock in Einstein's theory of relativity has generated as much effort at rational explanation among scientists as Zeno's paradoxes among philosophers.

But Christian theology, in striking contrast, has reflected and defended some pretty fundamental paradoxes: God's Trinitarian being as one in three (Nicea); the divine-human Christ of the Incarnation (Chalcedon); not to mention a divine-human

---

*For a rigorous criticism of Paul Tillich's systematic theology on this score as really philosophy of religion rather than Christian theology, see *The System and the Gospel* by Kenneth Hamilton (Grand Rapids, 1963).

book, the Bible, which tells us of God's sovereignty and man's responsibility in a way that leaves us with a paradox. Not all theologians, to be sure, have been happy with these paradoxes, but their efforts to resolve them have ended more often than not in heresy. Hence the church's rejection of every theology which reduces the paradoxes of the Christian faith to a rational synthesis.

Moving in toward the center of the discussion, I believe the lectures of Gorsuch focus the principle question  one must face in seeking to integrate the insights of psychology and a Christian view of man. I am not sure I can frame an adequate answer to the question, but I think I can state the question. It is just this: Is man a little lower than the angels, or a little higher than the animals? Is he in his essential being subject or object, person or thing? Put in this way in order to focus the issue, the matter is of course over-simplified. While a thoroughgoing reductionism would opt for a model of man as object, and pure idealism would conceive of man as transcendent spirit incarcerated, for the time being, in a body, Christians of every name would regard man as both object and subject, body and spirit. But in Christian theology the accent is on the spirit, that is, the personal self, viewed as a subject in what has been called an I-thou relationship with God and neighbor. In proportion, therefore, as one studies man as object, Christian theology is relatively indifferent to the results of such studies. And these results, by the same token, are a matter of precise description and quantitative, empirical measurement. Such, for example, are the findings in physiology with which medical science works. The structure and function of human organs, tissues, and cells, the analysis of processes of a physical and chemical sort by which these organs operate—all these matters have to do with man as object.

But as one moves from physiology to psychology and sociology, as the terms themselves imply, one is moving from the study of man as object to the study of man as subject in relationship to other subjects. Proportionately, therefore, the results of these studies are not simply a matter of precise description and quantitative measurement. Rather, these studies yield results that evoke judgments of value. Indeed, apart from such judgments of value, statistics and measurements in this area are largely jejune, if not meaningless. One may go even further and affirm that without value judgments, it is impossible to determine what is worth analysis and measurement in man's individual and social behavior.

The key theological concept which grounds all these judgments of value for the Christian theologian is the *imago Dei.* So far as man is subject, he is like God, copied from God, reflects God, and therefore is uniquely related to God and to his neighbor. This is true of all men by definition, whether they be related to God and neighbor negatively in sin or positively in grace. This theological view of man perceives every effort to reduce man, who is subject, to mere object, as the abolition of man. Man, for the Christian theologian, is not in his essential self a little higher than the animals but a little lower than the angels.

Another way of putting it is to say that the essential truth about man as person is grounded in the realm of transcendence. Man is the being who so transcends the realm of empirical causality as to be free, self-determined, and responsible. Therefore, to the degree his acts are truly human, they cannot be ultimately understood in terms of what is, but only of what ought to be. And between these two dimensions of imminence and transcendence, "is-ness" (*Sein*) and "ought-ness" (*Sollen*), there is a qualitative difference. Such then is the perspective from which I work as a theologian; I tend to see man as subject and to be suspicious of every approach to him which suggests that he is mere object. For me the great threat of psychology to a true and adequate understanding of man is that in its concern to be scientifically objective, psychology may reduce man to mere object. By the same token, Gorsuch, as a scientist, tends to find theology, if not a threat to the right understanding of man, in any case a perspective that is not very helpful, since he tends to see man as object whose behavior is to be studied empirically. In those areas where psychology and sociology have found it impossible to discover answers by analysis of empirical data, he would allow theology to speak. He tells us, for example, that "since psychology does not require one to assume either complete determinism or complete free will, we will be able to leave the question to the philosophers and theologians . . ." The theologian, however, will greet such a magnanimous gesture with a cool smile.

Perhaps the best opportunity afforded by Gorsuch's lectures for analyzing the manner in which the work of the psychologist and the theologian converge in their effort to understand man, though they are never looking through the same spectacles, is his handling of the question of man's moral turpitude from the vantage point of description, empirical measurement and casual explanation. The point of view is basically horizontal, immanental.

I, by contrast, an orthodox theologian, approach this question from the vantage point of a standard of right and wrong which I accept as a disclosure on God's part, in and through the history of Israel, of his will for man. This divine self-disclosure culminates in the life, death and resurrection of Jesus Christ, the Word made flesh, who was with God in the beginning and who is God (Jn. 1:1). Such a point of view is basically vertical, transcendental. Man's sinfulness is viewed as failure to measure up to the norm which God has given first through Moses the lawgiver and finally in Jesus Christ. Sin, therefore, is ultimately rebellion, revolt against God. In its primary form (original sin) this rebellion is a manifestation of pride, the desire to be like God; a perverseness which manifests itself toward one's neighbor as self-love, expropriating one's neighbor for one's own advantage rather than giving oneself to one's neighbor in loving service.

I do not mean to say that these two perspectives—the vertical and the horizontal—are mutually exclusive. The theological ethicist has much to learn from the data-oriented scientist. Take, for example, Gorsuch's analysis of social influence upon individual decision. The theological ethicist knows that no man is an island, that there is a solidarity of the race in evil, but the kind of precise measurement of this influence which is offered in the second lecture under the title "Man and Man" sharpens the point markedly.

Furthermore, the psychologist's research not only gives sharper definition to theological affirmations about the sinfulness of man, but it also corrects fallacies into which one may easily fall as a theologian. For example, one who approaches the question of racial prejudice from a theological perspective alone would almost surely reason that practicing Christians will show a minimum of prejudice, nominal Christians more prejudice, and non-Christians, especially those who are consciously so, maximum prejudice. But the data, which is a critical limiting factor for the theologian, does not bear out this conclusion. People with no religious commitment come out at about the same place as people with deep religious commitment. (See the section, Chapter IV, "Social Transcendence as a Function of Value Commitment.") In these and other illustrations that could be culled from the lectures, one sees the value of controlled empirical data in framing a theological judgment about human behavior, specifically culpable human behavior.

But one also needs to look at the other side of the picture, the side with which theology is concerned, in which the vertical perspective in the interpretation of man's moral failure is emphasized. It is here that the final issues are drawn. Gorsuch's treatment of the question of moral evil, *from this perspective,* I find less than satisfying. His lectures are marked by a tendency to reduce ethics to a descriptive rather than a normative science and to give an optimistic reading of man's moral ability by seeking a rational explanation of his sinful behavior. I stress the point that I am speaking about tendencies rather than specific affirmations in the lectures, though I shall cite some specific affirmations which reflect these tendencies. I recognize that these tendencies are consonant with a liberal theological stance in which there is little interest in atonement theory and salvation by grace because there is a basic optimism about man's moral potential and his ability to solve the problems created by his moral failure through rational insight and enlightened good will. I do not share this liberal theological stance.

Turning to the lectures, there is a section in Chapter III entitled "Man's Inhumane Treatment of Man." Gorsuch states that "evil" and "inhumane" are terms necessary if we are to have a complete description of human nature. The term "evil," he tells us, is used in the lecture as a psychological rather than a theological category. By this he means that his use of the term has a man to man reference only. He is not concerned with evil defined as willful disobedience to God, but defined as treatment of one's fellow man that increases injustice and injury in the world. I can only reply that Christian theology knows no distinction. He who treats his neighbor unjustly *is* disobedient to God.

In the section "Finite Judgments as a Source of Man's Inhumanity," Gorsuch makes an effort to show that man's inhumanity to man is sometimes a matter of poor judgment, as when thirty people in New York watched a man take half an hour to kill Kitty Geneviese. Researchers found upon inquiry that some of the by-standers assumed that someone else was helping or would soon do so. Others waited for someone to lead in group action. Due to these errors of judgment, Kitty lost her life. One wonders if it occurred to the psychological and sociological researchers that one of the effects of original sin is deceitfulness? To ask people, who should have helped another, why they did not do so and to suppose that they would tell the truth, the whole truth and nothing but the truth, is from the theologian's standpoint naive. When we do wrong we are never without excuse which we call a reason by which to palliate our peversity.

Besides ignorance, Gorsuch seeks to account for man's inhumanity by appealing to his moral immaturity. Because some people's development has failed, they do not make ethical decisions and treat others justly. He stresses the fact that the term immaturity is not defined value-wise but empirically by examining the difference between children and adults. Adults who still function at a child's level are labeled immature. This would surely seem to imply that such ethically retarded adults are not responsible for their moral deficiency. Gorsuch says as much, though in a somewhat circuitous manner:

> Inasmuch as ethically immature people are in positions of responsibility, then their amoral decisions will create many problems for others, problems which could be interpreted as evidence for the evil nature of mankind. If one appraises only acts, then the observable behavior of the ethically immature individual will be a strong argument for such constructs as original sin, every man's need for salvation and redemption, and the generally evil nature of man. A judgment of man's nature based upon the apparent intentions of immature people would also support this argument. When talking to a person who uses immature reasoning processes, one is impressed with his concern for his own gain, i.e. his selfishness. And the immature person who has not yet developed a sense of values will also be seen as having bad intentions. Such data would then support a negative view of mankind.
>
> Evidence for man's inhumane treatment of man which arises from immaturity raises an interesting question: Should we judge man by what some men are, by what men usually are, or by what man can be? If we judge man by what some men are, then serious attention must be given to the immature individual and the decision may be that man is inherently bad. On the other hand, if only those who are mature are examined, the picture shifts. The conclusion would probably be that mankind is basically good. In all likelihood, some of the differences among classical philosophers and theologians on the question of the goodness of man probably arise from their different views of immature adults.

I find such a paragraph scientifically imprecise and theologically superficial.*

Gorsuch next raises the question whether man is naturally aggressive. Again imprecision plagues the discussion. Is ag-

---

*Everyone recognizes, of course, that some people are retarded and as a result become physically adults while remaining intellectually and/or emotionally children. But such people may be very devout and moral or very impious and immoral in their life style. In the latter instance, they may be institutionalized. Yet though they are thus treated as no longer free agents, society does not hold them responsible; their incarceration is not an instance of retributative justice. I do not have the impression, however, that Doctor Gorsuch intends to limit the use of "immature" in the above discussion to such cases.

gressiveness wrong per se? Apparently not, since he speaks of that mild parental "aggression appropriate to a young child who 'needs' such treatment . . ." But the sort of aggressiveness he principally has in mind is an attitude which moves one to "acts injuring other people." All Christian theologians would surely agree with Gorsuch that such action can be evil, as when slave masters in a fit of pique beat their slaves until their lacerated flesh was bloody. But what if the slave was man enough to pick up the nearest club, resist his master and strike back with the intent of making it impossible for his master ever again to beat him or a fellow slave? Is such an act of aggression, which surely had as its primary intent "injuring another person," wrong?

I do not doubt, as a theologian, that acts of aggression can be learned and that the psychologist can frame certain principles of learning that throw light on how they are learned. For this information the theologian is grateful. But to say these "learning principles apply equally well to all species; even the gentle dove can be taught to be aggressive by simple Skinnarian procedures" is more confusing than helpful, in my judgment. Is it wrong for the psychologist to send the gentle dove to school and turn him into an aggressive dove? One smiles at such a question as ridiculous because the acts of doves, whether gentle or aggressive, are neither moral nor immoral. But then, why appeal to dove behavior in a discussion of the moral qualities of man's inhumanity to man? Even before Skinner learned how to educate doves, everybody had observed and knew full well that lions will kill each other fighting over a lioness or a zebra's carcass. But is this really "cannibalistic murder" as Gorsuch calls it, quoting the research of another psychologist? Surely such a conceit cannot have as its purpose to make the lion look bad, but to make man look good, or at least not so bad as the theologians, following the lead of Paul, Augustine, and Calvin, have tended to make him look. "There is no evidence," says Gorsuch, "that man is necessarily more aggressive than most of the other creatures on earth, for [concerning?] whom the term depraved is seldom used." Not only is the term seldom used, it is never so used, to my knowledge, by moral philosophers and theologians in such a context.

Finally, having related man to the animals, where the theologian would relate him to God, Gorsuch goes on to speak of the effect of environment on man's behavior. He cites the instance of boys in summer camp who found the pressure of competition in games the occasion for expressing hostile aggression toward one another. This aggression "arose solely as the means of obtaining a desirable end [winning the game] when no other means were available." But for the theological ethicist, a *desirable* end—winning the game—is not in itself a *good* end, save as it is achieved by superior play according to the rules of the game. However, from the psychologist's perspective, such "aggression is the result of man's striving for intrinsically good goals which happen to exclude other men achieving the same goals." The harm, we are told, brought to others is a "by-product" of this good goal seeking. For the Christian theologian, by contrast (the Jesuistic opponents of Pascal being excepted), there are no good goals to be so achieved. The end does not justify the means.* A goal which is achieved by harming others is a bad goal. Of course those who justify such attaining of a goal at the expense of others are, according to Gorsuch, using "pre-moral reasoning processes" which are the mark of immaturity.

Gorsuch concludes his discussion of man's inhuman acts as follows:

> The general conclusions from analyses of man's inhumanity is that man has no drives or goals which can only be satisfied at the expense of others. Instead, the drives and goals a person seeks may cause evil because he has no means of obtaining the goals without harming others. Our general results would suggest that there are three major causes of observed inhumane treatment of man by his fellow man: man's tendency toward judgmental errors, his failure

---

*The ends do not justfy the means in the sense that one cannot infer necessarily from the conclusion that an end is good, that any means which will achieve said good end, is itself good.

to approach problems with a mature ethical reasoning process, and the environmental situations which place him in competition with his fellow man to achieve the same goals.

A paragraph like this reminds one of a remark of Celia to Reilly in T. S. Eliot's *The Cocktail Party:*

> I have always been taught to disbelieve in sin.
> Oh, I don't mean that it was ever mentioned!
> But everything wrong, from our point of view,
> Was either bad form, or was *psychological.*

To be sure Gorsuch says, "But using social psychological research as a basis for maximizing the good in man does not mean that social institutions can be remade to remove all evil from the world." (p. 54) The late British philosopher C. E. M. Joad put it a bit more emphatically and, in my way of thinking, more accurately, when speaking of his conversion to the Christian faith. Animadverting on his pre-Christian thought, he observes that it was:

> "a little inadequate on the moral side. Sin and evil I dismissed," he says, "as the incidental accompaniments of man's imperfect development. . . The war opened my eyes to the impossibility of writing off what I had better call man's 'sinfulness' as a mere by-product of circumstances. The evil in man was due, I had been taught, either to economic circumstances (because people were poor, their habits were squalid, their tastes undeveloped, their passions untamed) or to psychological circumstances."

Being compelled to abandon this confidence in man's capacity for the good, Joad goes on to say that as a result he came to embrace "the hope offered in the Christian doctrine that God sent his Son into the world to save sinners." And having made such a choice he set his feet "on the steep and slippery path that leads to heaven." (Joad, 1948)

## CHAPTER VI

# Man in Society

H. NEWTON MALONY

GORSUCH'S EFFORT to induce man's nature from the findings of social psychology is a commendable enterprise. He attempts to remain the scientist throughout and to report only what research has found to be true. He avoids speculation where there is no evidence. He often admits a given subject has not been investigated and points the reader to future studies. He declines to pontificate outside his area of expertise. He claims to speak as a social psychologist who is limited by the available data on mid-twentieth century man. Further, he confines his conclusions to those regarding the nature of man as described by the contemporary evidence. His view is, thus, historically limited and conditioned by his own place and time. Further, he presents his deductions as descriptions rather than explanations, as if to suggest he knows *what* is so but not *why*. He defines his task as that of inductively seeking a pattern within the data and of being silent where there is no evidence to report.

Without yet attending to the content of his treatises, let it be said that the above description of method, if it be accurate, leaves the reactor both vague and confused. We are never clear as to what social psychology is nor as to what social psychologists do. Therefore, it is difficult to fully appreciate Doctor Gorsuch's method. At best we often are left with feeling social psychologists do what Doctor Gorsuch is doing and a social psychological view of man's nature is no more or less than Doctor Gorsuch has reported. His limitations regarding method and content play into such a reaction.

Admittedly, the above is somewhat of a caricature. Nevertheless, the reader would have benefited from some definitional statements delineating the concerns and approaches of social psychology. These would have made the task of interacting with him a clearer and more manageable one.

That he did not do so does not suggest to me he is unclear on these issues, however. I trust he agrees with Hollander (1971) in perceiving social psychology to be that scientific field which "directs its attention to *understanding* the influences producing regularities and diversities in human *social* behavior" (p. 3). Further, I think he would agree that social psychology attempts to understand both "The *individual* as a participant in social relations and . . . The social influences process underlying these relationships" (p. 4). Nevertheless, because he was not explicit in these matters he almost ignored the two most time-honored concerns of social psychology, i.e. motivation and influence.

Regarding motivation, Gorsuch notes that man is characterized by ". . . a self activating nature, a continuing curiosity and . . . a constant desire to analyze and understand." He further states, "man is a creature who is constantly trying to take his destiny into his own hands." However, these passing references do not provide a thorough discussion of man's motives, i.e. those forces that prompt his interactions with other persons. A clearer statement of the task of social psychology might have prevented this omission. Certainly, as I shall point out, motivation has been a perennial concern of social psychology (and social philosophy). I feel it holds some important cues concerning the nature of man.

Regarding social influence, Gorsuch seems solely concerned with the ways man conforms to or resists others. But as August Comte posed the paradox over a century ago "How is it that man *shapes* society and yet *is shaped* by it?" To be sure Gorsuch refers to the need for support systems that enhance post-conventional thinking but the model, even here, is that of passive man. He over-emphasizes man's powerlessness. The corrective I offer later in this essay is an appreciation for the influence persons have on groups. This, I feel, is a more balanced view which takes account of the interaction between an individual and society. It further provides for a more positive role for institutions than I feel Gorsuch allows.

Finally, I find in Gorsuch an illustration of his own analysis that man is unaware of how much his judgments depend on others. Some scientists have presumed they came to the task without presumptions. Gorsuch seems to imply this in spite of the fact that he acknowledges scientific paradigms dictate what the researcher looks for or considers important.

A view of human nature may be one of those assumptions that is pre-scientific. I think it is. Further, I would see Gorsuch as in need of becoming more explicit about his assumptions which he brings to the data. Therefore, I shall discuss these issues and report on the research in this area later in the chapter.

## DESCRIPTION AND ANALYSIS OF CONTENT

Again, Gorsuch's efforts to summarize the conclusions from social psychology regarding man's nature are commendable. They could be summarized by the following statements:

(1) Men seem to follow similar processes in the development of moral and ethical reasoning, i.e. they progress from pre-moral, anarchistic to conventional, socially acceptable thinking about right and wrong. Some men progress to a post-conventional level and reason on the basis of values that supersede the culture of which they are a part.

(2) Man's ability to make judgments is inadequate and is limited by his ability to gather information, to broaden his experience, to reason at the appropriate level, to reflect on his own weaknesses, to free himself from presumptions and involvment, to comprehend the complexity of situations, and to recognize meaningless data.

(3) Man, in general, conforms to the judgments of groups he is in and is unaware of how much he is influenced by other persons. Further, the more ambiguous and the more complex

the situation, the more man conforms to the group decision. Man's behavior will conform to the group he is in and he will be inconsistent in his behavior from one group to another. Man forms his groups by coincidence then later reflects the group norm without questioning them. Man's need for others makes him dependent on them.

(4) Man often treats his fellow man inhumanely because of his own limited ability to make decisions or because of the immaturity of his judgment. Often his inhumaneness is due to his inability to extricate himself from the influence of others.

(5) Man is adaptable and will behave more lovingly toward others where he sees models being concerned, where he is free to choose new alternatives, where he discusses moral dilemmas, where he is in a close-knit group whose purpose is doing good and where interactions with opposing groups is limited.

(6) Man is always striving to determine his own destiny. Where he feels responsible his behavior is related to his values. However, very often, he is not predictable for a variety of reasons including social pressure. Internalized values help man transcend social influence and cause him to be unpredictable. He becomes less dependent on group norms.

The above summary is brief. There are important omissions such as Gorsuch's treatment of leadership. Yet the gist of his arguments is intact. They call for some critical additions. First, there is a need to delineate more fully the ways in which basic assumptions about human nature influence behavior. Gorsuch only mentions this in a passing reference (cf. the reference to Crow and Hammond, 1957). It remains to be demonstrated just how these develop and whether they are shared within a group. But that they are related to behavior is a proven fact. Second, Gorsuch's view of how man comes to know what he knows, i.e. his epistemology, is highly individualistic. It emphasizes sensation over perception and absolute over social reality. Gorsuch often writes as if there is a real world beyond man's perception and the judgments of his fellows. An alternative view needs to be considered. Third, conformity seems to be simplistically presented. It is a complex process serving many purposes. It is not entirely negative, as Gorsuch implies. His appreciation for conformity is blinded by an over-emphasis on an individualistic ethic. Conformity needs reconsideration. It can be a force promoting transcendence and uniqueness. Finally, Gorsuch does not appreciate the value of groups and institutions. His discussion is limited to either a caution regarding their pressures or the use of them to support individual values. Perhaps this is an overstatement but it is fair to say that in general Gorsuch distrusts society and sees it as a necessary but frustrating force. More needs to be said about the possibility that groups can be structured to enhance individual initiative and the opportunity persons have to influence groups as well as be influenced by them.

The remainder of this essay will include discussions of several of the issues mentioned above. By and large, they should be conceived as supplements to Gorsuch rather than contradictives. I will not delimit myself as Gorsuch did, however, to available data. For good or ill, I intend to suggest hypotheses and offer interpretations which go beyond our current evidence.

## ASSUMPTIONS ABOUT HUMAN NATURE
### Assumptions Underlying the Scientific Task

It is widely acknowledged that basic assumptions dictate not only the events to be studied but also the facts to be observed. Gorsuch acknowledged this, in part. He suggests that a scientific theory (or paradigm) organizes the data so that it can be absorbed by a finite mind; identifies that which is relevant; is also an aid for deciding what research to pursue. He even acknowledges that: "The major differences between behavioristic psychologists such as Skinner and the humanistic psychology movements appear to be in their world views, which suggests that these broader constructs influence how man conducts his science."

However, it does not appear to be the case that Gorsuch acknowledges his own dependence on certain views of human nature. These will become clearer later in this section. Suffice it to say that there can be no atheoretical science and Gorsuch's intent to let the facts speak for themselves is no exception. Assumptions are always present. Even Skinner's pretense that "serendipity" (or the discovery of the un-sought-for) is possible has been called into question. Following rats who jump the maze does not make one free from basic assumptions about their nature and the processes by which rats learn.

## ASSUMPTIONS OR THEORIES MAN ALWAYS HAS WITH HIM
### Human Nature: A Persistent Concern of the Social Sciences

The nature of man, i.e. his persisting characteristics and guiding impulses, has been a perennial concern of the social philosophers throughout the centuries. This is no less true of their modern counterparts, the social scientists. This interest has expressed itself in two concerns: One, the search for a master motive, and, two, the attempt to understand how man is related to society.

### The Search for a Master Motive

In attempts to determine whether man was innately good or bad, philosophers since Aristotle have theorized about the extent to which man's behavior was determined by instinct and, if so, what kind? The most persistent tradition has seen man as basically hedonistic or pleasure seeking (e.g. Thomas Hobbes). Jeremy Bertham even proposed that man searched for pleasure at the expense of other men and that even altruistic acts were calculatedly self serving. Social contract views of society, as exemplified in Freud's *Group Psychology and the Analysis of the Ego* (1921), saw man as giving up part of his freedom in order to be protected against the self-centeredness of other men. Government, therefore, served a constraining and protective function. Of course, much of this point of view is also seen in the tenets of Darwinism.

No doubt self-centeredness is the dominant force in much

nodern psychology. Examples of this range from the self-psy-
:hology of Rogers, to the individual psychology of Adler to the
1umanistic psychology of Maslow.

While the search for a "master" motive is to some extent
passé, the assumption that man is primarily concerned with his
place, his status and his destiny is widely accepted. Certainly,
my formulation of man's motives into survival, satisfaction and
self-actualization (Malony, 1972) is based on this theme. Gorsuch
agrees with this as seen in his statement, ". . . man is a creature
constantly striving to take his destiny into his own hands."

More frequent attention to this basic assumption about
human motivation would have tempered the impression Gorsuch
often gives of detailing behavioral phenomena which is devoid
of rationale. His discussions of conformity, for example, seem
simplistic and do not clearly present man's behavior as guided
by self-concern. I am confident Gorsuch would not affirm Tarde's
laws of "imitation" which imply man copies other men simply
because he is created "suggestible." No, I feel he would agree
that man conforms because it serves his self-interest. Nevertheless, this necessary precondition is not referred to and thus the
reader is left somewhat confused.

## Man—Society Relations

Another aspect of man's nature that has evoked concern is
his relationship to society. Much like the heredity-environment
question is the issue of whether, and to what extent, man shapes,
or is shaped by, the society in which he lives. While Auguste
Comte posed the question, Gustave LeBon in his book *The Crowd*
(1897) gave the answer with which many social scientists agreed
until recently, namely, that man had a natural tendency to
imitate. This tendency overwhelmed his rational judgment when
he was in crowds and, thus, he was at the mercy of the "group
mind." It was as if man lost his autonomy and became subject to
the passion of the crowd. LeBon's rationale was a modern expression of Plato's conception that the masses were dominated
by feelings and needed the philosopher kings, who were ruled

by reason, to rule them. It is interesting that the assumption that man lost control of himself in groups permeated psychology in general to the extent that social and abnormal psychology were often grouped together. For example, *The Journal of Abnormal and Social Psychology* was published as late as 1965.

Three forces have altered scholars' views of man's relationship to society. One is the growing willingness to accept emotions as trustworthy and valid bases for action. The human relations movement encourages expression of feeling on the presumption that the greater danger is to be hyper-rational and deny emotions. Second, there is a growing opinion that man is not frustrated but fulfilled by others (cf. Sullivan, 1953). This is a positive view of man as essentially a social being. Others do not prevent him from reaching his goals. Human relationships are the prime goals for which man exists according to this position (cf. Cooley, 1922). Finally, the studies of leadership and social influence (e.g. Hollander, 1964) have demonstrated that man is not simply the victim of the groups to which he belongs but that they, in turn, are a function of the influence he exerts.

Gorsuch seems to affirm the older point of view, namely, that man looses his rationality in groups and thus man should resist society's influence if he is to live a transcendent life. It appears to be an over-emphasis on individual rationality coupled with a distrust of society.

These somewhat dated presuppositions color much of what Gorsuch has to say and confound his conclusions, in my opinion. He suggests man must divest himself of the influence of convention. He has a negative view of society.

## Current Research on Philosophies of Human Nature

The last decade has produced a program of research designed to measure differences in person's views toward human nature (Wrightsman, 1974). In a review of this endeavor, he (Wrightsman) notes the difference between the view of man implicit in *Lord of the Flies* and *Coral Island*. In the former a negative, pessimistic outlook of man under stress is given while in the latter, which incidentally poses the same stranded-on-a-tropical-island situation, a positive, more hopeful view is proposed.

These and many other sources led Wrightsman to propose six substantive dimensions of beliefs about human nature.

*Trustworthiness versus Untrustworthiness*—This is an indication of the extent to which one believes persons to be honest and responsible as opposed to immoral and irresponsible.

*Altruism versus Selfishness*—This is a measure of the extent to which one sees persons as basically self-centered or concerned for others.

*Independence versus Conformity to Group Pressures*—This is a judgment of the extent to which persons conform to the pressures of groups and authority or resist them.

*Strength of Will and Rationality versus External Locus of Control and Irrationality*—This is a judgment of persons' ability to control their own destiny as opposed to being pushed along by outside forces without understanding their own motivation.

*Complexity versus Simplicity*—This is a dimension which distinguishes between the view that man is complicated and hard to understand as opposed to being simple and easy to comprehend.

*Similarity versus Variability*—This is a judgment of the extent to which persons are unique or alike.

A reliable and construct valid scale to measure these dimensions has been developed by Wrightsman (1964). It has been widely utilized in research over the past decade (cf. Wrightsman and Hearn, 1971). Gorsuch himself participated in a factor analysis designed to empirically confirm the logical factors suggested by Wrightsman (Nottingham, Gorsuch and Wrightsman, 1970). It is interesting that Gorsuch did not mention this research.

Among the studies which suggest views toward human nature related to behavior is my dissertation (Malony, 1964) which found a small but significant correlation between a positive view of human nature (a combination of the first four dimensions of the Philosophy of Human Nature Scale) and a tendency for pastoral care behavior to be rated more like the ideal. Since the Rating Scale which was used on the written responses to typical pastoral care situations was patterned after the Rogerian Therapeutic Model of empathy, congruence and warmth, it would seem that a more positive, hopeful outlook toward human nature prompted more approach behavior on the part of the pastors who were studied. The reverse was also true. The more negative the view of human nature the more cold and withdrawn was the pastor.

It has likewise been found that guidance counselors have more positive views of human nature than medical students (Wrightsman, 1974). Other research suggested that those who trusted others in the Prisoner's Dilemma Game were more likely to be positive in their view of human nature than those who did not (Wrightsman, 1966).

Although it is true as Gorsuch suggests that the evidence is not consistent that views of human nature and behavior are related, it is most likely a case of our methodological naiveté rather than error in our judgment.

## Gorsuch's Basic Presuppositions

I would like to predict that if we were to administer the Philosophy of Human Nature Scale (Wrightsman, 1964) to Gorsuch he would score high on untrustworthiness, selfishness, conformity, external locus of control, irrationality, simplicity and similarity. In short, he appears to have a negative view of man. In phrase form, I perceive his assumptions to be:

(a) man at his best is reasonable, but

(b) society frustrates and confuses man, and, since

(c) conformity is what man inevitably does,

(d) true morality is to transcend group pressure.

I will attempt to show how these assumptions permeate Gorsuch's treatise. Hopefully some viable alternatives will be proposed.

## EPISTEMOLOGY AND SOCIAL INTERACTION

How does man know what he knows? What are the processes whereby one comes to know something and the procedures wherein one validates this knowledge against some standard? These are the questions of epistemology.

A discussion of these issues is critical since Gorsuch places such weighty emphasis on the finitude of man's decisions and judgments. In fact, one could classify him as a "probable pessimist" but "possible optimist" with regard to the ability of man to know the truth. This means he doubts conventional man's ability to make true judgments but trusts the solitary individual who has ideals to reason his way to truth. He is, thus, a pessimist but also an optimist.

He seems to model his total approach on correcting the "personal equation." It may be remembered that the helper Kinnebrook was fired from his job at Greenwich Laboratory in 1796 because it was discovered that he was always off a few seconds in assessing the time it took a star to traverse the grid. Although Kinnebrook lost his job, it later became common to correct for personal errors in judgment. This was done by adding to or subtracting from the assessment a constant equal to the average number of seconds an individual was in error over a period of time. This correction thus purified the judgment by removing the error variance due to personal differences in reaction time. Gorsuch follows this model. He gives a devastating analysis of the error factors in man's decision making then suggests ways man can refine his judgments.

Most of his suggestions are in the scientific tradition of Kinnebrook's personal equation, e.g. acknowledge your presuppositions and involvment, set up judgment procedures, resist conformity, repeat the judgment, seek an outside standard or norm.

It is in reference to this last suggestion, i.e. the outside norm, that more needs to be said. The presumption here is that there is, in fact, a real world (of facts and ideals) outside man which can apprehended through the use of purified reason. There is room to question this presumption especially in regard to complex and ambiguous questions where Gorsuch says man has the most trouble. One might question both whether there are in fact ultimate answers to these questions outside of man and whether, if there be such answers, man can get at them through a purified reason. It just may be that a more pessimistic view than Gorsuch gives is in order. Man may be unable to extricate himself from personal involvment *particularly* in complex and ambiguous situations. Moreover, there may be no ultimate reality outside of man to which man can refer. He may, in fact, have to trust the social process, or the "community of faith," as it were. This Gorsuch seems unwilling to do. Further elaboration of these points will follow.

## Sensation and Perception

Man's experience of reality begins with sensation but does not end there. It continues with perception. Perception is what the mind does with sensations which come to it through stimulation of the sense organs. This "what" that the mind does has been a concern of philosophers long before and since Immanuel Kant. It was Kant, however, who proposed that the mind contained innate categories which it used to organize these sensations. Thus, it categorized everything as occurring at some place or some time and as being made of some substance or caused by some previous event. Kant had a nondynamic view of perception. It is now acknowledged that the mind not only categorizes but selectively attends to some sensations and not to others, brings meaning to events in terms of past experience and functions to guide one toward his goals. The perceptual sets persons take with them are not so much innate, as Kant postulated, but are a function of person's interactions in the past and their yearnings for the future. Perception is inextricably involved in personal history.

Gorsuch seems to ignore perception and to act as if sensation was the critical process. Yet, in the words of William James, the world would be a "booming, buzzing confusion" were it not for perception. The sense organs function more or less indiscriminately. They send to the brain every sensation. It is the mind, i.e. the brain in action, that sorts and selects from among the sensations. I find a position that emphasizes pure sensation. to be very difficult to comprehend. To assume that we can purify perception and get behind it to reality, as I infer Gorsuch would have us do, seems an impossible task.

## Newtonian Epistemology Unwarranted

The history of the philosophy of science abounds with themes which keep repeating themselves. One such idea is grounded in the "great design" approach of Sir Issac Newton. His peace with the church was made by assuming that the reason of man was the tool whereby God's "great design" could be discovered. Thus a natural faith, grounded in the evolving pattern of creation discovered by the human mind, was proposed as a legitimate extension of faith based on revelation.

The important issue for our purposes is not the faith-reason controversy but the assumption that there is a natural order, or a reality, outside of man which man can understand through the use of his rational powers. Discovery is the correct word for this epistemological position. Reason is the means whereby the discovery takes place.

Hume, among others, questioned these assumptions. He suggested that we are unable to ascertain whether we are imposing or discovering an order on events. Inferences concerning cause and effect may be no more than artifacts of contiguity. Further, patterns themselves, e.g. the brown cow eating green grass and producing white milk, may be coincidences rather than illustrations of God's creative order. Order, Hume proposed, is an inference, not a discovery.

The ghosts of Newton and Hume are not dead. Many scientists still make Newtonian assumptions and ground their religious faith as well as their epistemology on them.

It would seem to me that in most of the areas with which social psychology is concerned a Newtonian epistemology is unwarranted. Gorsuch seems to decry the fact that man is dependent on his fellows in abstract and complex situations. Yet these may be the areas par excellence for social psychology. They may also be the areas in which the probability of discovering a reality outside is next to impossible.

The important judgments men must make are unlike the classification of rock strata in a hillside. These judgments about loyalty, love, values, meaning and ideals can scarcely be grounded in individual rational discoveries. Gorsuch seems to imply that there is a reality out there to be apprehended. He seems confident that even in the abstract and complex we can approach reality if we purify our reason enough. My opinion is that this Newtonian epistemology is questionable. I do not think that the important issues of human decision making can be thought of as quantitative extensions of such research as the Asch (1958) experiment in which the actual amount of autokinetic movement was always known. Nor do I agree that the Forer (1949) study of how a group of college students all made personal sense out of the same test data illustrates man's propensity for missing reality. In fact, the reality may have been in the consistency perceived by the students rather than in the inappropriate test protocol constructed by the experiment. Finally, in the Armstrong and Soelberg (1968) study of psychologists who made sense of factors based on an analysis of meaningless data, it is just as logical to presume the reality resides in their interpretations as in the meaninglessness of the original data. Both "meaning" and "meaningless" are inferences. Thus, again I state, a Newtonian epistemology seems unwarranted.

### Man Lives in a Social Reality

The only reality man has to refer his judgments to is a social one, i.e. the judgments of his fellow man. Gorsuch, in referring to Sherif and Sherif (1969) makes a gross understatement in saying, "The culture of which a person is a part does influence his concepts and behavior." This is truth that applies no less to the inability of certain Africans to experience the trapezoidal illusion (referred to in many general psychology textbooks) than to the place of women in life than to the ethics of the marketplace than to the proper mode of burying the dead. Man is historical, as Gorsuch has suggested. He is limited by the perspective of a given time and place. But this is more than his plight. It is his nature. Man is a social creature. He should exalt and use his finitude rather than deny or avoid it. It is just as easy to assume man is fulfilled as to assume he is frustrated by other persons. Rousseau's Emile would have been something less than man had he been reared in the forests away from the streets of Paris, according to this view. Man is not social by accident but by design!

As Mead (1934) and Cooley (1922) suggest, the prime skill of man may be his intuition rather than his reason. Intuition is the ability to emphasize, take the role of the other, see oneself through another and feel with others. This may be the key to the difference between the physical and human sciences, i.e. man's social existence and his ability to intuit. Thus a positive affirmation of man as living in the presence of social rather than inanimate reality is in order.

## Man's Finite Judgment Reconsidered

In light of the social reality model proposed above, the finiteness of man's judgment (referred to by Gorsuch in Chapters 2 and 3) should be reconsidered.

*Where is the real?:* Reality does not exist outside man, in a Newtonian sense, but in the agreed-upon judgments of his social group. For example, much modern theory in psychopathology suggests mental illness is the absence of a group with whom to share one's reality (cf. Millon, 1967, p. 19).

*Presumptions and involvment:* Contrary to what Gorsuch implies, it may be that reality can be apprehended *only* when one is involved and/or makes presumptions. Without involvement judgments make little sense and thus are not real. Reality, in a social sense, is a basis for action. The Sherif and Sherif (1969) study illustrates the point. *All* the judges were involved and used preconceptions. Would the sentences about Black persons have been more realistically rated by an unbiased judge? I think not. About all we could trust in this case would be that the judge was not invested in the task, thus, his ratings might be random and therefore meaningless. No, it probably takes involvement to be motivated in the judgment process. Accuracy is possibly the wrong term to apply to judgments. Judgments need to be understood in terms of the social realities they represent. Change in judgment would thus involve a change in social reality, i.e. one's groups, rather than a purifying of individual reason through such things as more information.

## Abstract and Complex Situations

Gorsuch notes that the more abstract and the more complex the situation, the more inaccurate and dependent man becomes. As stated before, *accuracy* may be the wrong term. But, *dependent* is correct. In a social reality man does rely more heavily on others as the situation becomes less clear or concrete.

Another manner of stating this fact is to say that as man approaches the limits of his ability to make sense out of his experience, he relies more and more on the truths given him by his fellows. This is not to say he accepts these truths without question but only that the situation goes beyond his rational capacities to comprehend. Thus, he has no place to turn at these times other than to the words of his fellow man who, in turn, have found the answers, or meanings, from others. This is often the case in passing down a tradition or a faith.

Karl Jasper speaks of these abstract-complex events as "boundary situations." The answers to these events often take the form of accepting what one is told and ceasing to try to make the conclusions fit a logical mode. Yet, these answers from the social world, i.e. others who surround man, often give purpose and meaning in a time of crisis. These answers, in turn, become the focus around which the more concrete decisions of everyday are made.

Thus, the abstract and complex may be the prime illustrations of what it means to be a man living in a social reality. As Gorsuch says, "the world in which man lives requires that he make complex decisions regardless of his ability to do so."

Comfort or accuracy at these times comes in knowing others agree to share the truth. An ancient Greek antiphonal hymn illustrates this point. A novitiate is standing at the bottom of a steep hill calling to the abbot of the monastery above. He is asking whether the experience in the Christian life is worth the climb. The abbot answers, "saints, apostles, prophets, martyrs answer yes." This was the only answer the abbot could give, i.e. point to a shared reality into which the newcomer could enter.

*Paradigms and theologies:* In reconsidering man's judgmental processes one omission in Gorsuch's treatment of paradigms and theologies needs noting, namely he did not indicate that their chief values lie in that they communicate a shared reality. Certainly this is true in science. A scientific model makes communication possible. Furthermore, if one accepts the assumptions of the model, he participates in a shared understanding of what is real. This is no less true of Theology. If one accepts the assumptions, he is able to communicate and he shares a reality. It is a social, not just an individual, event.

Thus, affirmation of the truth of a theology is not different qualitatively from that of a scientific theory. Both are concerned with abstract and complex questions. Both require making assumptions and both are buttressed by a community. Finally, both are based more on faith than on reason. One accepts and lives by them rather than logically proves them. Admittedly this is more an issue in theology than in science. The issue is still the same. While there may be Biblical evidence and scientific data, in truth such material only lends support to theology and to theory. It does not prove them. Theologies and theories are above all this. They are shared realities which have meaning because one is part of a community.

### Commitment Rather Than Tolerance

Gorsuch suggests in more than one place that as much information as possible should be sought in order to improve the basis for man's judgments. This may be more true to science than of religion, but even there it is an old maxim that theories are not proven or disproven. Nevertheless, it is true that theologies persist in the face of new evidence in a manner distinct from changes in scientific theory. Gorsuch's references to *When Prophecy Fails* (Festinger, et. al., 1956) merely illustrate what has been true of religious persons throughout the centuries, i.e. they hold onto their faith in the midst of the most adverse experiences.

Gorsuch completely equates paradigms and theologies; he cannot explain this persistence and sees it as just another error of conformity due to man's inability to extricate himself from the social process. Clear distinctions can be made, however. Scientific theories help man to understand the world, whereas theologies give meaning to his existence. The two are different endeavors.

It is no wonder that communities of faith tolerate many paradoxes in their experience. It is also no wonder that these groups ascribe ultimate validity to the sources of their faith, such as the Bible. Commitment rather than tolerance is the issue when the meaning of one's existence is at stake. New information serves as a corrective but never as a denial. The stakes are too high to do otherwise. Personal identity is in question.

Thus the community of faith, e.g. the church, brings persons into its reality and surrounds them with a group that sustains their commitment. One modern theologian, Karl Barth, has referred to this in theological terms as the "waiting church." He suggests that the responsibility of the church is to gather in worship, proclaim the faith and then wait for God through His Holy Spirit to bring the Word to life in the hearts of unbelievers. This is without doubt a theological statement of social process. The unbeliever is in the presence of believers. He is incorporated through conformity, i.e. an act of faith, into a social reality. The new convert is then sustained and supported by the believers who help him remain committed.

Had Gorsuch affirmed a more positive view of society he would have seen the value of conformity as a means to an end, i.e. the finding of a reality that gives purpose to life. It is felt that possibilities for transcendent, post-conventional living stem from, rather than by-pass, this process. The believer can be led through such persons as theological ethicists to see the implications of his faith for action. But they do not do so on the basis of abstract principles, as Gorsuch implies. The theologian and ethicist function as members of the community of faith. They are within, not without. Thus if man is to become transcendent, it must be by extending his understanding of what it means to be a member of the group, e.g. Christ's church, rather than to live by a set of rational ideals as Gorsuch implies. Conformity, thus, can serve individual uniqueness.

## Conformity, a Service to Individuality

Hollander (1971, p. 550.) notes that conformity is no simple process. It serves many purposes. Gorsuch, in his deemphasis of motivation, ignores the fact that motivation may well mean compliance without dependence, a desire to participate in the group and the search for the best ways to solve survival problems. He implies all conformity is directed toward acceptance and approval. Little wonder he pessimistically reports most persons use conventional moral reasoning without hope of transcending it.

An alternative is to trust individual motivation to be directed to something more than survival and satisfaction. Self-actualization (cf. Malony, 1972) can be thought of as the norm rather than the exception. Moreover, a further alternative is to trust the social process to support innovation. It is possible to look to the studies of leadership (cf. Hollander, 1971, p. 573) rather than the studies of nonconformity (Schachter, 1951) for a model. It could be that the reason the nonconforming individual in Schachter's research did not influence the group was because there had not been enough group life for him to build up credit which would allow for him to influence the group.

The credit referred to above is conformity. Hollander (1971, p. 573) has coined the term "idiosyncrasy credit" for the process whereby a person attains influence in a group. This influence allows for that person to lead others in either new means to old ends or new group goals. The group accords credit for past conformity. A person does in fact have the power to innovate if he will but use it. Conformity can serve individuality.

The church is probably the most viable of all institutions in which idiosyncrasy credit can function. This is true because it is a theological institution whose members are constantly being called beyond their own goals to a way of life befitting their faith. It is based on an ideal. Persons who are perceived as brothers in the faith will be listened to. Which leads me to the last point of this essay: *Society is not all bad.* No doubt many modern organizations inhibit and confine persons. Education is often thought of as the prime example of an institution which imprisons rather than frees man. Again, the research of Latané and Darley (1970), to which Gorsuch refers, seems to suggest that persons are much more recluctant to help a person in distress when they are in a group than when they are by themselves.

Other research, however, (Kogan and Wallach, 1964) indicates the opposite. People seem to be willing to take more risks when they are in a group. Many writers have alluded to this tendency of crowds to be impulsive (cf. LeBon, 1897). Most of them have perceived this tendency to be evil because it involved emotion. But what leads to lynch mobs could also lead to great innovation. The issue is not the emotion but the ideal of the leaders. In fact, as I have previously noted, emotion implies investment and the most important decisions require personal involvement.

The "Risky Shift" phenomenon may not exactly be comparable to the bystander situation. In the former, groups have been found to be more daring where the situation involved recommending economic risk with a possibility of great return.

In the case of bystander intervention, little or no return is probable save that of being a hero. In most cases there is the possibility of harm rather than gain. Also the situation is typically an unexpected emergency rather than a calculated decision. The question is: Can persons in groups come to the place where they act together for others without concern for their own welfare?

Again, I think the answer is yes if one is willing to trust the social process rather than be suspicious of it as Gorsuch tends to do. It should be possible to combine the best of McGuire's (1964) recommendations designed to induce resistance to temptation with Shephard's (1969) suggestions on how to create an organization that encourages uniqueness.

McGuire (1964) has been interested in studying ways persons can be trained to become committed to the extent that they resist conformity. It is interesting to note that all his recommendations involve making a person within one group resistant to the temptation to conform to another group. The very training itself is a social phenomenon. Three recommendations are critical: (1) Resistance is increased through a behavioral commitment; (2) resistance is increased through generalization of the belief to as many other beliefs as possible; and, (3) resistance is increased through rehearsal of situations where one may face temptation. A good group does all of these for its members. The Christian church at its best utilizes these procedures. It encourages commitment through a conversion experience. It encourages application of the faith through study. And, it often role-plays situations believers will face. It should be creating group members who will do more than conform to the world.

The observations of Shephard (1969) speak to this last point. There are many churches who fall into this trap of equating custom with the Christian ethic. These members will not see a conflict in such events as the Latané and Darley bystander situation or attitudes toward minorities (cf. Dittes, 1971). In brief, those groups where there is trust, mutual openness, and the ability to confront conflict create atmospheres in which persons can be innovative and still retain their group membership.

Groups of this type encourage individual initiative within the group context. These guidelines make post-conventional thinking (Kohlberg, 1968) a possibility.

Again, it appears that the church can be an institution that promotes innovation and individual expression because it pays allegiance to a theology that encourages individual response. A positive view of social process thus sees an institution such as the church as capable of making increasingly more risky decisions and allowing for individual uniqueness.

The history of the United Methodist Church is a case in point. John Wesley attempted to initiate innovation within the Church of England by taking the church to the people, i.e. to the mines, the hangings, and the homes. One could say that neither was the church of that day innovation producing enough nor was Wesley's idiosyncratic credit great enough to make his dream a reality. He had to leave the Church of England.

Yet, he established a church which encouraged resistance to worldly conformity through close knit weekly class meetings. He further encouraged a combination of reason and emotion by calling his followers to personal Christian experience and study. Patterning his rules after his own long search for assurance which came to an end in an experience on Aldersgate Street, he called for a religion of "the warm heart and the second mind." Thus he built resistance into persons' lives. Finally, he encouraged innovation by calling each person to "Godly piety," i.e. the exercise of religion in daily life. He left the group experience open and trusted his followers. He said, "If thy heart is as my heart, then give me thy hand." He asked for nothing else and left the witness to the individual.

This example of the United Methodist Church is probably but one of many examples of the wisdom of founders whose followers have lost the vision. Nevertheless it is a testimony to the positive power of a group to produce individuality via conformity.

## SUMMARY

In this essay I have challenged Gorsuch on several issues.

His lack of awareness of his own philosophy of human nature was noted. It was observed that he perceived man to be hyper-rational yet easily overwhelmed by emotional tendencies to conform. It was further observed that his suggestions for transcending man's suggestibility implied a negative view of the social process and a questionable belief that man could live abstract principles. A proposal for a more positive view of society was given. This view was seen to be based on a view of man as innately social. Lastly, correctives to Gorsuch's recommendations for enhancing man's judgmental powers were given. The functions of paradigms and theologies were suggested and the possibility of transcendence within the social process was suggested.

CHAPTER VII

# Three Exceptions
# To The Rule

RALPH D. WINTER

STREWN THROUGHOUT THE PAGES of these lectures are many fascinating items crying out for interaction and response. I must resist the temptation to make a series of mini-responses, however, so that I can deal more substantially with three basic matters.

## THE TOPIC IS ILLEGITIMATE

Just for the sake of discussion I would like to call the topic illegitimate, since it proposes to study an interdisciplinary hunk of reality from the perspective of a single discipline. I am aware that I am laying down an obligation that does not exist when a subject does not aim beyond any one discipline. It is not commonly voiced even when that happens. My reasoning is that the historic divisions between scholarly fields are hazy and highly artificial and that it is illegitimate to take notice of them wherever and whenever the specific subject being studied is dealt with by more than one field. This approach will allow me, in my first area of response, to grapple with the very idea of an interdisciplinary symposium, and to measure these lectures against that ideal.

Present fields of study, after all, are not the result of some omniscient person planning out in advance an array of areas of study that interlock faithfully in accord with the structure of reality, such that this array is both comprehensive and nonoverlapping. Thus as things stand in the pursuit of truth, interdisciplinary approaches are not a luxury but a necessity. Since truth is where you find it, it is a corollary that wherever the object of study is covered by more than one scholarly field, the truth is being sought by more than one group of scholars. This is why we have integration seminars at Fuller Theological Seminary. This is why, indeed, we have a School of Psychology which routinely draws input from both theology and psychology. The *raison d'etre* of the Fuller complex of schools (which also includes an anthropology-based School of World Missions), or for a university for that matter, is not a lust for the bizarre or the exotic. It reflects the fact that at least three groups of scholars are studying the nature of man, that they therefore belong on the same campus, and that they must of necessity compare notes *in order to be authentically scientific* even in their own fields.

This is not to say that these groups of scholars must compare notes in order to be acceptable in their respective professional associations. But success in the eyes of a single association is relative. For a scientist success is absolute only if the truth is discovered and correctly described. All of us who would seek scientifically to clarify the nature of reality must acknowledge a higher call than the social, cultural and historical contingencies which define the requirements of our respective professional associations.

The kind of science which creates this higher call is based on the belief that there is reality out there to be studied and that this reality is structured, orderly, susceptible of appreciation and description by man. Make no mistake, this is the usual kind of science. This somewhat novel definition merely stresses the basis of science rather than the methods characteristic of science, and explains why it is easier to be scientific in some areas than others. That is, science being the study of structural matter, it is plain why the "laws" of heredity were discovered before the symmetry of the sub-atomic particles. And it explains why anything both so complex and intangible as the nature of man would "take a little longer."

Most important for our discussion is the fact that this

definition of science allows for the possibility that the theologian may be as scientific as the social psychologist or anthropologist. The latter two may "try harder" and work more consciously to be scientific in *method*. But the degree of potential success (when we emphasize that science is made possible by the existence of describable, structured reality) is for all three the degree of success in *arriving* at the nature of reality. It is not measured by the degree of industry in applying one method or another in getting there.

One must hastily admit that Gorsuch has carefully explained, even in his subtitle — "A Social Psychological Perspective" — that he is not attempting to build on data other than that available in the literature of his field. At this point I have no quarrel with the way he proceeded on that basis. That will come later. Here *I am objecting to the very idea of a disciplinary treatment of an interdisciplinary subject.* In this connection, then, it is a curious fact that the lectures themselves warn that a limitation of data reduces the accuracy of human conclusions. It is thus particularly unfortunate that the data for the topic of these lectures would be limited to a single, historically (somewhat arbitrarily) defined area of scholarship.

These lectures also warn that social groupings greatly influence conclusions. Would it not then have been better for the study of the announced subject to have made a random sampling of data on the ethical nature of man from the literature of all the behavioral sciences instead of drawing exclusively and intentionally from one of them, when any one of these fields would tend to have a consistent bias? Perhaps one of the direct consequences of the fact that social groupings influence conclusions is precisely the conclusion (of a man at home in the grouping composed of social psychologists) that it is enough to study only the writings of those in his grouping! What we need is a "postconventional" social psychologist who is able and willing to break out of the limitations inherent in the professional group to whose social pressure he is primarily subject.

On the other hand, some will say, is it not enough even in

an interdisciplinary symposium to present fairly and clearly at least the consistent bias of one school of thought? I would like very much to say *yes*. I am driven to say *no*. The artificial fences between fields cannot forever be respected. They must be deliberately broken down. And when a significant topic is treated in more than one field the boundaries of the relevant "literature" must be determined by the topic not by any other consideration. We part ways with science itself if we do otherwise.

The stated assumption behind these remarks thus far has been the historical contingency of the existing fields of study. Is this not obvious? At times they have grown or changed with only glacial speed, but all change seems these days to be speeding up. Look where geographers have strayed in the last twenty years! Psychology itself has grown by leaps and bounds. Its branches seem to become more and more numerous. The number of students moving in the direction of psychology is expanding. As a matter of fact sociology, anthropology and psychology are all fairly young in the scholarly world. They are still bursting forth like three new denominations with their founding prophets and seers, their developing fissures and hair-splitting theologies!

This is not to doubt the historical *integrity* of these several groups of scholars and their holy writings, but this does not in any way qualify what we have said about their historical *contingency*. They did grow up like Topsy, and, as a result, their respective studies do focus to a considerable extent on the same acreage of reality. Now that the ecumenical era is fully upon us, we cannot go on like this. These behavioral science "denominations" may not be able to merge organically (many university mergers between sociology and anthropology departments have sprung apart after a trial marriage). Nevertheless, they must acknowledge that they study the same thing and that some sort of cross-fertilization of results is a necessity, not a luxury.

One final bit of evidence of intramural "field circumscribed" thinking is the semantic coloring of the words *psychology* and *psychological* as they are employed in these lectures. Undoubtedly psychologists on the whole try harder to be scientific in their methods than do philosophers and theologians, and it is thus reasonable for Gorsuch to suggest that psychology can be for them "a continuing corrective," due to the fact that psychology is a science. But even if the philosophers and theologians are only amateur scientists, it is by no means the case that scientific input in the study of the nature of man is the unique contribution of the psychologist. This reminds me of the long-standing assumption of medical "scientists" that the non-Western shaman or curer has no scientifically valid medicinal knowledge. What an embarrassment for the medical scientist to boast of scientific method while the shaman has the answer. In the same fashion the theologian may be the unscientific shaman simply because the truth is where you find it. And it is often found first by those who love the truth not just by those who utilize rigorous scientific methodology. In this sense the theologian may often be as well equipped as anyone else. We must never find ourselves choosing between the truth of science and the methods of science. We cannot therefore use *psychology* as a synonym for *science* and *theology* as a synonym for the *unscientific*.

Perhaps the best way to show the urgency of this first point is to move on to two other major areas of response which each illustrate the need for going beyond single-field presentations. Before that, however, one disclaimer. There has been no intention here to single out social psychologists as more or less guilty of intramural thinking than are those in the other behavioral sciences and in theology itself.

## ONE PRESUPPOSITION INTRODUCES A MASSIVE DISCREPANCY

Gorsuch must be given credit for making a serious attempt to establish the concept that at least certain aspects of man's nature are "culturally invariant." He acknowledges that this concept is not lightly to be assumed by saying, "Ethics and morality is a crucial area for evaluating if contemporary man has the same characteristics *regardless of his culture,* since ethical values are often assumed to be inconsistent across contemporary cultures." He provides data which support the belief that not only "the *process* used in moral reasoning" but also "the *contents* which are utilized in the reasoning process" are "relatively constant across cultures." (my italics)

There are several difficulties which immediately arise. First of all, if this cultural invariance is true, why then is it necessary for Gorsuch to limit his study to contemporary man? What is the significance of making clear, as he carefully does, that he is not taking into account any of the historical past but is concentrating only on contemporary phenomena? It is because he concedes that "historical conditions . . . influence (man's) characteristics." This is a startling concession. Does he not realize that the difference between an ancient Greek and a modern psychology professor is probably far less than the difference between either of these men and a contemporary Australian aborigine or a Point Barrow Eskimo? How can he think it possible to prove cultural invariance between vastly different modern contemporaries while conceding that there may not be invariance historically? That is, how logical is it to concede that man may well change across time but not across space? It is like admitting that clothing styles may change over a period of time but insisting that they are not different around the world at a given point in time.

Secondly, one is puzzled by the very purpose of proposing invariance. He apparently needs *to prove the cultural invariance of human nature* in order to be able to study the real nature of man. This is what he claims. And yet, there is a massive discrepancy between this concern and the fact that later on in his lectures he apparently needs to manifest the usefulness of social psychology by *proving precisely the variability of human nature* as the result of either genetic or cultural influences. If, in other words, he feels that it is necessary to show how human nature *can be changed,* why would he go to some length in his open words to maintain that this same aspect of human nature is invariant?

Thirdly, the most serious problem with the proposal of cultural invariance is that it flies in the face of an immense amount of anthropological data. The most primitive situation to which he refers (in British Honduras) turns out, nevertheless, to be one in which the people have already attached some value to "academic achievement." This sounds strangely unprimitive. Furthermore, to ask college students in foreign lands what they think about certain aspects of morality is a highly questionable approach to the basic problem, since college students may easily have picked up the very attitudes of the cultural complex of which the college itself is a part.

One is embarrassed by the very possibility that there is a tendency here (of psychologists in general?) to work in terms of an outdated concept of the cultural invariance of human nature, a concept that is a vestigial hold-over from a past in which, in all innocent provinciality, Western thinkers assumed that all aspects of the nature of the men they were studying was probably somehow universal. But if psychologists have not yet gone beyond such assumptions, anthropologists certainly have, and we thus have another illustration of the need for a given field of study to make itself aware of the fact that the same subject may simultaneously be under study by other people, in this case, people who have gathered far more data on the same subject, data which in the case of the variability of man would lead to quite different conclusions.

## A SECOND PRESUPPOSITION SKIRTS A SIGNIFICANT INSIGHT

A profound insight—for which these lectures allow but with which they do not successfully cope—is the increasing awareness among social scientists of a dual perception of man as an individual and man as a multi-individual phenomenon. No statement in the lectures is more pleasant to the eyes of a cultural anthropologist than one which comes into the lectures as little more than a passing remark: "The social nature of mankind is a construct needing thorough exploration by anyone who would seek to understand the human species. Indeed, it may be that one should not talk of the nature of man, but, instead, should talk of the nature of men." But Gorsuch does not follow through on this. As a social psychologist, he is dealing with groups at almost every point throughout his lecture, yet he seems to be looking at groups exclusively from the vantage point of their effect upon the individual. The above quotation is the only hint that any other perspective is possible. One must conclude that *social* psychology is by no means a shift from the study of the individual *psyche* to the study of social units of mankind, but merely the study of man as an individual as he is affected by society. Groups are important but they are not man. Worse still, the group, or society in general, turns out to be the enemy from which man must be freed to be redeemed.

Now this is quite a contrast from the perspective of the cultural anthropologist, who much more likely begins with the group as his starting point. It also clashes with the thinking of those missionary-anthropologist-theologians who are conversant with conditions around the world in which Christian faith is becoming adopted by groups—which are then called *churches.* Thus the missionary also sees the group as the permanent form man takes, and sees the redemption of men only as they are incorporated into the permanent, redemptive fellowship of the local churches. Psychologists seem always to befriend the individual against the group. They may temporarily concoct groups for the therapy of individuals, but they use groups up like Kleenex®. The group is impermanent; the individual is the goal, the focus. The individual has, of course, traditionally been the paying customer.

This contrast may be exaggerated, but it is not entirely artificial, and it would be a tragedy if our insight into the nature of man had to be looked at from only one of these two starting points. The very fact that conventional American thinking tends to treat man as purely an individual to be redeemed by psychology and/or theology means that both American psychologists and theologians will automatically tend to study man from the individualist starting point unless they have had some extensive extra-American cross-cultural experience. Only with this special experience will the group starting point become intellectually and emotionally acceptable.

How is this group starting point different? First of all, the anthropologist-missionary (call him the *missiologist*) does not derive from a vocational-professional tradition of individual paying customers; he is interested in the care and feeding of groups. Rightly or wrongly, individuals are in fact generally by-passed if they don't fit in. It is not a question of whether or not the individual can be better than the group but whether or not the individual can make the group better. Instead of blaming the group for the individual's problems, the tendency is to blame "unredeemed" individuals for the group's problems.

But this is too extreme. The missiologist does not merely envision the redeemed community surrounded by unredeemed individuals: it is surrounded by unredeemed groups as well. The missiologist has two basic plans—neither of which focuses on individuals. Either he starts a new community, which is a total alternative to the unredeemed world, or he tries to develop something new within the existing community. He won't give you a dime for the "lone believer" because he thinks the individual by himself can't make it, is too unstable. The point of all this is that the missiologist is working with one group or another, and these groups are ends, not means.

On the other hand, from the individualist starting point, Gorsuch sees man emerging from the womb as an immature individual who seeks immediate gratification, and if so judged would seem to be by nature selfish. But, he feels, this is unfair to man, since as individuals mature, most of them become less selfish, and once they achieve adult character, tend to be moral unless the group forces them to be inhumane. Man's innate goodness, he proposes, seems normally to appear with age (not with assimilation to a group), and this goodness can only have full freedom of development if it can escape the potentially dire influences of the group through the achievement of a behavior he calls "post-conventional." All of this is from the vantage point and, it would almost seem, strictly in defense of the individual. It is reminiscent of the "moral man, immoral society" theme.

Using the very same data, however, it is possible to posit almost the very reverse. Using the group as the starting point, the child is indeed selfish until he becomes adjusted to the ideals and interdependencies of the group, which universally requires group-serving not self-serving behavior. It is not the process of physically growing older that works this change, but the process of assimilation to the cultural complex of the group. This is the process whereby an ethnically Chinese baby becomes culturally Chinese, acquiring all the sensitivities and values inherent in one of the particular varieties of Chinese culture. Now, should this individual somehow wrest himself free from the acquired cultural pattern, his behavior (call it post-conventional if you like) may very well be inferior, not superior. What Gorsuch anticipates as superior, post-conventional morality, anthropologists simply label "deviation" and deviants are not generally known as would-be improvers of conventional morality. Indeed, as an example of individuals rising above the conventional morality, Redfield (1953, p. 130) cites the famous case of an Indian chieftan ending a long-standing pattern of annual ritual murder. But clearly this is a very rare case of the "transformation of ethical judgment" to something *superior*.

It almost seems that where Gorsuch finds adults doing non-conventional good things, he labels them *post-conventional,* and when he finds them doing non-conventional bad things, he applies the label *pre-conventional.* A mature adult with sufficient intellectual sophistication and emotional stamina to cheat on his income tax is thus pre-conventional. If a Jesuit priest schemes to immobilize Washington, he could be post-conventional. Both men are acting against society, but their values may or may not correspond, and to say that he is *post* who seeks "a long term, abstract goal" does not help greatly because this would seem to include both Napoleon and Hitler in the post-conventional group. It would seem that the immature/mature and selfish/selfless contrasts work nicely to help define the difference between pre-conventional and conventional behaviors but that they are not easily extrapolated into the difference between conventional and post-conventional behaviors.

The confusion lies in the failure to retain in view the essential dual perception of the nature of man as both individual and group. "Becoming mature" for the premoral person means, from the group starting point, accepting group norms rather than merely further growing up. This explains why social transcen-

dence, or post-conventional behavior, cannot be defined as becoming post-mature or super mature.

We must concede that Gorsuch is partially aware of the
group's role as the child moves from premoral to conventional
processes of thinking. The child must not only develop, following
puberty, "cognitive powers which enable him to abstract principles of behavior," but he needs to be "surrounded by a stimulating
environment which confronts him with choices that can only be
decided on the basis of abstract principles." He further notes that
those adults who "still use premoral thinking appear to have been
raised under inconsistent conditions where no principles are apparent in their environment." He does not perceive this "environment" as the highly structured phenomenon of "culture" about
which anthropologists talk.

The anthropologist sees a child growing up and assimilating
both a language and the larger cultural complex as a process of
exposure to a group rather than as simply the maturation or development of an individual. The individual "learns" the cultural
system just like he learns the cultural subsystem we call *language*.
The anthropologist will be very wary of concluding that a whole
lot of people in the black ghetto or the Puerto Rican ghetto seem
to use premoral processes of reasoning, for example. He will not
only point out that their "faulty" language is itself a highly developed system conventional to this sub-group, but will suspect
that the seemingly premoral thinking processes may similarly
belong to a highly-developed, internally consistent, logically abstract system of behavior that is actually conventional to these
people. In other words, what is one group's *conventional* can be
considered by another group *premoral*.

Where Gorsuch comes closest to the anthropologist's concept
of culture is in his references to *social support systems*. While his
very terminology here reduces it to something that affects individuals, his discussion of the need to be able to change these
systems is very valuable. His observation that religious social
support systems may be "conventionalistic" and "enslave people
rather than free them" is important. He acknowledges as "a topic
of great importance" the need for better understanding of "the

transactional development of group norms" and thus verges on the vast anthropological literature on "culture change" and "innovation," but he modestly observes that "social psychology is not as knowledgeable in this area as might be desired."

He feels "the church must go beyond social support systems to develop deeper belief and value commitments." That is, the church must be sure to develop not merely new and better social support systems, but always stress the need for people to weigh and evaluate the system itself. I have a feeling he would have every man become post-conventional, and accordingly he prefers "give and take discussions" rather than a "preaching or indoctrination approach" or settings involving "canned" responses. But the pervasive perspective in all of this is that there are *forces* (not the larger living reality of the group) that impinge in this or that way upon the *individual*.

Experimental psychology generally has dealt with laboratory animals that are—far more than man—creatures of instinct. Perhaps this background tends to bias all psychologists as they try to understand the nature of man.

As a final, perhaps overly drastic illustration of the tension between the individualistic starting point and the group starting point would be something like this: man is not like a handful of seeds thrown into a given social soil. Seeds are stunted by bad environment but their flowering is never formed or designed by the environment. The environment can only limit not create their full flowering. Man, however, is more nearly a "people" than an aggregate of individuals. The people, if anything, is itself the plant which grows as a living whole. The individual is in this sense an abstraction, simply part of his people. He cannot act, speak, or think apart from his people. There is no recorded example of an individual that has grown up apart from a group. He cannot be affected by his people like a seed is affected by soil conditions. The individual is part of a larger-than-individual organism; he is affected as part of a larger cell of life. To assume in any way that the individual can be understood in isolation is to skirt a significant insight—the dual perception of man as individual and as group.

CHAPTER VIII

# An Evaluation of The Nature of Man

DOUGLAS R. MATTHEWS

## THE PROBLEM OF PERSPECTIVE

RICHARD GORSUCH has taken on a prodigious assignment: Clarifying the nature of man from a social psychological perspective. He clearly articulates the ground rules for his venture at the outset. The task is seen as descriptive rather than explanatory. Furthermore, Gorsuch comes as social psychologist, not theologian. For him this means that his discussion is to be based on the data of science, i.e. empirical findings rather than philosophical/theological speculation. Although the distinctions between philosophy and psychology are recognized, he encourages cross-fertilization. The conclusions of the one, i.e. philosophy/theology, can be helpfully tempered by those of the other, i.e. the "science of psychology."

Gorsuch's intentions are admirable. As he explicitly defines the relation of social psychologist to philosopher, the separation is clear. However, as his essay unfolds, the distinctions between philosopher and scientist are blurred. A few illustrations are in order.

It is claimed that, "Society needs more uninvolved judges to help reflect on the proper course of action to be followed in almost every situation." The immediate context for the assertion is a discussion of the problem of finitude and judgmental error. The contention cannot be considered a descriptive statement. With the words, "Society *needs* . . ." (my italics) Gorsuch proffers prescription, not description. A value judgment is proposed. An imperative is given. Gorsuch wears the hat of social philosopher, not social scientist, according to his definition of science.

However, it might be argued that Gorsuch explicitly claimed the privilege of suggesting implications of social psychological investigation to areas beyond those particular boundaries. The objection is accepted. The problem at this point, then, is that Gorsuch has not clarified the hat that he wears.

Next, take the issue of evil. Gorsuch wisely considers that this is traditionally a problem lying beyond the grasp of science. With this caution in mind, he tries to bring it under the scientific microscope through re-definition. "Since the current discussion is focused on the psychological nature of man, the term evil is used as a psychological rather than a theological category. To say that man is evil means that man's treatment of his fellow man increases the amount of injustice and injury in the world." The difficulty hinges on the word "injustice." To write that an act is unjust is to assume that it ought not to have happened; it was wrong. A value judgment has thus been made. But science remains mute to such matters; the nature of her vocabulary is strictly descriptive. Again, intending to write from a social psychological perspective, Gorsuch has written from a social philosophical one instead.

Another example of Gorsuch's mixing of psychological with philosophical categories is found in his discussion of differences between immature and mature reasoning. Aside from the connotative problems with the term "immature," Gorsuch defines "immature" in terms of differences between the thinking of children and adults. As such, he stays within scientific psychological boundaries. But his discussion often slips beyond when he considers the mature to be the "good." Once again the words flow out of a social philosopher.

One more illustration comes with the consideration of the destiny of man. Several assumptions undergird this discussion. For one, he presumes that there is a possibility that men can rise above their historical circumstance to determine their own destiny. He also assumes that the morally mature, post-conventional, transcending person ought to decide the destiny of other, conventional men. These 'transcendants' are seen as most capable of making 'proper' decisions for others. Without responding to the content of these statements, the task here is merely to point out that they are value judgments generated from a particular social philosophical perspective.

To argue for the wide distinction between the science of psychology and philosophy raises several issues. For one, there is the repeated tendency within experimental psychology to forget its philosophical roots. Contemporary psychology owes much to those who seem so foreign now: Locke, Hobbes, Hume, and Kant. It appears that the infant scientific psychology is still trying too much to establish what it is, i.e. an objective discipline, by denying one of its parents, i.e. speculative philosophy. The admittedly vastly different methodologies ought (note the imperative!) not obliterate the sense of history; a spirit of communality rather than antagonism ought to be fostered. Historically, the relationship is much closer than present methodological distinctions would suggest.

A second more immediate issue is that philosophical presuppositions all too often form the hidden substructure of scientific inquiries. The problem lies in the failure of scientists to articulate their non-scientific assumptions. Further, the ensuing scientific findings often find eager reception; this is because of the authority that science commands in our culture. At the same time, the philosophical assumptions are unwittingly accepted as well as legitimized. What happens when a scientific psychologist fails to both articulate and recognize his presuppositions was demonstrated by John Watson. The famed behaviorist courageously rejected the prescientific concept of "mind." Mind was body. However, as Heidbreder (1931) contends, in attempting to reject mind/body dualism, he accepted it. Watson united with the enemy he set out to destroy. The front door had been successfully barricaded but not the back. What is more, descendant behaviorists with their 'black box mythology' often err in the same way, thus illustrating the tendency for history to perpetuate and legitimize its errors.

Matson (1966) rhetorically questions, "is it good science to ignore the origins and assumptions, the starting-point and reason for being of one's investigations? . . . And what is there left to social science by this self-denying ordinance other than the clerical performance of checking and tabulating, classifying and accounting?" (p. 79) It is suggested here that social science ought not to shudder in horror upon the recognition of its philosophical value commitments. Only through awareness of one's presuppositions can they be controlled in scientific enterprise. Only then can they serve the scientific task and not control it. Such awareness can well serve to remind the social psychologist of both the finiteness of his own efforts and his dependence upon the community of science.

The objection is not to Gorsuch having certain philosophical suppositions. Nor is it that he appears to be in search of their confirmation through scientific methodology. My concern is the mistaking of the philosophical for the scientific.

## THE OBJECTIVITY PROBLEM

*The possibilities of objective knowing.* Gorsuch considers a fundamental problem for man: Finitude. He suggests, "a basic characteristic of the nature of man is his fallible judgment." Various reasons are cited for the condition: limited information, failure to attend to relevant information, abstractness of situations, and inability to process information available adequately. He then presents certain prescriptions which would enable man to at least partially overcome the problem of fallible judgment, e.g. eliminating motivational involvement with the problem and establishing objective criteria to which all would give assent. At the same time, Gorsuch recognizes that the human situation all too often does not allow for decision postponement. Exigencies of the moment press for the blind leap rather than the studied step.

There is much to commend in the discussion of the infinite problem of finitude. A spirit of caution is kindled when the problem of judgmental errors (and judgmental errors of judgments) is recognized. Furthermore, the appeal for operational definitions to counter the opaque predicament caused by abstractions is not new but is noteworthy.

Problems arise with relation to the process of knowing. Specifically, they erupt with the affirmation that proper decisions are best made by those not personally involved. Gorsuch contends that "the nonpersonally involved individual will be a better judge since there is no need for him to transcend his desires." There appears to be at least two assumptions in the contention. Both are questionable. First, it is assumed that it is possible to be nonpersonally involved and second, that this is the optimal way of knowing.

As for the first, it may be possible to approach a problem while both detached from it and the issues clustering immediately around. However, from a practical standpoint, if a relatively accurate judgment is to be obtained, the resource person, i.e. judge, must be involved to some extent. Without interest in the matter, request for judgment would be met with polite decline. What is more, without a prior involvement with the particular subject matter, there would be a high probability of judgmental error. It would be better to call for judges not *excessively* involved ("excessive" would need operational clarification).

From another vantage point, it is more difficult to imagine an observer who is divorced from his cultural milieu. He may try to approach the problem as a disinterested observer. However, he approaches with a particular world view which will influence his perception of the data. He will organize that data into categories which, at least in part, generate from both past historical tradition and present historical conditions. Both the judge and the judgment are, inevitably, culturally contingent. As an illustration, it is impossible to imagine an "expert" witness on the abortion issue not to have experienced the implosion of media reaction, i.e. newspapers, journals, and television. This by itself is sufficient to kindle the biases and convictions. Further, specific judgment concerning a particular abortion would come in the context of certain assumptions. For example, the obligation of society to its particular members and the right of the individual for life are both inextricably bound to and informed by the cultural climate.

The difficulty of detachment with regard to the scientist has been articulated well by Polanyi (1964):

Viewed from the outside as we described him the scientist may appear as a mere truth-finding machine steered by intuitive sensitivity. But this view takes no account of the curious fact that he is himself the ultimate judge of what he accepts as true. His brain labors to satisfy its own demands according to criteria applied by its own judgment. It is like a game of patience in which the player has discretion to apply the rules to each as he thinks fit. Or, to vary the simile, the scientist appears acting here as detective, policeman, judge and jury all rolled into one. He apprehends certain clues as suspect; formulates the charges and examines the evidence both for and against it, admitting or rejecting such parts of it as he thinks fit, and finally pronounces judgment. While all the time, far from being neutral at heart, he is himself passionately interested in the outcome of the procedure . . . The scientist ought to be delighted when his theory, supported by a series of previous observations, appears to collapse in the light of his latest experiments. If he was wrong, then he has just escaped establishing a falsehood and been given a timely warning to turn in a new direction. But that is not how he feels. He is dejected and confused, and can only think of possible ways of explaining away the obstructive observation. (p. 38-39)

This point is not limited to the scientist alone but is most important here because few others strive for such "pure objectivity" as the scientist.

But if Gorsuch's first assumption, i.e. the possibilities of detachment, stands on shaky soil, what about his second? For the moment, grant that detachment is a possibility. Ought it to be the most desired way (attitude) of knowing? Not really. Personal, even passionate, involvement lies behind much of the progress in scientific enterprise. Mere recognition of the limitations to the understanding of a particular problem is not enough to propel new understandings. The recognition needs the seasoning of curiosity and desire. Satisfaction with that which is fails to ignite interest or excitement for what could be. The detached may well have the recognition but not the curiosity or desire necessary. The personally nonmotivated person does not move. Were the detached to be king in the land of progress with the involved as his subjects, we would still be waiting for the start of the scientific revolution.

Of course with personal involvement there is always the

possibility of disastrous errors. The bridge contractor decides to use a cheaper construction material in order to maximize profit margin. Stability is sacrificed for the sake of net earnings. The task of society is to set minimal standards necessary to preserve the safety of its population crossing that bridge. In so doing, an external check is placed upon the personally involved decision of the finite contractor. In science certain ground rules are established. For example experiments are described in such detail that they may be repeated by others. This points to the 'objective rule' policy advocated by Gorsuch as a way of ameliorating the problems associated with personal involvement.

*The possibilities of the objectively known.* In addition to unwarranted faith in the possibilities of objectively knowing, Gorsuch shows strong belief in the objectively known. He assumes that with both personal involvements at a minimum and all appropriate information available, proper fact-based decisions are then possible. However, if objective knowing is impossible, even more so is the objectively known.

Centuries ago Berkeley posited that, "to be is to be perceived." We only know as we experience, and, what we know is in part a product of our perceptual process. Nothing is discovered independent of the discoverer. In the present century, evidence from natural science has complemented this proposition. The "quantum revolution" has forced us to radically alter our mechanistic commitments as well as casting considerable doubt on the objective known (see Matson, 1966, p. 122f). Heisenberg's "indeterminacy" principle, generated from quantum theory, is important for discussion here. "The principle of indeterminacy is founded on the fact that we cannot observe the course of nature without disturbing it. This is a direct consequence of the quantum theory. (Sullivan, 1933, p. 70)." The intricate instruments designed to help man observe the state of sub-atomic matter altered it. The major consequence of the indeterminacy or uncertainty principle is that it "has closed the artificial gap between the knower and the known" . . . the thing observed is intimately bound up with the observer and his observation (Matson, 1966, p. 128).

From social science quarters comes further evidence of observer effects upon the observed. Rosenthal (1966) has studied the nature of interaction between human experimenter and human as well as non-human subjects. Unless specific precautions are taken, the results obtained are more likely a function of the experimenter's interaction with the subject than they are of the independent variable manipulated. Rosenthal considers the experimenter all too often to be a self-fulfilling prophet. "One prophecies an event, and the expectation of the event then changes the behavior of the prophet in such a way as to make the prophecied event more likely" (p. 129). Imagine a dog trainer claiming that his pet hound can count by patting his paw on the floor. He boasts of the remarkable ability Rover is able to display. Disbelievers stand amazed as they watch the event unfold. Rover counts. When his master says "Five, Rover! Five!", the precocious canine makes five deft strokes of the paw. What both the master and the audience failed to notice was the slight head movement of the trainer before each paw pat. In fact, Rover was not responding to the verbal command but to the head movement cues. Just as surely as Rover was responding to something other than the verbal cues, so was his master unaware of the powerful discriminative stimuli he was emitting. The self-fulfilling prophecy usually occurs without the prophet, i.e. the experimenter, being aware of it.

As clinical psychologists, we often find ourselves called upon to diagnose or evaluate some person's lifestyle. In order to accomplish this end, a battery of tests, both projective and non-projective, is usually given. The easy tendency, especially with objective tests from which quantitative results are obtained, is to ignore the effect of both the situation and our presence on those results. Yet, the effect is not only inescapable, it is also invaluable for our evaluation. The problem is that often the clinician fails to recognize that he is a part of the test stimuli situation. His role as clinical psychologist is clear. The role of the prophet remains hidden.

The preceding discussion is intended to cast doubt upon the belief in both objective knowing and knowing the objective. If the "facts" are necessary for proper decision, then it is also necessary to understand our inextricable bond with them. To make it very clear a distinction ought to be noted. The criticism of Gorsuch is not with "knowing" or the "known." Rather it is with Gorsuch's faith in both "objectively" knowing and the "objective" known.

But what then can we say? If men can be nothing other than personally involved in the decisions they make and if the 'facts' are never pure, what are the possibilities of judgment accuracy? In the first place, caution must be taken to avoid the demand for 'absolute' accuracy. Science has long since supplanted probability for truth statements. She feels comfortable with the penultimate (Gorsuch acknowledges this). Functional rather than absolute accuracy is a viable rule for decision making in general. Given the finitude of our circumstance, the possibility of error will always ride as passenger on the train of decision. Second, the reality that neither all nor, especially, one is free from judgment error suggests considering personal decisions in the context of community. The community is thus seen as a correcting agent. In so doing, the possibilities of proximate or functional accuracy are enhanced. For example, in science unless the research findings of one are replicated by others, their proximate accuracy value is seriously questioned. If one experimenter reports repeated findings of a particular chemical associated with particular bizarre behavioral manifestations but everyone else repeatedly fails to find it, the reported findings are discounted. The community, in this case science, disconfirms.

Finally, two terms (not new) important for the discussion are *representation* and *approximation*. We translate our experience into verbal symbols. These are not the concrete reality; they represent it. Furthermore, we refine these representations so that they better, but not perfectly, correspond with that which they are purported to represent. In other words, we proceed and progress through steadily improved approximations. Scientific enterprise can be described from this perspective: forging ahead through representations and approximations.

## MAN'S INHUMANITY

Gorsuch suggests several basic characteristics with regard to the nature of man. Of particular interest is his discussion of man's inhumanity to man. As he surveys the problem, several issues are telescoped in the one, e.g. finitude, constant ethical nature, the goodness or evil controversy, the relation of the individual to the group.

Gorsuch summarizes his position with these words:

> Our general results would indicate that there are three major causes of observed inhumane treatment of man by his fellow man: Man's tendency towards judgmental errors, his failure to approach problems with a mature ethical reasoning process, and the environmental situations which place him in competition with his fellow man to achieve the same goals.

Innate aggressive tendencies are rejected. The pressure of the group to magnify evil as well as maximize the good is also considered.

In his perusal of the human situation, Gorsuch pauses to consider man's bent for self-destruction. Although declining theological discussion, he nonetheless returns to the theological problem of good and evil. He asserts that whether or not one determines man to be innately "good" on the one hand or, innately "evil" on the other depends upon the data surveyed, i.e. the behavior of the post-conventionally moral or pre-conventionally moral, respectively. He goes on to suggest that, "In all likelihood, some of the differences among classical philosophers and theologians on the question of the goodness of man probably arises from their different views of immature adults." He seems to come to a "both/and" solution. Evil is recognized but so are the possibilities of the good.

In response to this understanding, several things can be said. For one, to speak of "the good" (or "the evil") is to make a value-judgment. The discussion has, then, shifted to philosophical and theological grounds.

It appears that Gorsuch is suggesting a natural theological approach to the problem of Original Sin. It would seem that the Fall is seen more as a stumble. Man was not completely tainted by the disaster of Eden. Apparently, the image, i.e. the good, survived the impact of the Fall; it is witnessed to in the post-conventionally moral person. Another way of looking at the issue is to see man as created in the image of God; the image is defined in terms of relationship rather than in optic qualities, i.e. goodness in man. Further, the Fall meant that that image, i.e. relationship between God and man, was broken. There is no way that man can restore that image by perfecting his inherent qualities, whether by reason or valuing processes. Whereas Gorsuch contends that there are three ways to look at man, i.e. good, bad, or both, this view says, "None of these." It does so because it starts from another ground—revelation rather than nature. It further contends that salvation or reconciliation does not reside in moral perfection but in the Divine disclosure in history, that is, Jesus Christ. This discussion is entertained not so much to raise the theological issue but to point to both a different theological posture and to show that, once again, philosophical/theological assumptions have crept into Gorsuch's social psychological perspective.

Gorsuch cites the Milgram series to buttress his claim that the propensity for evil is magnified in social or group situations. "Relying upon others for norms and behavior, people will follow bad norms as well as good. Once an unjust norm has been established, the group conformity effect tends to magnify and stabilize that injustice." In examining Milgram's results he alludes to the one-third that did not conform and claims: "It would therefore seem crucial to examine the nature of non-conformity to understand the characteristics of people who appear to transcend the impact of their social environment." Later he contends that those who did not conform were the post-conventionally moral, i.e. persons who decided "their own course of action rather than letting the environment determine it for them. These are people whom we would expect to be shaping their own destinies."

In the first place, the Milgram series (1963, 1964a, 1964b, 1965a, 1965b, and 1967) is far more complicated both in its design and in its interpretation than Gorsuch suggests. The original design, which is what Gorsuch describes, did obtain the results his essay indicates. However, even these are subject to a far more parsimonious explanation than Gorsuch indicates. The naive subject who refuses to comply with the experimenter's demands to continue is considered "disobedient." It is most important to remember that the terms "disobedience" and "obedience" define only the relationship between the experimenter and the naive subject. Rather than assume that the disobedient subject has transcended the situation, a more viable alternative is that he was obedient to the "learner-victim" (confederate subject) demands. It ought to be remembered that while the experimenter is demanding that the naive subject proceed, the confederate subject is literally screaming, "Hey! I don't want to do this anymore. My heart's starting to bother me!" (Earlier, as the confederate subject was being strapped in his chair, the confederate had casually mentioned his bad heart.) To ignore this crucial aspect of the Milgram situation by claiming that the disobedient subjects were acting on the basis of internal values transcending the situation is to fail to understand the Milgram experiment.

But there is not just one "most parsimonious" explanation of the events in the obedience series. A more complete view of the Milgram experiments is in order. "The crux of the study is to vary systematically the factors believed to alter the degree of obedience to the experimental commands, to learn under what conditions submission to authority is most probable and under what conditions defiance is brought to the fore." (Milgram, 1965a, p. 60) The essential variables manipulated were situation and locale. First, Milgram altered the immediate situation in a number of ways. He varied the proximity both between the experimenter and the naive subject and between the confederate subject and the naive subject. In one situation the subject was required to place the hand of the learner on the shock plate before punishment was administered. In another situation, he could only see, not hear, the learner-victim, and, obviously, there was no physical contact between them. In yet another situation the two subjects were close to each other while the experimenter remained distant, contacting the naive subject by telephone only.

The addition of two other confederate subjects to aid the naive subject in his "teaching" function was yet another situational variation. Second, Milgram manipulated the locale or setting in which the experiment took place. Wondering if the university context might have had some contaminating effect on the obedience obtained, he conducted the experiment in a business setting.

The results obtained in the particular situation Gorsuch cites (see Milgram, 1963), were only obtained under those particular conditions. Throughout the series, including an initial pilot study, obedience ranged from a high of 100 percent to a low of 23 percent *depending* upon the situation. In support of the hypothesis mentioned above, i.e. that the issue is "obedience to whom—experimenter or victim," the closer the naive subject was to the victim, the less compliant he was to the demands of the experimenter. Conversely, the more removed he was from the victim, the more obedience he demonstrated to the experimenter.

There are a number of factors Milgram cites in effort to explain the obedient behavior of subjects. It is most likely that no one, including "obedience to whom," will stand as the final explanation. Rather than describe every factor suggested by Milgram, a sample will be highlighted. First, there are a number of situational factors. For one,

> The meaning of any act can be altered by placing it in the appropriate context . . . By virtue of its articulation with the larger context of society, the psychological laboratory has a strong claim of legitimacy and evokes trust and confidence in those who perform there. An action such as shocking a victim, which in isolation appears evil, acquires a totally different meaning when placed in this setting. (Milgram, 1967, p. 6)

Second, the subject's perspective of both himself and his task is considered. Milgram notes: ". . . the tendency of the individual to become so absorbed in the narrow technical performance of the task that he loses sight of the broader consequences of his action." (1967, p. 5-6) Again, Milgram says: "The most common adjustment of thought in the obedient subject is merely to see himself as not responsible for his own actions. He divests himself of responsibility by attributing all initiative to the experimenter, to a legitimate authority." (1967, p. 6) Third, the naive subject's attitude towards the victim is also discussed. Again, a number of possibilities are raised including the devaluation of the victim by the naive teacher (Milgram, 1967, p. 7). This is a cognitive dissonnance approach. Finally, certain personality variables were measured, e.g. authoritarianism.

The writer's own understanding of the complex phenomena of the Milgram situation is yet another possibility. Whereas Milgram's explanation are "dyadic," i.e. the naive subject's relation to the experimenter or the naive subject's relation to the confederate subject, this hypothesis seeks to incorporate the three at once. It is predicated on Sarbin's (1970) role-theory. Some background is in order. Sarbin contends that all persons must locate themselves in at least four sets of ecologies, i.e. sets of interactions between the person and his environment. The four include self-maintenance, social, normative, and transcendental (1970, p. 90f). Each asks certain fundamental questions. Of particular interest are the latter three, i.e. "Who am I?" (social), "How well am I enacting my role?" (normative), and "How ought I relate to my fellow man?" (transcendental).

In the Milgram situation an immediate answer is understood to the social-ecological question, "Who am I," i.e. a subject in this psychological experiment. However, the specific parameters of that role are not readily apparent to the subject. He has to be instructed by the experimenter, e.g. in the operation of the shocking device. Even as the subject is coming to terms with the social-ecological variables, the normative is being experienced, "How well am I enacting my role?" ("How well am I working this confangled device?"). Given the nature of personal involvement, the subject is most likely to take considerable interest in his performance, and, furthermore, he most likely desires to do well. Quality of performance becomes important because of both *objective* and *attributed* demand.

It is suggested, therefore, that the subject is primarily involved in two sets of ecological happenings defined as social and normative. It is further proposed that, especially in the early procedure, transcendental issues are not readily reared. This is due, in part, to the fact that the subject is still learning the specific role parameters and, in part, to the reality that the accomplice-victim does not complain in those early moments.

With this in mind, three points are proposed. First, the ethical or transcendental question ("What is my obligation to the learner-victim?") is covertly reared prior to disengagement/ disobedience. Second, not only must the transcendental tension be experienced, it must become prepotent for disengagement. Third, the continuing thrust of social and normative ecological demands tends to profoundly suppress the transcendental. To this extent obedience persists.

It should be clear that the social and normative issues conflict with the transcendental in the Milgram situation. It should be further clarified that resolution of the conflict is not necessary for the subject to become disobedient, i.e. refuse to further comply with the experimenter. Unresolved cognitive dissonance (e.g. "I must comply with the experimenter's demands since I'm committed to it," while at the same time, "I am inflicting much pain on a fellow human being . . . and, besides, his heart!") is likely to be experienced by *both* obedient and disobedient subjects. Whether or not a particular subject continues to comply is a function of the two polarities: Social/normative demand versus the transcendental, and experimental authority versus victim demand experienced.

One obvious implication of the preceding discussion is that the inference that disobedience is a function of post-conventional moraltiy is rather suspect. The importance of personal value commitment is greatly exaggerated.

Another has to do with the "nature" of the ethically post-conventional. They are depicted as both transcending the group, and, yet still influenced by it. They are uneasy social creatures. This is especially so when they are in conventional group settings. One of Gorsuch's important and unquestioned assumptions is that of post-conventional *consistency*. They maximize the humane possibilities in all situations. The identification of the post-conventional person may not always be consistent, but not so the post-conventional person himself. The morally mature person never acts against his most basic values. He fulfills the Kantian imperative categorically! As he maximizes his own good, he automatically does the same for others. However, the Milgram series tends to disconfirm rather than confirm the consistency hypothesis. Disobedience is a function of the person in a particular situation. To the extent that conclusions from this monumental series are proximally accurate, the transcendent, post-conventionally-moral man hypothesis crumples.

But before we lay 'him' to final rest, some further comments are in order. Gorsuch stretches hard rules of consistency in order to preserve his consistent post-conventional moralist. He writes, "An individual begins to transcend the group when he has an internalized normative system. It is lack of clear personal values that lead man to being so heavily influenced by people around him." He later adds,

> It should be noted that the socially transcendent person is more capable of transcending group influences but that his transcendence is not infinite. A person's social setting provides him with his basic guidelines for living, with his norms for non-critical areas, and sets limits on how he can pursue his destiny.

We feel the post-conventional's fragility. Let us assume that Gorsuch is correct in affirming the consistency of the post-conventional in "critical value" dimensions. One of the problems here has to do with the distinction between the conventional and post-conventional value content; he assumes a radical discontinuity. The movement from level II to level III is a large leap, not a small step. In order to posit this Gorsuch has to assume that only "noncritical" norms are internalized. He has to go through extreme acrobatics of logic in order to preserve the purity of those "critical" values. He appears to sense the problems involved were he to admit that critical values, as well, are no more than group values internalized. As it is, he fails to explain how those critical contents came into being. At best he seems to affirm that they could not be a product of social process. Were it to be demonstrated that even those critical values are the result of social learning process and thus the continuity between the conventional and post-conventional admitted, serious problems would ensue. Either the pedestal upon which the post-conventional person stands would have to be removed or it would have to be broadened to hold the conventionally moral. With the theme of radical discontinuity discontinued, Gorsuch's morally mature persons could no longer be seen as the sole social saviors, i.e. transactors. Furthermore, were it demonstrated that there was continuity of content between levels II and III, not only would the "discrete level" model be wholly inaccurate in terms of content, it would tend to render the "level model" for process irrelevant as well. The only "value" in keeping it would be that the post-conventional person would possibly be more consistent in applying group norms, now internalized, in specific situations. For him the norms of the group might be immediately apparent, whereas the conventional man may well need external (social) clarification. Aside from this, Gorsuch fails to explain (describe) how the post-conventional person comes to that very personal, humanistic set of critical values.

## SUMMARY

This critique has focused on three problems in the Gorsuch essay: 1.) the confusion between psychological and philosophical perspectives; 2.) unwarranted faith in the objective; 3.) the explanation of man's inhumanity to man. There are others: Gorsuch's assumption that the church is culture free, the failure to take seriously the broader cultural context in the discussion of social influences, and the subtle antagonism implied between the individual and the group. Nonetheless, he has boldly tackled the social nature of man issue. His desire to make psychological findings useful, i.e. applying them to the church, is commendable. The value of his essay will be realized when it generates more precise representations and approximations in the "nature of man" reflections. Finally, the Gorsuch judgments suffer from the very problem of finitude he so aptly defines.

## CHAPTER IX

# Not Either-Or But Both-And

HENRY B. VENEMA

## EMPIRICAL SCIENCE AND PHILOSOPHICAL SPECULATION

IN THE INTRODUCTION Gorsuch remarks that the nature of man has been studied by theologians and philosophers for many centuries. He implies that they were less than successful and, therefore, at the present time it is most appropriate to study the nature of man as elucidated by the discoveries of the social sciences. Gorsuch points out that each age has tried to understand man in those terms and symbols most familiar to it. Every age has struggled with its own models to capture the meaning of man.

The twentieth century is a time of unprecedented importance for the social sciences. During this century we have been profoundly influenced by the work of anthropologists, sociologists and psychologists. However I believe that it is impossible to reason—as Gorsuch seems to do—that these sciences can now take the place of the work of philosophers and theologians and make their contribution to the understanding of man apart from the contribution made by many thinkers in centuries past.

The history of thought demonstrates rather clearly that man is a complex being. A thoroughgoing understanding of human nature probably demands the contribution of every scientist and philosopher. No single science can provide the complete answer to the complex questions of human existence. I agree with the implication that the contribution of the social sciences is long overdue and needs now to be made with vigor and cogency. Whereas we have long suffered from, as well as benefited by, the speculations of thinkers, now is the time also to enlarge our perspective of ourselves with the empirical efforts of the social scientist.

Gorsuch rightly notes that psychology alone cannot determine why human nature came to be the way it is nor how long it will continue this way. Each science can thus at best provide only a partial look at man with the result that a healthy skepticism about anyone's absolute claims is a genuine asset. In the concluding section of the first lecture Gorsuch returns to the role of psychology in the total perspective on man and he comments that, because of every man's finitude, the psychologist's contribution can serve as a continuing corrective to the thinking of the theologian and philosopher. This prevents their work from becoming sheerly speculative and unrelated to the data of human experience. Hopefully at the same time, the theologian and philosopher can assist the psychologist with a broader perspective and a more humanistic attitude towards man. Examples of these broader issues are the question of man's identity in the infinite universe, the meaning and purpose of human life, and man's relationship to his environment.

## CONSTANCY AND VARIABILITY IN HUMAN NATURE

In addition to the problem of the role of the social sciences, the lectures raise the problem of human nature. They present evidence to support the contention that man's nature is consistent and constant at least in moral reasoning processes and ethical content. Gorsuch is careful to note that his argument is intended to support only the nature of contemporary man and his cross-cultural evidence is limited to the ethical nature of contemporary man.

Does it make sense to talk about human nature? Gorsuch thinks that it does, notwithstanding the strong cultural relativism that has been sweeping cultural anthropology for the past several decades. However, in the effort to offset the tide of cultural relativism Gorsuch tends to relegate the fantastic variability of man in his cultural expressions to a secondary role and does not seem to consider this variability a part of human nature. It appears that, for Gorsuch, human nature lies primarily in the identification of certain consistent characteristics of man. It is in this connection that he concludes that in at least two respects human nature is the same everywhere. These characteristics are man's ability to reason ethically and the content of these ethical decisions.

Research might highlight many other areas where man is consistent too, but Gorsuch has singled out these two areas. The implication is that the essence of human nature lies in consistency or cultural invariance in regard to certain traits.

It appears that Gorsuch is attempting to defend against the presumptuous claims of the cultural relativists who maintain, on the basis of the remarkable differences in cultural expression of man, that there is no such thing as human nature. Gorsuch rightly notes that the relativity of man has received a great deal of attention over the past several decades in the studies of anthropologists and ethnologists. These crosscultural studies have jarred our Western arrogance which denigrated almost every cultural expression which did not measure up to our standards as primitive and savage. Against the background which has long assumed that human nature is consistent along Western cultural lines, the shock of the work of the cultural relativists is at least understandable, though it is hardly the final answer to the problem of man. Absolutizing the differences is as damaging as finalizing the similarities. Gorsuch's line of reasoning based on his own research and that of others provides a needed corrective to thoroughgoing relativism.

These two sides of human existence, constancy and variability, must be held in balance. The issue is not resolved by choosing consistency as representative of the nature of man since variability is equally part of each one of us. Man's nature is bipolar. This bipolarity resides in both consistent characteristics and enormous adaptability. The cultural relativists did not do away with human nature. They only highlighted one facet of it. Thus the solution to the problem is not Gorsuch's implied attempt to reestablish the validity of talking about human nature because research has shown that there are some identifiable invariants across cultures. Rather a more adequate approach to the problem is the frank recognition that man is extremely adaptable to his environment and that he presents almost endless variations on basic themes in different cultural settings. The variability is as much a part of us as the constancies.

Consistency and variation are interacting processes in every man. To absolutize relativity is to forget its original meaning of "being related to" which suggests that relativity is related to underlying themes. At the same time the latter are shaped and molded by the variant demands of individual personalities and changing environments.

Thus my response is twofold. I believe along with Gorsuch that the contribution of the social sciences must be added to the efforts of past philosophers and scientists in the endeavor to understand man. Today is a most appropriate time for the social sciences to make their contributions simply because they have finally come into their own, not because they will present a more adequate or more valid picture of man. Secondly, in the context of these lectures I believe that human nature does not reside exclusively in crosscultural ethical invariance but that the nature of man includes the variety of cultural expression to which different personality and environment have brought him.

## OBJECTIVE INPUT AND SUBJECTIVE KNOWLEDGE IN DECISION MAKING

In the first lecture Gorsuch deals with a basic issue: Man's finitude. His point is clear: Man is finite and his finitude limits his ability to make accurate judgments about his situation. Thus the problem is epistemological. The issue is one of knowing enough to make good decisions. If man has insufficient knowledge or information, caution is required in decision making. A certain tentativeness and readiness to re-evaluate is crucial for both scientific advance and personal growth. Gorsuch shows that man's judgment is inadequate because he seldom gets all the facts relevant to a particular decision. He further notes that even if man were able to obtain all the relevant information, it is unlikely that he could process all the data to comprehend the situation correctly.

Man's inability to make accurate judgments in the face of new information is increased by previous learning and knowledge which prevent a fresh assessment of a new situation. Furthermore, Gorsuch argues that personal involvement is a serious hindrance in decision making because such involvement biases our judgment resulting in inaccuracy. On a still different level, the difficulty is exacerbated by the fact that we can make only finite judgments about our own finite judgments.

Granted the serious limitations imposed by man's finitude, the questions are, "Can we do any differently in making our decisions?," "What can be done to improve the accuracy of judgment?," "Are there ways and means to get around stereotypes and personal involvement and finite judgments about finite judgments?" Gorsuch presents several ways in which these difficulties can be minimized. He suggests, for example, that personal involvement can be offset by establishing objective decision rules which can be applied by another individual who does not have a strong personal involvement in the particular matter in question. Such an arrangement works admirably in some instances such as the testing of a new drug. But, how can such objectively established rules be applied by an impartial judge in a highly personal situation such as the choice of a spouse or the selection of a career? In these kinds of problems can personal value commitment or any other deep personal involvement be eliminated or minimized? Should such involvement even be eliminated?

Along with Gorsuch, I am suggesting that personal involvement in most situations is inescapable. However, to try and eliminate the personal involvement of the persons making the decisions may mean a serious reduction in the information needed to make some kind of decision. Consequently a more generally applicable strategy might be to try and understand the nature of personal involvement, to assess its impact for distortion in decision making, rather than to try and eliminate it. Again, the solution to the problem is not to neutralize a person's individual values but to complement his stance by objective criteria. To make an accurate decision we need *all* the information we can get. We also need to know the potential for distortion due to either objective or subjective factors in all our decisions.

Thus, in my estimation, the response sets to which Gorsuch refers are our best friends in meeting the world of new information, provided they are reasonably flexible and open. Without them the world would remain a booming, buzzing confusion for us. The risk is that our response sets will shut out essential, new information and thus seriously impair our ability to make accurate judgments. Therefore, the fundamental problem for man is to keep an open and flexible mind offsetting the tendency to rigidity and ossification.

Gorsuch further argues that, for proper judgments to be made, man must be able to step outside of his emotional involvements. He reasons that, given the same information, the person who is not emotionally involved will be able to make a more accurate judgment. The question is: Does the person who is not emotionally involved ever have the same information? Can man ever escape his biases? A more treacherous difficulty is lack of awareness of biases. Regardless of the level of a man's understanding of his presuppositions and predilections they inevitably exert extensive influence in his judgments.

The insistence by scientists that objectivity or emotional noninvolvement is the hallmark of genuine scientific work has led us to the illusion that total objectivity is possible and attainable. This seems to lead for many scientists to a rather concerted effort to deny or suppress their personal biases in their work. The other side of the coin used to emphasize the illusion of objectivity is to denigrate every situation where objectivity is obviously impossible or undesirable as unscientific. In recent years a significant literature has evolved to counteract this illusion of scientific objectivity (*cf.* Bakan, 1969; Farson, 1965; Maslow, 1966; Orne, 1962; Rosenthal, 1968; Rychlak, 1968). In all of these writings, to a greater or lesser degree, the authors' intention is to demonstrate that the person of the scientist is very much involved in the decisions he makes relative to his science. The authors are well acquainted with the arguments for scientific objectivity but they see this attitude also as a serious limitation to achieving full knowledge of man and his affairs. Orne and Rosenthal, for example, both show that in scientific experiments the issue of personal involvement is complicated by personal bias. The experimenter not only has to manage his own preconceptions and biases but he also has to take into account the attitudes and presuppositions of the subject.

These considerations lead me to the conclusion that the requirement of objectivity in the pursuit of accurate judgments is impossible to achieve and even undesirable. Where knowledge about human beings is concerned it is incumbent on the scientist to be ready to measure and account for all of the information available. Even apart from psychological research the problem of this kind of emotional involvement seems best managed by a frank recognition of the measure of involvement and to allow this involvement to complement the judgment of objective observers. For example in designing more humane prisons it would be foolhardy to ignore the input of inmates and guards. Similarly in deciding the issue of abortion it would be unwise to disregard the opinions of the persons most involved, namely, women.

In policy making the information available needs to be sought, both that from impartial judges and that of highly involved persons. Accuracy of judgment is enhanced by the careful consideration of all the relevant input.

In his discussion of this issue Gorsuch seems to be reacting to situations where too many decisions are made on the basis of bias. To offset such a one-sided approach he is pleading for more objectivity and critical judgment in sensitive areas of policy making and ethical issues. It is my contention that man can thrive on input from both sides and that accuracy of judgment is significantly improved by both subjective and objective standards.

On a deeper level, personal involvement in our decisions is inevitable because in the final analysis every judgment we make is made against the background of our personal value structure, personal presuppositions, or personal paradigms. Our emotional biases and response sets form a significant and influential part of the world view which each man constructs for himself. On an individual level every man operates with the kinds of paradigms Kuhn (1962) has described in the practice of science. These individual paradigms organize incoming data and assist one in responding to the constant flow of stimulation.

The world view developed by the individual also includes a personal theology because every man attempts to respond to the ultimate questions of his life. Articulating individual "religious" experience is an important part of life which results from the search for the meaning of existence. Judgments about the ultimate concerns in life may not be very accurate. Nevertheless every man theologizes. Again, the issue is to learn ways to help man appreciate the meaning of life and to enhance or increase the truth value of his personal theology. Thus on the deeper level, a person's emotional and cognitive involvement in all the judgments he makes is equivalent to his basic stance toward life or his personal philosophy of life.

One of the functions of both theology and psychology is to assist man in clarifying both the content and role of his presuppositions. Both disciplines thus can contribute to the explanation of man's behavior. If theology is to make this contribution along with psychology, it has to become related to the data appropriate to its concern. In this connection Gorsuch rightly suggests that a major task of theology is to organize and interpret relevant religious experience. In Christian theology the constant thrust is to examine contemporary experience in the light of Biblical revelation. The data base for Christian theology is twofold: Contemporary man's "religioning" process and Scripture.

## MAN'S GROUP MEMBERSHIP AND TRANSCENDENCE

The second and third lectures are concerned with two intimately related issues of man's relationship to the group and his transcendence of the group. The second lecture is devoted entirely to an examination of the impact and extent of man's social relationships. Gorsuch illustrates how values and ethics are socially shaped and developed and he concludes that ethics need to be viewed as a group function. He also states that the customary moral issue debated by ethicists, that of the individual acting alone, is a straw man issue because such a situation never really exists.

In this connection Gorsuch's distinction between what an individual feels is happening and what he actually does is an apt one. For example, we have been taught to live with the widespread myth that independence of thought and action is a high value goal. We talk about self-made men and we behave as though communal influences and social opportunities had nothing to do with advancement in business or industry. There is little recognition, let alone appreciation, for the societal context that makes free enterprise and individualism possible.

On the other hand, many times we believe that we act independently when our decisions clearly reflect the response patterns and norms or values of our support group. In both instances, that of the rising successful executive and the self-confessed nonconformist, genuine independence is a myth. As a result we are culturally only minimally familiar with the depth and beneficence of social networks. We could benefit as a society from the social issues raised by Gorsuch in the second lecture.

Against the background of his strong insistence on man's social nature in the second lecture, Gorsuch's return to man's individual destiny is noteworthy. Man's achievement of his destiny is limited by the conformity to his social setting. Furthermore he says that, as long as man conforms extensively to the group, his destiny will be a function of the group. Man needs to transcend the group at least partially to be able to say that he has had a hand in shaping his own destiny. This analysis raises several interesting issues. It appears that some men have a better destiny than others. Those who transcend the group are apparently more felicitous or at least more powerful in their destiny. On the other hand, Gorsuch comments that most men never rise above conventional or conforming morality. That being the case, is it meaningful to search for ways to improve the destiny of the group? Moreover, does the person who conforms to the group have no hand in shaping his destiny at all? In other words, is the privilege of shaping destiny reserved for the elite among us?

It seems that this issue of shaping destiny is also commonly

viewed in static terms or in exclusivistic categories. Those who
are able to transcend the group shape destiny. Those who never
transcend the group do not shape their destiny and are likely to
be the hapless victims of group destiny shapers. In my view, the
destiny issue is another example of man's bipolarity. In many
ways man's existence is elliptical with dual foci. Most men at
some point in their lives experience transcendence of their
group. At the same time, man never escapes the group influence
because even his feeling of transcendence is related to his experience of his group and his environment. The feeling of rising
above the group is not usually construed in terms of leaving the
group behind or abandoning it except perhaps in the case of
outright mystics. Ordinarily, the benefits derived from a
transcendent experience are fed back into the group for its
growth and development. Man's social nature and his individuality are not mutually exclusive concepts—they are dual foci of
human existence around which every man moves.

For many years personality theorists and ethicists have tried
to teach us that personality and ethics are highly individualized.
Gorsuch has demonstrated admirably how man is socially conditioned and shaped in terms of his personality and ethics. My
remarks in response to his earlier points suggested that comple-
mentation of one viewpoint by another is essential for completing
our understanding of man's finitude and his social nature. In the
discussion of man's destiny a similar complement is needed to
indicate that man's destiny also is not exclusively a function of
the individual but also of the group to which he belongs.

It is interesting to note that the best analysis of human conflict and aggression is in terms of group conflict. Gorsuch cites
supporting evidence that intergroup aggression is a by-product
of competition for goals. The rule is simple. When several groups
are competing for the same goal, the groups will eventually conflict with one another since there are only a limited number of
goals that are worth pursuing. If one group beats the other to
the treasure a fight ensues and if someone is harmed in the fray,
that is an unfortunate but nevertheless inevitable by-product. If
we take Gorsuch's analysis of moral behavior and apply it to a

group setting, the conclusion is that groups behave regrettably premorally, that is, on behalf of short-range, selfish goals. Any cursory glance at man's history on the earth will confirm this conclusion. There is of course a question whether such an extrapolation from individual moral behavior to group moral behavior is valid. I believe that the jump is valid in terms of Gorsuch's discussion of the social nature of ethics. He concludes that ethics is a group function.

If such intergroup conflict is the result of competition for goals and thereby is illustrative of premoral behavior, then the questions are, "Can groups be taught to behave more conventionally and even post-conventionally in terms of preeminent ethical principles?" and "Can groups develop morally?" It seems that such a development is needed for the survival of the world and even of man himself. It could be argued that the contemporary world has evolved to the point where at least a conventional morality among the various nation groups is essential to prevent further global conflict and possible destruction. Nations have to begin to learn to abide by the rules of the world community. Moreover, and more importantly, the world community has to establish a kind of global morality through its leadership. The charter of the United Nations is an initial attempt to establish some agreements and rules that will help the nations of the world to live in peace and justice. Yet ethical conventionalization has not progressed very far in the past thirty years.

The relationship between this discussion about teaching conventional morality to the world community and the role of the church is an intimate one. If premoral behavior is evident in selfish short-term goal seeking; if conventional moral reasoning is characterized by conformity to rules; and if post-conventional morality is exemplified by adherence to underlying principles, then the church is the first community to appear in the world which could be called a post-conventional community. The New Testament teaches that the church is a live model of the life to come. The church is the new community where the old rules no longer apply. It is the community where the principle of brotherly love is to be applied and lived. Love is Christ's gift to the church and in the same way, love is intended to be the church's gift to the world. The church is committed first of all to living by two principles, i.e. love of God and love of neighbor. It is not primarily committed to meeting group goals.

From the history of the church it is obvious that the church has not become what its Lord has said it would be. Nevertheless the church carries the promise and the hope that, if this new morality is to be visible at all today, it will be within its confines. I do not mean hereby to suggest that the contemporary form of the church is the best place where the new life will be evident. Perhaps it would be better to say that wherever we find the new life of love and hope lived out by people, there is the church.

Gorsuch points out in his lectures that all too often religious bodies require nothing further than adherence to the rules and norms of the particular denomination. He recognizes that the church all too often has been a stifling instead of a liberating environment. Only seldom has the church provided the individual believer with the context where he can avoid neither the challenge nor the need to develop his own response. If the church were able to live out what it is intended to be, it would be a strong influence on the rest of the world by giving leadership in developing the emerging world community. At the same time it would be an attractive group to which to belong.

Gorsuch gives a number of suggestions to churches to make them more effective. He says, for example, that the church must go beyond social support systems to develop deeper belief and value commitments. The person deeply committed to values is the socially transcendent person. He is also the person who exercises the greatest influence on his group for moral good.

## THEOLOGICAL AND PSYCHOLOGICAL ISSUES

Another issue raised by Gorsuch's discussions in the second and third lectures involves two minor remarks indicating his willingness to surrender the final decision on man's goodness or depravity and his freedom or determinism to the theologians. It is noteworthy that Gorsuch does not relinquish the privilege of analyzing man's nature from a social psychological perspective to the theologians. Apparently he feels that as a psychologist he can make a significant contribution to our understanding of human nature. But he just begs off as a psychologist on the issues of freedom and determinism and man's evil or good nature.

My problem is how to distinguish between a psychological and a theological question. What standards does one use? If the theologian, on the basis of his examination of present day man in terms of Biblical revelations should conclude that man is basically corrupt, is this conclusion more valid than if the psychologist looking over the same territory comes to the opposite conclusion? They cannot both be correct although they could both be wrong. My point is to suggest that the social psychologist does have a significant contribution to make on these problems. In my view neither the theologian nor the psychologist can decide these issues finally. In the final analysis the resolution of these problems lies in the commitment made by the believer. The task of both theologian and psychologist is to clarify the issue as much as possible so that the believer can choose wisely and can thus have a mature faith.

## SUMMARY

The lectures are approached critically from a viewpoint of complementarity. The reactions in this paper follow a theme which attempts to bring balance of perspective to what seemed to be onesided viewpoints in the lectures themselves.

Thus I reason that human nature cannot be adequately described by highlighting only its constancy. Changeability and variation are as much a part of human nature as unchanging characteristics. Both perspectives are needed for a complete understanding of man. Further, in contrast to the heavily stressed need for objective input in the lectures, I suggest that man's ability to make decisions can be enhanced by taking subjective awareness into account as well.

Similarly, the problem of man's individuality and his social conditioning cannot be resolved by pitting one perspective against the other. We are neither totally self-made men nor are we exclusively socially conditioned. Both perspectives are needed for a comprehensive understanding of man's life as it is lived in the world.

I attempt to further the presentation of the lectures with regard to intergroup conflict and aggression by relating the discussion to the political realities of the world community and the church. Finally, I believe that both the psychologist and the theologian have important contributions to make in elaborating upon the issues confronting man today.

CHAPTER X

# Summative Discussion[*]

RICHARD L. GORSUCH

WHEN A SET OF COMPLEX IDEAS are communicated in a limited length of time, miscommunication will generally occur. In part, such miscommunication arises from variations in the meanings of key words, particularly across disciplines, but it also lies in the finite judgments of both the speaker and the listener. In an attempt to communicate a major point, the speaker may unintentionally give a distorted picture of his own position. In listening to a lecture, certain points will act as keys for the listener which unlock a whole train of thought which, while stimulating, distracts the listener from gaining a well-rounded understanding of the lecture. But the Finch Lecture Series format allows for responses so that the lecturer can better understand how others receive his message. The present discussion of the responses will, hopefully, reduce the number of misunderstandings so that the similarities and differences between my position and that of the respondents become clearer.

Since this postscript is aimed at clarifying my position, it will not be a summary of the initial lectures. Many, if not most, of the points of the lectures were not disputed by the respondents; these points will seldom be discussed in this discussion. It is therefore assumed that the reader will re-examine the lectures so that the importance of major points not discussed here is noted.

## BASIC ASSUMPTIONS

In the opening lecture, the point was made that a social-

---

[*]An earlier version of this response was critiqued by Dr. Kenneth Lawrence, to whom this writer is indebted.

psychological perspective was being adopted. As Malony and Matthews point out, a scientific perspective has definite philosophical assumptions. One can broaden their statements to say that every perspective has certain philosophical assumptions, for it is impossible to build any position without some bedrock upon which to stand. Tillich makes this point explicitly regarding the circular nature of theology, and it is recognized by virtually every philosopher of science. Therefore, by stating that a social-psychological perspective is adopted, one implicitly states a set of assumptions, including the value of truth, the desire to focus on individuals, the advisability of using the scientific method, the importance of examining the impact of other people and the social context, the fact that the integration of research is my own, and that the "facts" are "facts" within this context.

Given the three-hour limit on the amount of material which could be presented, it was also necessary to make certain assumptions about the audience. One such assumption was that we would be restricted to the English language. On first reading, that assumption may not seem important, but given the work of Whorf (1956) and others it may occasionally be more important than we realize. Using another linguistic system could—but not necessarily would—lead directly to a somewhat different description of humanity. Another assumption was that the audience could readily distinguish between descriptive verbs such as 'is' and proscriptive verbs such as 'should'. With an audience sophisticated in both psychology and theology, there would seem to be no need to point out that the descriptive and the proscriptive involve scientific and ethical statements respectively.

The lectures would probably have benefited from a more explicit statement of the philosophical and theological values which were used at several points. One such assumption that I generally make, noted elsewhere (Gorsuch, 1973) and mentioned in the lectures, is that the characteristics of the adult are *generally* more desirable than the characteristics of the child, although this point needs to be held in tension with the point that some characteristics easily identifiable in children are more desirable than the characteristics of many adults.† For example, the assumption that adult characteristics are generally desirable is easily made in the area of skills and has been found useful in the area of moral and ethical development.

An additional assumption needed beyond that of maturation is as follows: If individuals consistently choose one particular value process when they understand and can utilize *all* the value processes, then that value process can be assumed to be better unless the results are radically different from the conclusions of philosophers and theologians. An examination of the empirical literature for those characteristics which meet these assumptions identifies attributes such as an advanced stage of moral judgment where the person is in transaction with the group rather than being dominated by or independent of it, being considerate of others and reducing injustice.

Hence, these two assumptions were utilized as a philosophical basis for those parts of the lectures where psychology interacted with philosophy and theology and where "shoulds" seemed of interest.‡ In developing the lectures, these assumptions were not discussed since it was felt that most people would agree that they are a reasonable point of departure and the attributes selected appropriate. An additional problem is that such a discussion would have seriously reduced the amount of time which could have been given to the announced topic.

---

†Whenever it is suggested that we accept adult characteristics over those of children, Jesus' statements about the value of children are brought forth. While I do feel that children occasionally show very worthwhile characteristics that adults should emulate, it is also true that these are the exception rather than the rule. This is shown by the fact that Jesus did not begin his ministry while he was a child but waited till some thirty years of age, and that he selected all of his disciples from among adults and not children. While remembering the value of children's characteristics serves as a useful corrective, we must not imply that children's characteristics are always more desirable than those of adults.

‡I feel they are more sophisticated than Malony's "since (c) conformity is what man inevitably does, (d) true morality is to transcend group pressure." This would be odd reasoning since the assumption needed for this logic to hold is that "things should be the opposite of what they are."

## SOCIAL PSYCHOLOGY AND THE NATURE OF MAN

With only an occasional sojourn into the application of the value assumptions noted above, the lectures were designed to explicate the contribution of social psychology to the discussion of the nature of humanity. A social-psychological approach was taken for several reasons. First, the need is there. Discussions of the nature of man are often solely from philosophical, theological or anthropological points of view and generally ignore the volumes of studies conducted by social psychologists. Second, it is doubtful that any individual scholar can adequately treat the topic of humanity's nature from a multi-disciplinary view within a three-hour time limit, so it seemed more profitable to move social psychology from its hidden niche out into the arena of discussion about the nature of humanity. By such a move, it is hoped that interdisciplinary dialogue between psychologists and others traditionally concerned with this topic will be encouraged, to the benefit of all. Winter is perfectly correct that a broader, interdisciplinary view of the nature of man is highly desirable. I look forward to Winter's giving us examples of either the interdisciplinary approach he recommends or of anthropologic data relevant to the topics discussed in social psychology.

As Jewett points out, the psychological perspective on the nature of man needs to interact with other disciplines such as theology. For example, views which stress man as subject and views which may—but not necessarily do—reduce man to "mere object" will need to be thoroughly debated and explored in future discussions. It is apparent that the data of psychology need to be involved in these explorations even as it is also true that the data of theology add unique dimensions to those discussions.*

---

*It is unfortunate that Jewett misinterpreted my comment on leaving the question of determinism and free will to the philosophers and theologians. I did not mean that psychologists would have been able to answer the question better, since they are definitely unqualified to do so. Rather, my point was that we were fortunate an answer to that question was not required in our psychological discussion because (a) psychologists are poorly qualified to answer it, and (b) it is still debated in theological and philosophical circles. Hopefully, the

(continued)

The discussion was centered on the nature of contemporary humanity, as Winter notes, because of the nature of social psychology. The research in social psychology has all been conducted within the contemporary era. While enough of the research has been cross-cultural to indicate that there is a reasonable likelihood that cross-cultural similarities exist as well as cross-cultural differences, none of the research has been conducted across a long enough historical period to eliminate the hypothesis that man is constantly changing. To have stated that a social-psychological perspective was being used and then either to have implied that we could generalize back 3000 years or to have utilized extensive historical data would have been contradictory. However, Winter's logic and observations are good and produces the *hypothesis* that we should be able to generalize historically as well. Social psychology has yet to produce any data to contribute to an evaluation of that hypothesis.

Approaching the nature of humanity as a discussion of the psychological nature of contemporary mankind has the additional advantage of suggesting that people are not frozen. Regardless of whether or not humanity had different psychological characteristics at some time in the past, people may be different in the future. Whether those changes are progressive or regressive would need to be evaluated, but, since the possibility of a variety of changes is there, it is possible for the changes to be progressive. Insomuch as we can build our own destiny, it is hoped that we will have enough sense to make the changes progressive. Such changes may alter characteristics which have been stable for eons.

From the cross-cultural research which has been conducted, the tentative conclusion is that there is more variability within each culture in the characteristics of people than there is across cultures. The first lecture provided data on this conclusion from research concerning value content and processing, an area generally thought to be shot through with cross-cultural differences.

(continued from facing page)
   question will be better clarified and possibly resolved before it becomes crucial to psychological discussions.

While this research still has methodological limitations and is only across contemporary cultures, it is a conclusion which some anthropologists have long supported (e.g. Linton, 1952). Note, however, that *this conclusion is primarily about the psychological nature of people and not about situations or behavior.* Although ecological psychology is in its infancy, it does appear that many cultures exist under a limited set of situational conditions which are radically different from those of other cultures and which produce the differences in behavior reported by anthropologists. For example, the Eskimos of Northern Alaska exist in a radically different situation than the Caribs of British Honduras, the Blacks of American ghettos, or South Sea islanders. The major cultural differences observed in behavior are, I suspect, due more to the differences arising from variations in situations than to the psychological differences in people, including their values.

The high variability within each culture suggests that it is difficult to discuss the characteristics of people unless the variability is discussed also. For that reason, the lectures explicitly set forth dimensions of individual differences which seem essential in the discussion of the nature of humanity. Such an approach implicitly recognizes the fact that mankind's variability must be examined critically and taken into account in developing a total perspective on the nature of man. That is, *one of the more important universal characteristics is that people are variable along certain predictable lines.* The lectures therefore do not deny variability in man but rather deny uniformity within any particular culture of man and suggest that those who hold that "all South Sea islanders look alike" simply have not looked close enough.

## FINITUDE AND OBJECTIVE JUDGMENT

Jewett asked what was meant by the term "finite" and how that dimension related to the distinction between concrete and abstract. "Finite" was used essentially as it is defined in dictionaries, i.e. as having bounds or defined limits. The concrete and well-defined are examples of the finite, since limits are identified and set. The term "abstract" is, however, ambiguous at this point. It can mean either that which is "(1) considered apart from concrete existence or specification thereof" or "(2) theoretical, that is, not applied or practical" (Davies, 1973). The term abstract was used in the former sense rather than the latter.

We can illustrate the distinction between the two interpretations of the term abstract by reference to logic and mathematics. The concepts and modes of relationship expressed by these disciplines are abstract only in the second sense of the term: they are theoretical and do not directly involve a particular instance. However, the success of mathematics and logic is based on the fact that the elements and modes of relationship are exceptionally well-defined and specified, and thus have clearly defined boundaries. In this sense, logic and mathematics are excellent examples of how man takes an area which was of too great magnitude for his limited capabilities and "finitizes it." By establishing a set of well-defined boundaries for each term and clearly defined methods of proof, humanity has brought the not-so-finite down to his level. Since man has "finitized" this area, his judgments are relatively clear and accurate within that system.

Before logic and mathematics were finitized, little progress was made. One scholar could argue for the exact opposite of that which another scholar supported. This could occur because the ambiguities in the situation allowed other factors than just the logic of the situation to be influential. It is in situations with insufficient finiteness that distortions can be reduced by making the subject matter more finite.

From Kuhn's analysis, it appears that the advances of science result from finitizing the elements of our existence. In part, this has occurred through objectively defining terms so that the terms become well bounded and can therefore be dealt with unambiguously. In part, it is also through the use of blind techniques which take the scientist out of the situation as much as possible. In astronomy, for example, the camera-paced-by-a-clock method has replaced the eye-at-the-telescope-and-watch-in-the-hand approach which, as is well known, produced discrepant results depending upon whose eye and whose watch were involved. The same type approaches are being adapted in psychology to reduce the Rosenthal, or experimenter, effect in research studies.

Matthews and Venema made many of the points mentioned in the last paragraph. They and Malony also stated that complete objectivity is not possible. This is certainly true. Even in the most objective experiment, someone must identify which variables to examine, which to ignore, the research designs which are relevant, the statistics utilized, and which results should be reported to others in what detail. The impossibility of achieving complete objectivity is still another reason why humanity must consider all of its judgments fallible and open to biases such as were discussed previously.

But at this point, I have problems with both Matthews' and Malony's discussions. Although they show that greater objectivity is desirable in researching the problem of the psychological nature of man, they then argue that complete objectivity is not possible and leave the impression that we should give up any concern for objectivity. To assume that because we cannot be completely objective we should be subjective will only increase the difficulties in reaching accurate conclusions. While I agree that complete objectivity is never possible, the distinction between the relatively objective and relatively subjective is nevertheless a crucial one when discussing the implications of man's finitude. Through using well-defined categories, blind procedures, and replications by others with different involvements, it is possible to take large steps from the subjective in the direction of the objective. Inasmuch as those steps are taken, a person then receives the feedback on his decisions and judgments which enables him to learn from his past experience and to improve those decisions and judgments. While it is good that we never feel that we have become completely objective— for such feelings would preclude further recognition and correction of the biases in our judgments—it is good only so long as it encourages us to become *more* objective.

Venema presents another viewpoint on subjectivity in decision making which probably arises from a difference in definitions. He states that the accuracy of judgments is likely to be improved through the utilization of both subjective and objective data. It would be interesting to evaluate the evidence pro and con on this particular question, particularly since such an evaluation would enable us to understand better what is meant by the terms accurate, subjective, and objective, and what mixture of objectivity and subjectivity is profitable under what conditions.

From the perspective of the lectures, objectivity occurs when several observers from a variety of perspectives but given the same information come to the same conclusions. Subjectivity is, then, where the personal perspectives of the observers predetermine the conclusion regardless of any information that the person is given, or where the utilization of information is so idiosyncratic that identical conclusions are never reached. But the term subjective can be used in other ways as well, as for example, when subjective is often used to refer to personal feelings and emotions. If the latter is Venema's definition of subjective, then it is obvious that the subjective elements (i.e. personal feelings) are involved in all major decisions.

Under the definitions which I tended to use in the lectures, personal feelings could be either objective or subjective elements in a major decision. If these feelings can never be made known to another in such a manner that the other person agrees that they exist or if they prevent the evaluation of legitimate evidence relevant to the decision, then they cannot be objective. Purely personal feelings in this sense, however, appear to be rare. An outside observer can often readily identify the feelings which a person has by simply observing his behavior. In addition, interviewing the person to evaluate his feelings is one of the objective approaches to the analysis of feelings.

Feelings are crucial elements in making a career decision or selecting a marriage partner provided they are evaluated on a relatively objective basis. From a Rogerian perspective, the counselor helps the patient see his feelings by acting as a sounding board. From these clinical perspectives, only as a person becomes truly in touch with his real feelings—i.e., takes a relatively objective look at his own emotional reactions—can he make appropriate decisions. So long as the person remains subjective—and therefore does not, for example, cross-check how he thinks he feels with his actual visceral and behavioral reactions—then he never truly knows what his feelings actually are. Therefore, by decreasing what I have termed the subjective elements, courses of action will be selected which are in keeping with our emotional needs. Note again, however, my limited definition of the term subjective and the fact that an objectively based decision generally necessitates a serious evaluation of feelings and emotions.

The question of objectivity and accuracy of judgment is philosophically complicated because, as Malony notes, we assumed the existence of an outside reality in those discussions. Without assuming an outside reality, no theory or conclusion could be judged correct or incorrect, and, therefore, there would be no need to evaluate any judgments or conclusions. Ever since my first high school experiences with Descarte's discussion of the proofs of reality, I have been firmly convinced that objective reality can never be proved and that anyone writing from a scientific perspective can be automatically challenged at this point. On the other hand, everyone who crosses a street, buys a car with idiosyncratic starting characteristics, attempts to help patients, or analyzes a set of data to test his hypotheses realizes that our experience includes elements over which we have little apparent control regardless of our perspective or the perspective of our particular subculture. These elements give rise to many basic facts, such as being awake is different than being asleep and food is necessary to live, which are recognized in every culture. Therefore, science has made the reasonable assumption that some outside reality—apart from the highly important social reality—exists to which we can relate to some unknown degree.

I have made and shall continue to make that assumption. It then allows the use of a term such as "correct judgment" even though we may be ultimately limited to only indicating that one judgment is closer to that category than another.

Being objectively oriented, the social-psychological perspective from which I write stresses the importance of relating data and evidence to decisions. While I am not sure if I can objectively distinguish "purified" reason from "unpurified" reason, the connotations of that term render it unsuitable in this context. Rather, reason is a tool which man utilizes to create a rational system which helps him "understand" and predict events around him. The success of the rational system is testified to by the dictaphone which I am using, the chair in which the reader is probably sitting, and the host of items which every contemporary American uses in his daily life. The fact that science is a human task, and therefore as finite and fallible as are humanity's reasoning powers, is also testified to by the problems such as pollution and occasional attempts to deny the emotional side of human existence.

The task of making judgments more objective to overcome the limits of man's finitude does imply that personal involvements need to be carefully examined for the biases they may introduce. There is considerable evidence, as noted in the lectures and in the responses, that personal involvement disrupts accuracy of judgments and hence needs to be minimized. As the respondents have pointed out, one needs to interpret this statement from a balanced perspective. Motivation is essential to becoming involved in and completing any task, and therefore the scholar concerned with a particular topic must indeed be motivated to solve it. But at that point the careful scholar identifies techniques and procedures which will minimize *his* impact upon the results so that the information that he needs to reach conclusions will be unbiased by his initial position. To obtain such unbiased, unambiguous results is the entire task of scientific method.

In the present era, it seems that there is no lack of motivation for involvement with tasks, but as Rosenthal and others have shown, the greater problem seems to be the recognition of the subtle ways in which our own biases may influence the information which we use to reach conclusions. And where biases cannot be overcome in any other way, it is the scholar's responsibility to approach the topic from each of the several possible perspectives so that the results which hold true regardless of perspective can be identified and the results which require one to adopt a distinctive perspective to be meaningful will be highlighted. This is one meaning of the statement that "A good scholar can find three sides for every two-sided argument."

## INTERPERSONAL INFLUENCE

When writing these lectures, I unfortunately forgot about a study on preaching whose results were being passed through the grapevine a few years ago. This study was rumored to have found that the examples used in a sermon communicated more to the hearers than did either the preacher's direct statements or his interpretations of those illustrations. In discussing interpersonal influence, the most dramatic and readily available illustrations are those which show man's negative influence on man. It seems that these illustrations may have communicated more than I intended. The result was that it appeared that I thought man lost his rationality in groups (cf. Malony), an impression which I wish to correct at this point.

The major point of the section on interpersonal influence was that people do influence each other to a surprising extent. As noted in the case of the "risky shift" phenomenon in groups, the group influence can be either toward more conservative or more liberal conclusions and may either help or hinder the reaching of correct decisions (Cartwright, 1973). Therefore, *group influence per se is neutral*. It only becomes good or bad as a function of what it does under particular circumstances. Indeed, while the impact of a group may sometimes be negative, it can often be positive, and the entire last section of the second lecture was an attempt to further specify conditions which will encourage that positive impact.

Malony's and Winter's basic position that "society is not all

bad" is a good corrective to my over-reliance on negative examples. Humanity is a social creature, a fact which we cannot
deny and still be a part of the human race. Therefore, rejecting
society is inappropriate and restructuring aspects of society to
increase the positive impact of people upon people is to be
stressed. This was dealt with at length in the latter part of lecture two and is again noted in lecture three where it is suggested
that the church must go beyond conventionalistic social support
systems to help people develop deeper belief and value commitments, the result of which is a person in *transaction with* the
groups of which he is a part. Psychologists, of course, focus on
the *person* in the group process whereas anthropology and sociology focus on the *group* consisting of persons (and this is in
spite of the fact that research-producing psychologists receive
pay from institutions or from the groups with whom they con-
sult).

Perhaps my better balanced example of interpersonal influence was that of the impact of teachers and peers on a child's
value development. There we found that some children shifted
in one direction and some in another. Those who shifted in the
first direction did so because their peer group and teacher support were in that direction; the others did not shift in that direction because their own position and peer group support was
antithetical to such a shift. In this single study, we have examples of shifts in both directions which are readily interpreted
as a function of group influences. Whether one wishes to identify
the modal shift as good or bad is an independent question.

The Milgram studies are a classical example of the influence of others upon a person's behavior, an influence which
is deemed unwanted according to the values most people hold.
But I did not quote the study to suggest that interpersonal influence is *only* negative but to, instead, stress that the influence
can be important. These studies do show that influence quite
dramatically. Indeed, in studies following Milgram's original
ones and which Matthews quotes, the fact of the social influence
is further shown. Matthews notes that the average subject of

the experiment would shock the other person if he was standing close to the experimenter but would not shock him if he was standing close to the "learner" who is begging not to be shocked. Thus the behavior of the average participant was a direct function of the person to whom the subject was physically closest, and seldom from the person's own ideas or values. (It is surprising that Matthews recognizes that the experiments show that "the issue is obedience to whom" but misses the fact that one of the main reasons for my quoting the Milgram studies was to show that people are influenced by other people.)

However, I did not, as Matthews suggests, "contend" that higher levels of moral judgment played a role in reducing the social influence in the Milgram studies; instead, I *stated,* on the basis of current evidence, that the phenomenon occurs. My reference at this point was research where the subjects who participated in the original Milgram studies were interviewed. As noted in the lectures, those who resisted conforming in the original setting were predominantly those at the post-conventional level of moral judgment. Therefore, to refute my statement Matthews must show a methodological flaw in this and similar studies (e.g. Bock and Warren, 1972) or show that it was a chance finding which does not replicate. If he is able to prove either point, then I shall happily state that the reported result was misleading or nonreplicable. But until that time, the truth of the statement stands regardless of who makes it or how we feel about it. A post-conventional approach to moral judgments is seldom found, but when it occurs, it tends to override the social influences in the Milgram studies.

The follow-up research on the Milgram participants further clarifies another point. Malony suggests that I feel people conform simply because they are "suggestible." I would hold that suggestibility is part of the story, a position well-documented by the social learning theory research on modeling (Bandura, 1969), and also hold that imitation is only one source of interpersonal influence. Sometimes people conform because it is in their own self-interest, as Malony suggests, but the stages of moral development suggest an additional reason: Some people turn to others for their norms of what is appropriate. This conventionalism is a rational approach where it is argued that norms are completely relative and solely a function of the group and that one's prime responsibility is to be a "good boy." The conventionalists are those whom one would expect to be highly influenced by the experimenter in the typical Milgram situation, a hypothesis which is supported by Kohlberg's research. Other reasons for conforming to the group can be suggested—such as the fact that a majority vote is more likely to be accurate in many situations than the individual's decision—but were not dealt with in depth since the lecture is concerned more with the description of humanity than with explanatory theories of why we are like we are.

## MAN: GOOD OR EVIL

In approaching a problem as basic, emotionally laden, and lacking finiteness as whether humanity is basically good or evil, it is likely that a person's underlying position will determine the outcome more than does the data; on this score, it seems that the second lecture struck a reasonable balance. The evidence for the balance is that the arguments were rejected by Jewett because he felt they assumed man was good whereas they were critiqued by Malony for assuming that man was bad. Jewett sees the discussion as basically from a rational, liberal vantage point which, if not denying, ignores concepts of man's fall from grace, his need for atonement, and the role of the sacrifice of Christ. On the other hand, Malony feels confident that my scores on the Philosophy of Human Nature Scale would show I saw humanity as being untrustworthy, selfish, conforming and having all the other "bad" characteristics evaluated by these scales.*

---

*For those interested, my scores on the Philosophy of Human Nature Scale show a relatively average profile which sees man as neither extremely trustworthy or untrustworthy, nor conforming or non-conforming, with the sole exception of the altruism scale where I scored considerably higher than others.

(continued)

While one's personal views do often determine the outcome of a scholar's argument, an attempt was made to reduce that element by only presenting positions which I see as supported by methodologically sound data. The references in the lectures were quoted to illustrate and document that research, and to provide greater meaning for the concepts. As a result, I do not feel frozen to these positions since it is always possible that new and better data may highlight limits in the present research which were not previously obvious.

Part of the reason why many may feel that a speaker's assumptions will predetermine his position on the question of the nature of man's goodness and evil is the difficulty in separating theological from psychological questions, as Venema notes. I see Jewett approaching this topic theologically. Jewett's theological orientation defines the question of man's good or evil nature as consisting primarily of his relationship with God and of being answerable only by revelation. Since the only legitimate arguments are theological and since, for him, the question has already been answered, it is no surprise that my psychologically oriented discussion makes no sense to him. For a scientific question to be a question, one must be willing to consider other options than one's current position and to frame the question so that empirical data will help decide the question. Jewett's position explicitly prevents either of these two conditions from being met and therefore prevents the arguments from being meaningful to him.

The psychological question being asked in lecture two was concerned with the sources of evil which can be readily observed in interpersonal relationships and explicitly excluded man's relationship with God. The discussion is limited to human interrelationships because the perspective adopted for the lectures is a

---

(continued from page 187)

An additional personal note is that I have never found the concept of atonement to be personally meaningful to me or important in my theology although I do recognize the centrality of the doctrine in Christian doctrine; however, man's estrangement from God is extremely meaningful as is the Adam-Eve-snake-apple event and the love of God expressed through Christ.

psychological one and psychology is not the discipline which examines man-God interrelationships. With the concern of the lecture being a person's interrelationships with others, the discussion is more limited than that of Jewett and Matthews who are also concerned with man's relationship with God.

For a complete understanding of the goodness and evil in humanity, it seems apparent that both person to person and person to God relationships need to be thoroughly analyzed, and that the analysis needs to include the relevant aspects of contemporary psychology. For this reason, I shall continue to argue that the complete analysis of the nature of humanity, which would be too lengthy to attempt in three hours of lecture, needs to be interdisciplinary so that it can examine at least psychological and theological aspects. The theological aspects have a long history of analysis, but we are only beginning the psychological analysis. Therefore, it behooves psychologists to bring the relevant research into the discussion so that it can then be integrated as appropriate with other disciplines.

Since humanity is a social creature, there is always a definite and strong place for social relationships that cannot be ignored. While Malony's example of Wesley's impact is somewhat individualistic and may be ignoring some strong group processes, it is probably a good example of a conventional to post-conventional person transacting with a group where his positive impact is, for the new follower, increased because of the nature of the social support system.

From a psychological understanding of interpersonal relationships, including the conditions under which that relationship maximizes evil and the conditions under which it maximizes good, it is then possible to talk of a social support system which will help man reduce the amount of evil in interpersonal relationships. As was assumed in the latter part of the second lecture and as Malony explicitly points out, group influences are useful in this task. This is well illustrated through the stages of moral judgment. It is only as one enters into group relationships of a significant nature that a person can move from the pre-conventional to the conventional stage. Without living in the group-oriented conventional stage, it is impossible to move to the post-conventional stage. As noted in lecture three, the post-conventional stage does *not* mean the person functions independently of groups but rather means that he transacts with groups instead of conforming to them, i.e. the person holds his own ideas with sufficient self-confidence so that he influences the group in addition to the group influencing him.


## POST-CONVENTIONAL MAN AND SOCIETY

Post-conventional thinking develops when an individual realizes that simply adopting the norms of the group of which he is a member presents problems. These problems include that of resolving intergroup conflict on any basis other than pure self-interest or immediate group participation, and that arising from multiple group memberships which may demand that the individual act simultaneously in several incompatible ways. The results are concepts such as "inalienable rights" and the need for justice and love for all regardless of who they are or where they came from. This is the level which research has found to be characteristic of some adults but which, unlike the prior two levels, is never found in children.

The person whose moral judgment processes function at the post-conventional level is just as limited by his finitude as are other people. For this reason, a post-conventional thinker will not necessarily come to the same conclusion in the same situation as another post-conventional person, nor will either be necessarily consistent. In the research studies, the post-conventional thinker is identified as the person whose *modal* judgment is at the post-conventional level but where some conventional thinking usually still occurs. It is also true that conventional thinkers will occasionally use post-conventional thinking, but they are not called post-conventional thinkers because they ordinarily and customarily use conventional thought processes. Therefore, the post-conventional are not assumed to be consistent nor to maximize humane possibilities in all situations. Indeed, the latter question of maximizing the humane possibilities is an empirical one independent of the measurement operation identifying the level of thought processes. While the preliminary evidence does suggest that post-conventional people will tend to create more humane situations (as defined by the philosophical assumptions noted earlier) than those at other levels of thinking, the final decision can only be based on extensive empirical data.

Winter has suggested that the pre-/post-conventional distinction is a tautological one arising from definitions of the good, a suggestion which is only of limited usefulness. The labels preconventional and post-conventional have little to do with philosophical assumptions about the nature of the good but are simply descriptive of *when* the levels occur in normal development. The pre-conventional level occurs before the child is either capable of, or in the habit of, thinking in the conventional mode. The postconventional stage is empirically defined as that which occurs after the person has come to understand and utilize conventional thought processes, and has not been found in children. There is little relationship to the nature of the good in the definitions of these stages since the stages are defined on a relatively empirical and objective process-oriented basis. It is only by later research and analysis that it is found, for example, that people traditionally seen as good in our society are at the post-conventional stage, whereas individuals such as Hitler and Eichmann are found to be at lower stages (Kohlberg, 1969, p. 382f). The phrase "found to be" refers to empirical scoring of statements which these individuals have made, a procedure which makes it somewhat more objective and thus less dependent on biases. Therefore, the biases that Winter suggests may be pervading this discussion are relatively minor.

It is easy to see why Winter developed his interpretation; many of the widely read psychologists and anthropologists who discuss these issues do proceed on just the basis that Winter has suggested. One way to reduce the domination by one's biases is to use clearly and objectively defined variables in statistical analyses, a procedure utilized by the studies quoted in these lectures.

In lecture three, post-conventional humanity was presented as transcending groups, a position Venema ably summarized: "In many ways man's existence is elliptical with dual foci." While man transcends his group,

> at the same time he never escapes the group influence because even his feeling of transcendence is related to his experience of his group and his environment. The feeling of rising above the group is not usually construed in terms of leaving the group behind or abandoning it except perhaps in the case of outright mystics. Ordinarily, the benefits derived from a transcendent experience are fed back into the group for its growth and development. Man's social nature and his individuality are not mutually exclusive concepts; they are dual foci of human existence . . .

for the post-conventionalist.

The primary difference between the post-conventional and conventional person is that the post-conventional thought processes are not *dominated* by concerns of what the group thinks but *also* involve the person's internalized values. Because the post-conventional person is a part of the group in the full sense of that term, the post-conventional person often builds up the "idiosyncratic credit" noted by Malony which is so essential to the ongoing transaction with the group. (The pre-conventionalist could be characterized as focusing only on himself while the conventionalist flip-flops between focusing solely on himself and focusing solely on the group.)

Unfortunately, not everyone clearly perceived the fact that post-conventional humanity is still finite and social. Matthews speaks as if the post-conventional person is against the group and must function completely independent thereof. But there is nothing inherently *anti*-conventional in the post-conventional person, for to transcend is not necessarily to oppose or to be opposite of the group. Instead, the post-conventional person is in a transaction with the group where his personal values and norms function as an independent input along with the input from the group, and out of which a synthesis arises. Several of the other respondents also seemed to perceive the post-conventional individual as an individualistic angel, possibly because of the term transcendent. For this reason, I would now use the term transaction more frequently in the discussion of the topics included in lecture three and down-play the term transcendent. By doing so, the fact that the post-conventional person is a social creature in the full sense of that term might be more clearly seen.

## CONCLUDING COMMENTS

A number of major points were not discussed in depth in either the responses or this reply. These undiscussed points include the consistent nature of man's ethical systems across contemporary cultures, the finiteness of human decisions, theology and science as human attempts to piece together experience, human needs for social support systems, psychology's side-stepping of the free will-determinism controversy, the suggestions for helping people become more transactional, and the openness of humanity's future. While a lack of discussion does not mean each respondent agrees with each of these points, neither does it mean the points are unimportant. The decision of the importance of each of the major points will depend on their usefulness in particular settings.*

Since I initially wrote the lectures, Cattell (1972) has published a book which would have helped shape the last lecture if it had been available. While he takes a social Darwinistic

---

*Presenting the lectures, discussing them with the members of the Fuller community, receiving the respondents' reactions, and replying to these has been an interesting experience. Most interesting was the fact that several respondents utilized virtually no data and seemed to ignore the fact that I was attempting to summarize the status of a body of research rather than present my assumptions per se. It is indeed easy to suggest another position is "superficial" or "dominated by presuppositions" when no evidence is needed or given to support that claim and when it is not open to empirical verification.

While living within one's assumptions is a comfortable world, it is not the world in which I, as a social scientist, desire to live. The positions suggested here are as open to empirical verification as they could be currently made. While this is not as empirical as we would hope to see such discussions in the future, it is a start in that direction and will hopefully be revised on the basis of demonstrations showing the inadequacy of the data or because of new data which has not yet been taken into account.

position which would not be acceptable in many theological circles, he nevertheless suggests procedures for the development of social and feedback systems which can help maximize the good and which can help man take destiny into his own hands. I recommend the book highly. If you are opposed to social Darwinism, simply ignore those elements and ask how Cattell's suggestions would help man shape his own destiny through the use of empirical research. I am sure you will find the discussion interesting.

In concluding, the reader would do well to remember that I and the respondents stand within our historical conditions of finitude and thus are far from infallible. None of us can be taken as ultimate oracles of an ultimate truth. I hope that you, the reader, will utilize these materials to further develop your own concepts of the nature of man while remembering that you too join us in being finite, fallible creatures.

# Questions and Answers

## QUESTIONS FOLLOWING LECTURE #1

MODERATOR: I was sitting there trying to assimilate all of the information that Dr. Gorsuch so articulately presented, and realized as I was doing so that I was making finite judgments about his information. But then, of course, I realized that I was making a finite judgment about making a finite judgment . . . .

Do you have any questions?

QUESTIONER #1: I would like to ask Doctor Gorsuch to speak a little bit more about what you mean by *accurate decision* in the ethical reasoning of man. I want to make sure that you identified man's being finite with his being subjective in his judgment.

GORSUCH: Let me speak to the latter question first. I would not equate finitude with subjectivity in judgment by any common definition of subjective. For example, a scientist tends to be objective, but how much he is actually objective—and particularly, whether or not you can ever be *completely* objective—depends upon your definition of the term. But even if man is relatively objective, he is still finite in his judgmental powers. He has tools that help him to overcome that finitude, for example, computers. Data analyses help to expand his judgmental powers, but even these are still finite and, even more importantly, they are contingent upon man's finite judgment about what to enter into them. And so I would say that subjectivity and finitude are distinct.

I'm not quite sure where I used the phrase "correct ethical decisions." I tend to avoid such phrases wherever possible; I'll have to check over my manuscript. Can you comment more about the context in which I said that?

QUESTIONER: You talked about man's ethical reasoning, and you also said that man is finite because he is not able to take all the factors into consideration when he makes judgments. Therefore, his decisions may not be accurate. So I just want to know what is meant by "accurate decision in ethical reasoning."

GORSUCH: The research on accuracy of decisions has not been in the area of ethical and moral reasoning. It has been in other areas. But I think we can easily extrapolate from that and say that no matter what criterion you want to use, judgments will often be inaccurate. The same conditions producing inaccuracy in other areas will probably also produce inaccuracies in the area of moral and ethical development.

QUESTIONER #2: I'm a little confused about man's viewpoint of mankind being determined largely by his judgments. My question then is: Educationally speaking, are we moving toward an improvement of his viewpoint of mankind or are we endeavoring to look more toward his judgments? Or, to put it another way, does that not reduce the whole educational process to a theological base? Is not a viewpoint of mankind a theological question?

GORSUCH: I would not limit it to theology but would involve philosophy also. The only data I do know of concerning education and man's view of himself suggests that college students' views of the nature of man have become more sceptical in the past ten years. Larry Wrightsman at Peabody College has been collecting philosophy of human nature data for about ten or fifteen years, and his data show a definite move toward scepticism, which might, of course, be one reason for student activism. So there have been some real changes, but we don't know the role of education in those changes. We need to do several things. One is that we need to look much more closely at our bases, such as theological bases, for our views of man, and we need to be more concerned about them in our educational process. We also need to teach people more about how to make accurate judgments about other people. Our efforts in these directions are not too successful because we don't know a lot about how to do it yet.

QUESTIONER #3: I didn't quite follow the discussion toward the last because I couldn't get a clear concept of what your distinction was between a paradigm and a hypothesis. I wonder if you would expand on this a little bit more in order to help us understand.

GORSUCH: The closest relationship in science is between a paradigm and a theory. Generally, we talked about scientific theories, and a theory is when propositions are set out with appropriate corollaries defined by operational measures. You then draw your hypothesis from the theory in terms of the corollaries via the operational measures and apply the results in an appropriate data situation to test your hypothesis. The theory view of science has then held that the theories were accepted or rejected because of the facts found in such studies.

The actual practice of science has not been in that manner; that is, theories have not really been accepted or rejected because they led to confirmed hypotheses or they led to unsupportable hypotheses. Therefore, Kuhn suggests that we suppliment "theory" with the concept "paradigm" in order to point to the fact that sets of scientific constructs often serve a different purpose than we have been taught in our textbooks. The scientist who is actually in the field uses a paradigm, that is, a set of scientific constructs and models for doing research, to decide what research is relevant and what research is not important. He does relate the paradigm to data and, eventually, contradictory data may lead to rejection of the paradigm.

But a paradigm or theory may also be rejected for other reasons which have nothing to do with its truth value. Perhaps as a simple example we might point to the fact that for centuries one set of theories suggested that the earth was round while another set suggested that the earth was flat. *Conclusive* evidence on the difference between these two theories only occurred when the astronauts went up. Why then did we reject the theory that the world was flat? Because scientists found it more useful to think of it as round. You might say it was more fun for their research. It, to them, led to a simpler integration of the data, and it led to some interesting research. So they accepted that as a paradigm because of its usefulness in their scientific lives, not because it was more accurate.

QUESTIONER #4: I'm bothered a little bit by Doctor Gorsuch's scepticism, by his doubt about all of us. I got the feeling that I didn't know if I even wanted to think because maybe I was thinking incorrectly. I thought perhaps that was wrong and I was incorrect, so I didn't know what to do. I am going to ask him if he will help me now. Is what I am doing now worth anything? Am I fooling everybody and mainly myself? Is this all a joke? Am I really carrying on at all? Could you help me here with my subjective problem?

GORSUCH: In the lectures, I moved from talking about the finiteness of man's judgment to talking about the role of paradigms and world views. That is, man does confront an infinite universe with only finite capabilities. We are forced to make decisions which we know are probably wrong. And it is likely that they are wrong, but we still have to make those decisions. That's our existential predicament.

What do we do in response to the predicament? We develop paradigms, we develop world views, we develop theologies. I would hope that we would remember that significant elements of these are probably wrong. And I would suggest that we need to keep all of these theories as concrete as possible, as applied to our life experiences as possible, and as open to correction by our continuing life experiences as possible. While none of us *talk* as if our judgments are finite—and I don't either, since it makes more interesting conversation—nevertheless that is so. Some theologies become too abstract and too far removed from religious experience to have much chance of helping anybody relate to their lives or to have much chance to be corrected by our experiences. I would hope that theologians, philosophers, clinicians, and other people who are in areas with highly abstract data would keep in mind the fact that they need to be looking for ways to check their ideas against some sort of experience. They need to be asking what the purposes of their concepts are and, therefore, what experiences can help them maximize those purposes. But it is an existential predicament; even though we make finite theological judgments and they are often wrong, we still must make them and somehow we must live with them.

QUESTIONER: That was really the question I was asking: can I trust my experiences? Can I have any faith, either in the uniqueness of my experiences or the generality of my experiences? Would I need to trust them only if everybody else has the same experience?

GORSUCH: History suggests that we do not all have the same experiences, and that we do not always interpret the same experience the same way. But I would suggest that if we cannot find at least a significant group of others who have had similar experiences and interpret them in similar ways, we are probably wrong. Now, this is what the person classified as paranoid refuses to do. He is the only one who thinks that "all these electrical gadgets are out to get him." He fails to use other people's experience as a check for the validity of his own. Since he goes way out on a limb, we call him "crazy." Maybe he isn't, who knows? But we *call* him crazy, and it seems to be the best paradigm for mankind in general to assume that he is.

Now this discussion does not deny that we may have our

own unique experiences and that we may learn considerably from them in terms of our existential situation, but it would suggest that we ought to view our own ideas somewhat sceptically and check them out in the most meaningful ways that we can. This is where the church has always been concerned with a host of witnesses—both past, present, and future—and why the church has seldom been willing to establish any one person as the definer of doctrine. Only in the last hundred years has this happened, with the Pope being defined as infallible. All other church doctrines that I know suggest that it is only the host of witnesses that have any chance of a successful judgment. They refuse to base doctrine upon one person's unique experiences, although one person's unique experiences might be used as an illumination for others. But even in order for that to occur, the individual experience must be integrated with other people's religious experiences so that it becomes a meaningful event for many.

QUESTIONER #5: Significant areas of our judgments may be wrong. Can you also say that significant areas of our judgment may be right?

GORSUCH: Yes. I did not stress correct judgments because most people will assume they are right. Therefore, the major point of the lecture had to question that judgment so as to free people to critically examine their own judgments.

QUESTIONER: Is there any way of determining the degree of rightness or wrongness of our judgments?

GORSUCH: This depends upon the area in which we are. For example, research referred to in the selection of graduate students for psychology programs led to some very interesting data on how accurate human judgments are. This required some sophisticated research procedures and an objective criterion. In areas where there is a criterion, rightness and wrongness exist, and those criteria are, of course, provided by one's world view. Ultimately, I suspect we can never transcend our world view. There are some definite limitations here, some circularities. We must make some assumptions even to get into the process.

I'm not too worried about the circularity in defining criteria of correct judgments because mankind has been accurate enough to survive for several million years, and therefore I would suggest we'll be accurate enough to survive a while longer. How much longer depends upon the accuracy of our judgments about international warfare and the role of atomic weapons.

QUESTIONER: Can we believe that the area of our accuracy is increasing?

GORSUCH: I think so. But here I would simply rely upon technological types of evidence. We are able to do more things now, and that is obvious evidence. It is, of course, in the more scientific realms where we can note progress, that is, realms where we have a criterion of accuracy. In other realms where it is more difficult to get criteria of accuracy, it is an open question as to whether or not we know more about what we know, than in the past. And it is a real problem. Perhaps it suggests that more disciplines need to establish criteria for accuracy to evaluate how well they are doing.

Establishing criteria was what I suggested for the area of Biblical criticism. For example, one could set up an experimental model where people integrate letters as you think were done in Paul's time. Then see whether or not your suggested procedures for Biblical analysis will separate out the experimental letters before applying the procedures to the New Testament. A procedure such as that would enable us to check how good the procedures are. It does mean a lot of work and that we will find out we are often wrong. Being wrong then means more work. Evaluating our procedures also means more openness to rejection of our own ideas in which we are ego-involved, and that is dangerous and difficult to do. I am very sympathetic because the scholar is putting his whole reputation on the line.

But until we begin attempting to hurdle such problems, we cannot expect progress.

QUESTIONER #6: I am very interested in the implication of some of your theological statements, which are somewhat scary. Certainly, they are put to us in extreme caution. For example, if we are talking about God, I gather from what you say that finite man has to be very careful about making a judgment about God because he may fail to realize he is finite. So if one is concerned with a proposition dealing with God—for example, God will damn the soul or deny life to the unjust—which comes by revelation, I think you'd say man would have to be very careful about his remembering his finiteness in order to dispute that statement because God might know more about this than he does.

GORSUCH: Yes, and particularly in terms of ethical matters which is where I tried to draw that out. For example, there have been arguments that one cannot say that good is defined as the will of God. We have to define it independently and find out whether God's will is good or not. I can't quite buy that because one would need to assume that we are able to have the highest levels of ethical reasoning in order to stand in judgment over God's ethical reasoning. But we may not be able to even comprehend God's ethical reasoning. So I think it is legitimate to define the will of God as good and say man's concepts of the good have to stand under the judgment of that rather than vice-versa.

QUESTIONER: Let me take this a step further. How could we ever verify a theological proposition, such as saying God denies life to the unjust? Does this mean that to make that kind of theological statement is exceedingly risky for me because now, as a finite person, I have to be aware of my lack of capability to get objectivity? It really raises the question of how you establish the truth value of theological statements.

GORSUCH: I do feel a world view is necessary—and I include theology as a type of world view—because we have to operate as if we knew the answer to that question. While we need to remember that our judgment about that question may be inaccurate, we still have to make our best bet. And there's where we need all the critical facilities we can bring to bear on the question.

In theology, we might point out that you have the problem of authority. What is a revelation from God? How do we know if it is a revelation from God? But at times we must make the decision. We must say, in essence, "Here I stand; I can do no other." It is man's existential predicament. He is not given faith on a platter. But I would still like to recognize that we can't be dogmatic either. Other theologies *may* be correct, even though we disagree with them and even though we bet on our own.

QUESTIONER #7: I'd like to get back to what was said earlier. I have a problem. In terms of my limited reading of the history of science, quite frequently one person with the idea turns out to be the right one in the end. I recall many cases when a person stood out against the crowd, against the judgment of the group and was finally proved right. It seems to me that in these cases the element of time comes into it. You haven't dealt, as I remember, with the element of time in judgments for criteria about judgments. Would you like to comment on that?

GORSUCH: To answer that question, let's consider a hypothetical case. Let's say we have a scientific area and thirty different theories that are relevant to it. One of these theories is bound to be better than others. Which one we don't know. Well, let's say that a partially incorrect theory becomes adopted for a while. What happens in the area? Later on they find out that they are wrong, and they go back to the better one. But in doing so they almost never pay attention to the first person who proposed the theory. The reason why they come to the one which is more correct is because some inconsistencies keep appearing in the data and somebody comes up with the theory.

One person may well be right over the group, but if we have no data to know whether or not he is right I don't know what we can do about it. It's just one of those predicaments. And that's why we have to remain open, I think, to a wide variety of ideas until there is fairly conclusive data that rejects some of them.

Perhaps I should add one other statement about science. If there is anything that science has shown us, it has shown us that all theories are wrong. Practically every theory that has ever been proposed has been ultimately proved to be wrong in some major respect. And our best prediction for any current theory is that, sooner or later, somebody is going to prove it wrong and replace it. So it is hard for me to talk of an ultimately correct theory.

MODERATOR: Thank you, Doctor Gorsuch. I have exceeded my bounds. I know that there are at least three of you whose hands I saw who have questions and you might be able to impose on Doctor Gorsuch after the meeting tonight. We have two more days and I am sure, in the context of those times, we will have considerable discussion along the way.

## QUESTIONS FOLLOWING LECTURE #3

MODERATOR:After the last two lectureships and lectures, there was a time of question-answer opportunity. We've discovered in reevaluating these experiences in the past that the audience is divided into three groups: those that have premoral thought processes during the question-answer period, and they ask questions and then answer them. They talk to themselves. There are those who don't say anything and they are conventional thought processes persons; then there are those that ask questions that someone else asked them to and they are also conventional. And then there are those who ask questions interacting with the lecturer that indicates that they are in the advanced group of post-conventionals. I have one or two of those questions at hand, but I'll let you present your own. We have no microphone in the audience so if you'll rise to your feet and speak clearly, I'll repeat your question so all can hear.

QUESTIONER #1 (Moderator repeating): There is a request that Doctor Gorsuch comment further on the work of B. F. Skinner, with reference to the lecture.

GORSUCH: Skinner's work can be broken into two different categories. One is his work as a psychologist and the other is his work as a philosopher. I think his psychology work is quite good, indeed excellent. He has found a number of principles of learning theory which are quite applicable to pigeons and probably young children. They are also applicable in many situations to adults. And this work is helpful for a complete science of psychology.

On the other hand, one has Skinner as a paradigm builder and philosopher. Here, I have less agreement with him. For example, he is one of those who adopts the deterministic position. But then he goes on to help man shape his own destiny. I think there is a basic incompatibility there.

I do feel that Skinner in practice is often misunderstood and misinterpreted, that people respond more to this determinism and less to what he is trying to do. And what he is trying to do is to help man learn that which influences him so that he can take charge of that which influences him. When he is speaking in that vein, I am in agreement with him.

QUESTIONER #2: The request is that Doctor Gorsuch will respond with reference to his categories and social analyses to the work of John Wesley, particularly pertaining to the small class groups.

GORSUCH: I would interpret the small class groups as a deliberate attempt to build a social support system for the

individuals involved, and a fairly successful one, which probably utilized principles we would now refer to as membership
group-reference group distinctions to help class members maintain their distinct value systems when going back into society.
The result was the formation of mutually supportive groups.

Perhaps I might also mention the Methodist circuit rider
as a paradigm or classical example of the clergy's role. Here
you have an outside individual who maintains ties with the
greater church community while being in transaction with the
individual groups to help them transcend their own local situation by becoming tied to the norms of the entire church. The
clergymen themselves, by the fact that they were riding circuit,
were possibly more effective than the pastor in the individual
church. On their circuits they probably found social support
for some of their positions in one setting that they may not
have had in other settings. Therefore, their social support system was more diffuse and not limited just to their congregation,
so you had less of the "going-native" effect that one observes
among pastors.

QUESTIONER #3: I'm supposed to repeat the question. Doctor
Gorsuch, will you repeat it as you heard it, and then answer?

GORSUCH: What I heard being asked was whether or not social
support system should not be social support systems, and how
a conventional type person handles the different norms that
arise from the different groups.

That's a good point. The social support system should be
viewed as an integrated group of sub-systems. Now how does an
individual reconcile the various norms, various conflicts? Often,
he really doesn't. That is, the norms of the different groups
are in different settings. When the person is a football player
and he plays football, he sees how much he can shake up the
opposing team in keeping with the norms of the football team.
But when he goes into another setting and he is not playing
football, he has another set of norms which he follows. True

conflicts may be solved by dropping some of the groups or by forming one's own norms, i.e. becoming post-conventional.

QUESTIONER #4: Once again I defer to you.

GORSUCH: The gist of the question seems to be: How can the church avoid the problem of being only conventionalist and help people become post-conventionalist in a real sense? Might not this happen by, or be best brought about by, not building a solid social support system?

This is a real problem, as I commented earlier. The fact is we really don't have a whole lot of data on how post-conventional people develop, and until we get that data it's going to be difficult to decide how we can respond to questions such as these. That's one reason I'm in psychological research, because I'm not at all sure we do know how to do it. We don't even know if everybody can become post-conventional, we don't know what that means if they do, or what sort of groups would result. There are all sorts of problems there on an empirical basis that need to be tackled, and I am glad we are aware of them. And perhaps we have not been as aware of them in the past.

The one danger of going out immediately to turn all our conventional people in churches to post-conventionalism is the fact that we might flub it so badly that they would all become preconventionalists instead. It seems that if one gets discouraged with the fact that a group really doesn't, have any conventionalistic norms and if he does not get practice in abstracting and building normative systems, then he may well give up completely and conclude that it's all relative (which is a very common comment in our society). So you have dangers both ways— of trapping people in the conventionalistic system, or of throwing them out of the conventionalistic system. But it does seem reasonably sure that it is necessary to pass through conventionalism to reach postconventionalism.

QUESTIONER #5: GORSUCH: The question is how I deal with the highly idiosyncratic prophetic souls of history.

In terms of our categories, they would tend to be those who are able to transcend the group norms. Now, transcending the group norms may not always be good or always bad. But most of those whom we call prophetic people are those whom we currently assume were good. Many of the prophetic people have not been influential in their societies because the conventional norms went against them, which is one reason why we often remember them as martyrs, as outcasts, and so forth.

But even these people need social support. Perhaps this is one reason why one famous prophetic soul gathered twelve people around him. By doing so, he began building his own social support system. Now I think a lesson might be learned from this. One way to maintain one's own prophetic stance might be to build up his own social support system.

QUESTIONER #6: In order for a pastor to generate self- or socially-transcendent committed parishoners, should he attempt to do this in terms of a one-to-one or small group interaction, or may he effectively do it in terms of a large group, in perhaps by classical preachment from the pulpit?

GORSUCH: I would suggest that this in part depends upon the homogeneity of the group. If you have a very homogeneous group, then you can hope to do a lot by preaching. I do think that we underrate preaching quite often. In Rokeach's study, there was found a shifting of values to more commitment from preaching, although the people did not recognize it as such and were, therefore, perhaps more open to it. Rokeach spent perhaps five minutes talking to these college students in a large group setting. That's all. And a year and a half later, there was a differential rate of response to appeal from the NAACP for funds between the experimental and control groups. Nevertheless, I suspect that the heterogenous makeup of most congregations means more progress could be made by working with small groups, that is, by attempting to move small groups forward into a deeper commitment to values or to postconventional thinking. In answering this question, I should also point out that we have two different paradigms in this area. One is concerned with being deeply committed to values and the other is concerned with the reasoning processes. The procedure necessary to produce deep commitment to values may be more applicable to preaching type situations than small group sessions. I have implied that they might both ultimately be the same—which makes it easy to talk about—but we really have no data on it.

QUESTIONER #7: Are there any studies on the nature of support groups in terms of being good, bad, indifferent? For example, is a support group by nature defensive and negative, or can a support group be introductory and neutral with new ideas and values?

GORSUCH: Whenever we get into terms such as "good, bad, indifferent, effective, ineffective," I immediately start wondering how we define those terms. A psychologist, when he defines them, is bringing in philosophical and theological presuppositions, and I would like those definitions to be obvious and open so that they can be discussed by everyone. Having pointed to the problem, I'll use some of my own definitions and go on.

I suppose that there is a sense in which a social support system has to be concerned with itself to remain a social system. Hence, there is always a bit of selfishness or institutionalism involved in groups. To accomplish their goals, they must first be a group, and so challenges to their groupness will be tackled first.

I tend to feel that everyone needs social support systems, and therefore the question is how we can make them more effective, not whether or not they are effective. Certainly, any group changes and changes rapidly under proper conditions, although we think of institutions and groups as set in their ways. But just let one of these institutions be seriously challenged by some new and outside force and you'll see them change, and change rapidly, for their own survival. So they can introduce new norms and the like—we just don't know much about the conditions which lead them to introduce new norms. That is, we really don't know much about how we shape up institutions and social support systems. Perhaps the sociologist might have more to say to that.

Since this is the last question, I would like to say that both my wife and I have deeply appreciated the opportunity to come here and carry on these conversations and the hospitality of Fuller. Although I have been deeply interested in psychology and religion, one professionally has few opportunities to engage in relating these areas. This lecture series helps provide those opportunities for us; not only does the audience benefit, but the scholar also benefits. Thank you.

MODERATOR: Richard, I feel I speak for all of us in all of the three schools in saying that our gratitude is great to you, that you have stimulated us, and I hope that our responses will carry on and be stimulating to you as we engage in further dialogue. Thank you.

# REFERENCES

Allen, R. O., and Spilka, B.: Committed and consensual religion: A specification of religion-prejudice relationships. *Journal for the Scientific Study of Religion, 6*:191-206, 1967.

Armstrong, J. S., and Soelberg, P.: On the interpretation of factor analysis. *Psychol Bull, 70*:361-364, 1968.

Asch, S. E.: Effects of group pressure upon the modification and distortion of judgments. In E. E. Maccoby et al (Eds.): *Readings in Social Psychology.* New York, Henry Holt & Co., 1958, pp. 174-183 and Holt, Rinehart and Winston, Inc., 1963.

Bakan, D.: *On Method.* San Francisco, Jossey Bass, 1969.

Bandura, A., and Walters, R. H.: *Social Learning and Personality Development.* New York, Holt, Rinehart and Winston, Inc., 1963.

Barker, R. G., and Gump, P. V.: *Big school, small school.* Stanford, California, Stanford University Press, 1964.

Berelson, B., and Steiner, G. A.: *Human Behavior: An Inventory of Scientific Findings.* New York, Harcourt, Brace, and World, 1964.

Bock, D. C., and Warren, N. C.: Religious belief as a factor in obedience to destructive commands. *Review of Religious Research, 12*:185-191, 1972.

Bowers, W. L.: Normative constraints on deviant behavior in the college context. *Sociometry, 31*(4):370-385, 1968.

Bowlby, J.: *Maternal care and mental health.* World Health Organization Monograph Series, No. 2., 1952.

Bull, N. J.: *Moral Judgment from Childhood to Adolescence.* Beverly Hills, California, Sage, 1969.

Carlin, J.: *Lawyer's Ethics.* New York, Russell Sage Foundation, 1966.

Cartwright, D.: Determinants of scientific progress: The case of research on the risky shift. *Am Psychol, 28*:222-231, 1973.

Cattell, R. B.: *A New Morality from Science: Beyondism.* New York, Pergamon, 1972.

Comfort, A.: *The Nature of Human Nature.* New York, Harper and Row, 1966.

Cooley, C. H.: *Human Nature and the Social Order.* New York, Scribners, 1902 (Rev. ed. 1922).

Crow, W. J., and Hammond, K. R.: The generality of accuracy and response sets in interpersonal perception. *J Abnorm Psychol, 54*:384-390, 1957.

Davies, P.: *The American Heritage Dictionary of the English Language,* New York, Dell, 1973.

Dawes, R. M.: *The superiority of random linear combinations to real judges.* Paper presented at the annual meeting of the Society for Multivariate Experimental Psychology, 1972.

Dittes, J. E.: Religion, prejudice and personality. In M. P. Strommen (Ed.): *Research on Religious Development.* New York, Hawthorn, 1971, pp. 355-390.

Doniger, S. (Ed.): *The Nature of Man in Theological and Psychological Perspective.* New York, Harper and Row, 1962.

Farson, R. F.: *Science and Human Affairs.* Palo Alto, California, Science and Behavior Books, 1965.

Festinger, L., Riecken, H. W., and Schachter, S.: *When Prophecy Fails.* Minneapolis, University of Minnesota Press, 1956.

Festinger, L., Schachter, S., and Back, K.: *Social Pressures in Informal Groups.* New York, Harper and Row, 1950.

Fishbein, M.: Attitude and the prediction of behavior. In M. Fishbein (Ed.): *Readings in Attitude Theory and Measurement.* New York, Wiley, 1967, pp. 477-492.

Forer, B. R.: The fallacy of personal validations: A classroom demonstration of gullibility. *J Abnorm Soc Psychol, 44:*118-123, 1949.

Freud, S.: *Group Psychology and the Analysis of the Ego.* New York, Norton, 1961. (Originally published: 1921.)

Goldfarb, W.: Infant rearing as a factor in foster home replacement. *J Exp Ed, 12:*162-167, 1943.

Gorsuch, R. L.: *Value Conflicts in the School Setting.* Final report, August, 1971, George Peabody College for Teachers, Project #9-427, Office of Education, Department of Health, Education and Welfare. ERIC Document (Ed. 057 410).

Gorsuch, R. L.: Moral education from a psychological view of man as an ethical being. *The Educational Forum,* Sept., 1973, pp. 169-178.

Gorsuch, R. L., and Aleshire, D.: Christian faith and ethnic tolerance: a review and interpretation of research, *J Sci Study Rel, 13:*281-307, 1974.

Gorsuch, R. L., and Barnes, M. L.: Stages of ethical reasoning and moral norms of Carib youths. *J Cross Cul Psychol, 4:*283-301, 1973.

Gorsuch, R. L., and Smith, R. A.: Changes in college students' evaluation of moral behavior: 1969 versus 1939, 1949, and 1958. *J Personal Soc Psychol, 24*(3): 381-391, 1972.

Greeley, A. M., and Gockel, G. L.: The religious effects of parochial education. In Strommen, M. P. (Ed.): *Research on Religious Development.* New York, Hawthorn Books, 1971, pp. 264-301.

Haan, N., Smith, B., and Block, J.: Moral reasoning of young adults' political-social behavior, family background, and personality correlates. *J Personal Soc Psychol, 10*:183-201, 1968.

Hare, R. M.: Theology and falsification. In Flew, A., and MacIntyre, A. (Eds.): *New Essays in Philosophical Theology.* London, S.C.M. Press, 1955, pp. 99-103.

Harlow, H. F.: The heterosexual affectional system in monkeys. *Am Psychol, 17*:1-9, 1962.

Hartshorne, H., and May, M.: *Studies in Deceit,* Vol. 1. *Studies in the Nature of Character.* New York, Macmillan, 1928.

Hartshorne, H., May, M., and Maller, J.: *Studies in Service and Self-Control,* Vol. 2. *Studies in the Nature of Character.* New York, Macmillan, 1929.

Heidbreder, E.: *Seven Psychologies.* New York, Appleton-Century-Crofts, 1933.

Hick, J.: *Faith and Knowledge.* (2nd ed.) Ithaca, Cornell University Press, 1966.

Hollander, E. P.: *Leaders, Groups and Influence.* New York, Oxford University Press, 1964.

Hollander, E. P.: *Principles and Methods of Social Psychology.* (2nd ed.) New York, Oxford University Press, 1971.

Holtzman, W. H., and Sells, S. B.: Prediction of flying success by clinical analysis of test protocols. *J Abnor Soc Psychol, 49*:485-490, 1954.

Jessor, R., Graves, T. D., Hanson, R. D., and Jessor, S. C.: *Society, Personality and Deviant Behavior.* New York, Holt, Rinehart and Winston, 1968.

Joad, C. E. M.: The faith of great scientists. In *The American Weekly.* The Hearst Publishing Co., Inc., 1948.

Johnson, R. N.: *Aggression in Man and Animals.* Philadelphia, W. B. Saunders, 1972.

Kogan, N., and Wallach, M. A.: *Risk Taking: A Study in Cognition and Personality.* New York, Holt, Rinehart and Winston, 1964.

Kohlberg, L.: The child as a moral philosopher. *Psychology Today, 2*(4): 25-30, 1968.

Kohlberg, L.: Stage and sequence: The cognitive-developmental approach to socialization. In Goslin, D. A. (Ed.): *Handbook of Socialization Theory and Research.* Chicago, Rand McNally, 1969, pp. 347-480.

Kohn, M. L.: *Class and Conformity: A Study in Values.* Homewood, Illinois, Dorsey Press, 1969.

Kuhn, T. S.: *The Structure of Scientific Revolutions.* Chicago, University of Chicago Press, 1962.

Latané, B., and Darley, J.: *The Unresponsive Bystander: Why Doesn't He Help?* New York, Appleton-Century-Crofts, 1970.

LeBon, G.: *The Crowd: A Study of the Popular Mind.* (2nd Ed.) London, T. F. University, 1897.

Lenski, G.: *The Religious Factor: A Sociologist's Inquiry.* (Rev. Ed.) New York, Anchor Books, Doubleday and Company, 1963.

Linton, R.: Universal ethical principles: An anthropological view. In Ansken, R. (Ed.): *Moral Principles of Action.* New York, Harper, 1952.

Luchins, A. S.: Experimental attempts to minimize the impact of first impressions. In Hovland, C. I. (Ed.): *The Order of Presentation in Persuasion.* New Haven, Yale University Press, 1957, pp. 62-75.

Malony, H. N.: Human nature, religious belief and pastoral care. Unpublished doctoral dissertation, George Peabody College, Nashville, Tennessee, 1964.

Malony, H. N.: Motivation and management: The M & M's of the pastor's task. *Theology News and Notes,* 18(4):16-20, 1972.

Maslow, A. H.: *The Psychology of Science.* Chicago, Henry Regney Co., 1966.

Matson, F. W.: *The Broken Image.* Garden City, New York, Anchor Books, 1966.

McGuire, W. J.: Persistence of the resistance to persuasion induced by various types of prior belief defenses. *J Abnor Soc Psychol,* 64:241-248, 1962.

McGuire, W. J.: Inducing resistance to persuasion. In L. Berkowitz (Ed.): *Advances in Experimental Social Psychology,* Vol. 1. New York, Academic Press, 1964, pp. 191-229.

Mead, G. H.: *Mind, Self and Society.* Chicago, University of Chicago Press, 1934.

Milgram, S.: Behavioral study of obedience. *J Abnorm Soc Psychol,* 67(4):371-378, 1963.

Milgram, S.: Group pressure and action against a person. *J Abnorm Soc Psychol,* 19(11):848-852, 1964a.

Milgram, S.: Issues in the study of obedience: A reply to Baumrind. *Am Psychol,* 19(11):848-852, 1964b.

Milgram, S.: Liberating effects of group pressure. *J Personal Soc Psychol,* 1(2):127-134, 1965a.

Milgram, S.: Some conditions of obedience and disobedience to authority. *Human Relations,* 18:57-76, 1965b.

Milgram, S.: The compulsion to do evil. *Patterns of Prejudice,* 1(6):3-7, 1967.

Millon, T. (Ed.): *Theories of Psychopathology.* Philadelphia, W. B. Saunders, 1967.

Moberg, D.: Religious practices. In Strommen, M. P. (Ed.): *Research on Religious Development.* New York, Hawthorn Books, 1971, pp. 551-598.

Munsinger, H.: *Human Quality Control.* Pacific Palisades, California, Goodyear Publishing, 1972.

Newcomb, T. M., Koenig, L. E., Flacks, R., and Warwick, D. P.: *Persistence and Change: Bennington College and its Students after Twenty-Five Years.* New York, Wiley, 1967.

Nottingham, J., Gorsuch, R. and Wrightsman, L. S.: Factoral replication of the theoretically derived subscales of the Philosophy of Human Nature Scale. *J Soc Psychol, 81*:129-130, 1970.

Orne, M. T.: On the social psychology of the psychological experiment: With particular reference to demand characteristics and their implications. *Am Psychol, 17*:776-783, 1962.

Penelhum, T.: *Religion and Rationality: An Introduction to the Philosophy of Religion.* New York, Random House, 1971.

Polanyi, M.: *Science, Faith and Society.* London, Oxford University Press, 1964.

Radhakrishan, S., and Raju, P. T. (Eds.): *The Concept of Man.* London, Tinling, 1960.

Redfield, R.: *The Primitive World and its Transformations.* Ithaca, Cornell University Press, 1953.

Rokeach, M.: Long-range experimental modification of values, attitudes, and behavior. *Am Psychol, 26*:453-459, 1971.

Rosenhan, D.: Some origins of concern for others. In Rosenhan, D., and London, P. (Eds.): *Theory and Research in Abnormal Psychology.* New York, Holt, Rinehart and Winston, 1969. pp. 491-507.

Rosenthal, R.: *Experimenter Effects in Behavioral Research.* New York, Appleton-Century-Crofts, 1966.

Rosenthal, R., and Jacobson, L.: *Pygmalion in the Classroom.* New York, Holt, Rinehart, and Winston, 1968.

Rychlak, J. F.: *A Philosophy of Science for Personality Theory.* Boston, Houghton Mifflin, 1968.

Schachter, S.: Deviation, rejection, and communication. *J Abnorm Soc Psychol, 46*:190-207, 1951.

Schwartz, S.: Words, deeds, and the perception of consequences and responsibility in action situations. *J Personal Soc Psychol, 10*:232-242, 1968.

Seller, J.: *Public Ethics.* New York, Harper and Row, 1970.

Shamsavari, F.: *The moral development of Iranian village boys.* Unpublished M.A. thesis, George Peabody College, 1973.

Shephard, H. A.: Innovation resisting and innovation producing organizations. In Bennis, W. G., Benne, K. D., and Chin, R. (Eds.): *The Planning of Change.* New York, Holt, Rinehart, Winston, 1969, pp. 519-525.

Sherif, M.: *The Psychology of Social Norms.* New York, Harper Torchbooks, 1966. (Originally published:1936)

Sherif, M., and Hovland, C. I.: *Social Judgment*. New Haven, Yale University Press, 1961.

Sherif, M., and Sherif, C. W.: *Reference Groups: Exploration Into the Conformity and Deviation of Adolescents*. New York, Harper and Row, 1964.

Sherif, M., and Sherif, C. W.: *Social Psychology*. New York, Harper and Row, 1969.

Siegel, A. E., and Siegel, S.: Reference groups, membership groups and attitude change. *J Abnorm Soc Psychol*, 55:360-364, 1957.

Sinsheimer, R. L.: The prospect for designed genetic change. *Am Sci* 57:134-142, 1969.

Skinner, B. F.: Beyond freedom and dignity. *Psychology Today*, 5(3):33-80, 1971.

Stern, G. G.: Personality environment interaction in large organizations. In Hunt, W. (Ed.): *Human Behavior and Its Control*. Cambridge, Mass., Schenkman Publishing, 1971, pp. 14-29.

Sullivan, H. S.: *The Interpersonal Theory of Psychiatry*. New York, W. W. Norton & Company, 1953.

Sullivan, J. W. N.: *The Limitations of Science*. New York, Viking Press, 1933.

Sullivan, P. R.: Influence of personal values on psychiatric judgment: A military example. *J Nerv Ment Dis*, 153(3):193-198, 1971.

Tomeh, A. K.: Patterns of moral behavior in two social structures. *Sociology and Social Research*, 55(2):149-160, 1971.

Tuddenham, R. D., and McBride, P. D.: The yielding experiment from the subject's point of view. *J Personal*, 27:259-271, 1959.

Turiel, E.: Development processes in the child's moral thinking. In Mussen, P., Langer, J., and Covington, N. (Eds.): *Trends and Issues in Developmental Psychology*, New York, Holt, Rinehart and Winston, 1969, pp. 97-133.

Walters, Sr. A., and Bradley, Sr. R.: Motivation and religious behavior. In Strommen, M. P. (Ed.): *Research on Religious Development*. New York, Hawthorn Books, 1971, pp. 599-651.

Whorf, B. L.: *Language, Thought and Reality*. New York, Wiley, 1956.

Wickler, W.: *The Sexual Code: The Social Behavior of Animal and Man*. Garden City, New Jersey, Doubleday, 1972.

Wrightsman, L. S.: Measurement of philosophies of human nature. *Psychological Reports*, 14:743-751, 1964.

Wrightsman, L. S.: Personality and attitudinal correlates of trusting and trustworthy behaviors in a two person game. *J Personal Soc Psychol*, 4:328-332, 1966.

Wrightsman, L. S.: *Assumptions About Human Nature: A Social Psychological Approach*. Monterey, Brooks-Cole, 1974.

Wrightsman, L. S.: *Social Psychology in the Seventies.* Monterey, Brooks-Cole, 1972b.

Wrightsman, L. S., and Hearn, B. S.: Annotated bibliography of research on the Philosophies of Human Nature Scale. Unpublished manuscript, Nashville, Tennessee, George Peabody College, 1971.

Yandell, K. E.: *Basic Issues in the Philosophy of Religion.* Boston, Allyn and Bacon, 1971.

# AUTHOR INDEX

# SUBJECT INDEX

**P**

Paradigms: 30-33, 97-98, 123.

Philosophies of human nature: 31-32, 114-117, 187.

Philosophy: *see* theology, psychology: social psychological perspective, assumptions.

Psychology, social psychological perspective: 4-6, 98-102, 107-109, 142-145, 159-160, 169-171, 173-178.

Psychology, social psychological perspective vs. interdisciplinary: 6, 130-134, 176.

**R**

Religious institutions: 54-62, 81-83, 124-125, 169-170.

Religious institutions, growth of: 61-62.

**S**

Situations, finiteness of: 24-29.

Social influence: 34-43, 83-89, 115-116, 117-122, 125-128, 135-141, 151-157, 184-187, 190-193.

Social support systems: 41-43, 54-62, 84-87.

Social transcendence: 69-87, 166-168, 184-193.

Social transcendence, development of: 77-83, 89-92.

Social transcendence, impact of: 84-89.

**T**

Theology: 30-33, 96-98, 123-125, 170-171, 176, 188-189.

**V**

Value commitment: cf. ethical content.

# DATE DUE

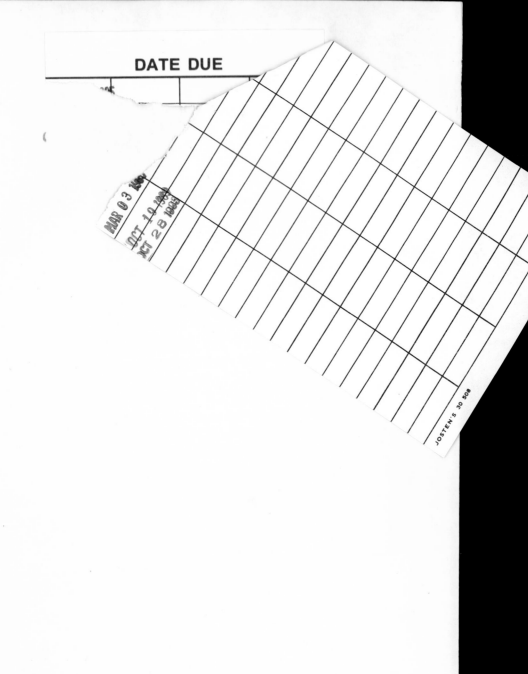

JOSTEN'S 30 508